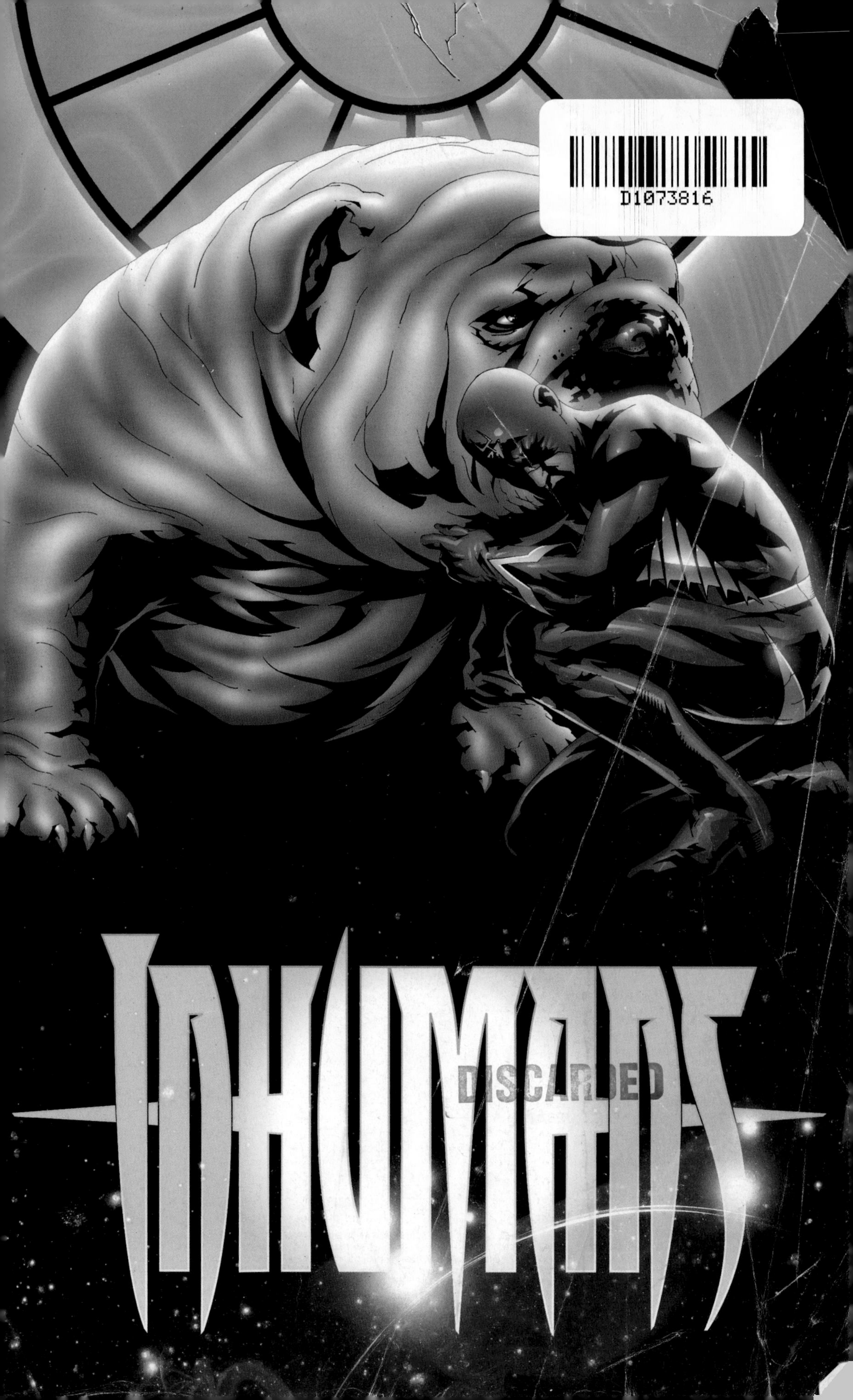
INHUMANS

COLLECTION EDITOR: **MARK D. BEAZLEY**
ASSISTANT MANAGING EDITOR: **ALEX STARBUCK**
EDITOR, SPECIAL PROJECTS: **JENNIFER GRÜNWALD**
SENIOR EDITOR, SPECIAL PROJECTS: **JEFF YOUNGQUIST**
RESEARCH & LAYOUT: **JEPH YORK**
PRODUCTION: **RYAN DEVALL**
BOOK DESIGN: **RODOLFO MURAGUCHI**

SVP PRINT, SALES & MARKETING: **DAVID GABRIEL**
EDITOR IN CHIEF: **AXEL ALONSO**
CHIEF CREATIVE OFFICER: **JOE QUESADA**
PUBLISHER: **DAN BUCKLEY**
EXECUTIVE PRODUCER: **ALAN FINE**

INHUMANS BY PAUL JENKINS & JAE LEE. Contains material originally published in magazine form as INHUMANS #1-12. Second edition. First printing 2015. ISBN# 978-0-7851-9749-2. Published by MARVEL WORLDWIDE, INC., a subsidiary of MARVEL ENTERTAINMENT, LLC. OFFICE OF PUBLICATION: 135 West 50th Street, New York, NY 10020. Copyright © 2015 MARVEL No similarity between any of the names, characters, persons, and/or institutions in this magazine with those of any living or dead person or institution is intended, and any such similarity which may exist is purely coincidental. **Printed in the U.S.A.** ALAN FINE, President, Marvel Entertainment; DAN BUCKLEY, President, TV, Publishing and Brand Management; JOE QUESADA, Chief Creative Officer; TOM BREVOORT, SVP of Publishing; DAVID BOGART, SVP of Operations & Procurement, Publishing; C.B. CEBULSKI, VP of International Development & Brand Management; DAVID GABRIEL, SVP Print, Sales & Marketing; JIM O'KEEFE, VP of Operations & Logistics; DAN CARR, Executive Director of Publishing Technology; SUSAN CRESPI, Editorial Operations Manager; ALEX MORALES, Publishing Operations Manager; STAN LEE, Chairman Emeritus. For information regarding advertising in Marvel Comics or on Marvel.com, please contact Jonathan Rheingold, VP of Custom Solutions & Ad Sales, at jrheingold@marvel.com. For Marvel subscription inquiries, please call 800-217-9158. **Manufactured between** 7/3/2015 and 8/10/2015 by R.R. DONNELLEY, INC., SALEM, VA, USA.

10 9 8 7 6 5 4 3 2 1

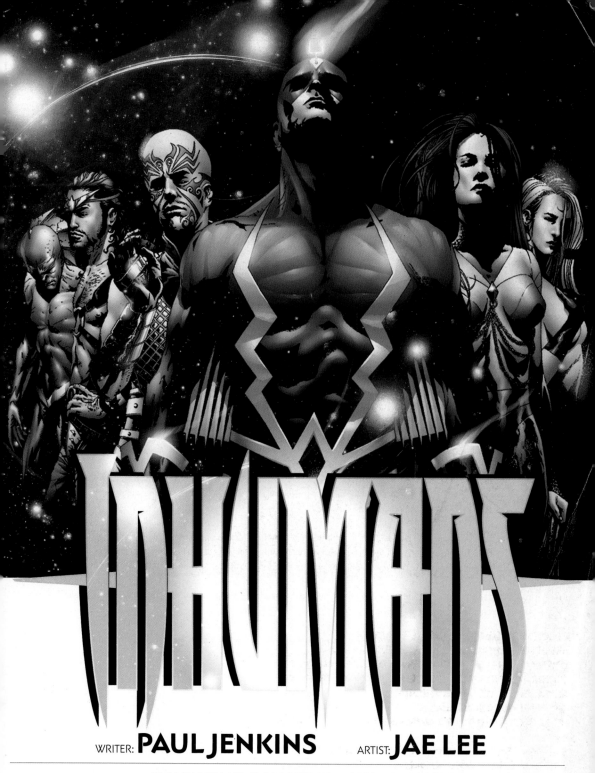

INHUMANS

WRITER: **PAUL JENKINS**　　　ARTIST: **JAE LEE**

COLORISTS: **DAVE KEMP, DAN KEMP** & **AVALON STUDIOS**

LETTERERS: **RICHARD STARKINGS** & **COMICRAFT'S DAVE LANPHEAR,
WES ABBOTT, LIZ AGRAPHIOTIS, SAIDA TEMOFONTE** & **JOHN GAUSHELL**

EDITORS:
JOE QUESADA &
JIMMY PALMIOTTI

MARVEL KNIGHTS
MANAGING EDITOR:
NANCI DAKESIAN

COVER ART:
JAE LEE &
AVALON STUDIOS

BACK COVER ART:
JAE LEE &
AVALON STUDIOS

SPECIAL THANKS TO **MIKE HANSEN**

INHUMANS CREATED BY **STAN LEE** & **JACK KIRBY**

INTRODUCTION

BY ALEX ROSS

I t's a great honor for me to introduce some of you to Paul Jenkins and Jae Lee's *Inhumans*. When this series was first published, I awaited each chapter with a mixture of eagerness, anticipation...and a little fear.

Let me explain: At the same time Paul and Jae were planning to put their mark on the Inhumans, Jim Krueger and I were planning to do the same in our futuristic series *Earth X*, and our treatment drew heavily upon the framework laid down decades ago by Jack Kirby and Stan Lee. The last thing we needed was a couple of young upstarts beating us to the punch or worse, doing something so self-consciously radical that it would confuse people who weren't sure how our future tied in with their present.

In fact, what they did was radical...but it wasn't a problem. With *Inhumans*, Jenkins and Lee tell a story that bears only the slightest resemblance to the stories of Kirby and Lee. In the process, they created something quite captivating and inspirational, and provided insight that most of us — and by "us" I mean those folks who've admired Lee and Kirby's Inhumans for years — had never even considered. Their drastically realistic view honors and even enriches the original material by showing us sides of the characters that we never knew existed. Paul's Black Bolt, for instance, is treated with cool detachment, bringing new insight to the stereotypical "strong-but-silent team leader." The brothers' love-hate relationship is treated with such charm and believability that it calls to mind the characters in Dumas' *Man in the Iron Mask*. The little touches — like Reed Richards' appearing on a talk show — bring the tale into our world, making it "real" in a way precious few comic books have.

Jae Lee's artwork, too, is as far from Jack Kirby's larger-than-life look as one can get. I've been a fan of Jae's for some time and particularly enjoyed seeing him work at incorporating elements of reality into his work. The result is that he's come back to Marvel with a new graphic sense that sets him apart from the majority of artists working in comics today.

In a sense, I had the good fortune to work alongside the creation of *Inhumans*. Maybe that's why I feel a certain kinship to what Paul and Jae have done.

Whatever the case may be, I'm quite in awe of it. And if you're familiar with Kirby and Lee's Inhumans — or if you're coming to these characters for the first time — I'll bet you will be, too. Enjoy.

Alex Ross
2000

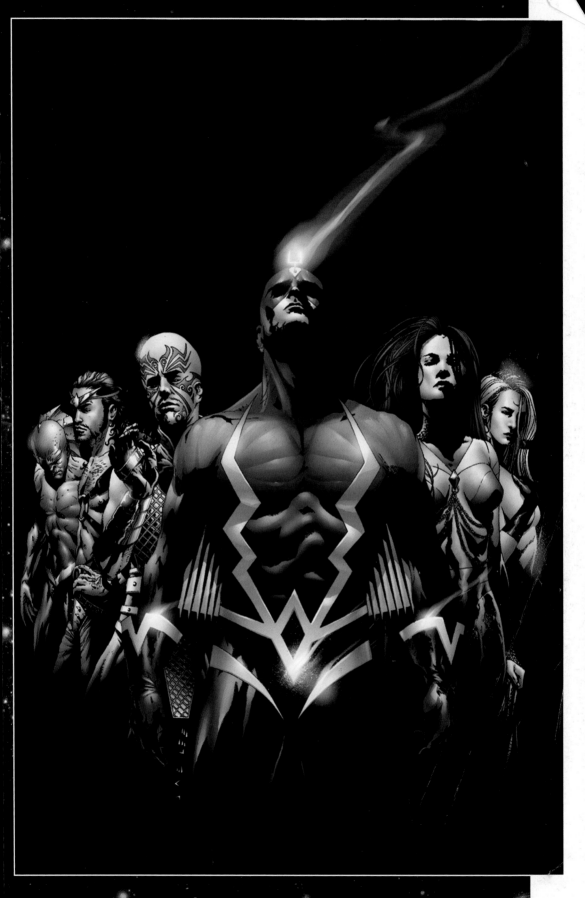

INHUMANS #1

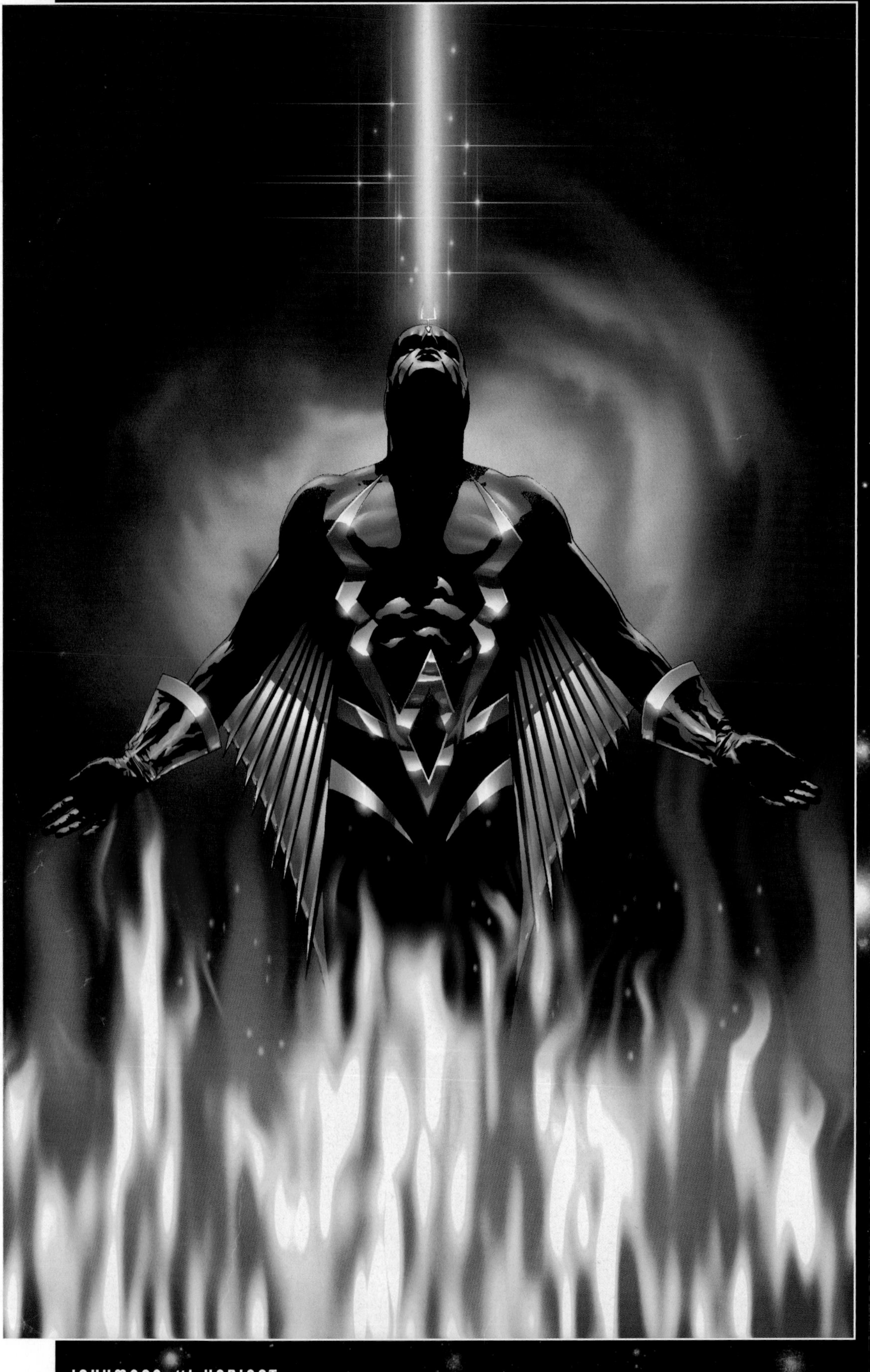

INHUMANS #1 VARIANT

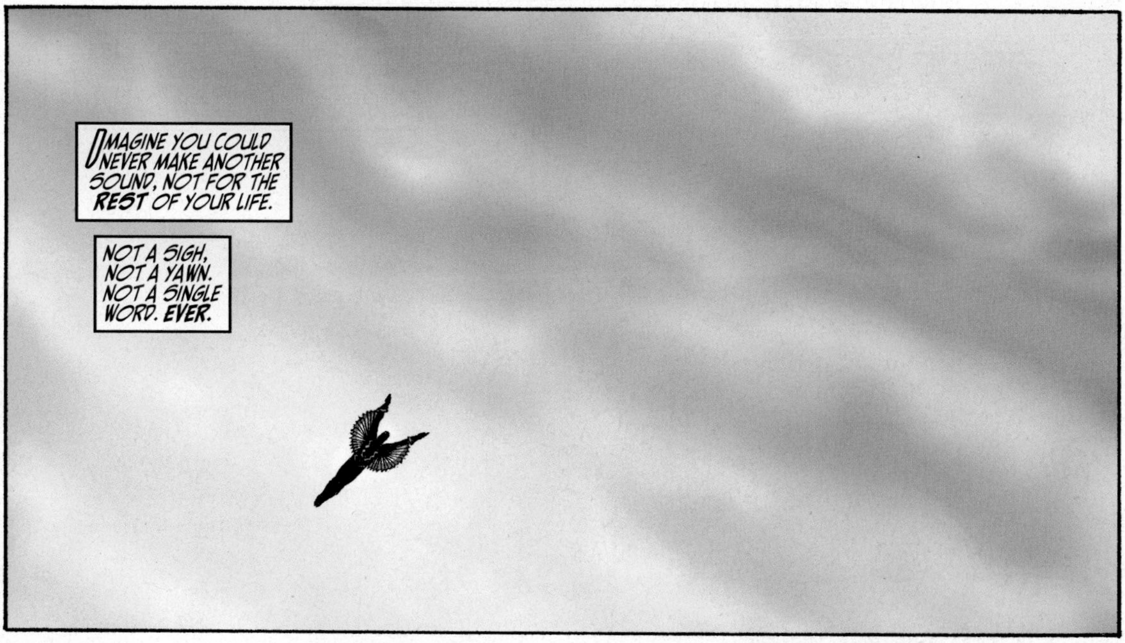
IMAGINE YOU COULD NEVER MAKE ANOTHER SOUND, NOT FOR THE REST OF YOUR LIFE.
NOT A SIGH, NOT A YAWN. NOT A SINGLE WORD. EVER.

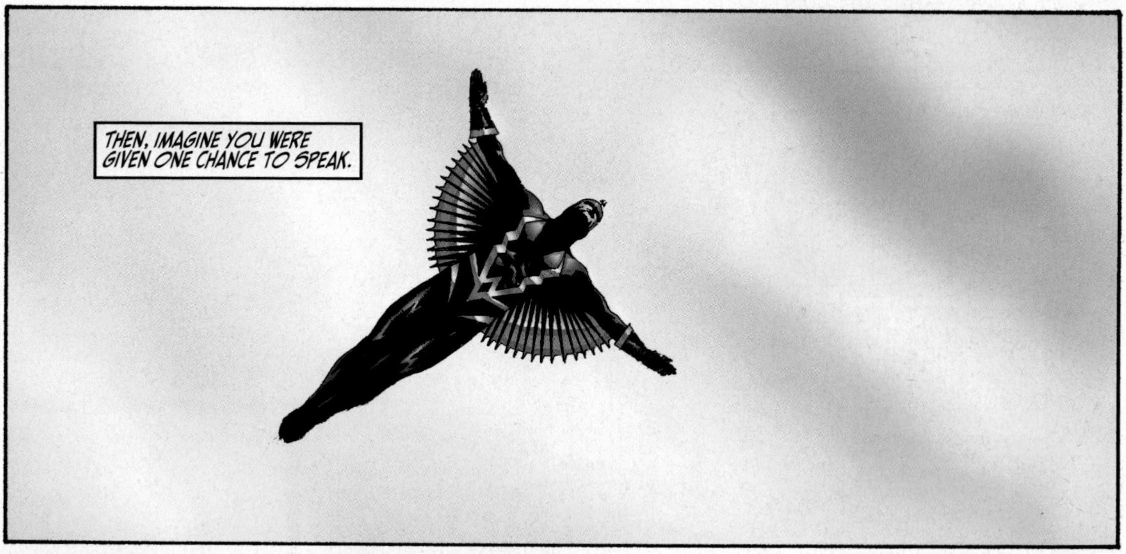
THEN, IMAGINE YOU WERE GIVEN ONE CHANCE TO SPEAK.

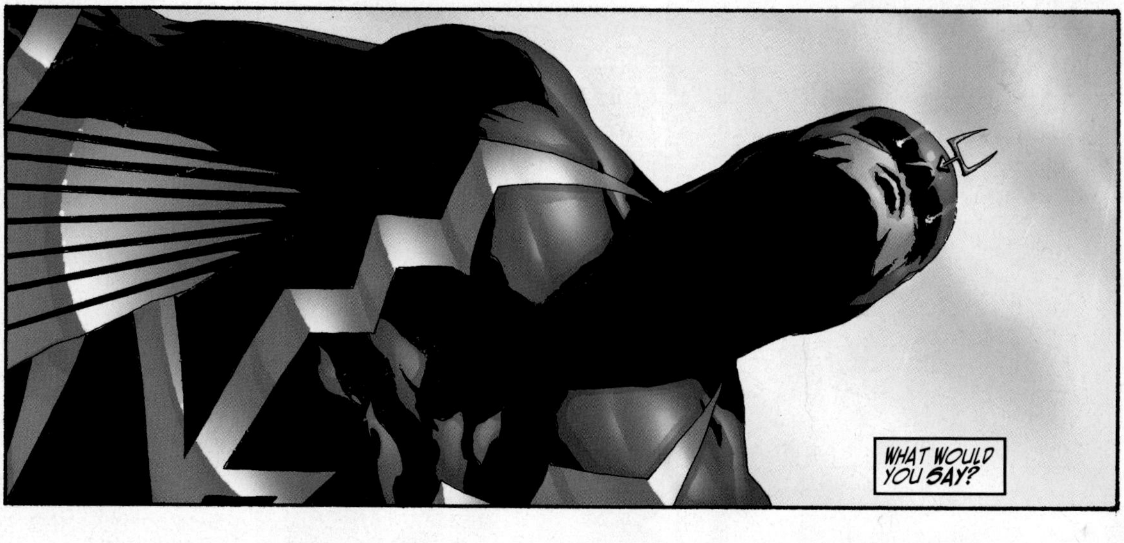
WHAT WOULD YOU SAY?

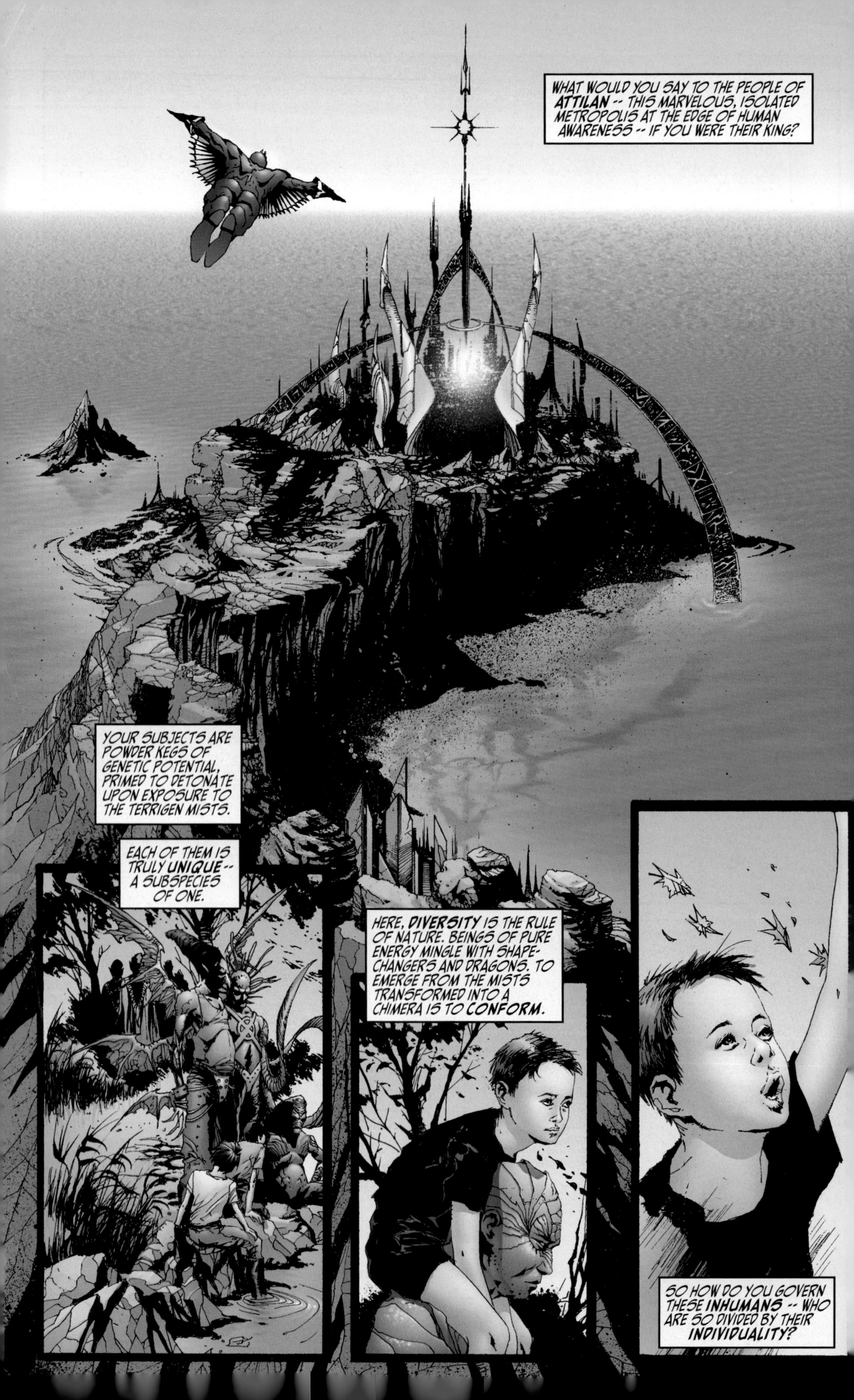

WHAT WOULD YOU SAY TO THE PEOPLE OF ATTILAN -- THIS MARVELOUS, ISOLATED METROPOLIS AT THE EDGE OF HUMAN AWARENESS -- IF YOU WERE THEIR KING?
YOUR SUBJECTS ARE POWDER KEGS OF GENETIC POTENTIAL, PRIMED TO DETONATE UPON EXPOSURE TO THE TERRIGEN MISTS.
EACH OF THEM IS TRULY UNIQUE -- A SUBSPECIES OF ONE.
HERE, DIVERSITY IS THE RULE OF NATURE. BEINGS OF PURE ENERGY MINGLE WITH SHAPE-CHANGERS AND DRAGONS. TO EMERGE FROM THE MISTS TRANSFORMED INTO A CHIMERA IS TO CONFORM.
SO HOW DO YOU GOVERN THESE INHUMANS -- WHO ARE SO DIVIDED BY THEIR INDIVIDUALITY?

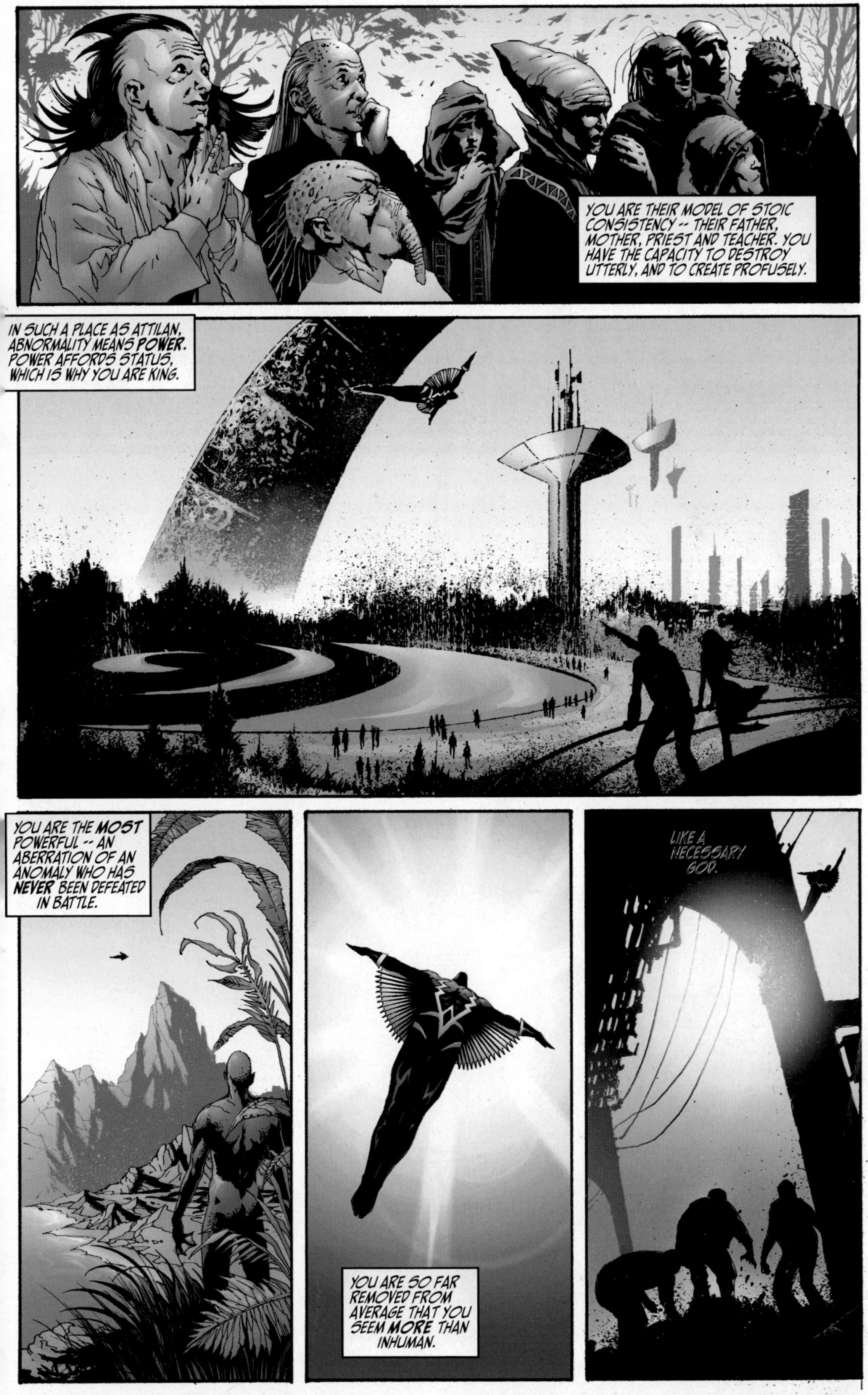
YOU ARE THEIR MODEL OF STOIC CONSISTENCY -- THEIR FATHER, MOTHER, PRIEST AND TEACHER. YOU HAVE THE CAPACITY TO DESTROY UTTERLY, AND TO CREATE PROFUSELY.
IN SUCH A PLACE AS ATTILAN, ABNORMALITY MEANS **POWER**. POWER AFFORDS STATUS, WHICH IS WHY YOU ARE KING.
YOU ARE THE **MOST** POWERFUL -- AN ABERRATION OF AN ANOMALY WHO HAS **NEVER** BEEN DEFEATED IN BATTLE.
YOU ARE SO FAR REMOVED FROM AVERAGE THAT YOU SEEM **MORE** THAN INHUMAN.
LIKE A NECESSARY GOD.

YOU MIGHT WELL SPEAK OF THE IRONY IN THIS. BUT TO DO SO WOULD RESULT IN CATASTROPHE.

BECAUSE YOUR VOICE IS SO RESONANT THAT IT REACHES INTO SOME NAMELESS, DISTANT SONIC RANGE. YOUR SLIGHTEST WHISPER HAS THE POWER TO LEVEL MOUNTAINS.

IN TRUTH, YOUR PEOPLE WOULD SCARCELY HEAR YOUR WORDS...

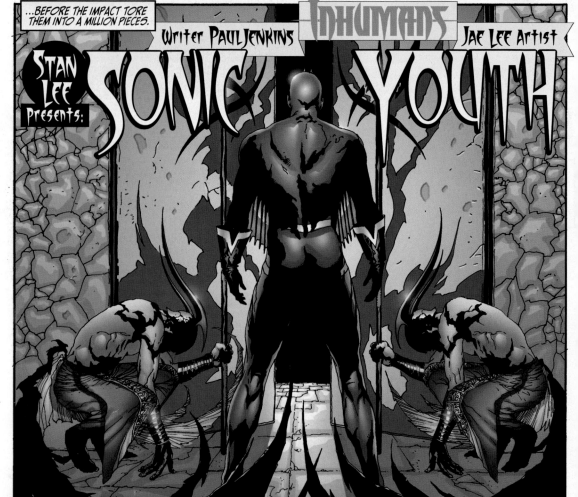

...BEFORE THE IMPACT TORE THEM INTO A MILLION PIECES.

INHUMANS

Writer PAUL JENKINS   Jae Lee Artist

STAN LEE Presents: SONIC YOUTH

AVALON STUDIOS
Colors

RS & COMICRAFT/DL
Letters

QUESADA & PALMIOTTI
Editors

NANCI DAKESIAN
Managing Editor

BOB HARRAS
Editor in Chief

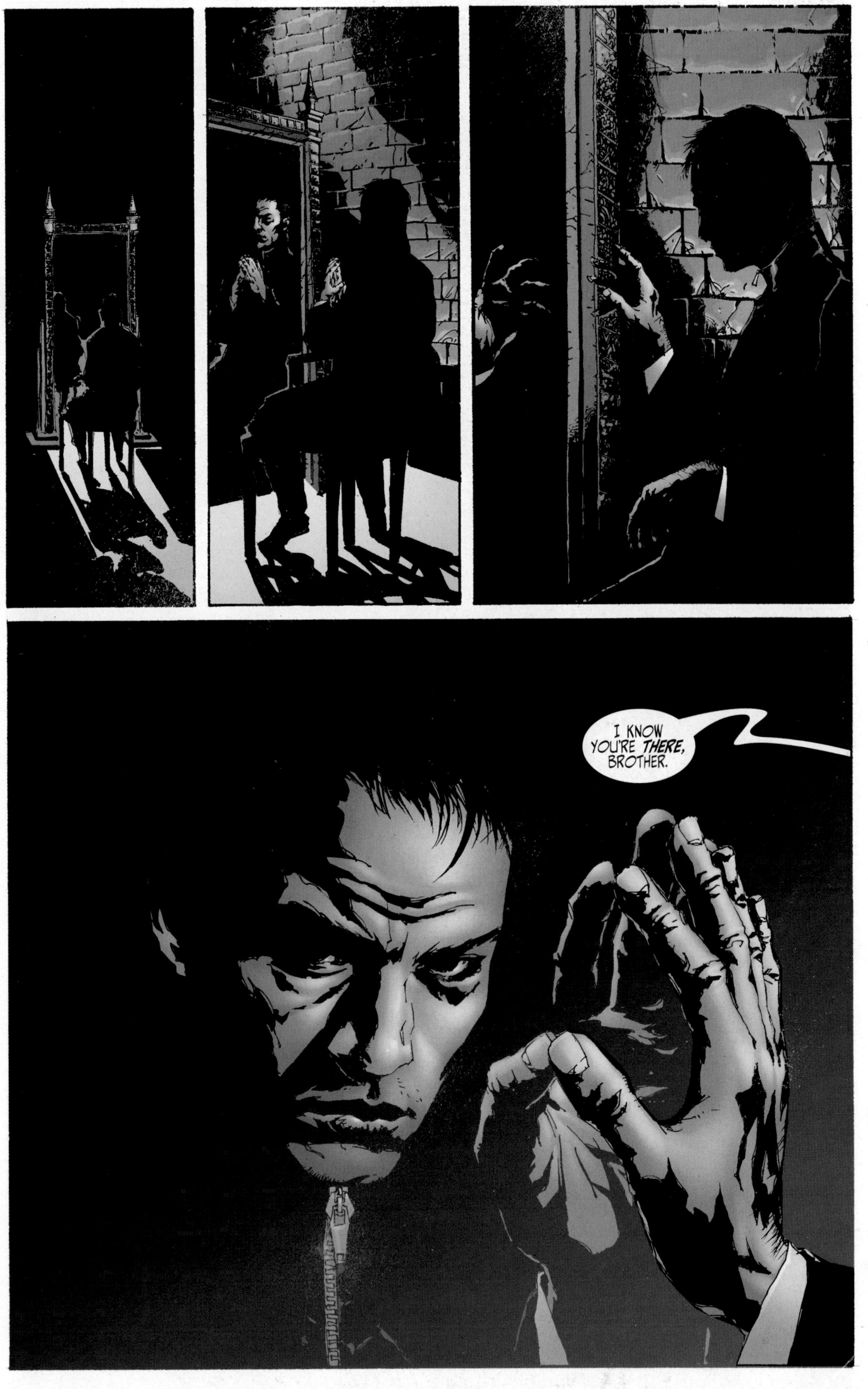
I KNOW YOU'RE THERE, BROTHER.

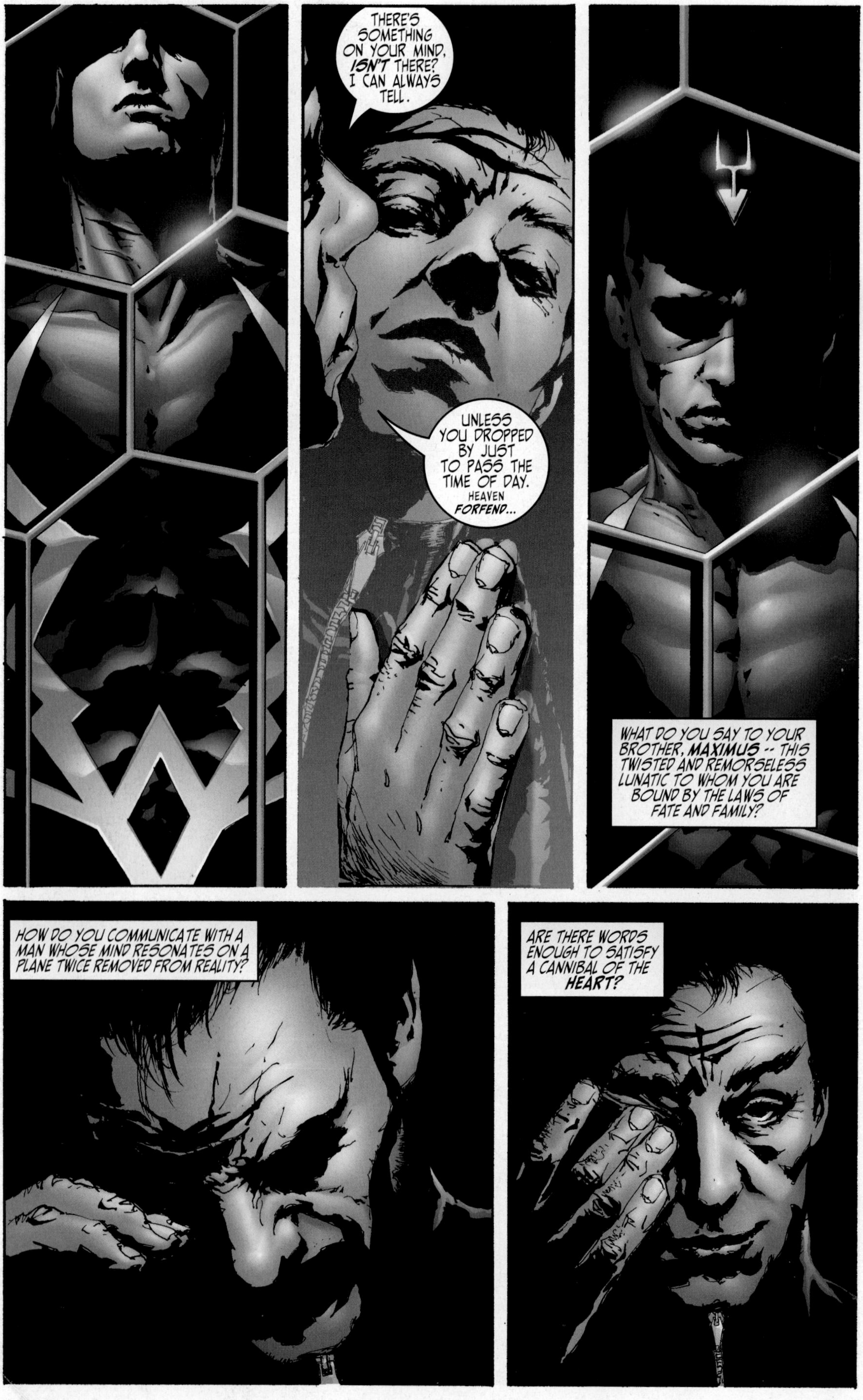
THERE'S SOMETHING ON YOUR MIND, ISN'T THERE? I CAN ALWAYS TELL.
UNLESS YOU DROPPED BY JUST TO PASS THE TIME OF DAY. HEAVEN FORFEND...
WHAT DO YOU SAY TO YOUR BROTHER, MAXIMUS -- THIS TWISTED AND REMORSELESS LUNATIC TO WHOM YOU ARE BOUND BY THE LAWS OF FATE AND FAMILY?
HOW DO YOU COMMUNICATE WITH A MAN WHOSE MIND RESONATES ON A PLANE TWICE REMOVED FROM REALITY?
ARE THERE WORDS ENOUGH TO SATISFY A CANNIBAL OF THE HEART?

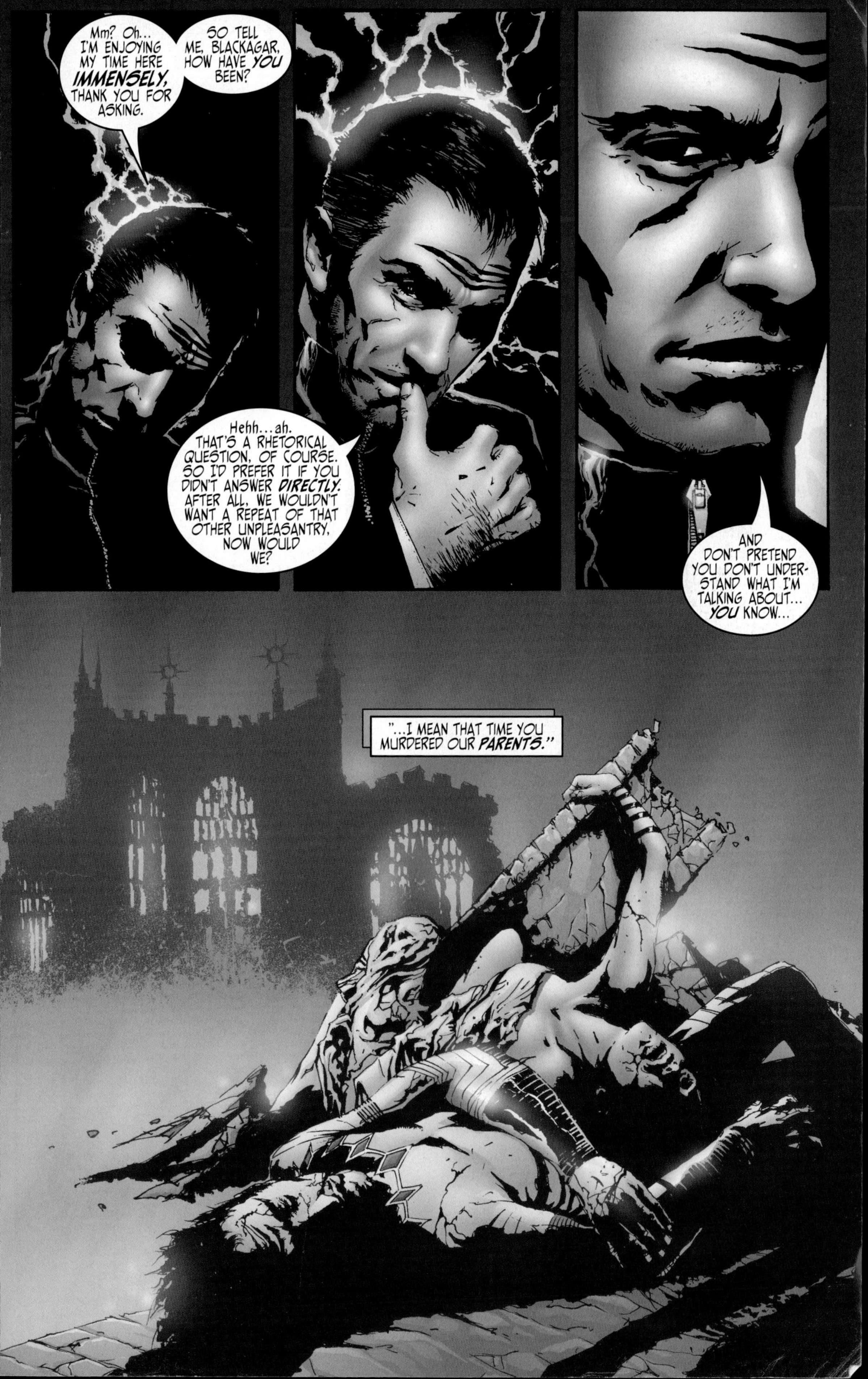
Mm? Oh... I'M ENJOYING MY TIME HERE IMMENSELY, THANK YOU FOR ASKING.
SO TELL ME, BLACKAGAR, HOW HAVE YOU BEEN?
Hehh...ah. THAT'S A RHETORICAL QUESTION, OF COURSE. SO I'D PREFER IT IF YOU DIDN'T ANSWER DIRECTLY. AFTER ALL, WE WOULDN'T WANT A REPEAT OF THAT OTHER UNPLEASANTRY, NOW WOULD WE?
AND DON'T PRETEND YOU DON'T UNDER-STAND WHAT I'M TALKING ABOUT... YOU KNOW...
"...I MEAN THAT TIME YOU MURDERED OUR PARENTS."

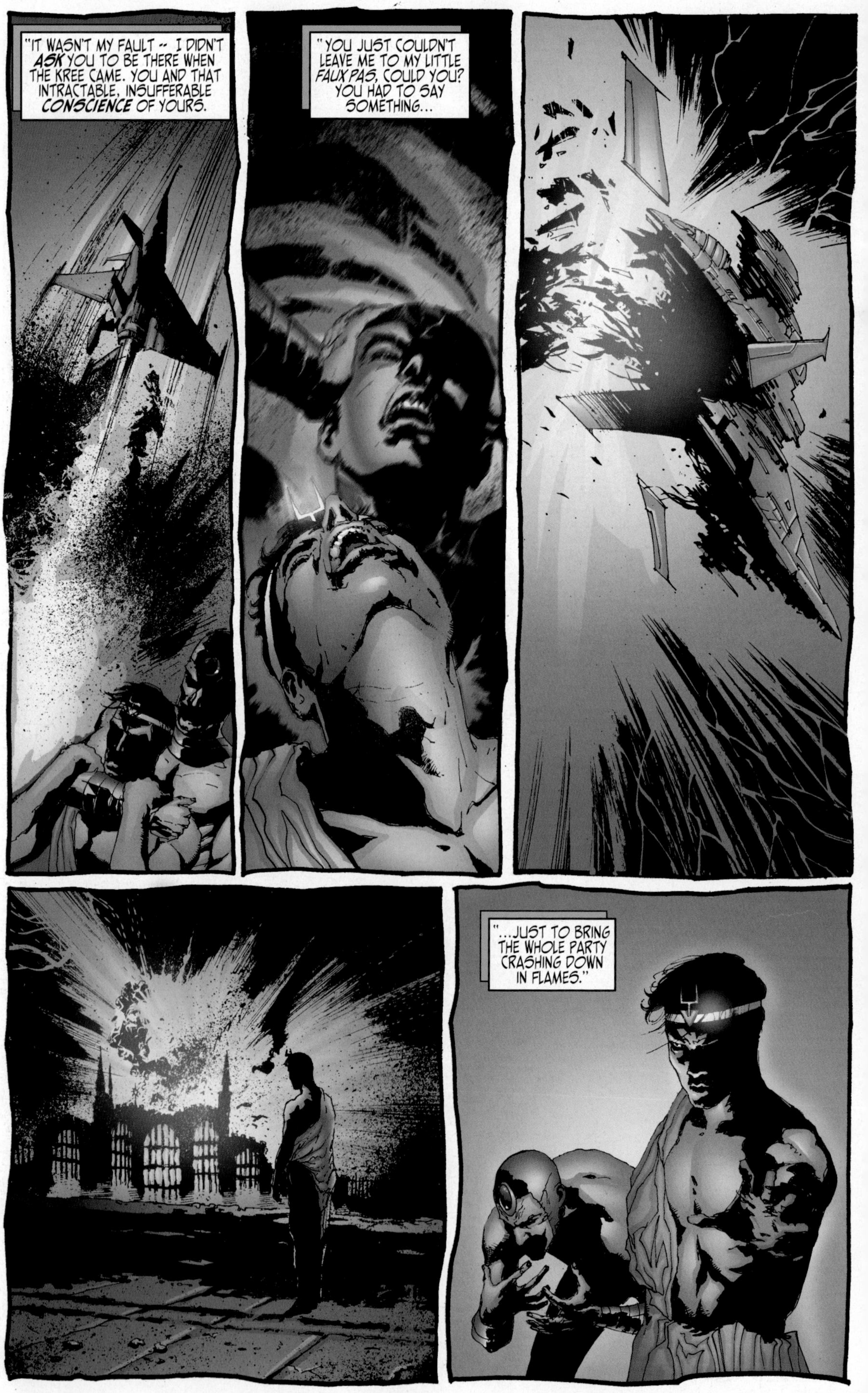
"IT WASN'T MY FAULT -- I DIDN'T ASK YOU TO BE THERE WHEN THE KREE CAME. YOU AND THAT INTRACTABLE, INSUFFERABLE CONSCIENCE OF YOURS.
"YOU JUST COULDN'T LEAVE ME TO MY LITTLE FAUX PAS, COULD YOU? YOU HAD TO SAY SOMETHING...
"...JUST TO BRING THE WHOLE PARTY CRASHING DOWN IN FLAMES."

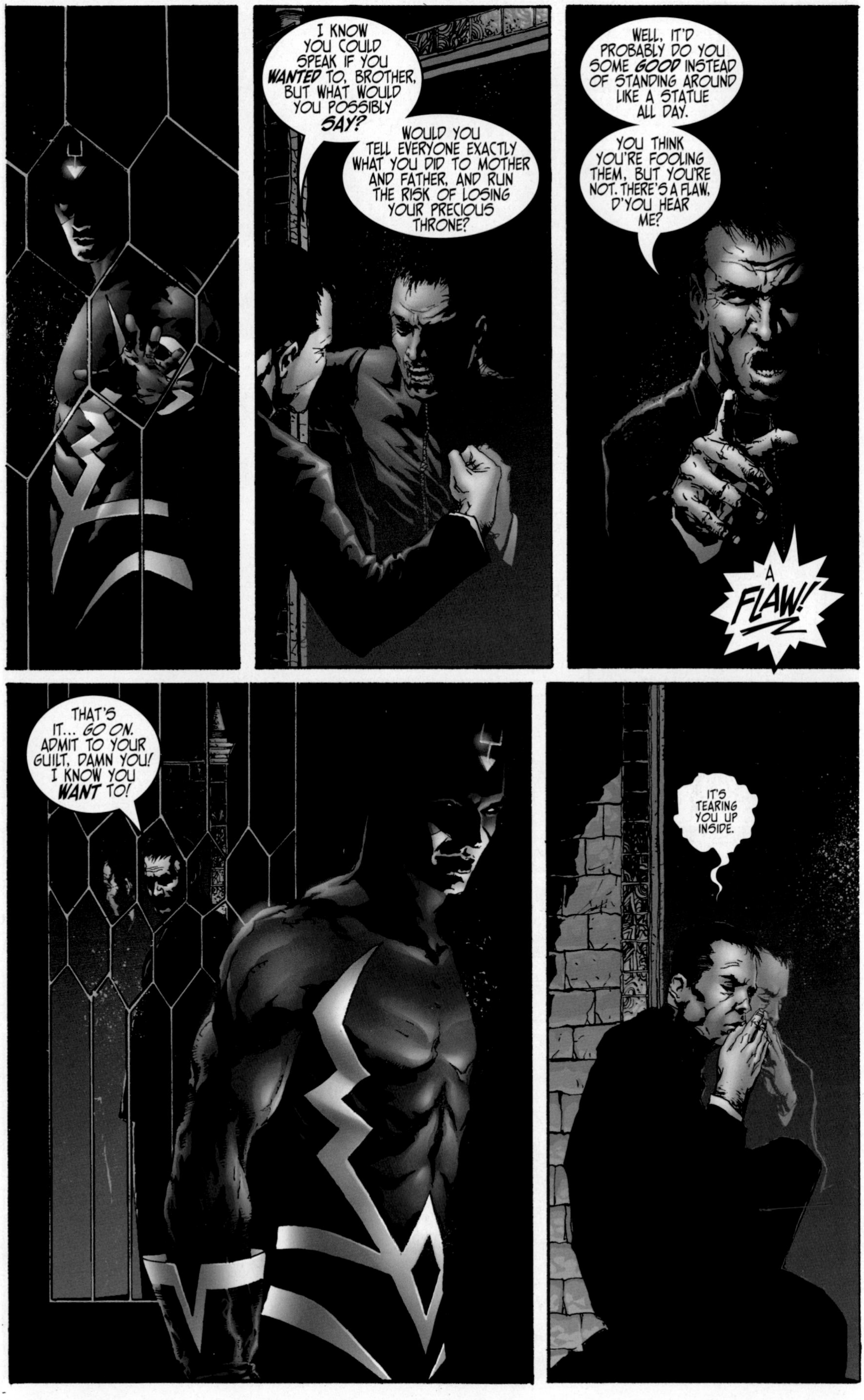
I KNOW YOU COULD SPEAK IF YOU WANTED TO, BROTHER, BUT WHAT WOULD YOU POSSIBLY SAY?
WOULD YOU TELL EVERYONE EXACTLY WHAT YOU DID TO MOTHER AND FATHER, AND RUN THE RISK OF LOSING YOUR PRECIOUS THRONE?
WELL, IT'D PROBABLY DO YOU SOME GOOD INSTEAD OF STANDING AROUND LIKE A STATUE ALL DAY.
YOU THINK YOU'RE FOOLING THEM, BUT YOU'RE NOT. THERE'S A FLAW, D'YOU HEAR ME?
A FLAW!
THAT'S IT... GO ON. ADMIT TO YOUR GUILT, DAMN YOU! I KNOW YOU WANT TO!
IT'S TEARING YOU UP INSIDE.

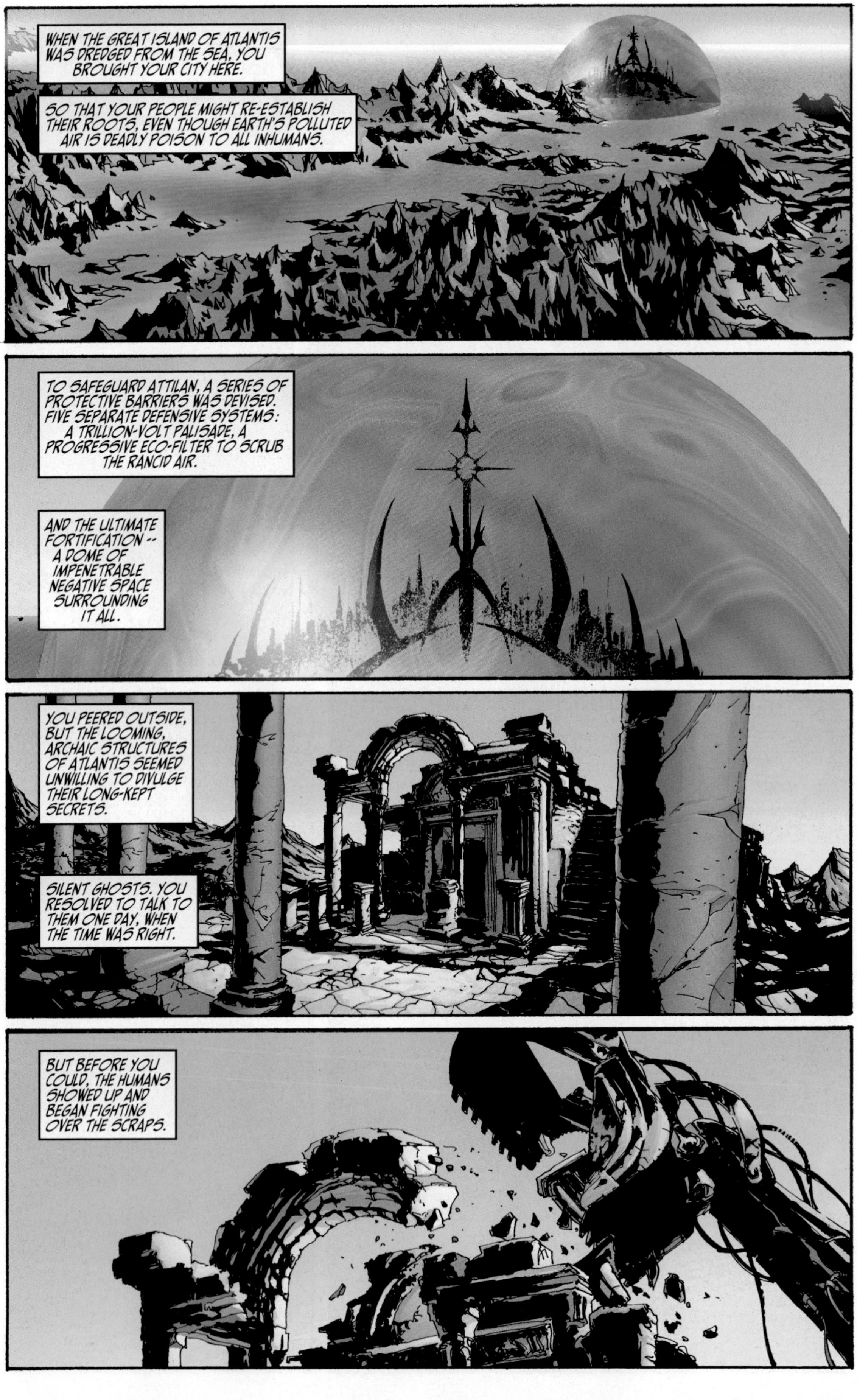
WHEN THE GREAT ISLAND OF ATLANTIS WAS DREDGED FROM THE SEA, YOU BROUGHT YOUR CITY HERE.
SO THAT YOUR PEOPLE MIGHT RE-ESTABLISH THEIR ROOTS, EVEN THOUGH EARTH'S POLLUTED AIR IS DEADLY POISON TO ALL INHUMANS.
TO SAFEGUARD ATTILAN, A SERIES OF PROTECTIVE BARRIERS WAS DEVISED. FIVE SEPARATE DEFENSIVE SYSTEMS: A TRILLION-VOLT PALISADE, A PROGRESSIVE ECO-FILTER TO SCRUB THE RANCID AIR.
AND THE ULTIMATE FORTIFICATION -- A DOME OF IMPENETRABLE NEGATIVE SPACE SURROUNDING IT ALL.
YOU PEERED OUTSIDE, BUT THE LOOMING, ARCHAIC STRUCTURES OF ATLANTIS SEEMED UNWILLING TO DIVULGE THEIR LONG-KEPT SECRETS.
SILENT GHOSTS. YOU RESOLVED TO TALK TO THEM ONE DAY, WHEN THE TIME WAS RIGHT.
BUT BEFORE YOU COULD, THE HUMANS SHOWED UP AND BEGAN FIGHTING OVER THE SCRAPS.

WHERE THEY ARE ARROGANT, THEY ARE NOBLE; DIVISIVE AND YET CAPABLE OF UNQUESTIONING LOYALTY.

THEY HIDE THEIR COMPASSION BENEATH HOSTILITY.

THEY ARE OZONE EATERS. EACH OF THEM HARBORS AN APOCALYPTIC ARRAY OF VIRUSES AND BACTERIAL INFECTIONS, TO WHICH THEY HAVE A HERCULEAN RESISTANCE.

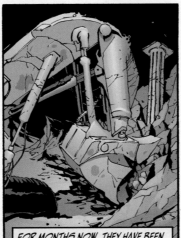

FOR MONTHS NOW, THEY HAVE BEEN RAKING THE ANCIENT ISLAND FOR METAL AND MINERALS. INTERNATIONAL CONGLOMERATES, SUPPORTED BY THE OCCUPYING PORTUGUESE ARMY.

WHATEVER YOU SAY TO THEM, IT HAD BETTER BE *GOOD.* BECAUSE THESE HUMANS, WHO BRING PESTILENCE, DISEASE AND DECAY TO YOUR PEOPLE, ARE *BACK.*

AND THEY'RE LESS THAN A MILE AWAY FROM YOUR BORDER.

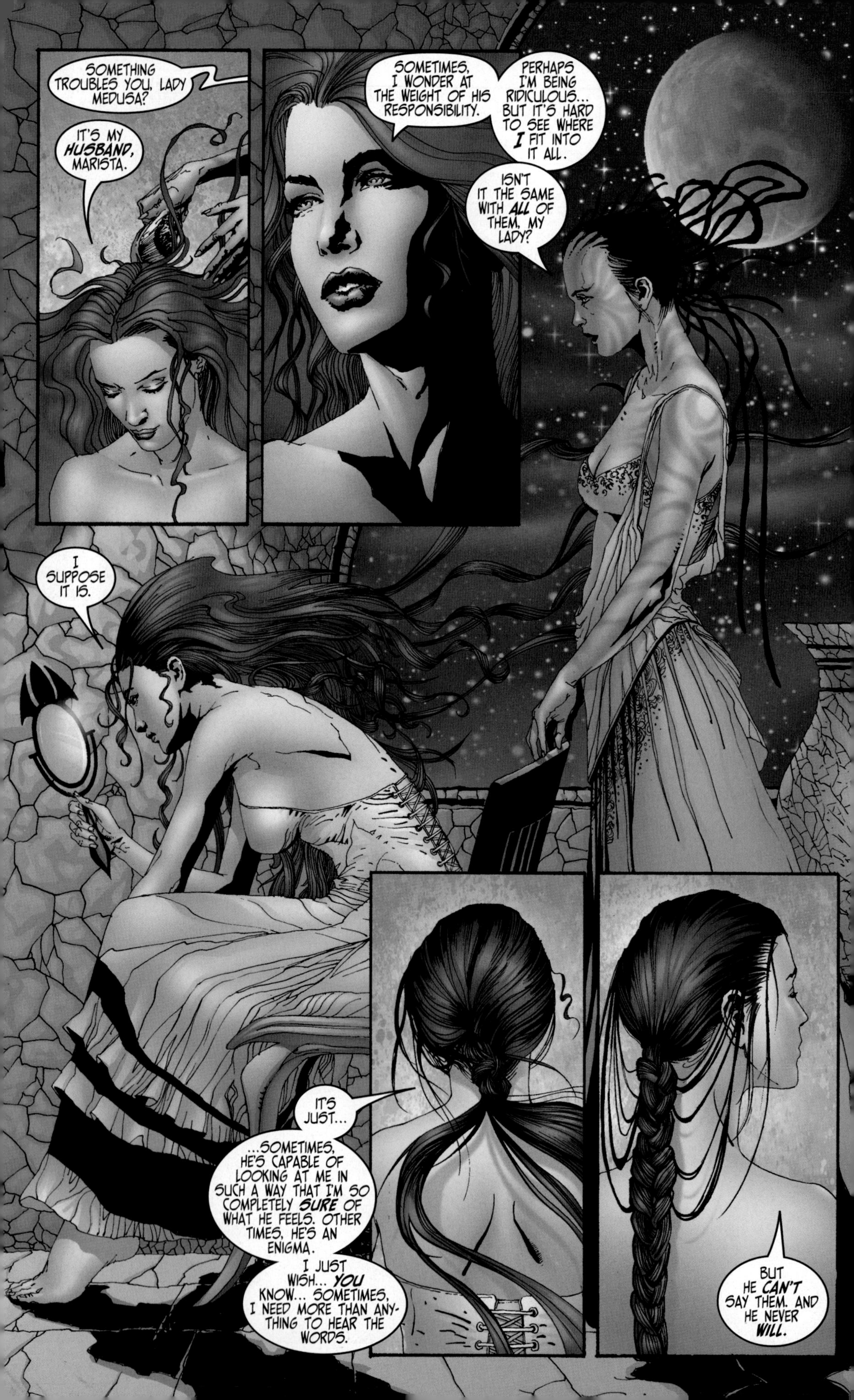
SOMETHING TROUBLES YOU, LADY MEDUSA?
IT'S MY HUSBAND, MARISTA.
SOMETIMES, I WONDER AT THE WEIGHT OF HIS RESPONSIBILITY.
PERHAPS I'M BEING RIDICULOUS... BUT IT'S HARD TO SEE WHERE I FIT INTO IT ALL.
ISN'T IT THE SAME WITH ALL OF THEM, MY LADY?
I SUPPOSE IT IS.
IT'S JUST...
...SOMETIMES, HE'S CAPABLE OF LOOKING AT ME IN SUCH A WAY THAT I'M SO COMPLETELY SURE OF WHAT HE FEELS. OTHER TIMES, HE'S AN ENIGMA.
I JUST WISH... YOU KNOW... SOMETIMES, I NEED MORE THAN ANY-THING TO HEAR THE WORDS.
BUT HE CAN'T SAY THEM. AND HE NEVER WILL.

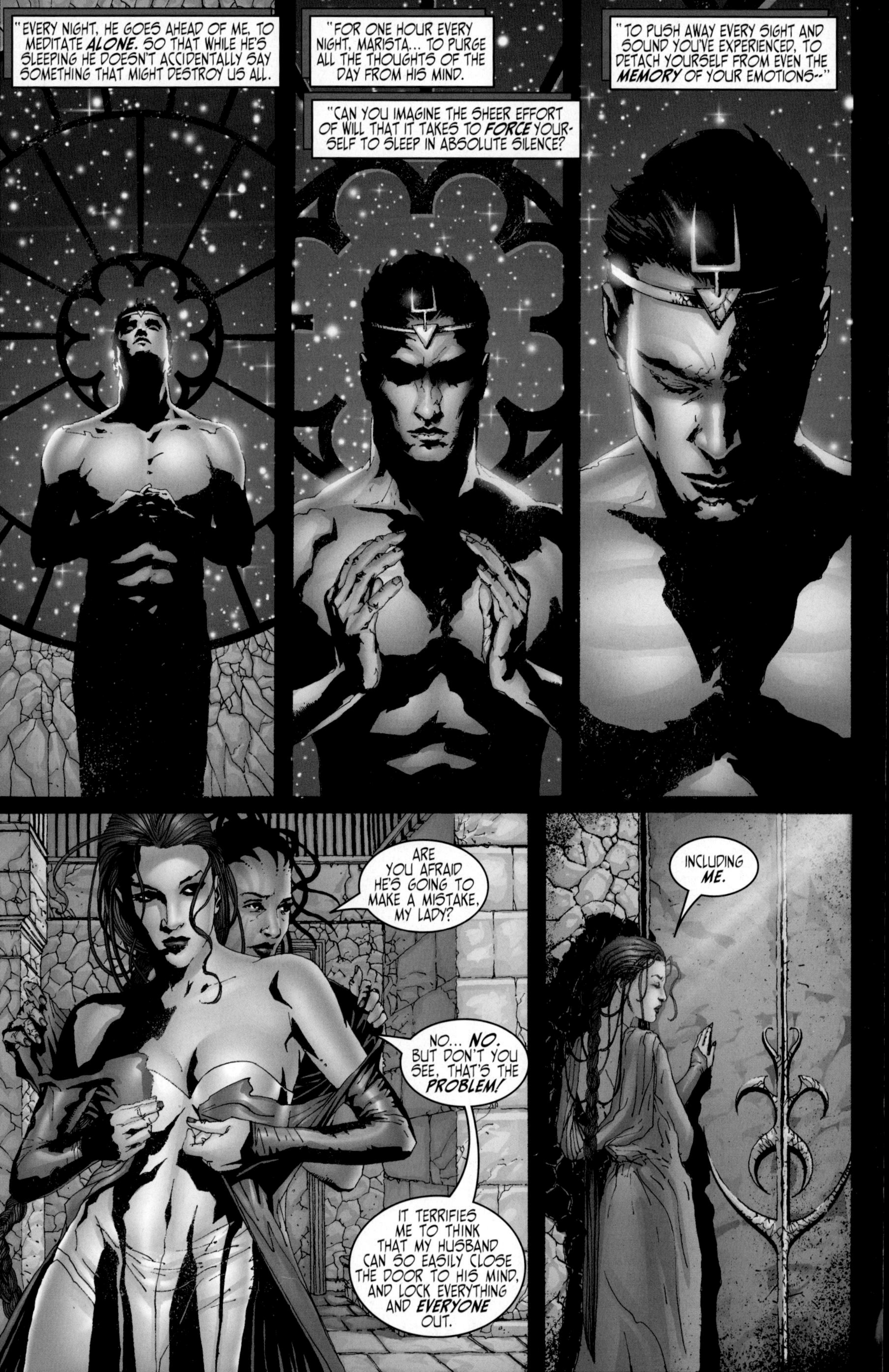
"EVERY NIGHT, HE GOES AHEAD OF ME, TO MEDITATE ALONE. SO THAT WHILE HE'S SLEEPING HE DOESN'T ACCIDENTALLY SAY SOMETHING THAT MIGHT DESTROY US ALL.
"FOR ONE HOUR EVERY NIGHT, MARISTA... TO PURGE ALL THE THOUGHTS OF THE DAY FROM HIS MIND.
"CAN YOU IMAGINE THE SHEER EFFORT OF WILL THAT IT TAKES TO FORCE YOURSELF TO SLEEP IN ABSOLUTE SILENCE?
"TO PUSH AWAY EVERY SIGHT AND SOUND YOU'VE EXPERIENCED, TO DETACH YOURSELF FROM EVEN THE MEMORY OF YOUR EMOTIONS--"
ARE YOU AFRAID HE'S GOING TO MAKE A MISTAKE, MY LADY?
NO... NO. BUT DON'T YOU SEE, THAT'S THE PROBLEM!
IT TERRIFIES ME TO THINK THAT MY HUSBAND CAN SO EASILY CLOSE THE DOOR TO HIS MIND, AND LOCK EVERYTHING AND EVERYONE OUT.
INCLUDING ME.

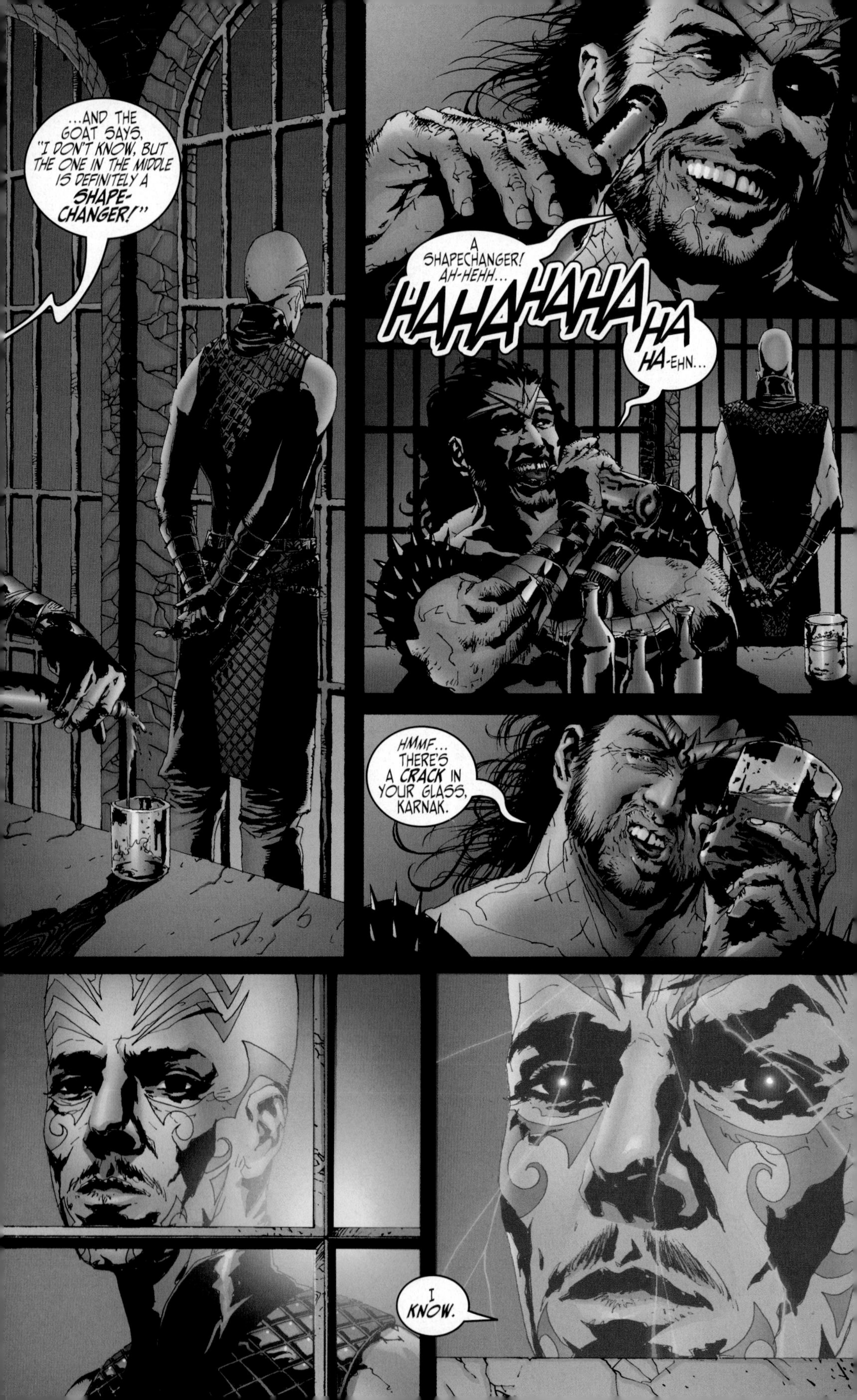
...AND THE GOAT SAYS, "I DON'T KNOW, BUT THE ONE IN THE MIDDLE IS DEFINITELY A SHAPE-CHANGER!"
A SHAPECHANGER! AH-HEHH... HAHAHAHAHAHA HA-EHN...
HMMF... THERE'S A CRACK IN YOUR GLASS, KARNAK.
I KNOW.

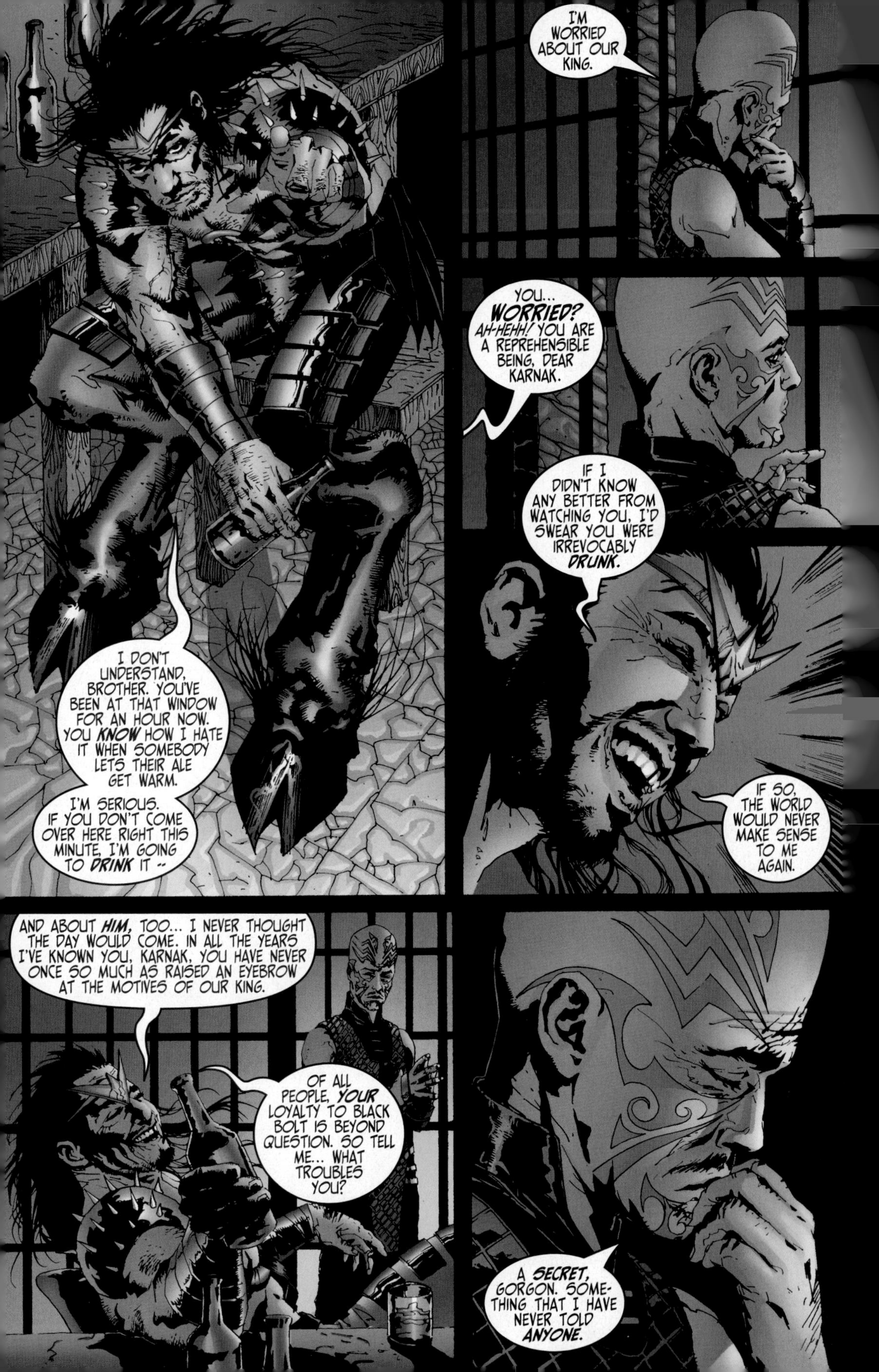
I DON'T UNDERSTAND, BROTHER. YOU'VE BEEN AT THAT WINDOW FOR AN HOUR NOW. YOU KNOW HOW I HATE IT WHEN SOMEBODY LETS THEIR ALE GET WARM.
I'M SERIOUS. IF YOU DON'T COME OVER HERE RIGHT THIS MINUTE, I'M GOING TO DRINK IT --
I'M WORRIED ABOUT OUR KING.
YOU... WORRIED? AH-HEHH! YOU ARE A REPREHENSIBLE BEING, DEAR KARNAK.
IF I DIDN'T KNOW ANY BETTER FROM WATCHING YOU, I'D SWEAR YOU WERE IRREVOCABLY DRUNK.
IF SO, THE WORLD WOULD NEVER MAKE SENSE TO ME AGAIN.
AND ABOUT HIM, TOO... I NEVER THOUGHT THE DAY WOULD COME. IN ALL THE YEARS I'VE KNOWN YOU, KARNAK, YOU HAVE NEVER ONCE SO MUCH AS RAISED AN EYEBROW AT THE MOTIVES OF OUR KING.
OF ALL PEOPLE, YOUR LOYALTY TO BLACK BOLT IS BEYOND QUESTION. SO TELL ME... WHAT TROUBLES YOU?
A SECRET, GORGON. SOMETHING THAT I HAVE NEVER TOLD ANYONE.

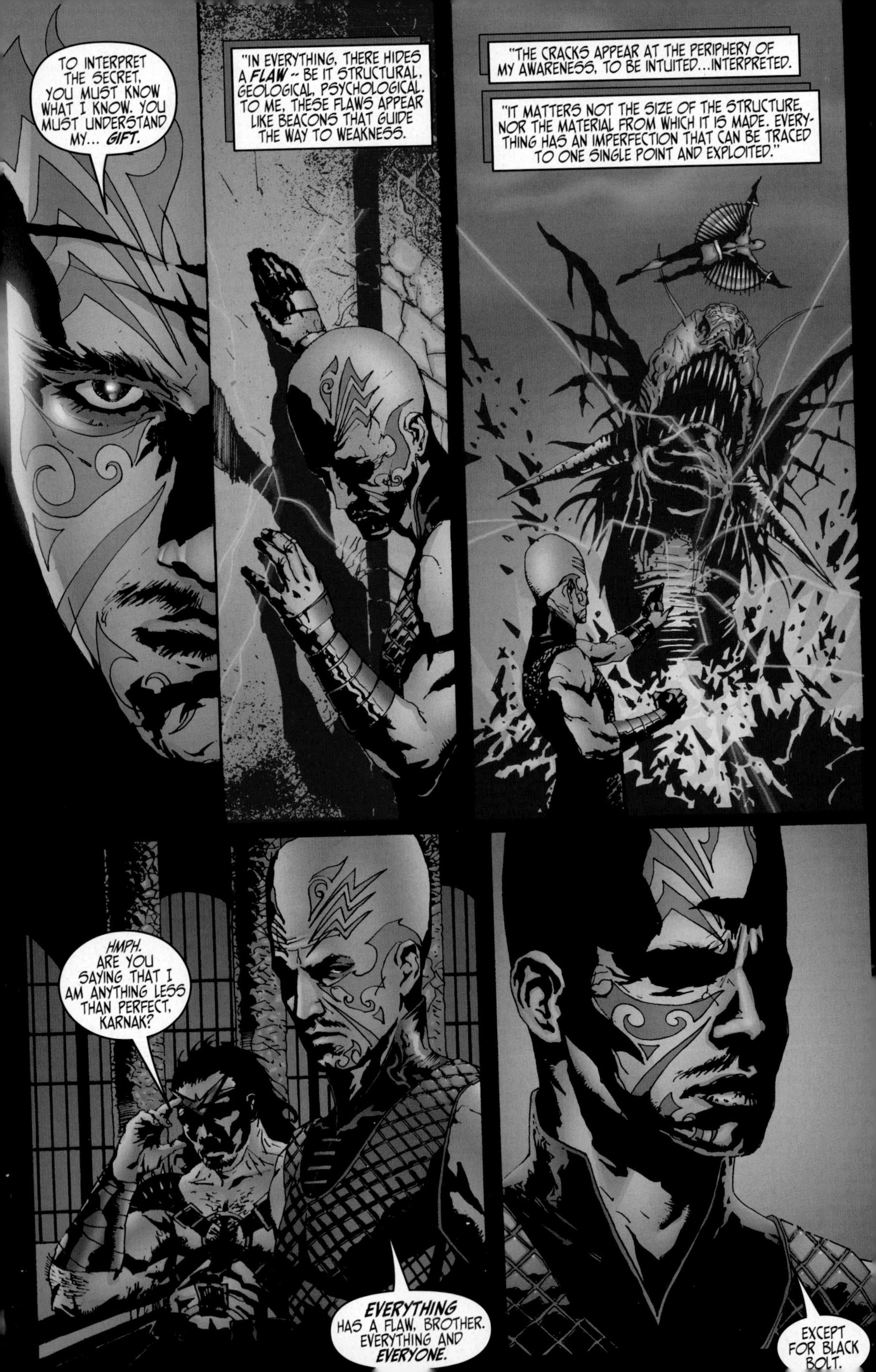
TO INTERPRET THE SECRET, YOU MUST KNOW WHAT I KNOW. YOU MUST UNDERSTAND MY... GIFT.
"IN EVERYTHING, THERE HIDES A FLAW -- BE IT STRUCTURAL, GEOLOGICAL, PSYCHOLOGICAL. TO ME, THESE FLAWS APPEAR LIKE BEACONS THAT GUIDE THE WAY TO WEAKNESS.
"THE CRACKS APPEAR AT THE PERIPHERY OF MY AWARENESS, TO BE INTUITED...INTERPRETED.
"IT MATTERS NOT THE SIZE OF THE STRUCTURE, NOR THE MATERIAL FROM WHICH IT IS MADE. EVERYTHING HAS AN IMPERFECTION THAT CAN BE TRACED TO ONE SINGLE POINT AND EXPLOITED."
HMPH. ARE YOU SAYING THAT I AM ANYTHING LESS THAN PERFECT, KARNAK?
EVERYTHING HAS A FLAW, BROTHER. EVERYTHING AND EVERYONE.
EXCEPT FOR BLACK BOLT.

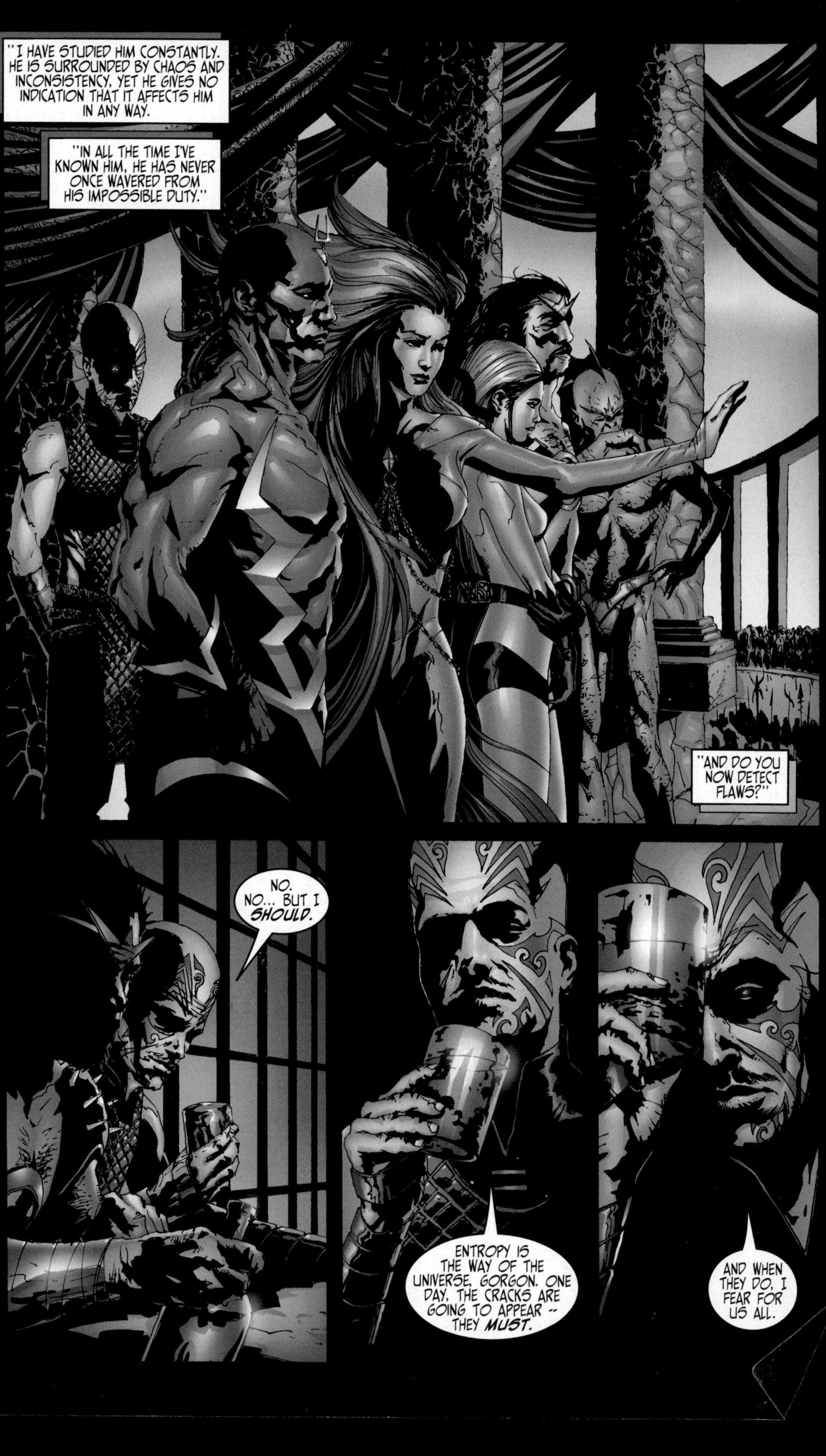
"I HAVE STUDIED HIM CONSTANTLY. HE IS SURROUNDED BY CHAOS AND INCONSISTENCY, YET HE GIVES NO INDICATION THAT IT AFFECTS HIM IN ANY WAY.
"IN ALL THE TIME I'VE KNOWN HIM, HE HAS NEVER ONCE WAVERED FROM HIS IMPOSSIBLE DUTY."
"AND DO YOU NOW DETECT FLAWS?"
NO. NO... BUT I SHOULD.
ENTROPY IS THE WAY OF THE UNIVERSE, GORGON. ONE DAY, THE CRACKS ARE GOING TO APPEAR -- THEY MUST.
AND WHEN THEY DO, I FEAR FOR US ALL.

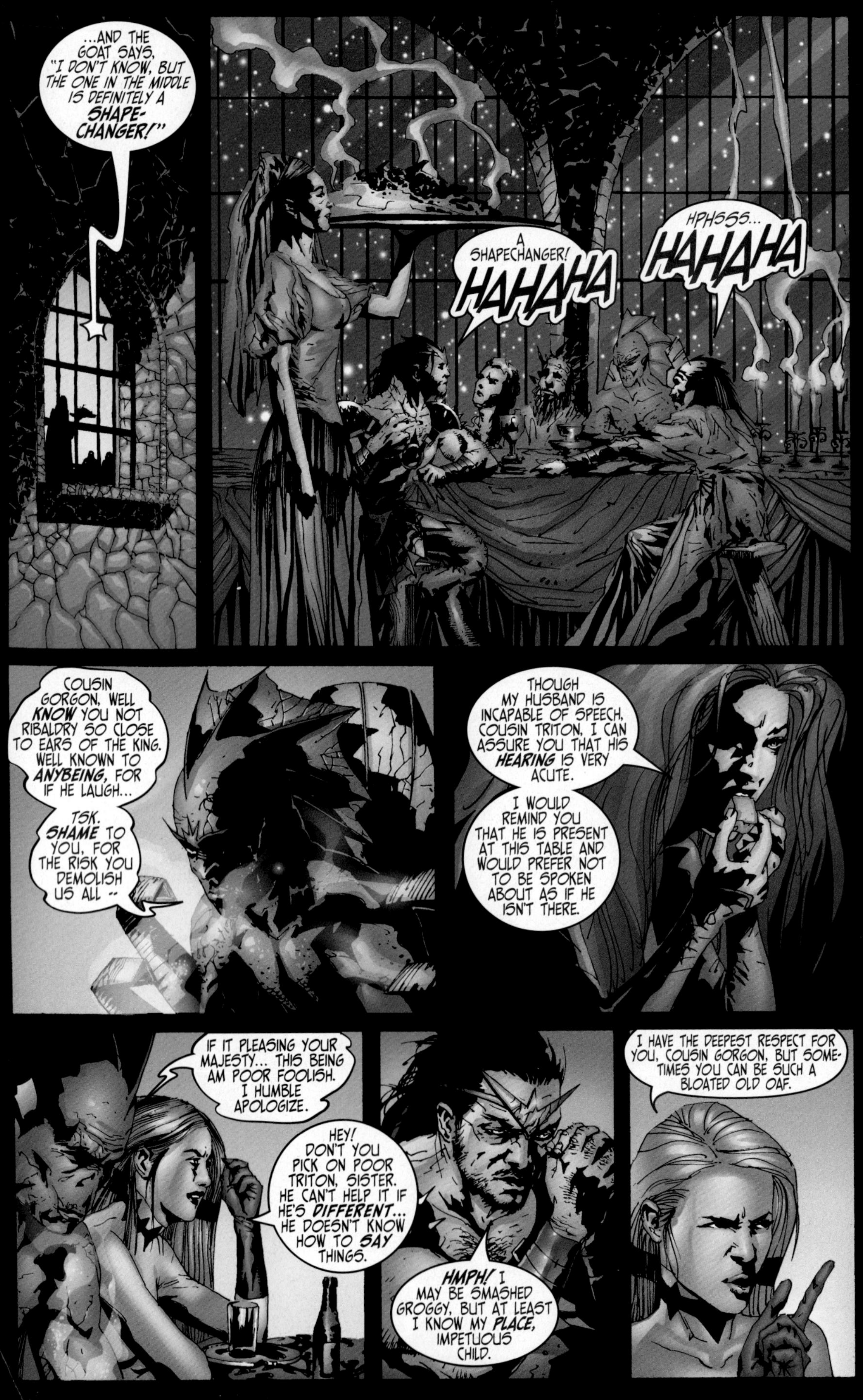
...AND THE GOAT SAYS, "I DON'T KNOW, BUT THE ONE IN THE MIDDLE IS DEFINITELY A SHAPE-CHANGER!"
A SHAPECHANGER! HAHAHA
HPHSSS... HAHAHA
COUSIN GORGON, WELL KNOW YOU NOT RIBALDRY SO CLOSE TO EARS OF THE KING. WELL KNOWN TO ANYBEING, FOR IF HE LAUGH...
TSK. SHAME TO YOU, FOR THE RISK YOU DEMOLISH US ALL --
THOUGH MY HUSBAND IS INCAPABLE OF SPEECH, COUSIN TRITON, I CAN ASSURE YOU THAT HIS HEARING IS VERY ACUTE.
I WOULD REMIND YOU THAT HE IS PRESENT AT THIS TABLE AND WOULD PREFER NOT TO BE SPOKEN ABOUT AS IF HE ISN'T THERE.
IF IT PLEASING YOUR MAJESTY... THIS BEING AM POOR FOOLISH. I HUMBLE APOLOGIZE.
HEY! DON'T YOU PICK ON POOR TRITON, SISTER. HE CAN'T HELP IT IF HE'S DIFFERENT... HE DOESN'T KNOW HOW TO SAY THINGS.
HMPH! I MAY BE SMASHED GROGGY, BUT AT LEAST I KNOW MY PLACE, IMPETUOUS CHILD.
I HAVE THE DEEPEST RESPECT FOR YOU, COUSIN GORGON, BUT SOME-TIMES YOU CAN BE SUCH A BLOATED OLD OAF.

WHAT WOULD YOU SAY IF YOU COULD ONLY SAY JUST ONE SIMPLE PHRASE FOR THE REST OF YOUR LIFE?

WHAT WOULD YOU TELL THE PEOPLE AROUND YOU WHO ARE YOUR SUBJECTS, YOUR COUSINS, YOUR ALLIES?

RRR

PTOO

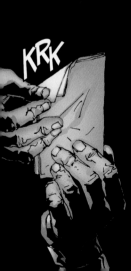

KRK

SORRY.

WHAT WOULD YOU SAY?

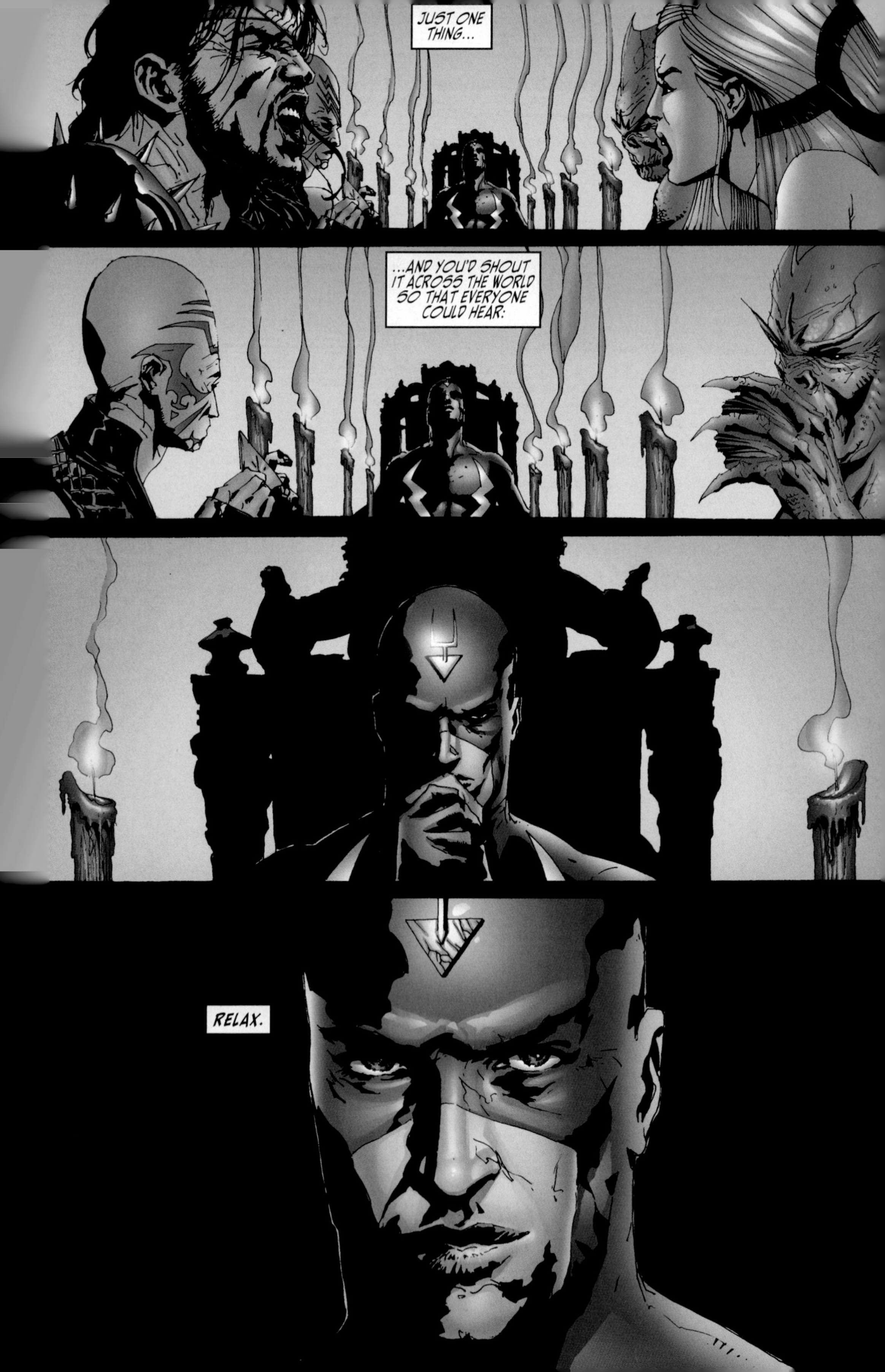
JUST ONE THING...
...AND YOU'D SHOUT IT ACROSS THE WORLD SO THAT EVERYONE COULD HEAR:
RELAX.

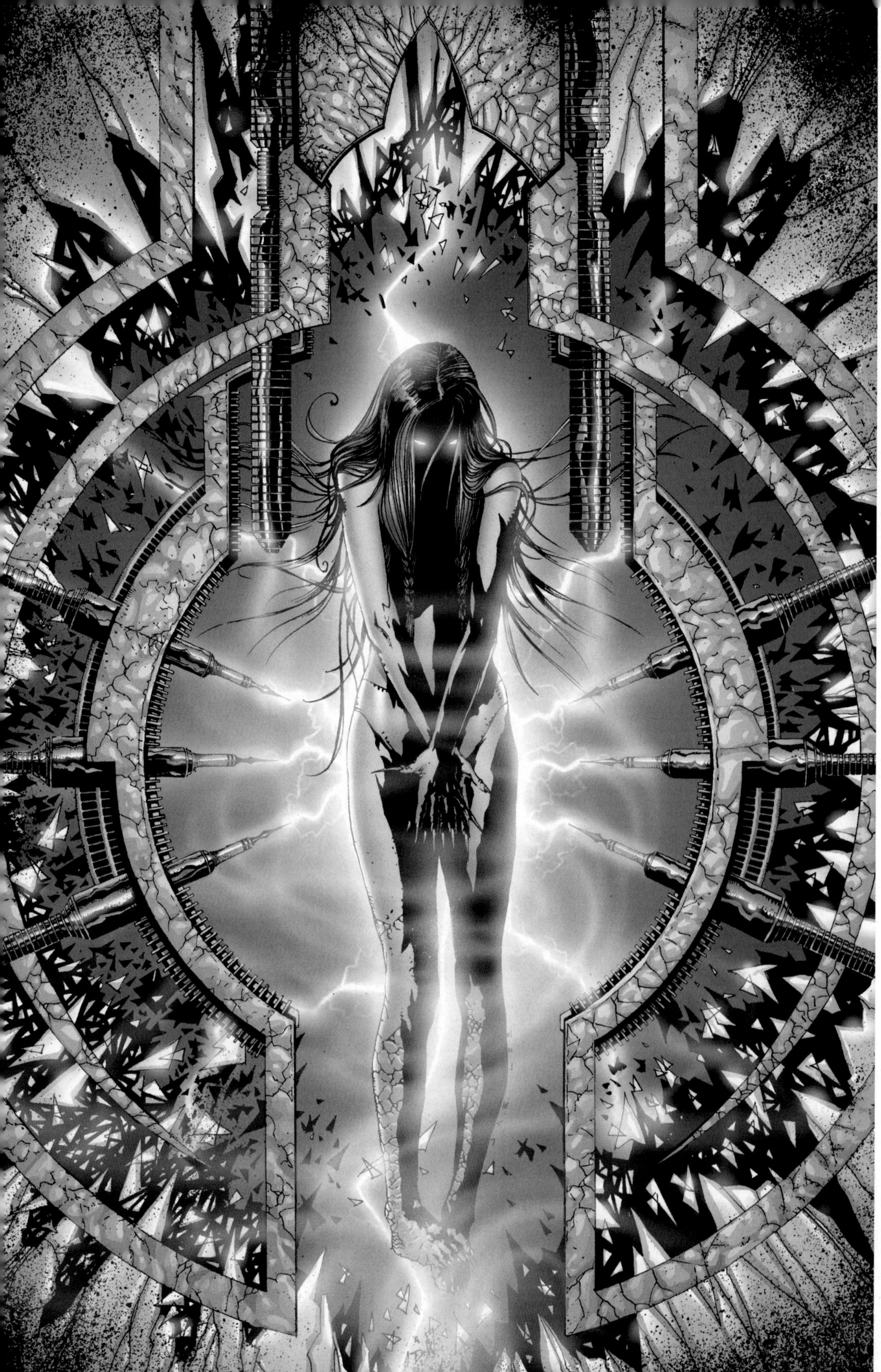

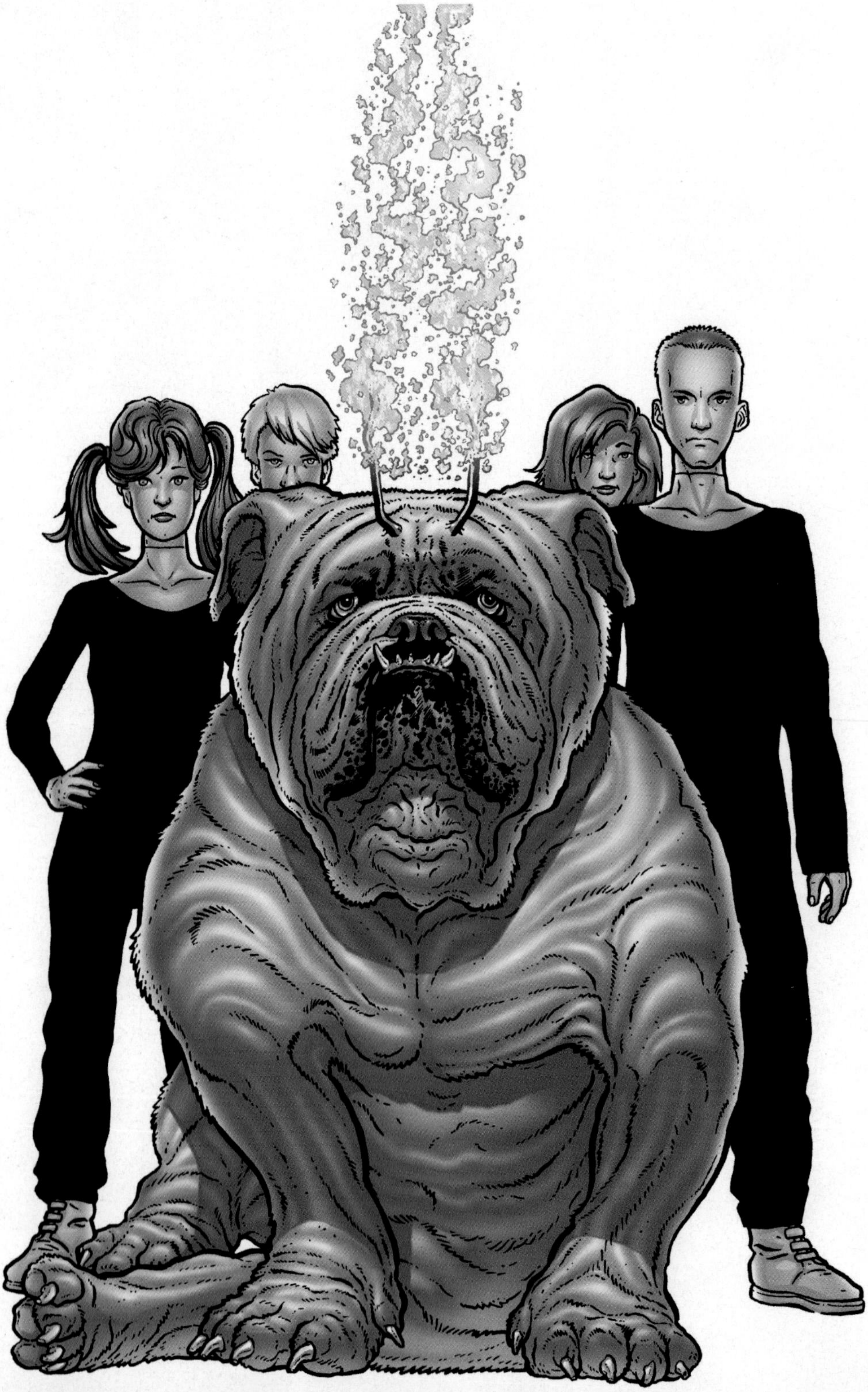

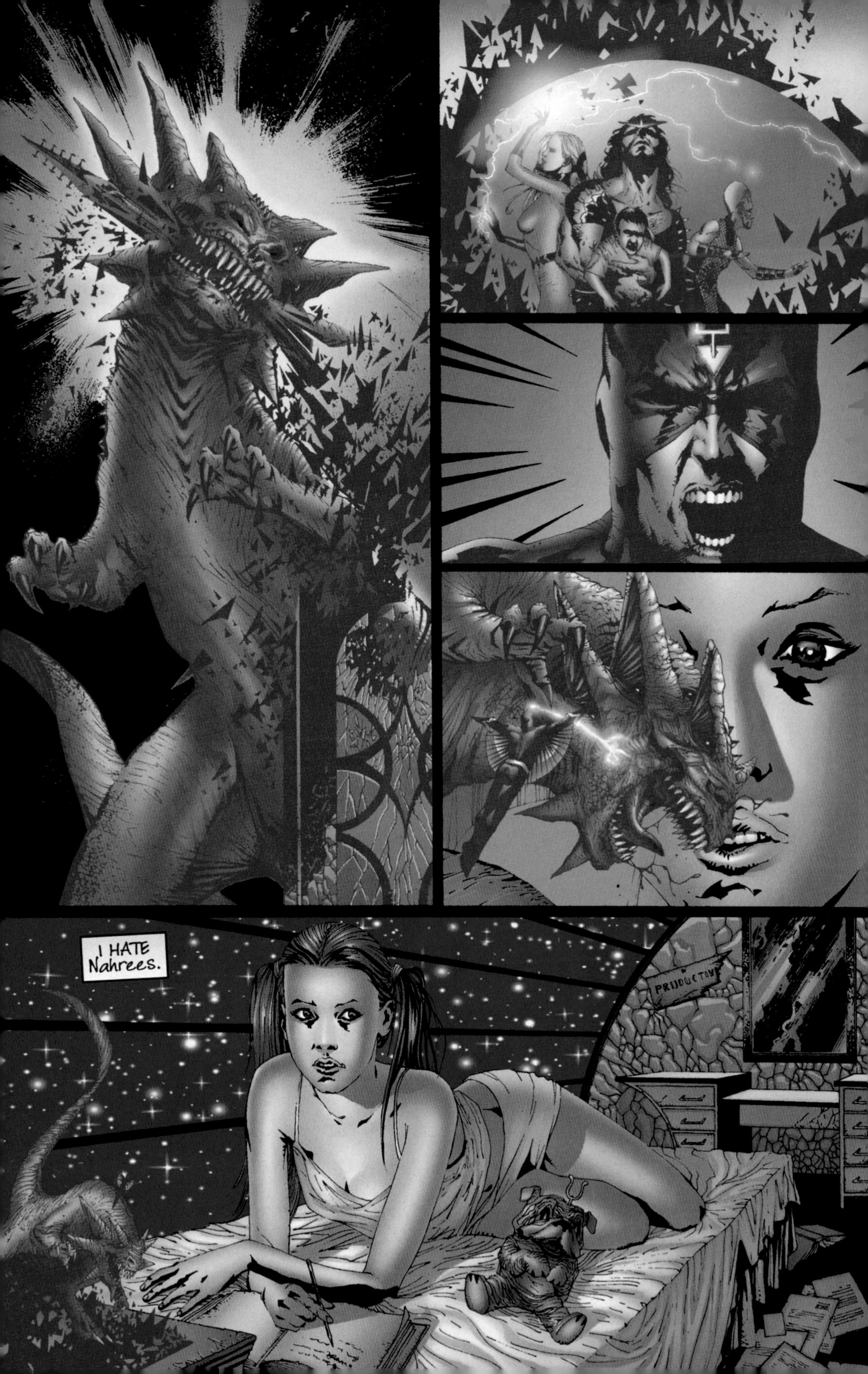
I HATE
Nahrees.

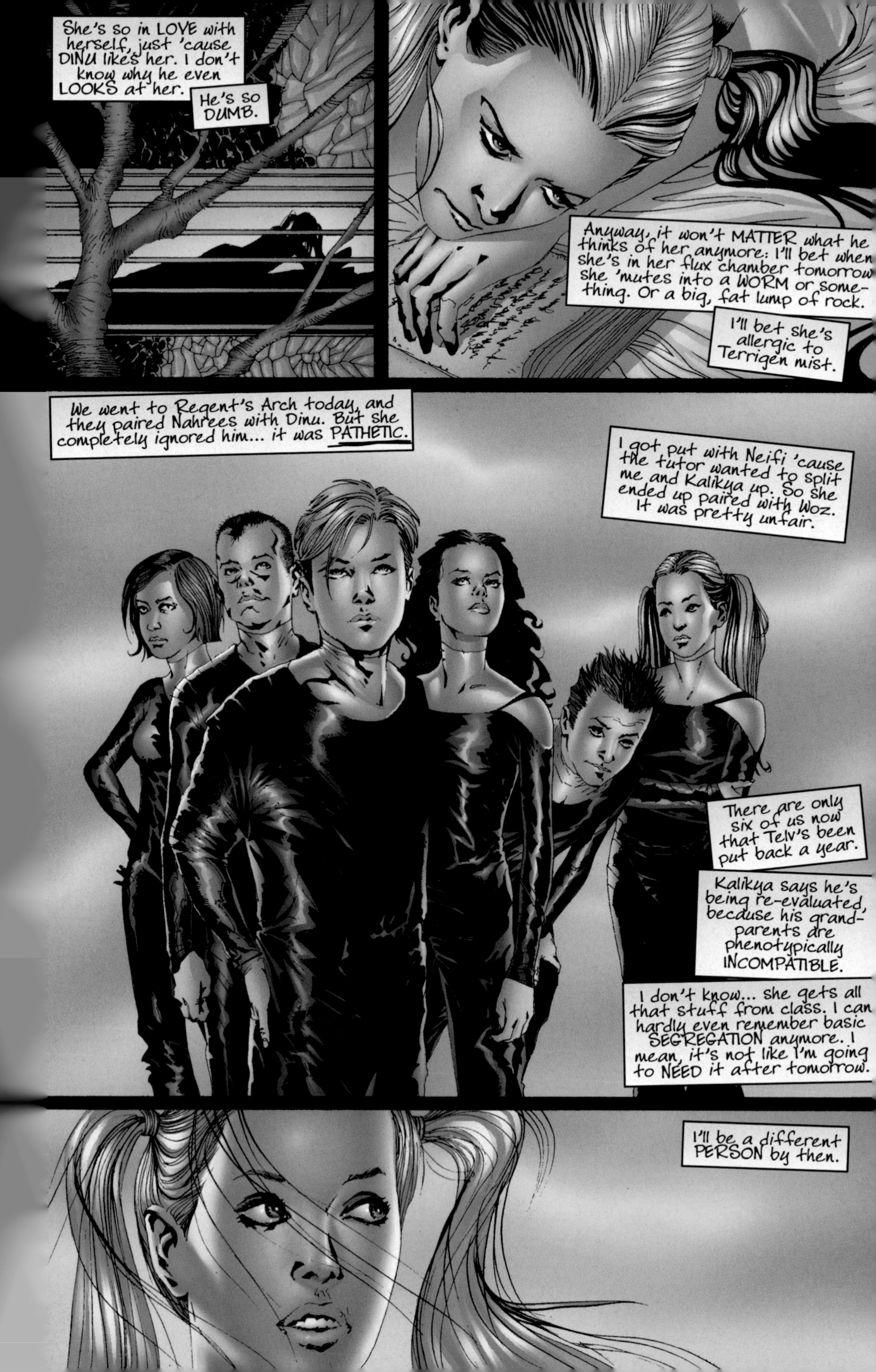
She's so in LOVE with herself, just 'cause DINU likes her. I don't know why he even LOOKS at her.
He's so DUMB.
Anyway, it won't MATTER what he thinks of her anymore: I'll bet when she's in her flux chamber tomorrow she 'mutes into a WORM or something. Or a big, fat lump of rock.
I'll bet she's allergic to Terrigen mist.
We went to Regent's Arch today, and they paired Nahrees with Dinu. But she completely ignored him... it was PATHETIC.
I got put with Neifi 'cause the tutor wanted to split me and Kalikya up. So she ended up paired with Woz. It was pretty unfair.
There are only six of us now that Telv's been put back a year.
Kalikya says he's being re-evaluated, because his grand-parents are phenotypically INCOMPATIBLE.
I don't know... she gets all that stuff from class. I can hardly even remember basic SEGREGATION anymore. I mean, it's not like I'm going to NEED it after tomorrow.
I'll be a different PERSON by then.

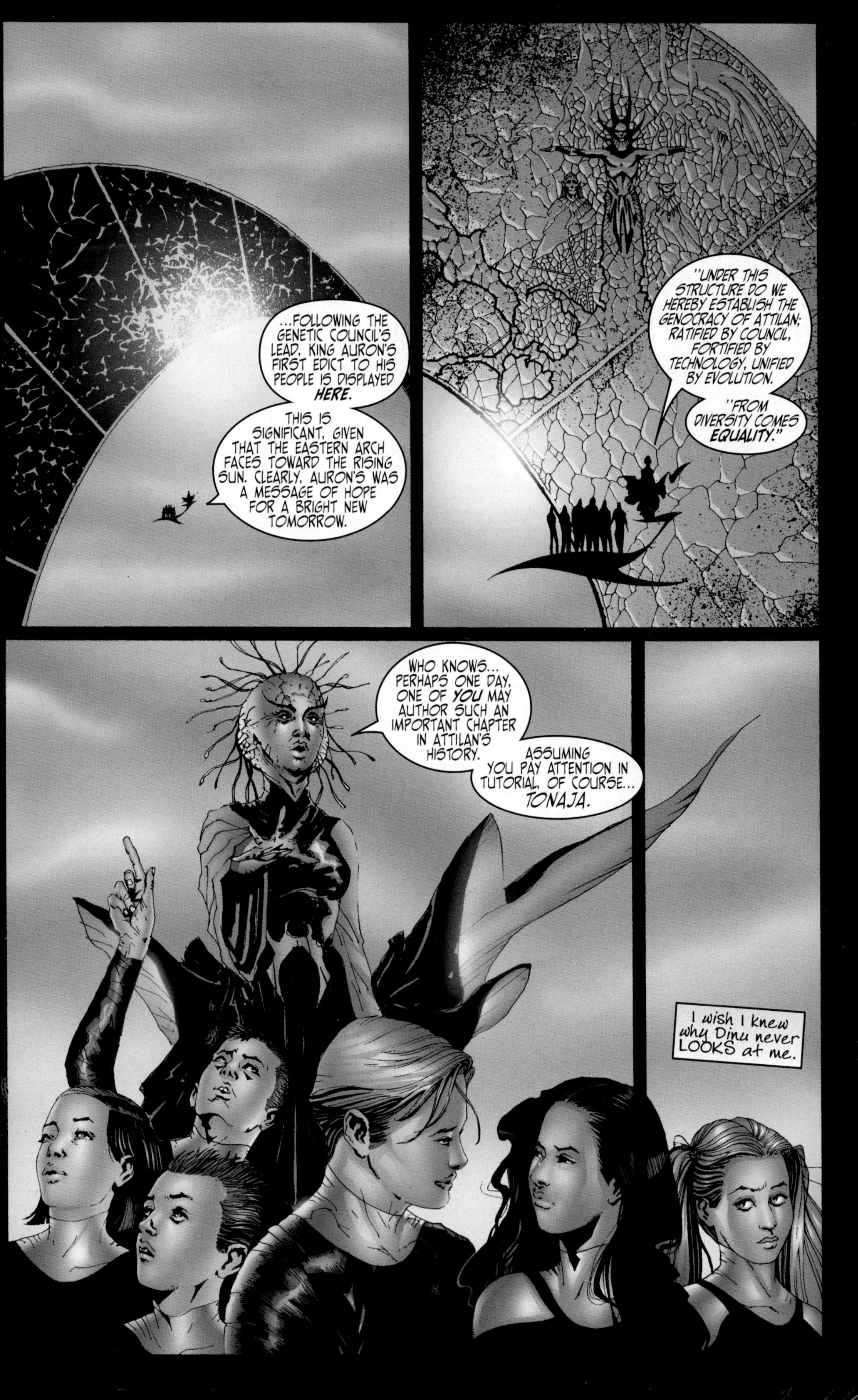
...FOLLOWING THE GENETIC COUNCIL'S LEAD, KING AURON'S FIRST EDICT TO HIS PEOPLE IS DISPLAYED HERE.
THIS IS SIGNIFICANT, GIVEN THAT THE EASTERN ARCH FACES TOWARD THE RISING SUN. CLEARLY, AURON'S WAS A MESSAGE OF HOPE FOR A BRIGHT NEW TOMORROW.
"UNDER THIS STRUCTURE DO WE HEREBY ESTABLISH THE GENOCRACY OF ATTILAN: RATIFIED BY COUNCIL, FORTIFIED BY TECHNOLOGY, UNIFIED BY EVOLUTION.
"FROM DIVERSITY COMES EQUALITY."
WHO KNOWS... PERHAPS ONE DAY, ONE OF YOU MAY AUTHOR SUCH AN IMPORTANT CHAPTER IN ATTILAN'S HISTORY.
ASSUMING YOU PAY ATTENTION IN TUTORIAL, OF COURSE... TONAJA.
I wish I knew why Dinu never LOOKS at me.

It's 'cause my nose is too big. Maybe I'll get lucky or something, and it'll disappedr completely.

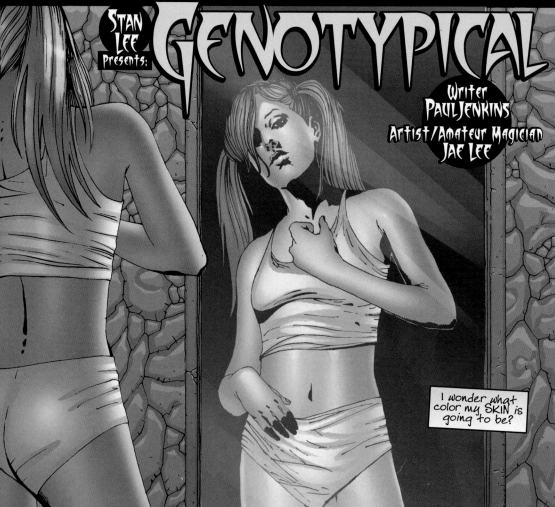

STAN LEE presents: GENOTYPICAL

Writer PAUL JENKINS

Artist/Amateur Magician JAE LEE

I wonder what color my SKIN is going to be?

DAVE KEMP/AVALON
Colorist, Gent, Toff

RS & COMICRAFT/DL
Calligraphers

QUESADA & PALMIOTTI
Keepers of the Myth

NANCI DAKESIAN
Keeping Jae on his Toes

BOB HARRAS
High Priest

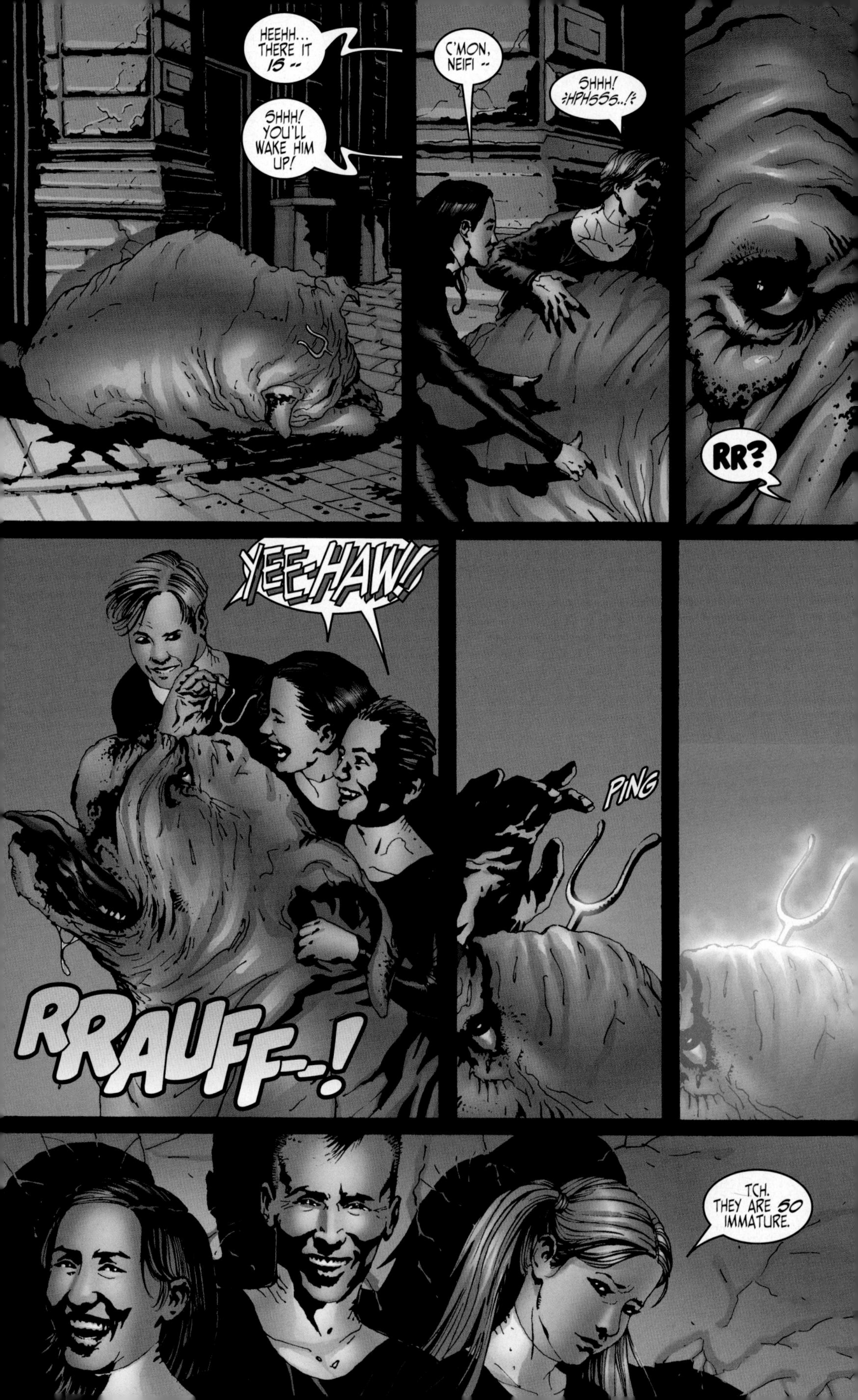
HEEHH... THERE IT IS --
SHHH! YOU'LL WAKE HIM UP!
C'MON, NEIFI --
SHHH! ;HPHSSS..!;
RR?
YEE-HAW!!
RRAUFF--!
PING
TCH. THEY ARE SO IMMATURE.

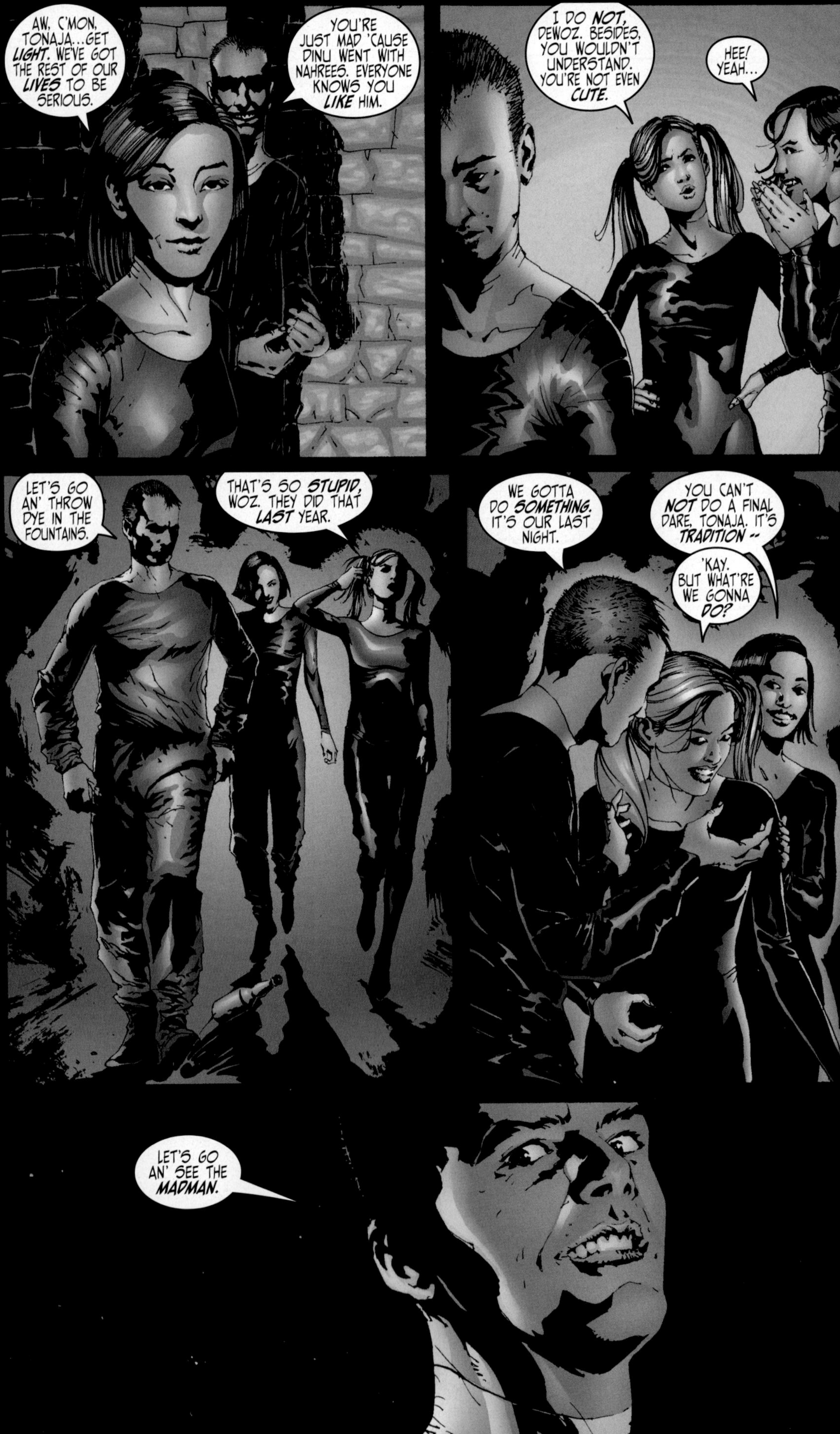
AW, C'MON, TONAJA...GET LIGHT. WE'VE GOT THE REST OF OUR LIVES TO BE SERIOUS.
YOU'RE JUST MAD 'CAUSE DINU WENT WITH NAHREES. EVERYONE KNOWS YOU LIKE HIM.
I DO NOT, DEWOZ. BESIDES, YOU WOULDN'T UNDERSTAND. YOU'RE NOT EVEN CUTE.
HEE! YEAH...
LET'S GO AN' THROW DYE IN THE FOUNTAINS.
THAT'S SO STUPID, WOZ. THEY DID THAT LAST YEAR.
WE GOTTA DO SOMETHING. IT'S OUR LAST NIGHT.
YOU CAN'T NOT DO A FINAL DARE, TONAJA. IT'S TRADITION --
'KAY. BUT WHAT'RE WE GONNA DO?
LET'S GO AN' SEE THE MADMAN.

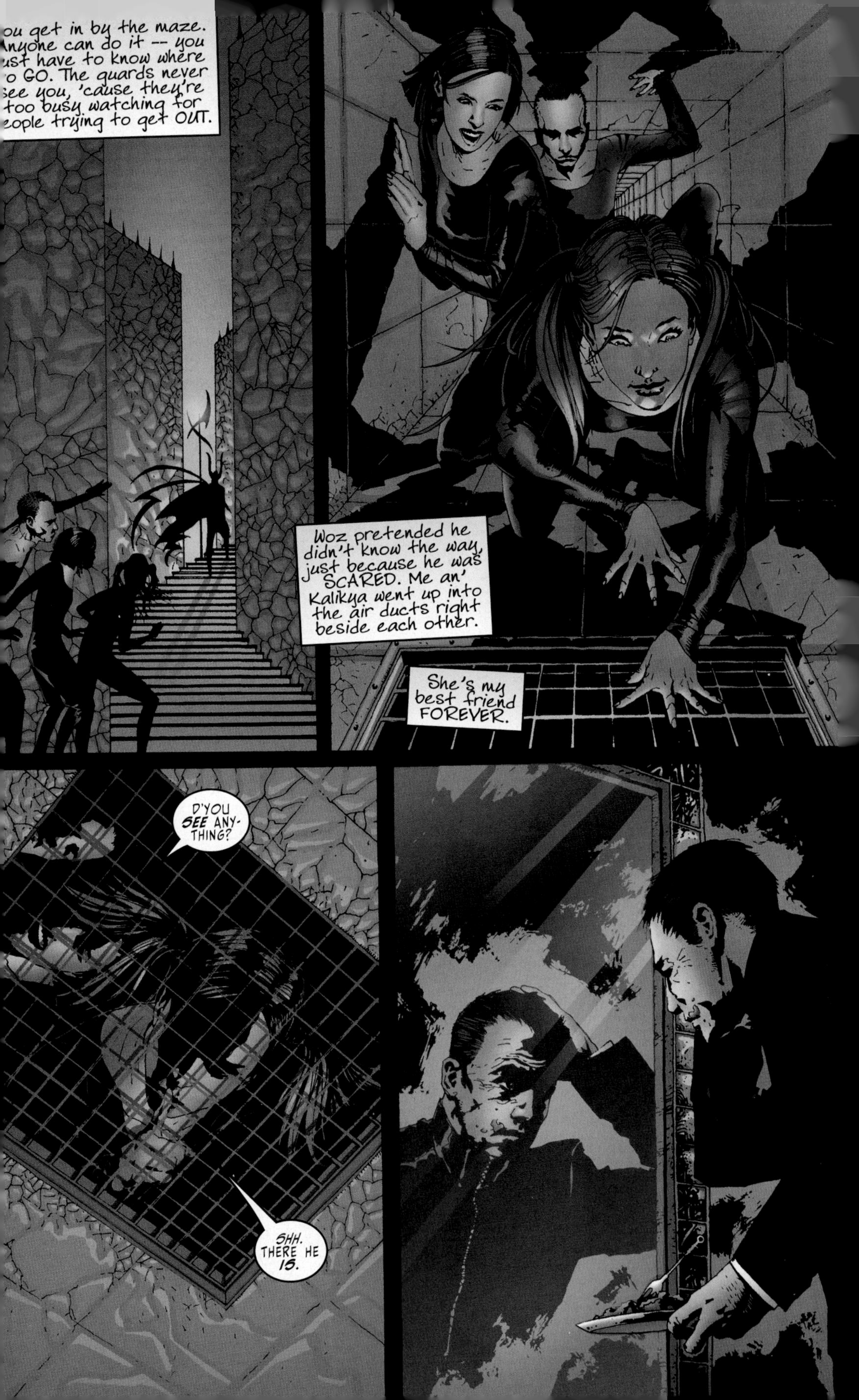
ou get in by the maze. Anyone can do it -- you ust have to know where o GO. The guards never see you, 'cause they're too busy watching for eople trying to get OUT.
Woz pretended he didn't know the way, just because he was SCARED. Me an' Kalikya went up into the air ducts right beside each other.
She's my best friend FOREVER.
D'YOU SEE ANY-THING?
SHH. THERE HE IS.

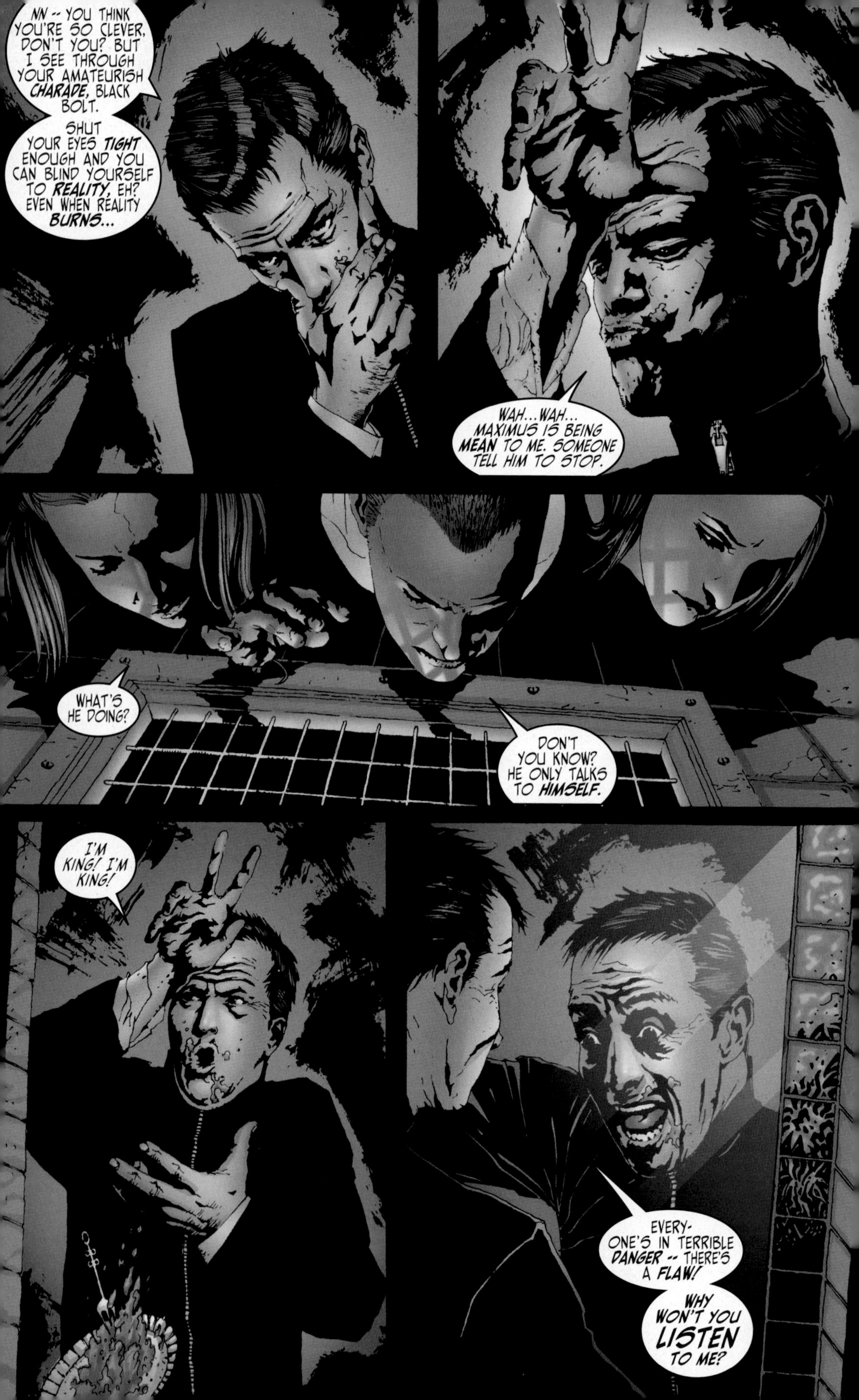
NN -- YOU THINK YOU'RE SO CLEVER, DON'T YOU? BUT I SEE THROUGH YOUR AMATEURISH CHARADE, BLACK BOLT.
SHUT YOUR EYES TIGHT ENOUGH AND YOU CAN BLIND YOURSELF TO REALITY, EH? EVEN WHEN REALITY BURNS...
WAH...WAH... MAXIMUS IS BEING MEAN TO ME. SOMEONE TELL HIM TO STOP.
WHAT'S HE DOING?
DON'T YOU KNOW? HE ONLY TALKS TO HIMSELF.
I'M KING! I'M KING!
EVERY-ONE'S IN TERRIBLE DANGER -- THERE'S A FLAW!
WHY WON'T YOU LISTEN TO ME?

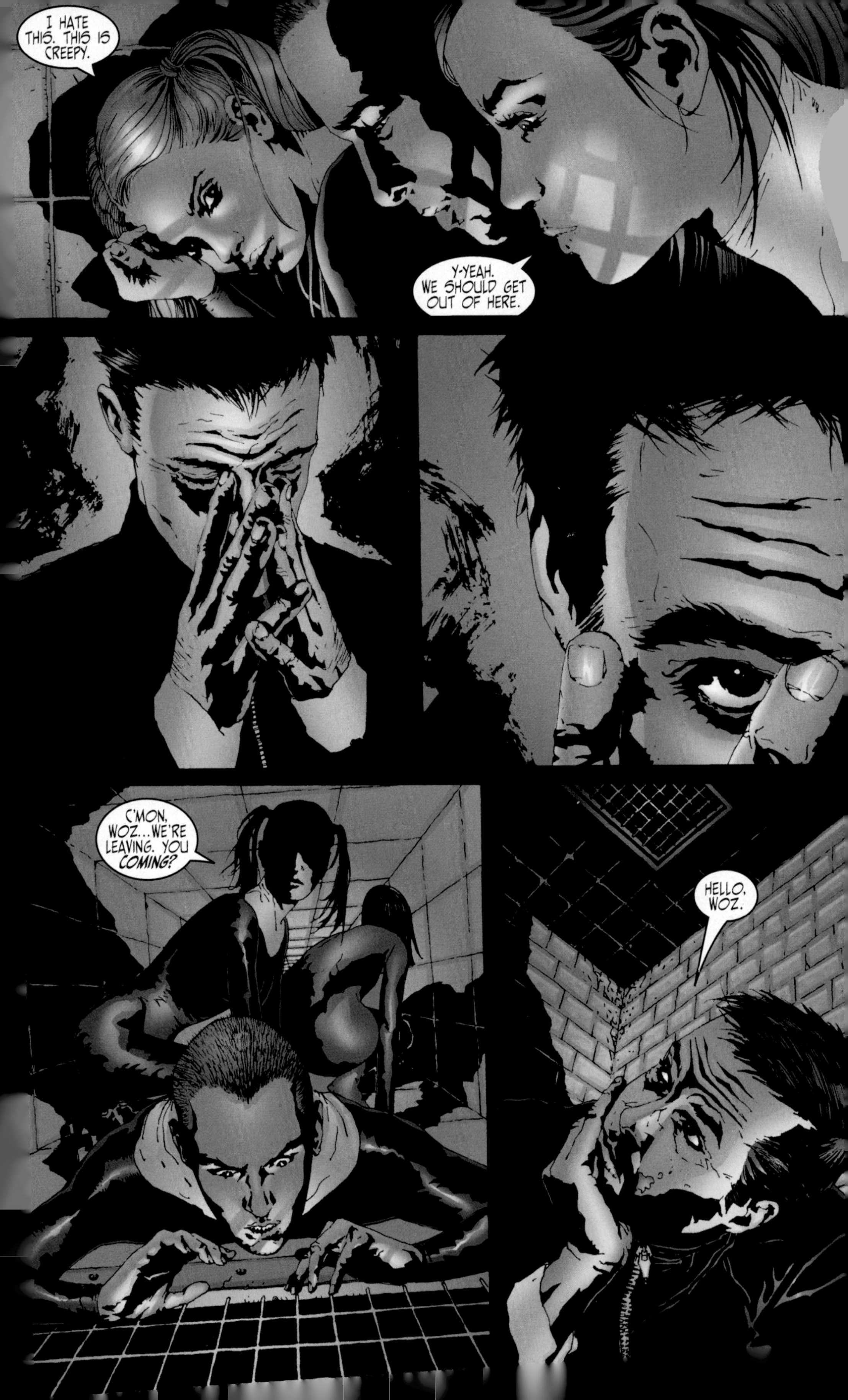
I HATE THIS. THIS IS CREEPY.
Y-YEAH. WE SHOULD GET OUT OF HERE.
C'MON, WOZ...WE'RE LEAVING. YOU *COMING?*
HELLO, WOZ.

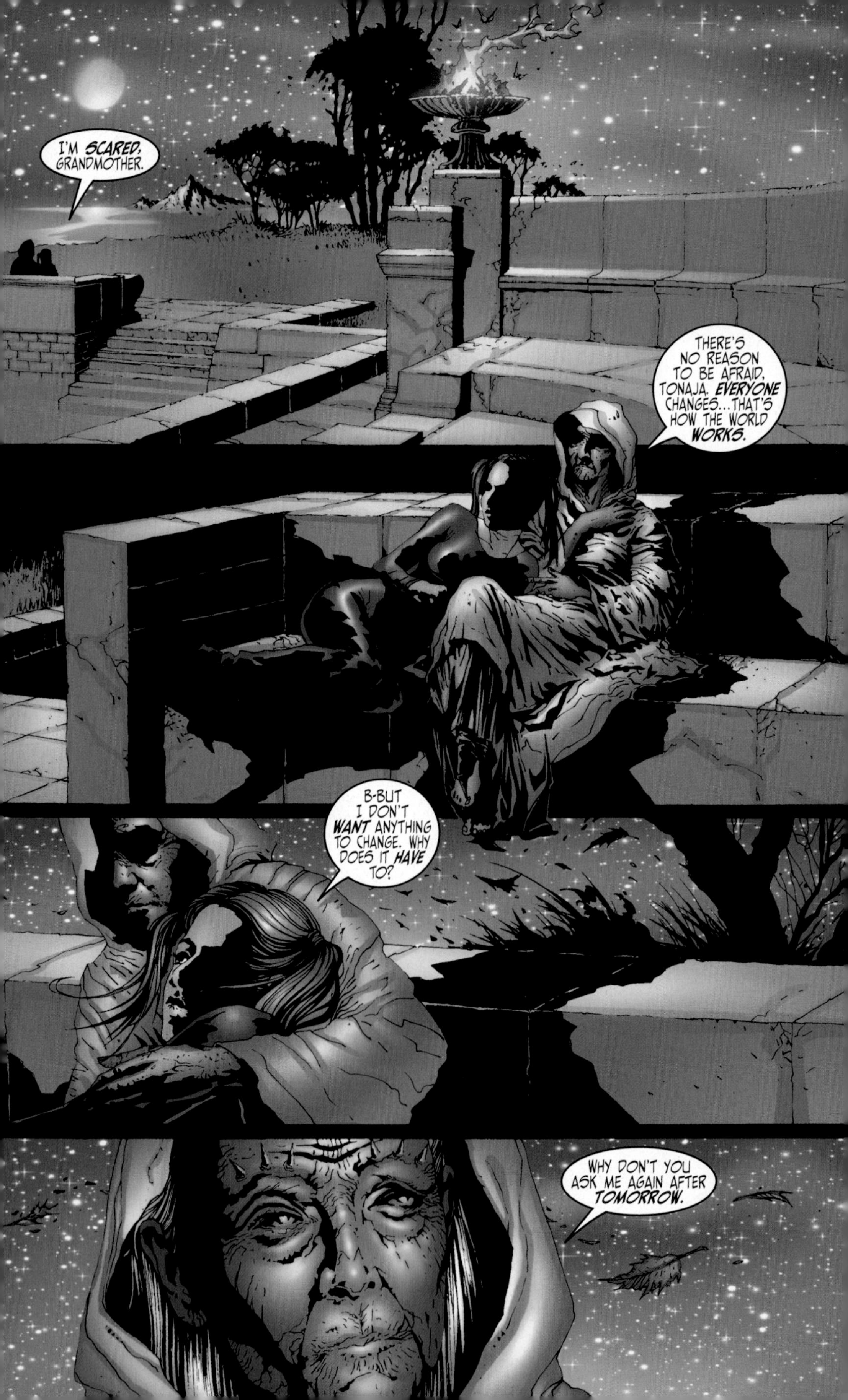
I'M SCARED, GRANDMOTHER.
THERE'S NO REASON TO BE AFRAID, TONAJA. EVERYONE CHANGES...THAT'S HOW THE WORLD WORKS.
B-BUT I DON'T WANT ANYTHING TO CHANGE. WHY DOES IT HAVE TO?
WHY DON'T YOU ASK ME AGAIN AFTER TOMORROW.

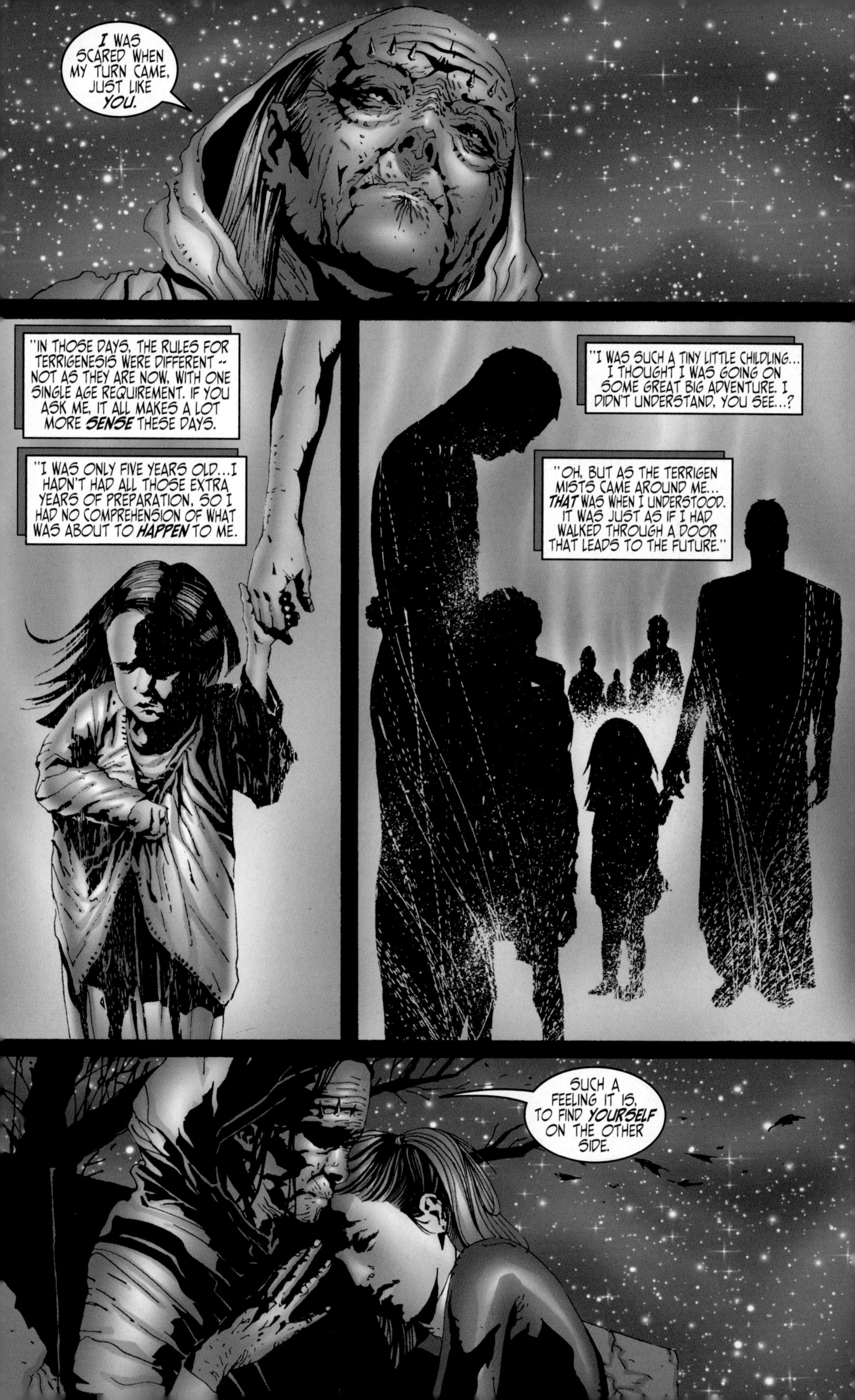
I WAS SCARED WHEN MY TURN CAME, JUST LIKE YOU.
"IN THOSE DAYS, THE RULES FOR TERRIGENESIS WERE DIFFERENT -- NOT AS THEY ARE NOW, WITH ONE SINGLE AGE REQUIREMENT. IF YOU ASK ME, IT ALL MAKES A LOT MORE SENSE THESE DAYS.
"I WAS ONLY FIVE YEARS OLD...I HADN'T HAD ALL THOSE EXTRA YEARS OF PREPARATION, SO I HAD NO COMPREHENSION OF WHAT WAS ABOUT TO HAPPEN TO ME.
"I WAS SUCH A TINY LITTLE CHILDLING... I THOUGHT I WAS GOING ON SOME GREAT BIG ADVENTURE. I DIDN'T UNDERSTAND, YOU SEE...?
"OH, BUT AS THE TERRIGEN MISTS CAME AROUND ME... THAT WAS WHEN I UNDERSTOOD. IT WAS JUST AS IF I HAD WALKED THROUGH A DOOR THAT LEADS TO THE FUTURE."
SUCH A FEELING IT IS, TO FIND YOURSELF ON THE OTHER SIDE.

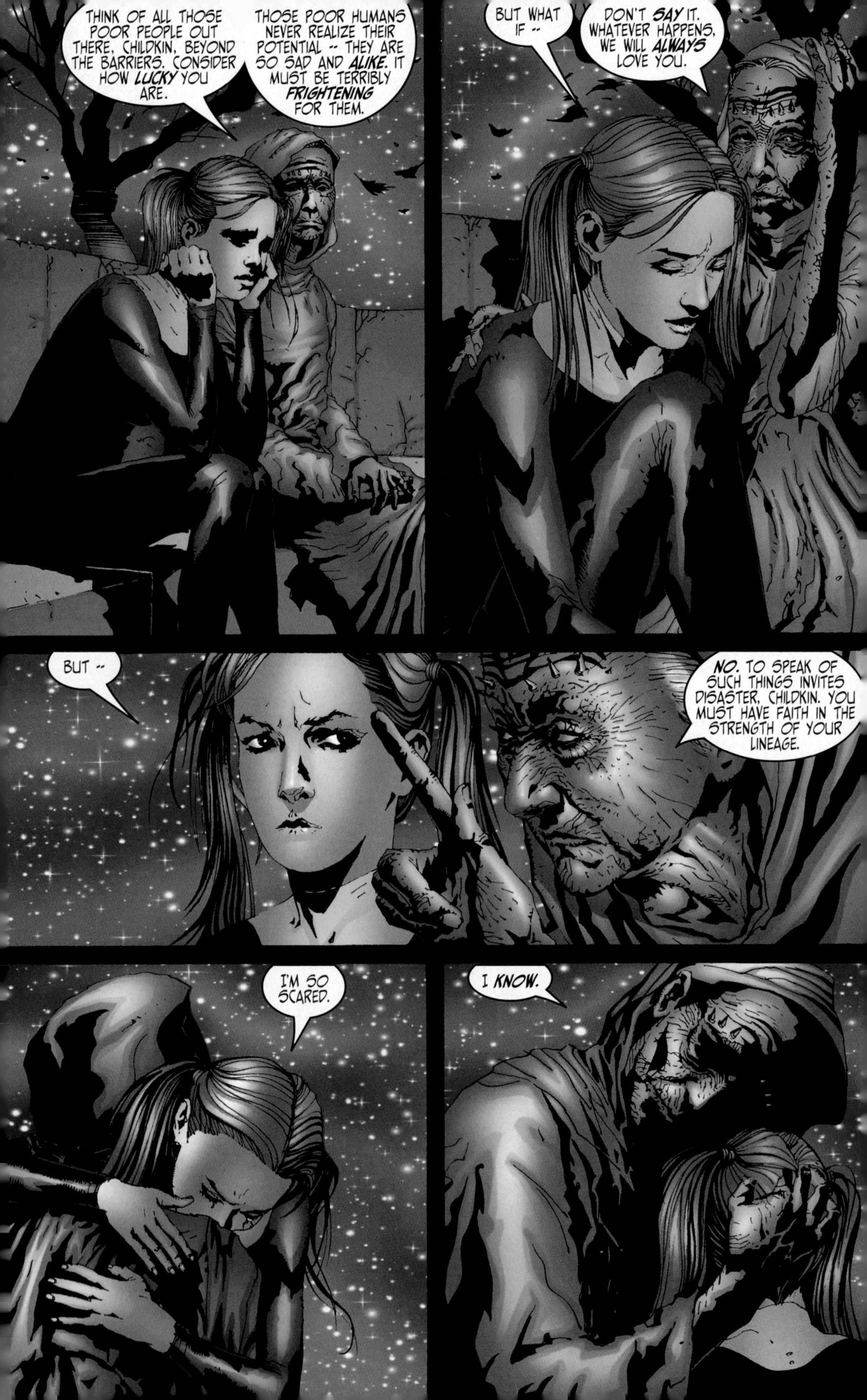
THINK OF ALL THOSE POOR PEOPLE OUT THERE, CHILDKIN, BEYOND THE BARRIERS. CONSIDER HOW LUCKY YOU ARE.
THOSE POOR HUMANS NEVER REALIZE THEIR POTENTIAL -- THEY ARE SO SAD AND ALIKE. IT MUST BE TERRIBLY FRIGHTENING FOR THEM.
BUT WHAT IF --
DON'T SAY IT. WHATEVER HAPPENS, WE WILL ALWAYS LOVE YOU.
BUT --
NO. TO SPEAK OF SUCH THINGS INVITES DISASTER, CHILDKIN. YOU MUST HAVE FAITH IN THE STRENGTH OF YOUR LINEAGE.
I'M SO SCARED.
I KNOW.

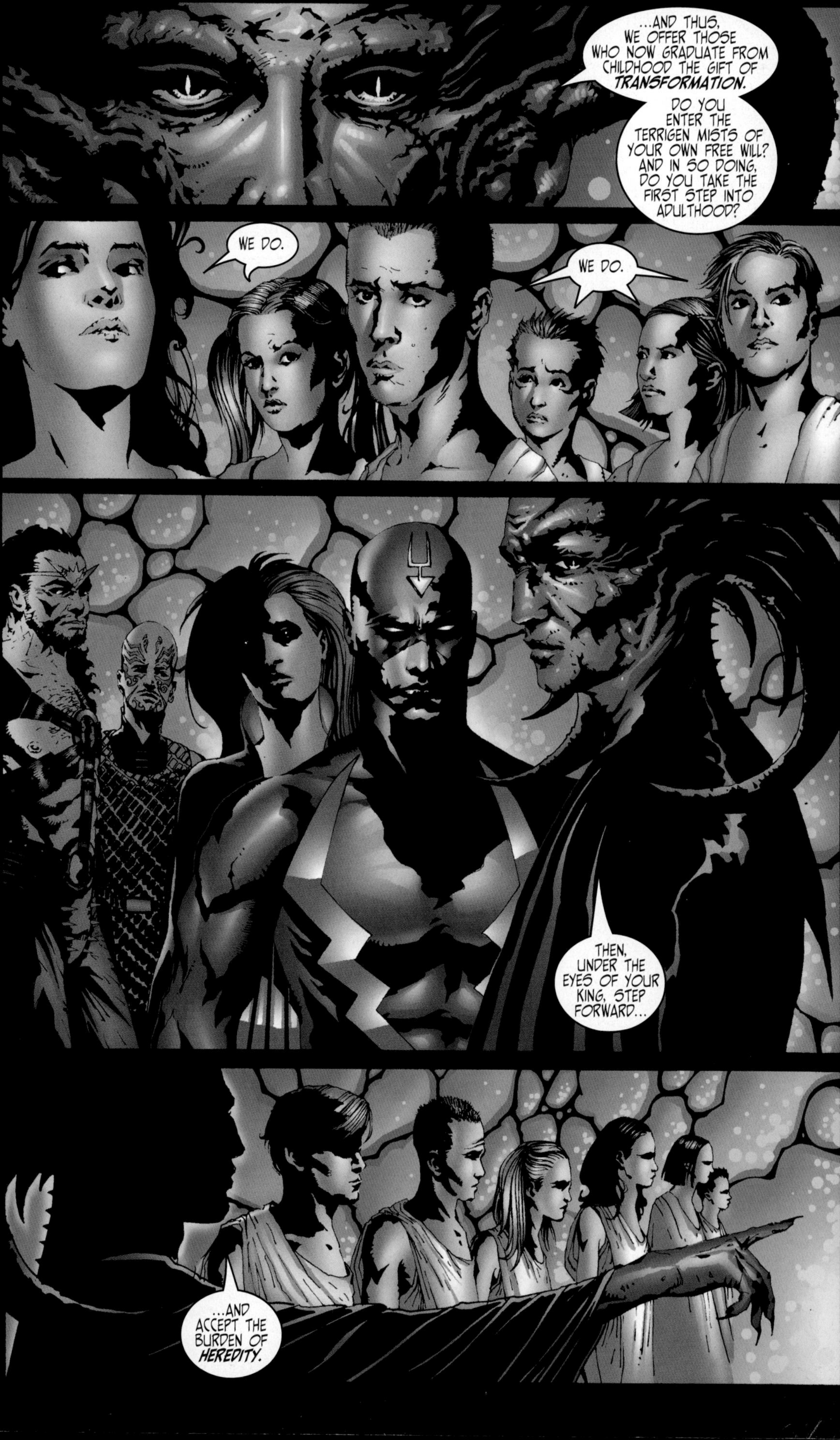
...AND THUS, WE OFFER THOSE WHO NOW GRADUATE FROM CHILDHOOD THE GIFT OF TRANSFORMATION.
DO YOU ENTER THE TERRIGEN MISTS OF YOUR OWN FREE WILL? AND IN SO DOING, DO YOU TAKE THE FIRST STEP INTO ADULTHOOD?
WE DO.
WE DO.
THEN, UNDER THE EYES OF YOUR KING, STEP FORWARD...
...AND ACCEPT THE BURDEN OF HEREDITY.

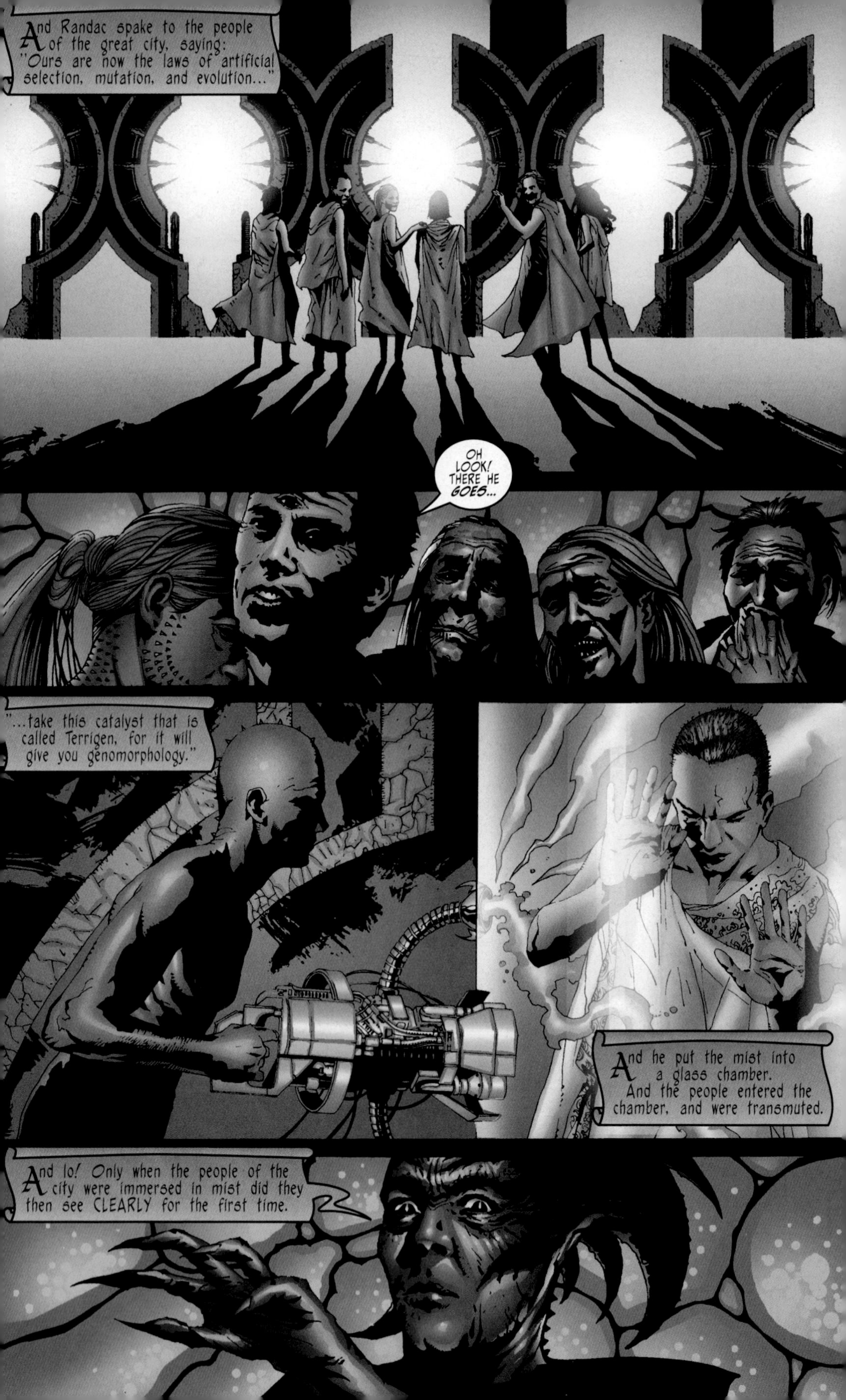
And Randac spake to the people of the great city, saying: "Ours are now the laws of artificial selection, mutation, and evolution..."
OH LOOK! THERE HE GOES...
"...take this catalyst that is called Terrigen, for it will give you genomorphology."
And he put the mist into a glass chamber. And the people entered the chamber, and were transmuted.
And lo! Only when the people of the city were immersed in mist did they then see CLEARLY for the first time.

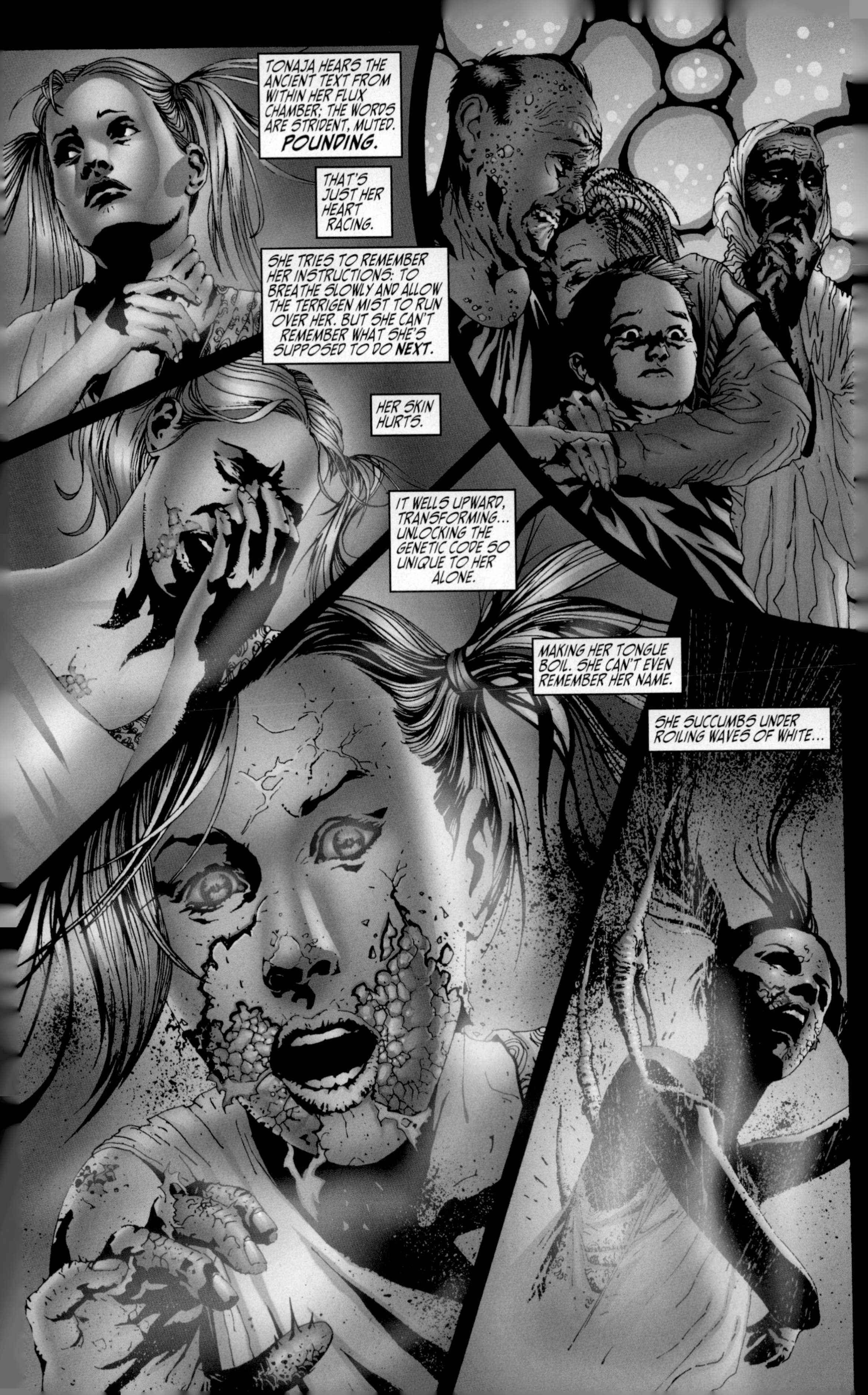
TONAJA HEARS THE ANCIENT TEXT FROM WITHIN HER FLUX CHAMBER; THE WORDS ARE STRIDENT, MUTED. **POUNDING.**
THAT'S JUST HER HEART RACING.
SHE TRIES TO REMEMBER HER INSTRUCTIONS: TO BREATHE SLOWLY AND ALLOW THE TERRIGEN MIST TO RUN OVER HER. BUT SHE CAN'T REMEMBER WHAT SHE'S SUPPOSED TO DO **NEXT.**
HER SKIN HURTS.
IT WELLS UPWARD, TRANSFORMING... UNLOCKING THE GENETIC CODE SO UNIQUE TO HER ALONE.
MAKING HER TONGUE BOIL. SHE CAN'T EVEN REMEMBER HER NAME.
SHE SUCCUMBS UNDER ROILING WAVES OF WHITE...

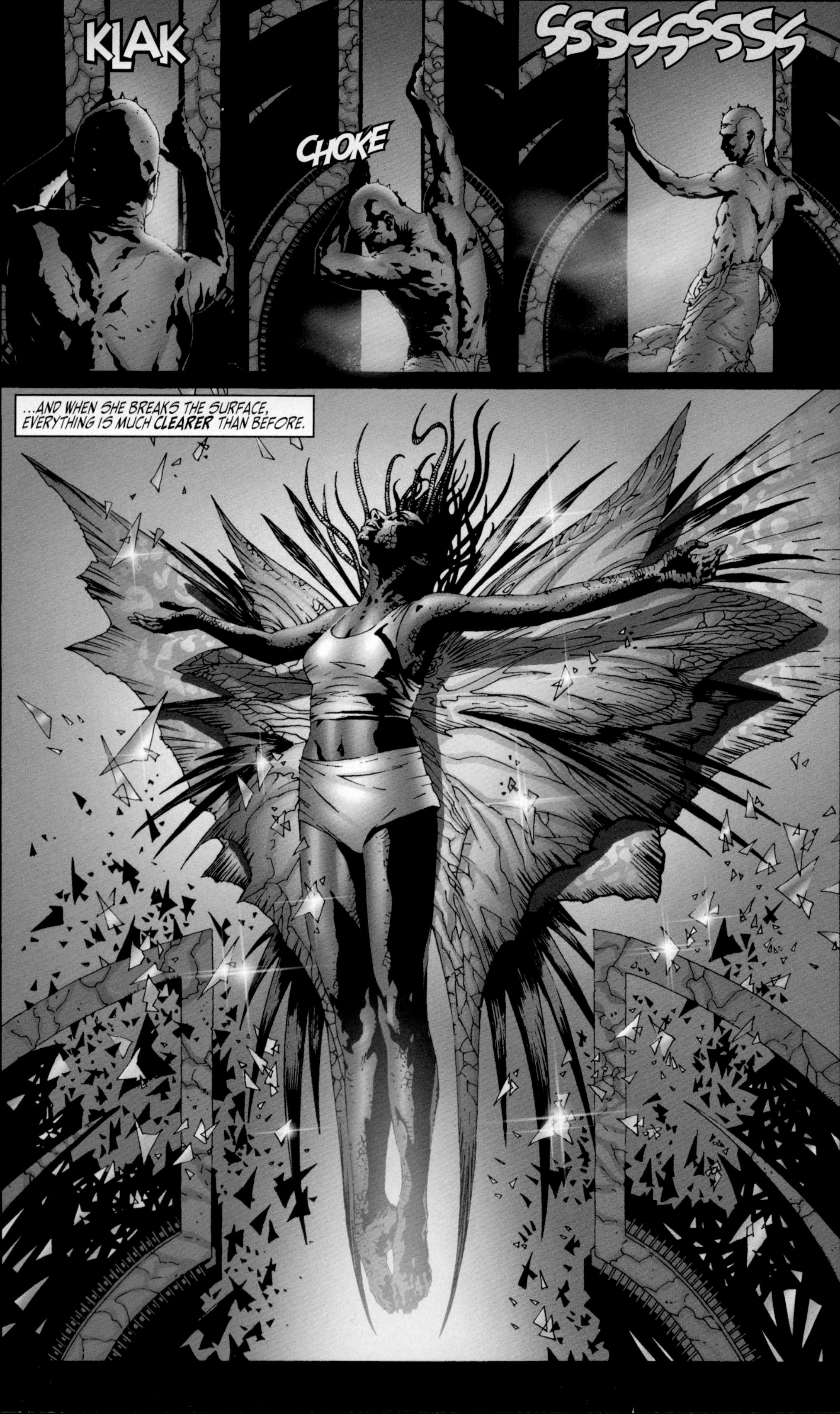
KLAK
CHOKE
SSSSSSSSS
...AND WHEN SHE BREAKS THE SURFACE, EVERYTHING IS MUCH CLEARER THAN BEFORE.

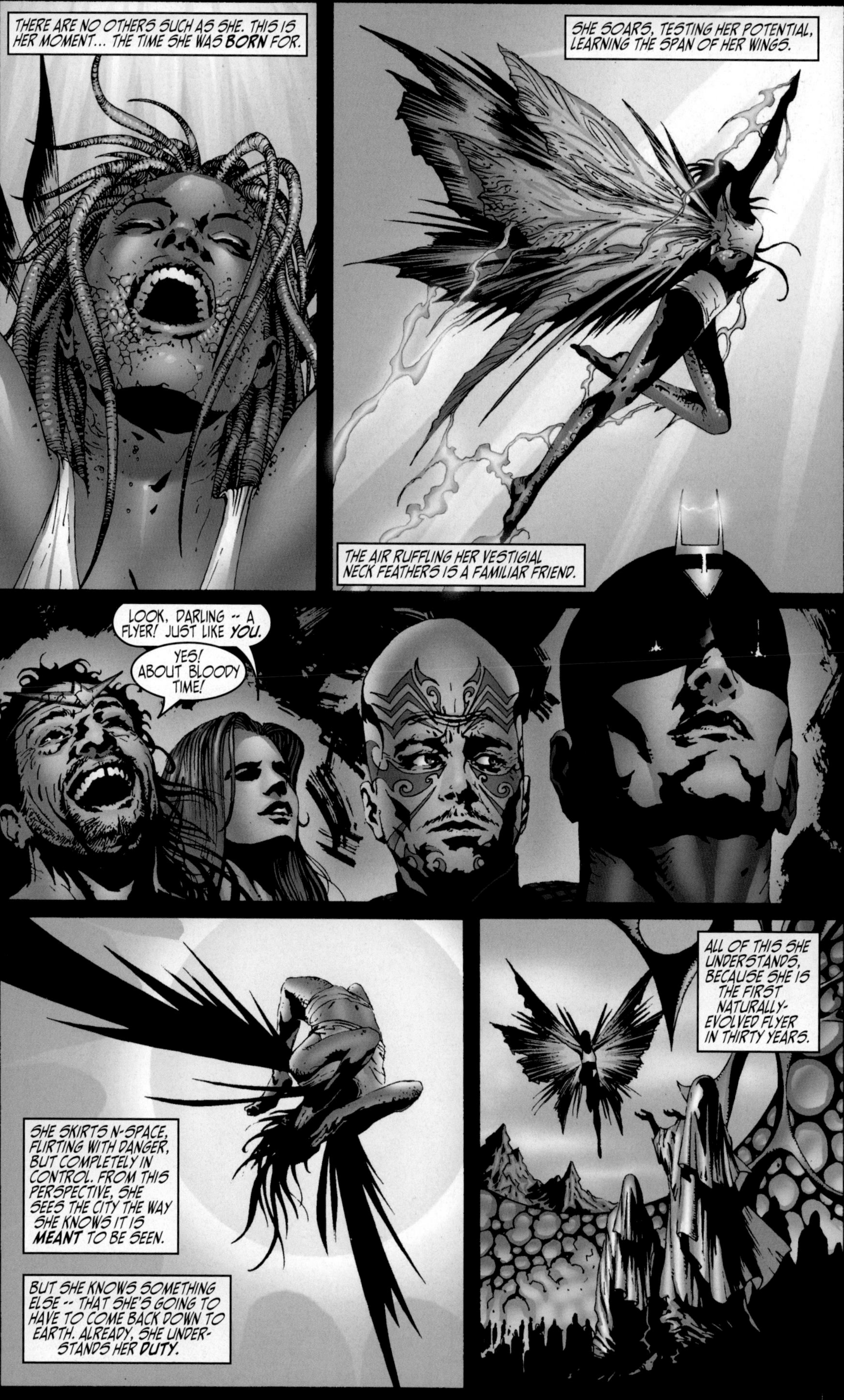
THERE ARE NO OTHERS SUCH AS SHE. THIS IS HER MOMENT... THE TIME SHE WAS BORN FOR.
SHE SOARS, TESTING HER POTENTIAL, LEARNING THE SPAN OF HER WINGS.
THE AIR RUFFLING HER VESTIGIAL NECK FEATHERS IS A FAMILIAR FRIEND.
LOOK, DARLING -- A FLYER! JUST LIKE YOU.
YES! ABOUT BLOODY TIME!
SHE SKIRTS N-SPACE, FLIRTING WITH DANGER, BUT COMPLETELY IN CONTROL. FROM THIS PERSPECTIVE, SHE SEES THE CITY THE WAY SHE KNOWS IT IS MEANT TO BE SEEN.
BUT SHE KNOWS SOMETHING ELSE -- THAT SHE'S GOING TO HAVE TO COME BACK DOWN TO EARTH. ALREADY, SHE UNDERSTANDS HER DUTY.
ALL OF THIS SHE UNDERSTANDS, BECAUSE SHE IS THE FIRST NATURALLY-EVOLVED FLYER IN THIRTY YEARS.

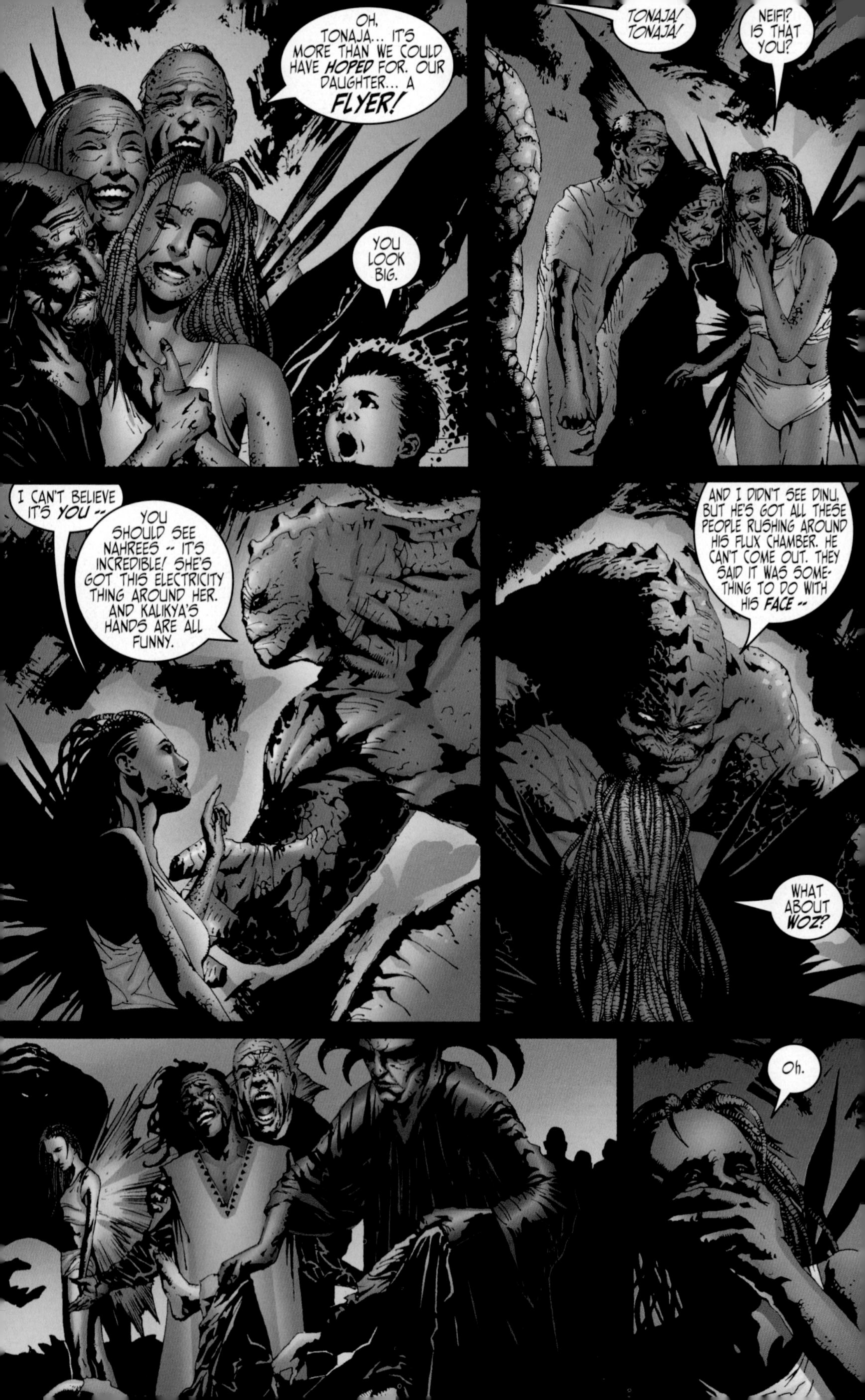
OH, TONAJA... IT'S MORE THAN WE COULD HAVE HOPED FOR. OUR DAUGHTER... A FLYER!
YOU LOOK BIG.
TONAJA! TONAJA!
NEIFI? IS THAT YOU?
I CAN'T BELIEVE IT'S YOU --
YOU SHOULD SEE NAHREES -- IT'S INCREDIBLE! SHE'S GOT THIS ELECTRICITY THING AROUND HER. AND KALIKYA'S HANDS ARE ALL FUNNY.
AND I DIDN'T SEE DINU, BUT HE'S GOT ALL THESE PEOPLE RUSHING AROUND HIS FLUX CHAMBER. HE CAN'T COME OUT. THEY SAID IT WAS SOMETHING TO DO WITH HIS FACE --
WHAT ABOUT WOZ?
Oh.

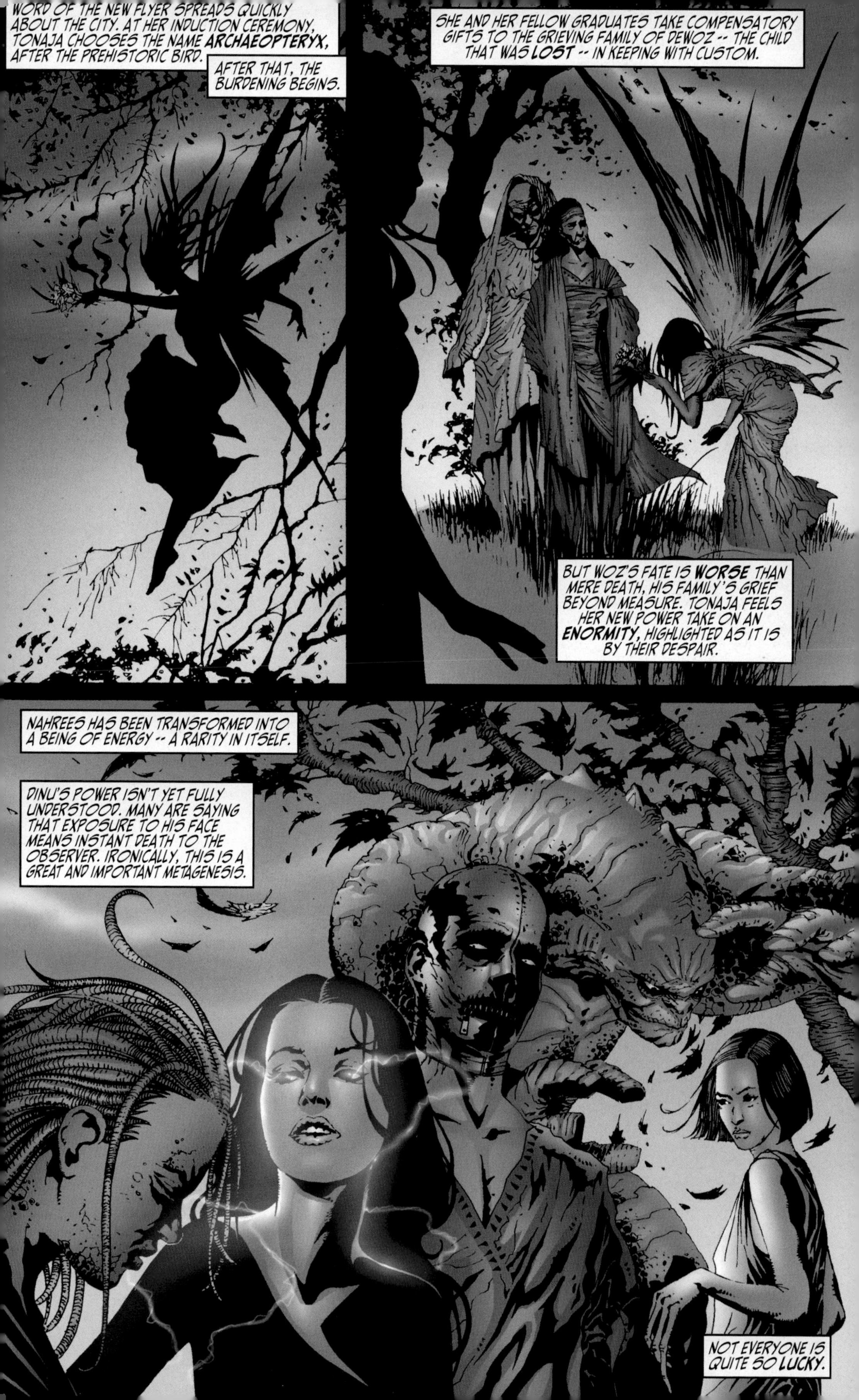
WORD OF THE NEW FLYER SPREADS QUICKLY ABOUT THE CITY. AT HER INDUCTION CEREMONY, TONAJA CHOOSES THE NAME ARCHAEOPTERYX, AFTER THE PREHISTORIC BIRD.
AFTER THAT, THE BURDENING BEGINS.
SHE AND HER FELLOW GRADUATES TAKE COMPENSATORY GIFTS TO THE GRIEVING FAMILY OF DEWOZ -- THE CHILD THAT WAS LOST -- IN KEEPING WITH CUSTOM.
BUT WOZ'S FATE IS WORSE THAN MERE DEATH, HIS FAMILY'S GRIEF BEYOND MEASURE. TONAJA FEELS HER NEW POWER TAKE ON AN ENORMITY, HIGHLIGHTED AS IT IS BY THEIR DESPAIR.
NAHREES HAS BEEN TRANSFORMED INTO A BEING OF ENERGY -- A RARITY IN ITSELF.
DINU'S POWER ISN'T YET FULLY UNDERSTOOD. MANY ARE SAYING THAT EXPOSURE TO HIS FACE MEANS INSTANT DEATH TO THE OBSERVER. IRONICALLY, THIS IS A GREAT AND IMPORTANT METAGENESIS.
NOT EVERYONE IS QUITE SO LUCKY.

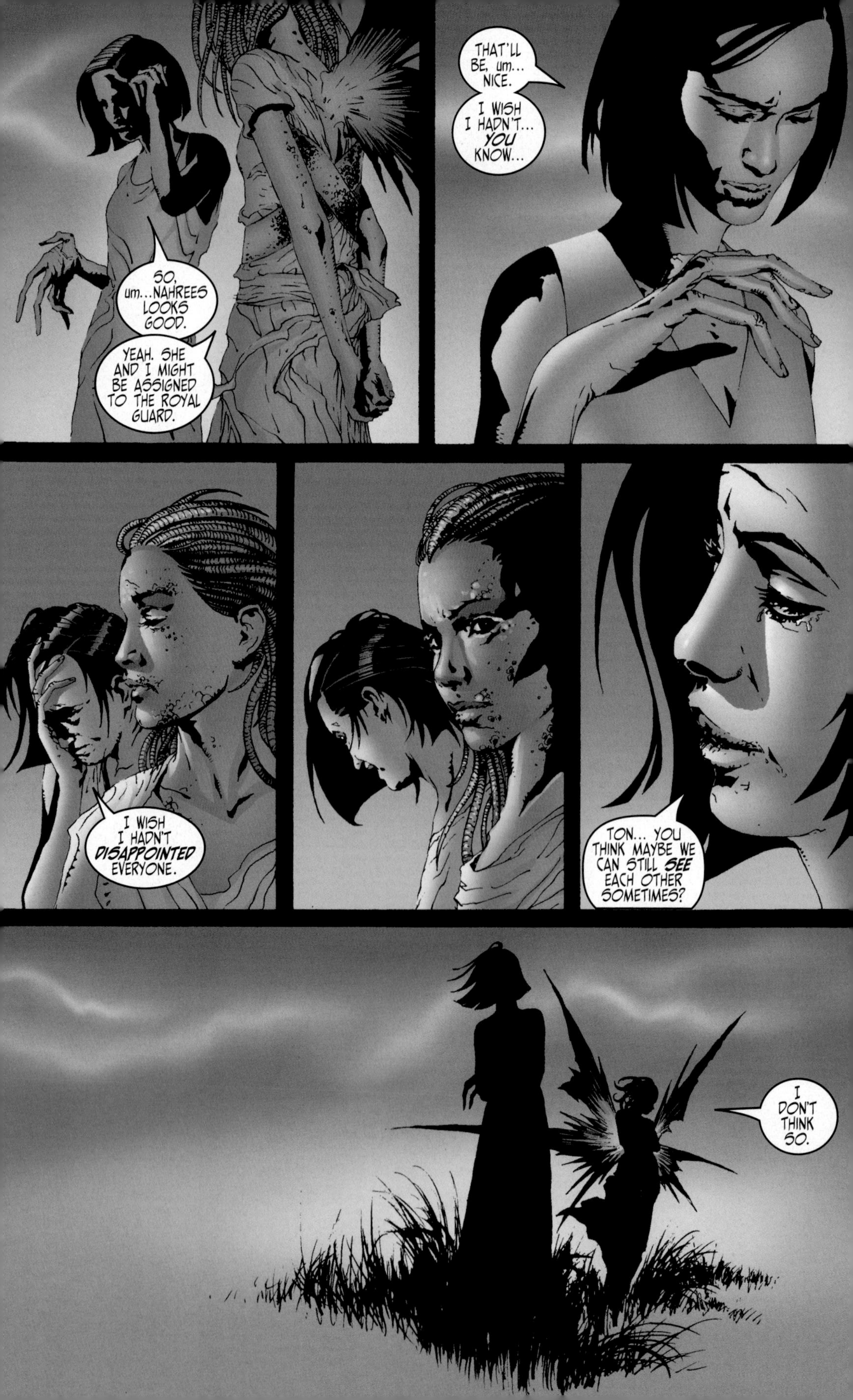
SO, um...NAHREES LOOKS GOOD.
YEAH. SHE AND I MIGHT BE ASSIGNED TO THE ROYAL GUARD.
THAT'LL BE, um... NICE.
I WISH I HADN'T... YOU KNOW...
I WISH I HADN'T DISAPPOINTED EVERYONE.
TON... YOU THINK MAYBE WE CAN STILL SEE EACH OTHER SOMETIMES?
I DON'T THINK SO.

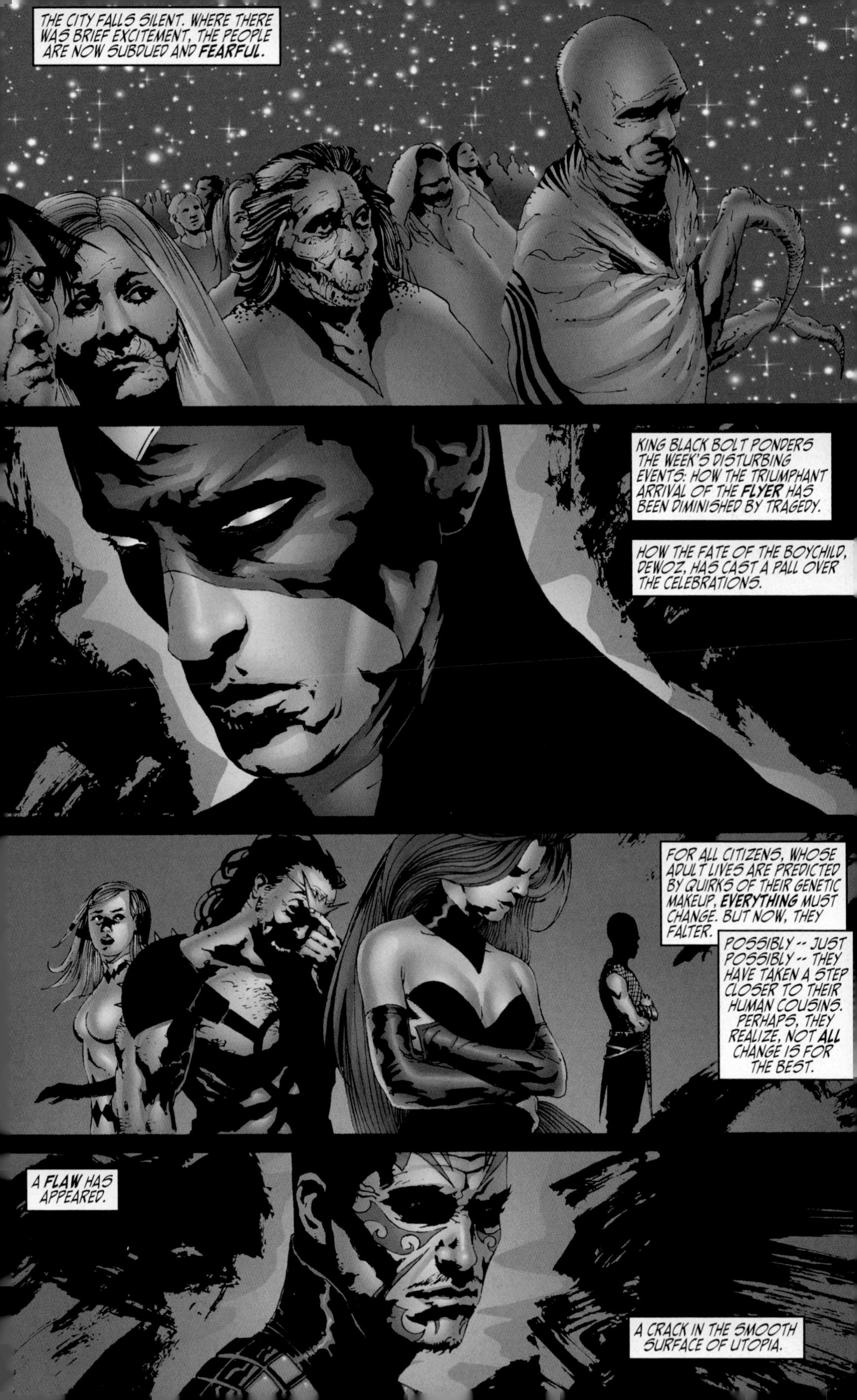
THE CITY FALLS SILENT. WHERE THERE WAS BRIEF EXCITEMENT, THE PEOPLE ARE NOW SUBDUED AND FEARFUL.
KING BLACK BOLT PONDERS THE WEEK'S DISTURBING EVENTS: HOW THE TRIUMPHANT ARRIVAL OF THE FLYER HAS BEEN DIMINISHED BY TRAGEDY.
HOW THE FATE OF THE BOYCHILD, DEWOZ, HAS CAST A PALL OVER THE CELEBRATIONS.
FOR ALL CITIZENS, WHOSE ADULT LIVES ARE PREDICTED BY QUIRKS OF THEIR GENETIC MAKEUP, EVERYTHING MUST CHANGE. BUT NOW, THEY FALTER.
POSSIBLY -- JUST POSSIBLY -- THEY HAVE TAKEN A STEP CLOSER TO THEIR HUMAN COUSINS. PERHAPS, THEY REALIZE, NOT ALL CHANGE IS FOR THE BEST.
A FLAW HAS APPEARED.
A CRACK IN THE SMOOTH SURFACE OF UTOPIA.

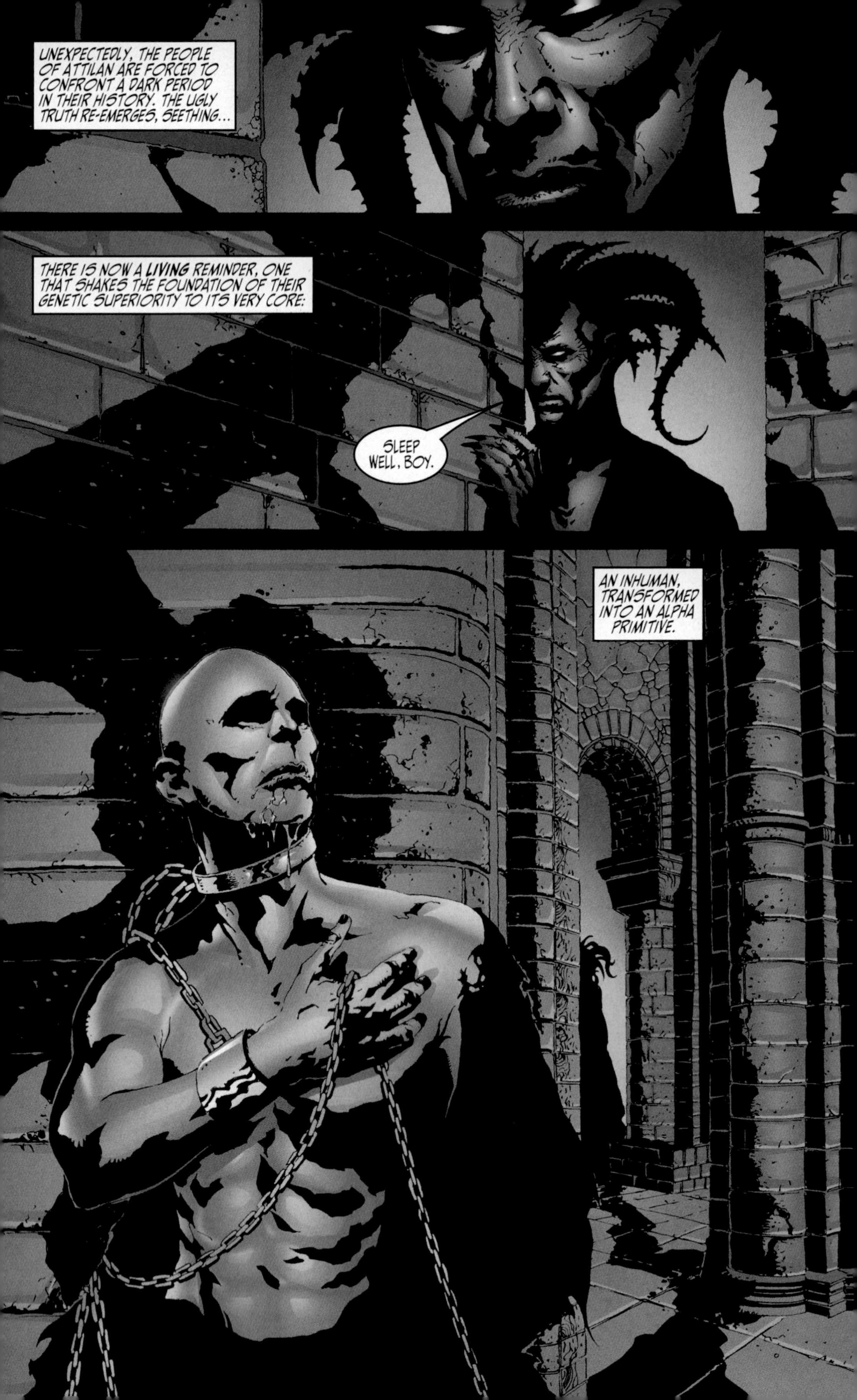
UNEXPECTEDLY, THE PEOPLE OF ATTILAN ARE FORCED TO CONFRONT A DARK PERIOD IN THEIR HISTORY. THE UGLY TRUTH RE-EMERGES, SEETHING...
THERE IS NOW A LIVING REMINDER, ONE THAT SHAKES THE FOUNDATION OF THEIR GENETIC SUPERIORITY TO ITS VERY CORE:
SLEEP WELL, BOY.
AN INHUMAN, TRANSFORMED INTO AN ALPHA PRIMITIVE.

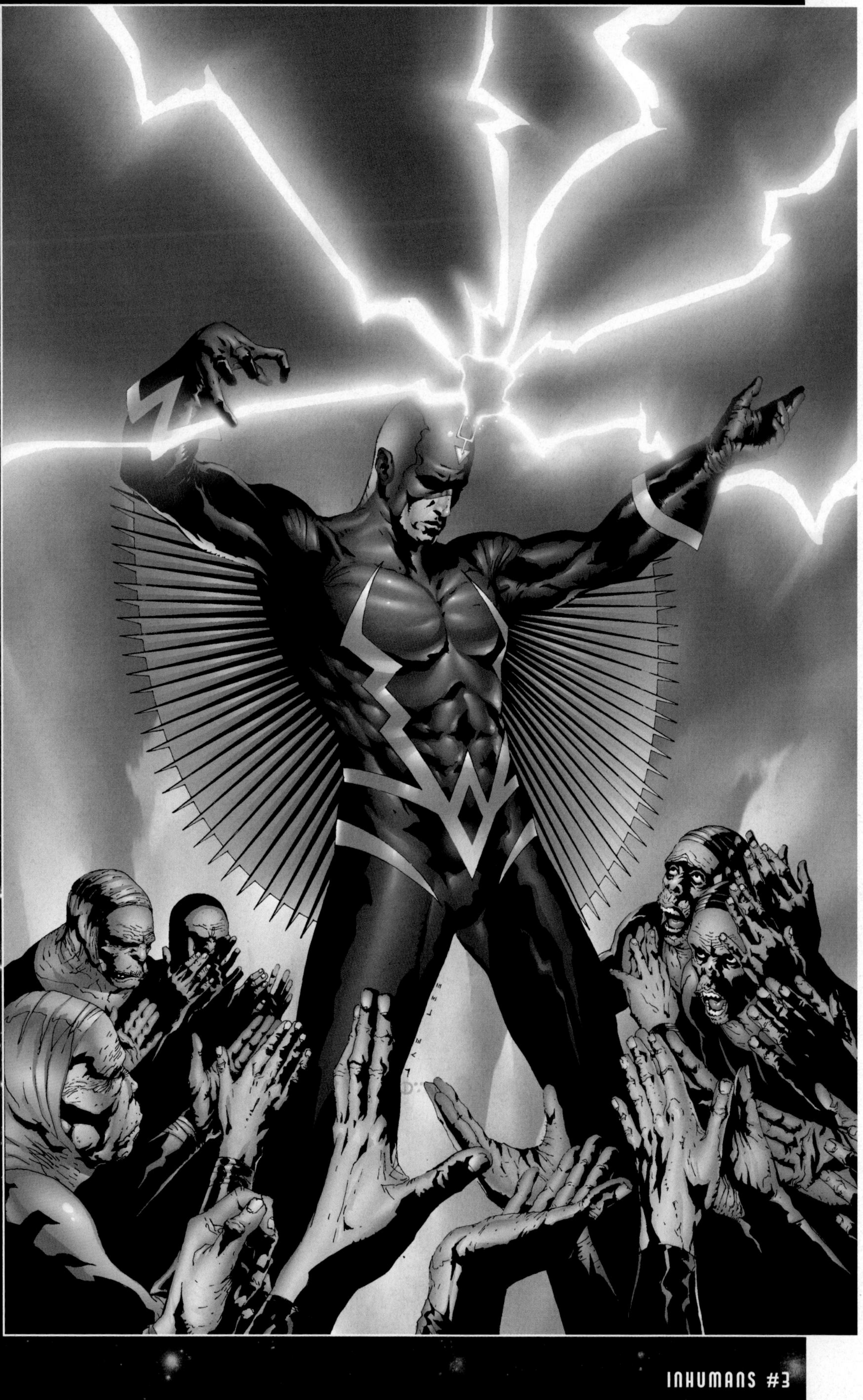

INHUMANS #3

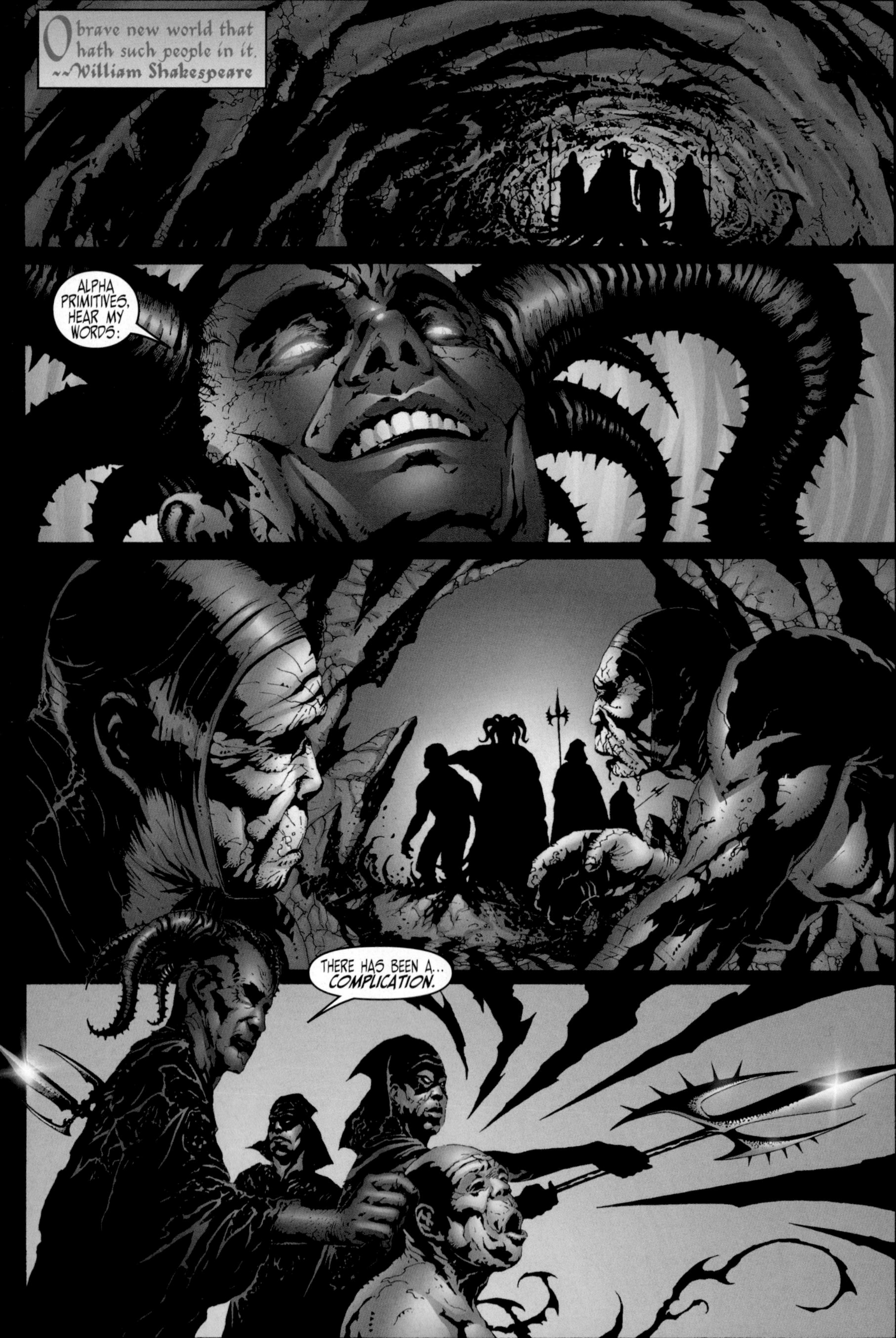
O brave new world that hath such people in it.
~~William Shakespeare
ALPHA PRIMITIVES, HEAR MY WORDS:
THERE HAS BEEN A... COMPLICATION.

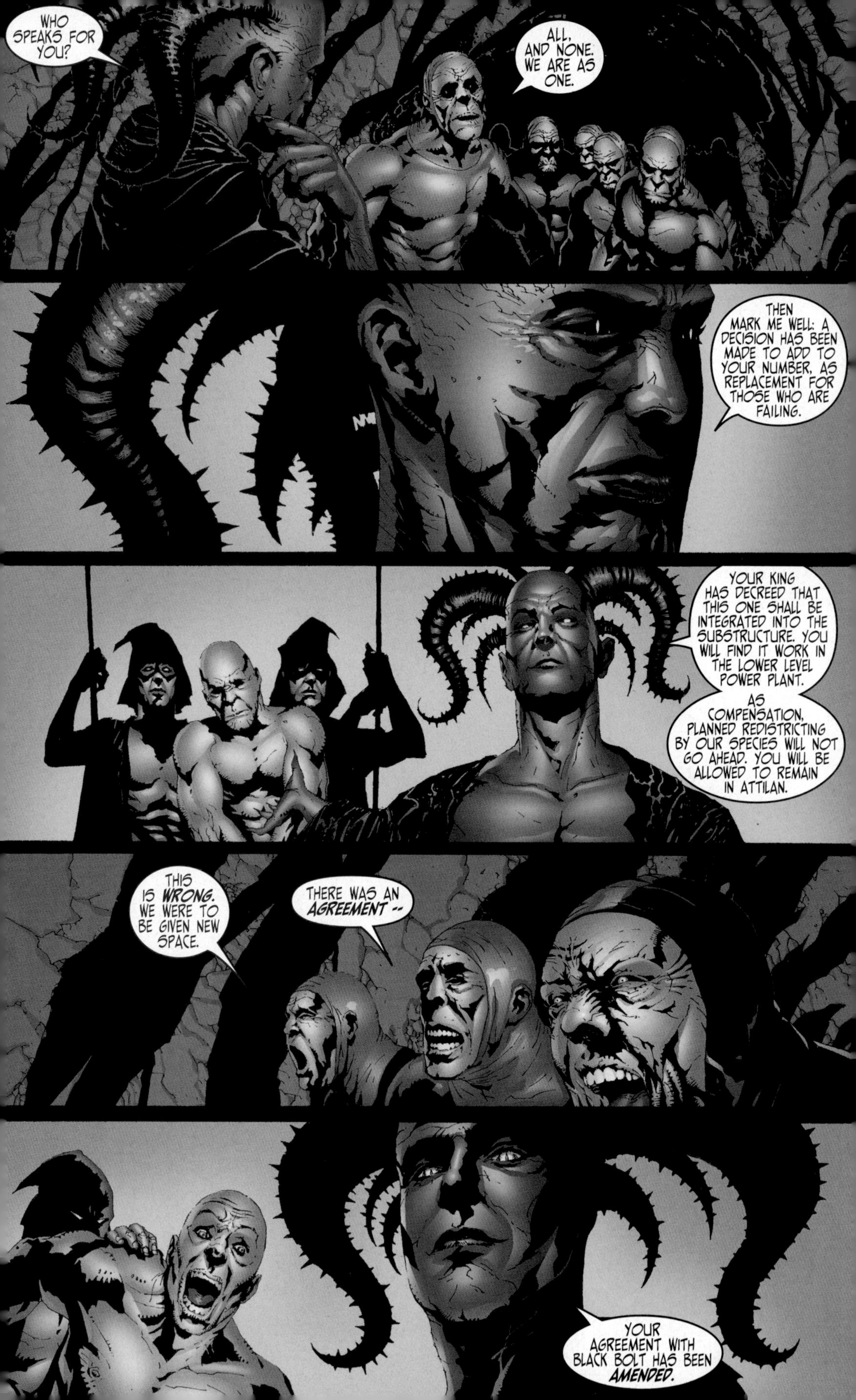
WHO SPEAKS FOR YOU?
ALL, AND NONE. WE ARE AS ONE.
THEN MARK ME WELL: A DECISION HAS BEEN MADE TO ADD TO YOUR NUMBER, AS REPLACEMENT FOR THOSE WHO ARE FAILING.
YOUR KING HAS DECREED THAT THIS ONE SHALL BE INTEGRATED INTO THE SUBSTRUCTURE. YOU WILL FIND IT WORK IN THE LOWER LEVEL POWER PLANT.
AS COMPENSATION, PLANNED REDISTRICTING BY OUR SPECIES WILL NOT GO AHEAD. YOU WILL BE ALLOWED TO REMAIN IN ATTILAN.
THIS IS **WRONG**. WE WERE TO BE GIVEN NEW SPACE.
THERE WAS AN **AGREEMENT** --
YOUR AGREEMENT WITH BLACK BOLT HAS BEEN **AMENDED**.

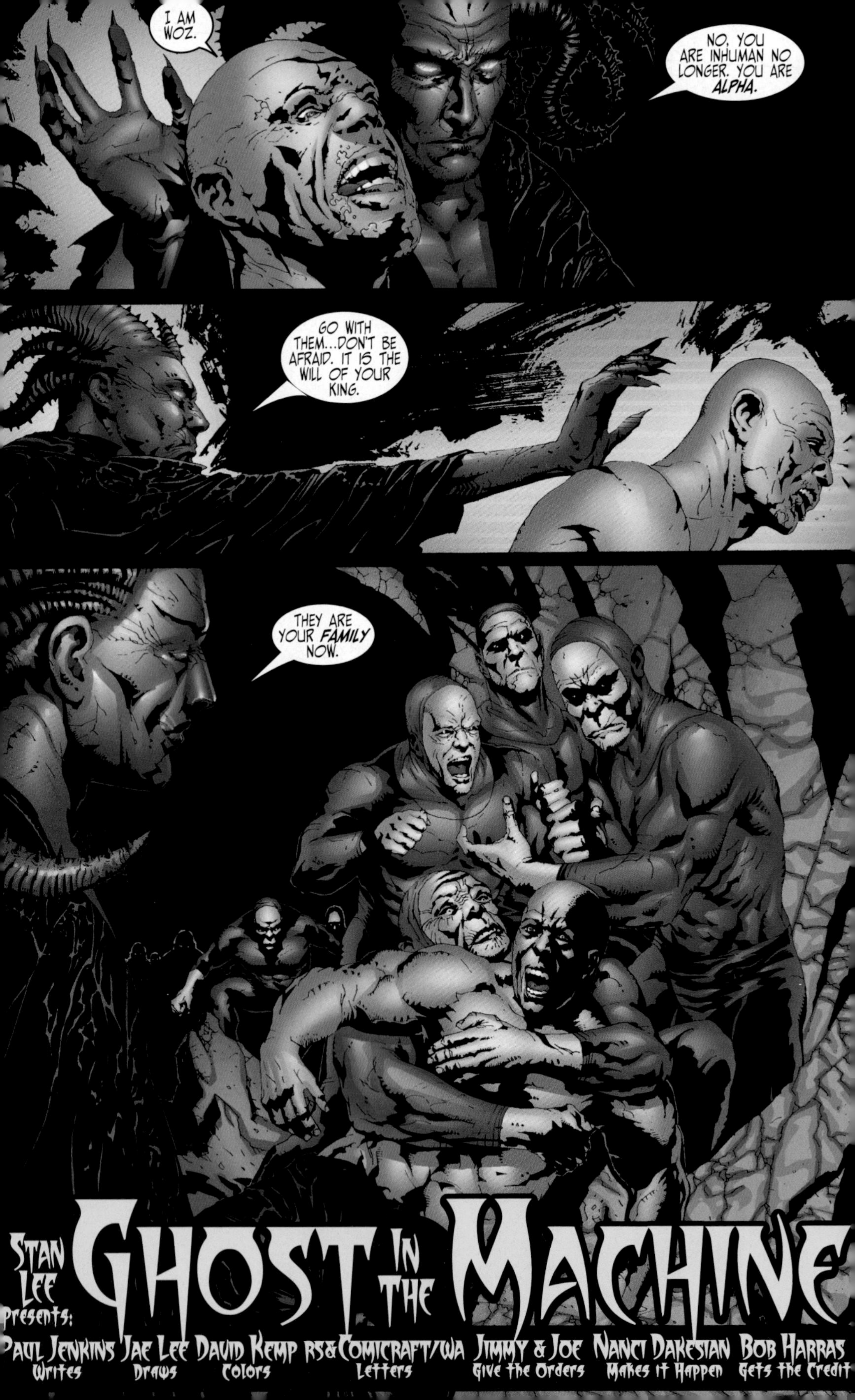

I AM WOZ.
NO, YOU ARE INHUMAN NO LONGER. YOU ARE *ALPHA*.
GO WITH THEM...DON'T BE AFRAID. IT IS THE WILL OF YOUR KING.
THEY ARE YOUR *FAMILY* NOW.
STAN LEE presents:
GHOST IN THE MACHINE
PAUL JENKINS Writes
JAE LEE Draws
DAVID KEMP Colors
RS&COMICRAFT/WA Letters
JIMMY & JOE Give the Orders
NANCI DAKESIAN Makes it Happen
BOB HARRAS Gets the Credit

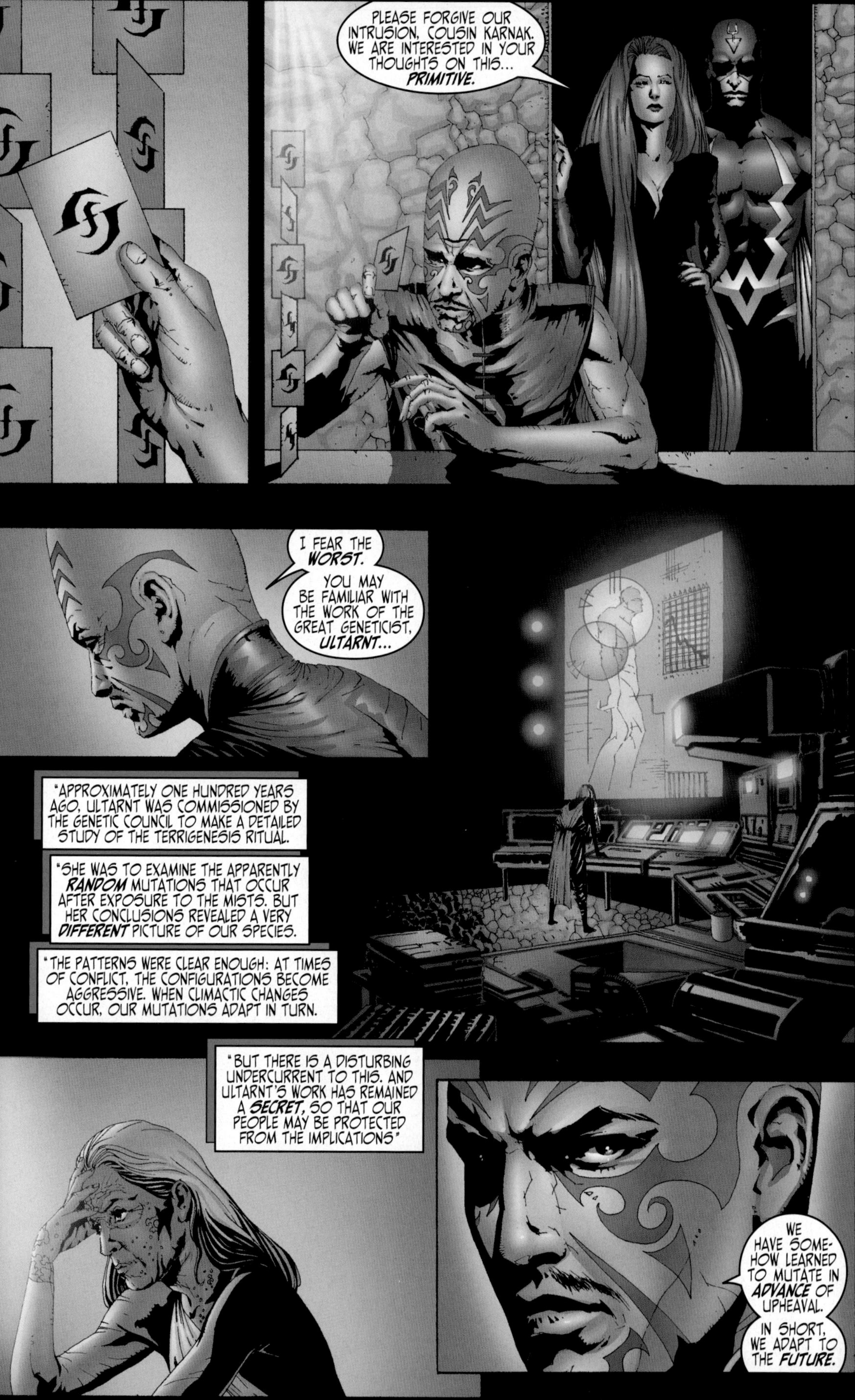
PLEASE FORGIVE OUR INTRUSION, COUSIN KARNAK. WE ARE INTERESTED IN YOUR THOUGHTS ON THIS... PRIMITIVE.
I FEAR THE WORST.
YOU MAY BE FAMILIAR WITH THE WORK OF THE GREAT GENETICIST, ULTARNT...
"APPROXIMATELY ONE HUNDRED YEARS AGO, ULTARNT WAS COMMISSIONED BY THE GENETIC COUNCIL TO MAKE A DETAILED STUDY OF THE TERRIGENESIS RITUAL.
"SHE WAS TO EXAMINE THE APPARENTLY RANDOM MUTATIONS THAT OCCUR AFTER EXPOSURE TO THE MISTS. BUT HER CONCLUSIONS REVEALED A VERY DIFFERENT PICTURE OF OUR SPECIES.
"THE PATTERNS WERE CLEAR ENOUGH: AT TIMES OF CONFLICT, THE CONFIGURATIONS BECOME AGGRESSIVE. WHEN CLIMACTIC CHANGES OCCUR, OUR MUTATIONS ADAPT IN TURN.
"BUT THERE IS A DISTURBING UNDERCURRENT TO THIS. AND ULTARNT'S WORK HAS REMAINED A SECRET, SO THAT OUR PEOPLE MAY BE PROTECTED FROM THE IMPLICATIONS"
WE HAVE SOMEHOW LEARNED TO MUTATE IN ADVANCE OF UPHEAVAL.
IN SHORT, WE ADAPT TO THE FUTURE.

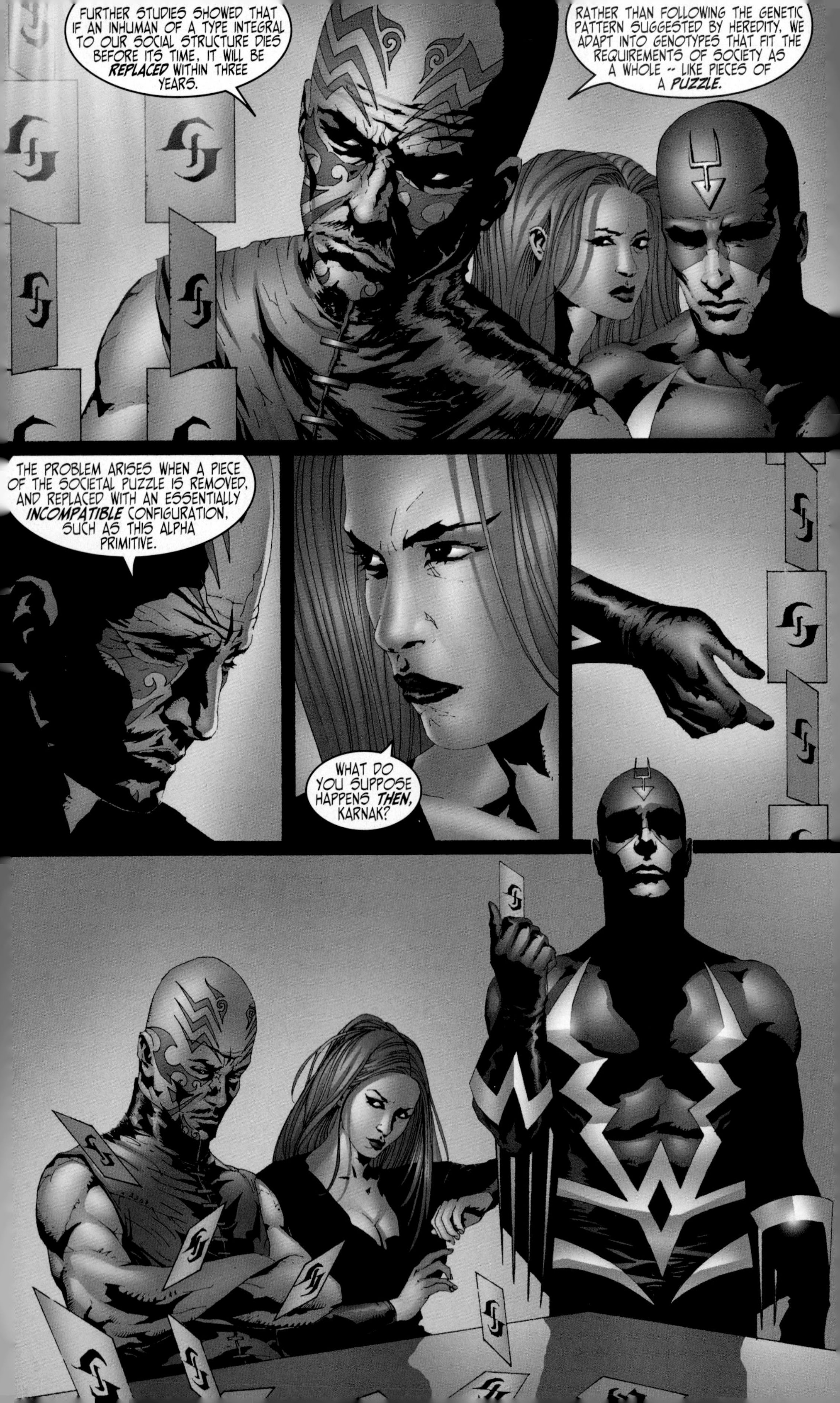
FURTHER STUDIES SHOWED THAT IF AN INHUMAN OF A TYPE INTEGRAL TO OUR SOCIAL STRUCTURE DIES BEFORE ITS TIME, IT WILL BE REPLACED WITHIN THREE YEARS.
RATHER THAN FOLLOWING THE GENETIC PATTERN SUGGESTED BY HEREDITY, WE ADAPT INTO GENOTYPES THAT FIT THE REQUIREMENTS OF SOCIETY AS A WHOLE -- LIKE PIECES OF A PUZZLE.
THE PROBLEM ARISES WHEN A PIECE OF THE SOCIETAL PUZZLE IS REMOVED, AND REPLACED WITH AN ESSENTIALLY INCOMPATIBLE CONFIGURATION, SUCH AS THIS ALPHA PRIMITIVE.
WHAT DO YOU SUPPOSE HAPPENS THEN, KARNAK?

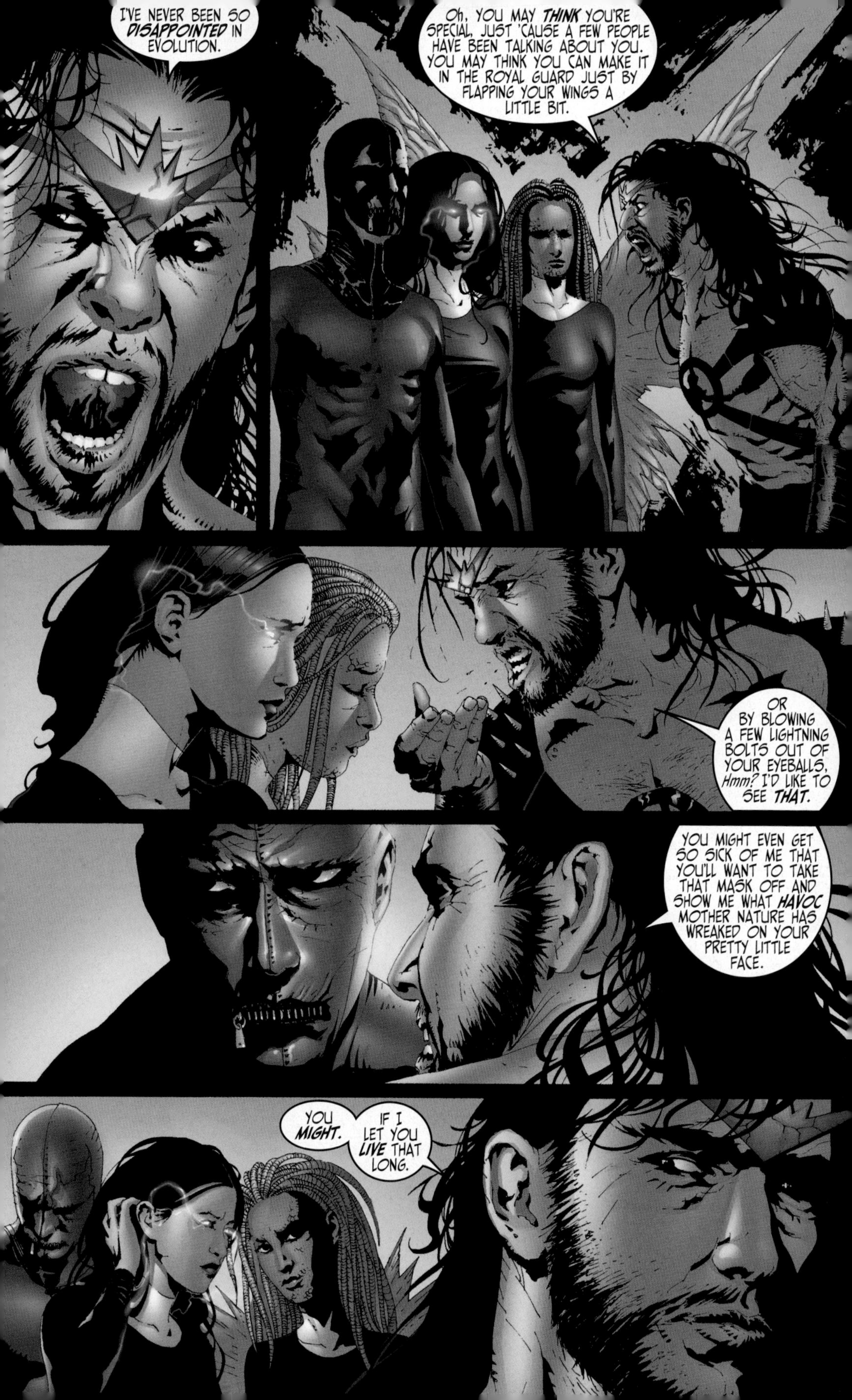
I'VE NEVER BEEN SO DISAPPOINTED IN EVOLUTION.
Oh, YOU MAY THINK YOU'RE SPECIAL, JUST 'CAUSE A FEW PEOPLE HAVE BEEN TALKING ABOUT YOU. YOU MAY THINK YOU CAN MAKE IT IN THE ROYAL GUARD JUST BY FLAPPING YOUR WINGS A LITTLE BIT.
OR BY BLOWING A FEW LIGHTNING BOLTS OUT OF YOUR EYEBALLS, Hmm? I'D LIKE TO SEE THAT.
YOU MIGHT EVEN GET SO SICK OF ME THAT YOU'LL WANT TO TAKE THAT MASK OFF AND SHOW ME WHAT HAVOC MOTHER NATURE HAS WREAKED ON YOUR PRETTY LITTLE FACE.
YOU MIGHT.
IF I LET YOU LIVE THAT LONG.

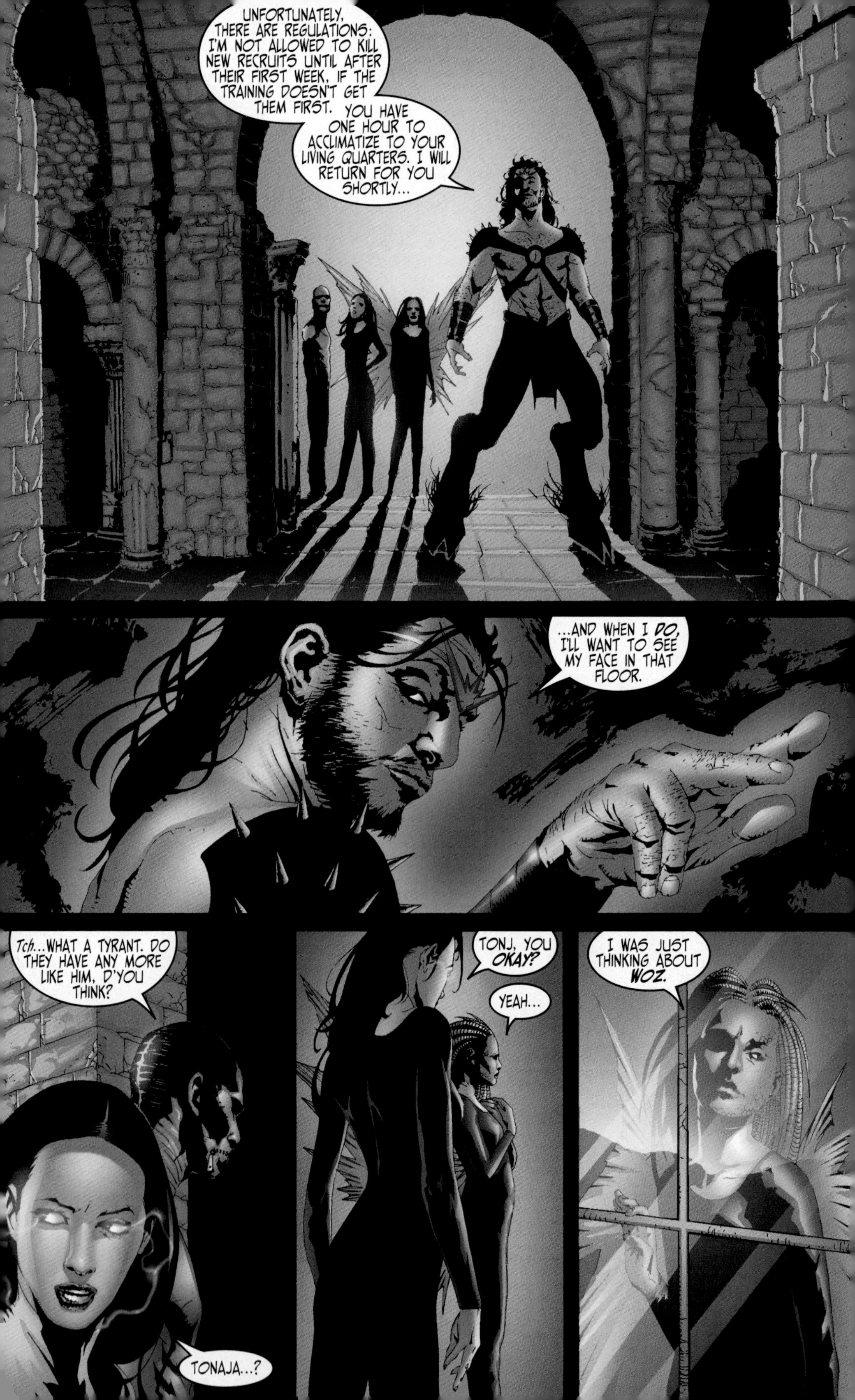
UNFORTUNATELY, THERE ARE REGULATIONS: I'M NOT ALLOWED TO KILL NEW RECRUITS UNTIL AFTER THEIR FIRST WEEK, IF THE TRAINING DOESN'T GET THEM FIRST.
YOU HAVE ONE HOUR TO ACCLIMATIZE TO YOUR LIVING QUARTERS. I WILL RETURN FOR YOU SHORTLY...
...AND WHEN I *DO*, I'LL WANT TO SEE MY FACE IN THAT FLOOR.
Tch...WHAT A TYRANT. DO THEY HAVE ANY MORE LIKE HIM, D'YOU THINK?
TONAJA...?
TONJ, YOU ***OKAY?***
YEAH...
I WAS JUST THINKING ABOUT ***WOZ.***

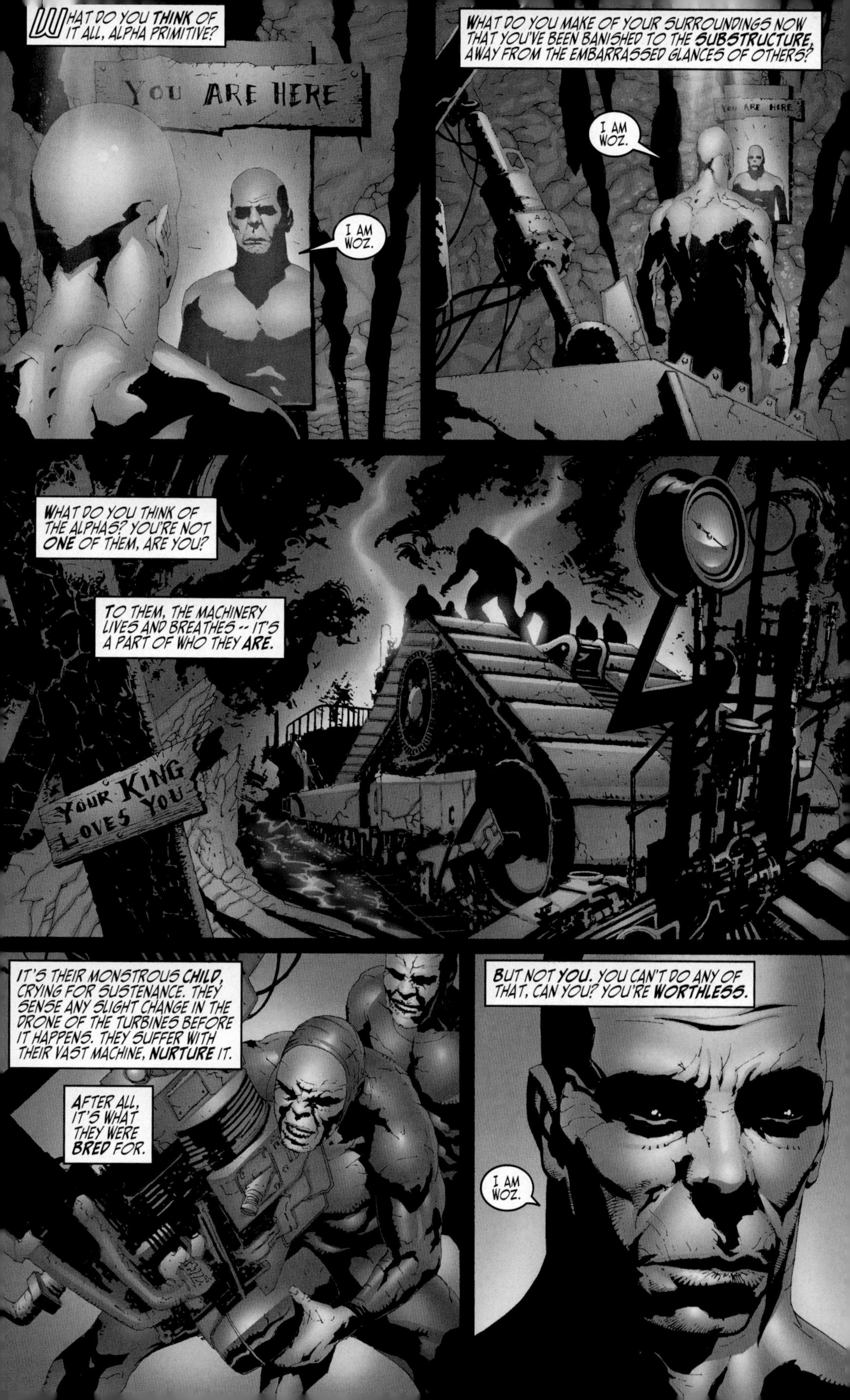
WHAT DO YOU THINK OF IT ALL, ALPHA PRIMITIVE?
YOU ARE HERE
I AM WOZ.
WHAT DO YOU MAKE OF YOUR SURROUNDINGS NOW THAT YOU'VE BEEN BANISHED TO THE SUBSTRUCTURE, AWAY FROM THE EMBARRASSED GLANCES OF OTHERS?
YOU ARE HERE
I AM WOZ.
WHAT DO YOU THINK OF THE ALPHAS? YOU'RE NOT ONE OF THEM, ARE YOU?
TO THEM, THE MACHINERY LIVES AND BREATHES -- IT'S A PART OF WHO THEY ARE.
YOUR KING LOVES YOU
IT'S THEIR MONSTROUS CHILD, CRYING FOR SUSTENANCE. THEY SENSE ANY SLIGHT CHANGE IN THE DRONE OF THE TURBINES BEFORE IT HAPPENS. THEY SUFFER WITH THEIR VAST MACHINE, NURTURE IT.
AFTER ALL, IT'S WHAT THEY WERE BRED FOR.
BUT NOT YOU. YOU CAN'T DO ANY OF THAT, CAN YOU? YOU'RE WORTHLESS.
I AM WOZ.

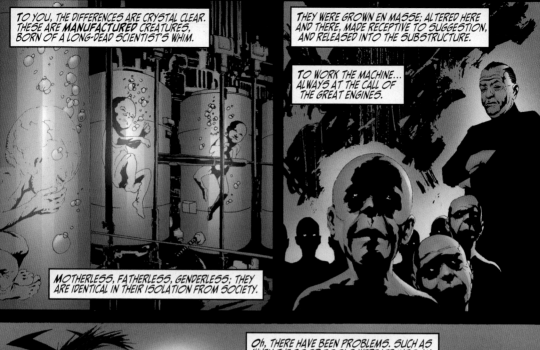

TO YOU, THE DIFFERENCES ARE CRYSTAL CLEAR. THESE ARE **MANUFACTURED** CREATURES, BORN OF A LONG-DEAD SCIENTIST'S WHIM.

THEY WERE GROWN EN MASSE; ALTERED HERE AND THERE, MADE RECEPTIVE TO SUGGESTION, AND RELEASED INTO THE SUBSTRUCTURE.

TO WORK THE MACHINE... ALWAYS AT THE CALL OF THE GREAT ENGINES.

MOTHERLESS, FATHERLESS, GENDERLESS; THEY ARE IDENTICAL IN THEIR ISOLATION FROM SOCIETY.

Oh, THERE HAVE BEEN PROBLEMS. SUCH AS WHEN THE POOR FOOLS WERE LED INTO AN UPRISING AGAINST THEIR "BENEFACTORS" -- THE CITIZENS OF ATTILAN.

GIVE A MORON JUST AN INKLING OF A NOTION THAT IT CAN BE FREE, AND IT'LL JUMP LIKE A DOG TO GRASP THE CONCEPT BY THE THROAT.

THEY'VE BEEN FREED, TO BE SURE, BUT WHAT **IS** FREEDOM TO THESE CREATURES? THEIR BREEDING GIVES THEM NO CHOICE BUT TO WORK THE MACHINE.

HERE THEY REMAIN, AND HERE THEY WILL **DIE** WHEN THERE ARE NO OTHERS TO REPLACE THEM.

DOWN IN THE SUBSTRUCTURE. OUT OF SIGHT. LIKE DIRT SWEPT UNDER THE RUG.

LIKE YOU.

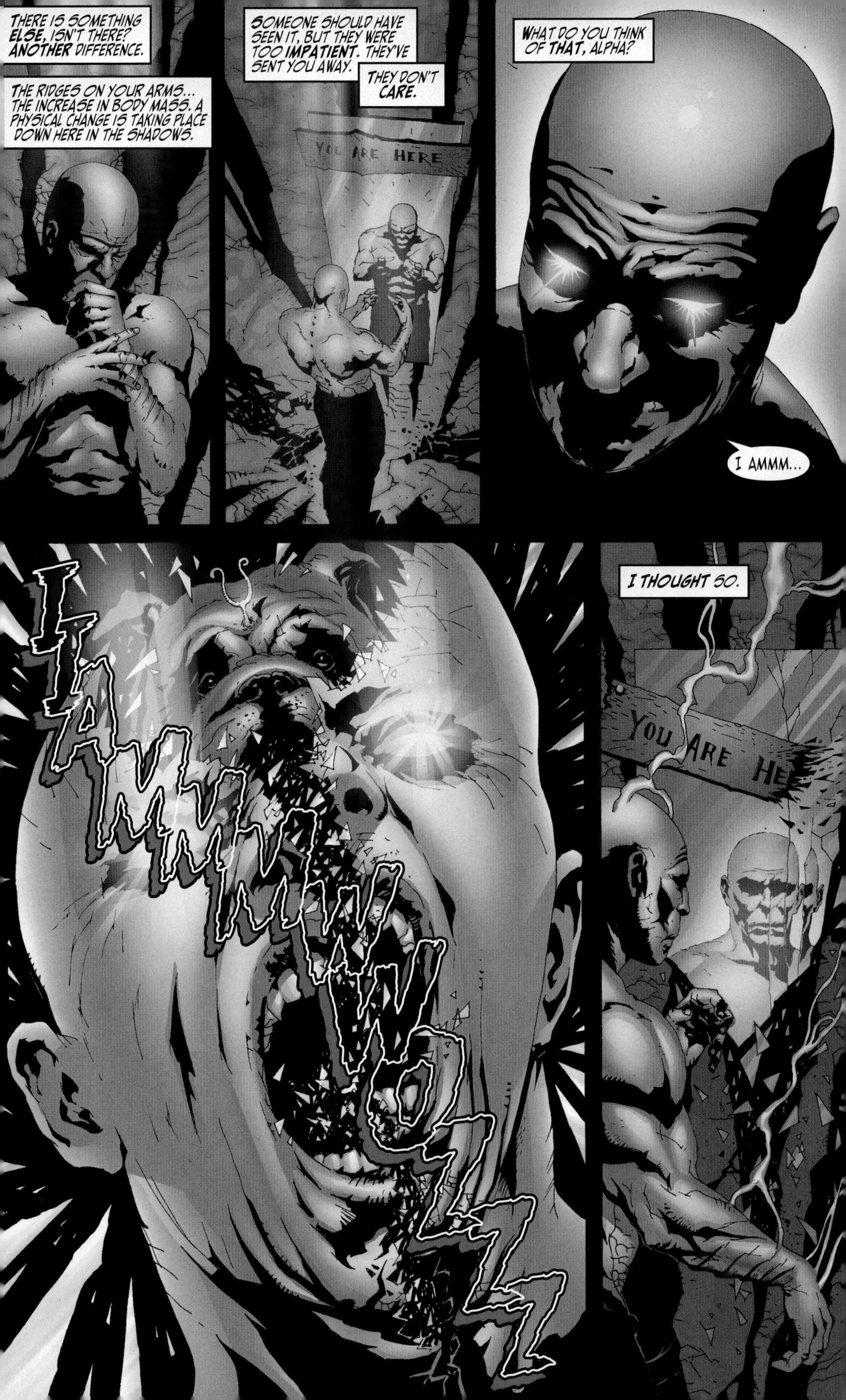
THERE IS SOMETHING ELSE, ISN'T THERE? ANOTHER DIFFERENCE.
THE RIDGES ON YOUR ARMS... THE INCREASE IN BODY MASS. A PHYSICAL CHANGE IS TAKING PLACE DOWN HERE IN THE SHADOWS.
SOMEONE SHOULD HAVE SEEN IT, BUT THEY WERE TOO IMPATIENT. THEY'VE SENT YOU AWAY.
THEY DON'T CARE.
YOU ARE HERE
WHAT DO YOU THINK OF THAT, ALPHA?
I AMMM...
I AMMMWOLLLZ
I THOUGHT SO.
YOU ARE HE

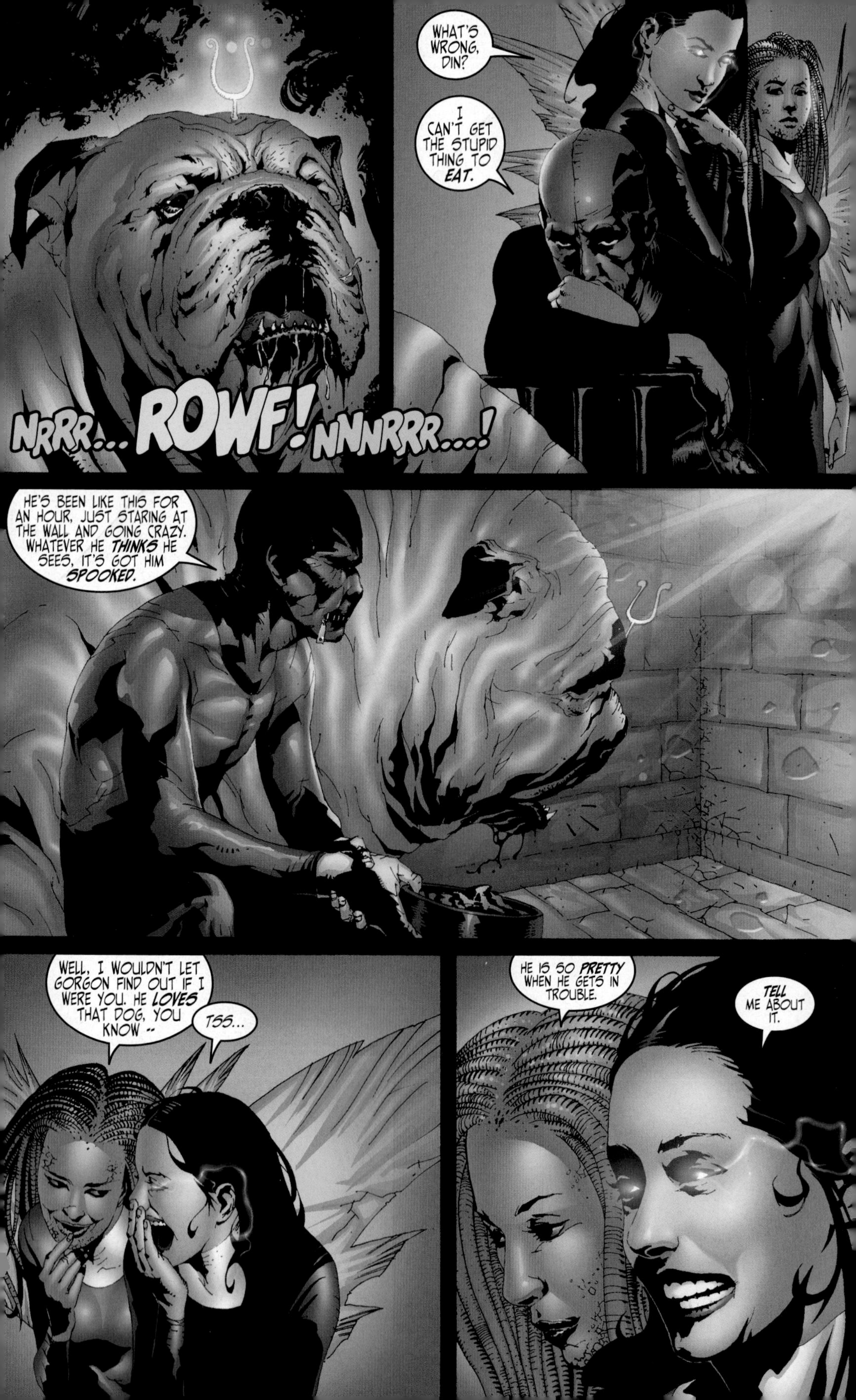
NRRR... ROWF! NNNRRR...!
WHAT'S WRONG, DIN?
I CAN'T GET THE STUPID THING TO EAT.
HE'S BEEN LIKE THIS FOR AN HOUR, JUST STARING AT THE WALL AND GOING CRAZY. WHATEVER HE THINKS HE SEES, IT'S GOT HIM SPOOKED.
WELL, I WOULDN'T LET GORGON FIND OUT IF I WERE YOU. HE LOVES THAT DOG, YOU KNOW --
TSS...
HE IS SO PRETTY WHEN HE GETS IN TROUBLE.
TELL ME ABOUT IT.

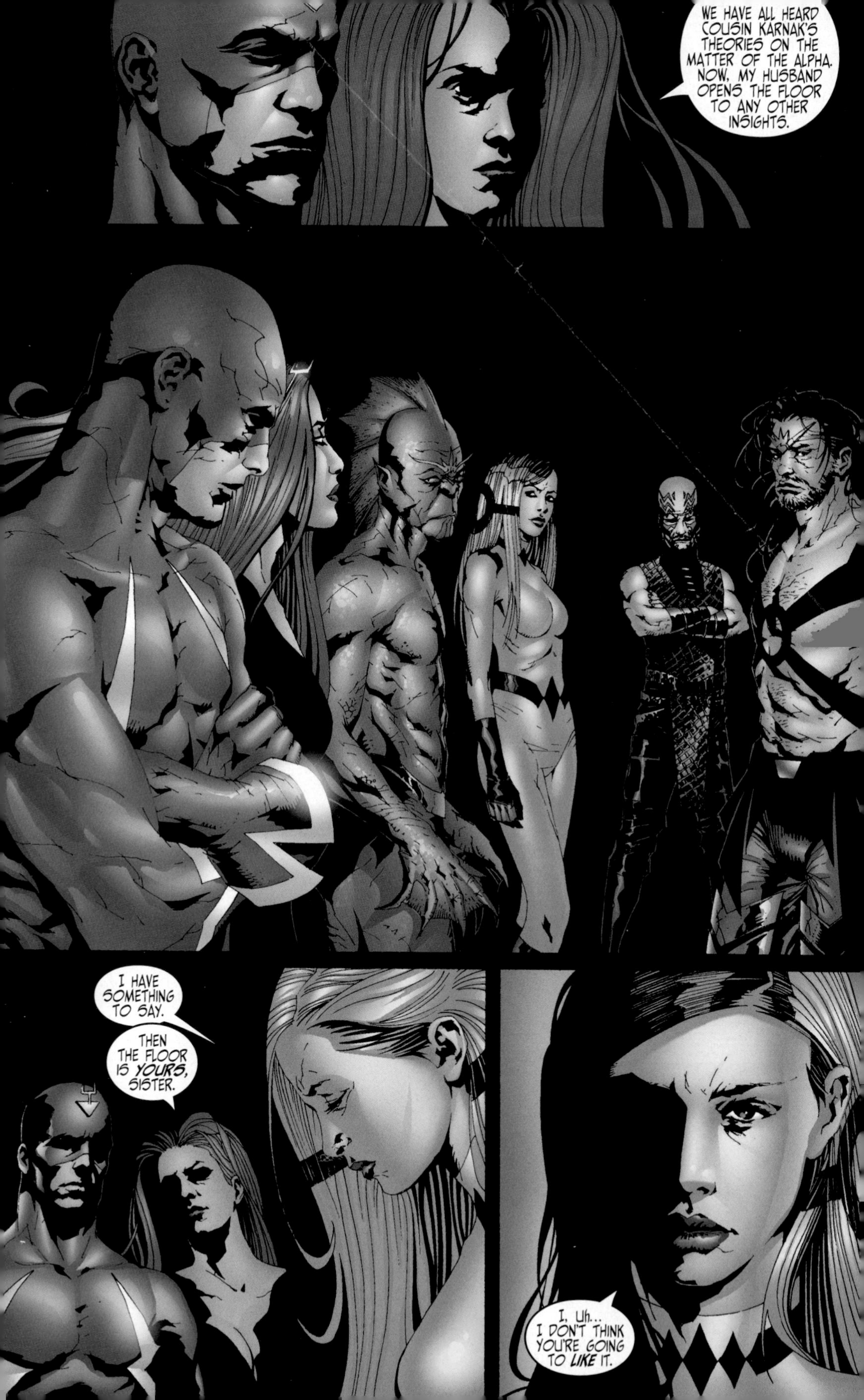
WE HAVE ALL HEARD COUSIN KARNAK'S THEORIES ON THE MATTER OF THE ALPHA. NOW, MY HUSBAND OPENS THE FLOOR TO ANY OTHER INSIGHTS.
I HAVE SOMETHING TO SAY.
THEN THE FLOOR IS *YOURS*, SISTER.
I, Uh... I DON'T THINK YOU'RE GOING TO *LIKE* IT.

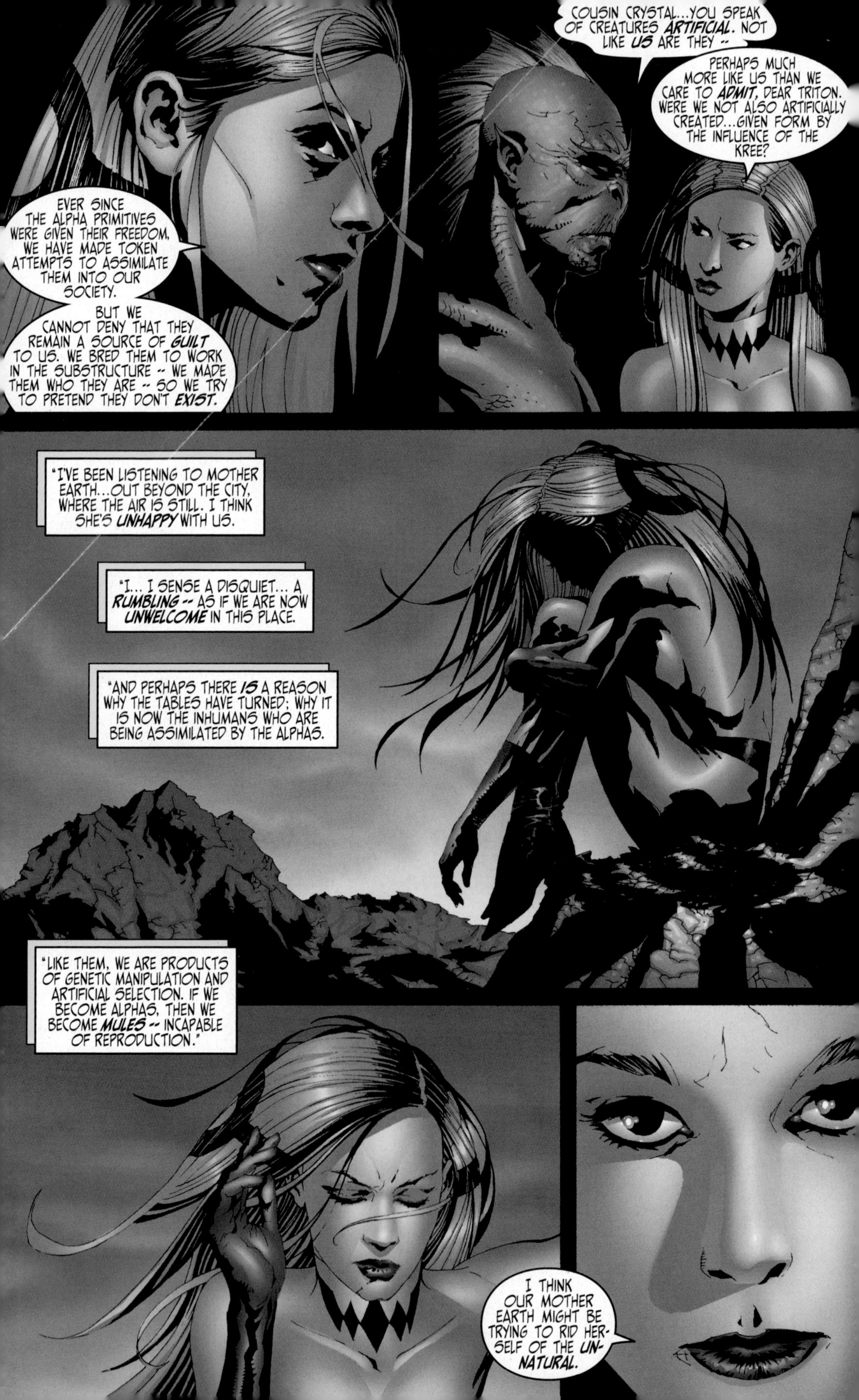
EVER SINCE THE ALPHA PRIMITIVES WERE GIVEN THEIR FREEDOM, WE HAVE MADE TOKEN ATTEMPTS TO ASSIMILATE THEM INTO OUR SOCIETY.
BUT WE CANNOT DENY THAT THEY REMAIN A SOURCE OF GUILT TO US. WE BRED THEM TO WORK IN THE SUBSTRUCTURE -- WE MADE THEM WHO THEY ARE -- SO WE TRY TO PRETEND THEY DON'T EXIST.
COUSIN CRYSTAL...YOU SPEAK OF CREATURES ARTIFICIAL. NOT LIKE US ARE THEY --
PERHAPS MUCH MORE LIKE US THAN WE CARE TO ADMIT, DEAR TRITON. WERE WE NOT ALSO ARTIFICIALLY CREATED...GIVEN FORM BY THE INFLUENCE OF THE KREE?
"I'VE BEEN LISTENING TO MOTHER EARTH...OUT BEYOND THE CITY, WHERE THE AIR IS STILL. I THINK SHE'S UNHAPPY WITH US.
"I... I SENSE A DISQUIET... A RUMBLING -- AS IF WE ARE NOW UNWELCOME IN THIS PLACE.
"AND PERHAPS THERE IS A REASON WHY THE TABLES HAVE TURNED; WHY IT IS NOW THE INHUMANS WHO ARE BEING ASSIMILATED BY THE ALPHAS.
"LIKE THEM, WE ARE PRODUCTS OF GENETIC MANIPULATION AND ARTIFICIAL SELECTION. IF WE BECOME ALPHAS, THEN WE BECOME MULES -- INCAPABLE OF REPRODUCTION."
I THINK OUR MOTHER EARTH MIGHT BE TRYING TO RID HER-SELF OF THE UN-NATURAL.

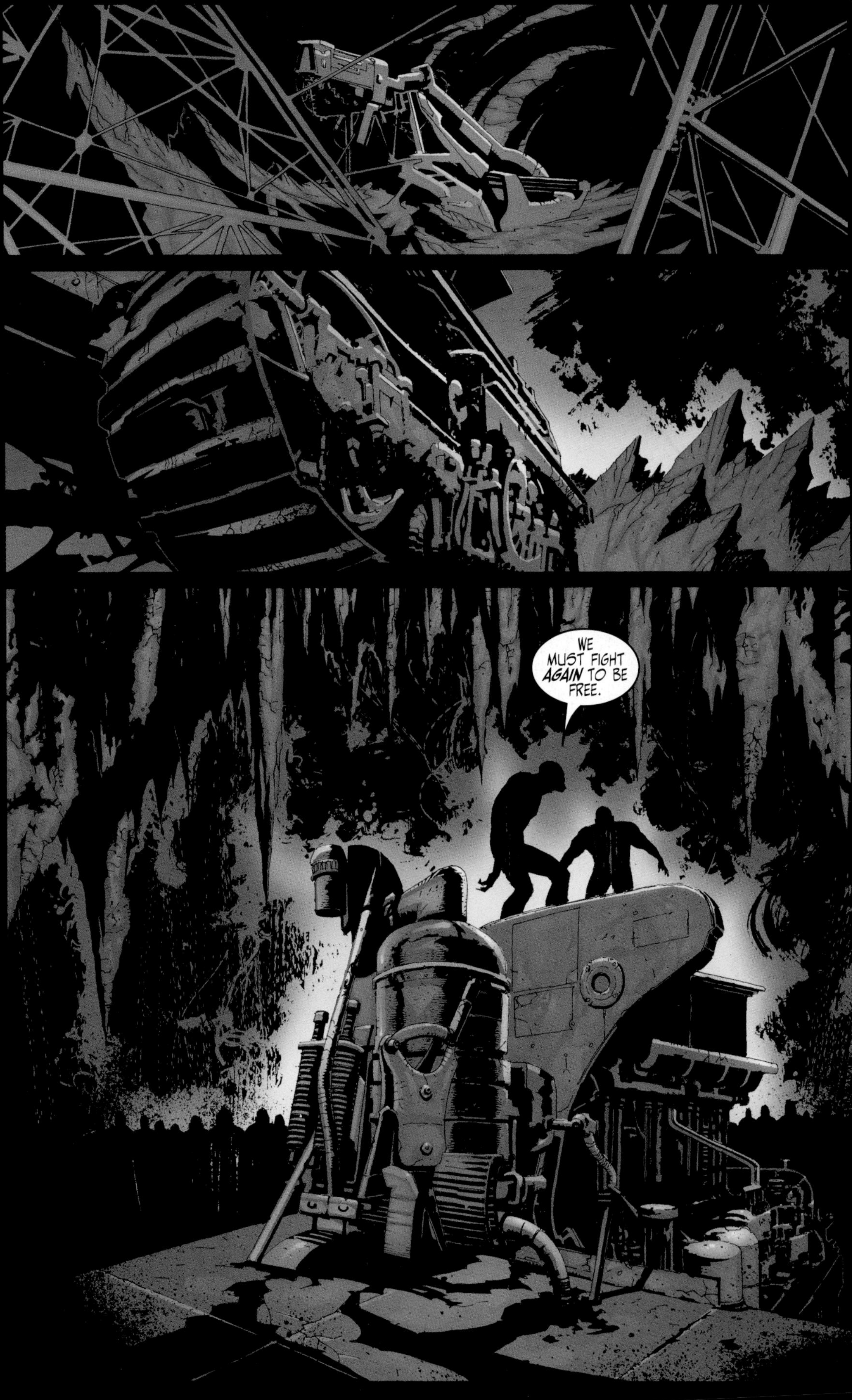
WE MUST FIGHT AGAIN TO BE FREE.

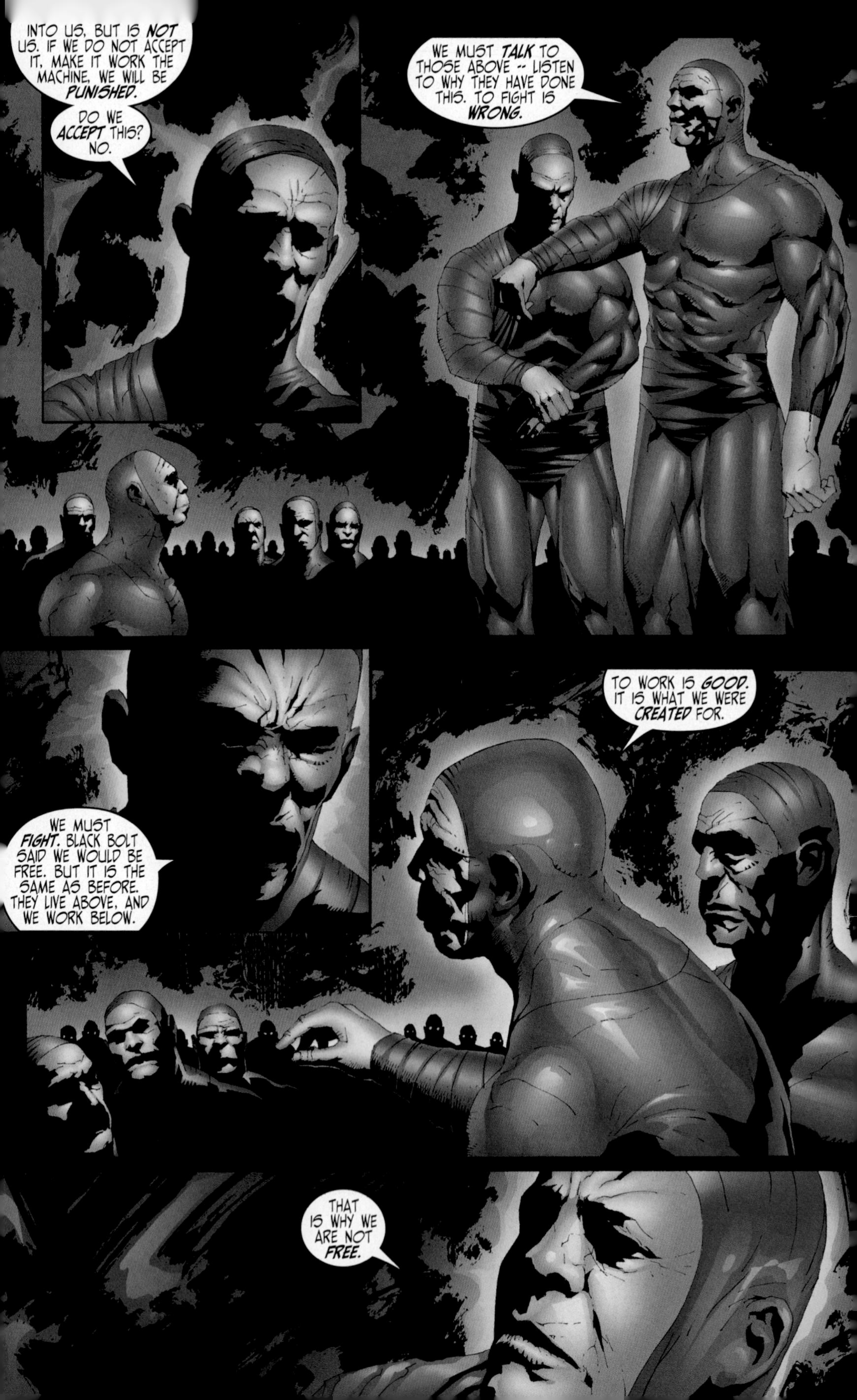

INTO US, BUT IS NOT US. IF WE DO NOT ACCEPT IT, MAKE IT WORK THE MACHINE, WE WILL BE PUNISHED.
DO WE ACCEPT THIS? NO.
WE MUST TALK TO THOSE ABOVE -- LISTEN TO WHY THEY HAVE DONE THIS. TO FIGHT IS WRONG.
WE MUST FIGHT. BLACK BOLT SAID WE WOULD BE FREE. BUT IT IS THE SAME AS BEFORE. THEY LIVE ABOVE, AND WE WORK BELOW.
TO WORK IS GOOD. IT IS WHAT WE WERE CREATED FOR.
THAT IS WHY WE ARE NOT FREE.

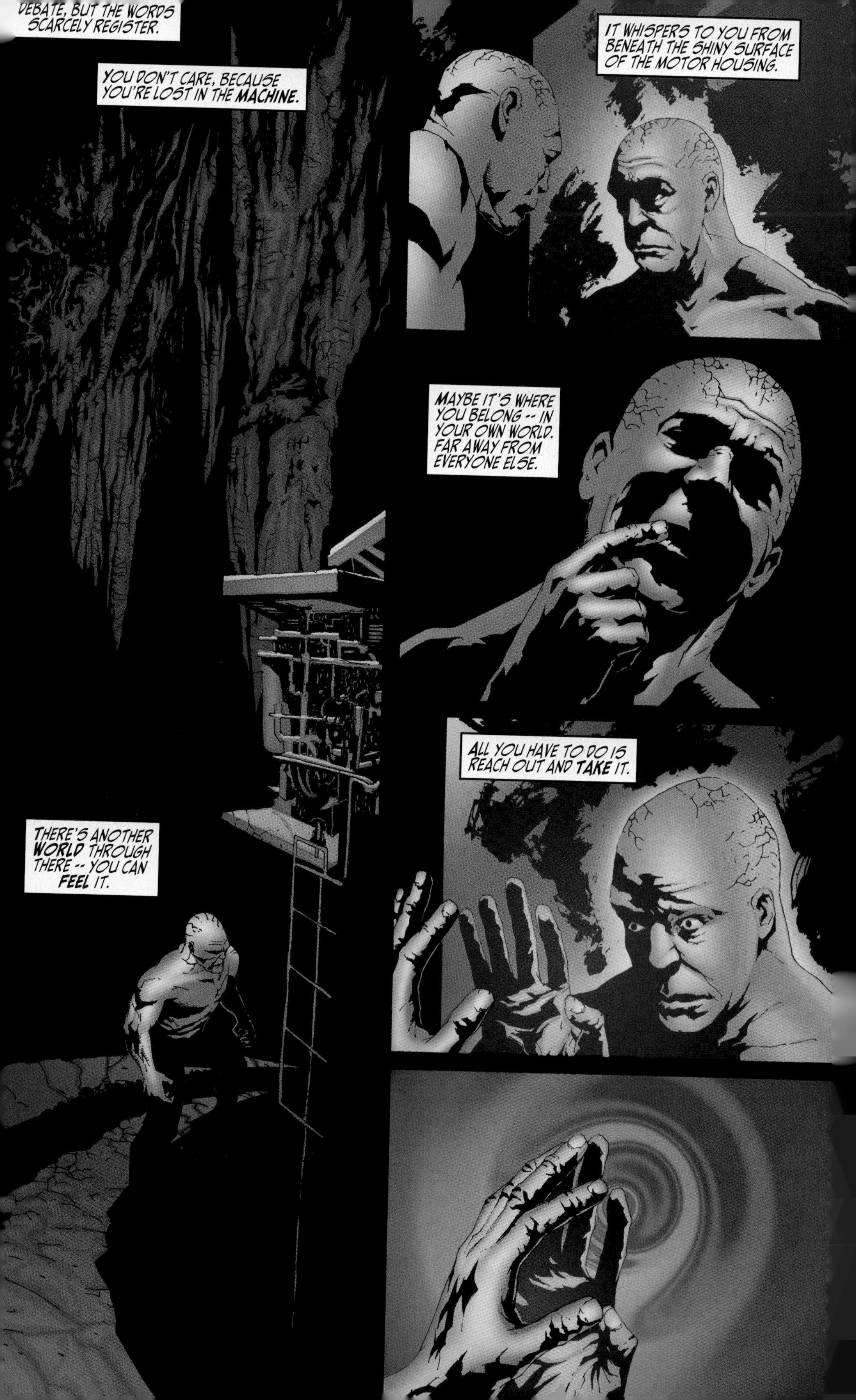
DEBATE, BUT THE WORDS SCARCELY REGISTER.
YOU DON'T CARE, BECAUSE YOU'RE LOST IN THE MACHINE.
IT WHISPERS TO YOU FROM BENEATH THE SHINY SURFACE OF THE MOTOR HOUSING.
MAYBE IT'S WHERE YOU BELONG -- IN YOUR OWN WORLD. FAR AWAY FROM EVERYONE ELSE.
THERE'S ANOTHER WORLD THROUGH THERE -- YOU CAN FEEL IT.
ALL YOU HAVE TO DO IS REACH OUT AND TAKE IT.

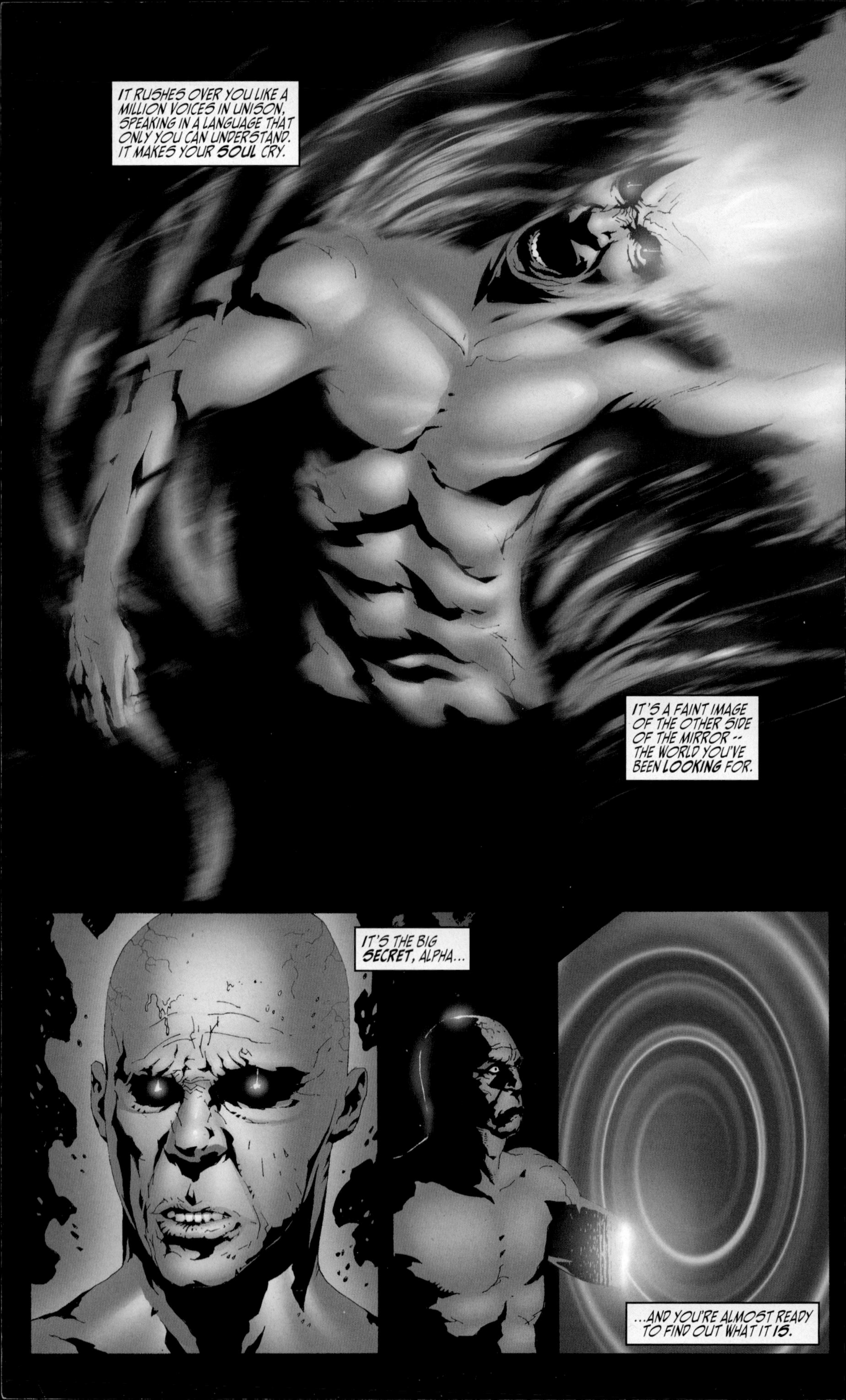
IT RUSHES OVER YOU LIKE A MILLION VOICES IN UNISON, SPEAKING IN A LANGUAGE THAT ONLY YOU CAN UNDERSTAND. IT MAKES YOUR SOUL CRY.
IT'S A FAINT IMAGE OF THE OTHER SIDE OF THE MIRROR -- THE WORLD YOU'VE BEEN LOOKING FOR.
IT'S THE BIG SECRET, ALPHA...
...AND YOU'RE ALMOST READY TO FIND OUT WHAT IT IS.

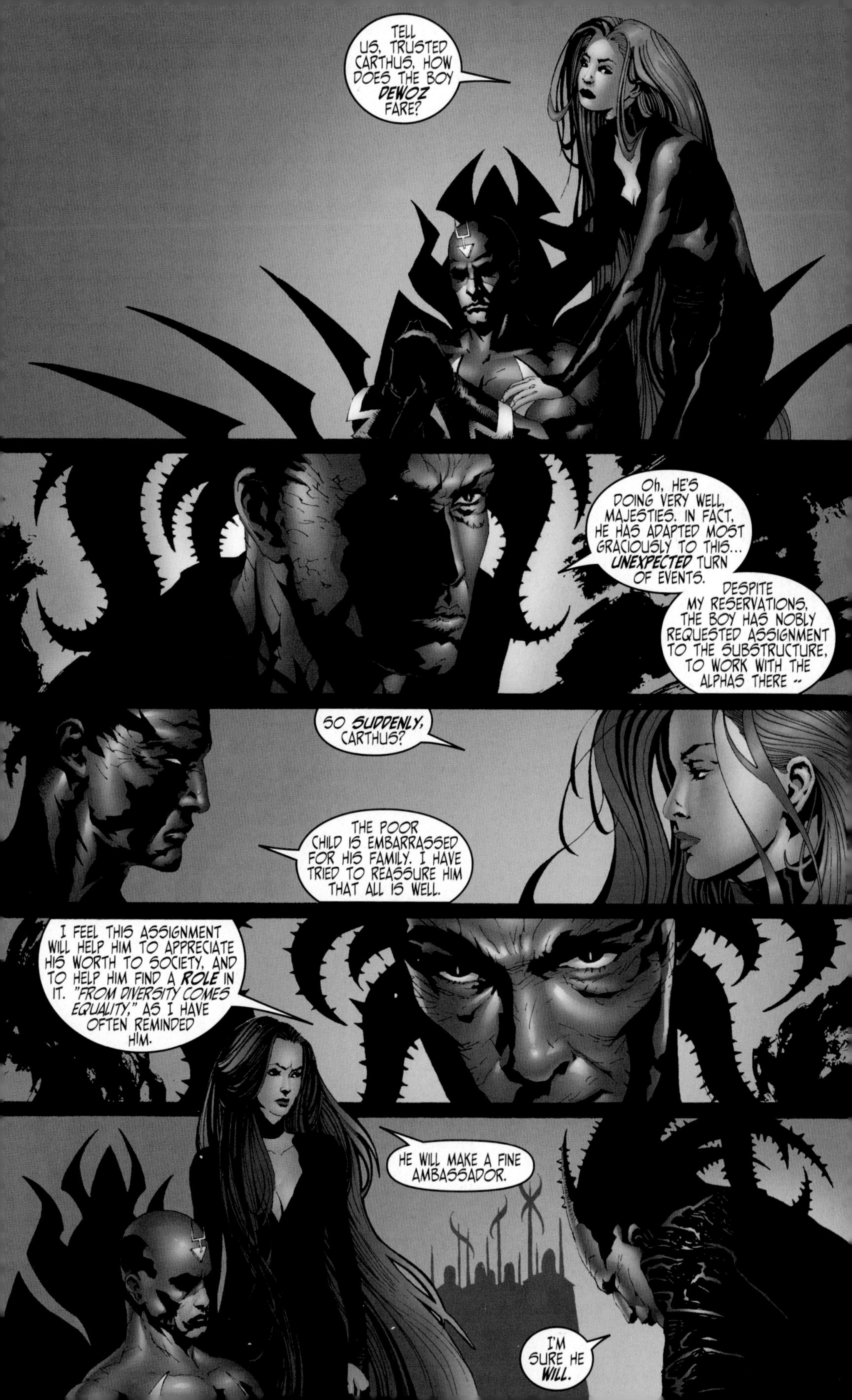
TELL US, TRUSTED CARTHUS, HOW DOES THE BOY DEWOZ FARE?
Oh, HE'S DOING VERY WELL, MAJESTIES. IN FACT, HE HAS ADAPTED MOST GRACIOUSLY TO THIS... UNEXPECTED TURN OF EVENTS.
DESPITE MY RESERVATIONS, THE BOY HAS NOBLY REQUESTED ASSIGNMENT TO THE SUBSTRUCTURE, TO WORK WITH THE ALPHAS THERE --
SO SUDDENLY, CARTHUS?
THE POOR CHILD IS EMBARRASSED FOR HIS FAMILY. I HAVE TRIED TO REASSURE HIM THAT ALL IS WELL.
I FEEL THIS ASSIGNMENT WILL HELP HIM TO APPRECIATE HIS WORTH TO SOCIETY, AND TO HELP HIM FIND A ROLE IN IT. "FROM DIVERSITY COMES EQUALITY," AS I HAVE OFTEN REMINDED HIM.
HE WILL MAKE A FINE AMBASSADOR.
I'M SURE HE WILL.

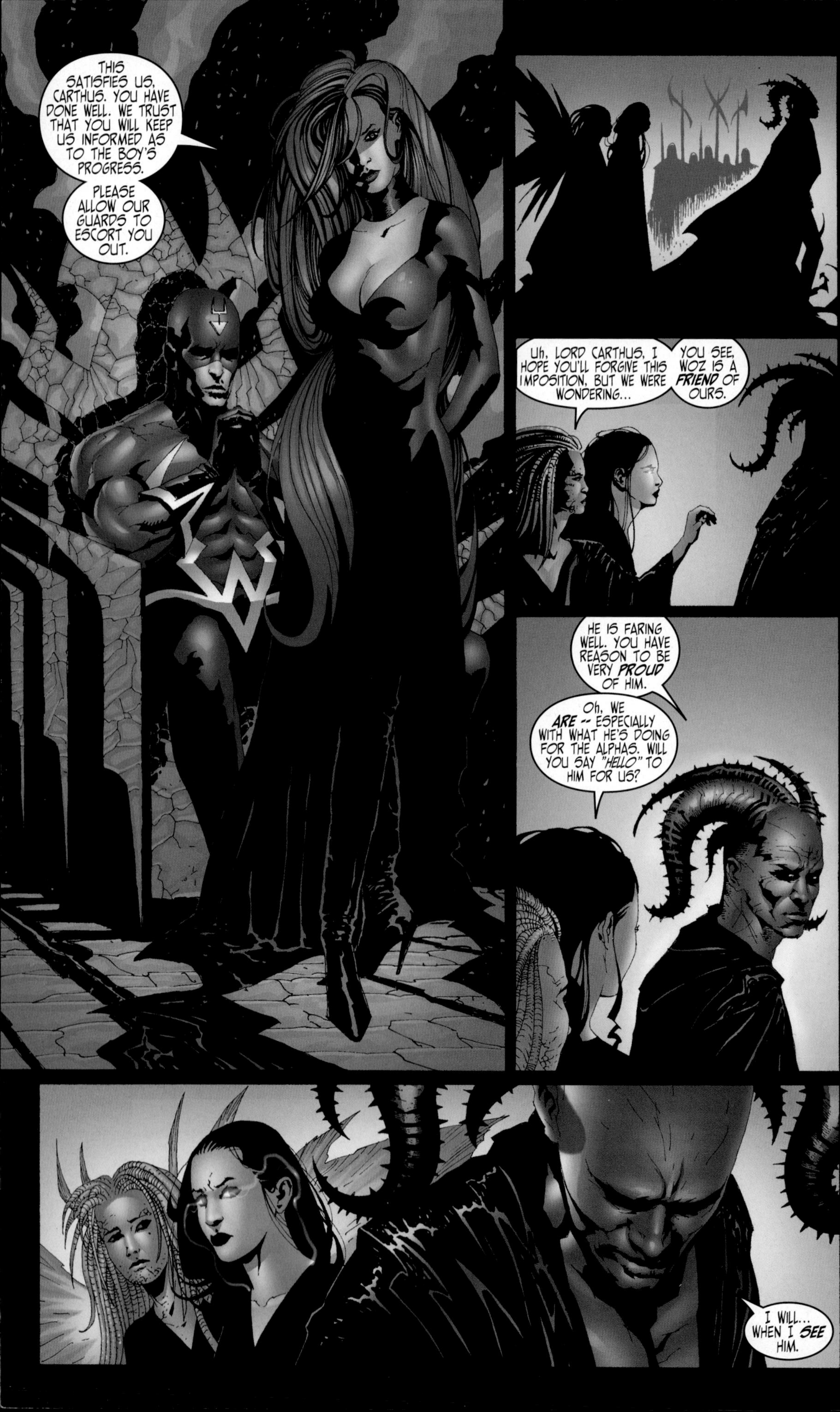
THIS SATISFIES US, CARTHUS. YOU HAVE DONE WELL. WE TRUST THAT YOU WILL KEEP US INFORMED AS TO THE BOY'S PROGRESS.
PLEASE ALLOW OUR GUARDS TO ESCORT YOU OUT.
Uh. LORD CARTHUS, I HOPE YOU'LL FORGIVE THIS IMPOSITION, BUT WE WERE WONDERING...
YOU SEE, WOZ IS A FRIEND OF OURS.
HE IS FARING WELL. YOU HAVE REASON TO BE VERY PROUD OF HIM.
Oh, WE ARE -- ESPECIALLY WITH WHAT HE'S DOING FOR THE ALPHAS. WILL YOU SAY "HELLO" TO HIM FOR US?
I WILL... WHEN I SEE HIM.

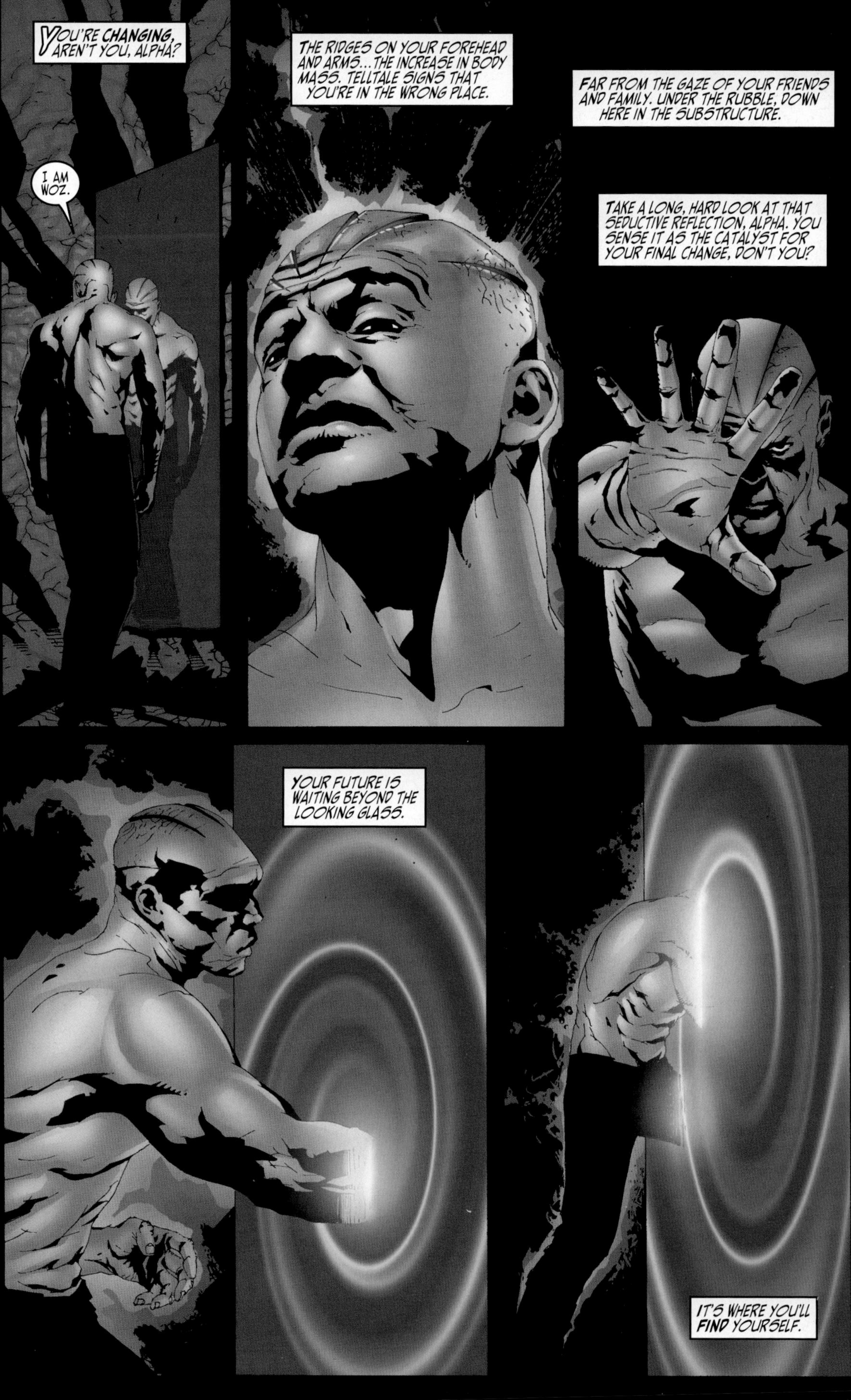
YOU'RE CHANGING, AREN'T YOU, ALPHA?
I AM WOZ.
THE RIDGES ON YOUR FOREHEAD AND ARMS... THE INCREASE IN BODY MASS. TELLTALE SIGNS THAT YOU'RE IN THE WRONG PLACE.
FAR FROM THE GAZE OF YOUR FRIENDS AND FAMILY. UNDER THE RUBBLE, DOWN HERE IN THE SUBSTRUCTURE.
TAKE A LONG, HARD LOOK AT THAT SEDUCTIVE REFLECTION, ALPHA. YOU SENSE IT AS THE CATALYST FOR YOUR FINAL CHANGE, DON'T YOU?
YOUR FUTURE IS WAITING BEYOND THE LOOKING GLASS.
IT'S WHERE YOU'LL FIND YOURSELF.

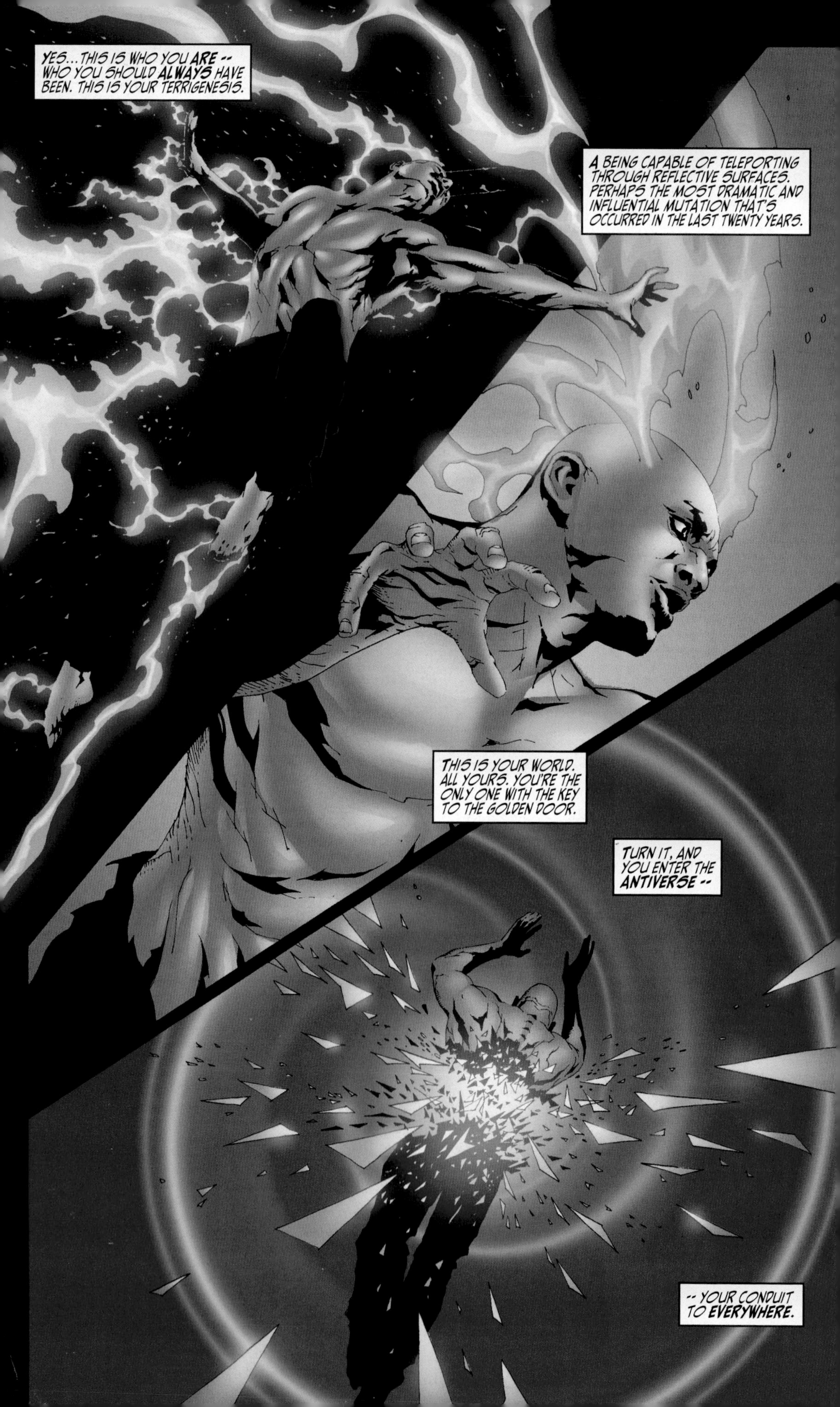
YES... THIS IS WHO YOU ARE -- WHO YOU SHOULD ALWAYS HAVE BEEN. THIS IS YOUR TERRIGENESIS.
A BEING CAPABLE OF TELEPORTING THROUGH REFLECTIVE SURFACES. PERHAPS THE MOST DRAMATIC AND INFLUENTIAL MUTATION THAT'S OCCURRED IN THE LAST TWENTY YEARS.
THIS IS YOUR WORLD. ALL YOURS. YOU'RE THE ONLY ONE WITH THE KEY TO THE GOLDEN DOOR.
TURN IT, AND YOU ENTER THE ANTIVERSE --
-- YOUR CONDUIT TO EVERYWHERE.

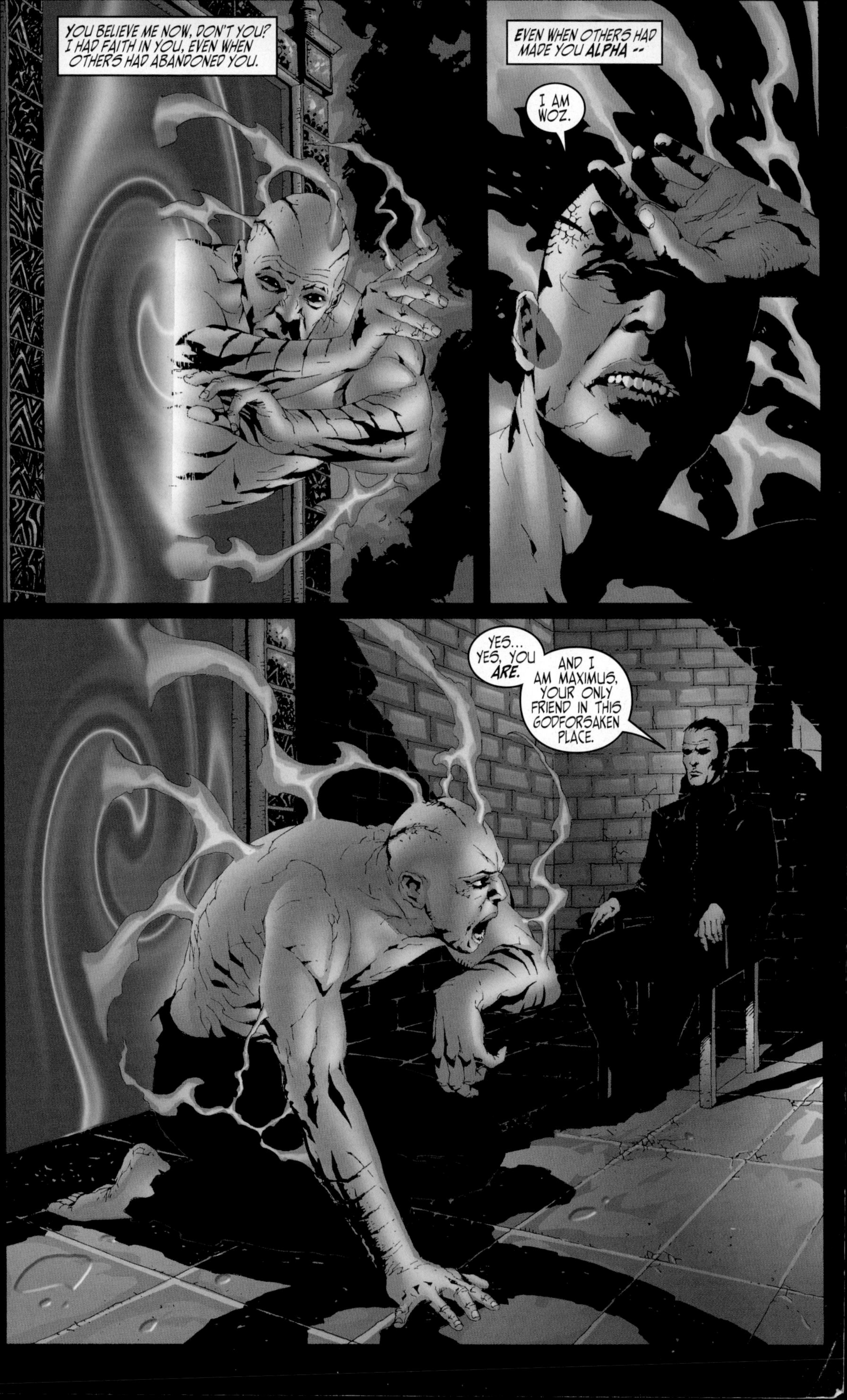
YOU BELIEVE ME NOW, DON'T YOU? I HAD FAITH IN YOU, EVEN WHEN OTHERS HAD ABANDONED YOU.
EVEN WHEN OTHERS HAD MADE YOU ALPHA --
I AM WOZ.
YES... YES, YOU ARE.
AND I AM MAXIMUS, YOUR ONLY FRIEND IN THIS GODFORSAKEN PLACE.

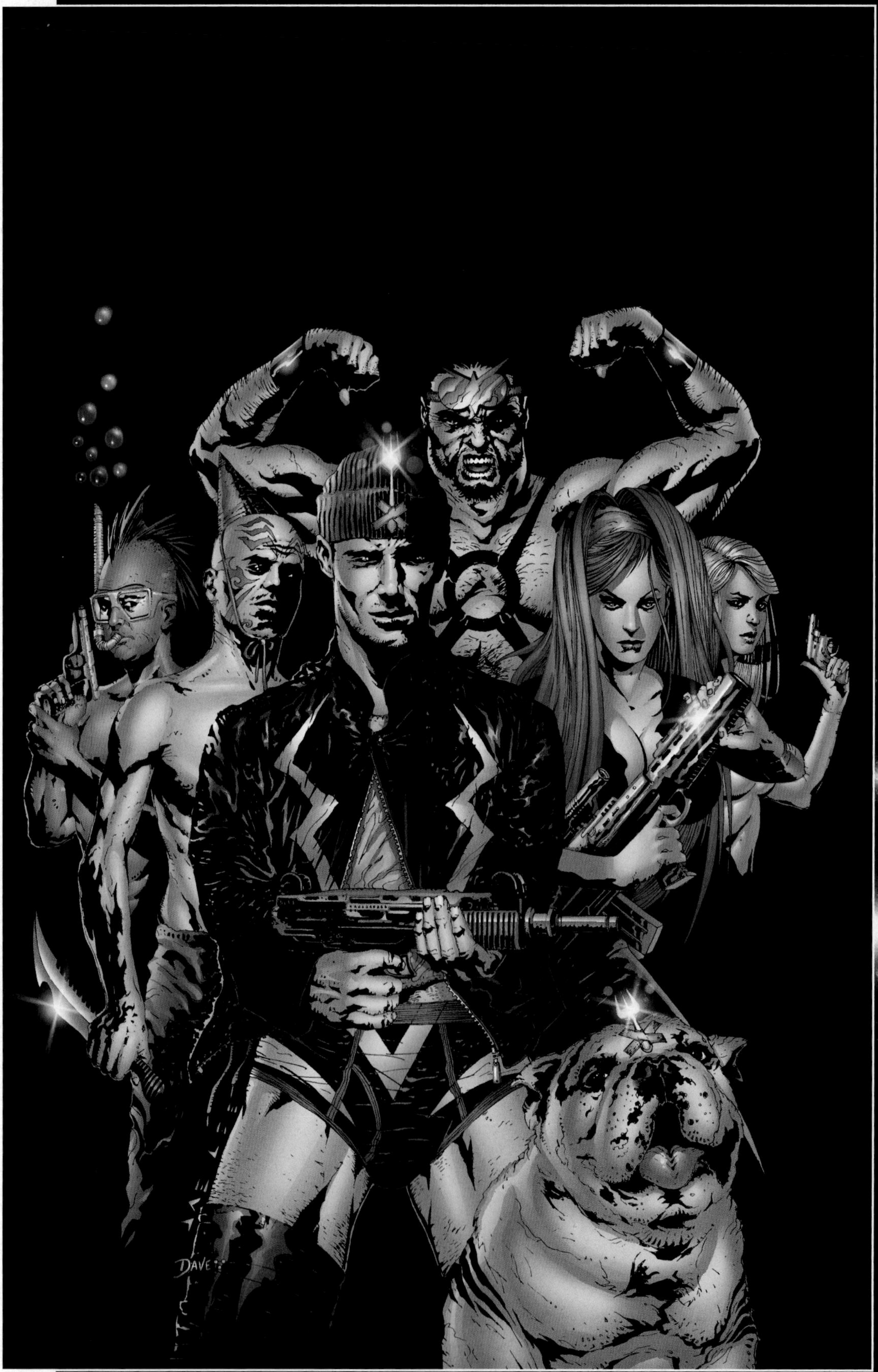

INHUMANS #4

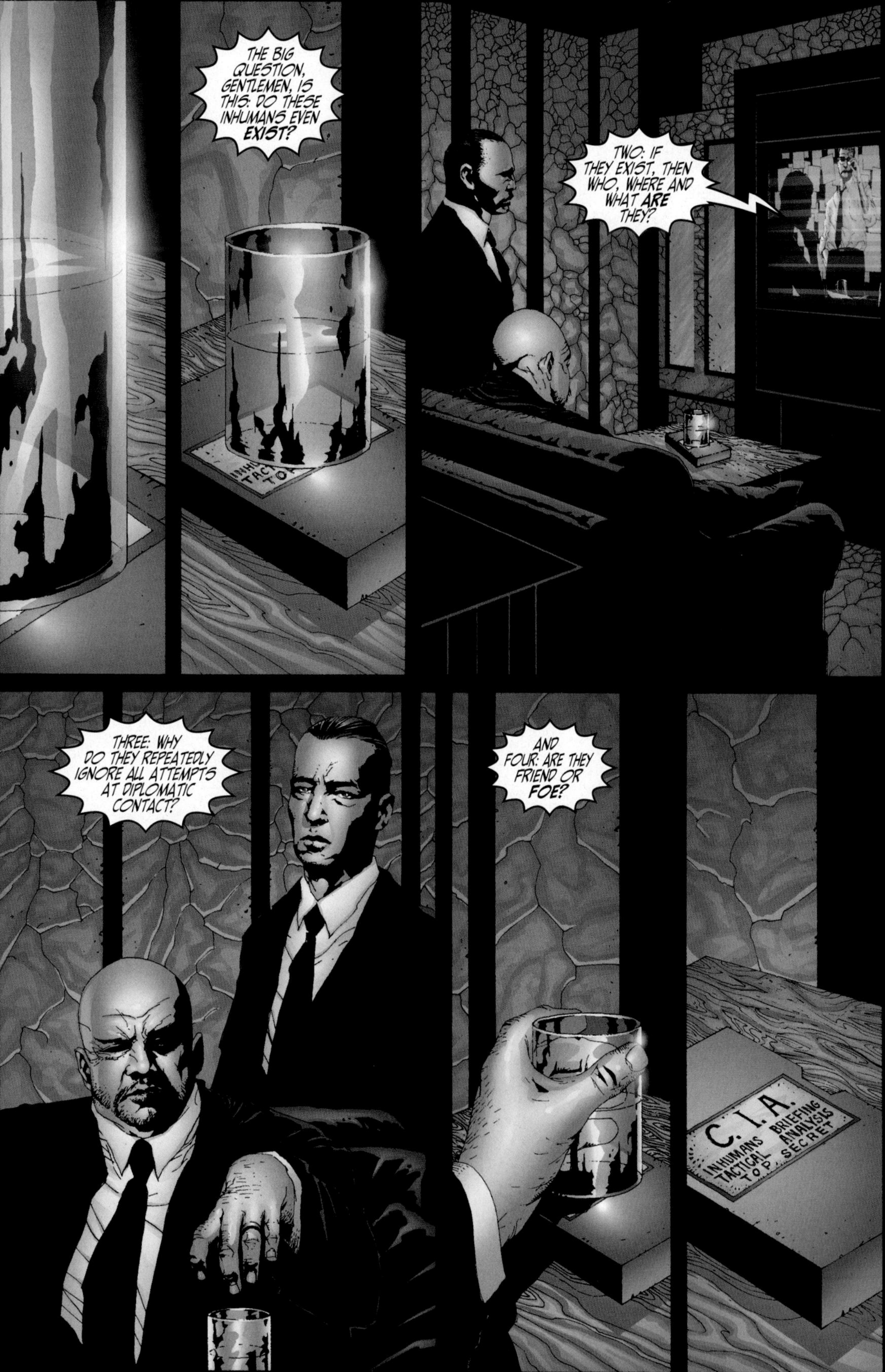
THE BIG QUESTION, GENTLEMEN, IS THIS: DO THESE INHUMANS EVEN **EXIST?**
TWO: IF THEY EXIST, THEN WHO, WHERE AND WHAT **ARE** THEY?
THREE: WHY DO THEY REPEATEDLY IGNORE ALL ATTEMPTS AT DIPLOMATIC CONTACT?
AND FOUR: ARE THEY FRIEND OR **FOE?**
C.I.A.
INHUMANS BRIEFING
TACTICAL ANALYSIS
TOP SECRET

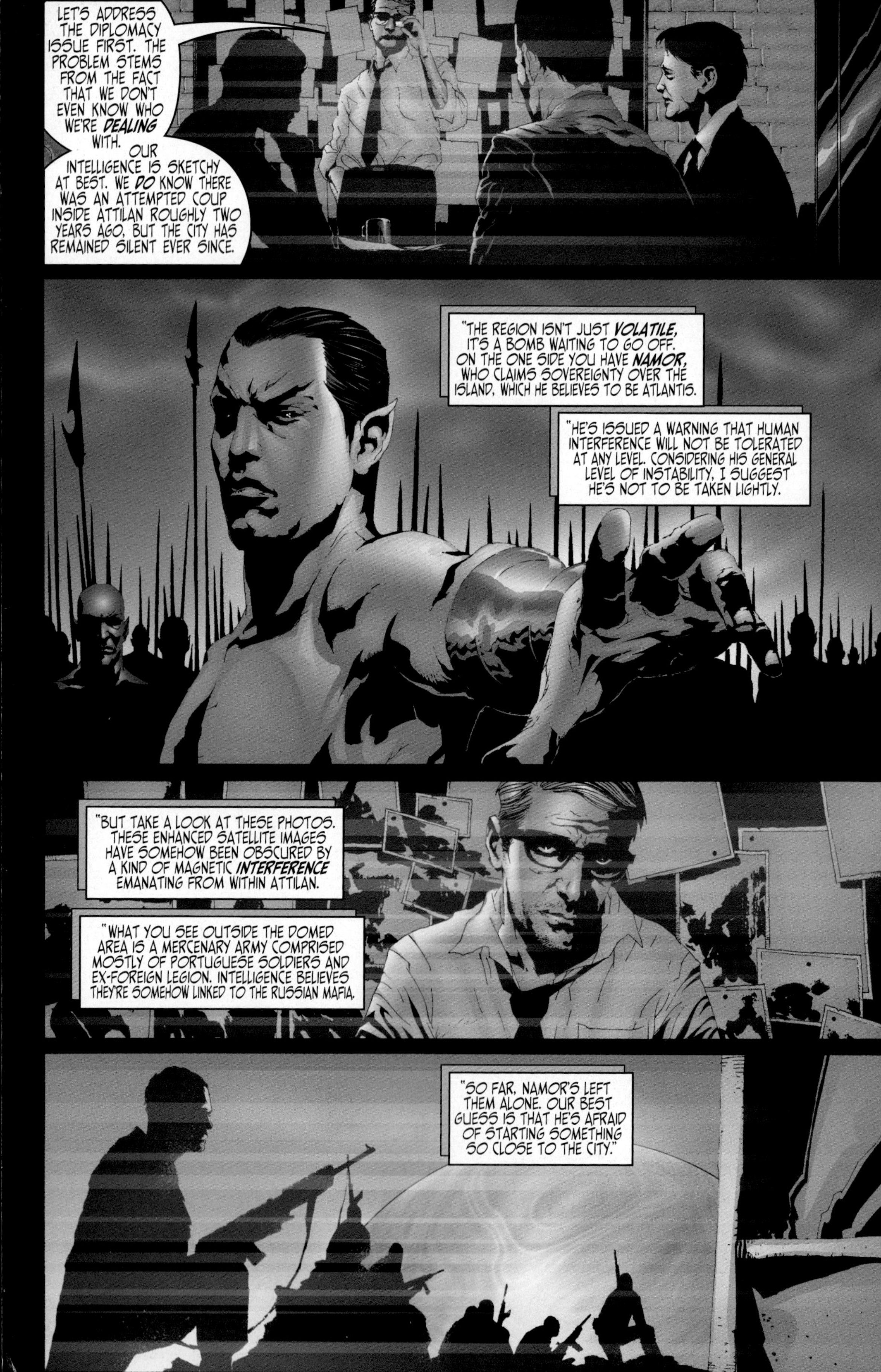
LET'S ADDRESS THE DIPLOMACY ISSUE FIRST. THE PROBLEM STEMS FROM THE FACT THAT WE DON'T EVEN KNOW WHO WE'RE DEALING WITH.
OUR INTELLIGENCE IS SKETCHY AT BEST. WE DO KNOW THERE WAS AN ATTEMPTED COUP INSIDE ATTILAN ROUGHLY TWO YEARS AGO, BUT THE CITY HAS REMAINED SILENT EVER SINCE.
"THE REGION ISN'T JUST VOLATILE, IT'S A BOMB WAITING TO GO OFF. ON THE ONE SIDE YOU HAVE NAMOR, WHO CLAIMS SOVEREIGNTY OVER THE ISLAND, WHICH HE BELIEVES TO BE ATLANTIS.
"HE'S ISSUED A WARNING THAT HUMAN INTERFERENCE WILL NOT BE TOLERATED AT ANY LEVEL. CONSIDERING HIS GENERAL LEVEL OF INSTABILITY, I SUGGEST HE'S NOT TO BE TAKEN LIGHTLY.
"BUT TAKE A LOOK AT THESE PHOTOS. THESE ENHANCED SATELLITE IMAGES HAVE SOMEHOW BEEN OBSCURED BY A KIND OF MAGNETIC INTERFERENCE EMANATING FROM WITHIN ATTILAN.
"WHAT YOU SEE OUTSIDE THE DOMED AREA IS A MERCENARY ARMY COMPRISED MOSTLY OF PORTUGUESE SOLDIERS AND EX-FOREIGN LEGION. INTELLIGENCE BELIEVES THEY'RE SOMEHOW LINKED TO THE RUSSIAN MAFIA.
"SO FAR, NAMOR'S LEFT THEM ALONE. OUR BEST GUESS IS THAT HE'S AFRAID OF STARTING SOMETHING SO CLOSE TO THE CITY."

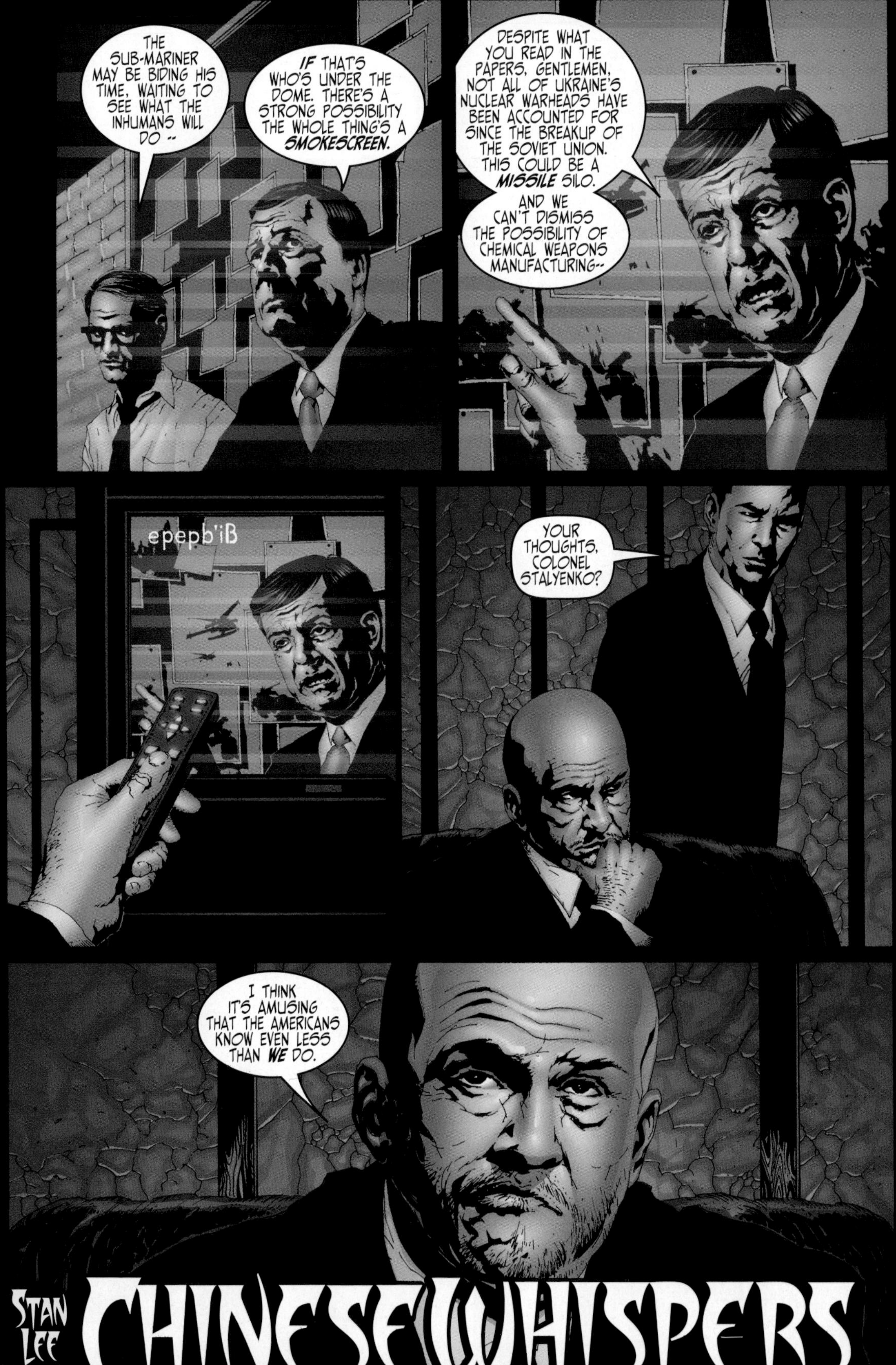
THE SUB-MARINER MAY BE BIDING HIS TIME, WAITING TO SEE WHAT THE INHUMANS WILL DO --
IF THAT'S WHO'S UNDER THE DOME. THERE'S A STRONG POSSIBILITY THE WHOLE THING'S A SMOKESCREEN.
DESPITE WHAT YOU READ IN THE PAPERS, GENTLEMEN, NOT ALL OF UKRAINE'S NUCLEAR WARHEADS HAVE BEEN ACCOUNTED FOR SINCE THE BREAKUP OF THE SOVIET UNION. THIS COULD BE A MISSILE SILO.
AND WE CAN'T DISMISS THE POSSIBILITY OF CHEMICAL WEAPONS MANUFACTURING--
epepb'iB
YOUR THOUGHTS, COLONEL STALYENKO?
I THINK IT'S AMUSING THAT THE AMERICANS KNOW EVEN LESS THAN WE DO.

Stan Lee Presents:

CHINESE WHISPERS

Paul Jenkins Wrote It Down | Jae Lee Drew It Out | David Kemp Colored It Up | RS&Comicraft/LA Lettered It Carefully | Joe & Jimmy Told it Right | Nanci Dakesian Passed it On | Bob Harras Misheard it

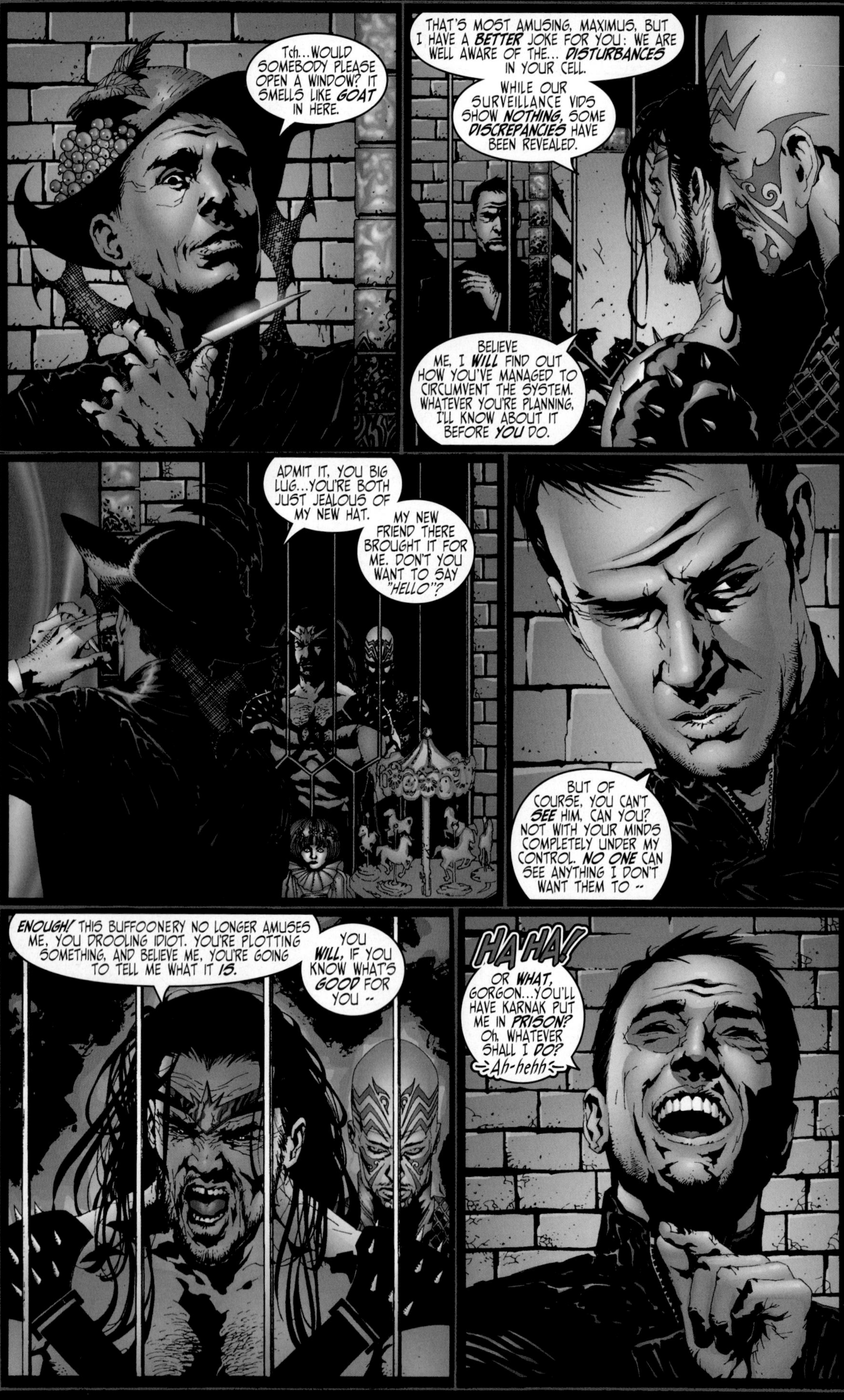
Tch...WOULD SOMEBODY PLEASE OPEN A WINDOW? IT SMELLS LIKE GOAT IN HERE.
THAT'S MOST AMUSING, MAXIMUS, BUT I HAVE A BETTER JOKE FOR YOU: WE ARE WELL AWARE OF THE... DISTURBANCES IN YOUR CELL.
WHILE OUR SURVEILLANCE VIDS SHOW NOTHING, SOME DISCREPANCIES HAVE BEEN REVEALED.
BELIEVE ME, I WILL FIND OUT HOW YOU'VE MANAGED TO CIRCUMVENT THE SYSTEM. WHATEVER YOU'RE PLANNING, I'LL KNOW ABOUT IT BEFORE YOU DO.
ADMIT IT, YOU BIG LUG...YOU'RE BOTH JUST JEALOUS OF MY NEW HAT.
MY NEW FRIEND THERE BROUGHT IT FOR ME. DON'T YOU WANT TO SAY "HELLO"?
BUT OF COURSE, YOU CAN'T SEE HIM, CAN YOU? NOT WITH YOUR MINDS COMPLETELY UNDER MY CONTROL. NO ONE CAN SEE ANYTHING I DON'T WANT THEM TO --
ENOUGH! THIS BUFFOONERY NO LONGER AMUSES ME, YOU DROOLING IDIOT. YOU'RE PLOTTING SOMETHING, AND BELIEVE ME, YOU'RE GOING TO TELL ME WHAT IT IS.
YOU WILL, IF YOU KNOW WHAT'S GOOD FOR YOU --
HA HA!
OR WHAT, GORGON...YOU'LL HAVE KARNAK PUT ME IN PRISON? Oh, WHATEVER SHALL I DO?
Ah-hehh

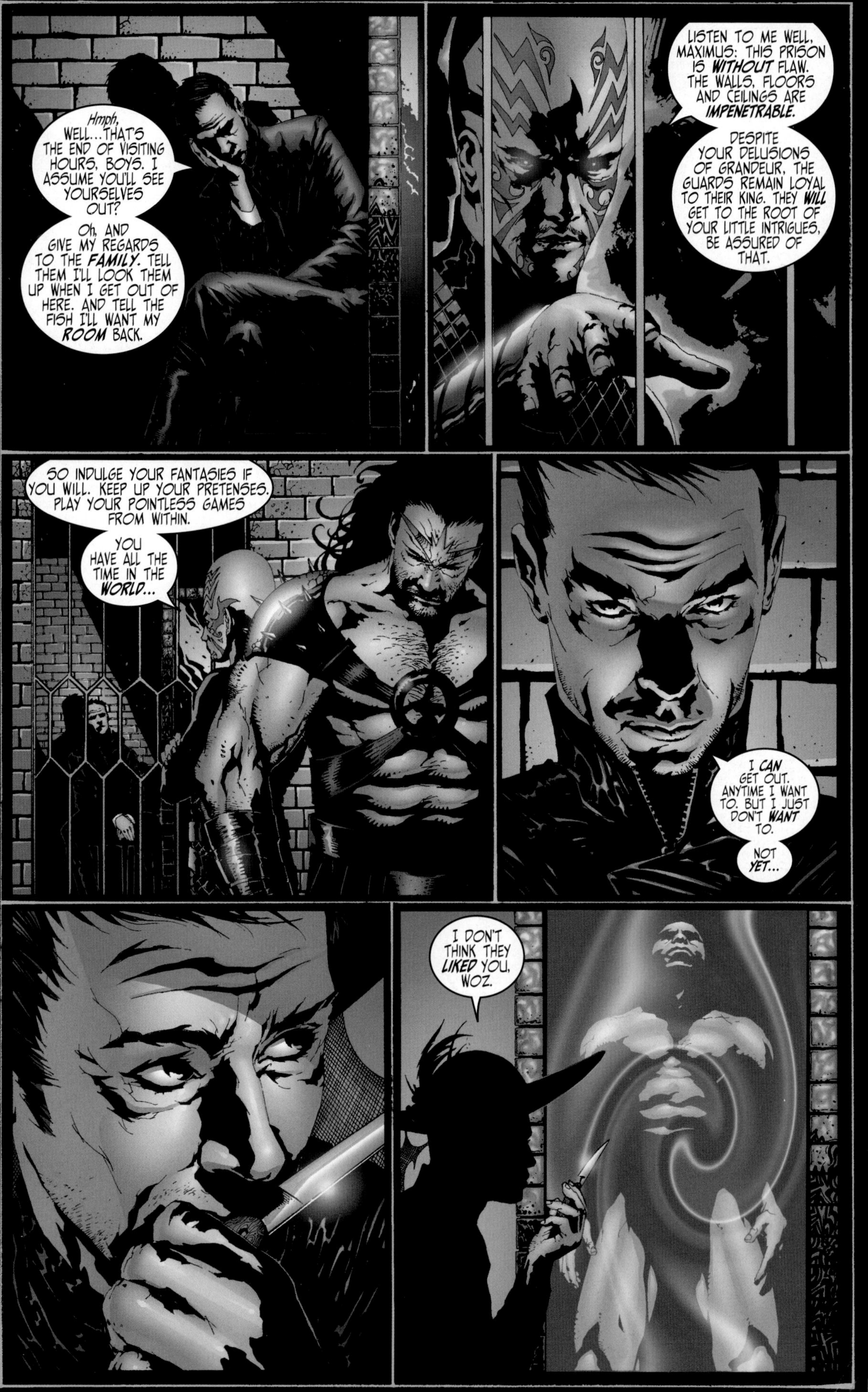
Hmph, WELL... THAT'S THE END OF VISITING HOURS, BOYS. I ASSUME YOU'LL SEE YOURSELVES OUT?
Oh, AND GIVE MY REGARDS TO THE FAMILY. TELL THEM I'LL LOOK THEM UP WHEN I GET OUT OF HERE. AND TELL THE FISH I'LL WANT MY ROOM BACK.
LISTEN TO ME WELL, MAXIMUS: THIS PRISON IS WITHOUT FLAW. THE WALLS, FLOORS AND CEILINGS ARE IMPENETRABLE.
DESPITE YOUR DELUSIONS OF GRANDEUR, THE GUARDS REMAIN LOYAL TO THEIR KING. THEY WILL GET TO THE ROOT OF YOUR LITTLE INTRIGUES, BE ASSURED OF THAT.
SO INDULGE YOUR FANTASIES IF YOU WILL. KEEP UP YOUR PRETENSES. PLAY YOUR POINTLESS GAMES FROM WITHIN.
YOU HAVE ALL THE TIME IN THE WORLD...
I CAN GET OUT. ANYTIME I WANT TO. BUT I JUST DON'T WANT TO.
NOT YET...
I DON'T THINK THEY LIKED YOU, WOZ.

I THINK THE FUNDAMENTAL QUESTION IS WHETHER WE CAN HOLD THESE INHUMANS -- IF THAT'S WHAT THEY *ARE* -- TO THE SAME STANDARDS AS *HUMANITY* --

YO, LISTEN...WE SAYIN' THEY ANY LESS THAN US 'CAUSE THEY *DIFFERENT?* 'CAUSE LAS' TIME I CHECK, WE KISSED *THAT* ATTITUDE GOODBYE A *LONG* TIME AGO.

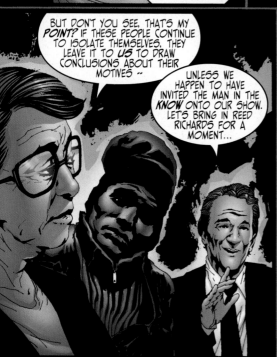

BUT DON'T YOU SEE, THAT'S MY *POINT?* IF THESE PEOPLE CONTINUE TO ISOLATE THEMSELVES, THEY LEAVE IT TO *US* TO DRAW CONCLUSIONS ABOUT THEIR MOTIVES --

UNLESS WE HAPPEN TO HAVE INVITED THE MAN IN THE *KNOW* ONTO OUR SHOW. LET'S BRING IN REED RICHARDS FOR A MOMENT...

REED, WE'VE ALL HEARD WILDLY INACCURATE RUMORS LINKING YOU WITH EVERYONE FROM MARILYN MANSON TO SPIDER-MAN TO THE CIA...

...BUT I HAVE IT ON GOOD AUTHORITY FROM MY FIVE-YEAR-OLD NEPHEW THAT YOU'VE BEEN *INSIDE* ATTILAN. SO, WHY THE COLD *SHOULDER?* AFRAID WE'LL STEAL THEIR WOMEN?

NO, I THINK THEY'RE DEATHLY AFRAID OF BEING INVITED TO APPEAR ON THIS SHOW.

HA HA

HA HA HA HA HA

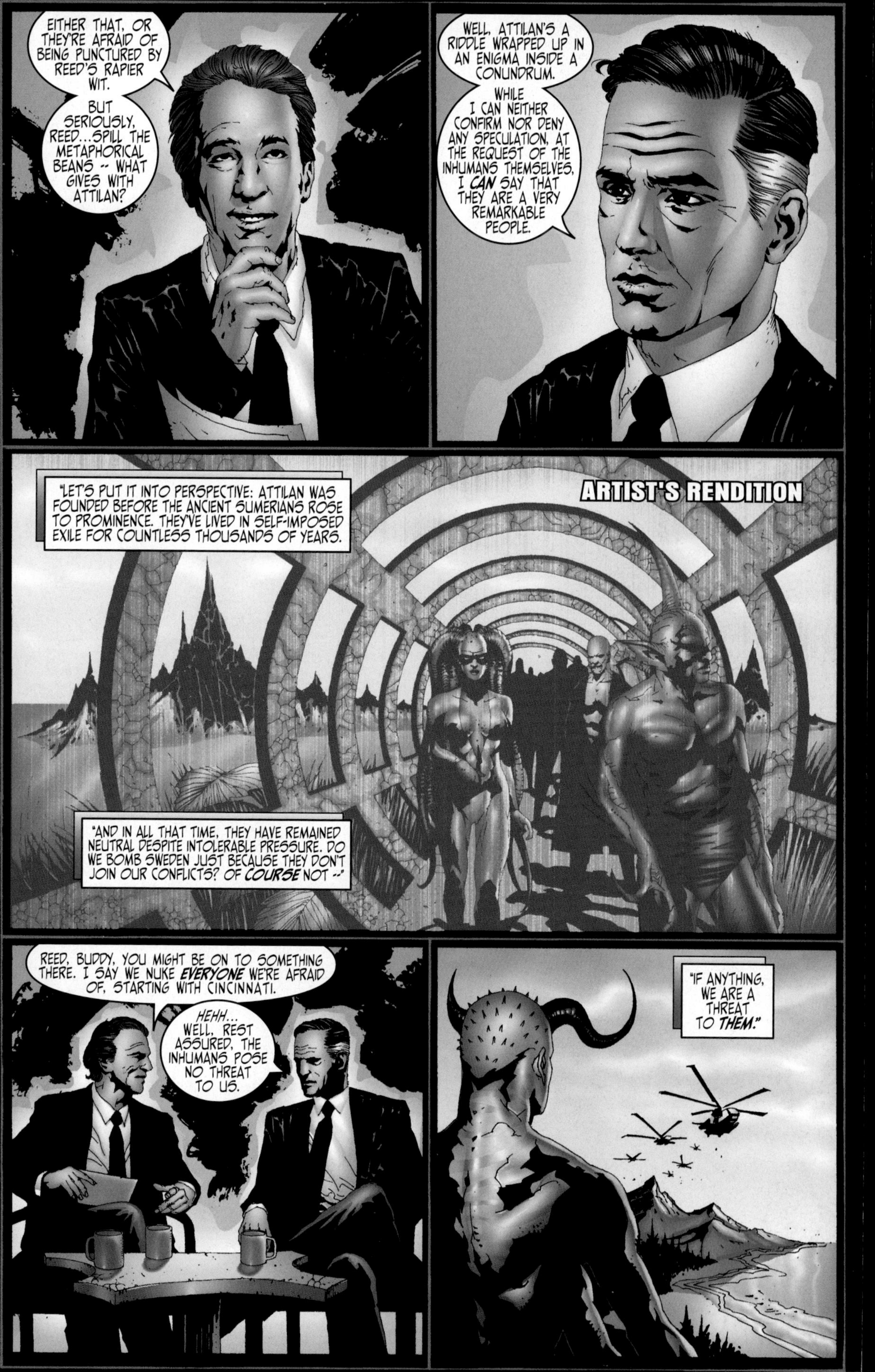
EITHER THAT, OR THEY'RE AFRAID OF BEING PUNCTURED BY REED'S RAPIER WIT.
BUT SERIOUSLY, REED...SPILL THE METAPHORICAL BEANS -- WHAT GIVES WITH ATTILAN?
WELL, ATTILAN'S A RIDDLE WRAPPED UP IN AN ENIGMA INSIDE A CONUNDRUM.
WHILE I CAN NEITHER CONFIRM NOR DENY ANY SPECULATION, AT THE REQUEST OF THE INHUMANS THEMSELVES, I CAN SAY THAT THEY ARE A VERY REMARKABLE PEOPLE.
"LET'S PUT IT INTO PERSPECTIVE: ATTILAN WAS FOUNDED BEFORE THE ANCIENT SUMERIANS ROSE TO PROMINENCE. THEY'VE LIVED IN SELF-IMPOSED EXILE FOR COUNTLESS THOUSANDS OF YEARS.
ARTIST'S RENDITION
"AND IN ALL THAT TIME, THEY HAVE REMAINED NEUTRAL DESPITE INTOLERABLE PRESSURE. DO WE BOMB SWEDEN JUST BECAUSE THEY DON'T JOIN OUR CONFLICTS? OF COURSE NOT --"
REED, BUDDY, YOU MIGHT BE ON TO SOMETHING THERE. I SAY WE NUKE EVERYONE WE'RE AFRAID OF, STARTING WITH CINCINNATI.
HEHH... WELL, REST ASSURED, THE INHUMANS POSE NO THREAT TO US.
"IF ANYTHING, WE ARE A THREAT TO THEM."

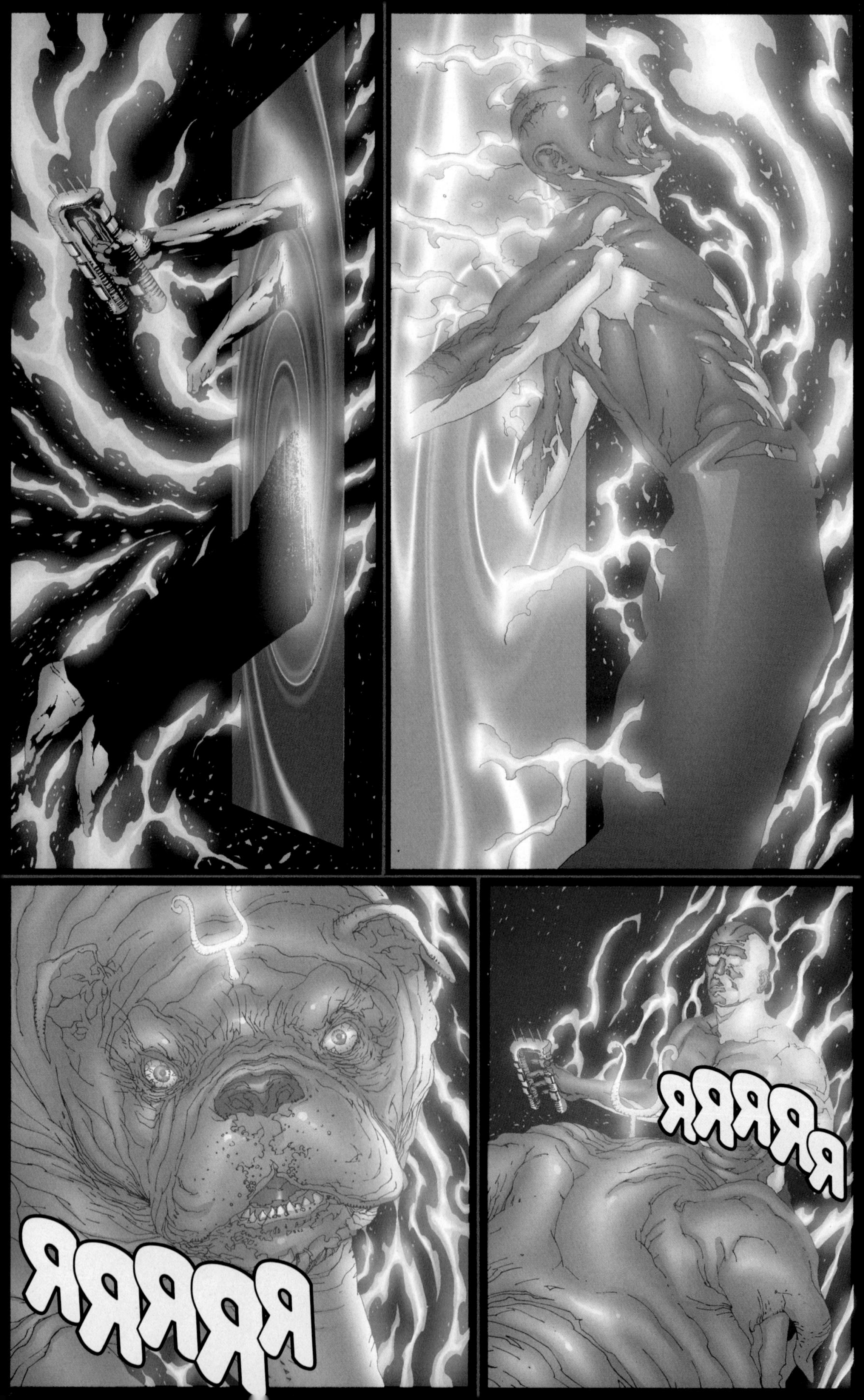
RRRRR
RRRRR

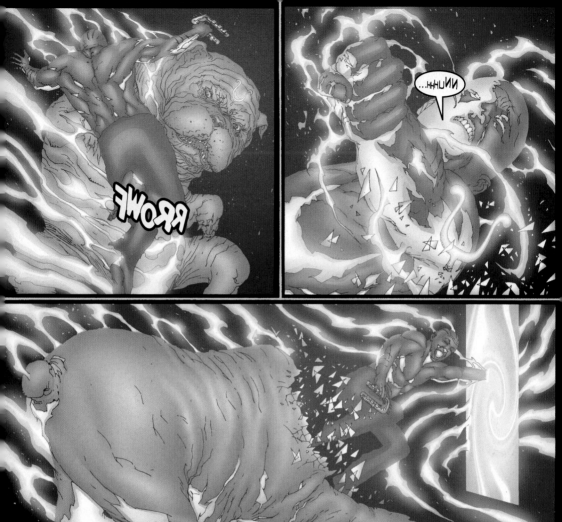

...HHHUNN..

ЯWOЯꟻ

Nnnuhh... DOG CHASE WOZ! DOG CHASE WOZ!

Hmm --?

YOU KNOW, WOZ, I THINK SOME *CURTAINS* WOULD BRIGHTEN THE PLACE UP A BIT...

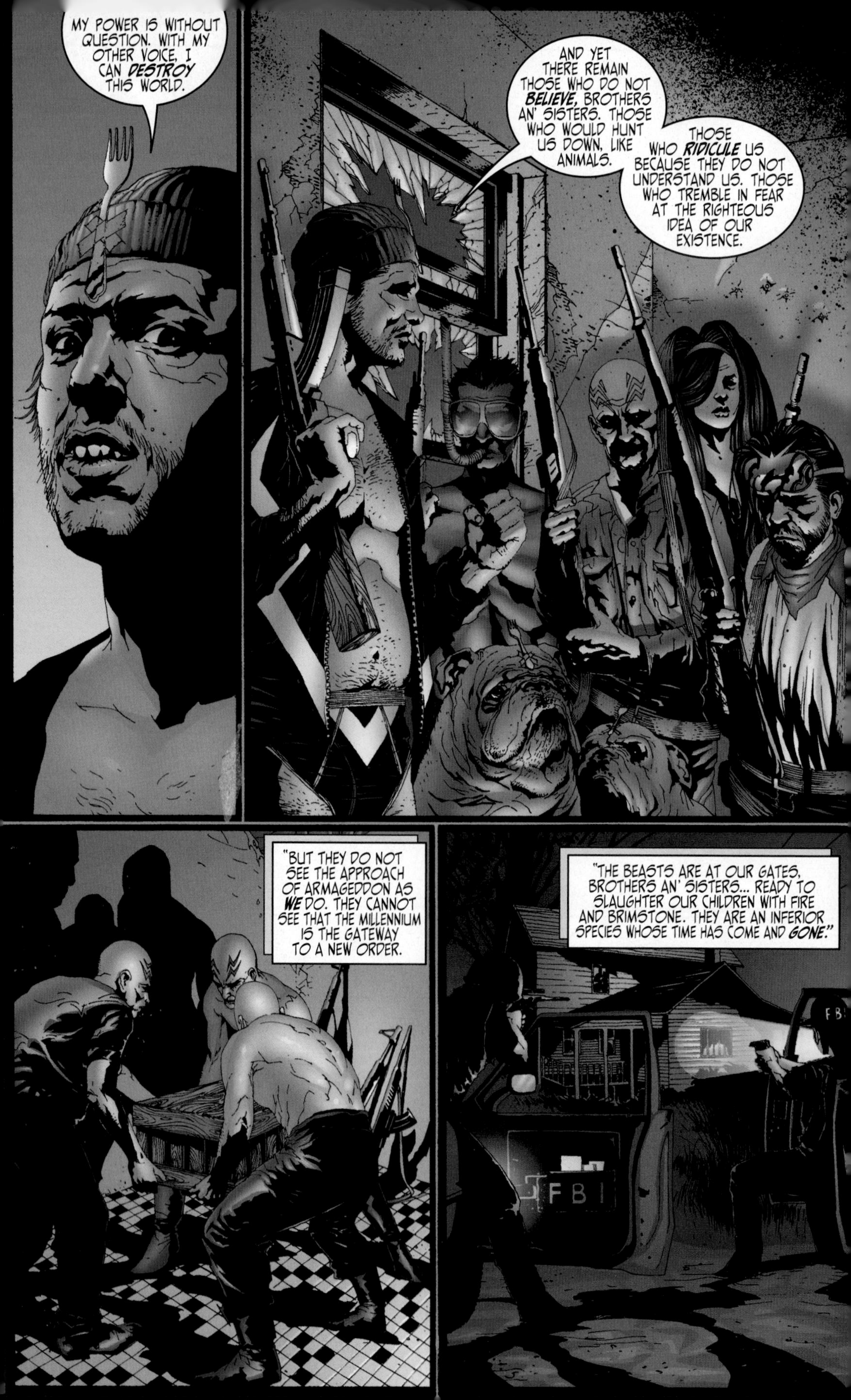
MY POWER IS WITHOUT QUESTION. WITH MY OTHER VOICE, I CAN DESTROY THIS WORLD.
AND YET THERE REMAIN THOSE WHO DO NOT BELIEVE, BROTHERS AN' SISTERS. THOSE WHO WOULD HUNT US DOWN, LIKE ANIMALS.
THOSE WHO RIDICULE US BECAUSE THEY DO NOT UNDERSTAND US. THOSE WHO TREMBLE IN FEAR AT THE RIGHTEOUS IDEA OF OUR EXISTENCE.
"BUT THEY DO NOT SEE THE APPROACH OF ARMAGEDDON AS WE DO. THEY CANNOT SEE THAT THE MILLENNIUM IS THE GATEWAY TO A NEW ORDER.
"THE BEASTS ARE AT OUR GATES, BROTHERS AN' SISTERS... READY TO SLAUGHTER OUR CHILDREN WITH FIRE AND BRIMSTONE. THEY ARE AN INFERIOR SPECIES WHOSE TIME HAS COME AND GONE."
FBI
FBI

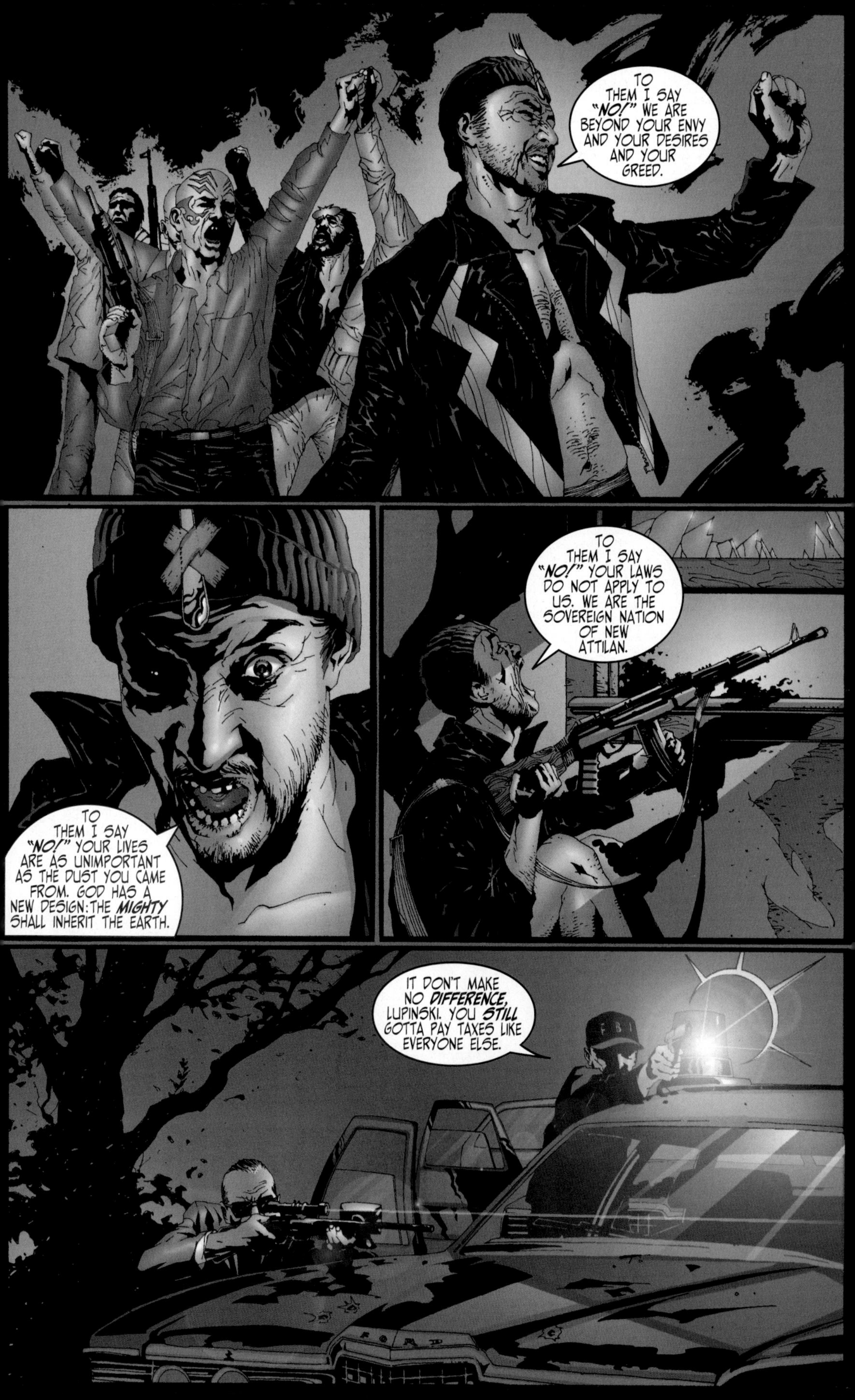
TO THEM I SAY "NO!" WE ARE BEYOND YOUR ENVY AND YOUR DESIRES AND YOUR GREED.
TO THEM I SAY "NO!" YOUR LIVES ARE AS UNIMPORTANT AS THE DUST YOU CAME FROM. GOD HAS A NEW DESIGN: THE MIGHTY SHALL INHERIT THE EARTH.
TO THEM I SAY "NO!" YOUR LAWS DO NOT APPLY TO US. WE ARE THE SOVEREIGN NATION OF NEW ATTILAN.
IT DON'T MAKE NO DIFFERENCE, LUPINSKI. YOU STILL GOTTA PAY TAXES LIKE EVERYONE ELSE.

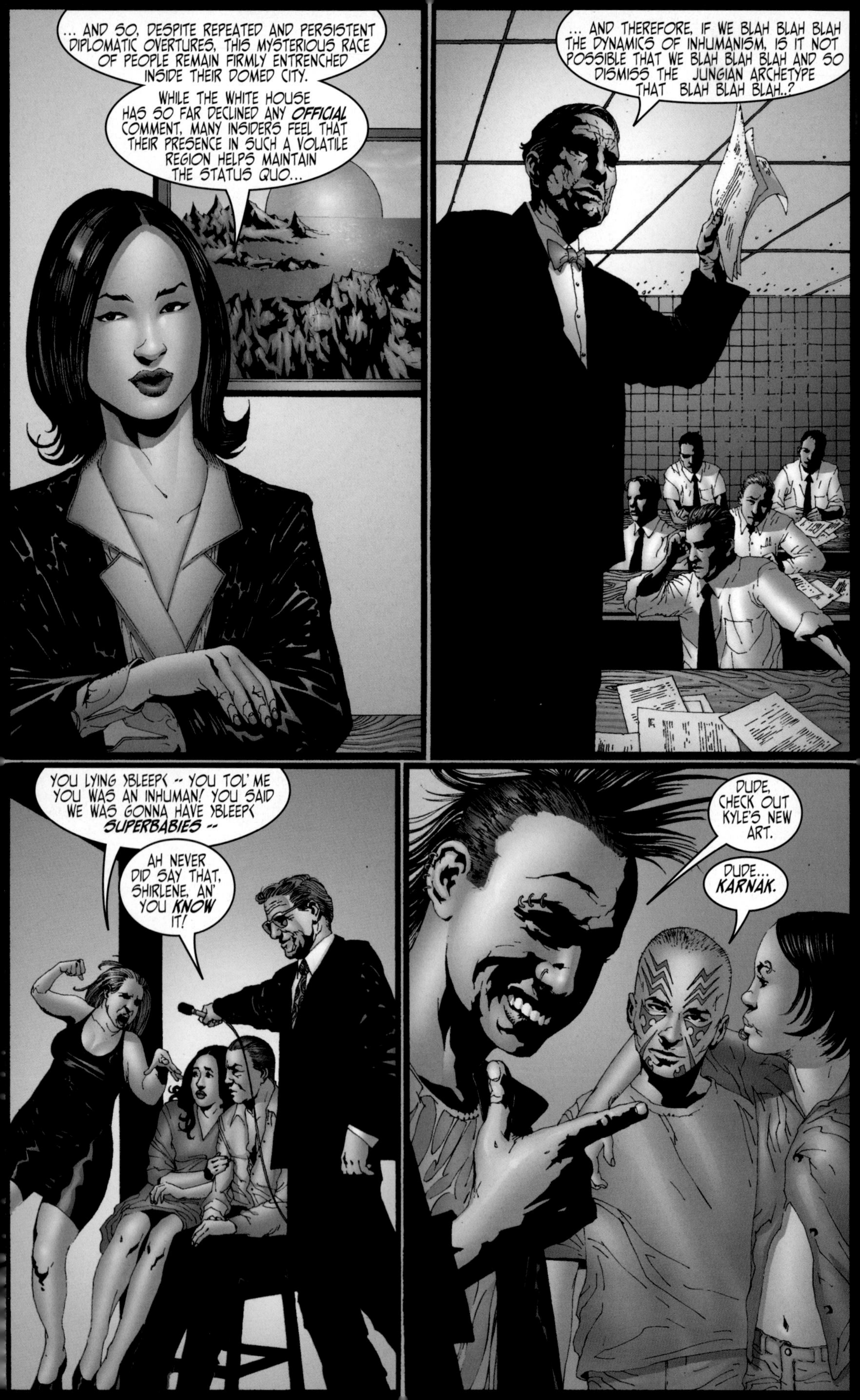
... AND SO, DESPITE REPEATED AND PERSISTENT DIPLOMATIC OVERTURES, THIS MYSTERIOUS RACE OF PEOPLE REMAIN FIRMLY ENTRENCHED INSIDE THEIR DOMED CITY.
WHILE THE WHITE HOUSE HAS SO FAR DECLINED ANY *OFFICIAL* COMMENT, MANY INSIDERS FEEL THAT THEIR PRESENCE IN SUCH A VOLATILE REGION HELPS MAINTAIN THE STATUS QUO...
... AND THEREFORE, IF WE BLAH BLAH BLAH THE DYNAMICS OF INHUMANISM, IS IT NOT POSSIBLE THAT WE BLAH BLAH BLAH AND SO DISMISS THE JUNGIAN ARCHETYPE THAT BLAH BLAH BLAH..?
YOU LYING >BLEEP< -- YOU TOL' ME YOU WAS AN INHUMAN! YOU SAID WE WAS GONNA HAVE >BLEEP< *SUPERBABIES* --
AH NEVER DID SAY THAT, SHIRLENE, AN' YOU *KNOW* IT!
DUDE, CHECK OUT KYLE'S NEW ART.
DUDE... *KARNAK.*

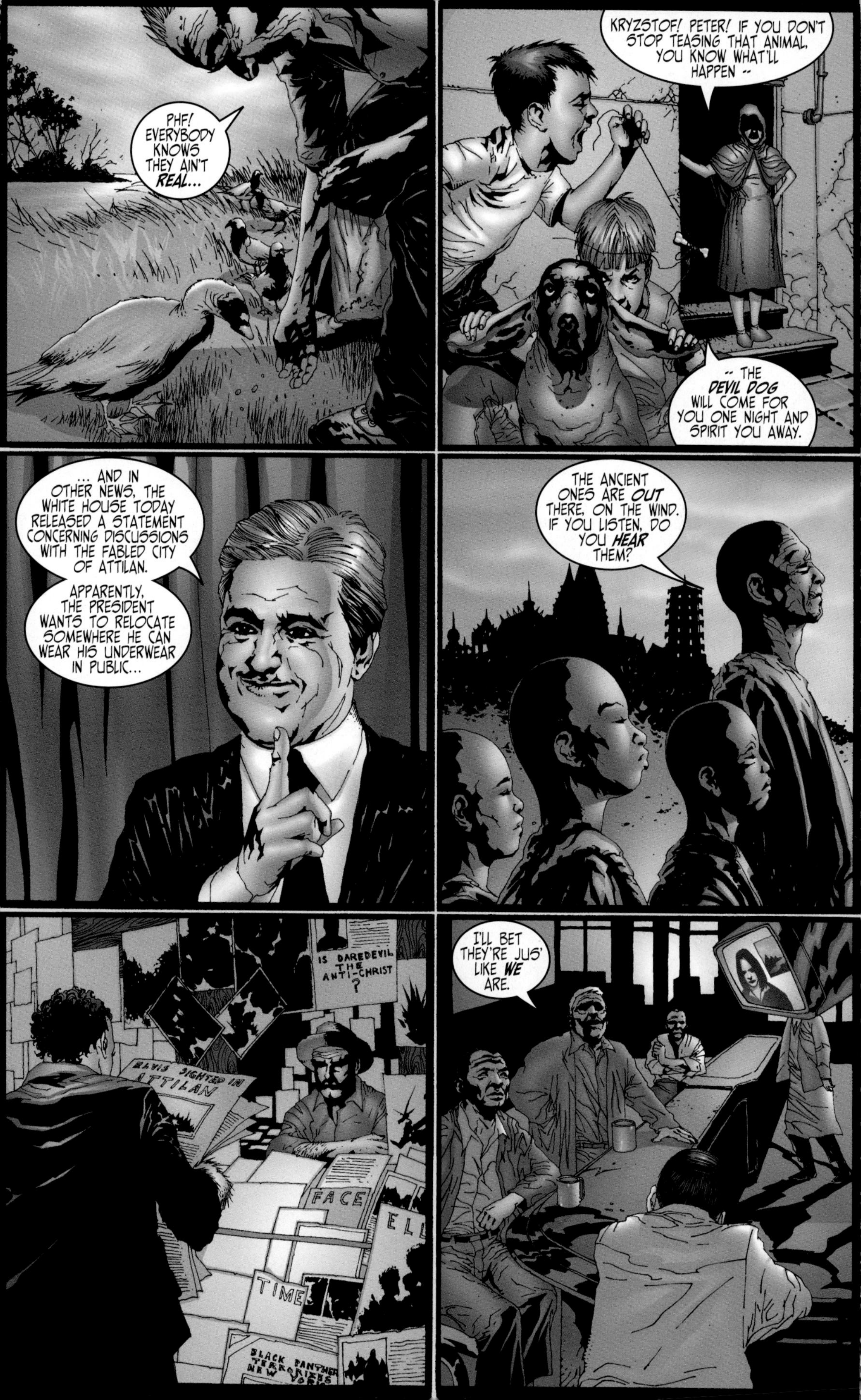
PHF! EVERYBODY KNOWS THEY AIN'T **REAL**...
KRYZSTOF! PETER! IF YOU DON'T STOP TEASING THAT ANIMAL, YOU KNOW WHAT'LL HAPPEN --
-- THE **DEVIL DOG** WILL COME FOR YOU ONE NIGHT AND SPIRIT YOU AWAY.
... AND IN OTHER NEWS, THE WHITE HOUSE TODAY RELEASED A STATEMENT CONCERNING DISCUSSIONS WITH THE FABLED CITY OF ATTILAN.
APPARENTLY, THE PRESIDENT WANTS TO RELOCATE SOMEWHERE HE CAN WEAR HIS UNDERWEAR IN PUBLIC...
THE ANCIENT ONES ARE **OUT** THERE, ON THE WIND. IF YOU LISTEN, DO YOU **HEAR** THEM?
IS DAREDEVIL THE ANTI-CHRIST ?
ELVIS SIGHTED IN ATTILAN
FACE
TIME
BLACK PANTHER TERRORIZES NEW YORK
I'LL BET THEY'RE JUS' LIKE **WE** ARE.

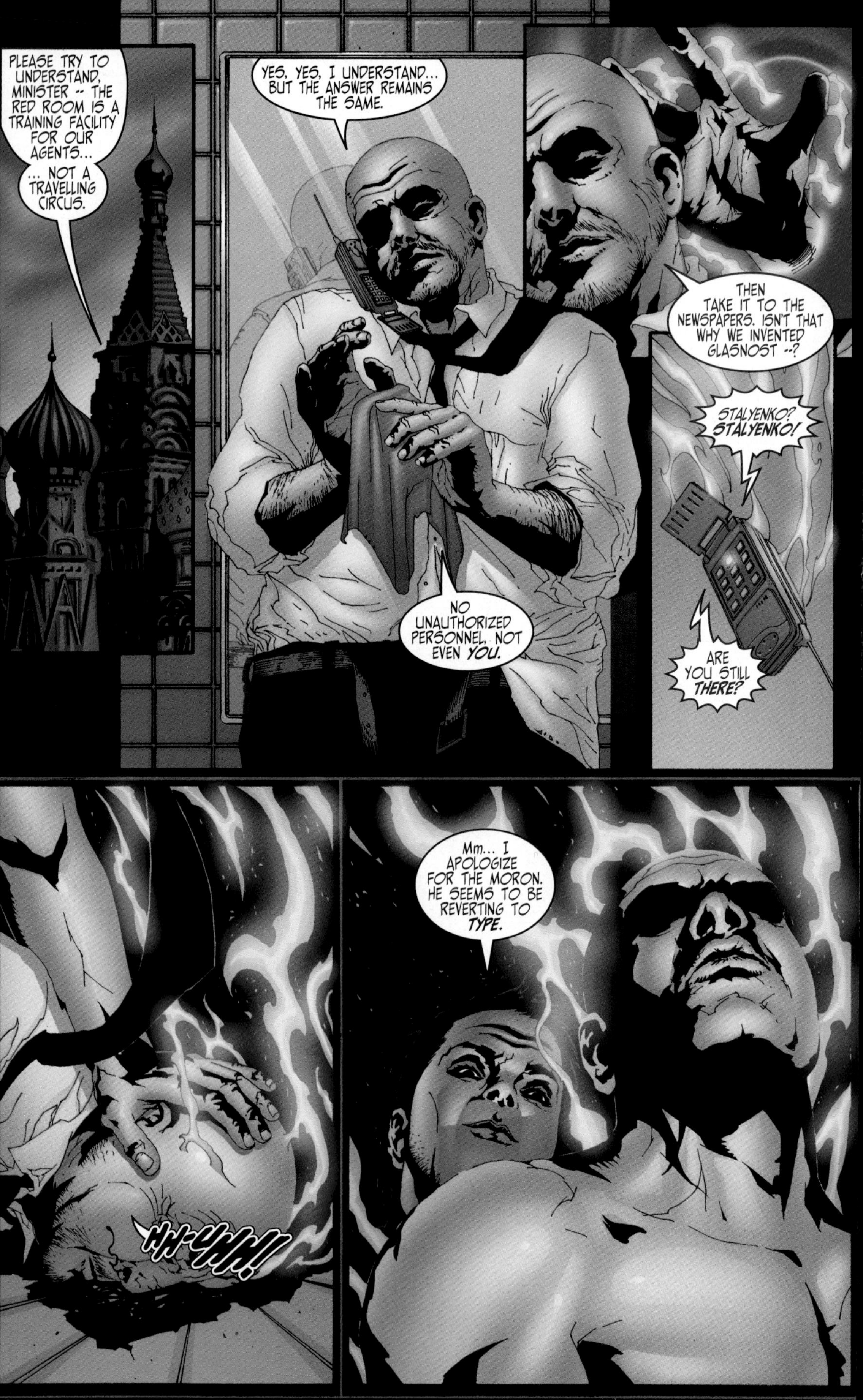
PLEASE TRY TO UNDERSTAND, MINISTER -- THE RED ROOM IS A TRAINING FACILITY FOR OUR AGENTS...
... NOT A TRAVELLING CIRCUS.
YES, YES, I UNDERSTAND... BUT THE ANSWER REMAINS THE SAME.
NO UNAUTHORIZED PERSONNEL, NOT EVEN YOU.
THEN TAKE IT TO THE NEWSPAPERS. ISN'T THAT WHY WE INVENTED GLASNOST --?
STALYENKO? STALYENKO!
ARE YOU STILL THERE?
HH-UHH!
Mm... I APOLOGIZE FOR THE MORON. HE SEEMS TO BE REVERTING TO TYPE.

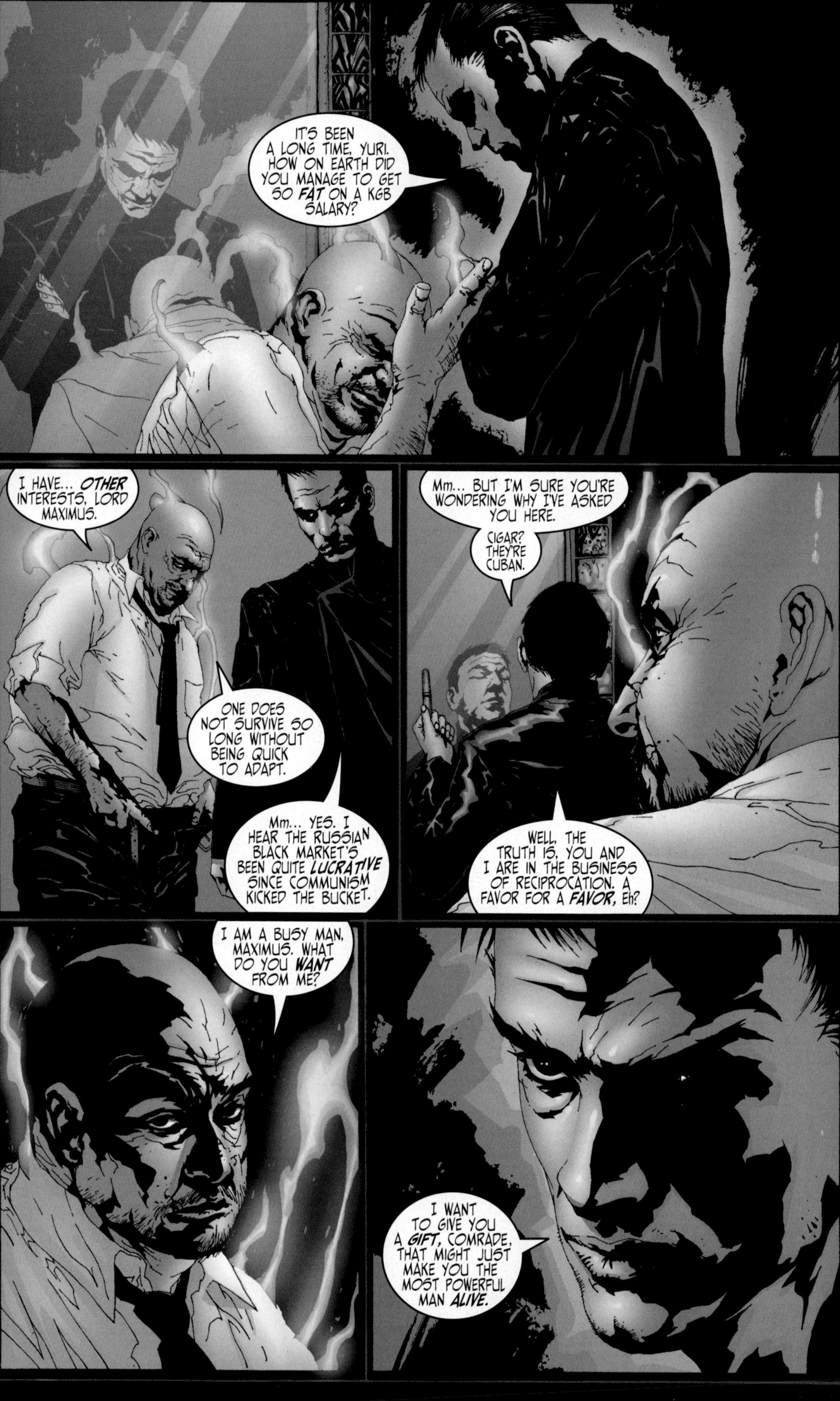
IT'S BEEN A LONG TIME, YURI. HOW ON EARTH DID YOU MANAGE TO GET SO FAT ON A KGB SALARY?
I HAVE... OTHER INTERESTS, LORD MAXIMUS.
ONE DOES NOT SURVIVE SO LONG WITHOUT BEING QUICK TO ADAPT.
Mm... YES. I HEAR THE RUSSIAN BLACK MARKET'S BEEN QUITE LUCRATIVE SINCE COMMUNISM KICKED THE BUCKET.
Mm... BUT I'M SURE YOU'RE WONDERING WHY I'VE ASKED YOU HERE.
CIGAR? THEY'RE CUBAN.
WELL, THE TRUTH IS, YOU AND I ARE IN THE BUSINESS OF RECIPROCATION. A FAVOR FOR A FAVOR, Eh?
I AM A BUSY MAN, MAXIMUS. WHAT DO YOU WANT FROM ME?
I WANT TO GIVE YOU A GIFT, COMRADE, THAT MIGHT JUST MAKE YOU THE MOST POWERFUL MAN ALIVE.

AND THE COST OF THIS... *"GIFT"*?

Oh. A MERE PITTANCE. WE'LL CONSIDER IT AN EQUAL TRADE.

AS YOU CAN SEE, I AM CURRENTLY INCARCERATED AGAINST MY WILL. REGRETTABLY, I HAVE BEEN USURPED FROM MY...->*Huff*<- **RIGHTFUL** POSITION AS MONARCH OF ATTILAN.

->*Huff*<- YOU CAN HELP ME GET MY NICE COMFORTABLE CHAIR BACK, YURI, AND I CAN GIVE YOU A TECHNOLOGICAL LEG-UP ON THE COMPETITION, SO TO SPEAK.

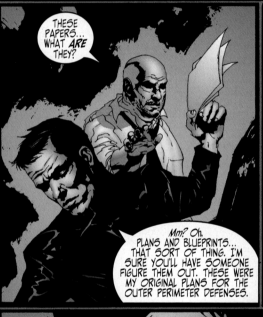

THESE PAPERS... WHAT *ARE* THEY?

Mm? Oh, PLANS AND BLUEPRINTS... THAT SORT OF THING. I'M SURE YOU'LL HAVE SOMEONE FIGURE THEM OUT. THESE WERE MY ORIGINAL PLANS FOR THE OUTER PERIMETER DEFENSES.

OF COURSE, NO DOUBT KARNAK HAS SEEN FIT TO MODIFY THE WHOLE THING.

Hmm... I HADN'T *THOUGHT* OF THAT.

EVEN IF I COULD FIND A WAY THROUGH THE PERIMETER DEFENSES, I WOULD GAIN *NOTHING* FROM IT. THE DOME IS IMPENETRABLE --

THE DOME IS MERELY A *DOORWAY*, YURI. ALL YOU NEED IS THE *KEY*.

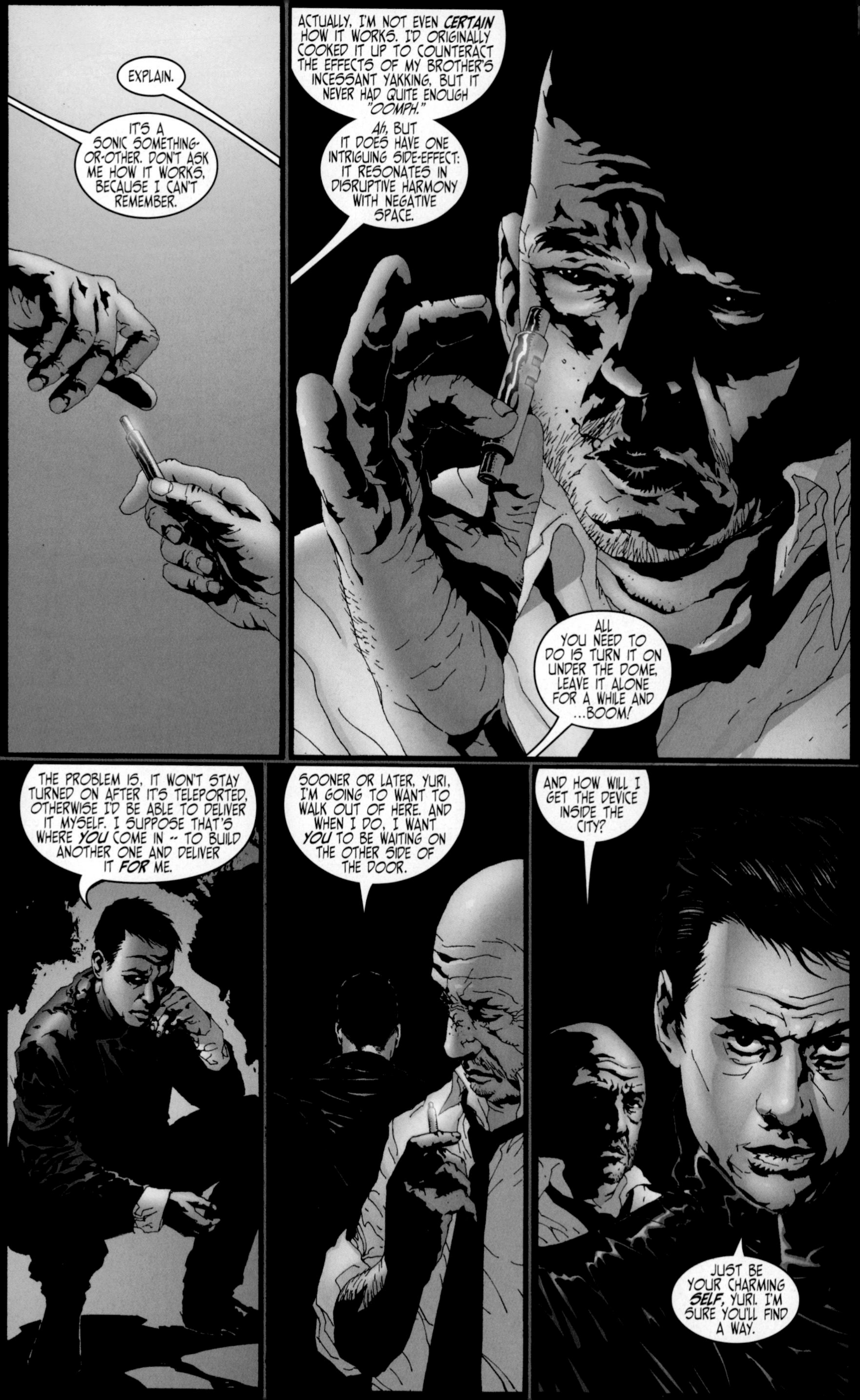
EXPLAIN.
IT'S A SONIC SOMETHING-OR-OTHER. DON'T ASK ME HOW IT WORKS, BECAUSE I CAN'T REMEMBER.
ACTUALLY, I'M NOT EVEN CERTAIN HOW IT WORKS. I'D ORIGINALLY COOKED IT UP TO COUNTERACT THE EFFECTS OF MY BROTHER'S INCESSANT YAKKING, BUT IT NEVER HAD QUITE ENOUGH "OOMPH."
Ah, BUT IT DOES HAVE ONE INTRIGUING SIDE-EFFECT: IT RESONATES IN DISRUPTIVE HARMONY WITH NEGATIVE SPACE.
ALL YOU NEED TO DO IS TURN IT ON UNDER THE DOME, LEAVE IT ALONE FOR A WHILE AND ...BOOM!
THE PROBLEM IS, IT WON'T STAY TURNED ON AFTER IT'S TELEPORTED, OTHERWISE I'D BE ABLE TO DELIVER IT MYSELF. I SUPPOSE THAT'S WHERE YOU COME IN -- TO BUILD ANOTHER ONE AND DELIVER IT FOR ME.
SOONER OR LATER, YURI, I'M GOING TO WANT TO WALK OUT OF HERE. AND WHEN I DO, I WANT YOU TO BE WAITING ON THE OTHER SIDE OF THE DOOR.
AND HOW WILL I GET THE DEVICE INSIDE THE CITY?
JUST BE YOUR CHARMING SELF, YURI. I'M SURE YOU'LL FIND A WAY.

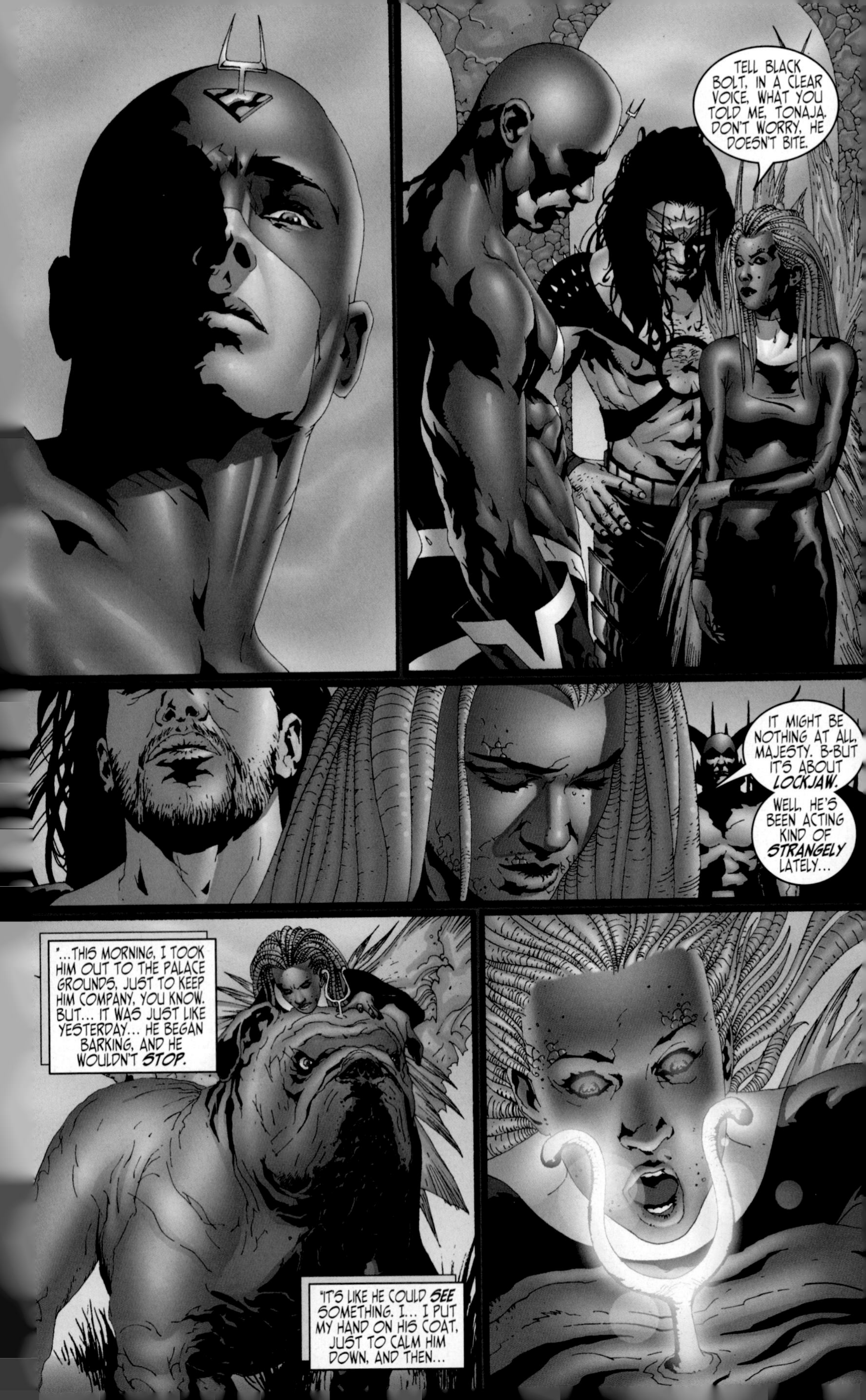
TELL BLACK BOLT, IN A CLEAR VOICE, WHAT YOU TOLD ME, TONAJA. DON'T WORRY, HE DOESN'T BITE.
IT MIGHT BE NOTHING AT ALL, MAJESTY. B-BUT IT'S ABOUT LOCKJAW.
WELL, HE'S BEEN ACTING KIND OF STRANGELY LATELY...
"...THIS MORNING, I TOOK HIM OUT TO THE PALACE GROUNDS, JUST TO KEEP HIM COMPANY, YOU KNOW. BUT... IT WAS JUST LIKE YESTERDAY... HE BEGAN BARKING, AND HE WOULDN'T STOP.
"IT'S LIKE HE COULD SEE SOMETHING. I... I PUT MY HAND ON HIS COAT, JUST TO CALM HIM DOWN, AND THEN...

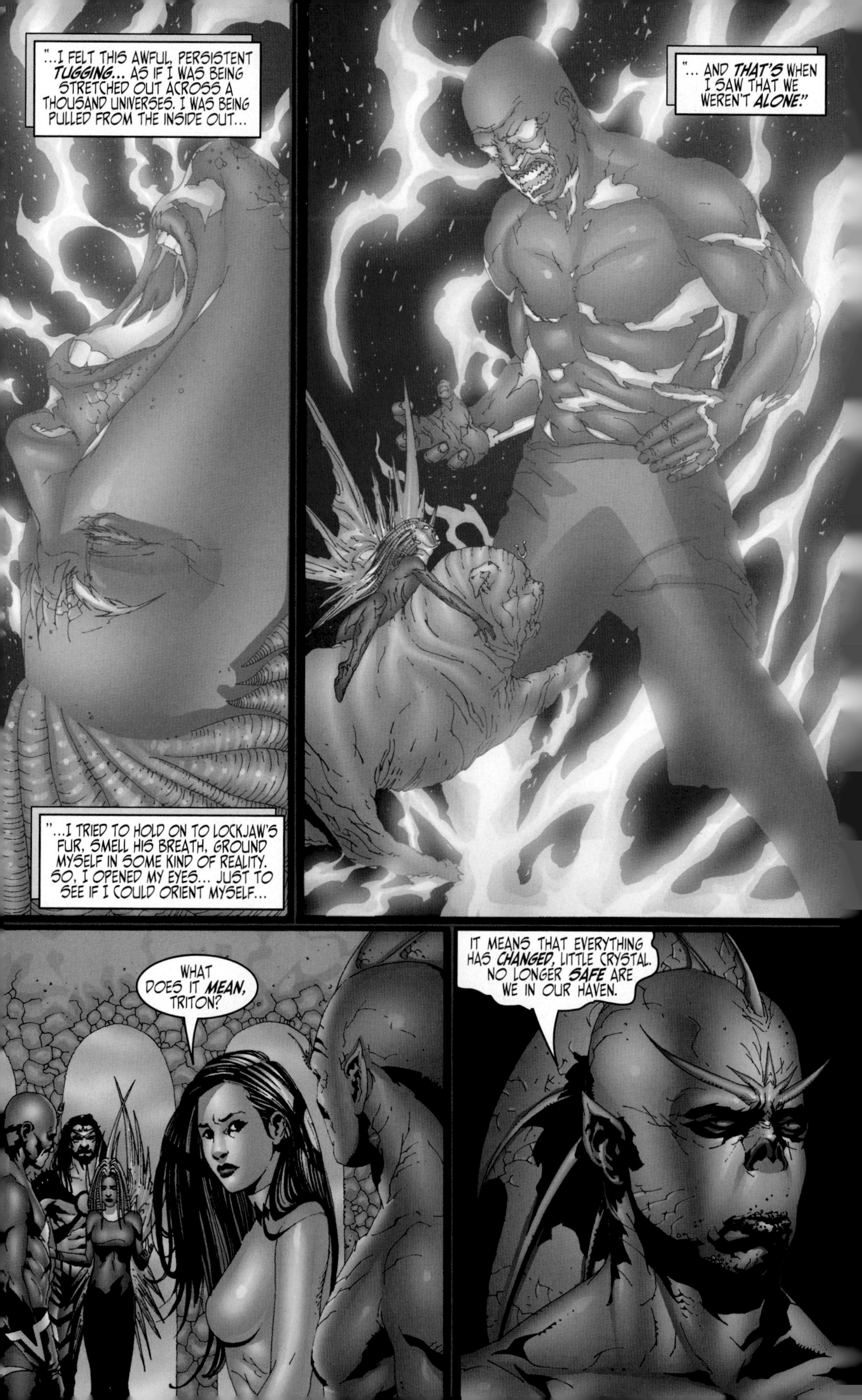
"...I FELT THIS AWFUL, PERSISTENT TUGGING... AS IF I WAS BEING STRETCHED OUT ACROSS A THOUSAND UNIVERSES. I WAS BEING PULLED FROM THE INSIDE OUT...
"...I TRIED TO HOLD ON TO LOCKJAW'S FUR, SMELL HIS BREATH, GROUND MYSELF IN SOME KIND OF REALITY. SO, I OPENED MY EYES... JUST TO SEE IF I COULD ORIENT MYSELF...
"... AND THAT'S WHEN I SAW THAT WE WEREN'T ALONE."
WHAT DOES IT MEAN, TRITON?
IT MEANS THAT EVERYTHING HAS CHANGED, LITTLE CRYSTAL. NO LONGER SAFE ARE WE IN OUR HAVEN.

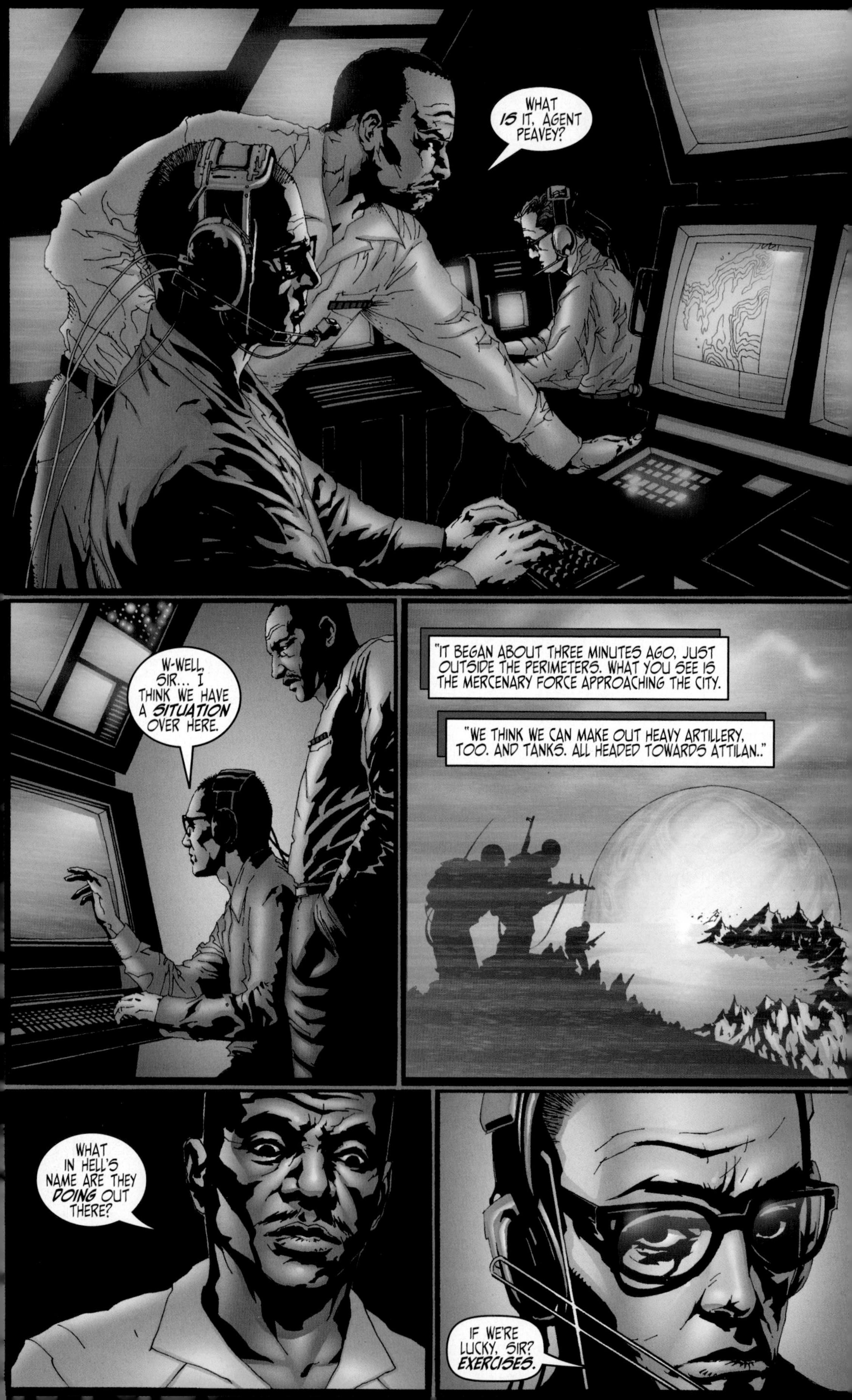

WHAT IS IT, AGENT PEAVEY?
W-WELL, SIR... I THINK WE HAVE A SITUATION OVER HERE.
"IT BEGAN ABOUT THREE MINUTES AGO, JUST OUTSIDE THE PERIMETERS. WHAT YOU SEE IS THE MERCENARY FORCE APPROACHING THE CITY.
"WE THINK WE CAN MAKE OUT HEAVY ARTILLERY, TOO. AND TANKS. ALL HEADED TOWARDS ATTILAN."
WHAT IN HELL'S NAME ARE THEY DOING OUT THERE?
IF WE'RE LUCKY, SIR? EXERCISES.

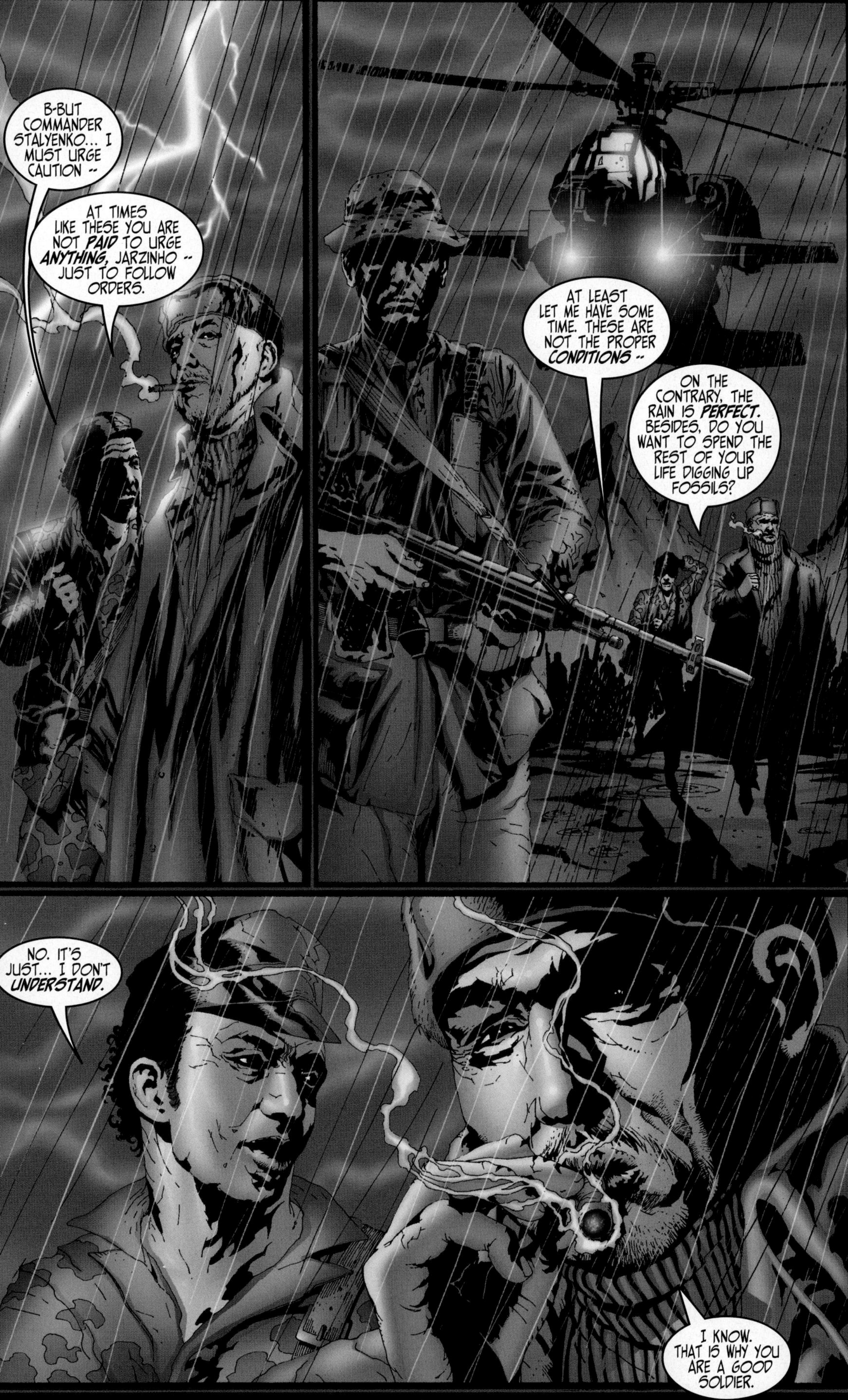
B-BUT COMMANDER STALYENKO... I MUST URGE CAUTION --
AT TIMES LIKE THESE YOU ARE NOT **PAID** TO URGE **ANYTHING**, JARZINHO -- JUST TO FOLLOW ORDERS.
AT LEAST LET ME HAVE SOME TIME. THESE ARE NOT THE PROPER **CONDITIONS** --
ON THE CONTRARY, THE RAIN IS **PERFECT**. BESIDES, DO YOU WANT TO SPEND THE REST OF YOUR LIFE DIGGING UP FOSSILS?
NO. IT'S JUST... I DON'T **UNDERSTAND**.
I KNOW. THAT IS WHY YOU ARE A GOOD SOLDIER.

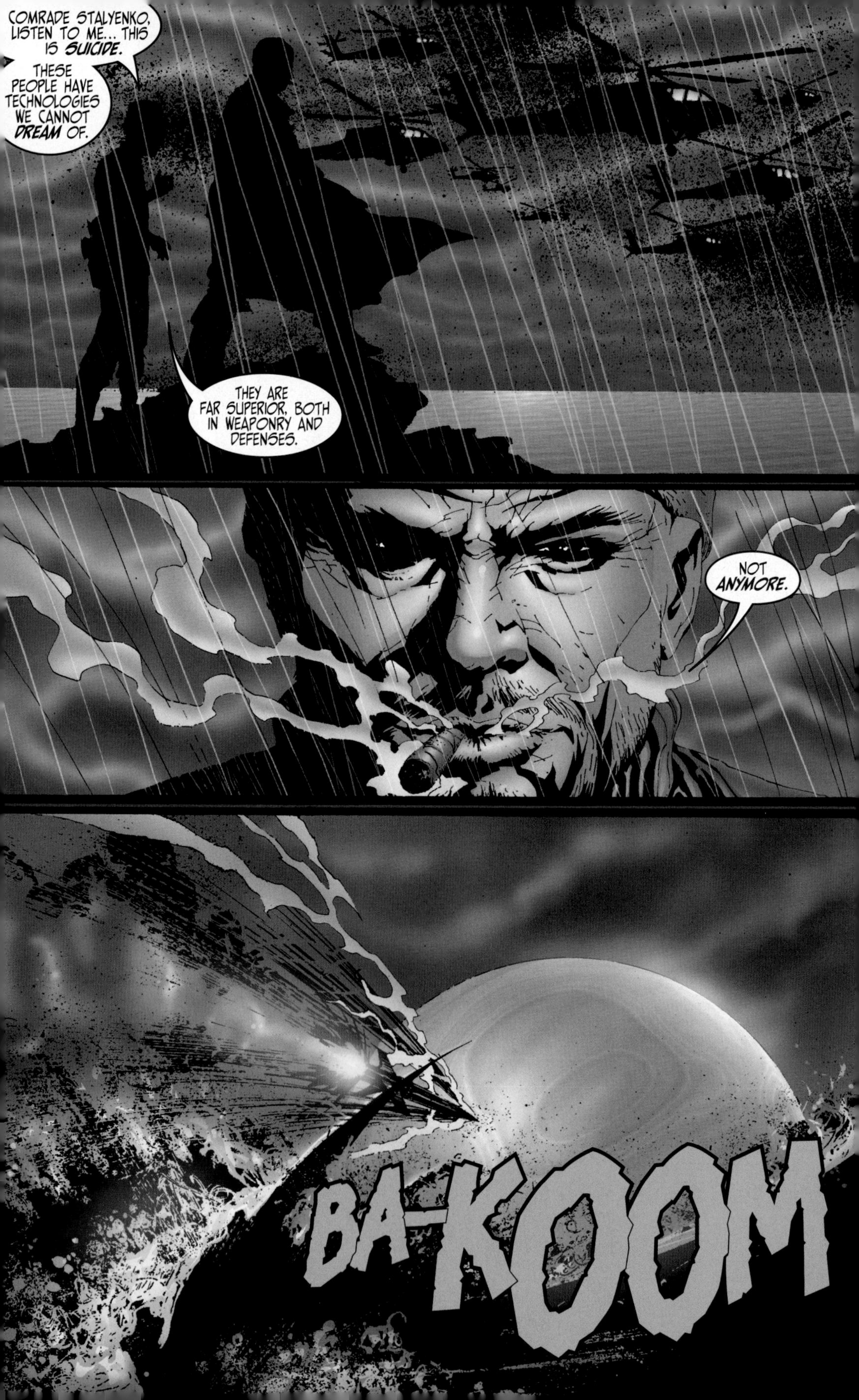

COMRADE STALYENKO, LISTEN TO ME... THIS IS SUICIDE.
THESE PEOPLE HAVE TECHNOLOGIES WE CANNOT DREAM OF.
THEY ARE FAR SUPERIOR, BOTH IN WEAPONRY AND DEFENSES.
NOT ANYMORE.
BA-KOOM

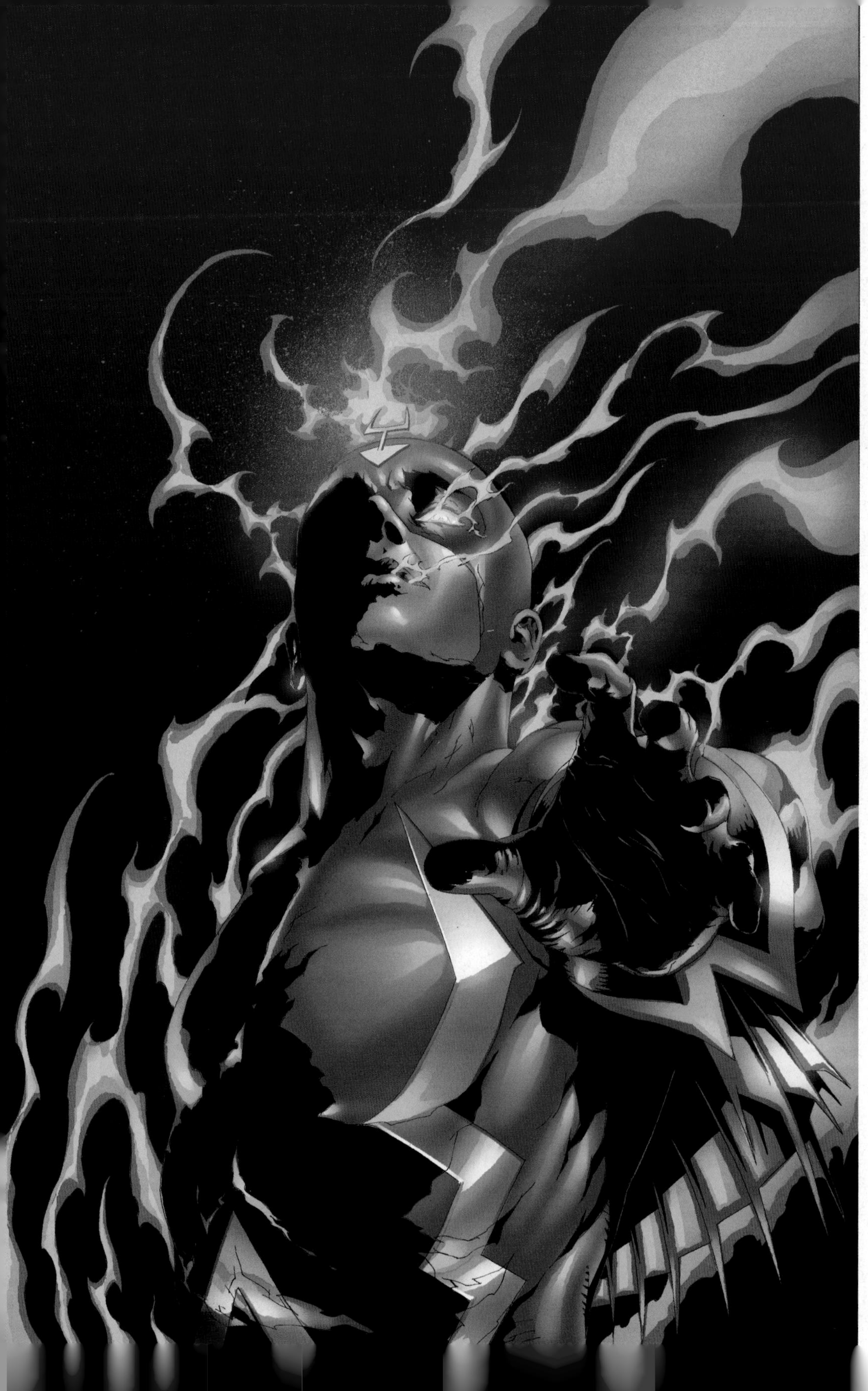

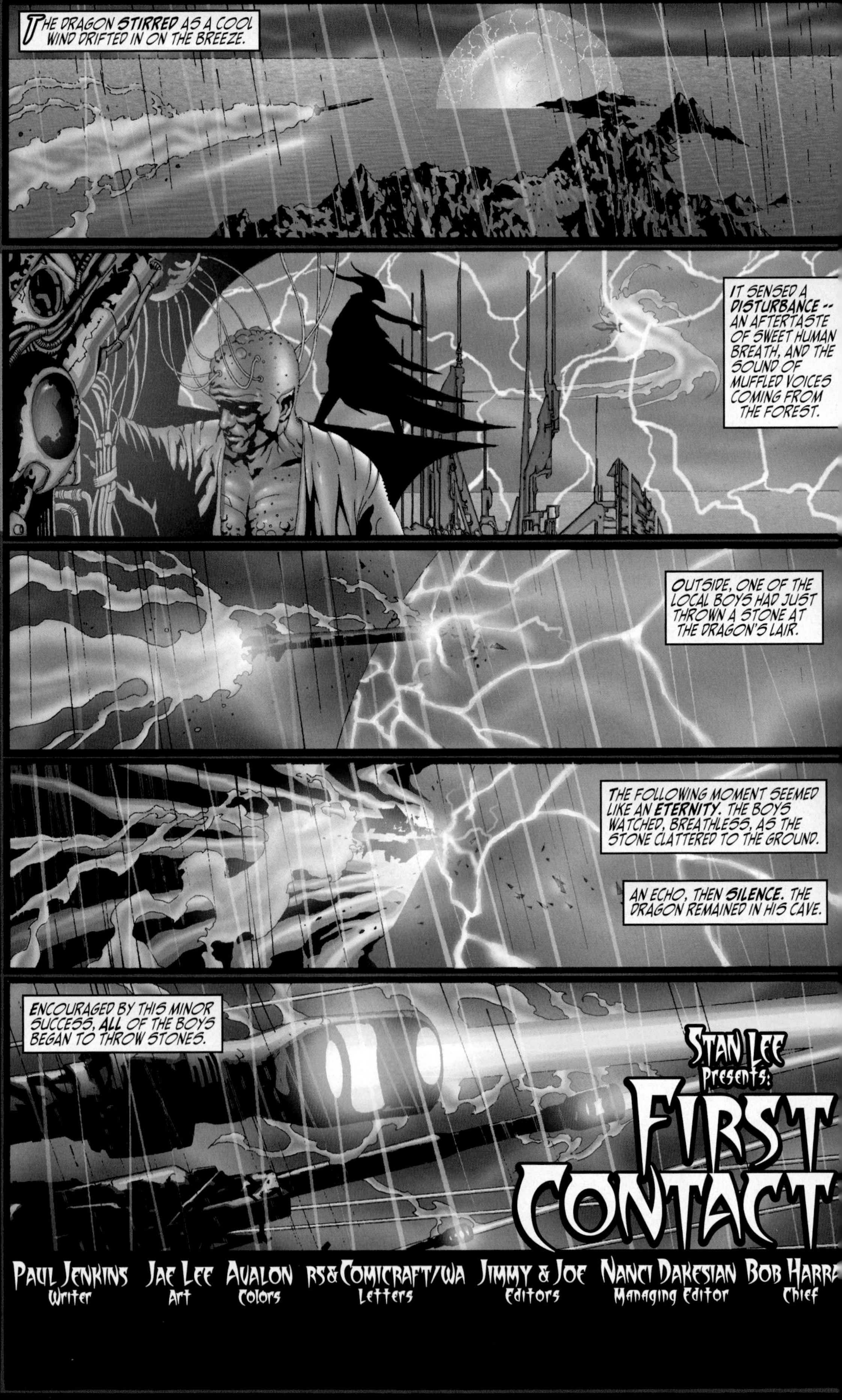
THE DRAGON STIRRED AS A COOL WIND DRIFTED IN ON THE BREEZE.
IT SENSED A DISTURBANCE -- AN AFTERTASTE OF SWEET HUMAN BREATH, AND THE SOUND OF MUFFLED VOICES COMING FROM THE FOREST.
OUTSIDE, ONE OF THE LOCAL BOYS HAD JUST THROWN A STONE AT THE DRAGON'S LAIR.
THE FOLLOWING MOMENT SEEMED LIKE AN ETERNITY. THE BOYS WATCHED, BREATHLESS, AS THE STONE CLATTERED TO THE GROUND.
AN ECHO, THEN SILENCE. THE DRAGON REMAINED IN HIS CAVE.
ENCOURAGED BY THIS MINOR SUCCESS, ALL OF THE BOYS BEGAN TO THROW STONES.
STAN LEE presents:
FIRST CONTACT
PAUL JENKINS Writer
JAE LEE Art
AVALON Colors
RS&COMICRAFT/WA Letters
JIMMY & JOE Editors
NANCI DAKESIAN Managing Editor
BOB HARRA Chief

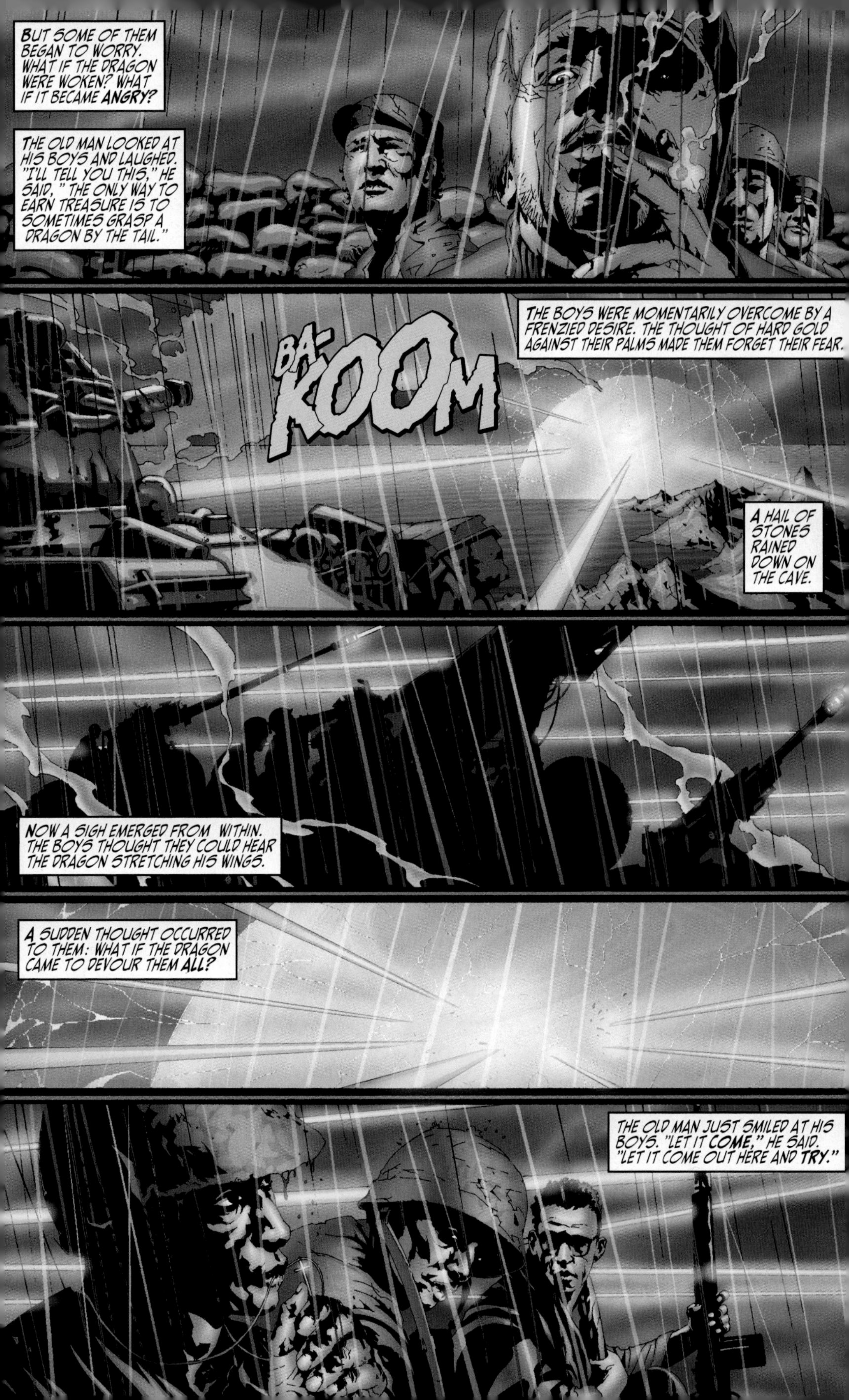
BUT SOME OF THEM BEGAN TO WORRY. WHAT IF THE DRAGON WERE WOKEN? WHAT IF IT BECAME ANGRY?
THE OLD MAN LOOKED AT HIS BOYS AND LAUGHED. "I'LL TELL YOU THIS," HE SAID, " THE ONLY WAY TO EARN TREASURE IS TO SOMETIMES GRASP A DRAGON BY THE TAIL."
THE BOYS WERE MOMENTARILY OVERCOME BY A FRENZIED DESIRE. THE THOUGHT OF HARD GOLD AGAINST THEIR PALMS MADE THEM FORGET THEIR FEAR.
BA-KOOM
A HAIL OF STONES RAINED DOWN ON THE CAVE.
NOW A SIGH EMERGED FROM WITHIN. THE BOYS THOUGHT THEY COULD HEAR THE DRAGON STRETCHING HIS WINGS.
A SUDDEN THOUGHT OCCURRED TO THEM: WHAT IF THE DRAGON CAME TO DEVOUR THEM ALL?
THE OLD MAN JUST SMILED AT HIS BOYS. "LET IT COME," HE SAID. "LET IT COME OUT HERE AND TRY."

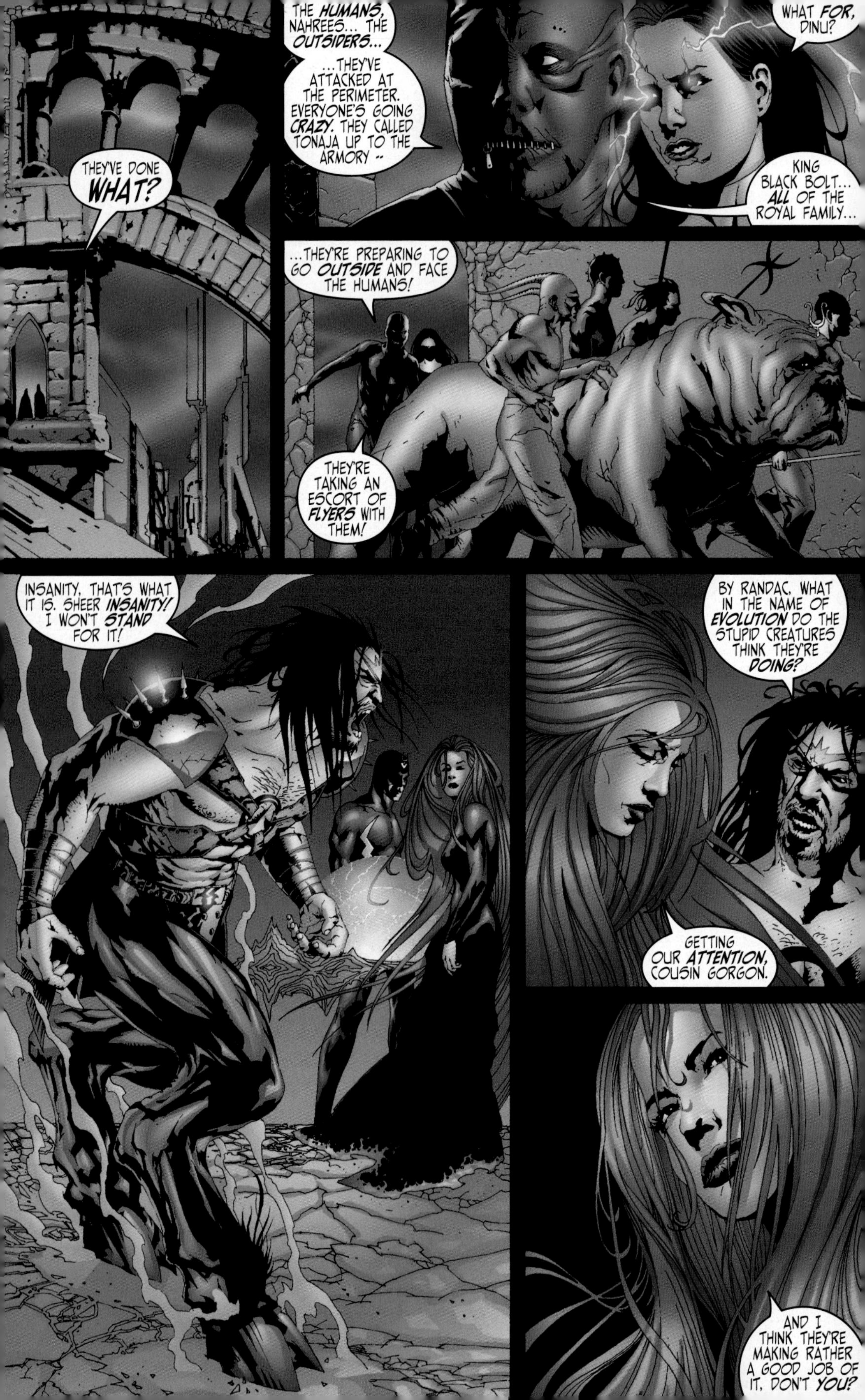
THEY'VE DONE WHAT?
THE HUMANS, NAHREES... THE OUTSIDERS...
...THEY'VE ATTACKED AT THE PERIMETER. EVERYONE'S GOING CRAZY. THEY CALLED TONAJA UP TO THE ARMORY --
WHAT FOR, DINU?
KING BLACK BOLT... ALL OF THE ROYAL FAMILY...
...THEY'RE PREPARING TO GO OUTSIDE AND FACE THE HUMANS!
THEY'RE TAKING AN ESCORT OF FLYERS WITH THEM!
INSANITY. THAT'S WHAT IT IS. SHEER INSANITY! I WON'T STAND FOR IT!
BY RANDAC, WHAT IN THE NAME OF EVOLUTION DO THE STUPID CREATURES THINK THEY'RE DOING?
GETTING OUR ATTENTION, COUSIN GORGON.
AND I THINK THEY'RE MAKING RATHER A GOOD JOB OF IT, DON'T YOU?

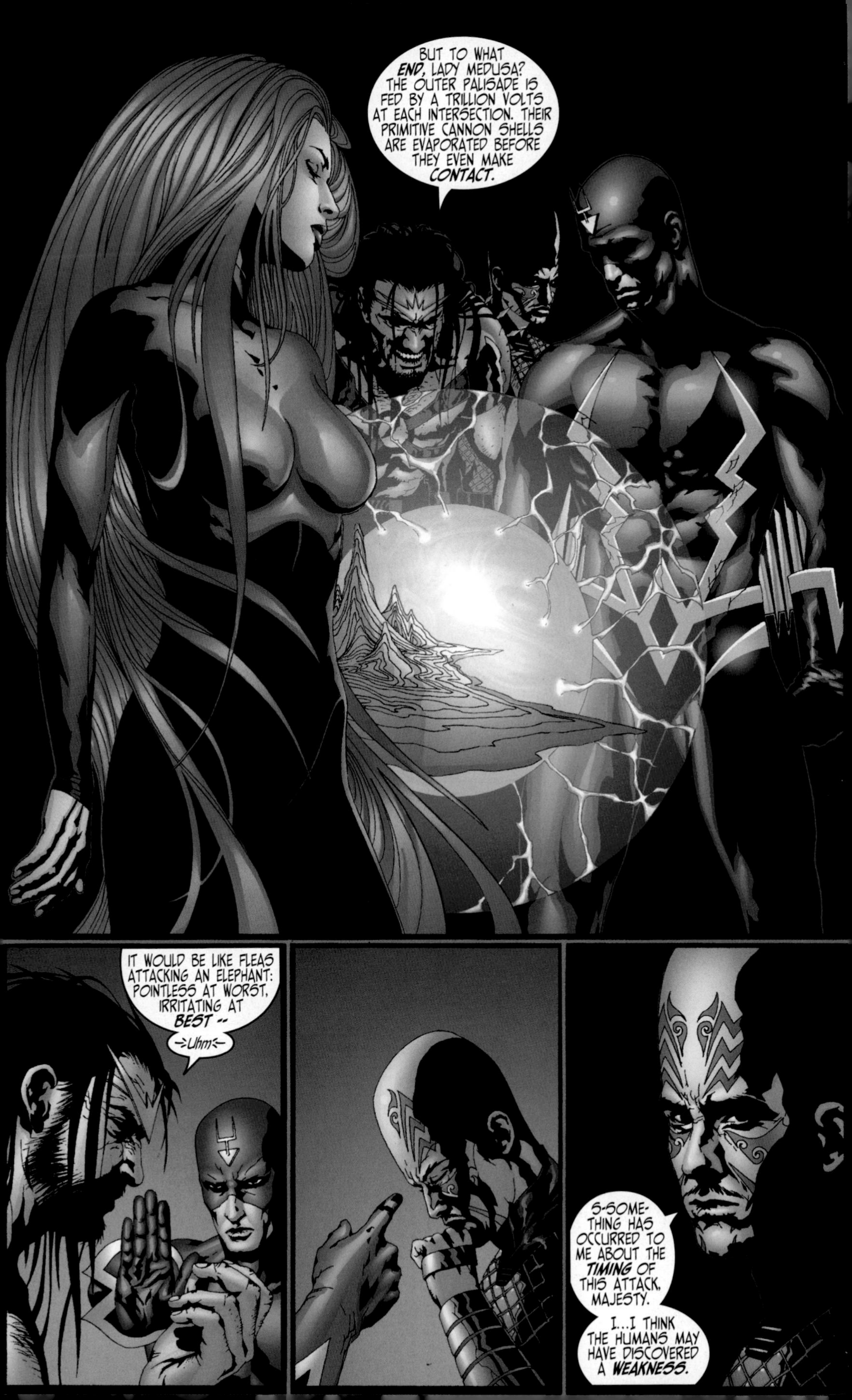
BUT TO WHAT END, LADY MEDUSA? THE OUTER PALISADE IS FED BY A TRILLION VOLTS AT EACH INTERSECTION. THEIR PRIMITIVE CANNON SHELLS ARE EVAPORATED BEFORE THEY EVEN MAKE CONTACT.
IT WOULD BE LIKE FLEAS ATTACKING AN ELEPHANT: POINTLESS AT WORST, IRRITATING AT BEST --
=Uhm=
S-SOMETHING HAS OCCURRED TO ME ABOUT THE TIMING OF THIS ATTACK, MAJESTY.
I...I THINK THE HUMANS MAY HAVE DISCOVERED A WEAKNESS.

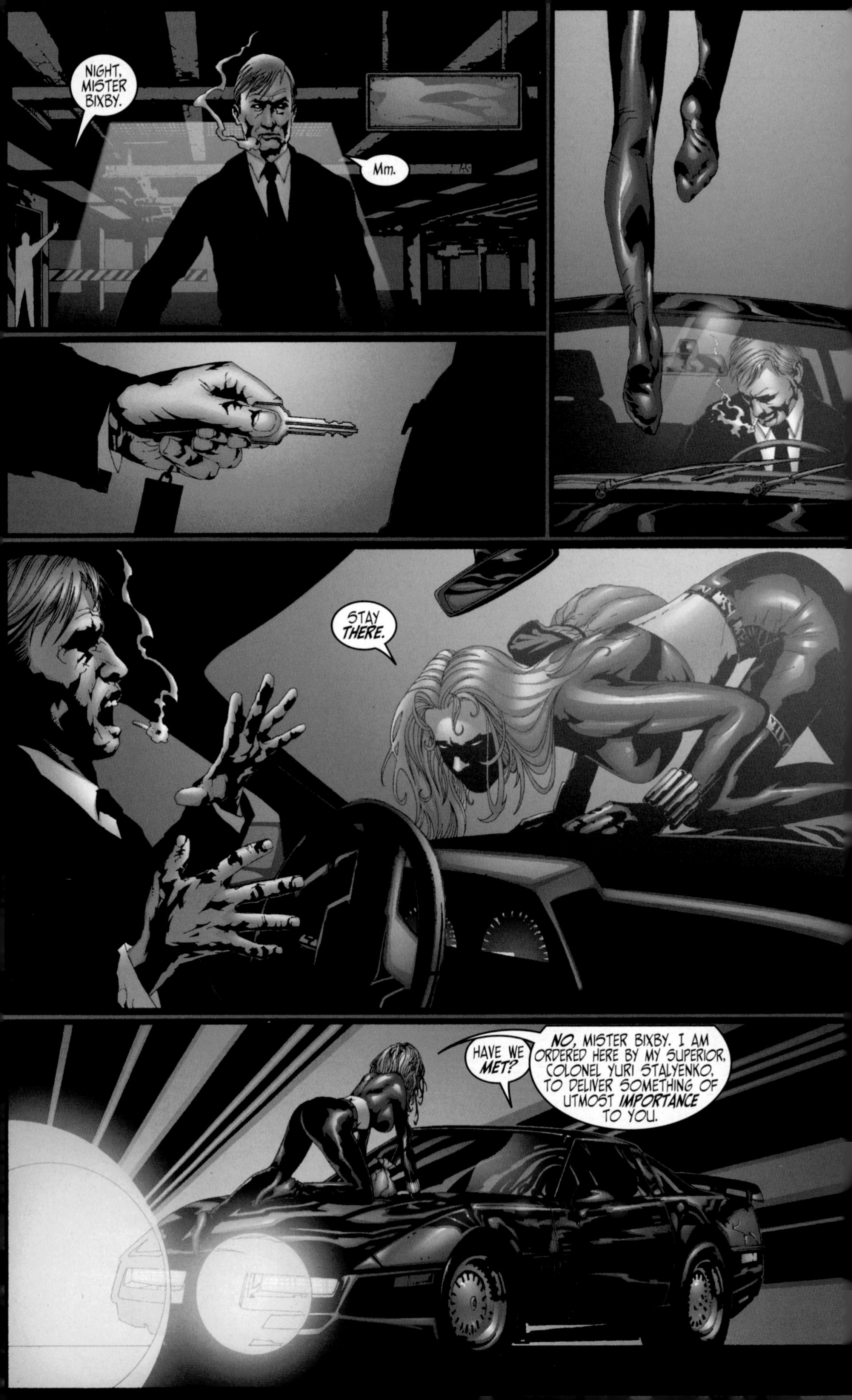
NIGHT, MISTER BIXBY.
Mm.
STAY *THERE.*
HAVE WE *MET?*
NO, MISTER BIXBY. I AM ORDERED HERE BY MY SUPERIOR, COLONEL YURI STALYENKO, TO DELIVER SOMETHING OF UTMOST *IMPORTANCE* TO YOU.

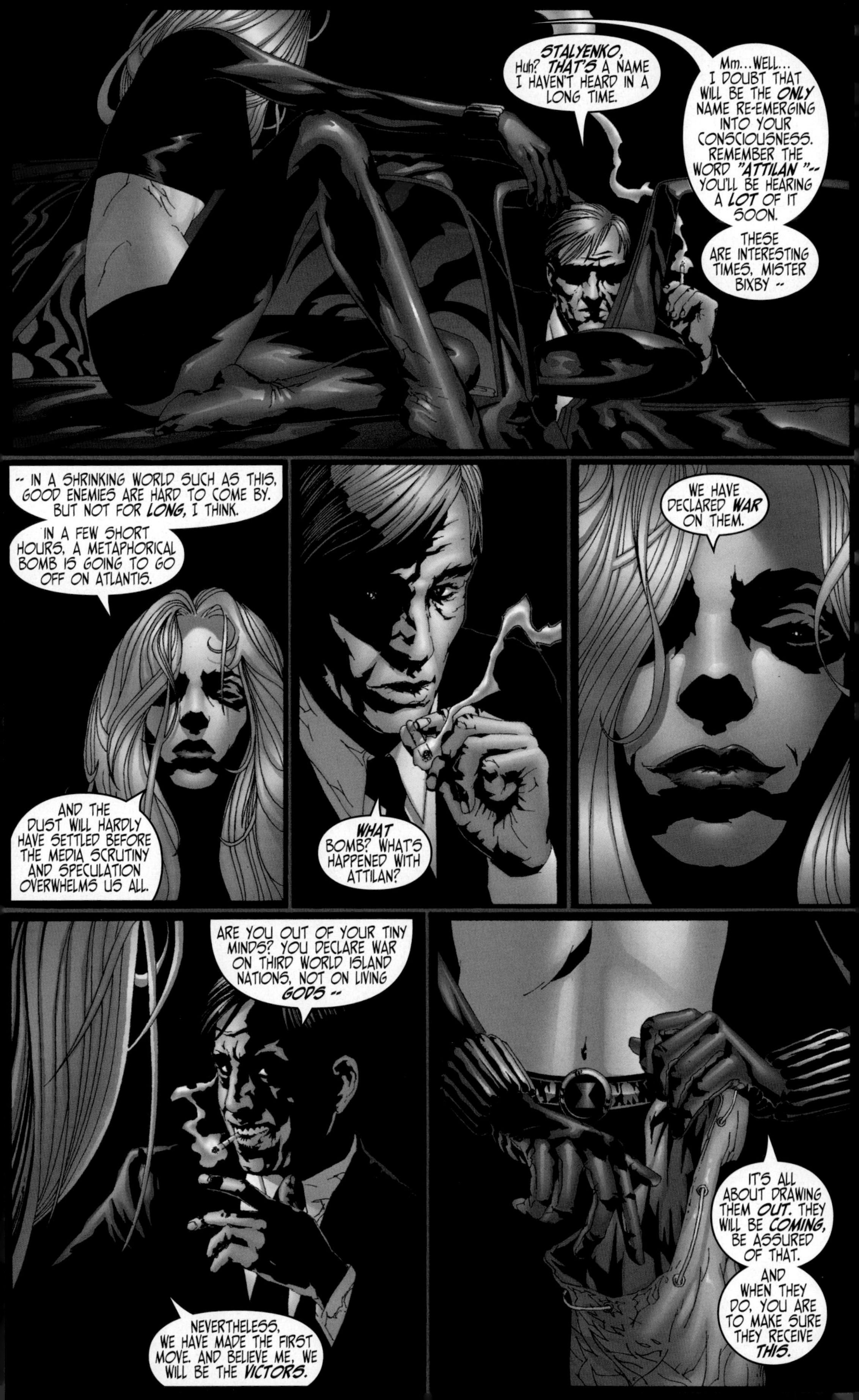
STALYENKO, Huh? THAT'S A NAME I HAVEN'T HEARD IN A LONG TIME.
Mm...WELL... I DOUBT THAT WILL BE THE ONLY NAME RE-EMERGING INTO YOUR CONSCIOUSNESS. REMEMBER THE WORD "ATTILAN"-- YOU'LL BE HEARING A LOT OF IT SOON.
THESE ARE INTERESTING TIMES, MISTER BIXBY --
-- IN A SHRINKING WORLD SUCH AS THIS, GOOD ENEMIES ARE HARD TO COME BY. BUT NOT FOR LONG, I THINK.
IN A FEW SHORT HOURS, A METAPHORICAL BOMB IS GOING TO GO OFF ON ATLANTIS.
AND THE DUST WILL HARDLY HAVE SETTLED BEFORE THE MEDIA SCRUTINY AND SPECULATION OVERWHELMS US ALL.
WHAT BOMB? WHAT'S HAPPENED WITH ATTILAN?
WE HAVE DECLARED WAR ON THEM.
ARE YOU OUT OF YOUR TINY MINDS? YOU DECLARE WAR ON THIRD WORLD ISLAND NATIONS, NOT ON LIVING GODS --
NEVERTHELESS, WE HAVE MADE THE FIRST MOVE. AND BELIEVE ME, WE WILL BE THE VICTORS.
IT'S ALL ABOUT DRAWING THEM OUT. THEY WILL BE COMING, BE ASSURED OF THAT.
AND WHEN THEY DO, YOU ARE TO MAKE SURE THEY RECEIVE THIS.

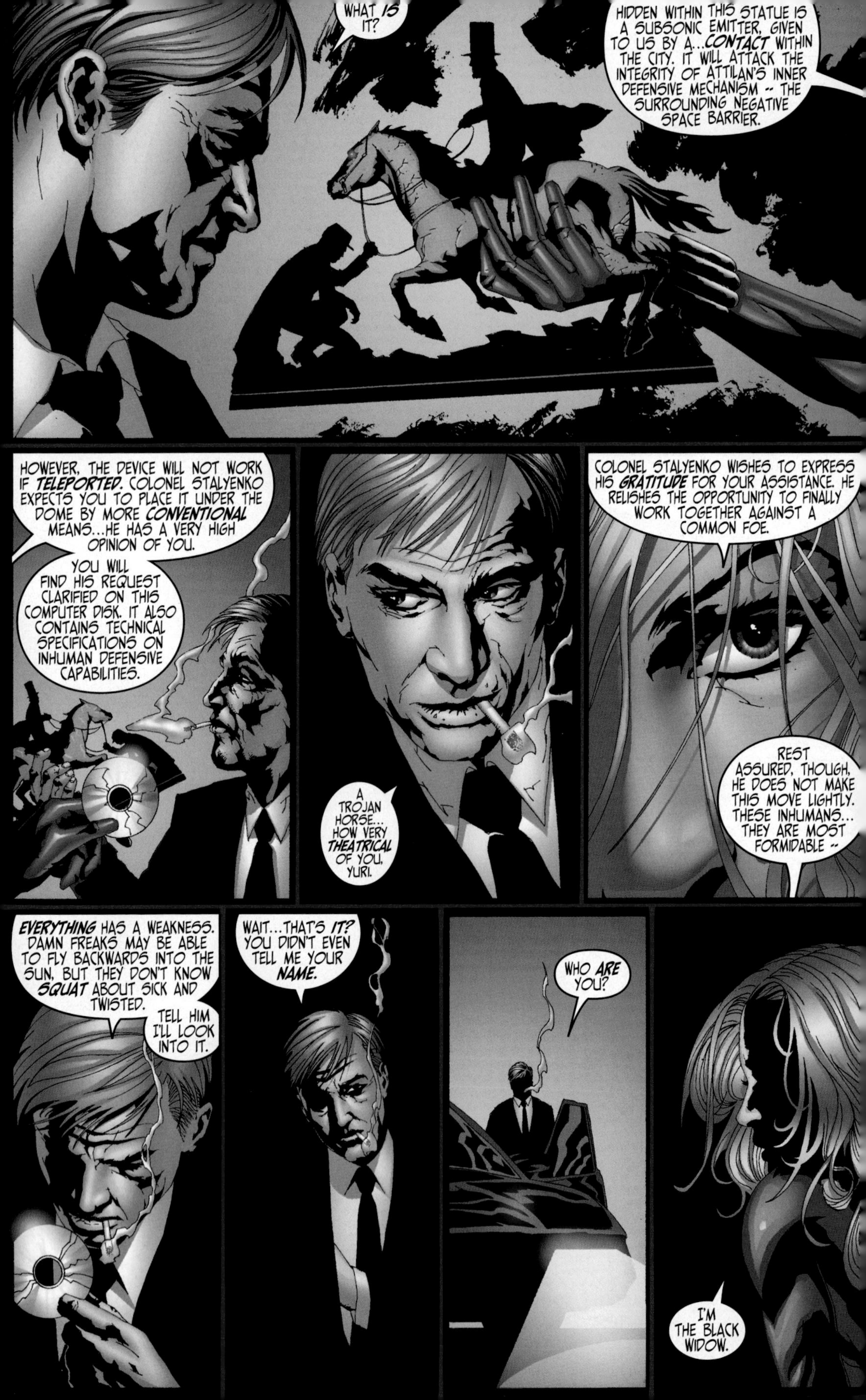
WHAT IS IT?
HIDDEN WITHIN THIS STATUE IS A SUBSONIC EMITTER, GIVEN TO US BY A...CONTACT WITHIN THE CITY. IT WILL ATTACK THE INTEGRITY OF ATTILAN'S INNER DEFENSIVE MECHANISM -- THE SURROUNDING NEGATIVE SPACE BARRIER.
HOWEVER, THE DEVICE WILL NOT WORK IF TELEPORTED. COLONEL STALYENKO EXPECTS YOU TO PLACE IT UNDER THE DOME BY MORE CONVENTIONAL MEANS...HE HAS A VERY HIGH OPINION OF YOU.
YOU WILL FIND HIS REQUEST CLARIFIED ON THIS COMPUTER DISK. IT ALSO CONTAINS TECHNICAL SPECIFICATIONS ON INHUMAN DEFENSIVE CAPABILITIES.
A TROJAN HORSE... HOW VERY THEATRICAL OF YOU, YURI.
COLONEL STALYENKO WISHES TO EXPRESS HIS GRATITUDE FOR YOUR ASSISTANCE. HE RELISHES THE OPPORTUNITY TO FINALLY WORK TOGETHER AGAINST A COMMON FOE.
REST ASSURED, THOUGH, HE DOES NOT MAKE THIS MOVE LIGHTLY. THESE INHUMANS... THEY ARE MOST FORMIDABLE --
EVERYTHING HAS A WEAKNESS. DAMN FREAKS MAY BE ABLE TO FLY BACKWARDS INTO THE SUN, BUT THEY DON'T KNOW SQUAT ABOUT SICK AND TWISTED.
TELL HIM I'LL LOOK INTO IT.
WAIT...THAT'S IT? YOU DIDN'T EVEN TELL ME YOUR NAME.
WHO ARE YOU?
I'M THE BLACK WIDOW.

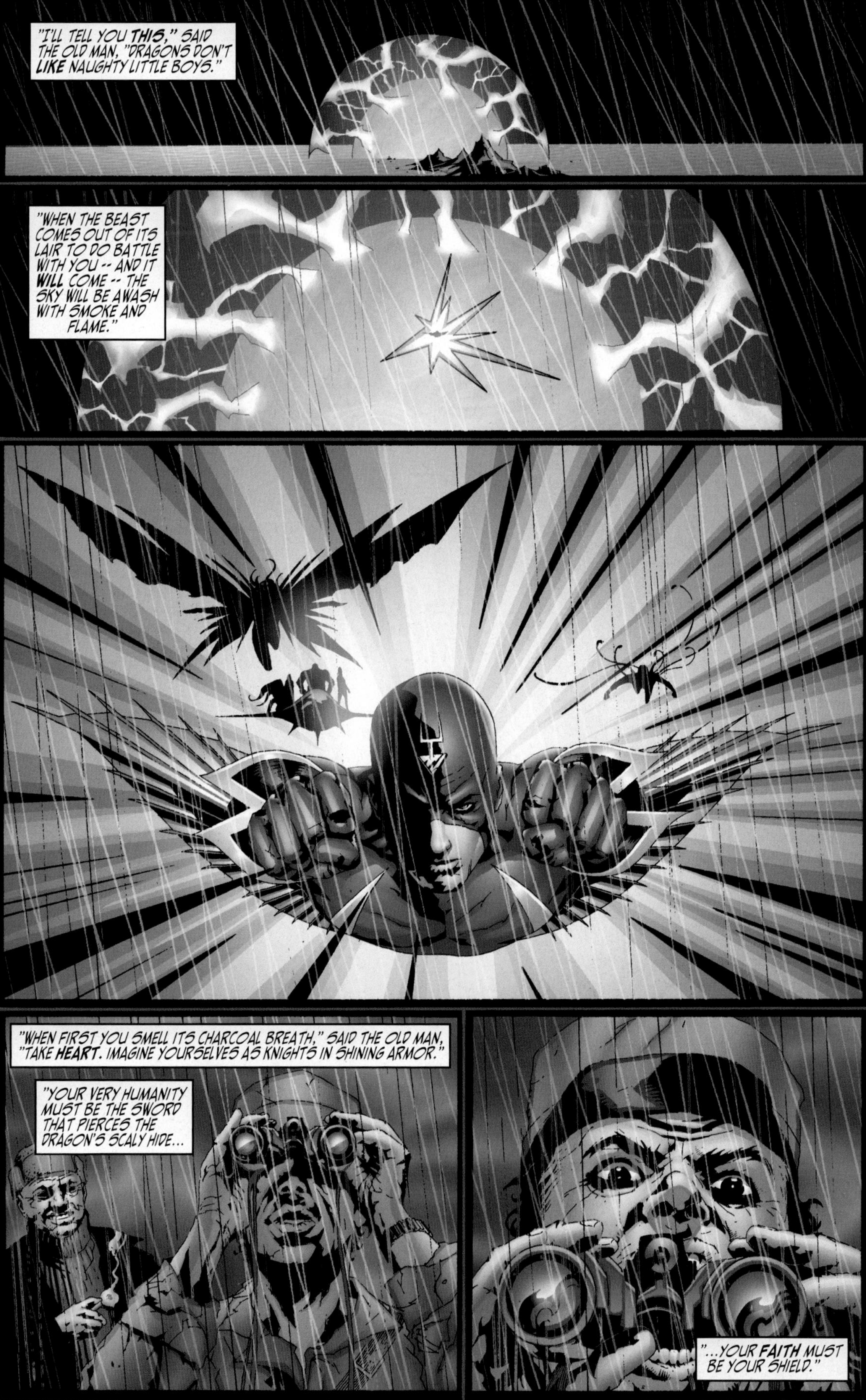
"I'LL TELL YOU THIS," SAID THE OLD MAN, "DRAGONS DON'T LIKE NAUGHTY LITTLE BOYS."
"WHEN THE BEAST COMES OUT OF ITS LAIR TO DO BATTLE WITH YOU -- AND IT WILL COME -- THE SKY WILL BE AWASH WITH SMOKE AND FLAME."
"WHEN FIRST YOU SMELL ITS CHARCOAL BREATH," SAID THE OLD MAN, "TAKE HEART. IMAGINE YOURSELVES AS KNIGHTS IN SHINING ARMOR."
"YOUR VERY HUMANITY MUST BE THE SWORD THAT PIERCES THE DRAGON'S SCALY HIDE...
"...YOUR FAITH MUST BE YOUR SHIELD."

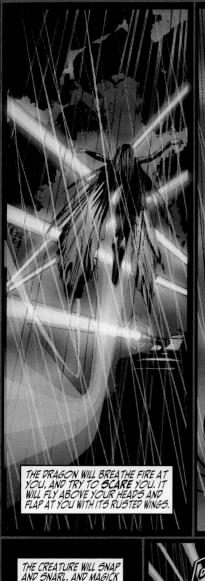

THE DRAGON WILL BREATHE FIRE AT YOU, AND TRY TO **SCARE** YOU. IT WILL FLY ABOVE YOUR HEADS AND FLAP AT YOU WITH ITS RUSTED WINGS.

WHEN YOU LOOK INTO ITS BLACK EYES, YOU WILL SEE THE FACE OF THE **DEVIL** HIMSELF -- UNFATHOMABLE AND MALICIOUS TO THE **CORE**.

THE CREATURE WILL SNAP AND SNARL, AND MAGICK YOU WITH ILLUSIONS UNFATHOMABLE...

BA-KOOM

...BUT YOUR GAZE WILL NEVER WAVER, BECAUSE YOU ARE TRUE OF HEART, AND PURE OF MIND AND SPIRIT.

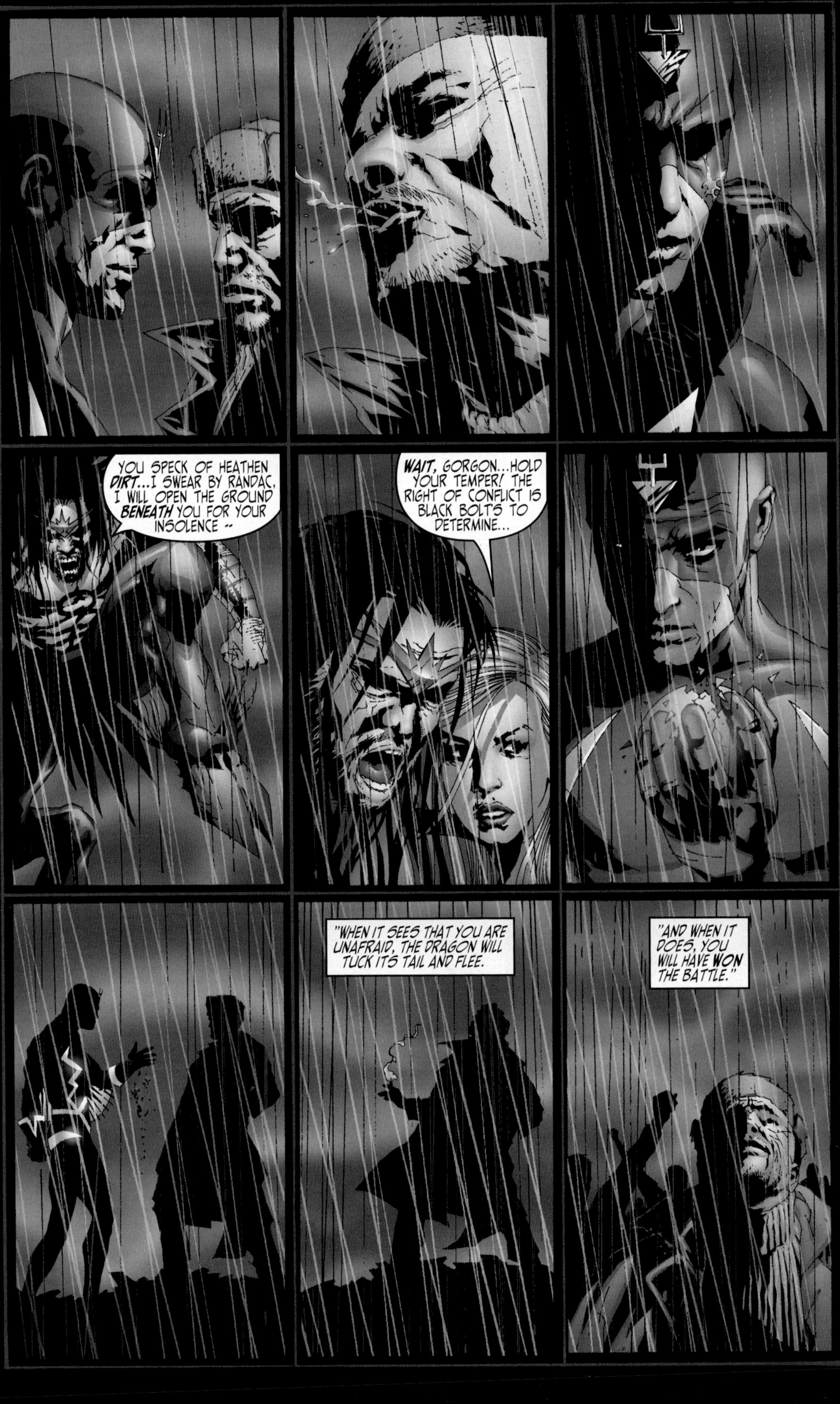
YOU SPECK OF HEATHEN DIRT...I SWEAR BY RANDAC, I WILL OPEN THE GROUND BENEATH YOU FOR YOUR INSOLENCE --
WAIT, GORGON...HOLD YOUR TEMPER! THE RIGHT OF CONFLICT IS BLACK BOLT'S TO DETERMINE...
"WHEN IT SEES THAT YOU ARE UNAFRAID, THE DRAGON WILL TUCK ITS TAIL AND FLEE.
"AND WHEN IT DOES, YOU WILL HAVE WON THE BATTLE."

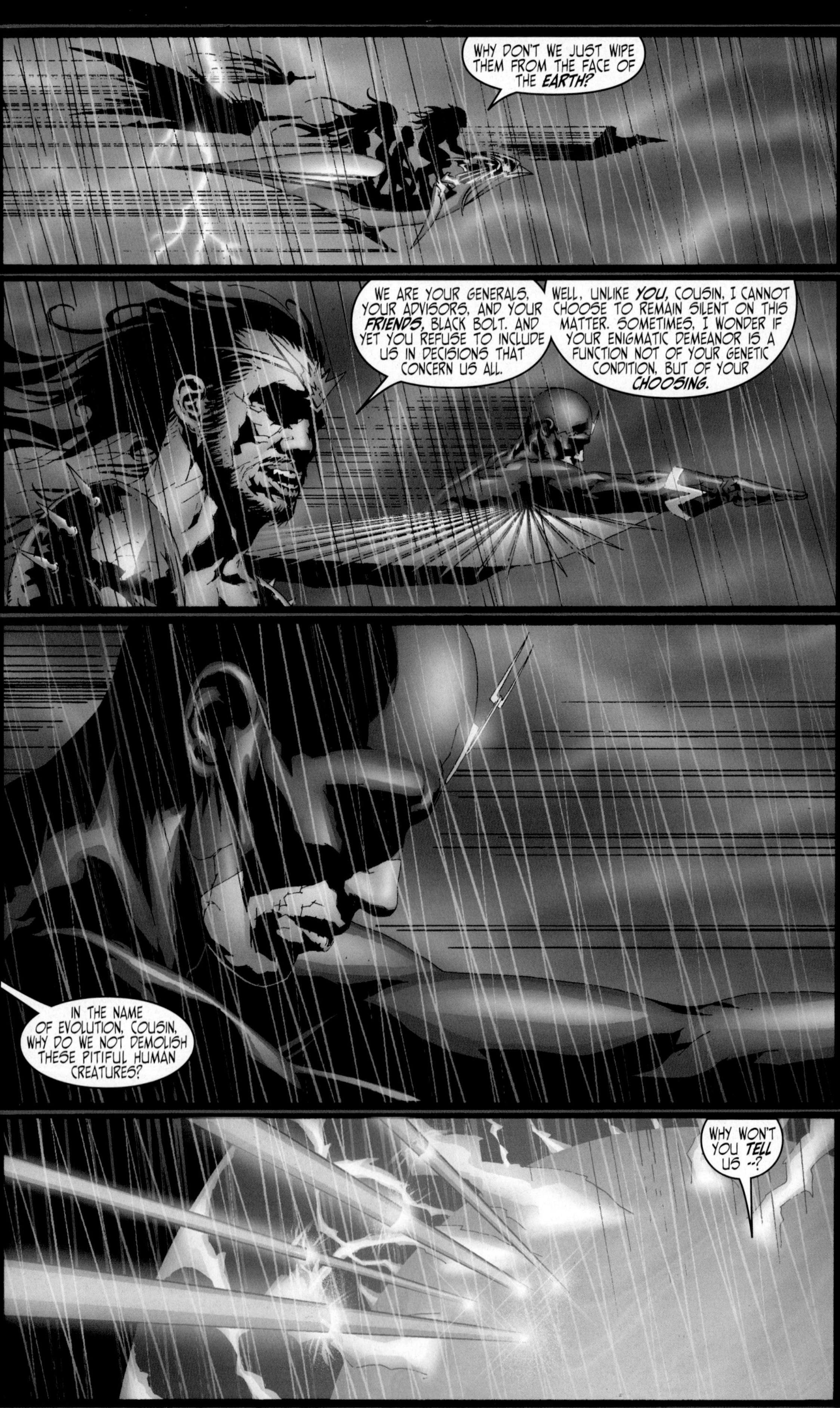
WHY DON'T WE JUST WIPE THEM FROM THE FACE OF THE EARTH?
WE ARE YOUR GENERALS, YOUR ADVISORS, AND YOUR FRIENDS, BLACK BOLT. AND YET YOU REFUSE TO INCLUDE US IN DECISIONS THAT CONCERN US ALL.
WELL, UNLIKE YOU, COUSIN, I CANNOT CHOOSE TO REMAIN SILENT ON THIS MATTER. SOMETIMES, I WONDER IF YOUR ENIGMATIC DEMEANOR IS A FUNCTION NOT OF YOUR GENETIC CONDITION, BUT OF YOUR CHOOSING.
IN THE NAME OF EVOLUTION, COUSIN, WHY DO WE NOT DEMOLISH THESE PITIFUL HUMAN CREATURES?
WHY WON'T YOU TELL US --?

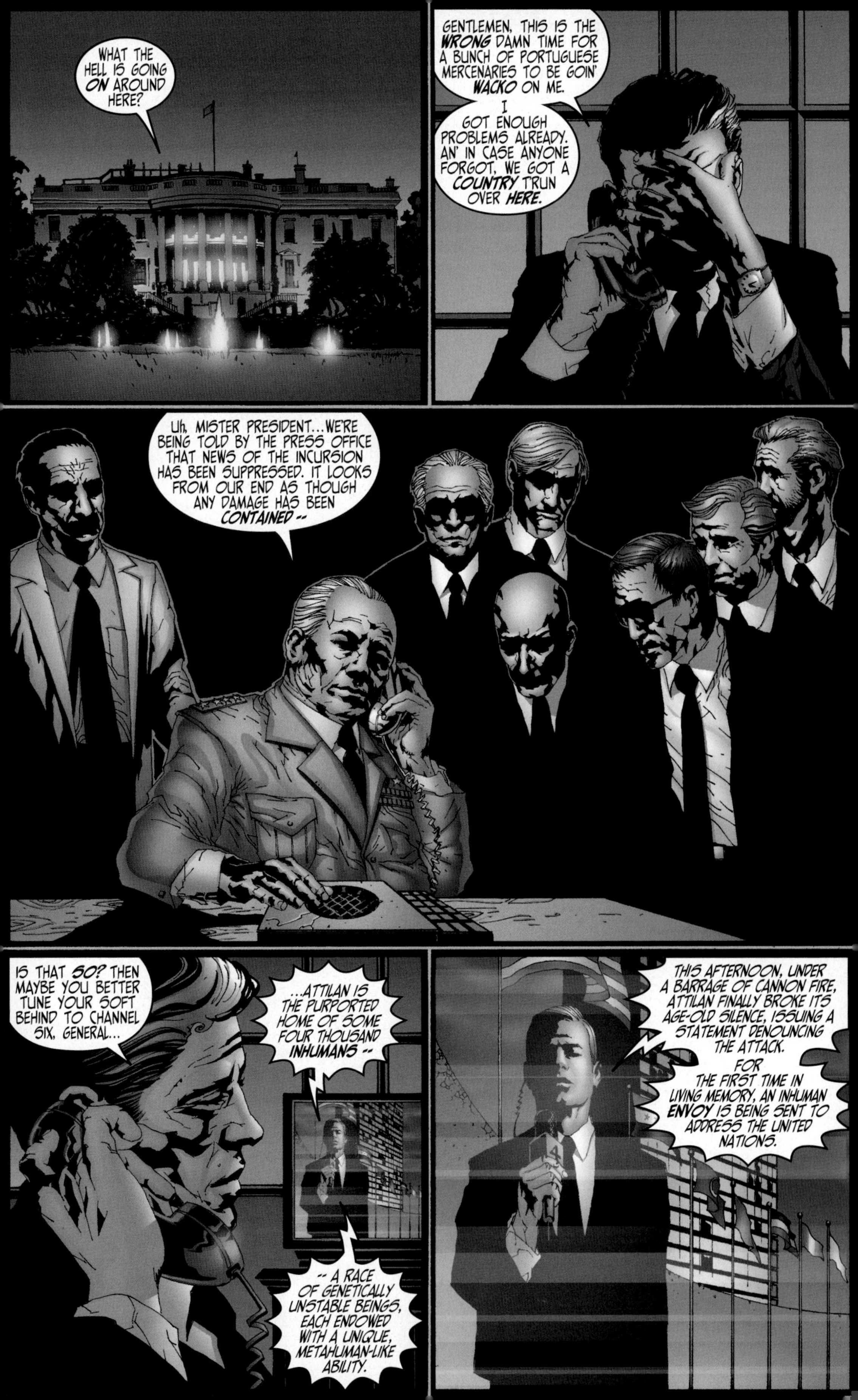
WHAT THE HELL IS GOING ON AROUND HERE?
GENTLEMEN, THIS IS THE WRONG DAMN TIME FOR A BUNCH OF PORTUGUESE MERCENARIES TO BE GOIN' WACKO ON ME.
I GOT ENOUGH PROBLEMS ALREADY. AN' IN CASE ANYONE FORGOT, WE GOT A COUNTRY T'RUN OVER HERE.
Uh, MISTER PRESIDENT...WE'RE BEING TOLD BY THE PRESS OFFICE THAT NEWS OF THE INCURSION HAS BEEN SUPPRESSED. IT LOOKS FROM OUR END AS THOUGH ANY DAMAGE HAS BEEN CONTAINED --
IS THAT SO? THEN MAYBE YOU BETTER TUNE YOUR SOFT BEHIND TO CHANNEL SIX, GENERAL...
...ATTILAN IS THE PURPORTED HOME OF SOME FOUR THOUSAND INHUMANS --
-- A RACE OF GENETICALLY UNSTABLE BEINGS, EACH ENDOWED WITH A UNIQUE, METAHUMAN-LIKE ABILITY.
THIS AFTERNOON, UNDER A BARRAGE OF CANNON FIRE, ATTILAN FINALLY BROKE ITS AGE-OLD SILENCE, ISSUING A STATEMENT DENOUNCING THE ATTACK.
FOR THE FIRST TIME IN LIVING MEMORY, AN INHUMAN ENVOY IS BEING SENT TO ADDRESS THE UNITED NATIONS.

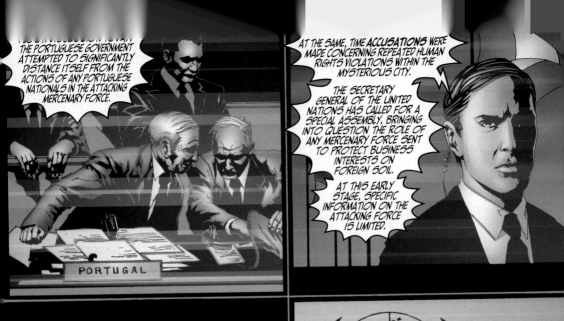

THE PORTUGUESE GOVERNMENT ATTEMPTED TO SIGNIFICANTLY DISTANCE ITSELF FROM THE ACTIONS OF ANY PORTUGUESE NATIONALS IN THE ATTACKING MERCENARY FORCE.

PORTUGAL

AT THE SAME, TIME ACCUSATIONS WERE MADE CONCERNING REPEATED HUMAN RIGHTS VIOLATIONS WITHIN THE MYSTERIOUS CITY.

THE SECRETARY GENERAL OF THE UNITED NATIONS HAS CALLED FOR A SPECIAL ASSEMBLY, BRINGING INTO QUESTION THE ROLE OF ANY MERCENARY FORCE SENT TO PROTECT BUSINESS INTERESTS ON FOREIGN SOIL.

AT THIS EARLY STAGE, SPECIFIC INFORMATION ON THE ATTACKING FORCE IS LIMITED.

THIS MAN --- COLONEL EDSON JARZINHO -- IS SAID TO COMMAND THE NEARLY TWELVE HUNDRED MEN ON ATLANTEAN SHORES. LITTLE INFORMATION ON THIS EX-POLITICAL PRISONER IS AVAILABLE TO THE PUBLIC.

A SPOKESMAN FOR LEXINGTON MINING CORPORATION -- PROSPECTING FOR VIBRANIUM IN THE REGION -- INSISTS THAT JARZINHO'S MERCENARIES HAVE ACTED OUTSIDE THE BOUNDARIES OF THEIR ORDERS.

GERMANY

SPAIN

IN THE MEANTIME, THE SITUATION REMAINS EXTREMELY TENSE, AND FOR NOW, SPECULATION MUST TAKE A BACK SEAT TO WONDERMENT...

...AS WE AWAIT THE AMBASSADOR OF AN ALIEN NATION, AND FIRST CONTACT.

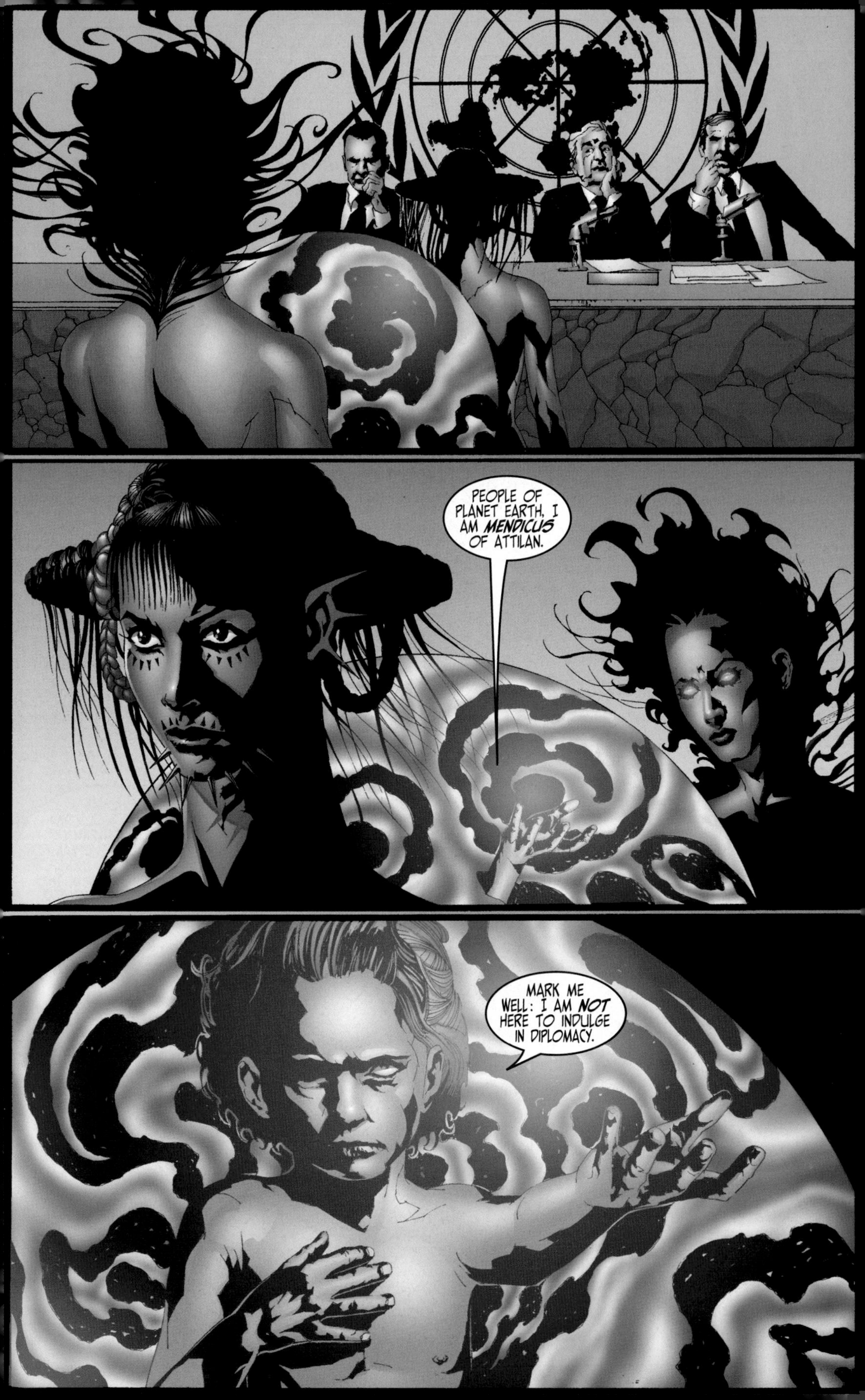
PEOPLE OF PLANET EARTH, I AM MENDICUS OF ATTILAN.
MARK ME WELL: I AM NOT HERE TO INDULGE IN DIPLOMACY.

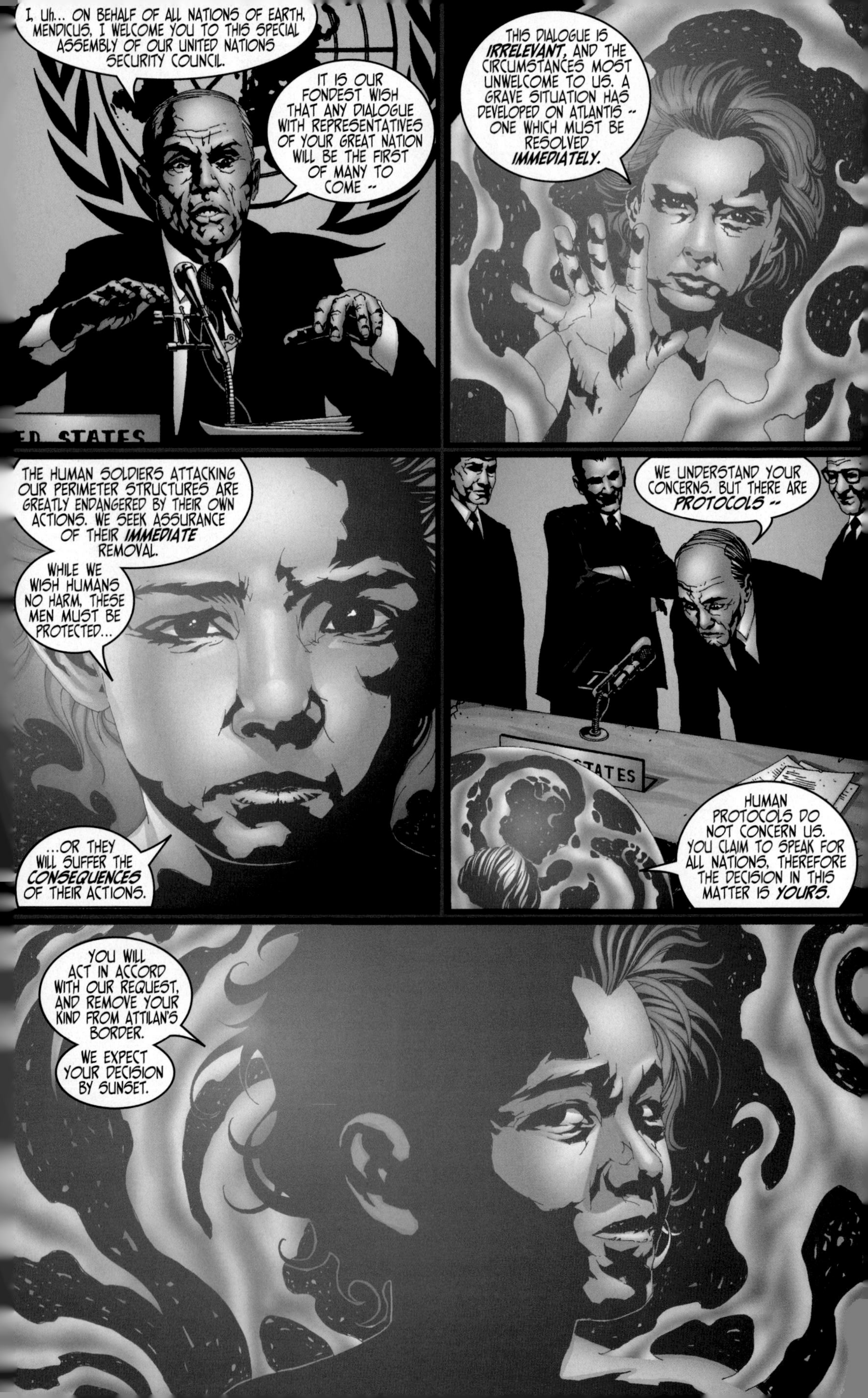
I, UH... ON BEHALF OF ALL NATIONS OF EARTH, MENDICUS, I WELCOME YOU TO THIS SPECIAL ASSEMBLY OF OUR UNITED NATIONS SECURITY COUNCIL.
IT IS OUR FONDEST WISH THAT ANY DIALOGUE WITH REPRESENTATIVES OF YOUR GREAT NATION WILL BE THE FIRST OF MANY TO COME --
THIS DIALOGUE IS IRRELEVANT, AND THE CIRCUMSTANCES MOST UNWELCOME TO US. A GRAVE SITUATION HAS DEVELOPED ON ATLANTIS -- ONE WHICH MUST BE RESOLVED IMMEDIATELY.
THE HUMAN SOLDIERS ATTACKING OUR PERIMETER STRUCTURES ARE GREATLY ENDANGERED BY THEIR OWN ACTIONS. WE SEEK ASSURANCE OF THEIR IMMEDIATE REMOVAL.
WHILE WE WISH HUMANS NO HARM, THESE MEN MUST BE PROTECTED...
...OR THEY WILL SUFFER THE CONSEQUENCES OF THEIR ACTIONS.
WE UNDERSTAND YOUR CONCERNS. BUT THERE ARE PROTOCOLS --
HUMAN PROTOCOLS DO NOT CONCERN US. YOU CLAIM TO SPEAK FOR ALL NATIONS, THEREFORE THE DECISION IN THIS MATTER IS YOURS.
YOU WILL ACT IN ACCORD WITH OUR REQUEST, AND REMOVE YOUR KIND FROM ATTILAN'S BORDER.
WE EXPECT YOUR DECISION BY SUNSET.

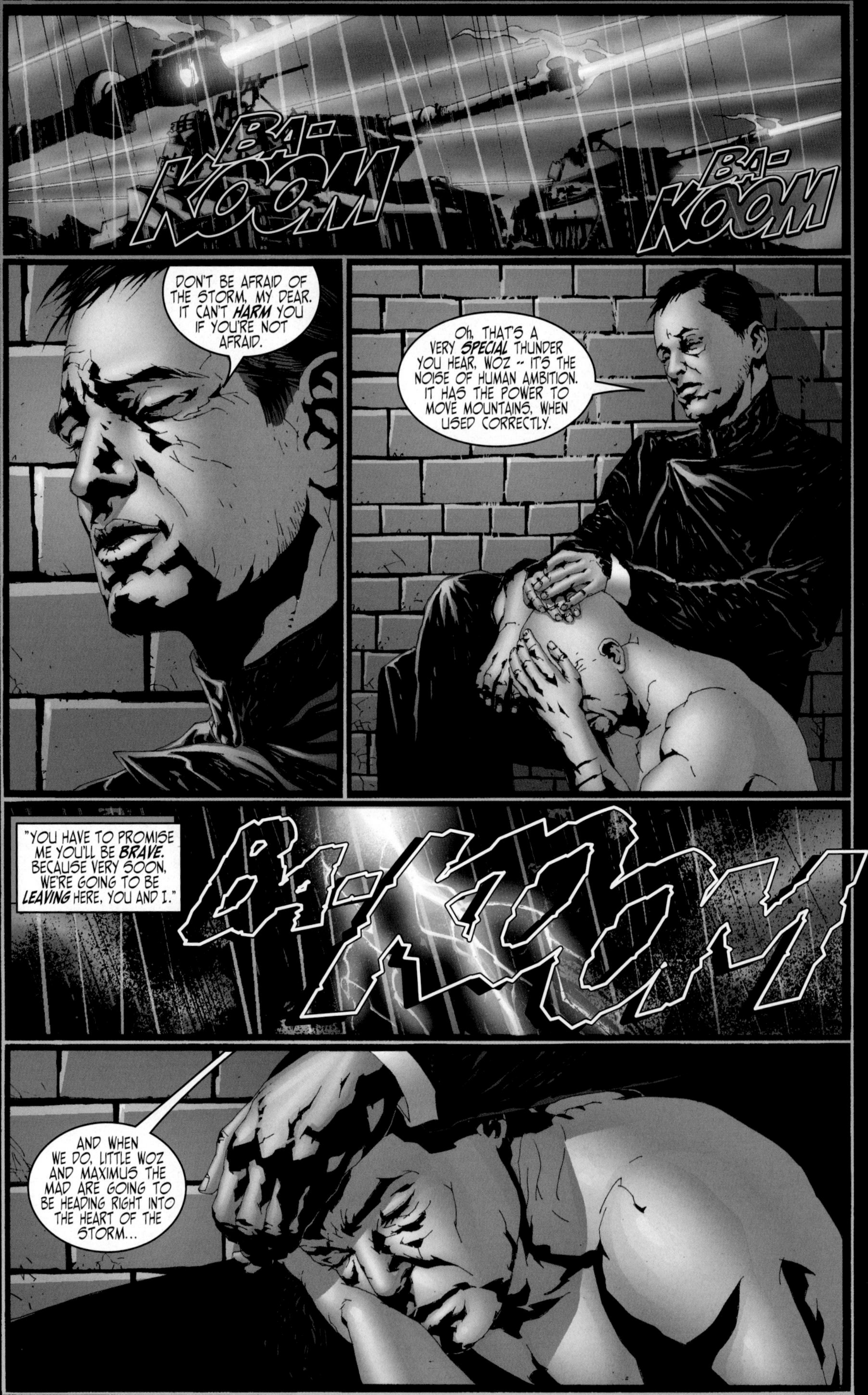
BA-KOOM
BA-KOOM
DON'T BE AFRAID OF THE STORM, MY DEAR. IT CAN'T HARM YOU IF YOU'RE NOT AFRAID.
Oh, THAT'S A VERY SPECIAL THUNDER YOU HEAR, WOZ -- IT'S THE NOISE OF HUMAN AMBITION. IT HAS THE POWER TO MOVE MOUNTAINS, WHEN USED CORRECTLY.
"YOU HAVE TO PROMISE ME YOU'LL BE BRAVE. BECAUSE VERY SOON, WE'RE GOING TO BE LEAVING HERE, YOU AND I."
BA-KOOM
AND WHEN WE DO, LITTLE WOZ AND MAXIMUS THE MAD ARE GOING TO BE HEADING RIGHT INTO THE HEART OF THE STORM...

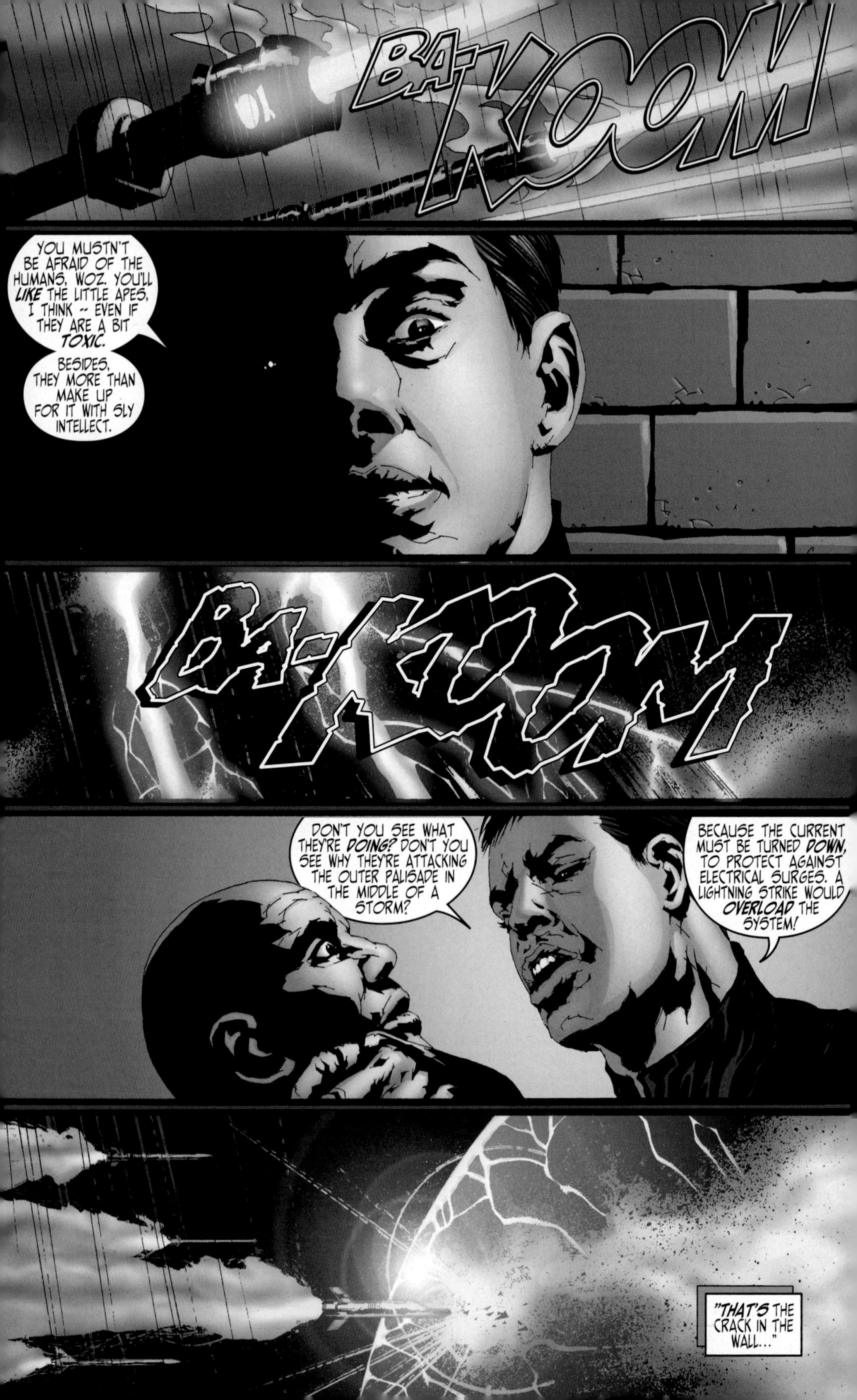
BA-NOOM!
YOU MUSTN'T BE AFRAID OF THE HUMANS, WOZ. YOU'LL LIKE THE LITTLE APES, I THINK -- EVEN IF THEY ARE A BIT TOXIC.
BESIDES, THEY MORE THAN MAKE UP FOR IT WITH SLY INTELLECT.
BA-KOOM
DON'T YOU SEE WHAT THEY'RE DOING? DON'T YOU SEE WHY THEY'RE ATTACKING THE OUTER PALISADE IN THE MIDDLE OF A STORM?
BECAUSE THE CURRENT MUST BE TURNED DOWN, TO PROTECT AGAINST ELECTRICAL SURGES. A LIGHTNING STRIKE WOULD OVERLOAD THE SYSTEM!
"THAT'S THE CRACK IN THE WALL..."

AMBASSADOR MENDICUS, I HAVE BEEN ASKED BY MY GOVERNMENT TO EXTEND A HAND OF FRIENDSHIP TO THE PEOPLE OF ATTILAN.

IN THESE DARK TIMES YOU CAN BE ASSURED OF *FULL* SUPPORT BY THE PEOPLE OF THE UNITED STATES OF AMERICA.

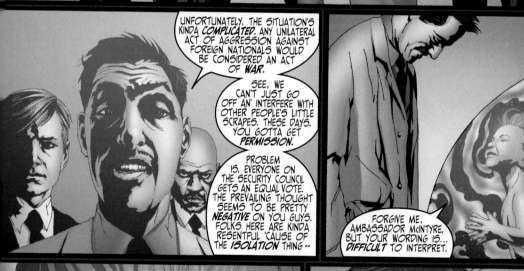

UNFORTUNATELY, THE SITUATION'S KINDA *COMPLICATED.* ANY UNILATERAL ACT OF AGGRESSION AGAINST FOREIGN NATIONALS WOULD BE CONSIDERED AN ACT OF *WAR.*

SEE, WE CAN'T JUST GO OFF AN' INTERFERE WITH OTHER PEOPLE'S LITTLE SCRAPES. THESE DAYS, YOU GOTTA GET *PERMISSION.*

PROBLEM IS, EVERYONE ON THE SECURITY COUNCIL GETS AN EQUAL VOTE. THE PREVAILING THOUGHT SEEMS TO BE PRETTY *NEGATIVE* ON YOU GUYS. FOLKS HERE ARE KINDA RESENTFUL 'CAUSE OF THE *ISOLATION* THING --

FORGIVE ME, AMBASSADOR McINTYRE, BUT YOUR WORDING IS... *DIFFICULT* TO INTERPRET.

ARE YOU SAYING YOU WILL NOT HELP US, EVEN THOUGH YOU SUPPORT US?

WE WISH ONLY FOR YOUR PEOPLE TO LEAVE. WE HAVE *NEVER* WISHED FOR CONTACT WITH YOU -- *THAT* IS WHY WE ARE ISOLATED FROM YOU.

WELL, THEN, I GUESS YOU CAN INTERPRET *THIS* PRETTY EASILY:

Y'ALL ARE ON YOUR OWN FOR NOW

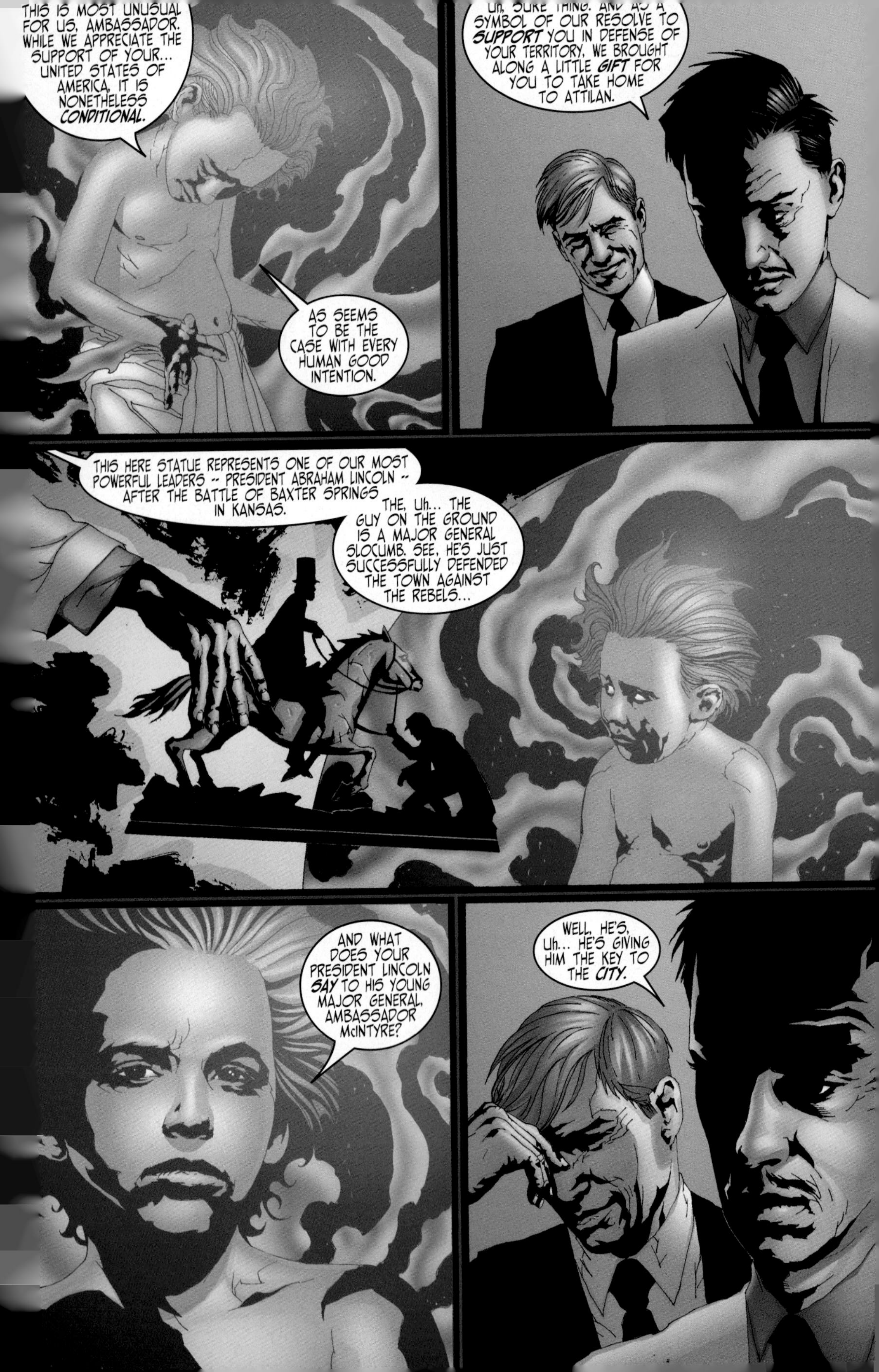
THIS IS MOST UNUSUAL FOR US, AMBASSADOR. WHILE WE APPRECIATE THE SUPPORT OF YOUR... UNITED STATES OF AMERICA, IT IS NONETHELESS CONDITIONAL.
AS SEEMS TO BE THE CASE WITH EVERY HUMAN GOOD INTENTION.
UH, SURE THING. AND AS A SYMBOL OF OUR RESOLVE TO SUPPORT YOU IN DEFENSE OF YOUR TERRITORY, WE BROUGHT ALONG A LITTLE GIFT FOR YOU TO TAKE HOME TO ATTILAN.
THIS HERE STATUE REPRESENTS ONE OF OUR MOST POWERFUL LEADERS -- PRESIDENT ABRAHAM LINCOLN -- AFTER THE BATTLE OF BAXTER SPRINGS IN KANSAS.
THE, UH... THE GUY ON THE GROUND IS A MAJOR GENERAL SLOCUMB. SEE, HE'S JUST SUCCESSFULLY DEFENDED THE TOWN AGAINST THE REBELS...
AND WHAT DOES YOUR PRESIDENT LINCOLN SAY TO HIS YOUNG MAJOR GENERAL, AMBASSADOR McINTYRE?
WELL, HE'S, UH... HE'S GIVING HIM THE KEY TO THE CITY.

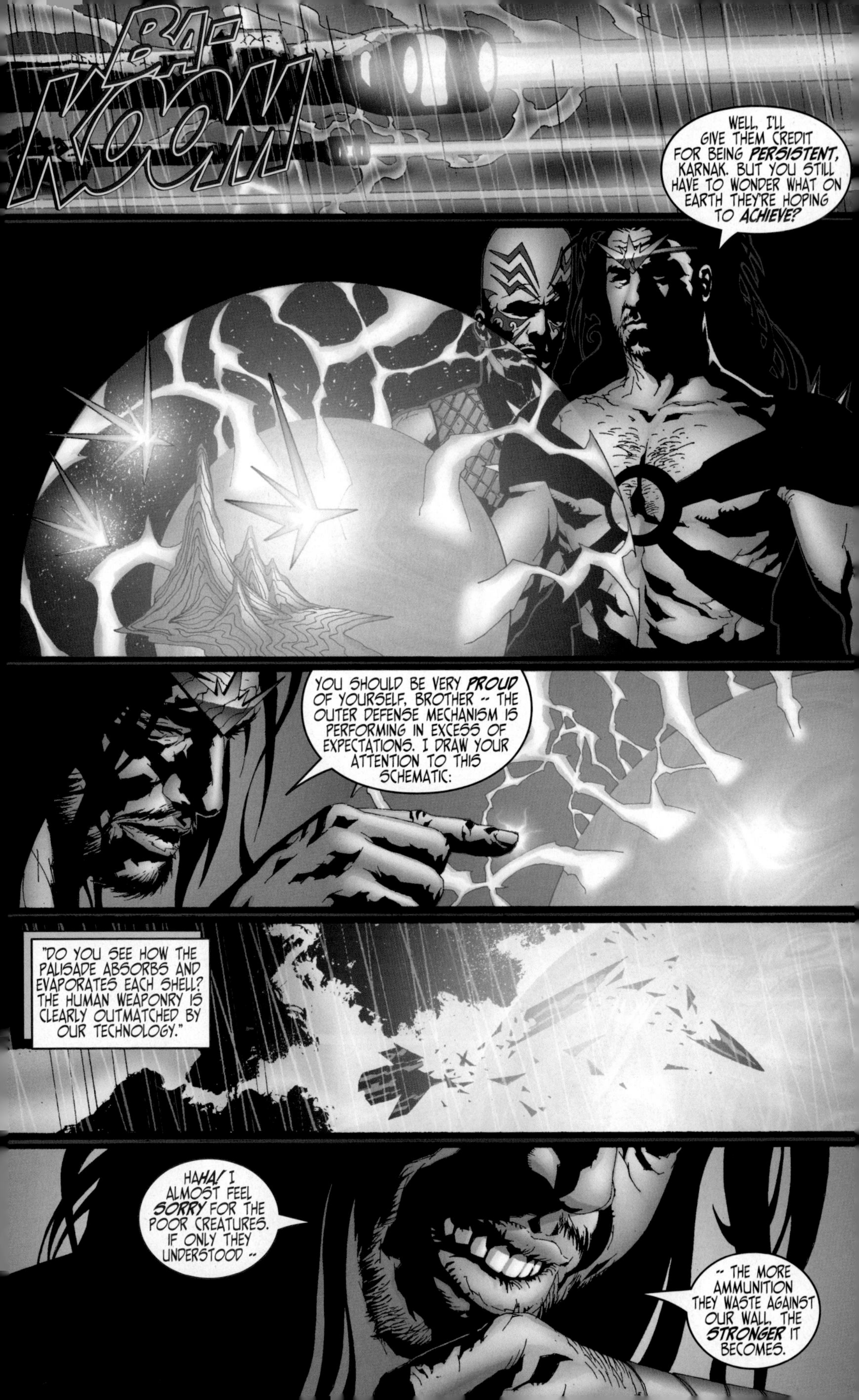
BA-NOOOM
WELL, I'LL GIVE THEM CREDIT FOR BEING PERSISTENT, KARNAK. BUT YOU STILL HAVE TO WONDER WHAT ON EARTH THEY'RE HOPING TO ACHIEVE?
YOU SHOULD BE VERY PROUD OF YOURSELF, BROTHER -- THE OUTER DEFENSE MECHANISM IS PERFORMING IN EXCESS OF EXPECTATIONS. I DRAW YOUR ATTENTION TO THIS SCHEMATIC:
"DO YOU SEE HOW THE PALISADE ABSORBS AND EVAPORATES EACH SHELL? THE HUMAN WEAPONRY IS CLEARLY OUTMATCHED BY OUR TECHNOLOGY."
HAHA! I ALMOST FEEL SORRY FOR THE POOR CREATURES. IF ONLY THEY UNDERSTOOD --
-- THE MORE AMMUNITION THEY WASTE AGAINST OUR WALL, THE STRONGER IT BECOMES.

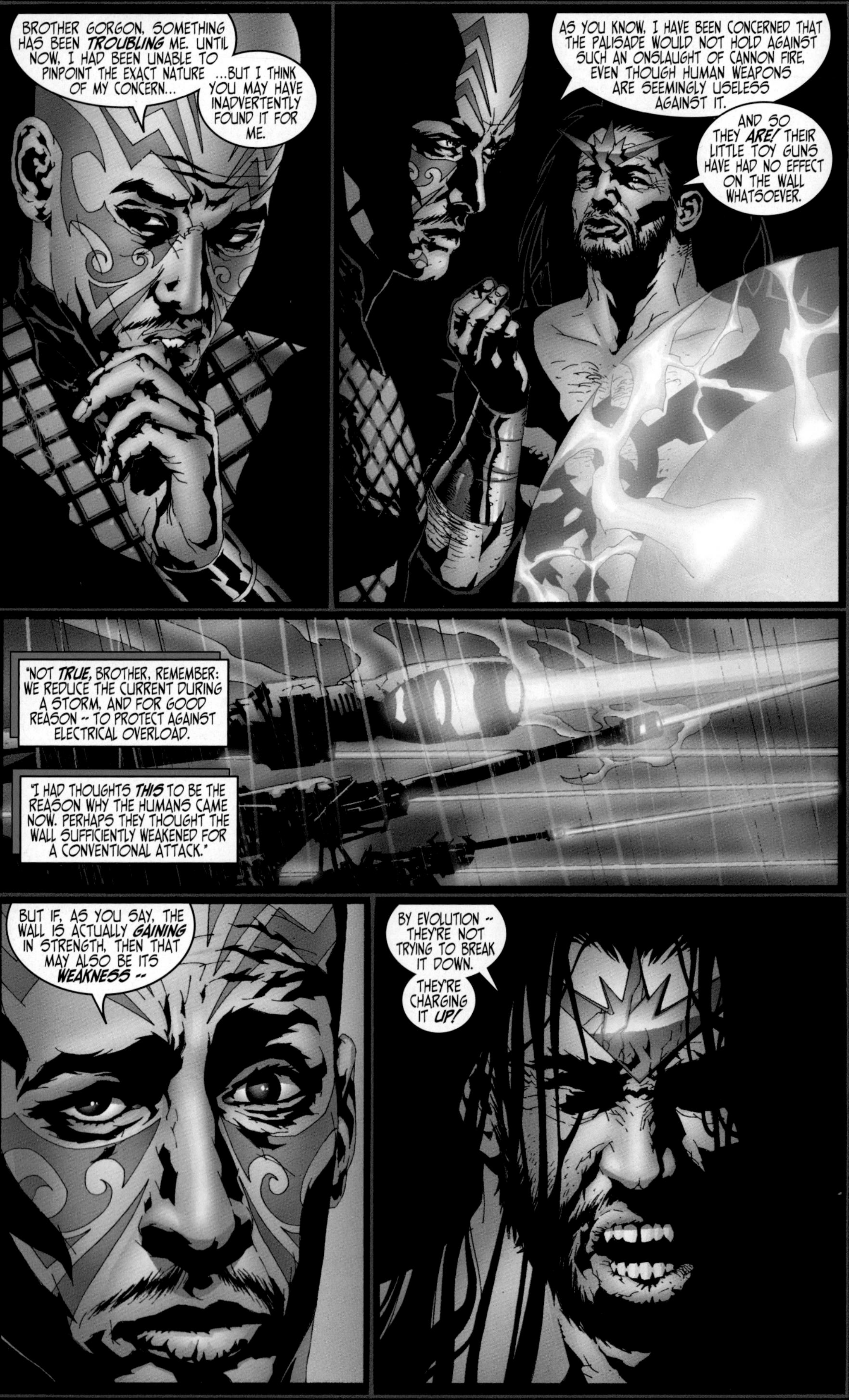
BROTHER GORGON, SOMETHING HAS BEEN TROUBLING ME. UNTIL NOW, I HAD BEEN UNABLE TO PINPOINT THE EXACT NATURE OF MY CONCERN...
...BUT I THINK YOU MAY HAVE INADVERTENTLY FOUND IT FOR ME.
AS YOU KNOW, I HAVE BEEN CONCERNED THAT THE PALISADE WOULD NOT HOLD AGAINST SUCH AN ONSLAUGHT OF CANNON FIRE, EVEN THOUGH HUMAN WEAPONS ARE SEEMINGLY USELESS AGAINST IT.
AND SO THEY ARE! THEIR LITTLE TOY GUNS HAVE HAD NO EFFECT ON THE WALL WHATSOEVER.
"NOT TRUE, BROTHER, REMEMBER: WE REDUCE THE CURRENT DURING A STORM, AND FOR GOOD REASON -- TO PROTECT AGAINST ELECTRICAL OVERLOAD.
"I HAD THOUGHTS THIS TO BE THE REASON WHY THE HUMANS CAME NOW. PERHAPS THEY THOUGHT THE WALL SUFFICIENTLY WEAKENED FOR A CONVENTIONAL ATTACK."
BUT IF, AS YOU SAY, THE WALL IS ACTUALLY GAINING IN STRENGTH, THEN THAT MAY ALSO BE ITS WEAKNESS --
BY EVOLUTION -- THEY'RE NOT TRYING TO BREAK IT DOWN.
THEY'RE CHARGING IT UP!

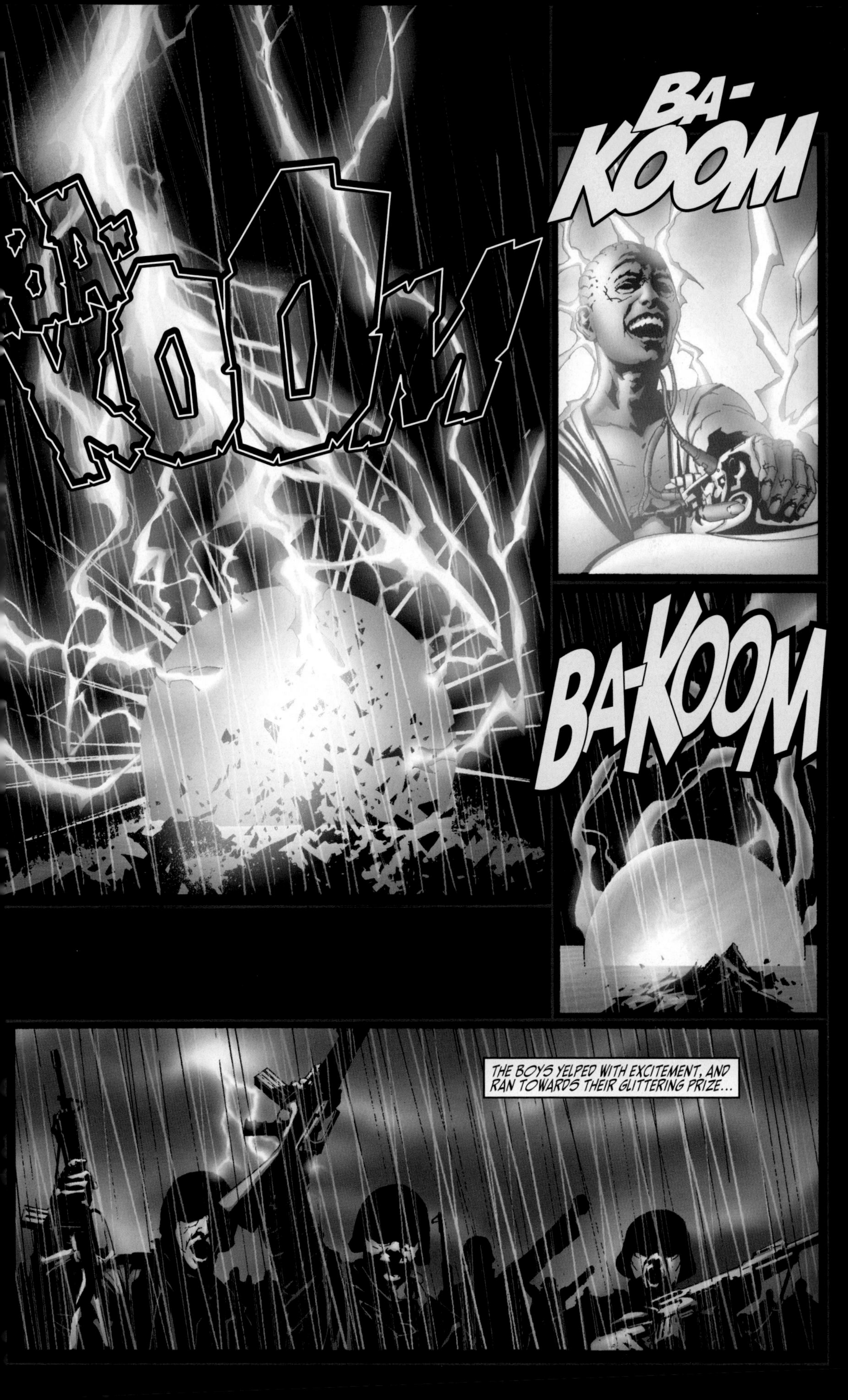
BA-KOOM
BA-KOOM
BA-KOOM
THE BOYS YELPED WITH EXCITEMENT, AND RAN TOWARDS THEIR GLITTERING PRIZE...

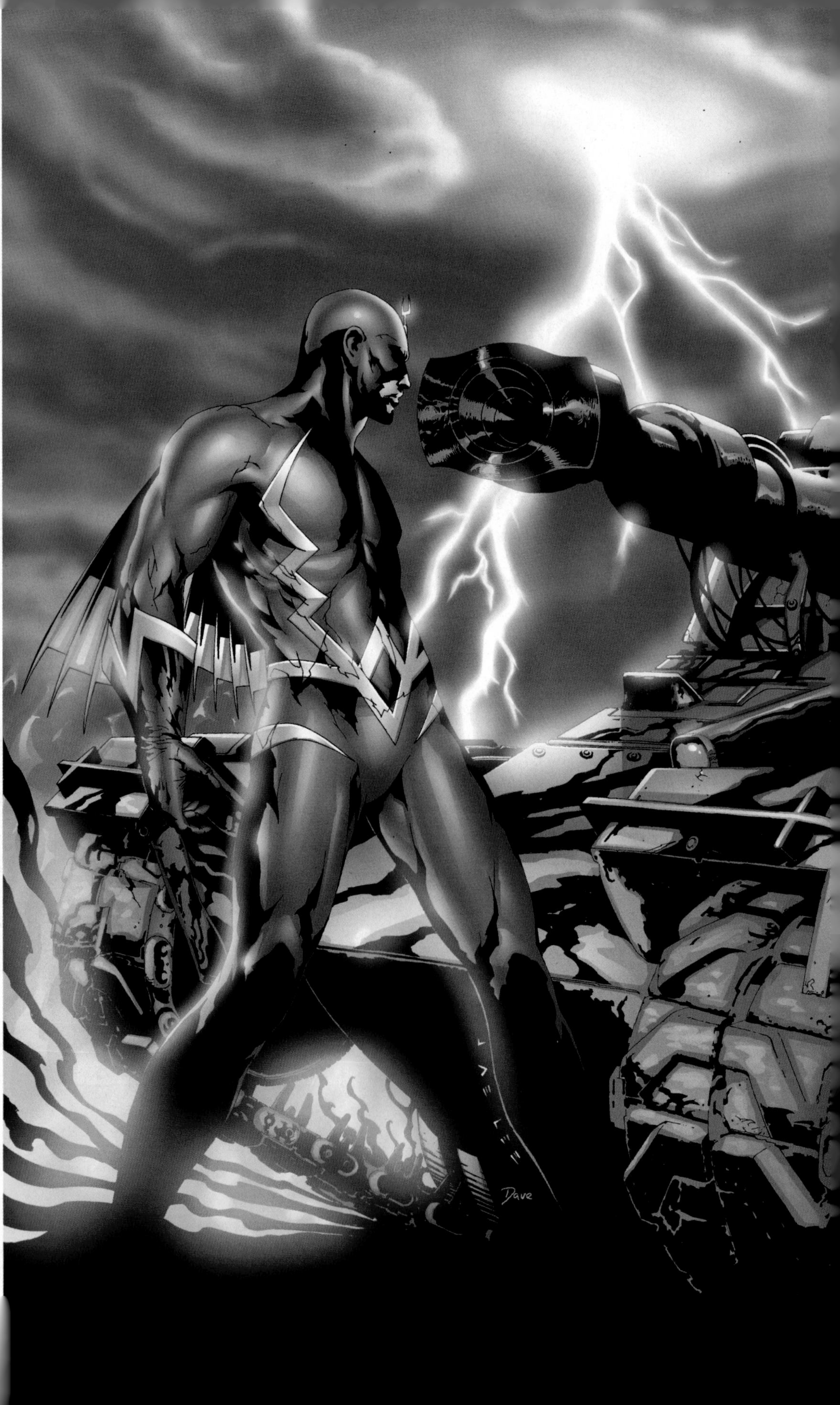
Dave

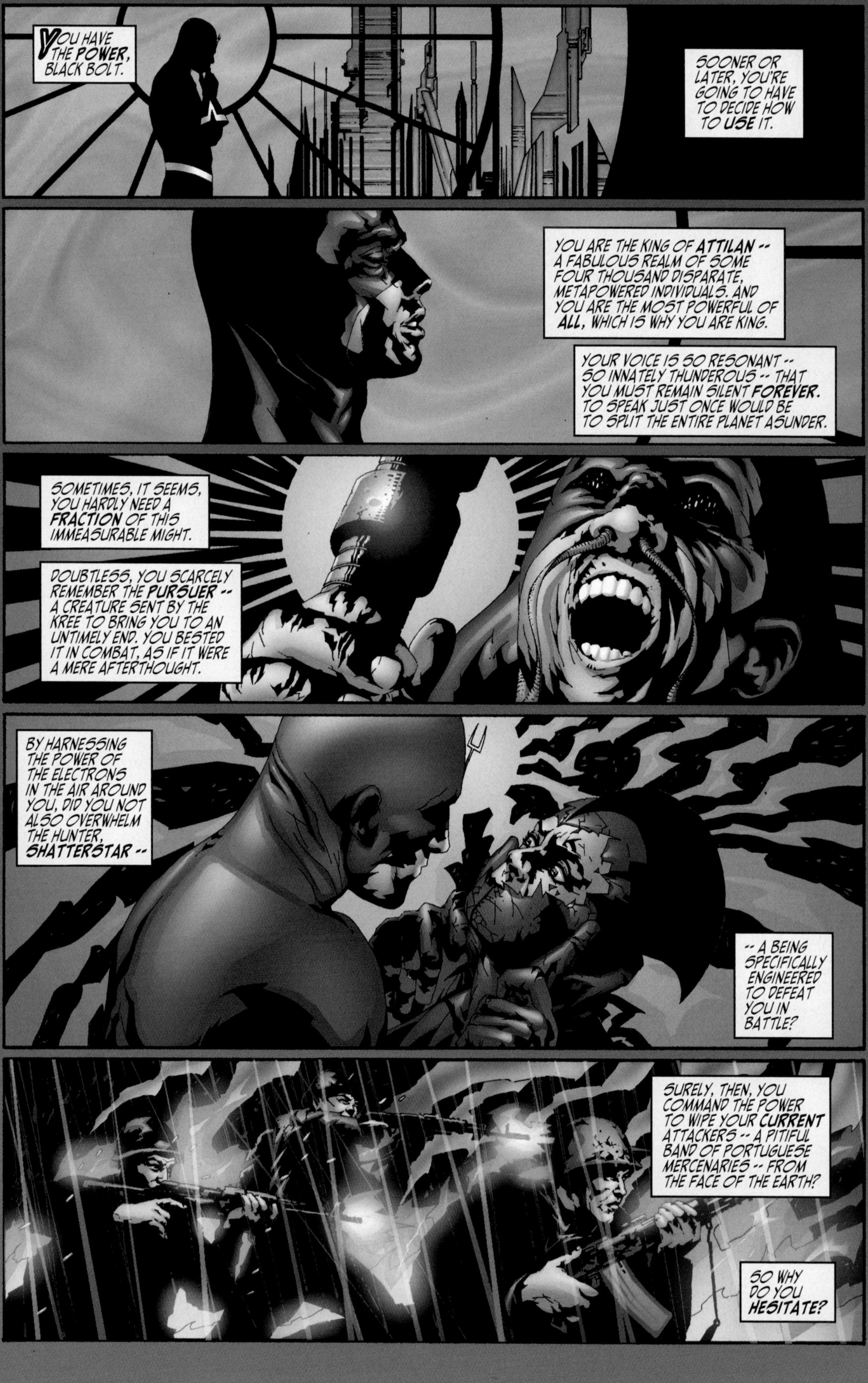
YOU HAVE THE POWER, BLACK BOLT.
SOONER OR LATER, YOU'RE GOING TO HAVE TO DECIDE HOW TO USE IT.
YOU ARE THE KING OF ATTILAN -- A FABULOUS REALM OF SOME FOUR THOUSAND DISPARATE, METAPOWERED INDIVIDUALS. AND YOU ARE THE MOST POWERFUL OF ALL, WHICH IS WHY YOU ARE KING.
YOUR VOICE IS SO RESONANT -- SO INNATELY THUNDEROUS -- THAT YOU MUST REMAIN SILENT FOREVER. TO SPEAK JUST ONCE WOULD BE TO SPLIT THE ENTIRE PLANET ASUNDER.
SOMETIMES, IT SEEMS, YOU HARDLY NEED A FRACTION OF THIS IMMEASURABLE MIGHT.
DOUBTLESS, YOU SCARCELY REMEMBER THE PURSUER -- A CREATURE SENT BY THE KREE TO BRING YOU TO AN UNTIMELY END. YOU BESTED IT IN COMBAT, AS IF IT WERE A MERE AFTERTHOUGHT.
BY HARNESSING THE POWER OF THE ELECTRONS IN THE AIR AROUND YOU, DID YOU NOT ALSO OVERWHELM THE HUNTER, SHATTERSTAR --
-- A BEING SPECIFICALLY ENGINEERED TO DEFEAT YOU IN BATTLE?
SURELY, THEN, YOU COMMAND THE POWER TO WIPE YOUR CURRENT ATTACKERS -- A PITIFUL BAND OF PORTUGUESE MERCENARIES -- FROM THE FACE OF THE EARTH?
SO WHY DO YOU HESITATE?

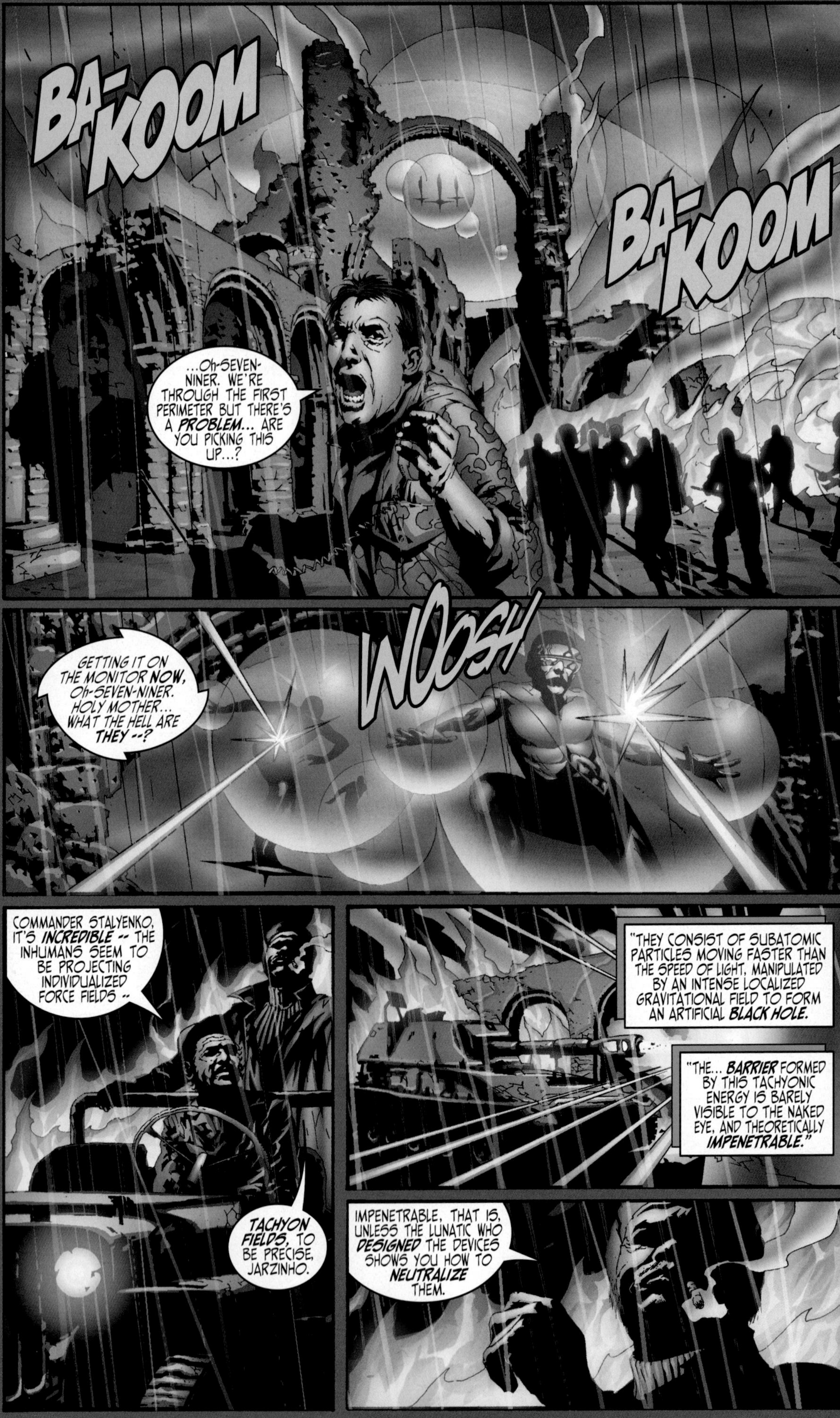
BA-KOOM
BA-KOOM
...Oh-SEVEN-NINER. WE'RE THROUGH THE FIRST PERIMETER BUT THERE'S A PROBLEM... ARE YOU PICKING THIS UP...?
WOOSH
GETTING IT ON THE MONITOR NOW, Oh-SEVEN-NINER. HOLY MOTHER... WHAT THE HELL ARE THEY --?
COMMANDER STALYENKO, IT'S INCREDIBLE -- THE INHUMANS SEEM TO BE PROJECTING INDIVIDUALIZED FORCE FIELDS --
TACHYON FIELDS, TO BE PRECISE, JARZINHO.
"THEY CONSIST OF SUBATOMIC PARTICLES MOVING FASTER THAN THE SPEED OF LIGHT, MANIPULATED BY AN INTENSE LOCALIZED GRAVITATIONAL FIELD TO FORM AN ARTIFICIAL BLACK HOLE.
"THE... BARRIER FORMED BY THIS TACHYONIC ENERGY IS BARELY VISIBLE TO THE NAKED EYE, AND THEORETICALLY IMPENETRABLE."
IMPENETRABLE, THAT IS, UNLESS THE LUNATIC WHO DESIGNED THE DEVICES SHOWS YOU HOW TO NEUTRALIZE THEM.

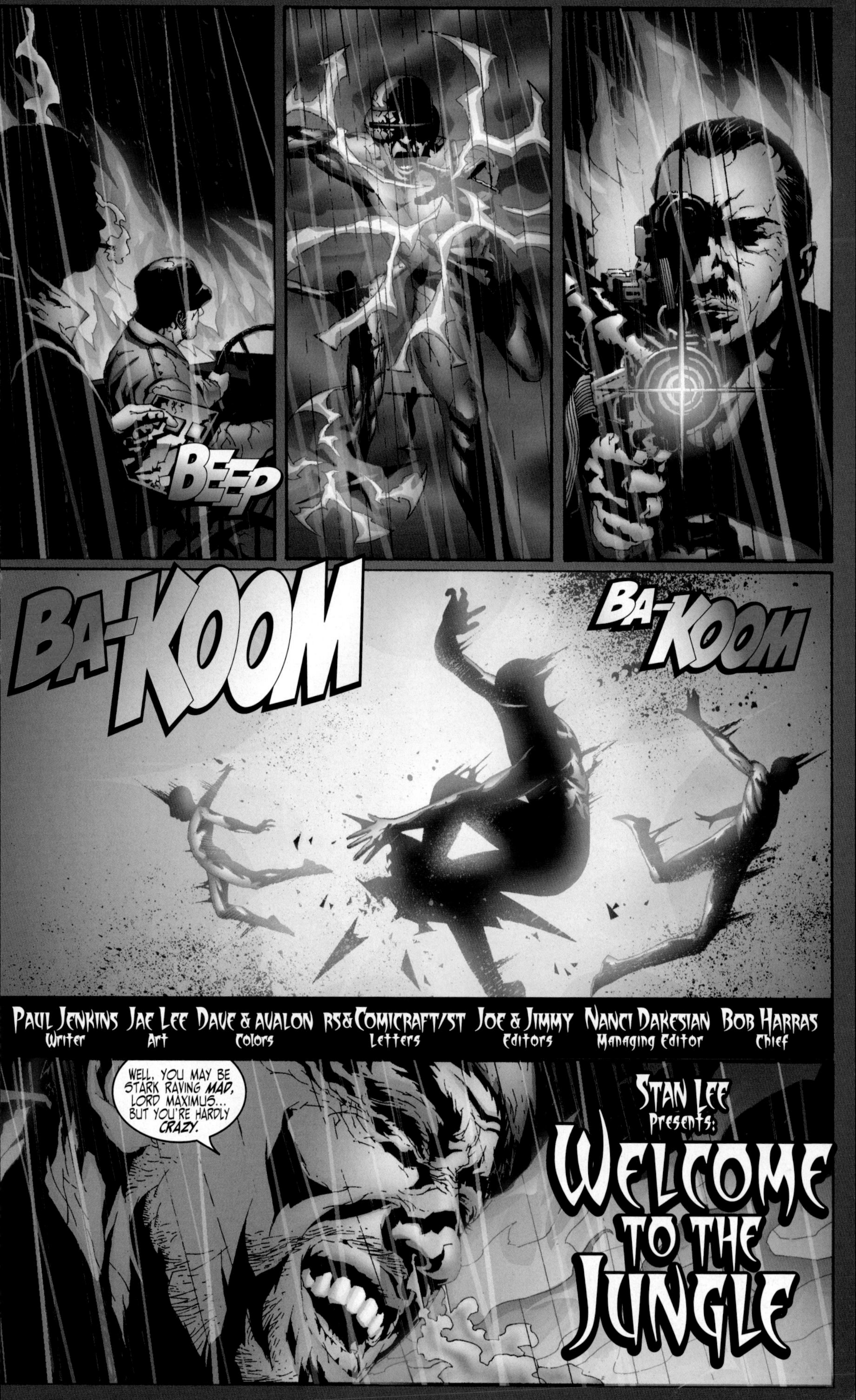
BEEP
BA-KOOM
BA-KOOM
PAUL JENKINS Writer
JAE LEE Art
DAVE & AVALON Colors
RS&COMICRAFT/ST Letters
JOE & JIMMY Editors
NANCI DAKESIAN Managing Editor
BOB HARRAS Chief
WELL, YOU MAY BE STARK RAVING MAD, LORD MAXIMUS... BUT YOU'RE HARDLY CRAZY.
STAN LEE Presents:
WELCOME TO THE JUNGLE

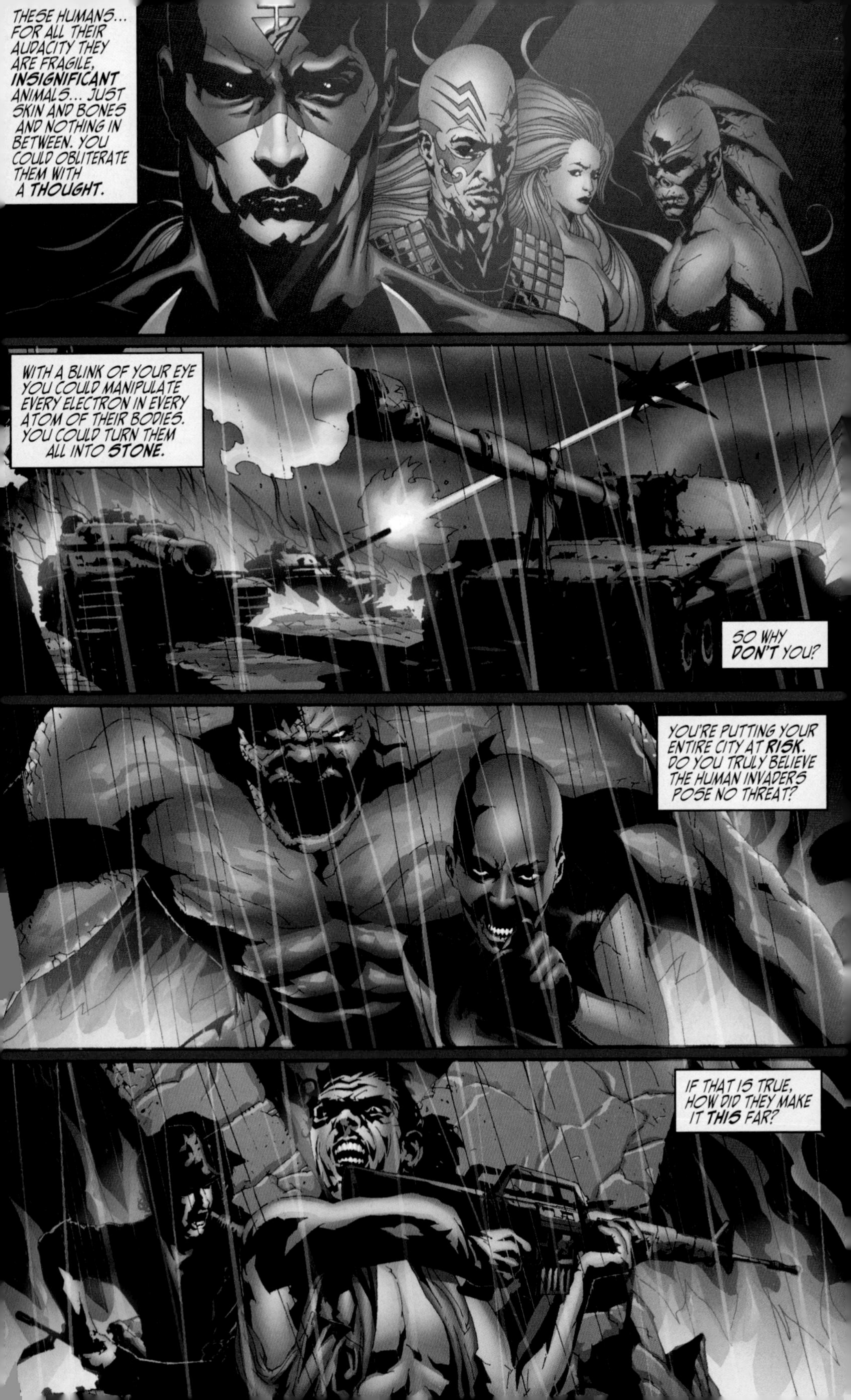
THESE HUMANS... FOR ALL THEIR AUDACITY THEY ARE FRAGILE, INSIGNIFICANT ANIMALS... JUST SKIN AND BONES AND NOTHING IN BETWEEN. YOU COULD OBLITERATE THEM WITH A THOUGHT.
WITH A BLINK OF YOUR EYE YOU COULD MANIPULATE EVERY ELECTRON IN EVERY ATOM OF THEIR BODIES. YOU COULD TURN THEM ALL INTO STONE.
SO WHY DON'T YOU?
YOU'RE PUTTING YOUR ENTIRE CITY AT RISK. DO YOU TRULY BELIEVE THE HUMAN INVADERS POSE NO THREAT?
IF THAT IS TRUE, HOW DID THEY MAKE IT THIS FAR?

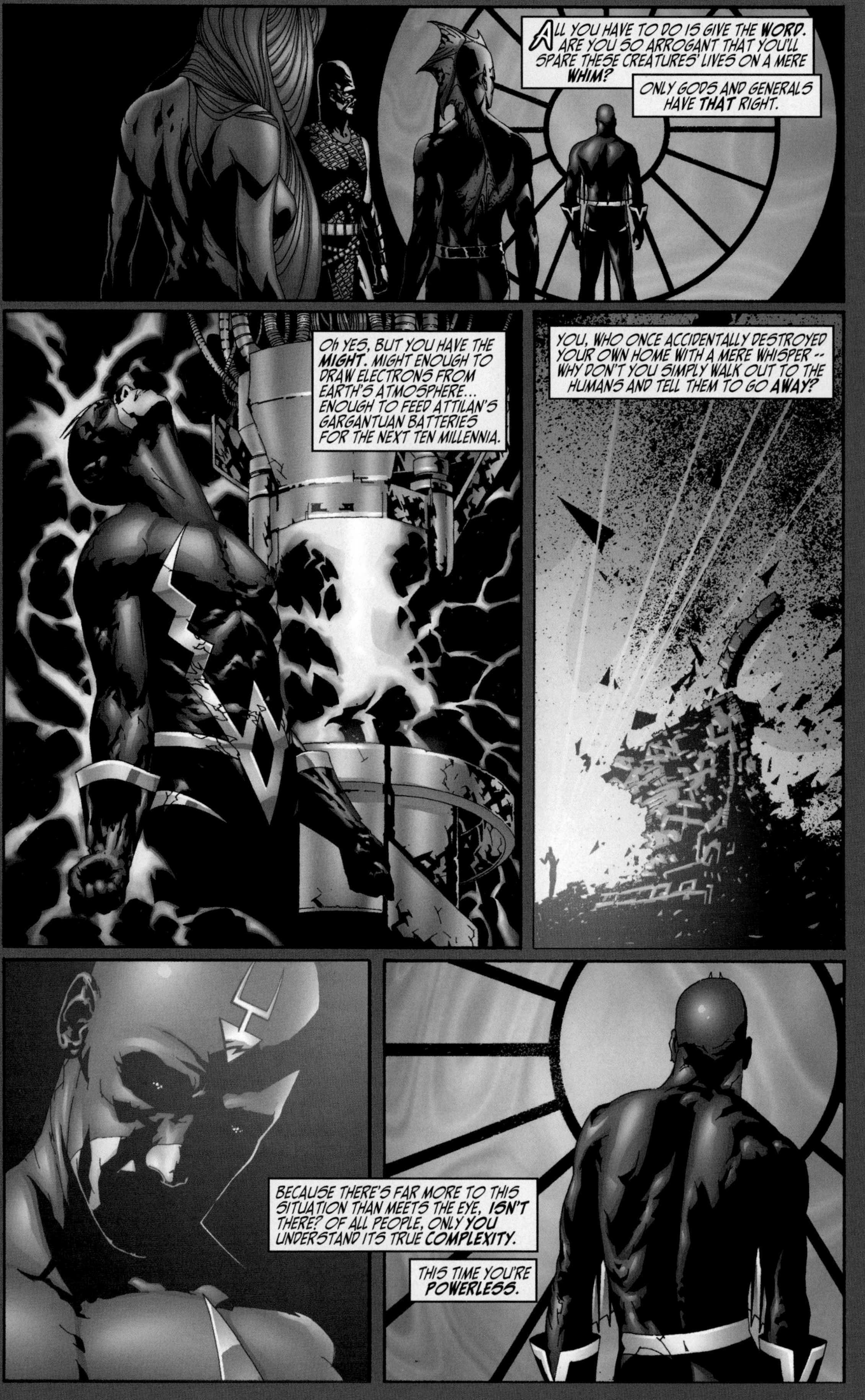
ALL YOU HAVE TO DO IS GIVE THE WORD. ARE YOU SO ARROGANT THAT YOU'LL SPARE THESE CREATURES' LIVES ON A MERE WHIM?
ONLY GODS AND GENERALS HAVE THAT RIGHT.
Oh YES, BUT YOU HAVE THE MIGHT. MIGHT ENOUGH TO DRAW ELECTRONS FROM EARTH'S ATMOSPHERE... ENOUGH TO FEED ATTILAN'S GARGANTUAN BATTERIES FOR THE NEXT TEN MILLENNIA.
YOU, WHO ONCE ACCIDENTALLY DESTROYED YOUR OWN HOME WITH A MERE WHISPER -- WHY DON'T YOU SIMPLY WALK OUT TO THE HUMANS AND TELL THEM TO GO AWAY?
BECAUSE THERE'S FAR MORE TO THIS SITUATION THAN MEETS THE EYE, ISN'T THERE? OF ALL PEOPLE, ONLY YOU UNDERSTAND ITS TRUE COMPLEXITY.
THIS TIME YOU'RE POWERLESS.

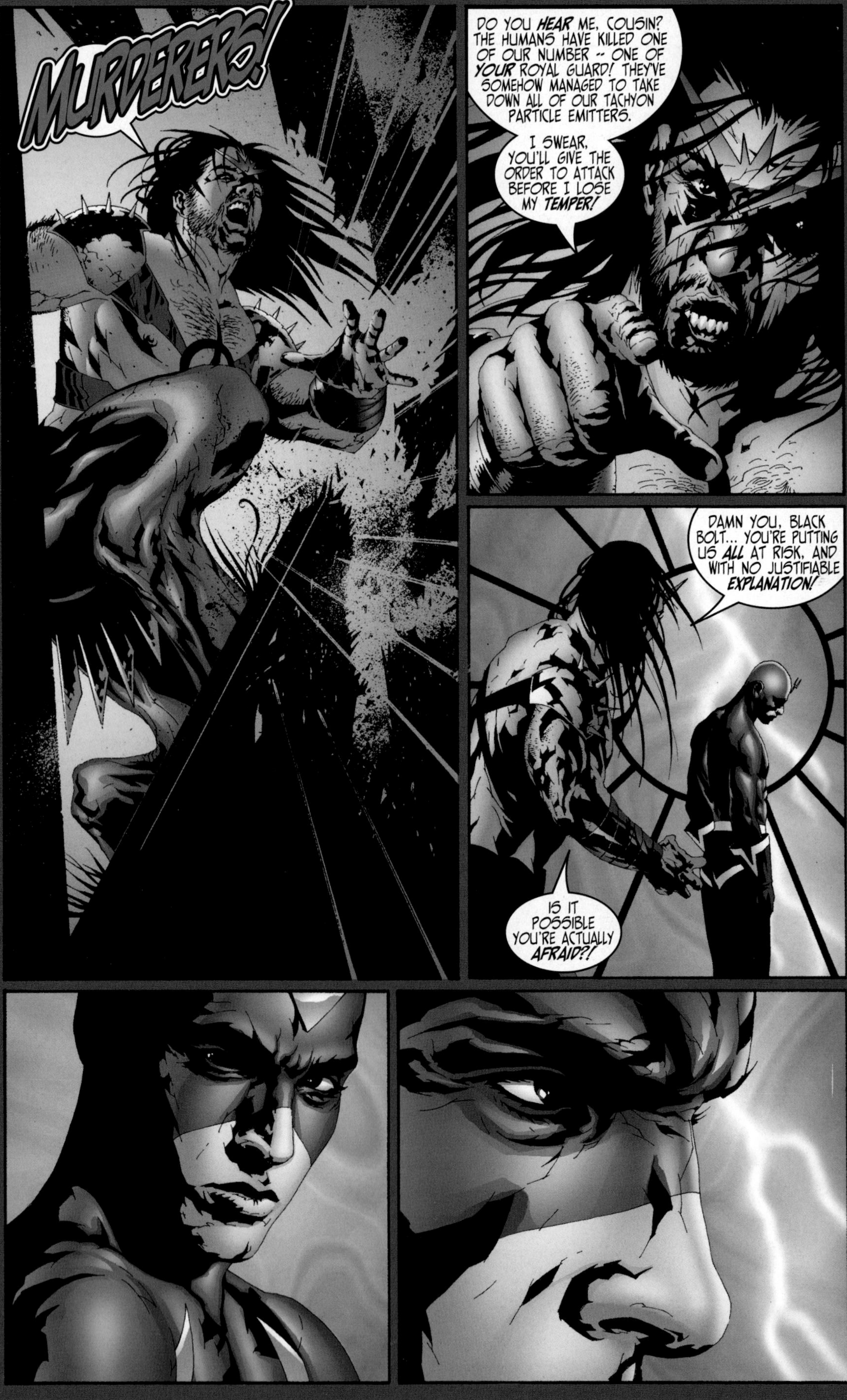
MURDERERS!
DO YOU HEAR ME, COUSIN? THE HUMANS HAVE KILLED ONE OF OUR NUMBER -- ONE OF YOUR ROYAL GUARD! THEY'VE SOMEHOW MANAGED TO TAKE DOWN ALL OF OUR TACHYON PARTICLE EMITTERS.
I SWEAR, YOU'LL GIVE THE ORDER TO ATTACK BEFORE I LOSE MY TEMPER!
DAMN YOU, BLACK BOLT... YOU'RE PUTTING US ALL AT RISK, AND WITH NO JUSTIFIABLE EXPLANATION!
IS IT POSSIBLE YOU'RE ACTUALLY AFRAID?!

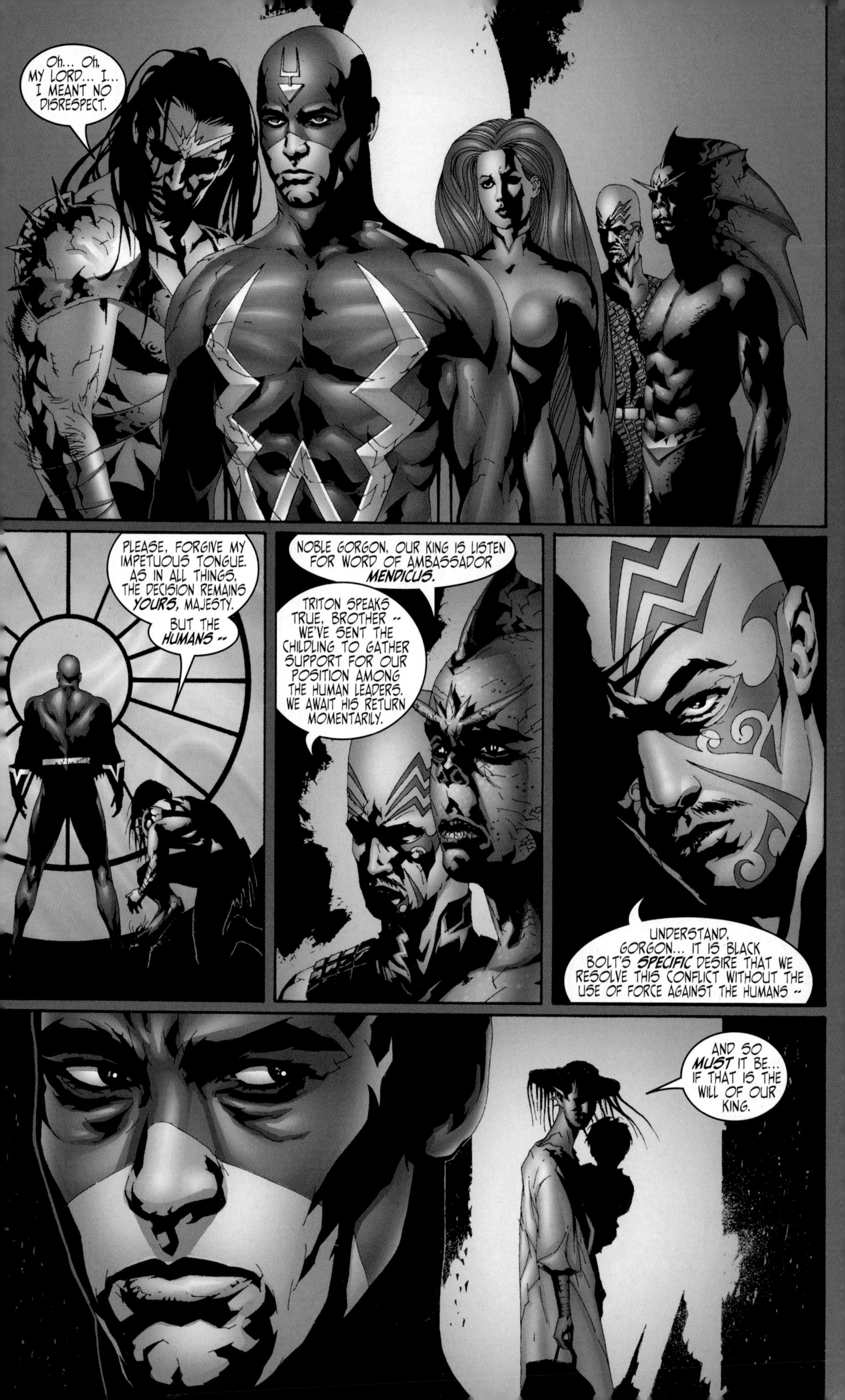
Oh... Oh, MY LORD... I... I MEANT NO DISRESPECT.
PLEASE, FORGIVE MY IMPETUOUS TONGUE. AS IN ALL THINGS, THE DECISION REMAINS YOURS, MAJESTY.
BUT THE HUMANS --
NOBLE GORGON, OUR KING IS LISTEN FOR WORD OF AMBASSADOR MENDICUS.
TRITON SPEAKS TRUE, BROTHER -- WE'VE SENT THE CHILDLING TO GATHER SUPPORT FOR OUR POSITION AMONG THE HUMAN LEADERS. WE AWAIT HIS RETURN MOMENTARILY.
UNDERSTAND, GORGON... IT IS BLACK BOLT'S SPECIFIC DESIRE THAT WE RESOLVE THIS CONFLICT WITHOUT THE USE OF FORCE AGAINST THE HUMANS --
AND SO MUST IT BE... IF THAT IS THE WILL OF OUR KING.

LORD MENDICUS, YOU'RE *WEARY* --

AMBASSADOR --?

PLEASE, MY LADY MEDUSA... A LITTLE FATIGUE IS HARDLY *FATAL*.

I COME WITH WORD FROM THE UNITED HUMAN NATIONS... THOUGH I FEAR IT WILL NOT BE TO YOUR LIKING.

THAT WILL BE ALL, ELEJEA. MY TASK IS TO REASON WITH HUMANS, NOT WITH OVERPROTECTIVE ATTENDANTS.

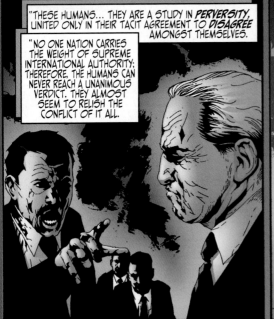

"THESE HUMANS... THEY ARE A STUDY IN *PERVERSITY*, UNITED ONLY IN THEIR TACIT AGREEMENT TO *DISAGREE* AMONGST THEMSELVES.

"NO ONE NATION CARRIES THE WEIGHT OF SUPREME INTERNATIONAL AUTHORITY; THEREFORE, THE HUMANS CAN NEVER REACH A UNANIMOUS VERDICT. THEY ALMOST SEEM TO RELISH THE CONFLICT OF IT ALL.

"AMBASSADOR McINTYRE OF THE UNITED AMERICAS HAS PLEDGED THE SUPPORT OF HIS NATION, AS HAVE THE AMBASSADORS OF BRITAIN, IRAQ AND ISRAEL.

"BUT THEY STAND *APART*, AS OTHER NATIONS REFUSE TO COME TO OUR AID. HUMANITY DOES NOT *TRUST* US, IT SEEMS."

WHATEVER COURSE OF ACTION WE TAKE, MAJESTIES, WE MUST TAKE IT *ALONE*.

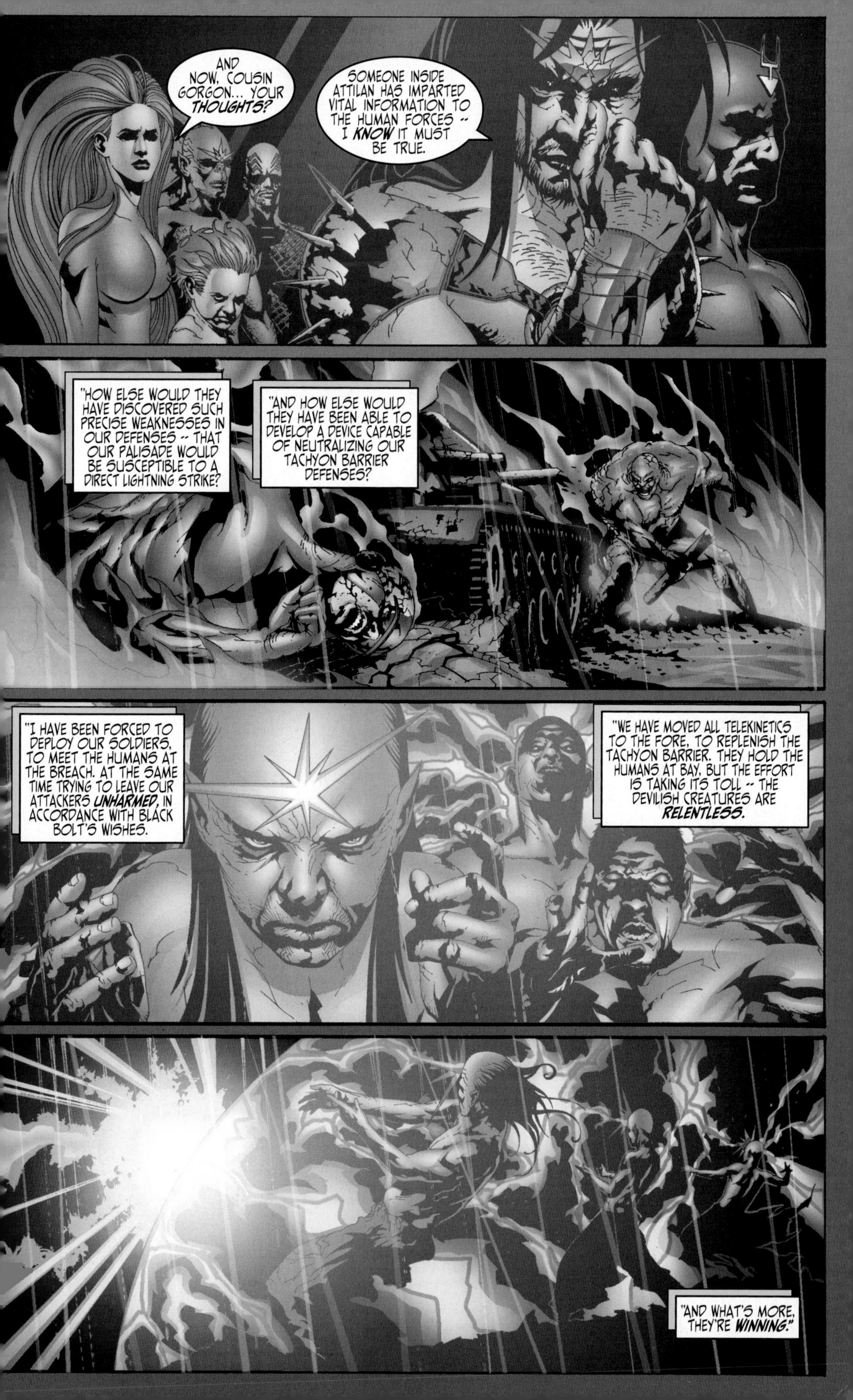
AND NOW, COUSIN GORGON... YOUR THOUGHTS?
SOMEONE INSIDE ATTILAN HAS IMPARTED VITAL INFORMATION TO THE HUMAN FORCES -- I KNOW IT MUST BE TRUE.
"HOW ELSE WOULD THEY HAVE DISCOVERED SUCH PRECISE WEAKNESSES IN OUR DEFENSES -- THAT OUR PALISADE WOULD BE SUSCEPTIBLE TO A DIRECT LIGHTNING STRIKE?
"AND HOW ELSE WOULD THEY HAVE BEEN ABLE TO DEVELOP A DEVICE CAPABLE OF NEUTRALIZING OUR TACHYON BARRIER DEFENSES?
"I HAVE BEEN FORCED TO DEPLOY OUR SOLDIERS, TO MEET THE HUMANS AT THE BREACH. AT THE SAME TIME TRYING TO LEAVE OUR ATTACKERS UNHARMED, IN ACCORDANCE WITH BLACK BOLT'S WISHES.
"WE HAVE MOVED ALL TELEKINETICS TO THE FORE, TO REPLENISH THE TACHYON BARRIER. THEY HOLD THE HUMANS AT BAY, BUT THE EFFORT IS TAKING ITS TOLL -- THE DEVILISH CREATURES ARE RELENTLESS.
"AND WHAT'S MORE, THEY'RE WINNING."

MISTER *BIXBY* -- I'M DELIGHTED YOU COULD JOIN US.

YEAH, WELL... AT LEAST *ONE* OF US IS HAVING A GOOD TIME. THIS PLACE STINKS; THE FOOD STINKS, THE AIR STINKS, AND WORST OF ALL... *I* STINK.

JESUS, *STALYENKO...* COULDN'T YOU HAVE PICKED A NICER PLACE TO COMMIT SUICIDE -- LIKE *HAWAII*, OR SOMETHING?

HOW WONDERFULLY *AMERICAN* OF YOU.

YOU KNOW, IN THE OLD DAYS I'D HAVE SET UP MY WAR ROOM IN SIBERIA -- *THEN* YOU WOULD HAVE REASON TO COMPLAIN ABOUT THE COLD.

YEAH, WELL... I'M NOT SO FRAIL I CAN'T UPHOLD MY END OF THE *BARGAIN,* COMMANDER. FOR WHICH I EXPECT TO BE WELL-*PAID* --

QUITE SO. AND THE *PRODUCT* --?

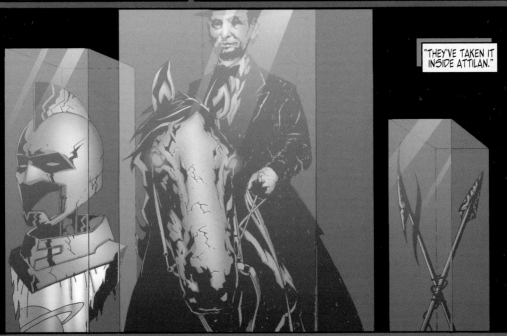

"THEY'VE TAKEN IT INSIDE ATTILAN."

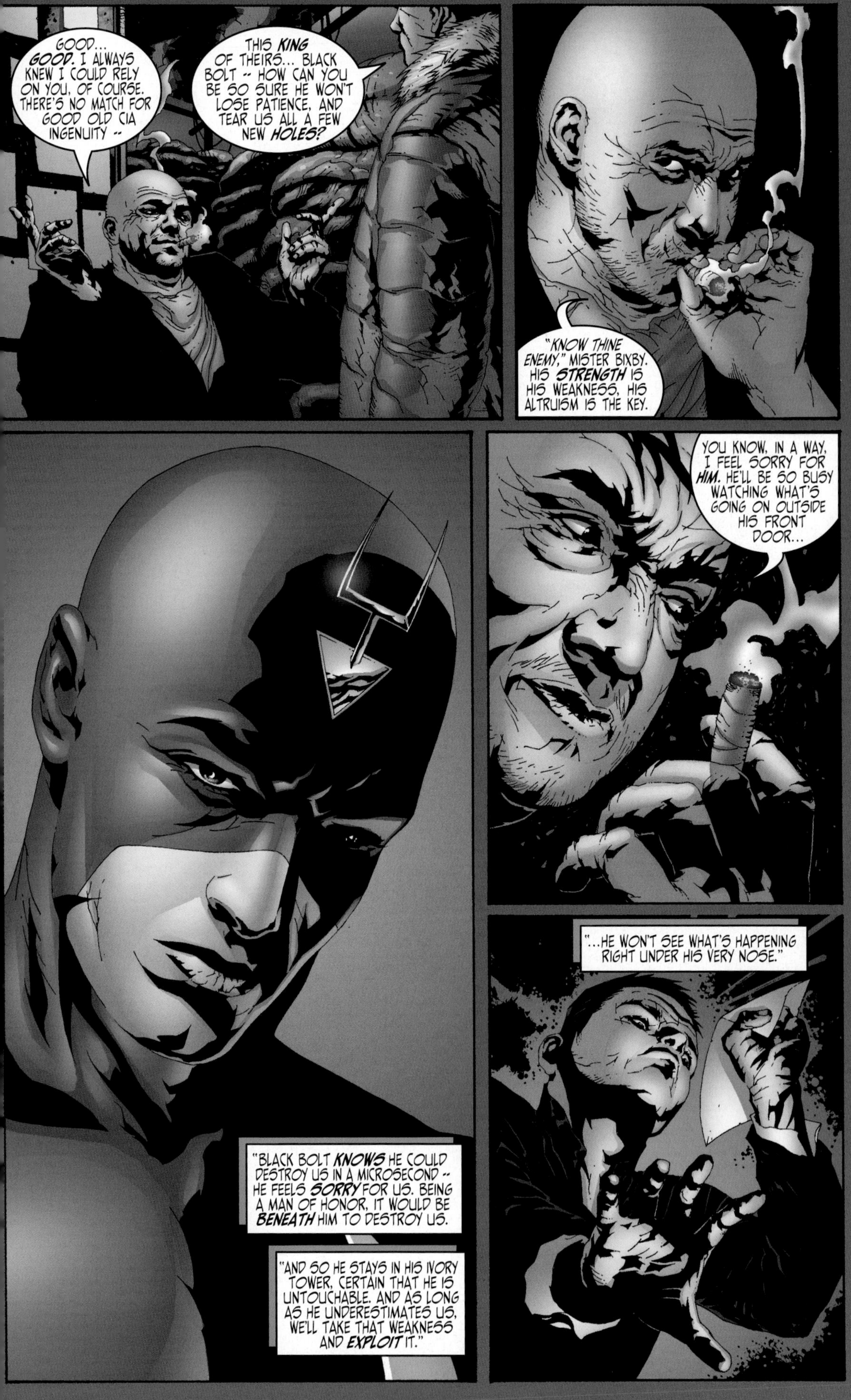
GOOD... GOOD. I ALWAYS KNEW I COULD RELY ON YOU, OF COURSE. THERE'S NO MATCH FOR GOOD OLD CIA INGENUITY --
THIS KING OF THEIRS... BLACK BOLT -- HOW CAN YOU BE SO SURE HE WON'T LOSE PATIENCE, AND TEAR US ALL A FEW NEW HOLES?
"KNOW THINE ENEMY," MISTER BIXBY. HIS STRENGTH IS HIS WEAKNESS, HIS ALTRUISM IS THE KEY.
YOU KNOW, IN A WAY, I FEEL SORRY FOR HIM. HE'LL BE SO BUSY WATCHING WHAT'S GOING ON OUTSIDE HIS FRONT DOOR...
"BLACK BOLT KNOWS HE COULD DESTROY US IN A MICROSECOND -- HE FEELS SORRY FOR US. BEING A MAN OF HONOR, IT WOULD BE BENEATH HIM TO DESTROY US.
"AND SO HE STAYS IN HIS IVORY TOWER, CERTAIN THAT HE IS UNTOUCHABLE. AND AS LONG AS HE UNDERESTIMATES US, WE'LL TAKE THAT WEAKNESS AND EXPLOIT IT."
"...HE WON'T SEE WHAT'S HAPPENING RIGHT UNDER HIS VERY NOSE."

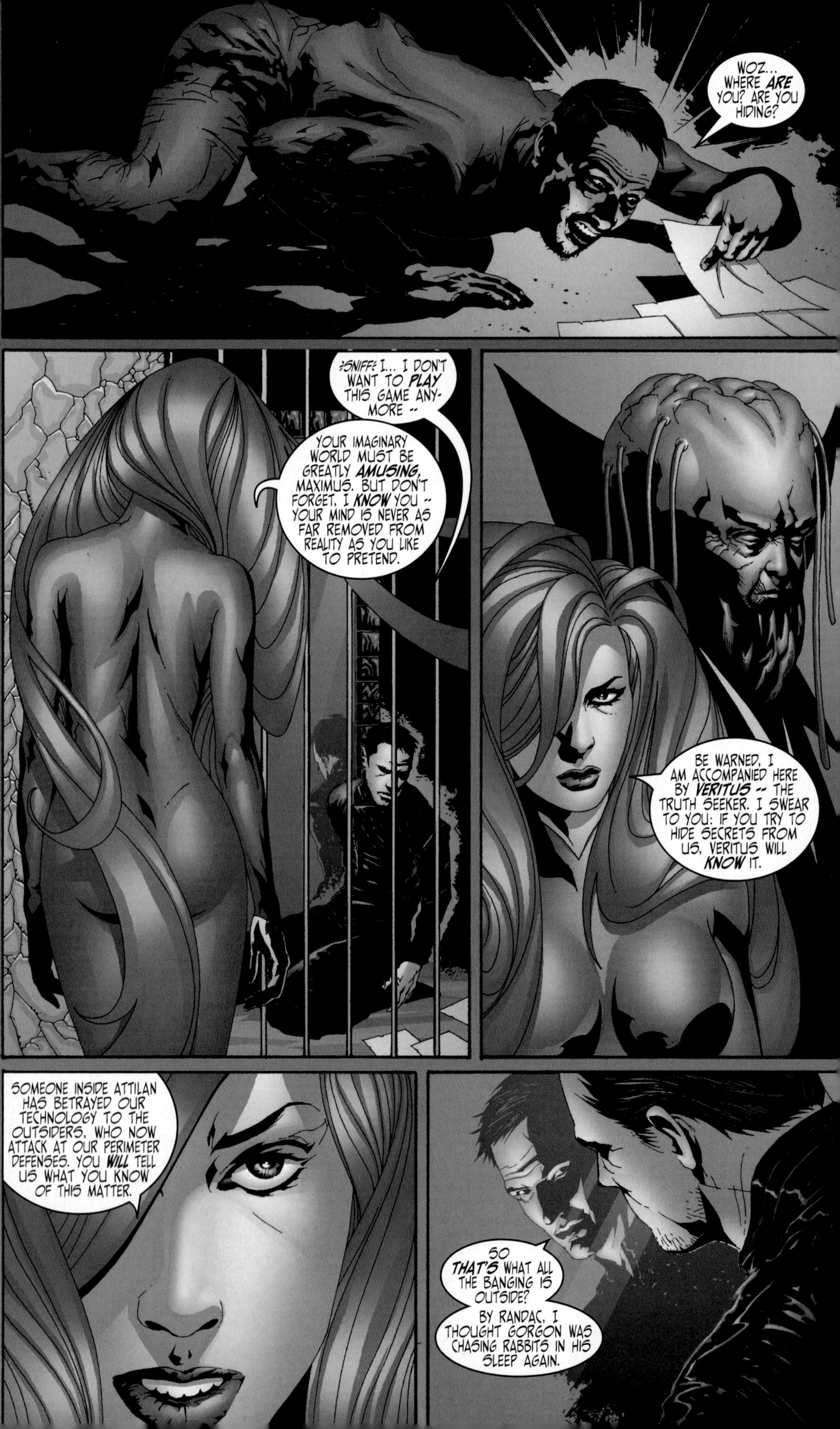
WOZ... WHERE ARE YOU? ARE YOU HIDING?
SNIFF I... I DON'T WANT TO PLAY THIS GAME ANY-MORE --
YOUR IMAGINARY WORLD MUST BE GREATLY AMUSING, MAXIMUS. BUT DON'T FORGET. I KNOW YOU -- YOUR MIND IS NEVER AS FAR REMOVED FROM REALITY AS YOU LIKE TO PRETEND.
BE WARNED. I AM ACCOMPANIED HERE BY VERITUS -- THE TRUTH SEEKER. I SWEAR TO YOU: IF YOU TRY TO HIDE SECRETS FROM US, VERITUS WILL KNOW IT.
SOMEONE INSIDE ATTILAN HAS BETRAYED OUR TECHNOLOGY TO THE OUTSIDERS, WHO NOW ATTACK AT OUR PERIMETER DEFENSES. YOU WILL TELL US WHAT YOU KNOW OF THIS MATTER.
SO THAT'S WHAT ALL THE BANGING IS OUTSIDE?
BY RANDAC, I THOUGHT GORGON WAS CHASING RABBITS IN HIS SLEEP AGAIN.

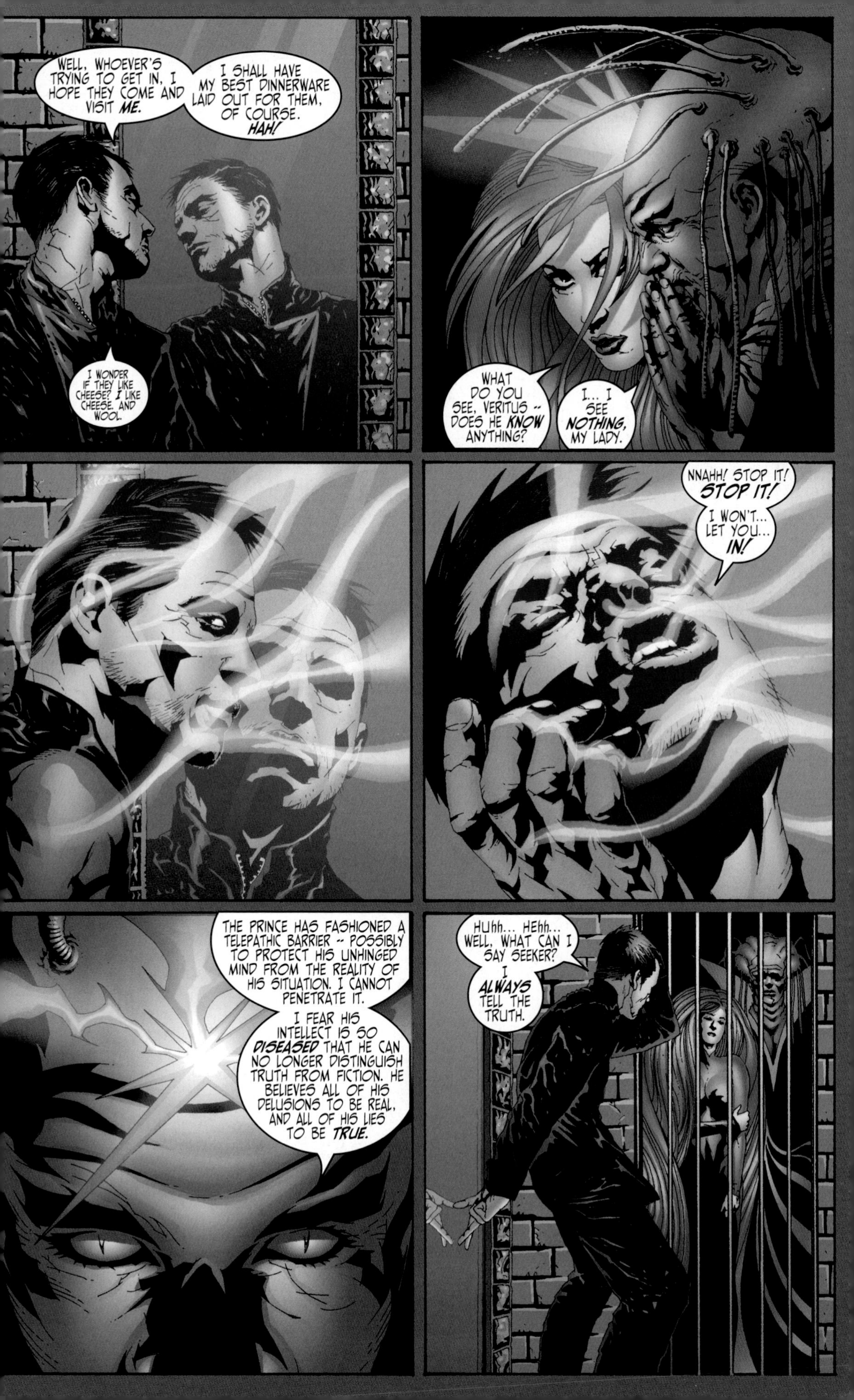

WELL, WHOEVER'S TRYING TO GET IN, I HOPE THEY COME AND VISIT ME.
I SHALL HAVE MY BEST DINNERWARE LAID OUT FOR THEM, OF COURSE. HAH!
I WONDER IF THEY LIKE CHEESE? I LIKE CHEESE. AND WOOL.
WHAT DO YOU SEE, VERITUS -- DOES HE KNOW ANYTHING?
I... I SEE NOTHING, MY LADY.
NNAHH! STOP IT! STOP IT!
I WON'T... LET YOU... IN!
THE PRINCE HAS FASHIONED A TELEPATHIC BARRIER -- POSSIBLY TO PROTECT HIS UNHINGED MIND FROM THE REALITY OF HIS SITUATION. I CANNOT PENETRATE IT.
I FEAR HIS INTELLECT IS SO DISEASED THAT HE CAN NO LONGER DISTINGUISH TRUTH FROM FICTION. HE BELIEVES ALL OF HIS DELUSIONS TO BE REAL, AND ALL OF HIS LIES TO BE TRUE.
Huhh... Hehh... WELL, WHAT CAN I SAY SEEKER?
I ALWAYS TELL THE TRUTH.

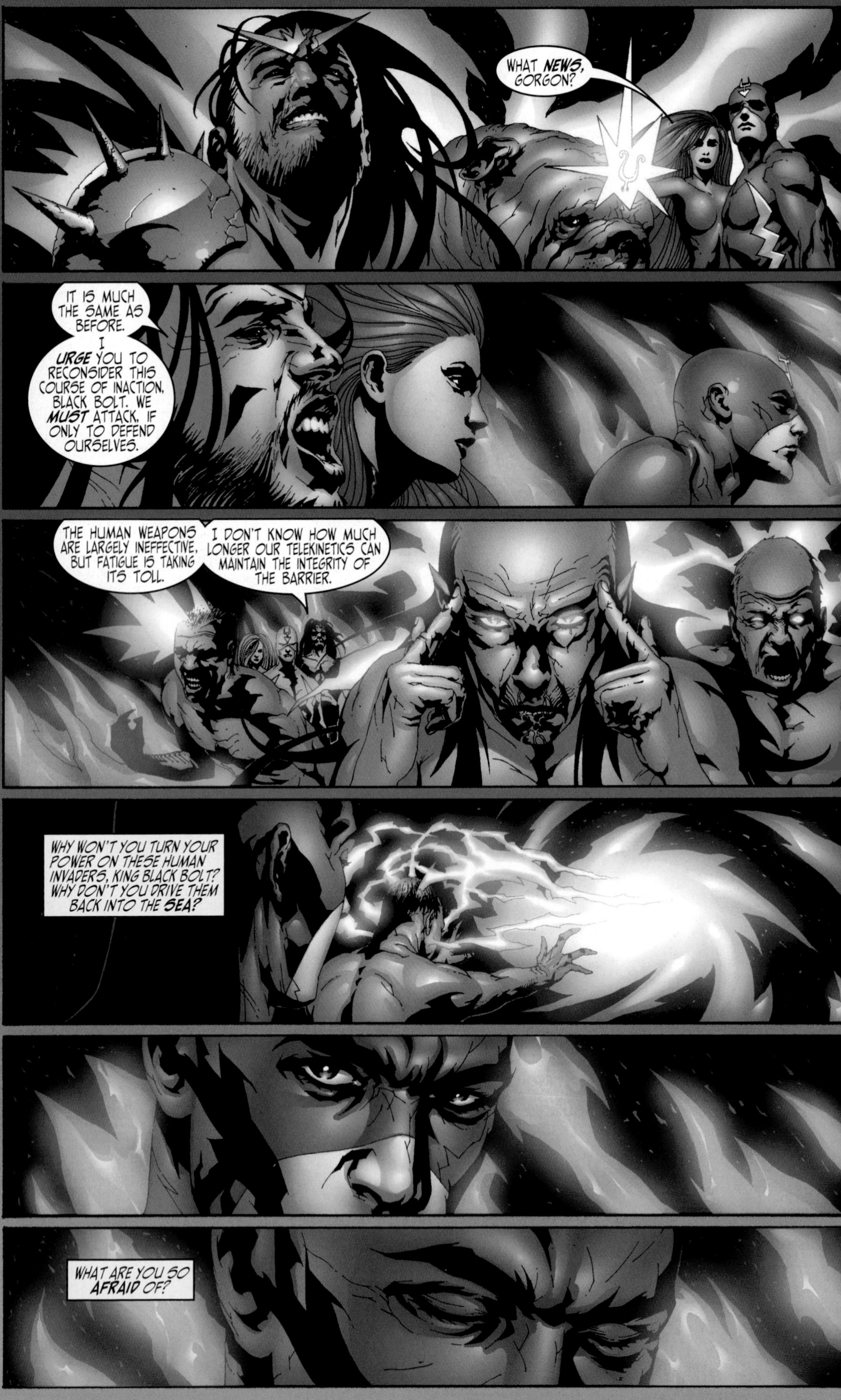
WHAT **NEWS,** GORGON?
IT IS MUCH THE SAME AS BEFORE.
I **URGE** YOU TO RECONSIDER THIS COURSE OF INACTION, BLACK BOLT. WE **MUST** ATTACK, IF ONLY TO DEFEND OURSELVES.
THE HUMAN WEAPONS ARE LARGELY INEFFECTIVE, BUT FATIGUE IS TAKING ITS TOLL.
I DON'T KNOW HOW MUCH LONGER OUR TELEKINETICS CAN MAINTAIN THE INTEGRITY OF THE BARRIER.
WHY WON'T YOU TURN YOUR POWER ON THESE HUMAN INVADERS, KING BLACK BOLT? WHY DON'T YOU DRIVE THEM BACK INTO THE **SEA?**
WHAT ARE YOU SO **AFRAID** OF?

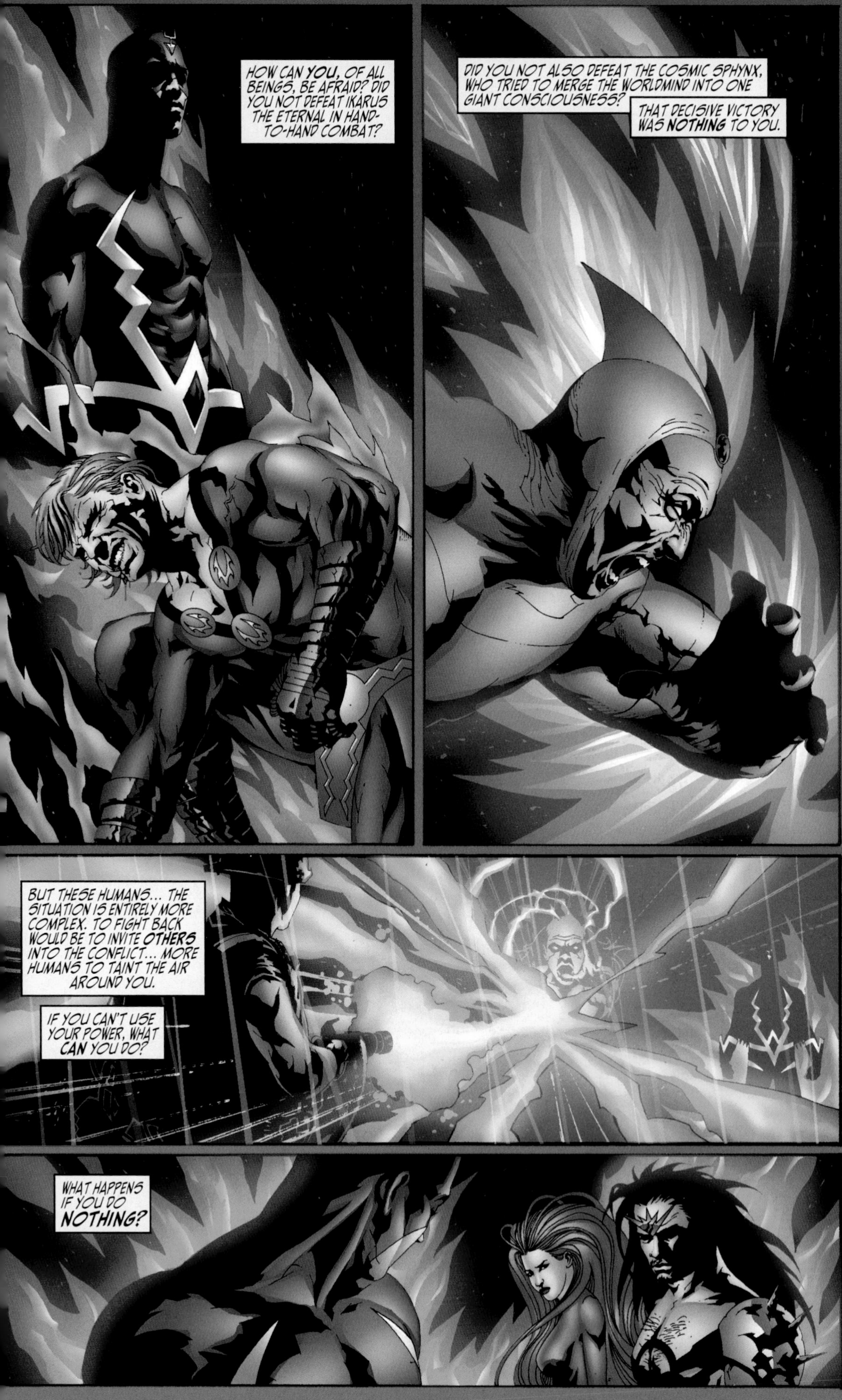
HOW CAN YOU, OF ALL BEINGS, BE AFRAID? DID YOU NOT DEFEAT IKARUS THE ETERNAL IN HAND-TO-HAND COMBAT?
DID YOU NOT ALSO DEFEAT THE COSMIC SPHYNX, WHO TRIED TO MERGE THE WORLDMIND INTO ONE GIANT CONSCIOUSNESS?
THAT DECISIVE VICTORY WAS NOTHING TO YOU.
BUT THESE HUMANS... THE SITUATION IS ENTIRELY MORE COMPLEX. TO FIGHT BACK WOULD BE TO INVITE OTHERS INTO THE CONFLICT... MORE HUMANS TO TAINT THE AIR AROUND YOU.
IF YOU CAN'T USE YOUR POWER, WHAT CAN YOU DO?
WHAT HAPPENS IF YOU DO NOTHING?

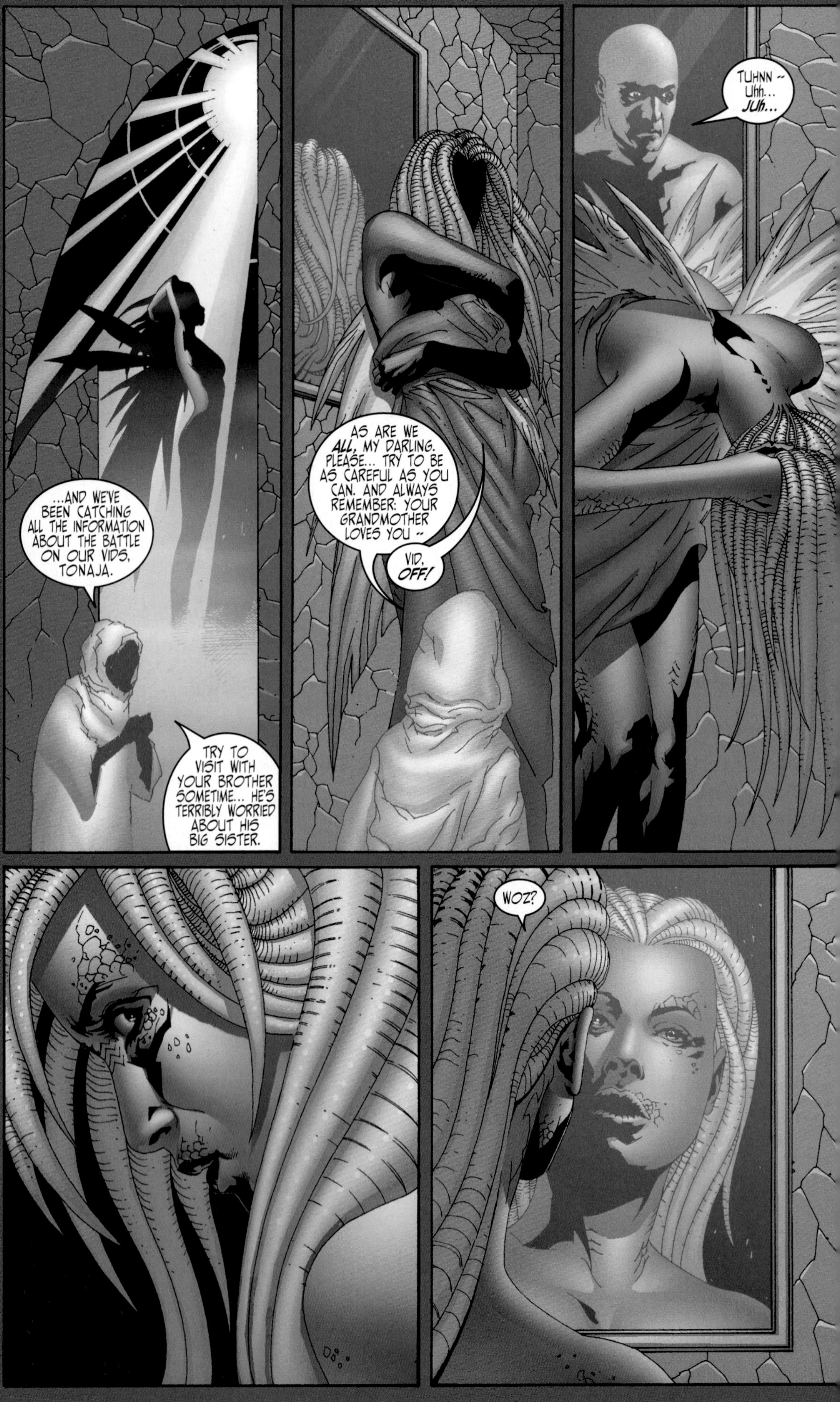
...AND WE'VE BEEN CATCHING ALL THE INFORMATION ABOUT THE BATTLE ON OUR VIDS, TONAJA.
TRY TO VISIT WITH YOUR BROTHER SOMETIME... HE'S TERRIBLY WORRIED ABOUT HIS BIG SISTER.
AS ARE WE ALL, MY DARLING. PLEASE... TRY TO BE AS CAREFUL AS YOU CAN. AND ALWAYS REMEMBER: YOUR GRANDMOTHER LOVES YOU --
VID, OFF!
TUHNN -- Uhh... JUH...
WOZ?

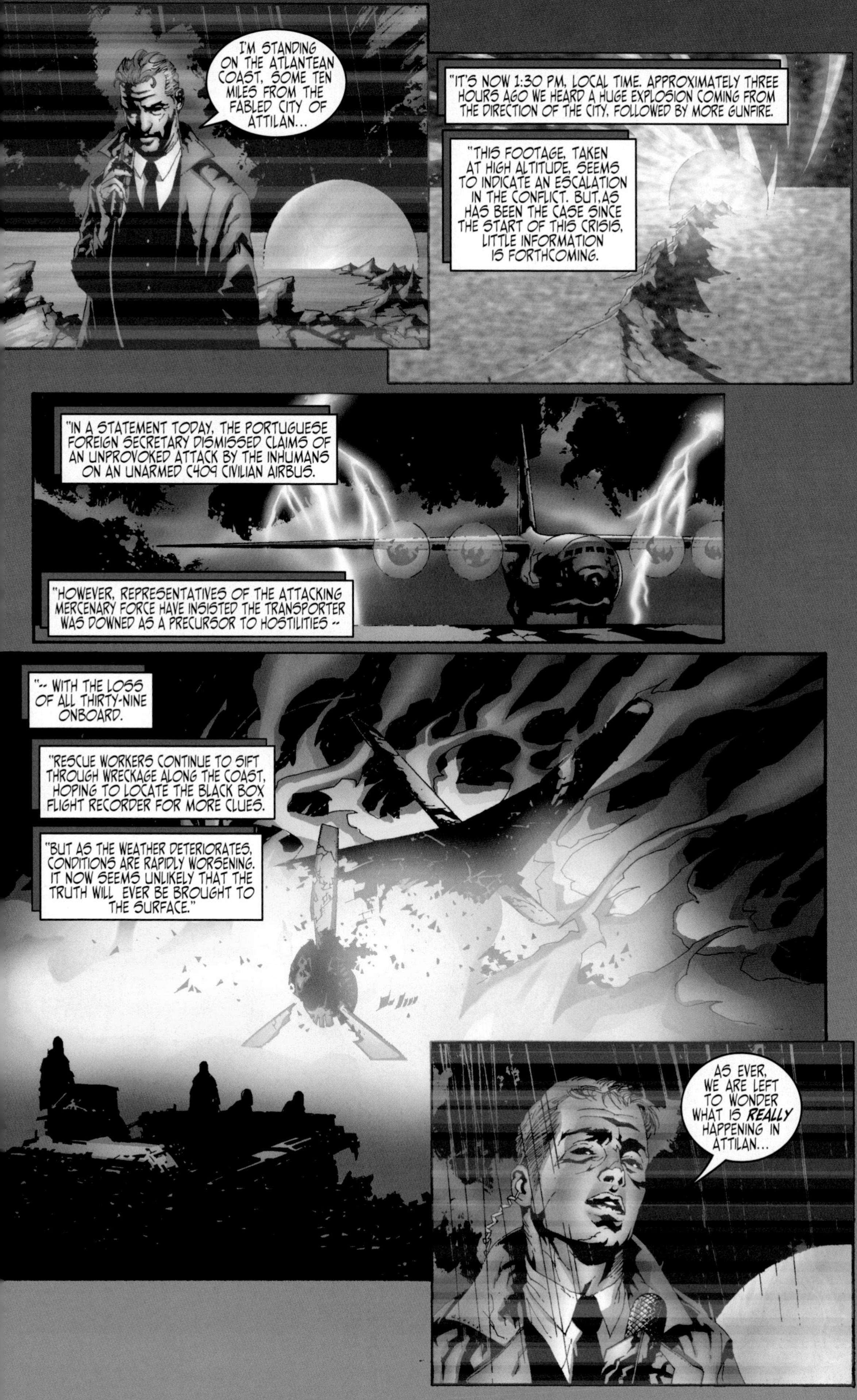
I'M STANDING ON THE ATLANTEAN COAST, SOME TEN MILES FROM THE FABLED CITY OF ATTILAN...
"IT'S NOW 1:30 PM, LOCAL TIME. APPROXIMATELY THREE HOURS AGO WE HEARD A HUGE EXPLOSION COMING FROM THE DIRECTION OF THE CITY, FOLLOWED BY MORE GUNFIRE.
"THIS FOOTAGE, TAKEN AT HIGH ALTITUDE, SEEMS TO INDICATE AN ESCALATION IN THE CONFLICT. BUT, AS HAS BEEN THE CASE SINCE THE START OF THIS CRISIS, LITTLE INFORMATION IS FORTHCOMING.
"IN A STATEMENT TODAY, THE PORTUGUESE FOREIGN SECRETARY DISMISSED CLAIMS OF AN UNPROVOKED ATTACK BY THE INHUMANS ON AN UNARMED C409 CIVILIAN AIRBUS.
"HOWEVER, REPRESENTATIVES OF THE ATTACKING MERCENARY FORCE HAVE INSISTED THE TRANSPORTER WAS DOWNED AS A PRECURSOR TO HOSTILITIES --
"-- WITH THE LOSS OF ALL THIRTY-NINE ONBOARD.
"RESCUE WORKERS CONTINUE TO SIFT THROUGH WRECKAGE ALONG THE COAST, HOPING TO LOCATE THE BLACK BOX FLIGHT RECORDER FOR MORE CLUES.
"BUT AS THE WEATHER DETERIORATES, CONDITIONS ARE RAPIDLY WORSENING. IT NOW SEEMS UNLIKELY THAT THE TRUTH WILL EVER BE BROUGHT TO THE SURFACE."
AS EVER, WE ARE LEFT TO WONDER WHAT IS *REALLY* HAPPENING IN ATTILAN...

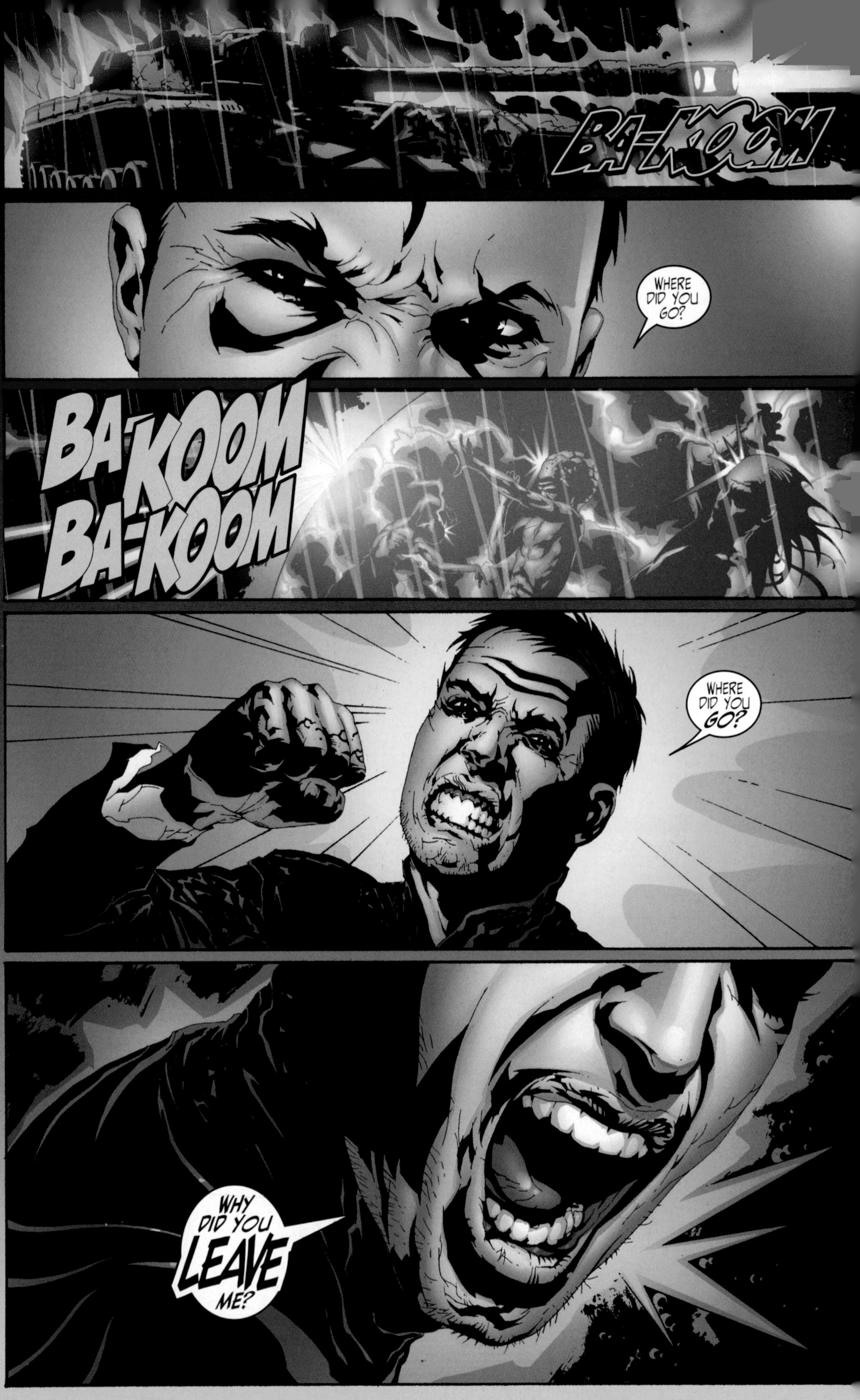
BA-KOOM
WHERE DID YOU GO?
BA-KOOM BA-KOOM
WHERE DID YOU GO?
WHY DID YOU LEAVE ME?

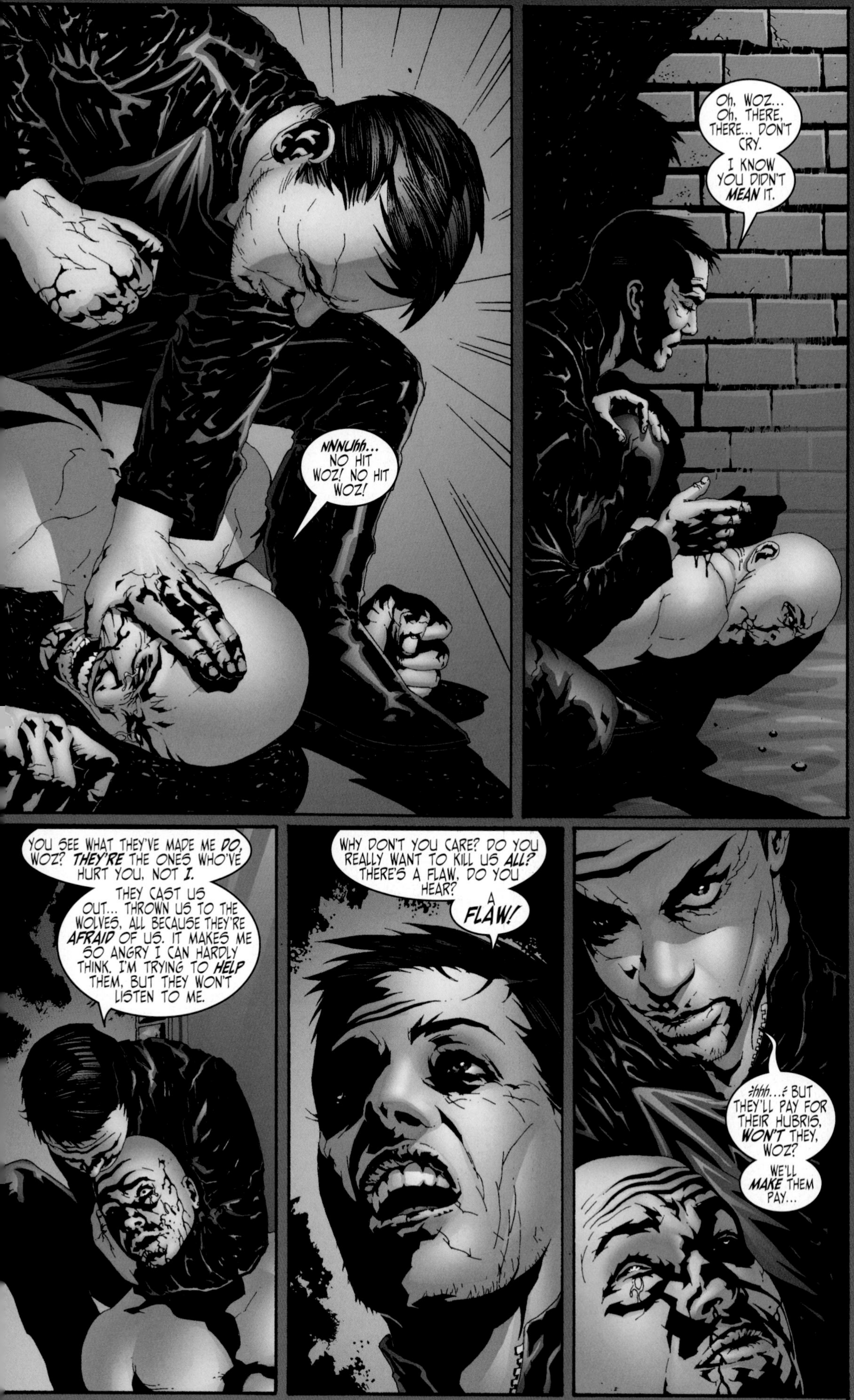
NNNUhh... NO HIT WOZ! NO HIT WOZ!
Oh, WOZ... Oh, THERE, THERE... DON'T CRY.
I KNOW YOU DIDN'T MEAN IT.
YOU SEE WHAT THEY'VE MADE ME DO, WOZ? THEY'RE THE ONES WHO'VE HURT YOU, NOT I.
THEY CAST US OUT... THROWN US TO THE WOLVES, ALL BECAUSE THEY'RE AFRAID OF US. IT MAKES ME SO ANGRY I CAN HARDLY THINK. I'M TRYING TO HELP THEM, BUT THEY WON'T LISTEN TO ME.
WHY DON'T YOU CARE? DO YOU REALLY WANT TO KILL US ALL? THERE'S A FLAW, DO YOU HEAR?
A FLAW!
shhh... BUT THEY'LL PAY FOR THEIR HUBRIS, WON'T THEY, WOZ?
WE'LL MAKE THEM PAY...

MY HUSBAND... YOUR PEOPLE AWAIT A DECISION. WHAT COURSE OF ACTION DO WE TAKE AGAINST THE HUMANS?

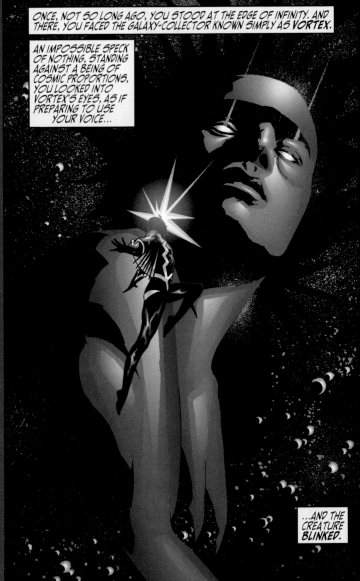

ONCE, NOT SO LONG AGO, YOU STOOD AT THE EDGE OF INFINITY. AND THERE, YOU FACED THE GALAXY-COLLECTOR KNOWN SIMPLY AS *VORTEX*.

AN IMPOSSIBLE SPECK OF NOTHING, STANDING AGAINST A BEING OF COSMIC PROPORTIONS, YOU LOOKED INTO VORTEX'S EYES, AS IF PREPARING TO USE YOUR VOICE...

...AND THE CREATURE BLINKED.

NOW, YOU UNDERSTAND HOW HE FELT.

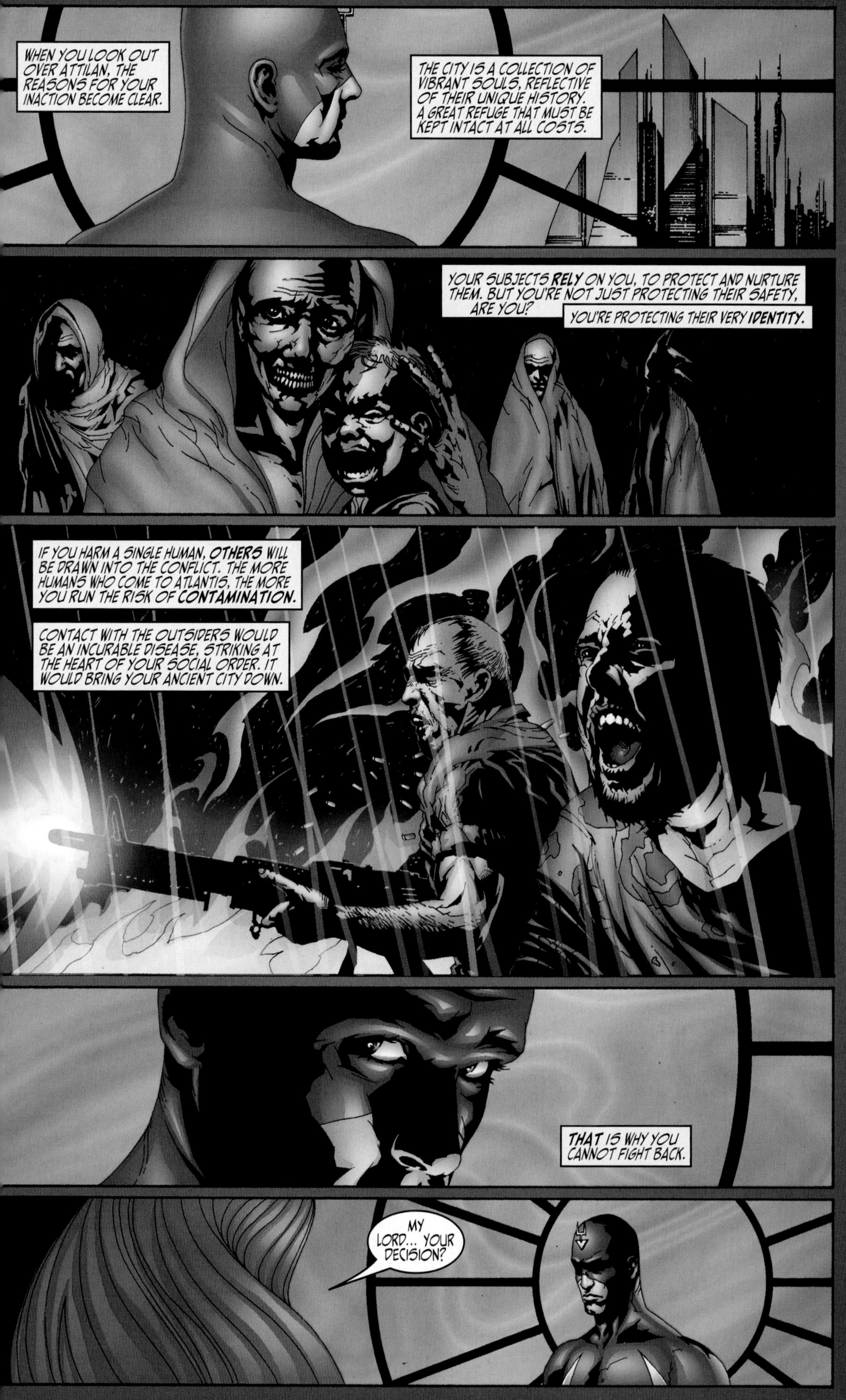
WHEN YOU LOOK OUT OVER ATTILAN, THE REASONS FOR YOUR INACTION BECOME CLEAR.
THE CITY IS A COLLECTION OF VIBRANT SOULS, REFLECTIVE OF THEIR UNIQUE HISTORY. A GREAT REFUGE THAT MUST BE KEPT INTACT AT ALL COSTS.
YOUR SUBJECTS RELY ON YOU, TO PROTECT AND NURTURE THEM. BUT YOU'RE NOT JUST PROTECTING THEIR SAFETY, ARE YOU?
YOU'RE PROTECTING THEIR VERY IDENTITY.
IF YOU HARM A SINGLE HUMAN, OTHERS WILL BE DRAWN INTO THE CONFLICT. THE MORE HUMANS WHO COME TO ATLANTIS, THE MORE YOU RUN THE RISK OF CONTAMINATION.
CONTACT WITH THE OUTSIDERS WOULD BE AN INCURABLE DISEASE, STRIKING AT THE HEART OF YOUR SOCIAL ORDER. IT WOULD BRING YOUR ANCIENT CITY DOWN.
THAT IS WHY YOU CANNOT FIGHT BACK.
MY LORD... YOUR DECISION?

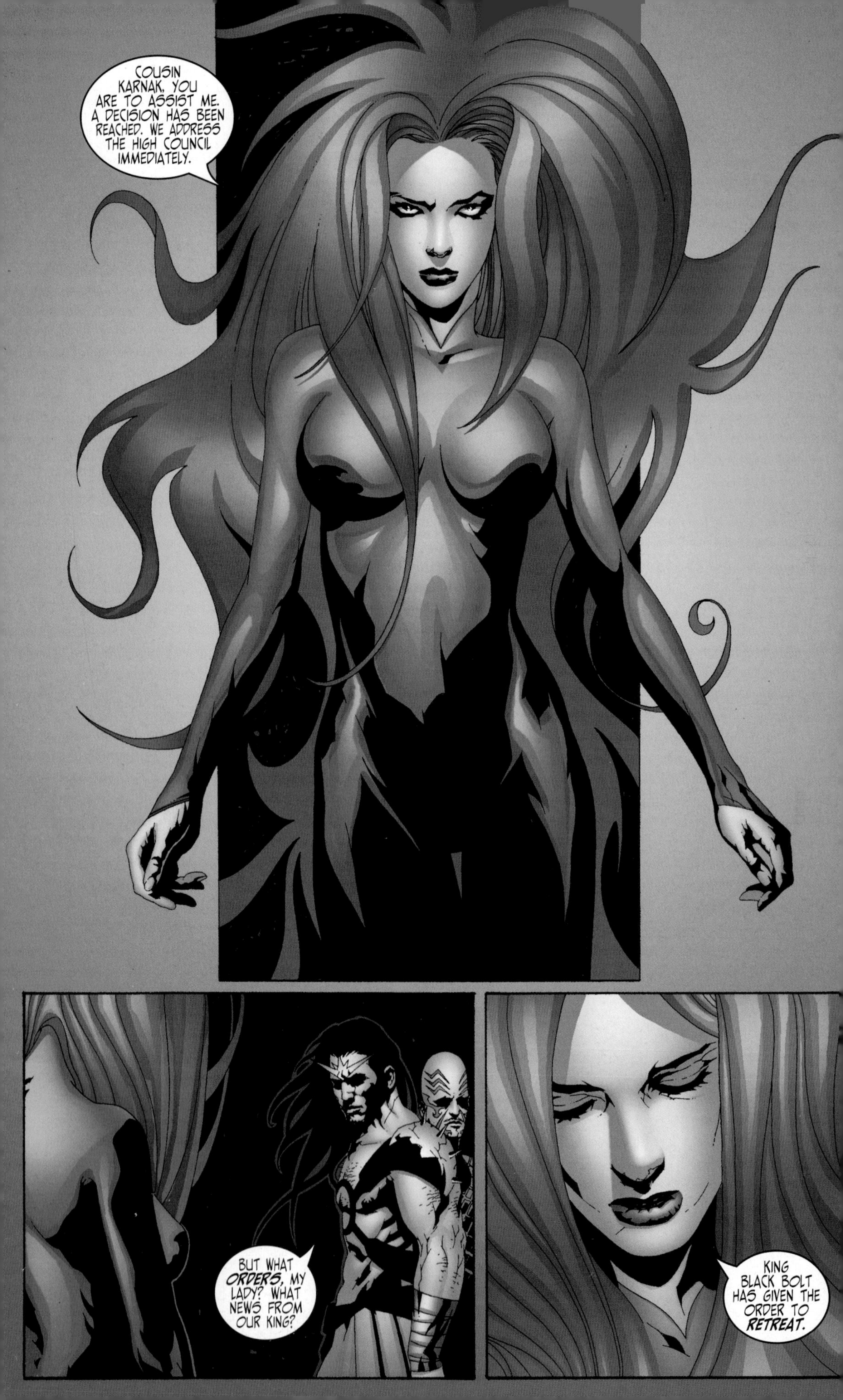
COUSIN KARNAK, YOU ARE TO ASSIST ME. A DECISION HAS BEEN REACHED. WE ADDRESS THE HIGH COUNCIL IMMEDIATELY.
BUT WHAT ORDERS, MY LADY? WHAT NEWS FROM OUR KING?
KING BLACK BOLT HAS GIVEN THE ORDER TO RETREAT.

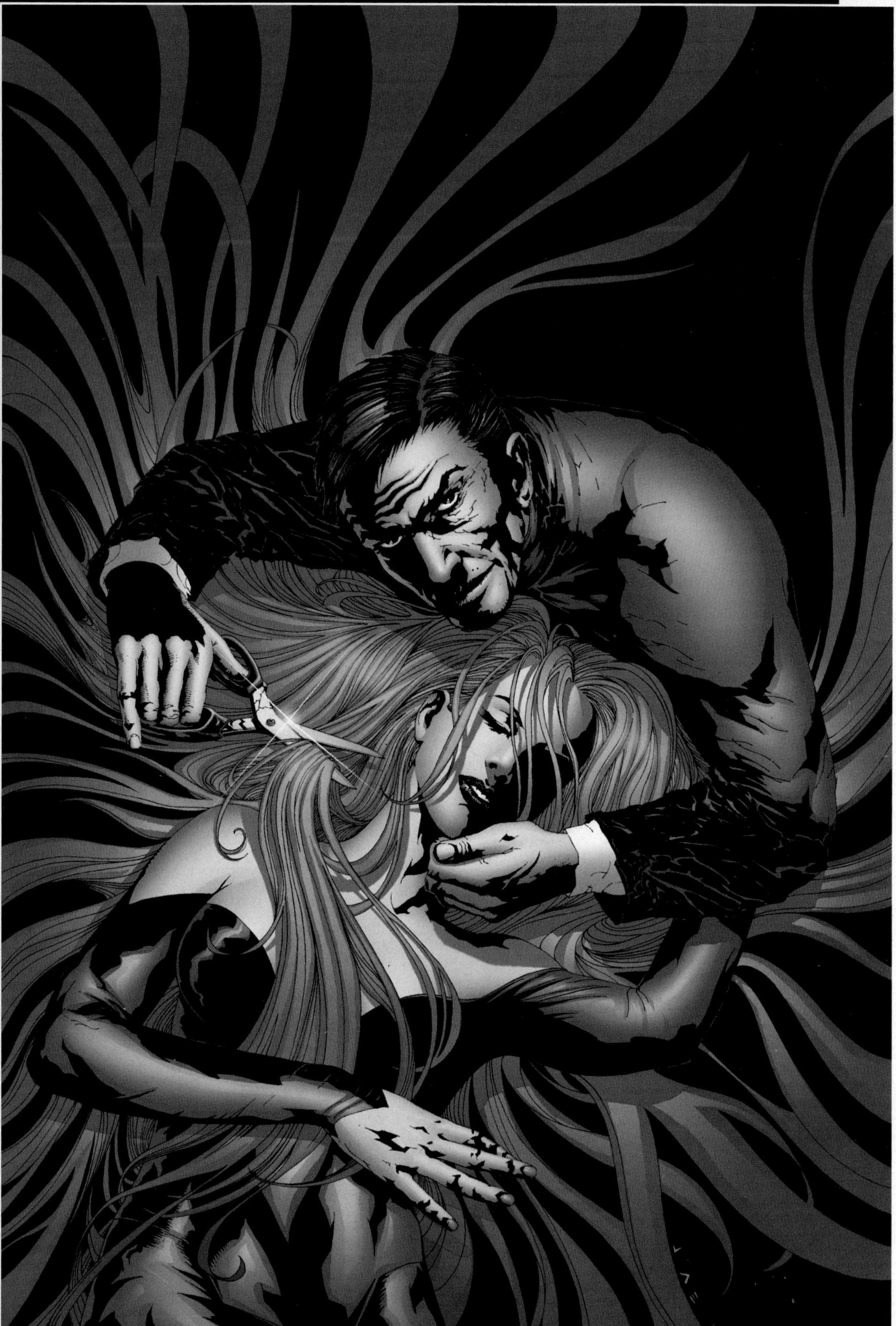

INHUMANS #7

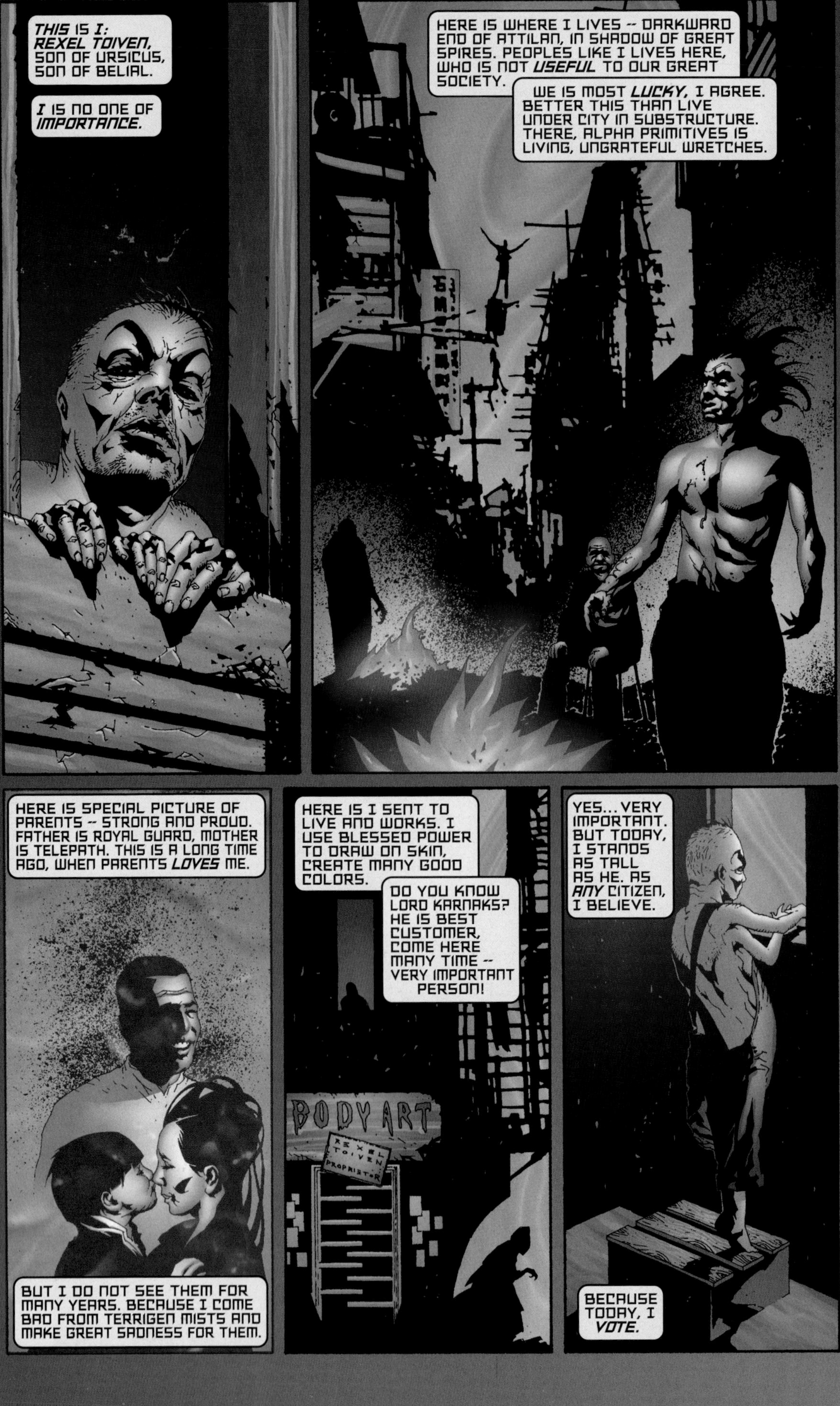
THIS IS I: REXEL TOIVEN, SON OF URSICUS, SON OF BELIAL.
I IS NO ONE OF IMPORTANCE.
HERE IS WHERE I LIVES -- DARKWARD END OF ATTILAN, IN SHADOW OF GREAT SPIRES. PEOPLES LIKE I LIVES HERE, WHO IS NOT USEFUL TO OUR GREAT SOCIETY.
WE IS MOST LUCKY, I AGREE. BETTER THIS THAN LIVE UNDER CITY IN SUBSTRUCTURE. THERE, ALPHA PRIMITIVES IS LIVING, UNGRATEFUL WRETCHES.
HERE IS SPECIAL PICTURE OF PARENTS -- STRONG AND PROUD. FATHER IS ROYAL GUARD, MOTHER IS TELEPATH. THIS IS A LONG TIME AGO, WHEN PARENTS LOVES ME.
BUT I DO NOT SEE THEM FOR MANY YEARS. BECAUSE I COME BAD FROM TERRIGEN MISTS AND MAKE GREAT SADNESS FOR THEM.
HERE IS I SENT TO LIVE AND WORKS. I USE BLESSED POWER TO DRAW ON SKIN, CREATE MANY GOOD COLORS.
DO YOU KNOW LORD KARNAKS? HE IS BEST CUSTOMER, COME HERE MANY TIME -- VERY IMPORTANT PERSON!
BODY ART
REXEL TOIVEN PROPRIETOR
YES... VERY IMPORTANT. BUT TODAY, I STANDS AS TALL AS HE. AS ANY CITIZEN, I BELIEVE.
BECAUSE TODAY, I VOTE.

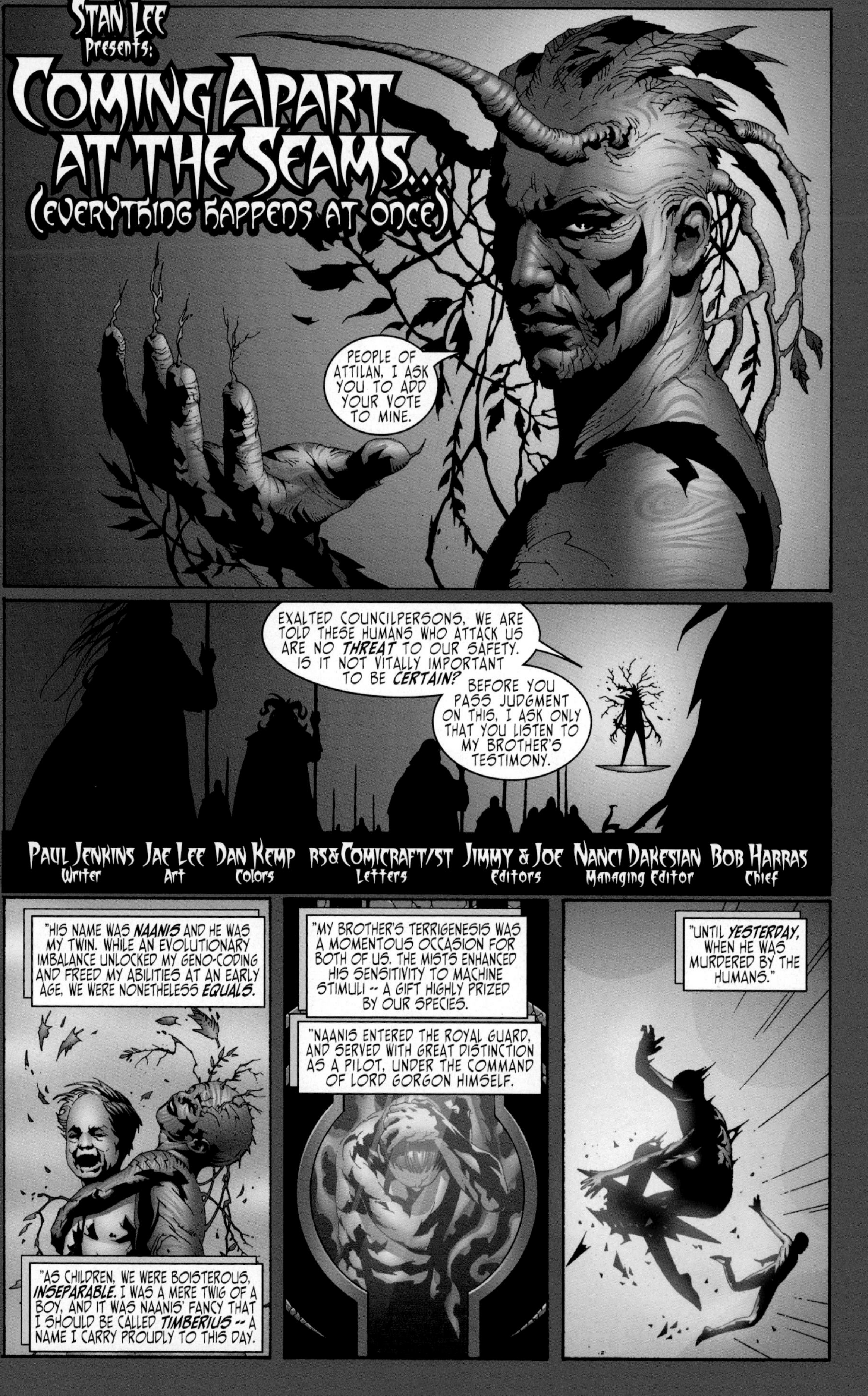
STAN LEE PRESENTS:
COMING APART AT THE SEAMS...
(EVERYTHING HAPPENS AT ONCE)
PEOPLE OF ATTILAN, I ASK YOU TO ADD YOUR VOTE TO MINE.
EXALTED COUNCILPERSONS, WE ARE TOLD THESE HUMANS WHO ATTACK US ARE NO THREAT TO OUR SAFETY. IS IT NOT VITALLY IMPORTANT TO BE CERTAIN?
BEFORE YOU PASS JUDGMENT ON THIS, I ASK ONLY THAT YOU LISTEN TO MY BROTHER'S TESTIMONY.
PAUL JENKINS Writer
JAE LEE Art
DAN KEMP Colors
RS&COMICRAFT/ST Letters
JIMMY & JOE Editors
NANCI DAKESIAN Managing Editor
BOB HARRAS Chief
"HIS NAME WAS NAANIS AND HE WAS MY TWIN. WHILE AN EVOLUTIONARY IMBALANCE UNLOCKED MY GENO-CODING AND FREED MY ABILITIES AT AN EARLY AGE, WE WERE NONETHELESS EQUALS.
"AS CHILDREN, WE WERE BOISTEROUS, INSEPARABLE. I WAS A MERE TWIG OF A BOY, AND IT WAS NAANIS' FANCY THAT I SHOULD BE CALLED TIMBERIUS -- A NAME I CARRY PROUDLY TO THIS DAY.
"MY BROTHER'S TERRIGENESIS WAS A MOMENTOUS OCCASION FOR BOTH OF US. THE MISTS ENHANCED HIS SENSITIVITY TO MACHINE STIMULI -- A GIFT HIGHLY PRIZED BY OUR SPECIES.
"NAANIS ENTERED THE ROYAL GUARD, AND SERVED WITH GREAT DISTINCTION AS A PILOT, UNDER THE COMMAND OF LORD GORGON HIMSELF.
"UNTIL YESTERDAY, WHEN HE WAS MURDERED BY THE HUMANS."

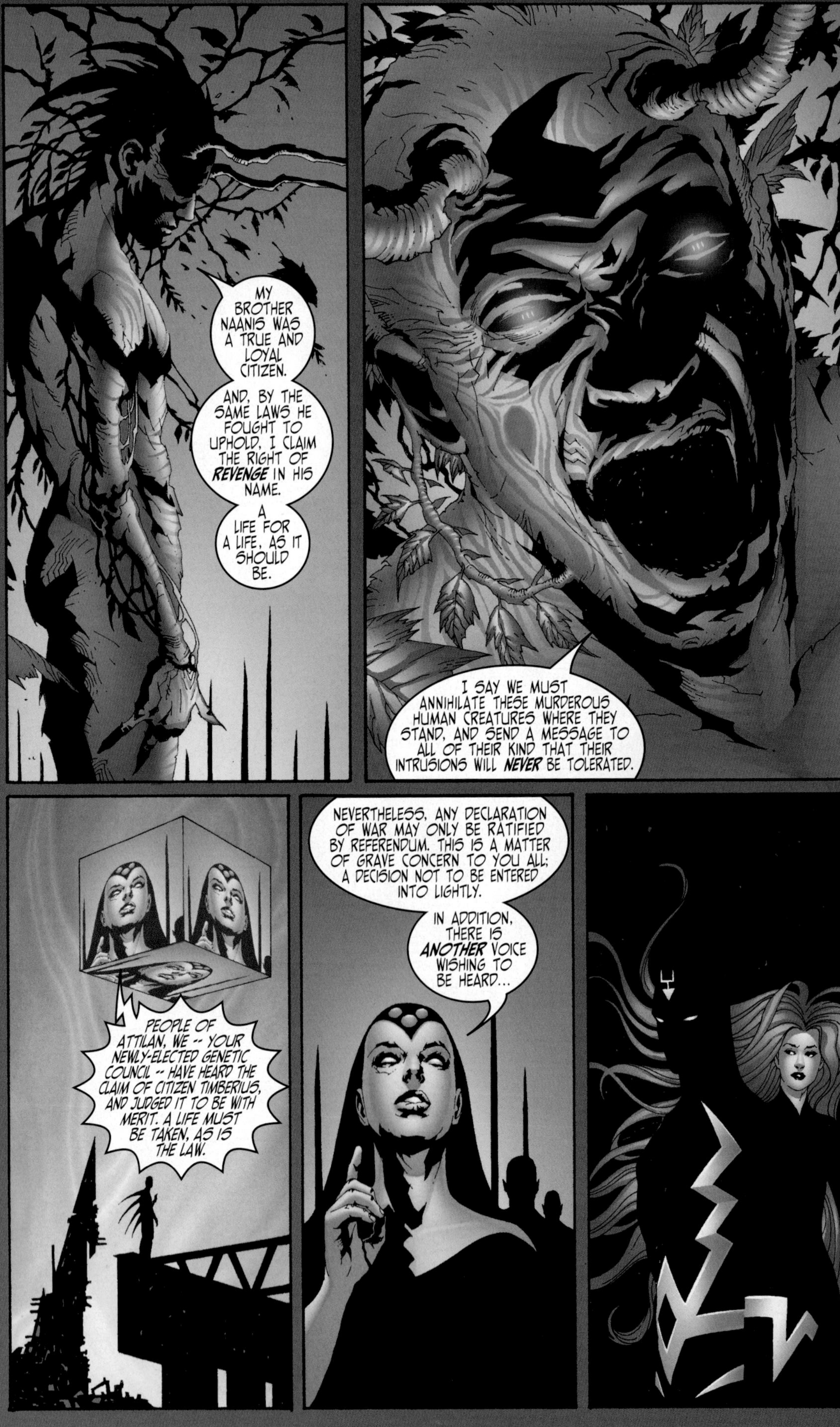
MY BROTHER NAANIS WAS A TRUE AND LOYAL CITIZEN.
AND, BY THE SAME LAWS HE FOUGHT TO UPHOLD, I CLAIM THE RIGHT OF **REVENGE** IN HIS NAME.
A LIFE FOR A LIFE, AS IT SHOULD BE.
I SAY WE MUST ANNIHILATE THESE MURDEROUS HUMAN CREATURES WHERE THEY STAND, AND SEND A MESSAGE TO ALL OF THEIR KIND THAT THEIR INTRUSIONS WILL **NEVER** BE TOLERATED.
PEOPLE OF ATTILAN, WE -- YOUR NEWLY-ELECTED GENETIC COUNCIL -- HAVE HEARD THE CLAIM OF CITIZEN TIMBERIUS, AND JUDGED IT TO BE WITH MERIT. A LIFE MUST BE TAKEN, AS IS THE LAW.
NEVERTHELESS, ANY DECLARATION OF WAR MAY ONLY BE RATIFIED BY REFERENDUM. THIS IS A MATTER OF GRAVE CONCERN TO YOU ALL; A DECISION NOT TO BE ENTERED INTO LIGHTLY.
IN ADDITION, THERE IS **ANOTHER** VOICE WISHING TO BE HEARD...

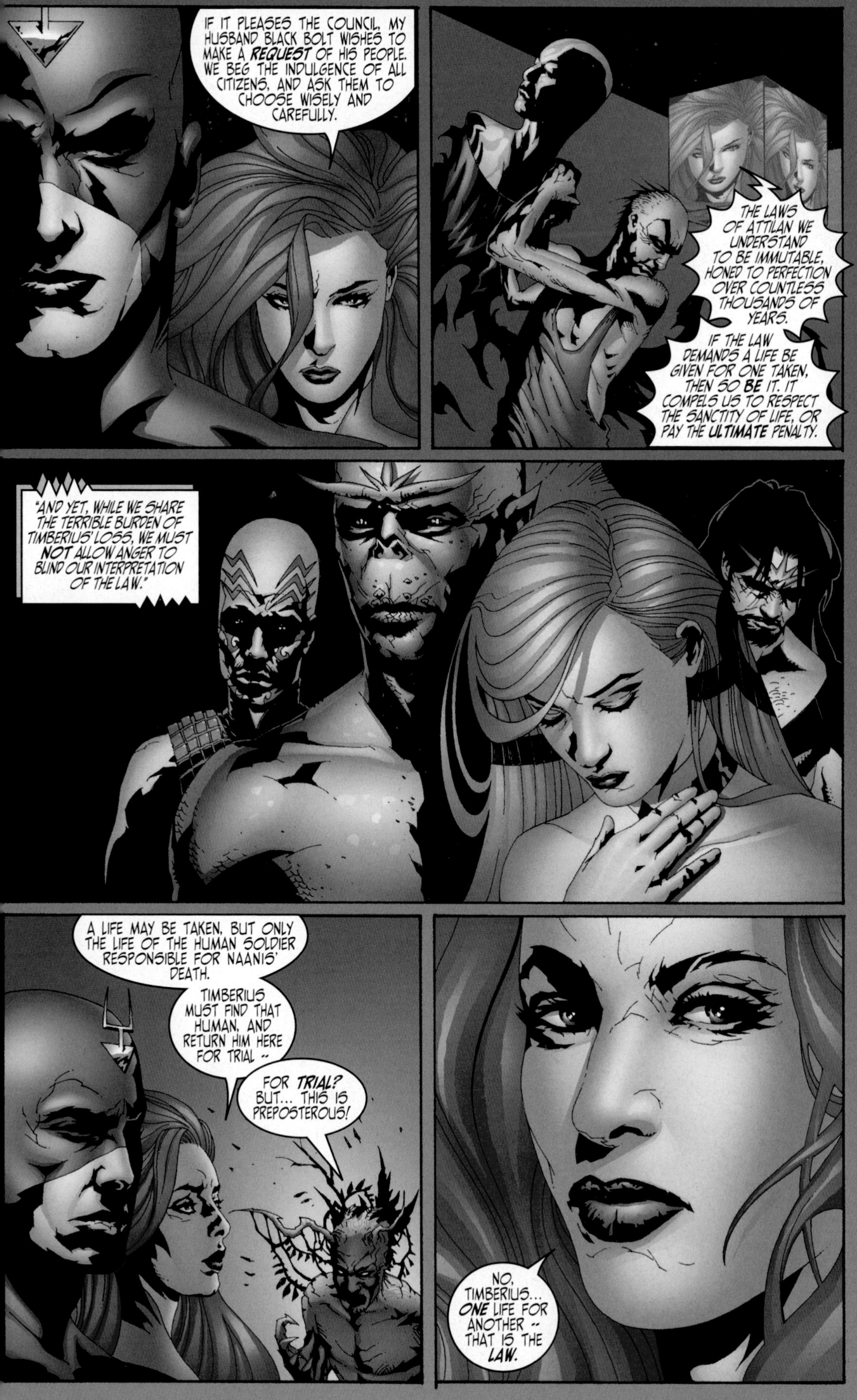

IF IT PLEASES THE COUNCIL, MY HUSBAND BLACK BOLT WISHES TO MAKE A **REQUEST** OF HIS PEOPLE. WE BEG THE INDULGENCE OF ALL CITIZENS, AND ASK THEM TO CHOOSE WISELY AND CAREFULLY.
THE LAWS OF ATTILAN WE UNDERSTAND TO BE IMMUTABLE, HONED TO PERFECTION OVER COUNTLESS THOUSANDS OF YEARS.
IF THE LAW DEMANDS A LIFE BE GIVEN FOR ONE TAKEN, THEN SO **BE** IT. IT COMPELS US TO RESPECT THE SANCTITY OF LIFE, OR PAY THE **ULTIMATE** PENALTY.
"AND YET, WHILE WE SHARE THE TERRIBLE BURDEN OF TIMBERIUS' LOSS, WE MUST **NOT** ALLOW ANGER TO BLIND OUR INTERPRETATION OF THE LAW."
A LIFE MAY BE TAKEN, BUT ONLY THE LIFE OF THE HUMAN SOLDIER RESPONSIBLE FOR NAANIS' DEATH.
TIMBERIUS MUST FIND THAT HUMAN, AND RETURN HIM HERE FOR TRIAL --
FOR **TRIAL?** BUT... THIS IS PREPOSTEROUS!
NO, TIMBERIUS... **ONE** LIFE FOR ANOTHER -- THAT IS THE **LAW.**

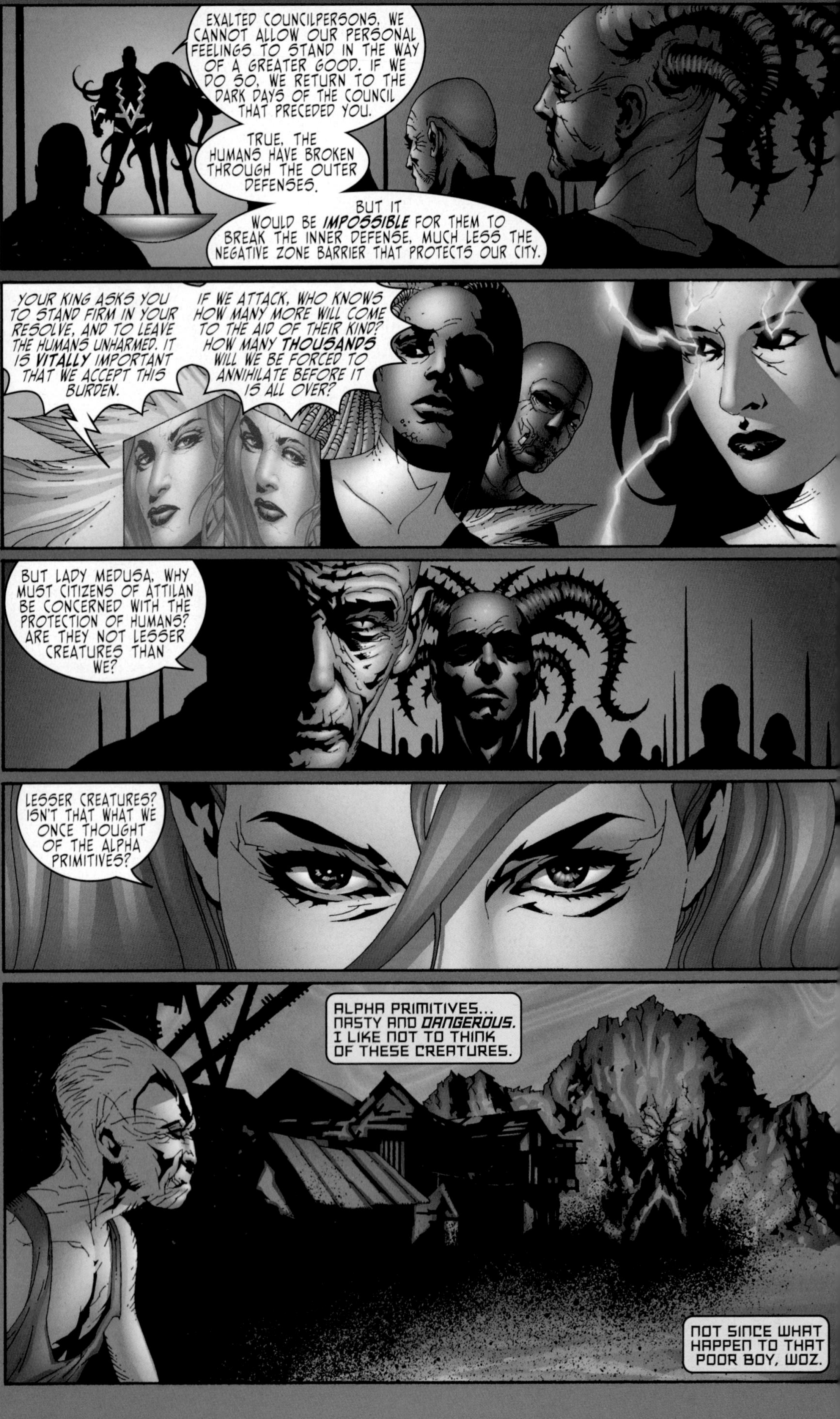
EXALTED COUNCILPERSONS, WE CANNOT ALLOW OUR PERSONAL FEELINGS TO STAND IN THE WAY OF A GREATER GOOD. IF WE DO SO, WE RETURN TO THE DARK DAYS OF THE COUNCIL THAT PRECEDED YOU.
TRUE, THE HUMANS HAVE BROKEN THROUGH THE OUTER DEFENSES.
BUT IT WOULD BE IMPOSSIBLE FOR THEM TO BREAK THE INNER DEFENSE, MUCH LESS THE NEGATIVE ZONE BARRIER THAT PROTECTS OUR CITY.
YOUR KING ASKS YOU TO STAND FIRM IN YOUR RESOLVE, AND TO LEAVE THE HUMANS UNHARMED. IT IS VITALLY IMPORTANT THAT WE ACCEPT THIS BURDEN.
IF WE ATTACK, WHO KNOWS HOW MANY MORE WILL COME TO THE AID OF THEIR KIND? HOW MANY THOUSANDS WILL WE BE FORCED TO ANNIHILATE BEFORE IT IS ALL OVER?
BUT LADY MEDUSA, WHY MUST CITIZENS OF ATTILAN BE CONCERNED WITH THE PROTECTION OF HUMANS? ARE THEY NOT LESSER CREATURES THAN WE?
LESSER CREATURES? ISN'T THAT WHAT WE ONCE THOUGHT OF THE ALPHA PRIMITIVES?
ALPHA PRIMITIVES... NASTY AND DANGEROUS. I LIKE NOT TO THINK OF THESE CREATURES.
NOT SINCE WHAT HAPPEN TO THAT POOR BOY, WOZ.

IF HUMANS AND ALPHAS IS ALIKE, THEN HUMANS IS *DANGEROUS.* I HAS MUCH CONCERN NOW.

BUT I HONOR WORD OF KING BLACK BOLT, WHO IS GOOD AND TRUE. WHAT IS I TO *DO?*

I KNOW NOT WHY HUMANS COME. THEY ATTACK WITHOUT REASON, AND BLACK BOLT SAY WE DO NOT FIGHT?

THIS IS GREAT LARGE THOUGHT, I DO NOT UNDERSTAND.

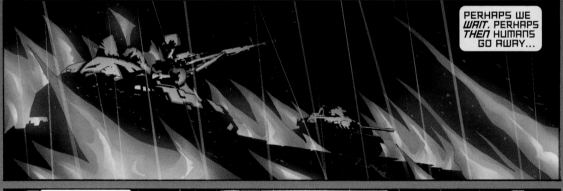

PERHAPS WE *WAIT.* PERHAPS *THEN* HUMANS GO AWAY...

NOW WHAT, COLONEL STALYENKO?

NOW, WE *WAIT.*

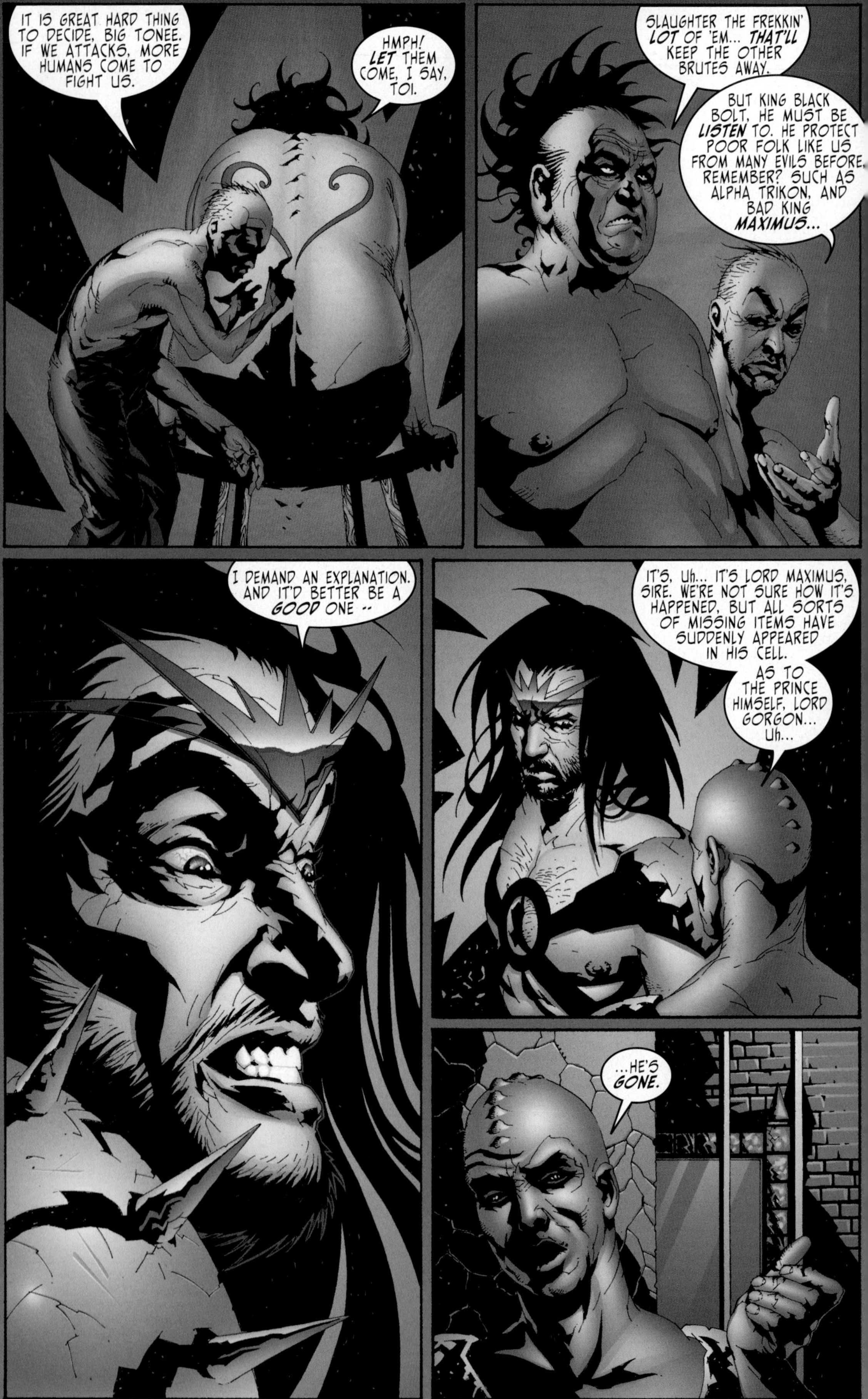

IT IS GREAT HARD THING TO DECIDE, BIG TONEE. IF WE ATTACKS, MORE HUMANS COME TO FIGHT US.
HMPH! LET THEM COME, I SAY, TOI.
SLAUGHTER THE FREKKIN' LOT OF 'EM... THAT'LL KEEP THE OTHER BRUTES AWAY.
BUT KING BLACK BOLT, HE MUST BE LISTEN TO. HE PROTECT POOR FOLK LIKE US FROM MANY EVILS BEFORE. REMEMBER? SUCH AS ALPHA TRIKON, AND BAD KING MAXIMUS...
I DEMAND AN EXPLANATION. AND IT'D BETTER BE A GOOD ONE --
IT'S, Uh... IT'S LORD MAXIMUS, SIRE. WE'RE NOT SURE HOW IT'S HAPPENED, BUT ALL SORTS OF MISSING ITEMS HAVE SUDDENLY APPEARED IN HIS CELL.
AS TO THE PRINCE HIMSELF, LORD GORGON... Uh...
...HE'S GONE.

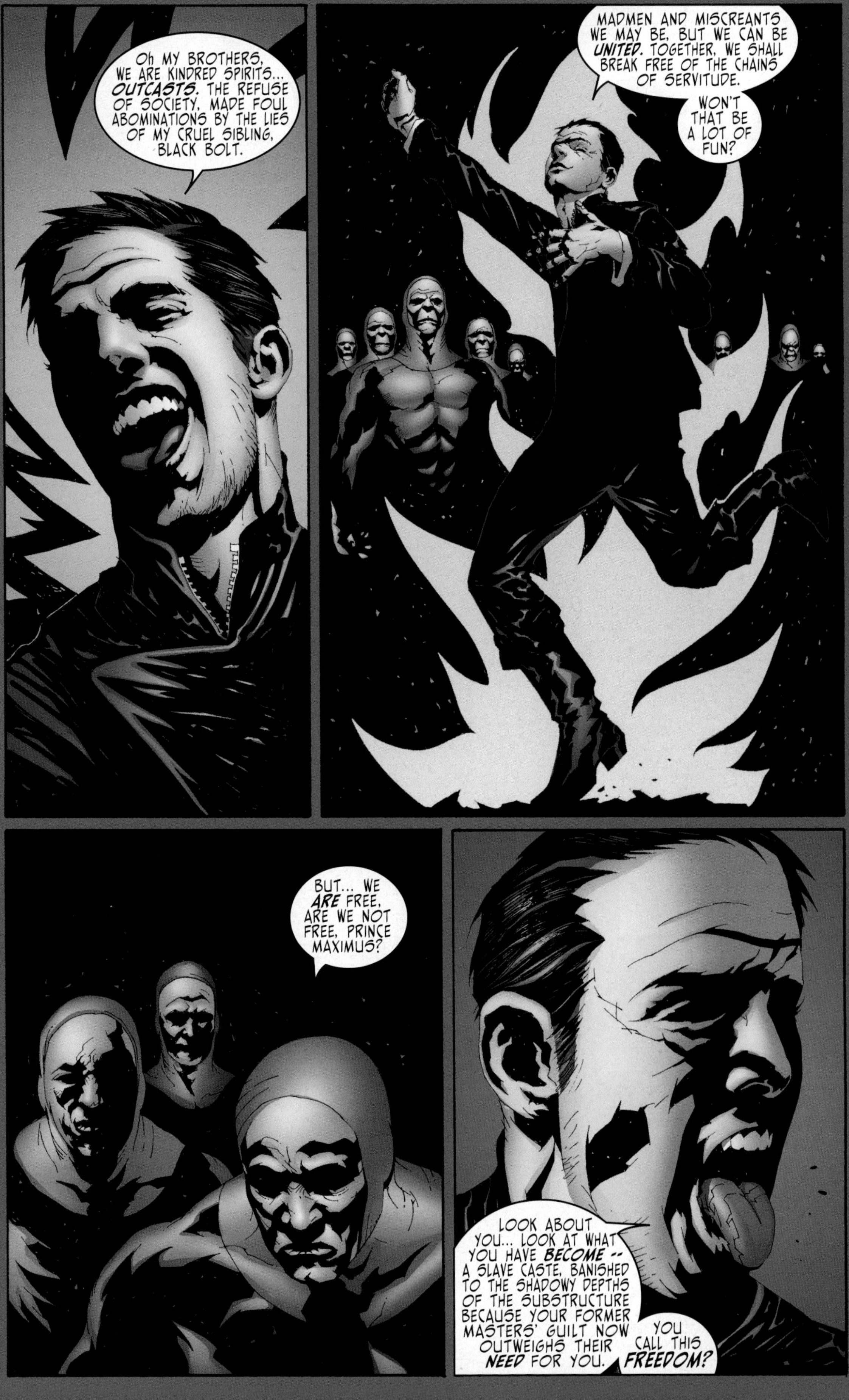
Oh MY BROTHERS, WE ARE KINDRED SPIRITS... OUTCASTS. THE REFUSE OF SOCIETY, MADE FOUL ABOMINATIONS BY THE LIES OF MY CRUEL SIBLING, BLACK BOLT.
MADMEN AND MISCREANTS WE MAY BE, BUT WE CAN BE UNITED. TOGETHER, WE SHALL BREAK FREE OF THE CHAINS OF SERVITUDE.
WON'T THAT BE A LOT OF FUN?
BUT... WE ARE FREE, ARE WE NOT FREE, PRINCE MAXIMUS?
LOOK ABOUT YOU... LOOK AT WHAT YOU HAVE BECOME -- A SLAVE CASTE, BANISHED TO THE SHADOWY DEPTHS OF THE SUBSTRUCTURE BECAUSE YOUR FORMER MASTERS' GUILT NOW OUTWEIGHS THEIR NEED FOR YOU.
YOU CALL THIS FREEDOM?

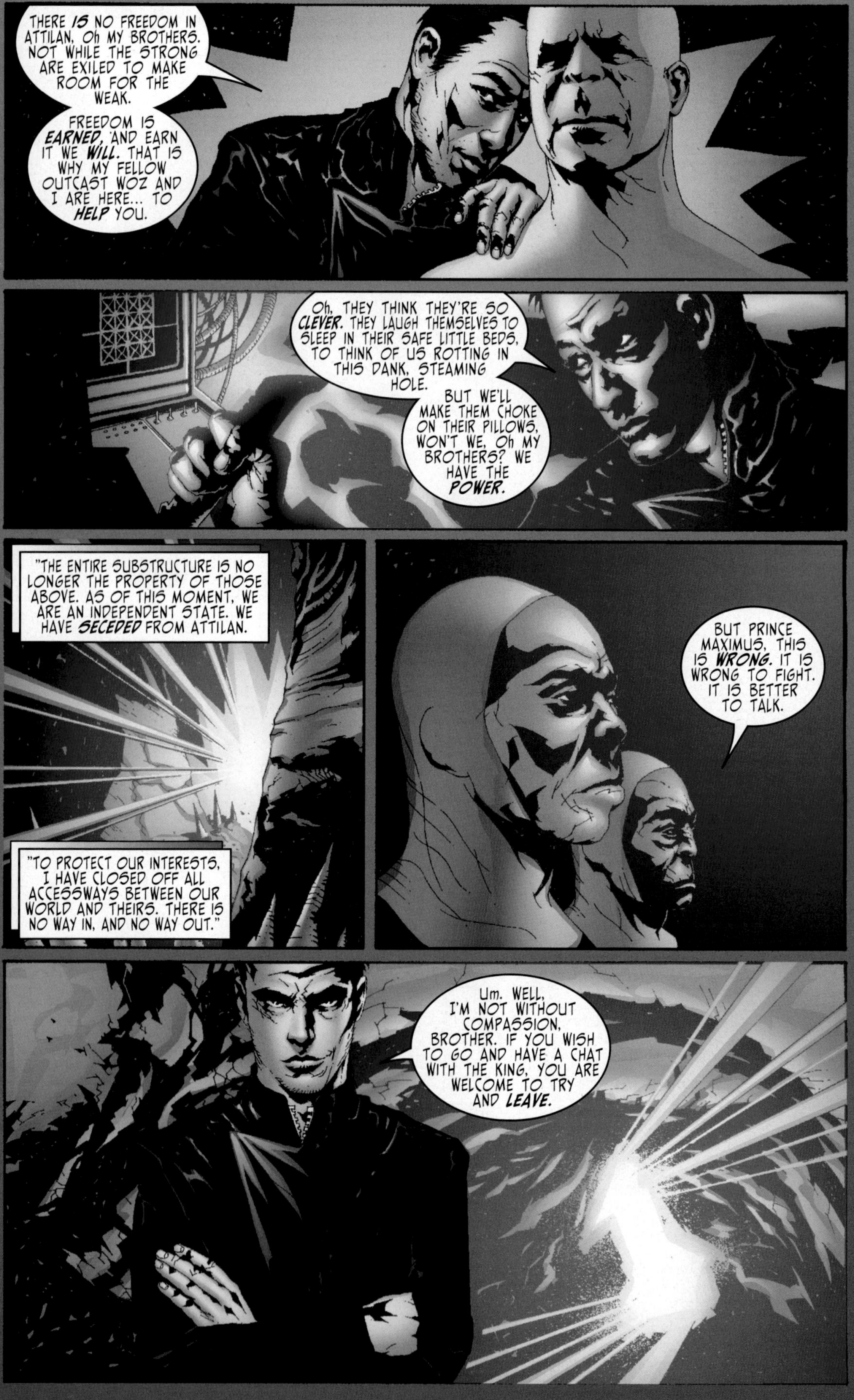
THERE IS NO FREEDOM IN ATTILAN, Oh MY BROTHERS. NOT WHILE THE STRONG ARE EXILED TO MAKE ROOM FOR THE WEAK.
FREEDOM IS EARNED, AND EARN IT WE WILL. THAT IS WHY MY FELLOW OUTCAST WOZ AND I ARE HERE... TO HELP YOU.
Oh, THEY THINK THEY'RE SO CLEVER. THEY LAUGH THEMSELVES TO SLEEP IN THEIR SAFE LITTLE BEDS, TO THINK OF US ROTTING IN THIS DANK, STEAMING HOLE.
BUT WE'LL MAKE THEM CHOKE ON THEIR PILLOWS, WON'T WE, Oh MY BROTHERS? WE HAVE THE POWER.
"THE ENTIRE SUBSTRUCTURE IS NO LONGER THE PROPERTY OF THOSE ABOVE. AS OF THIS MOMENT, WE ARE AN INDEPENDENT STATE. WE HAVE SECEDED FROM ATTILAN.
"TO PROTECT OUR INTERESTS, I HAVE CLOSED OFF ALL ACCESSWAYS BETWEEN OUR WORLD AND THEIRS. THERE IS NO WAY IN, AND NO WAY OUT."
BUT PRINCE MAXIMUS, THIS IS WRONG. IT IS WRONG TO FIGHT. IT IS BETTER TO TALK.
Um. WELL, I'M NOT WITHOUT COMPASSION, BROTHER. IF YOU WISH TO GO AND HAVE A CHAT WITH THE KING, YOU ARE WELCOME TO TRY AND LEAVE.

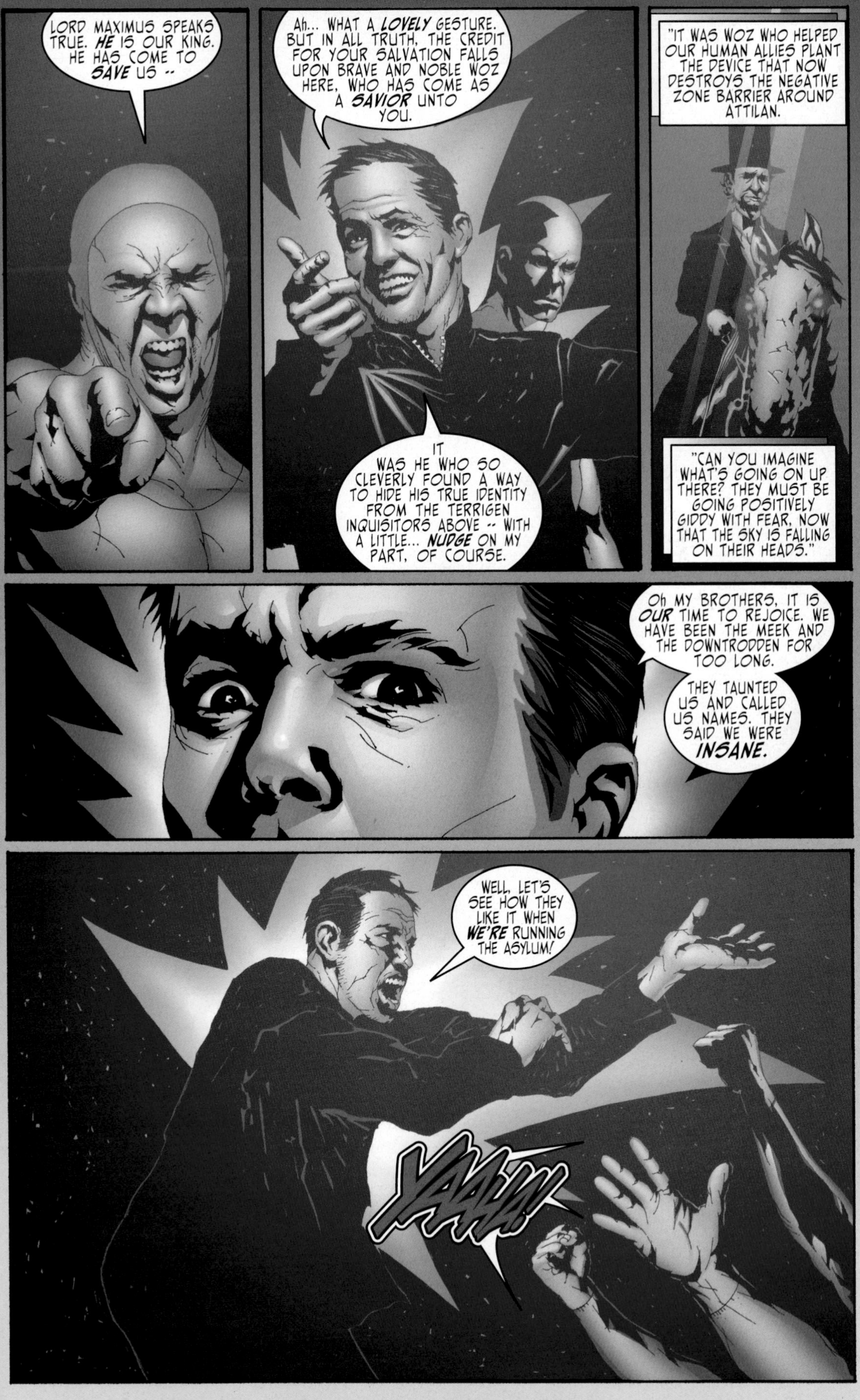
LORD MAXIMUS SPEAKS TRUE. HE IS OUR KING. HE HAS COME TO SAVE US --
Ah... WHAT A LOVELY GESTURE. BUT IN ALL TRUTH, THE CREDIT FOR YOUR SALVATION FALLS UPON BRAVE AND NOBLE WOZ HERE, WHO HAS COME AS A SAVIOR UNTO YOU.
IT WAS HE WHO SO CLEVERLY FOUND A WAY TO HIDE HIS TRUE IDENTITY FROM THE TERRIGEN INQUISITORS ABOVE -- WITH A LITTLE... NUDGE ON MY PART, OF COURSE.
"IT WAS WOZ WHO HELPED OUR HUMAN ALLIES PLANT THE DEVICE THAT NOW DESTROYS THE NEGATIVE ZONE BARRIER AROUND ATTILAN.
"CAN YOU IMAGINE WHAT'S GOING ON UP THERE? THEY MUST BE GOING POSITIVELY GIDDY WITH FEAR, NOW THAT THE SKY IS FALLING ON THEIR HEADS."
Oh MY BROTHERS, IT IS OUR TIME TO REJOICE. WE HAVE BEEN THE MEEK AND THE DOWNTRODDEN FOR TOO LONG.
THEY TAUNTED US AND CALLED US NAMES. THEY SAID WE WERE INSANE.
WELL, LET'S SEE HOW THEY LIKE IT WHEN WE'RE RUNNING THE ASYLUM!
YAAAA!

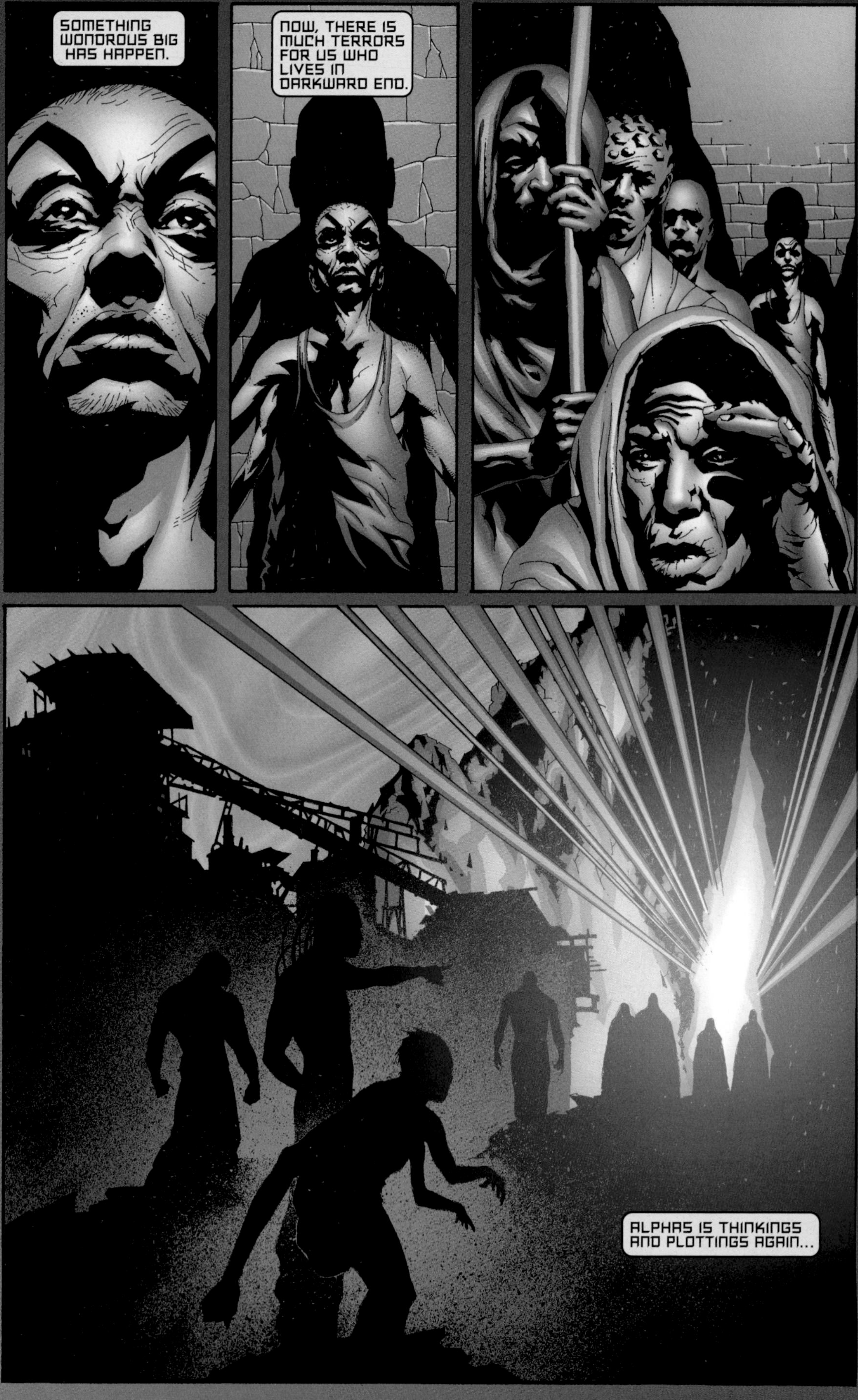
SOMETHING WONDROUS BIG HAS HAPPEN.
NOW, THERE IS MUCH TERRORS FOR US WHO LIVES IN DARKWARD END.
ALPHAS IS THINKINGS AND PLOTTINGS AGAIN...

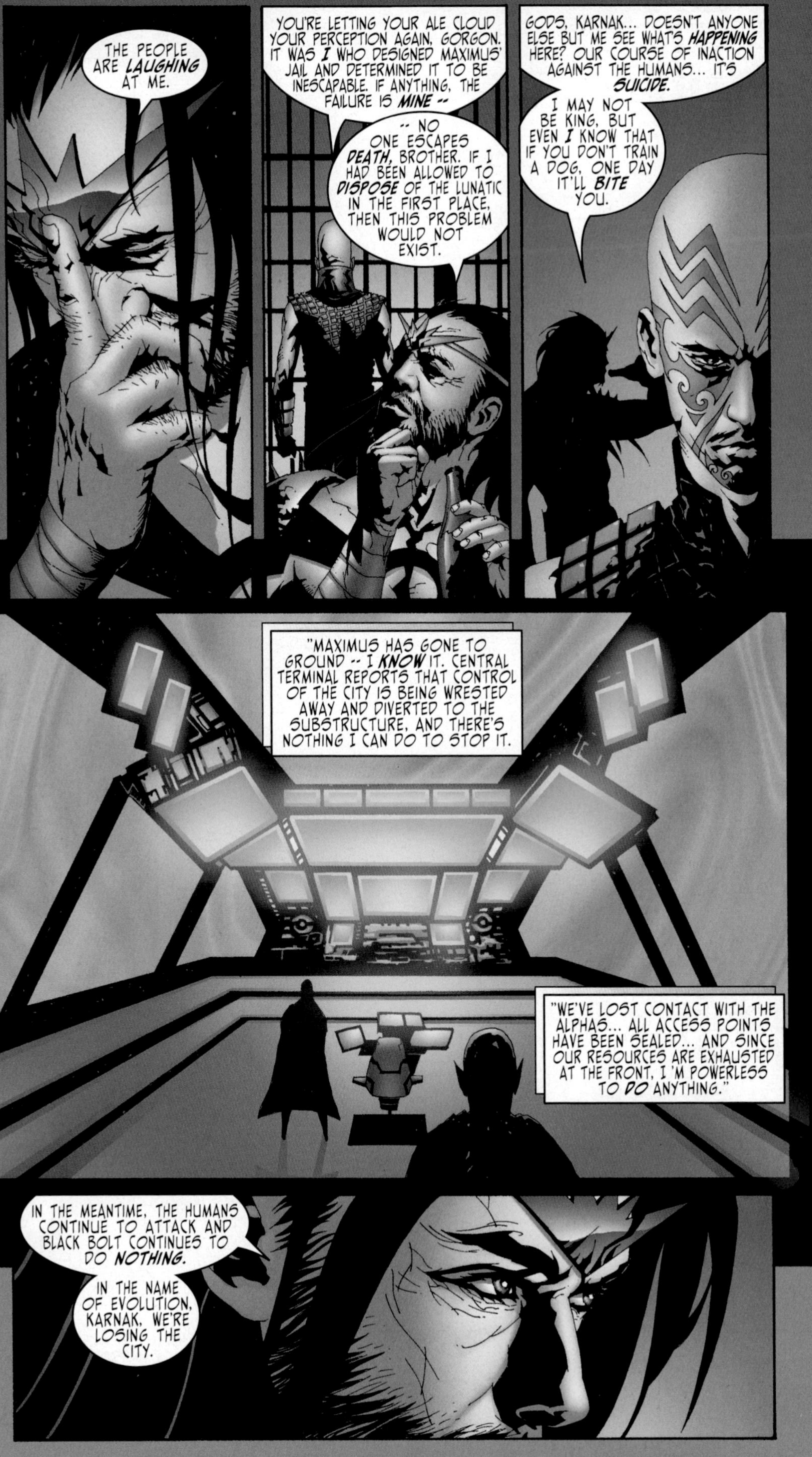
THE PEOPLE ARE LAUGHING AT ME.
YOU'RE LETTING YOUR ALE CLOUD YOUR PERCEPTION AGAIN, GORGON. IT WAS I WHO DESIGNED MAXIMUS' JAIL AND DETERMINED IT TO BE INESCAPABLE. IF ANYTHING, THE FAILURE IS MINE --
-- NO ONE ESCAPES DEATH, BROTHER. IF I HAD BEEN ALLOWED TO DISPOSE OF THE LUNATIC IN THE FIRST PLACE, THEN THIS PROBLEM WOULD NOT EXIST.
GODS, KARNAK... DOESN'T ANYONE ELSE BUT ME SEE WHAT'S HAPPENING HERE? OUR COURSE OF INACTION AGAINST THE HUMANS... IT'S SUICIDE.
I MAY NOT BE KING, BUT EVEN I KNOW THAT IF YOU DON'T TRAIN A DOG, ONE DAY IT'LL BITE YOU.
"MAXIMUS HAS GONE TO GROUND -- I KNOW IT. CENTRAL TERMINAL REPORTS THAT CONTROL OF THE CITY IS BEING WRESTED AWAY AND DIVERTED TO THE SUBSTRUCTURE, AND THERE'S NOTHING I CAN DO TO STOP IT.
"WE'VE LOST CONTACT WITH THE ALPHAS... ALL ACCESS POINTS HAVE BEEN SEALED... AND SINCE OUR RESOURCES ARE EXHAUSTED AT THE FRONT, I'M POWERLESS TO DO ANYTHING."
IN THE MEANTIME, THE HUMANS CONTINUE TO ATTACK AND BLACK BOLT CONTINUES TO DO NOTHING.
IN THE NAME OF EVOLUTION, KARNAK, WE'RE LOSING THE CITY.

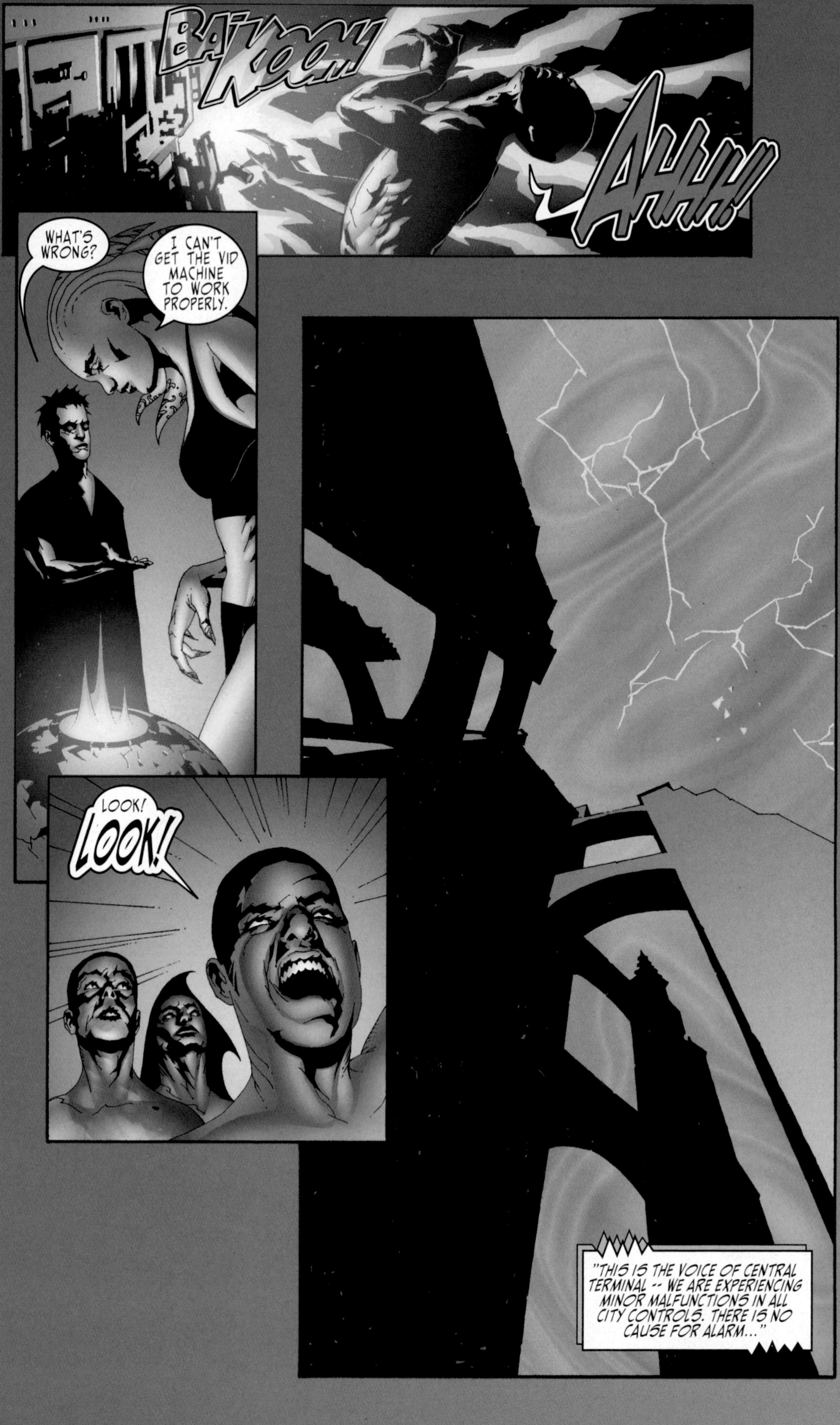
BA-KOOM
AHHH!!
WHAT'S WRONG?
I CAN'T GET THE VID MACHINE TO WORK PROPERLY.
LOOK!
LOOK!
"THIS IS THE VOICE OF CENTRAL TERMINAL -- WE ARE EXPERIENCING MINOR MALFUNCTIONS IN ALL CITY CONTROLS. THERE IS NO CAUSE FOR ALARM..."

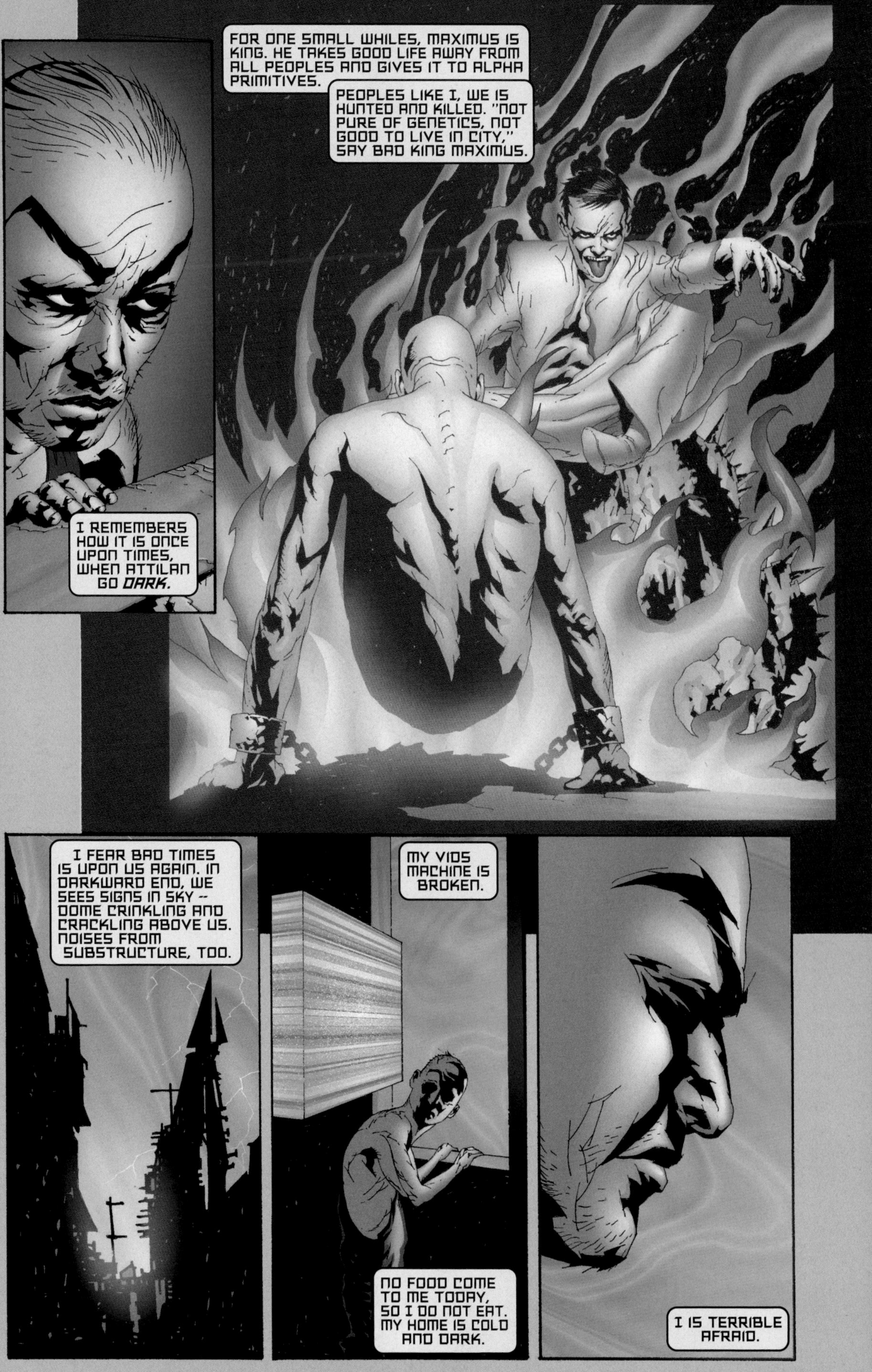
I REMEMBERS HOW IT IS ONCE UPON TIMES, WHEN ATTILAN GO *DARK*.
FOR ONE SMALL WHILES, MAXIMUS IS KING. HE TAKES GOOD LIFE AWAY FROM ALL PEOPLES AND GIVES IT TO ALPHA PRIMITIVES.
PEOPLES LIKE I, WE IS HUNTED AND KILLED. "NOT PURE OF GENETICS, NOT GOOD TO LIVE IN CITY," SAY BAD KING MAXIMUS.
I FEAR BAD TIMES IS UPON US AGAIN. IN DARKWARD END, WE SEES SIGNS IN SKY -- DOME CRINKLING AND CRACKLING ABOVE US. NOISES FROM SUBSTRUCTURE, TOO.
MY VIDS MACHINE IS BROKEN.
NO FOOD COME TO ME TODAY, SO I DO NOT EAT. MY HOME IS COLD AND DARK.
I IS TERRIBLE AFRAID.

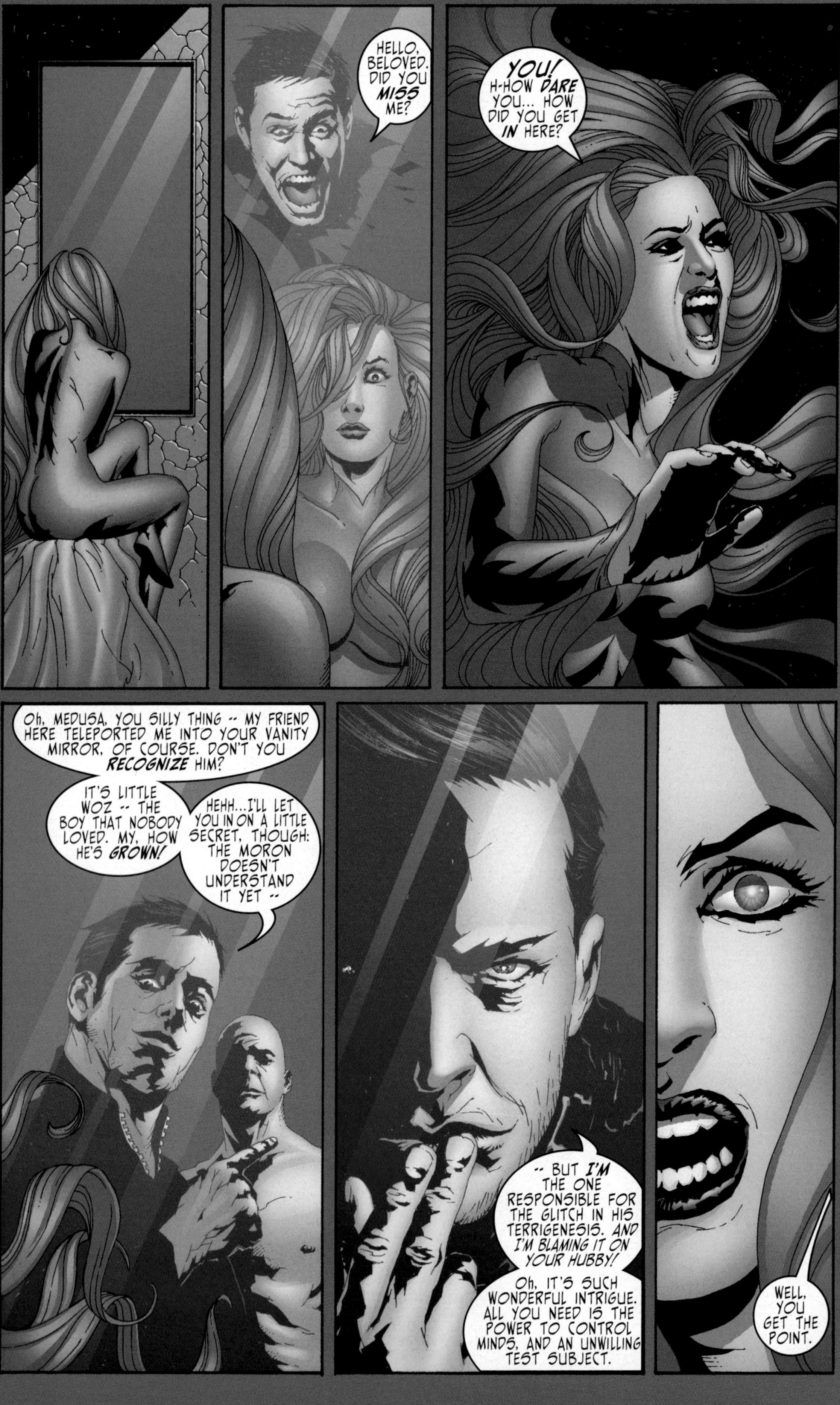
HELLO, BELOVED. DID YOU MISS ME?
YOU! H-HOW DARE YOU... HOW DID YOU GET IN HERE?
Oh, MEDUSA, YOU SILLY THING -- MY FRIEND HERE TELEPORTED ME INTO YOUR VANITY MIRROR, OF COURSE. DON'T YOU RECOGNIZE HIM?
IT'S LITTLE WOZ -- THE BOY THAT NOBODY LOVED. MY, HOW HE'S GROWN!
HEHH...I'LL LET YOU IN ON A LITTLE SECRET, THOUGH: THE MORON DOESN'T UNDERSTAND IT YET --
-- BUT I'M THE ONE RESPONSIBLE FOR THE GLITCH IN HIS TERRIGENESIS. AND I'M BLAMING IT ON YOUR HUBBY!
Oh, IT'S SUCH WONDERFUL INTRIGUE. ALL YOU NEED IS THE POWER TO CONTROL MINDS, AND AN UNWILLING TEST SUBJECT.
WELL, YOU GET THE POINT.

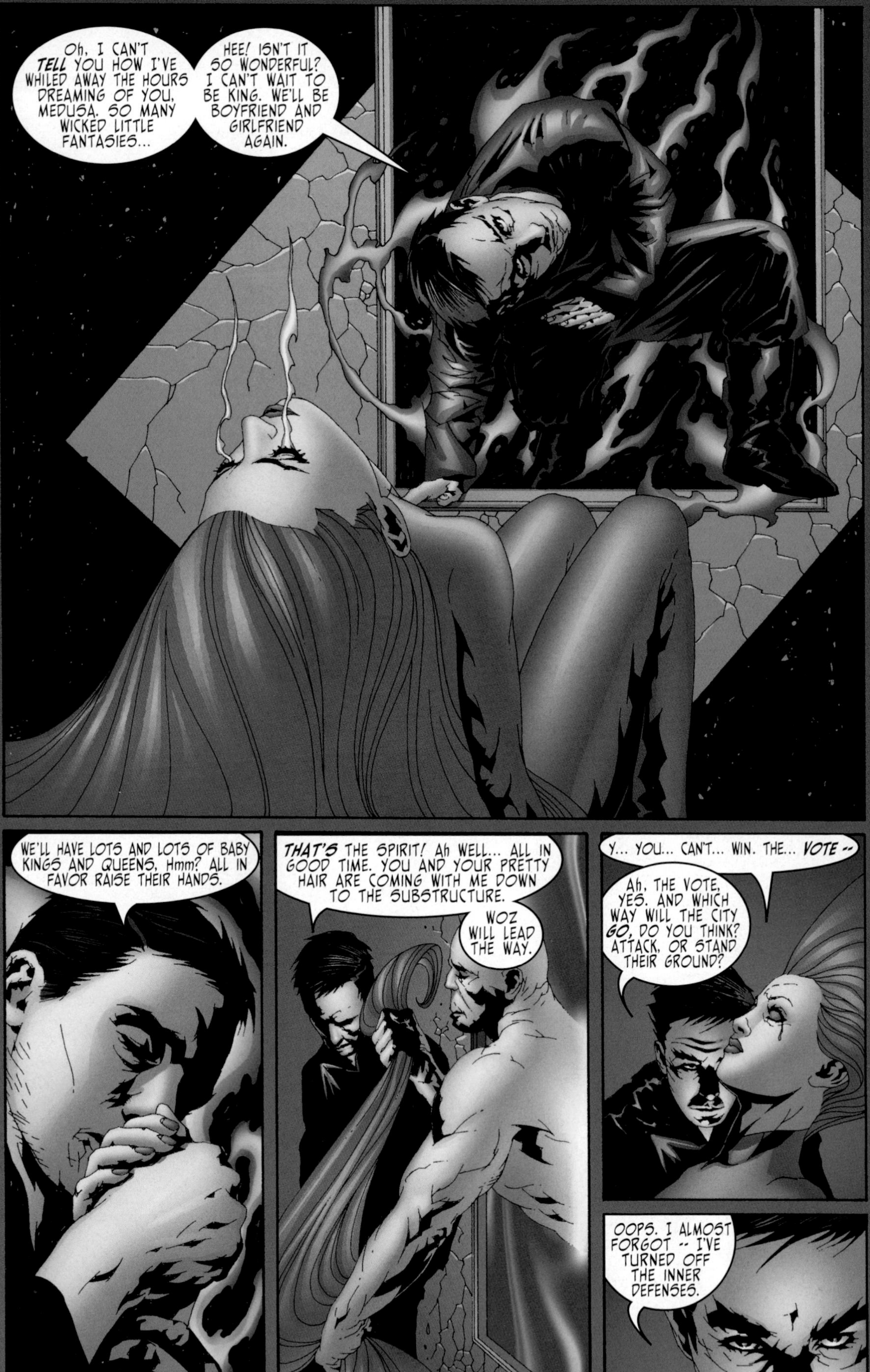
Oh, I CAN'T TELL YOU HOW I'VE WHILED AWAY THE HOURS DREAMING OF YOU, MEDUSA. SO MANY WICKED LITTLE FANTASIES...
HEE! ISN'T IT SO WONDERFUL? I CAN'T WAIT TO BE KING. WE'LL BE BOYFRIEND AND GIRLFRIEND AGAIN.
WE'LL HAVE LOTS AND LOTS OF BABY KINGS AND QUEENS, Hmm? ALL IN FAVOR RAISE THEIR HANDS.
THAT'S THE SPIRIT! Ah WELL... ALL IN GOOD TIME. YOU AND YOUR PRETTY HAIR ARE COMING WITH ME DOWN TO THE SUBSTRUCTURE.
WOZ WILL LEAD THE WAY.
Y... YOU... CAN'T... WIN. THE... VOTE --
Ah, THE VOTE, YES. AND WHICH WAY WILL THE CITY GO, DO YOU THINK? ATTACK, OR STAND THEIR GROUND?
OOPS. I ALMOST FORGOT -- I'VE TURNED OFF THE INNER DEFENSES.

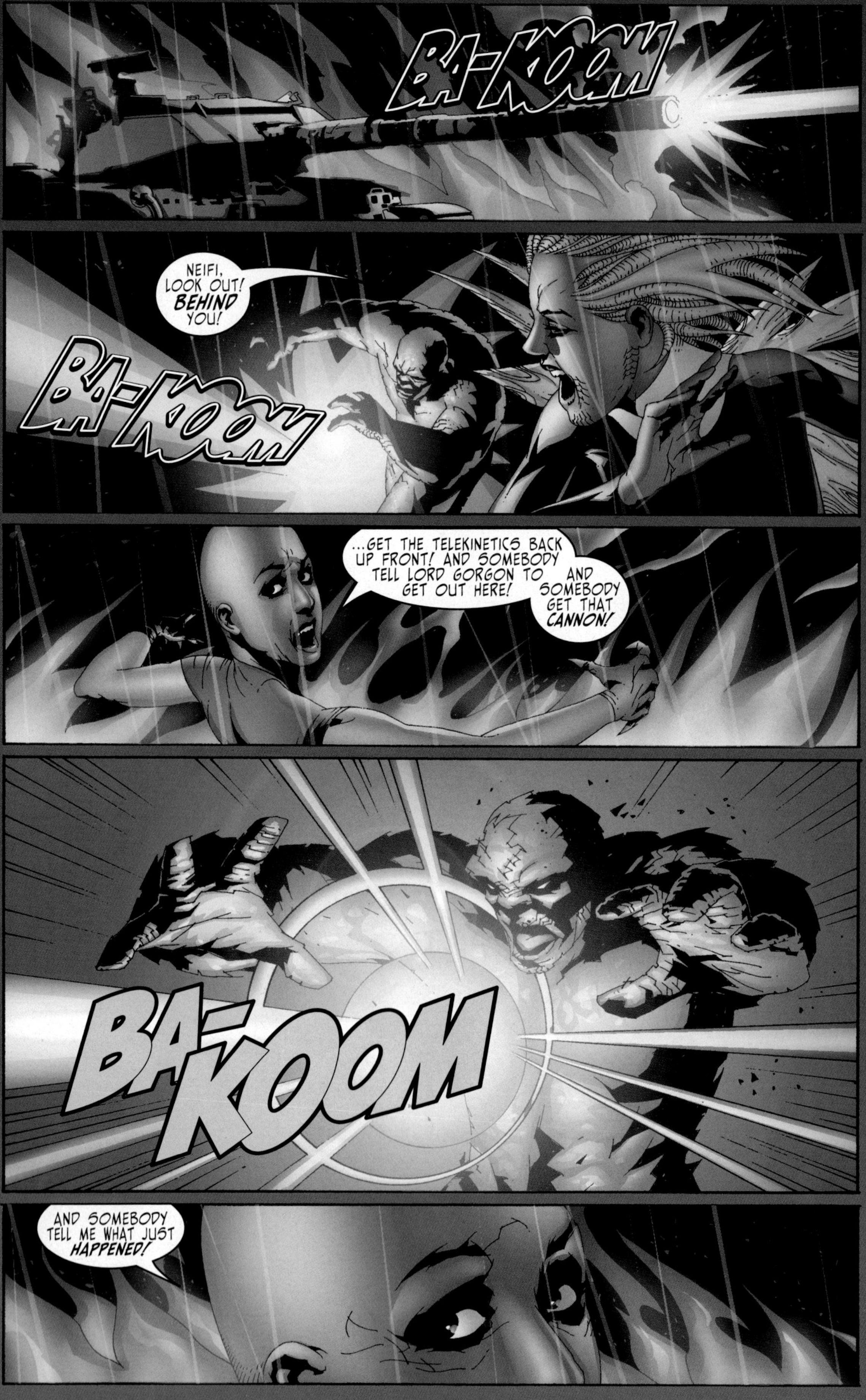
BA-KOOM
NEIFI, LOOK OUT! BEHIND YOU!
BA-KOOM
...GET THE TELEKINETICS BACK UP FRONT! AND SOMEBODY TELL LORD GORGON TO GET OUT HERE!
AND SOMEBODY GET THAT CANNON!
BA-KOOM
AND SOMEBODY TELL ME WHAT JUST HAPPENED!

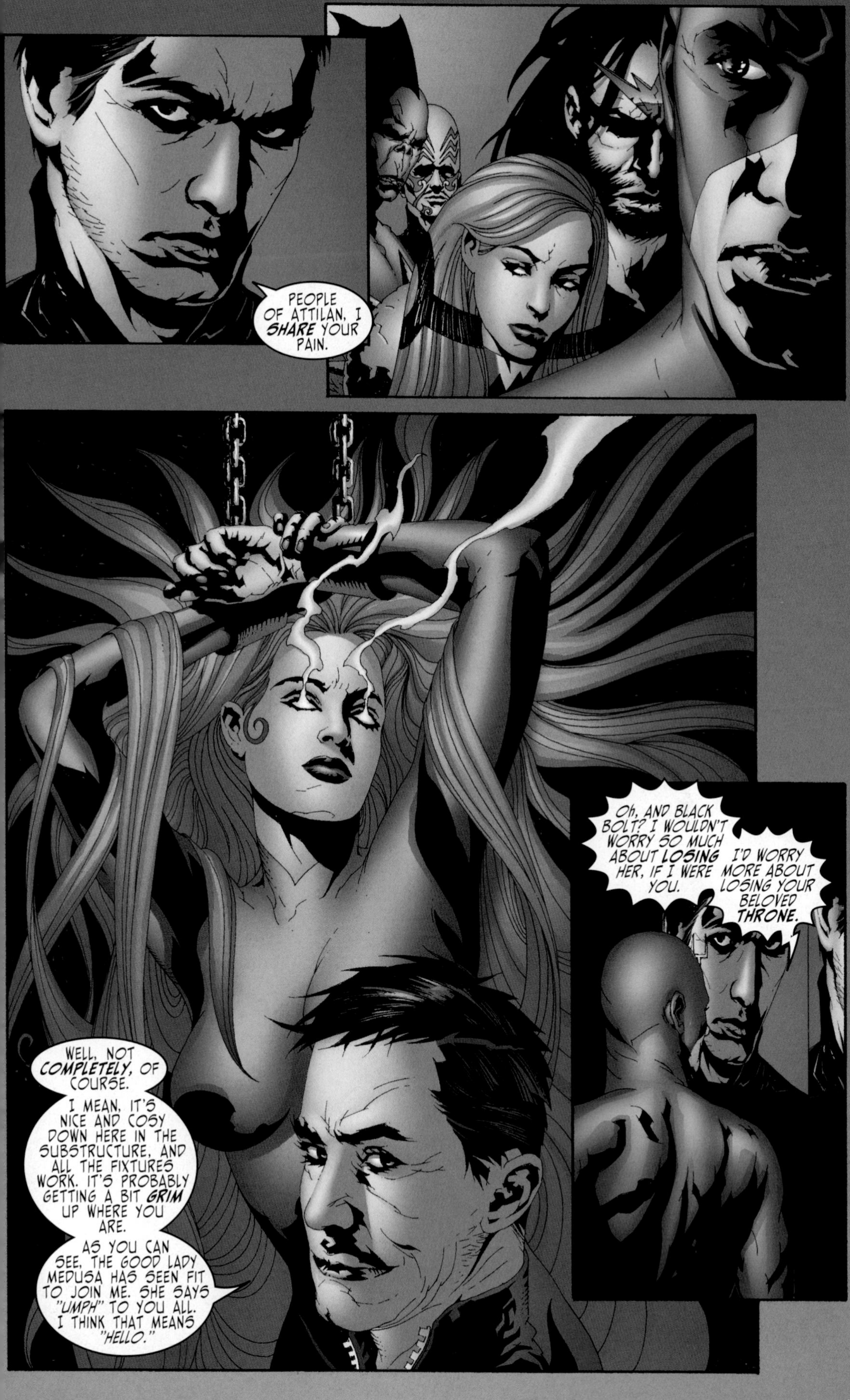
PEOPLE OF ATTILAN, I SHARE YOUR PAIN.
WELL, NOT COMPLETELY, OF COURSE.
I MEAN, IT'S NICE AND COSY DOWN HERE IN THE SUBSTRUCTURE, AND ALL THE FIXTURES WORK. IT'S PROBABLY GETTING A BIT GRIM UP WHERE YOU ARE.
AS YOU CAN SEE, THE GOOD LADY MEDUSA HAS SEEN FIT TO JOIN ME. SHE SAYS "UMPH" TO YOU ALL. I THINK THAT MEANS "HELLO."
Oh, AND BLACK BOLT? I WOULDN'T WORRY SO MUCH ABOUT LOSING HER, IF I WERE YOU.
I'D WORRY MORE ABOUT LOSING YOUR BELOVED THRONE.

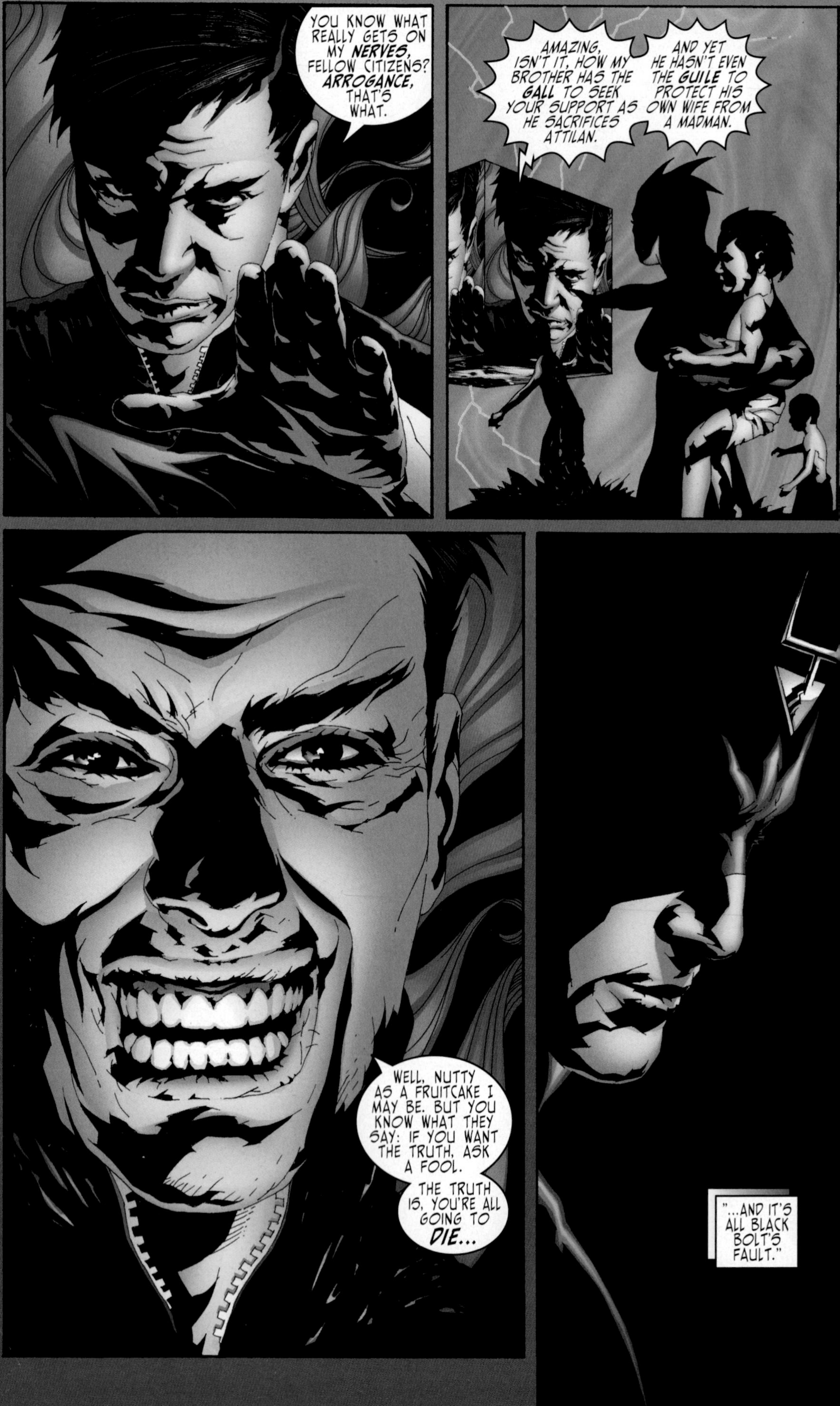

YOU KNOW WHAT REALLY GETS ON MY NERVES, FELLOW CITIZENS? ARROGANCE, THAT'S WHAT.
AMAZING, ISN'T IT, HOW MY BROTHER HAS THE GALL TO SEEK YOUR SUPPORT AS HE SACRIFICES ATTILAN.
AND YET HE HASN'T EVEN THE GUILE TO PROTECT HIS OWN WIFE FROM A MADMAN.
WELL, NUTTY AS A FRUITCAKE I MAY BE. BUT YOU KNOW WHAT THEY SAY: IF YOU WANT THE TRUTH, ASK A FOOL.
THE TRUTH IS, YOU'RE ALL GOING TO DIE...
"...AND IT'S ALL BLACK BOLT'S FAULT."

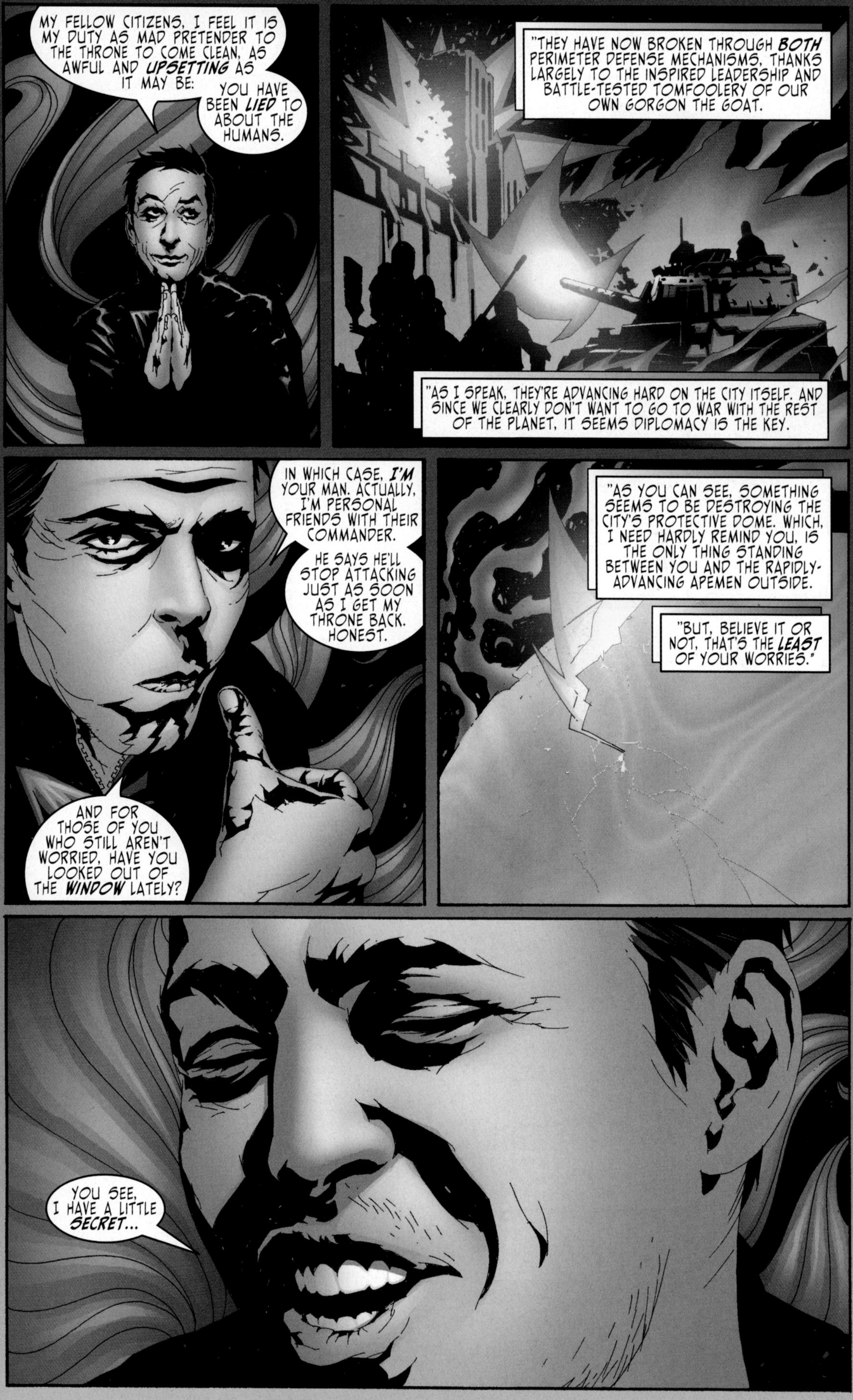

MY FELLOW CITIZENS, I FEEL IT IS MY DUTY AS MAD PRETENDER TO THE THRONE TO COME CLEAN, AS AWFUL AND UPSETTING AS IT MAY BE:
YOU HAVE BEEN LIED TO ABOUT THE HUMANS.
"THEY HAVE NOW BROKEN THROUGH BOTH PERIMETER DEFENSE MECHANISMS, THANKS LARGELY TO THE INSPIRED LEADERSHIP AND BATTLE-TESTED TOMFOOLERY OF OUR OWN GORGON THE GOAT.
"AS I SPEAK, THEY'RE ADVANCING HARD ON THE CITY ITSELF. AND SINCE WE CLEARLY DON'T WANT TO GO TO WAR WITH THE REST OF THE PLANET, IT SEEMS DIPLOMACY IS THE KEY.
IN WHICH CASE, I'M YOUR MAN. ACTUALLY, I'M PERSONAL FRIENDS WITH THEIR COMMANDER.
HE SAYS HE'LL STOP ATTACKING JUST AS SOON AS I GET MY THRONE BACK. HONEST.
AND FOR THOSE OF YOU WHO STILL AREN'T WORRIED, HAVE YOU LOOKED OUT OF THE WINDOW LATELY?
"AS YOU CAN SEE, SOMETHING SEEMS TO BE DESTROYING THE CITY'S PROTECTIVE DOME. WHICH, I NEED HARDLY REMIND YOU, IS THE ONLY THING STANDING BETWEEN YOU AND THE RAPIDLY-ADVANCING APEMEN OUTSIDE.
"BUT, BELIEVE IT OR NOT, THAT'S THE LEAST OF YOUR WORRIES."
YOU SEE, I HAVE A LITTLE SECRET...

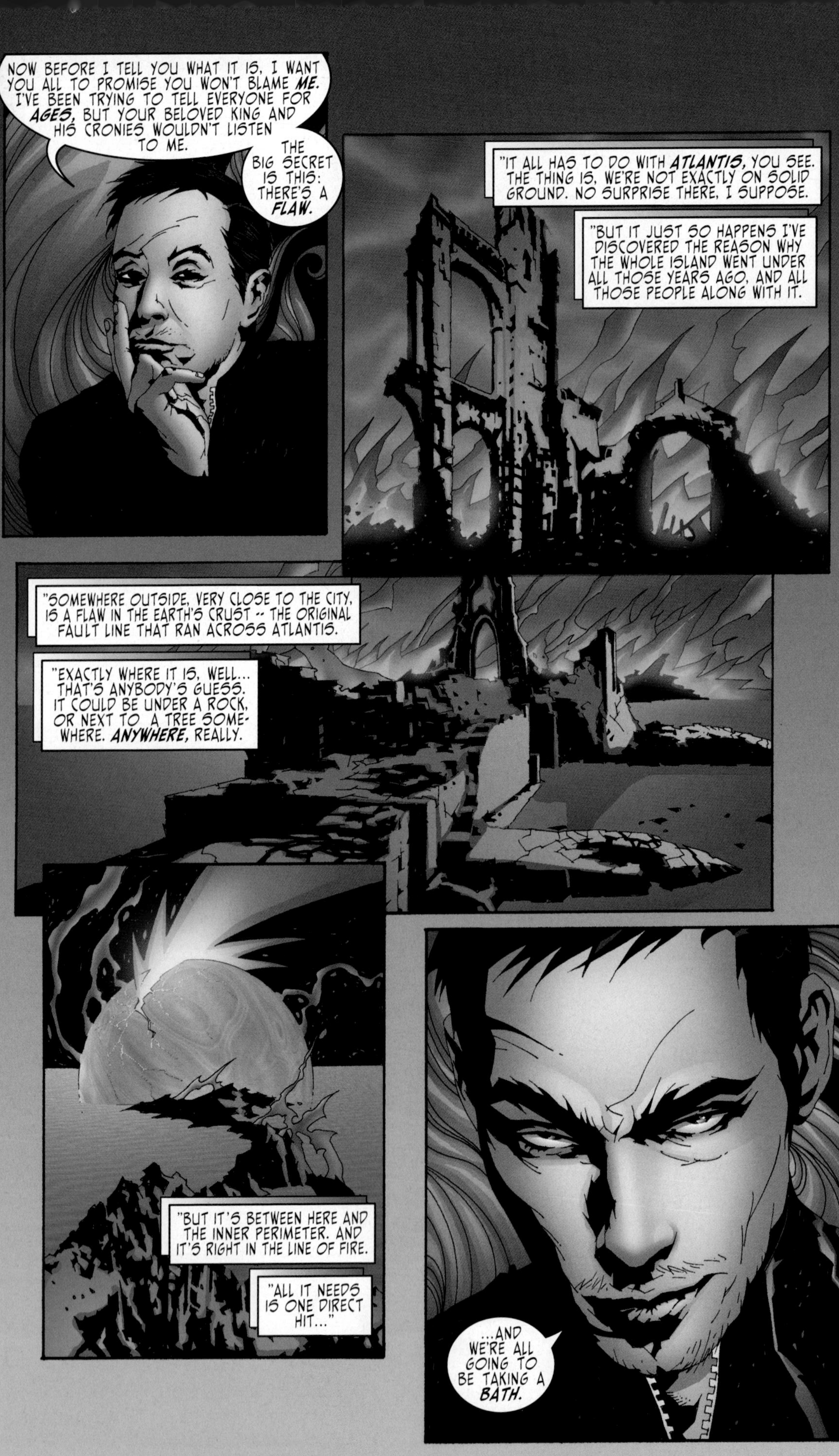
NOW BEFORE I TELL YOU WHAT IT IS, I WANT YOU ALL TO PROMISE YOU WON'T BLAME ME. I'VE BEEN TRYING TO TELL EVERYONE FOR AGES, BUT YOUR BELOVED KING AND HIS CRONIES WOULDN'T LISTEN TO ME.
THE BIG SECRET IS THIS: THERE'S A FLAW.
"IT ALL HAS TO DO WITH ATLANTIS, YOU SEE. THE THING IS, WE'RE NOT EXACTLY ON SOLID GROUND. NO SURPRISE THERE, I SUPPOSE.
"BUT IT JUST SO HAPPENS I'VE DISCOVERED THE REASON WHY THE WHOLE ISLAND WENT UNDER ALL THOSE YEARS AGO, AND ALL THOSE PEOPLE ALONG WITH IT.
"SOMEWHERE OUTSIDE, VERY CLOSE TO THE CITY, IS A FLAW IN THE EARTH'S CRUST -- THE ORIGINAL FAULT LINE THAT RAN ACROSS ATLANTIS.
"EXACTLY WHERE IT IS, WELL... THAT'S ANYBODY'S GUESS. IT COULD BE UNDER A ROCK, OR NEXT TO A TREE SOMEWHERE. ANYWHERE, REALLY.
"BUT IT'S BETWEEN HERE AND THE INNER PERIMETER. AND IT'S RIGHT IN THE LINE OF FIRE.
"ALL IT NEEDS IS ONE DIRECT HIT..."
...AND WE'RE ALL GOING TO BE TAKING A BATH.

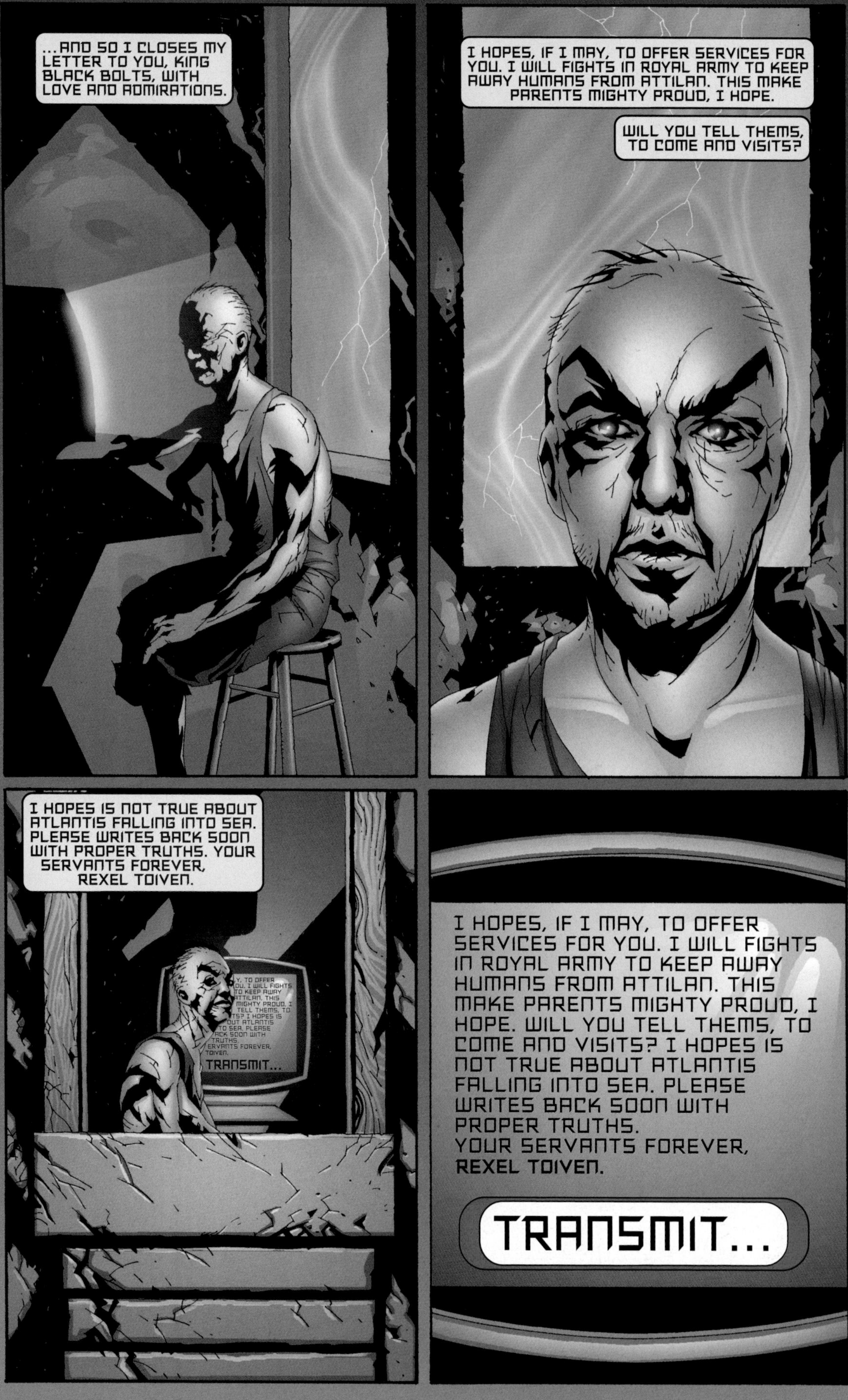
...AND SO I CLOSES MY LETTER TO YOU, KING BLACK BOLTS, WITH LOVE AND ADMIRATIONS.
I HOPES, IF I MAY, TO OFFER SERVICES FOR YOU. I WILL FIGHTS IN ROYAL ARMY TO KEEP AWAY HUMANS FROM ATTILAN. THIS MAKE PARENTS MIGHTY PROUD, I HOPE.
WILL YOU TELL THEMS, TO COME AND VISITS?
I HOPES IS NOT TRUE ABOUT ATLANTIS FALLING INTO SEA. PLEASE WRITES BACK SOON WITH PROPER TRUTHS. YOUR SERVANTS FOREVER, REXEL TOIVEN.
TRANSMIT...
I HOPES, IF I MAY, TO OFFER SERVICES FOR YOU. I WILL FIGHTS IN ROYAL ARMY TO KEEP AWAY HUMANS FROM ATTILAN. THIS MAKE PARENTS MIGHTY PROUD, I HOPE. WILL YOU TELL THEMS, TO COME AND VISITS? I HOPES IS NOT TRUE ABOUT ATLANTIS FALLING INTO SEA. PLEASE WRITES BACK SOON WITH PROPER TRUTHS.
YOUR SERVANTS FOREVER,
REXEL TOIVEN.
TRANSMIT...

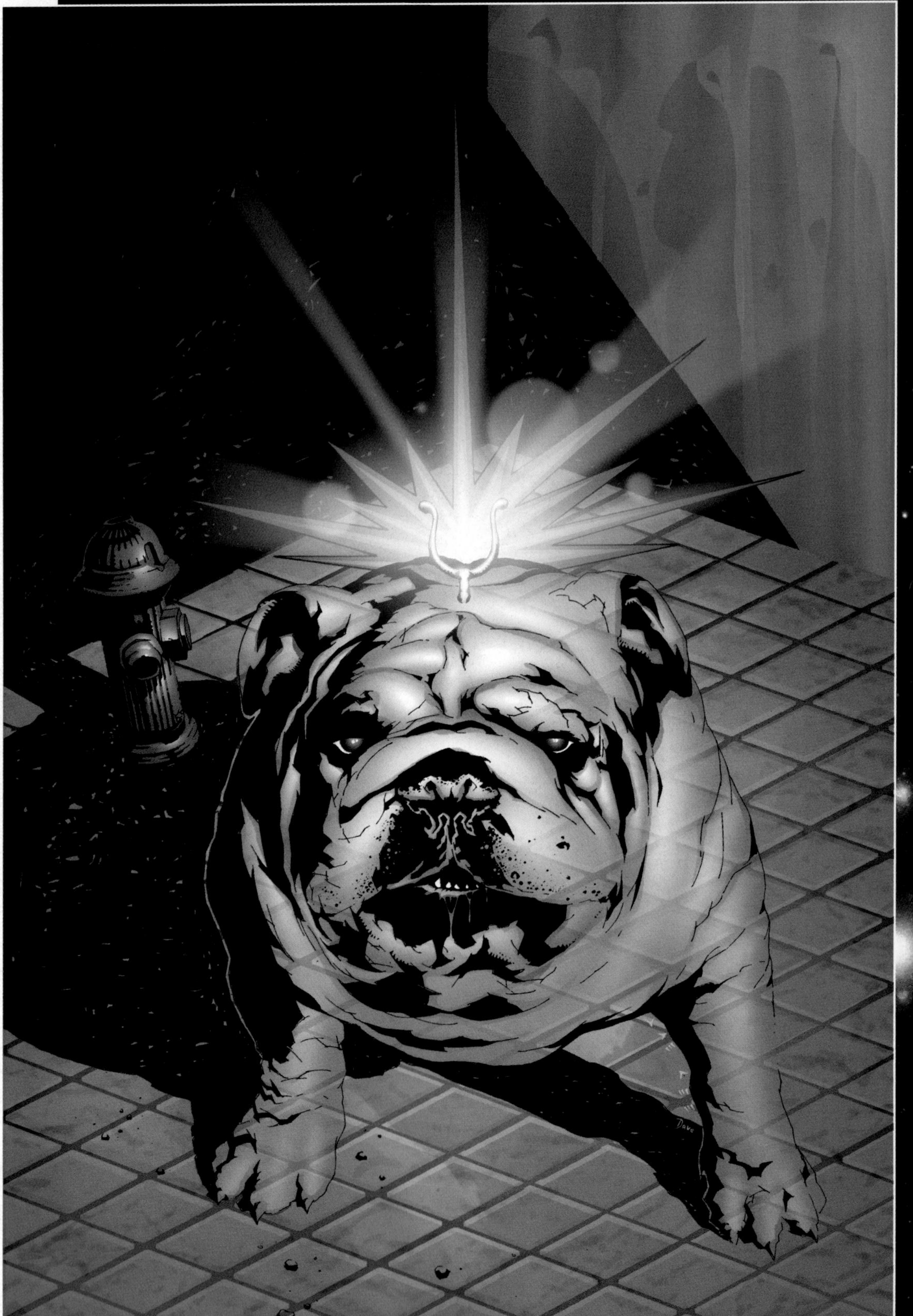
Dave

LOOK... YOU CAN SEE THE *SKY!*

IT'S SO STRANGE... SO *UGLY.*

THE HUMANS ARE RESPONSIBLE -- THEY'VE POISONED THE AIR. WHO *KNOWS* WHAT THEY'LL DO TO US IF MAXIMUS LETS THEM IN --?

IT'LL BE *BLACK BOLT'S* FAULT. I *STILL* DON'T UNDERSTAND WHY WE CAN'T FIGHT BACK.

DADDY, I'M FRIGHTENED... IS IT TRUE WE'RE ALL GOING TO *DROWN?*

HUSH, CHILD -- OUR KING WILL HAVE A PLAN TO SAVE US.

"""""""""
"""""""""""
""""""""""
""""""
"""""""

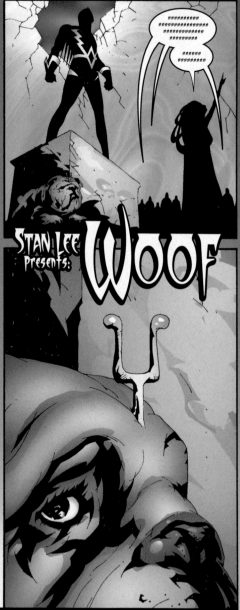

STAN LEE presents: WOOF

PAUL JENKINS
BARKING MAD

JAE LEE
BARKING UP THE WRONG TREE

BROTHERS KEMP
LICKING HIS PRIVATES

RS & COMICRAFT/ST
LEARNING NEW TRICKS

JOE & JIMMY
WHINING

NANCI DAKESIAN
BARKING OUT ORDERS

BOB HARRAS
LIVING A DOG'S LIFE

PEOPLE NOISY BARK BARK... SLEEP IS GONE. SCRATCHITY-SCRATCH.

URFF

DOG GO OUTSIDE...

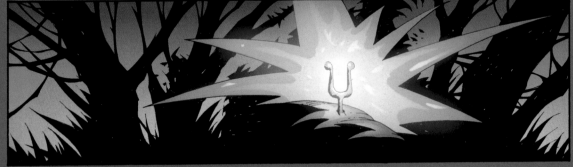

SNFF

SNFF SNFF

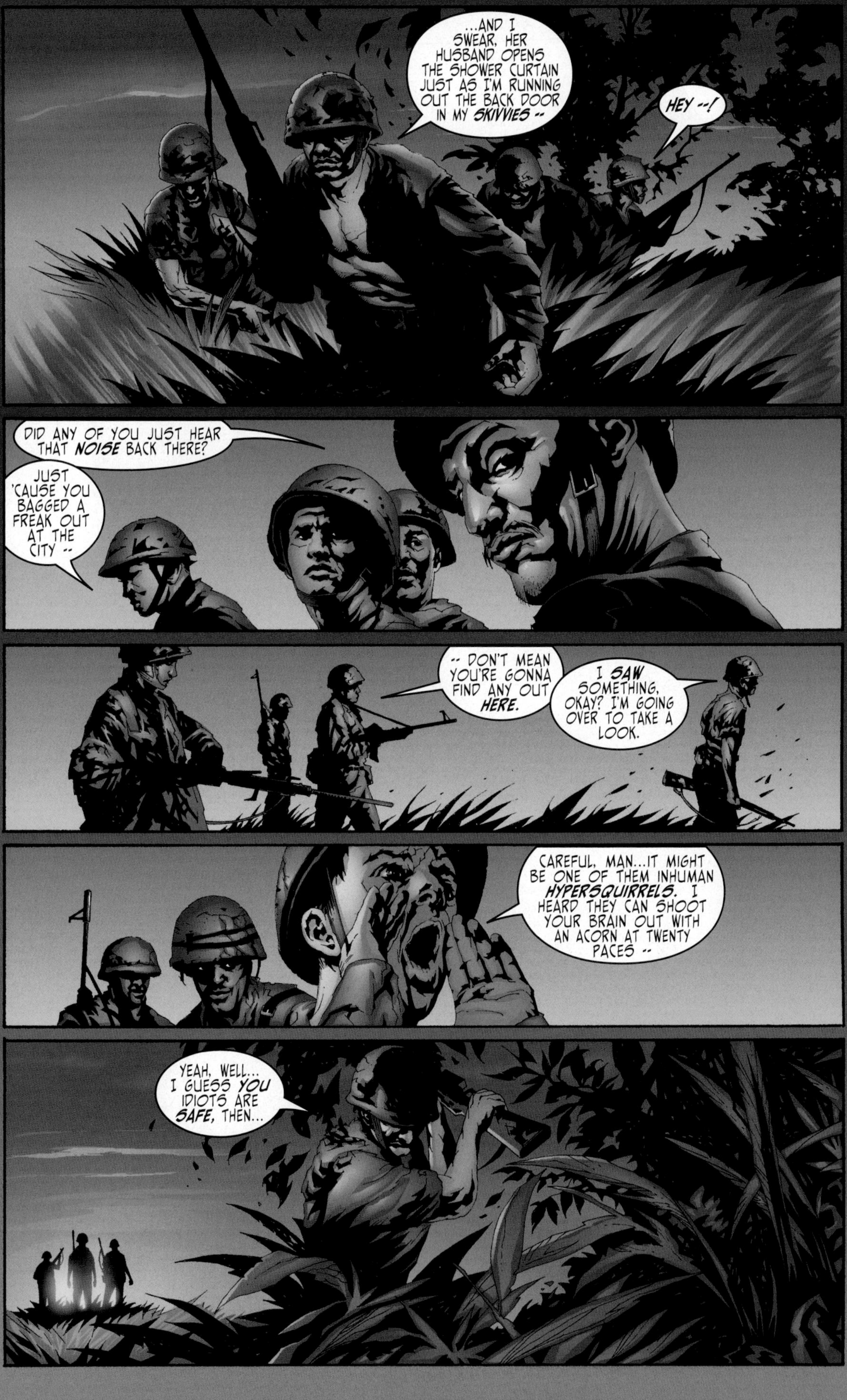
...AND I SWEAR, HER HUSBAND OPENS THE SHOWER CURTAIN JUST AS I'M RUNNING OUT THE BACK DOOR IN MY SKIVVIES --
HEY --!
DID ANY OF YOU JUST HEAR THAT NOISE BACK THERE?
JUST 'CAUSE YOU BAGGED A FREAK OUT AT THE CITY --
-- DON'T MEAN YOU'RE GONNA FIND ANY OUT HERE.
I SAW SOMETHING, OKAY? I'M GOING OVER TO TAKE A LOOK.
CAREFUL, MAN...IT MIGHT BE ONE OF THEM INHUMAN HYPERSQUIRRELS. I HEARD THEY CAN SHOOT YOUR BRAIN OUT WITH AN ACORN AT TWENTY PACES --
YEAH, WELL... I GUESS YOU IDIOTS ARE SAFE, THEN...

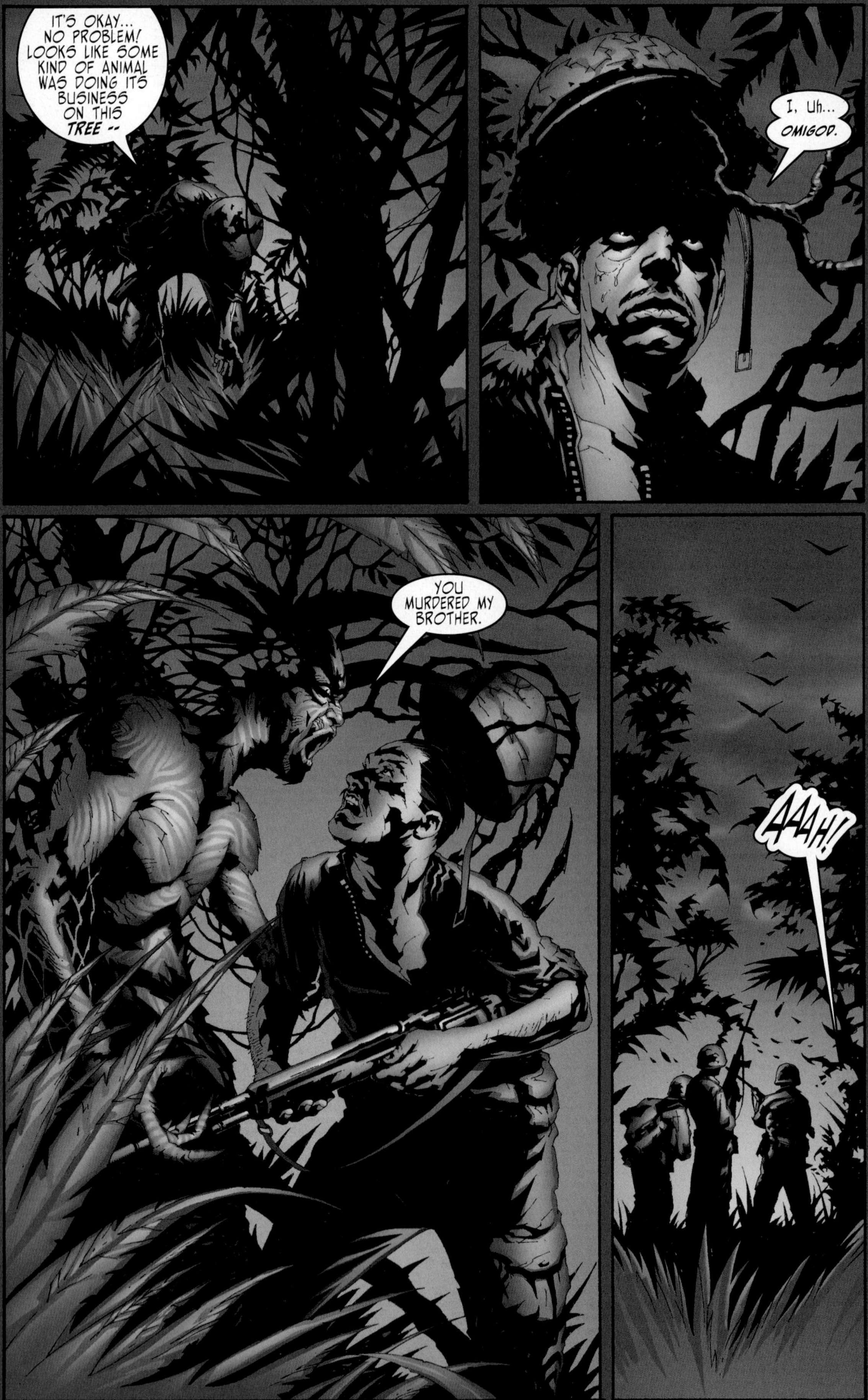
IT'S OKAY... NO PROBLEM! LOOKS LIKE SOME KIND OF ANIMAL WAS DOING ITS BUSINESS ON THIS TREE --
I, Uh... OMIGOD.
YOU MURDERED MY BROTHER.
AAAH!

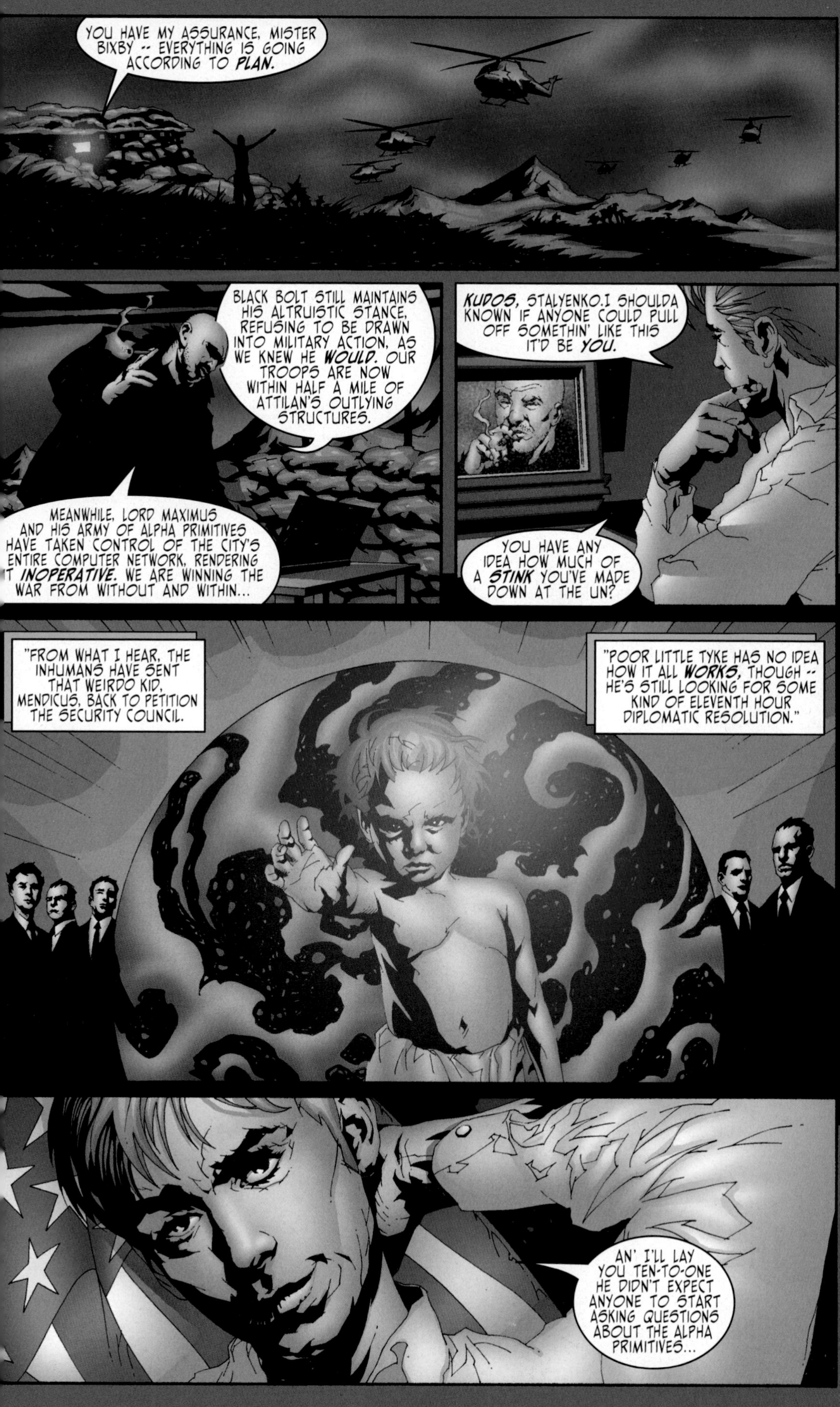

YOU HAVE MY ASSURANCE, MISTER BIXBY -- EVERYTHING IS GOING ACCORDING TO PLAN.
BLACK BOLT STILL MAINTAINS HIS ALTRUISTIC STANCE, REFUSING TO BE DRAWN INTO MILITARY ACTION, AS WE KNEW HE WOULD. OUR TROOPS ARE NOW WITHIN HALF A MILE OF ATTILAN'S OUTLYING STRUCTURES.
MEANWHILE, LORD MAXIMUS AND HIS ARMY OF ALPHA PRIMITIVES HAVE TAKEN CONTROL OF THE CITY'S ENTIRE COMPUTER NETWORK, RENDERING IT INOPERATIVE. WE ARE WINNING THE WAR FROM WITHOUT AND WITHIN...
KUDOS, STALYENKO. I SHOULDA KNOWN IF ANYONE COULD PULL OFF SOMETHIN' LIKE THIS IT'D BE YOU.
YOU HAVE ANY IDEA HOW MUCH OF A STINK YOU'VE MADE DOWN AT THE UN?
"FROM WHAT I HEAR, THE INHUMANS HAVE SENT THAT WEIRDO KID, MENDICUS, BACK TO PETITION THE SECURITY COUNCIL.
"POOR LITTLE TYKE HAS NO IDEA HOW IT ALL WORKS, THOUGH -- HE'S STILL LOOKING FOR SOME KIND OF ELEVENTH HOUR DIPLOMATIC RESOLUTION."
AN' I'LL LAY YOU TEN-TO-ONE HE DIDN'T EXPECT ANYONE TO START ASKING QUESTIONS ABOUT THE ALPHA PRIMITIVES...

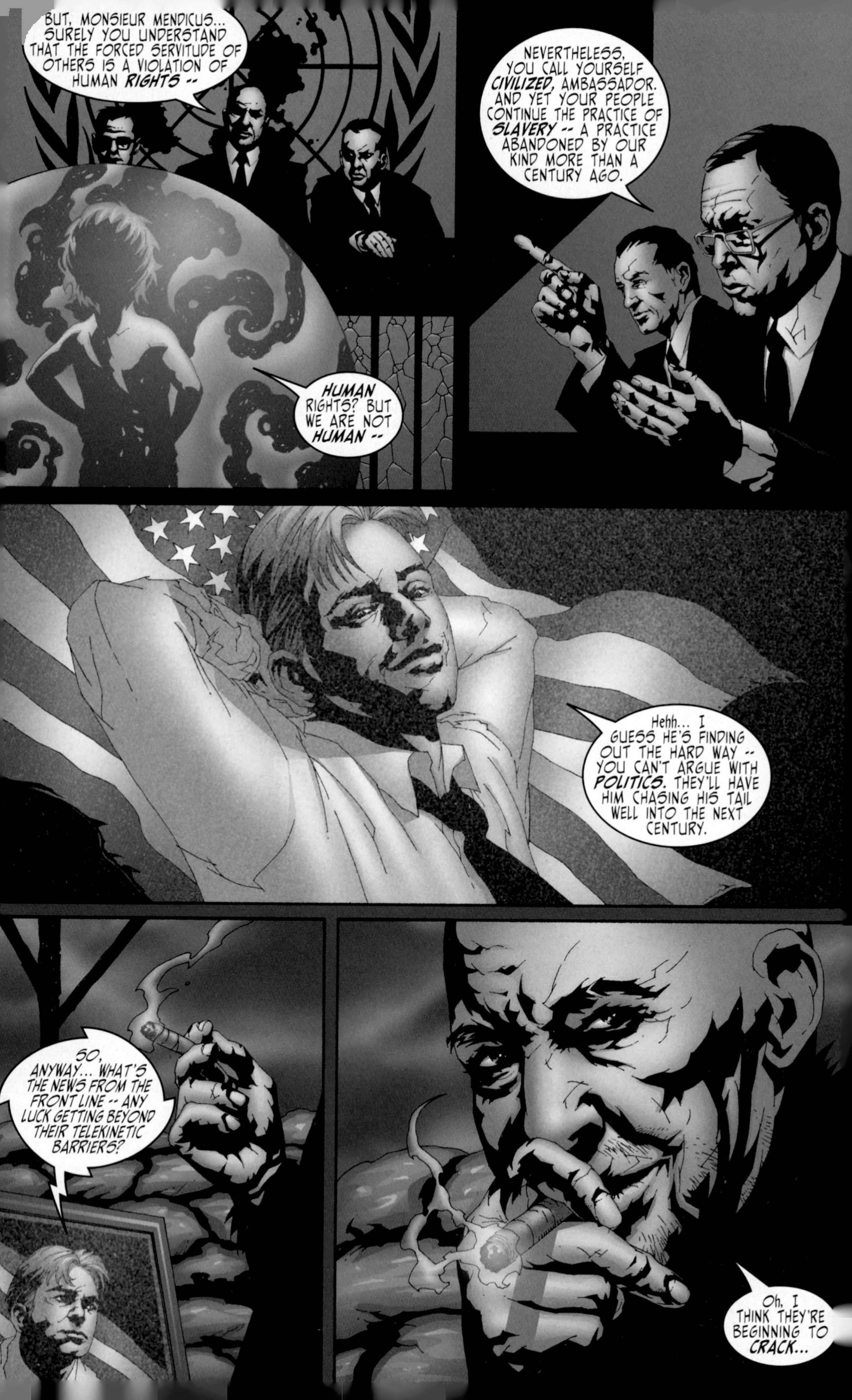
BUT, MONSIEUR MENDICUS... SURELY YOU UNDERSTAND THAT THE FORCED SERVITUDE OF OTHERS IS A VIOLATION OF HUMAN RIGHTS --
HUMAN RIGHTS? BUT WE ARE NOT HUMAN --
NEVERTHELESS, YOU CALL YOURSELF CIVILIZED, AMBASSADOR. AND YET YOUR PEOPLE CONTINUE THE PRACTICE OF SLAVERY -- A PRACTICE ABANDONED BY OUR KIND MORE THAN A CENTURY AGO.
Hehh... I GUESS HE'S FINDING OUT THE HARD WAY -- YOU CAN'T ARGUE WITH POLITICS. THEY'LL HAVE HIM CHASING HIS TAIL WELL INTO THE NEXT CENTURY.
SO, ANYWAY... WHAT'S THE NEWS FROM THE FRONT LINE -- ANY LUCK GETTING BEYOND THEIR TELEKINETIC BARRIERS?
Oh, I THINK THEY'RE BEGINNING TO CRACK...

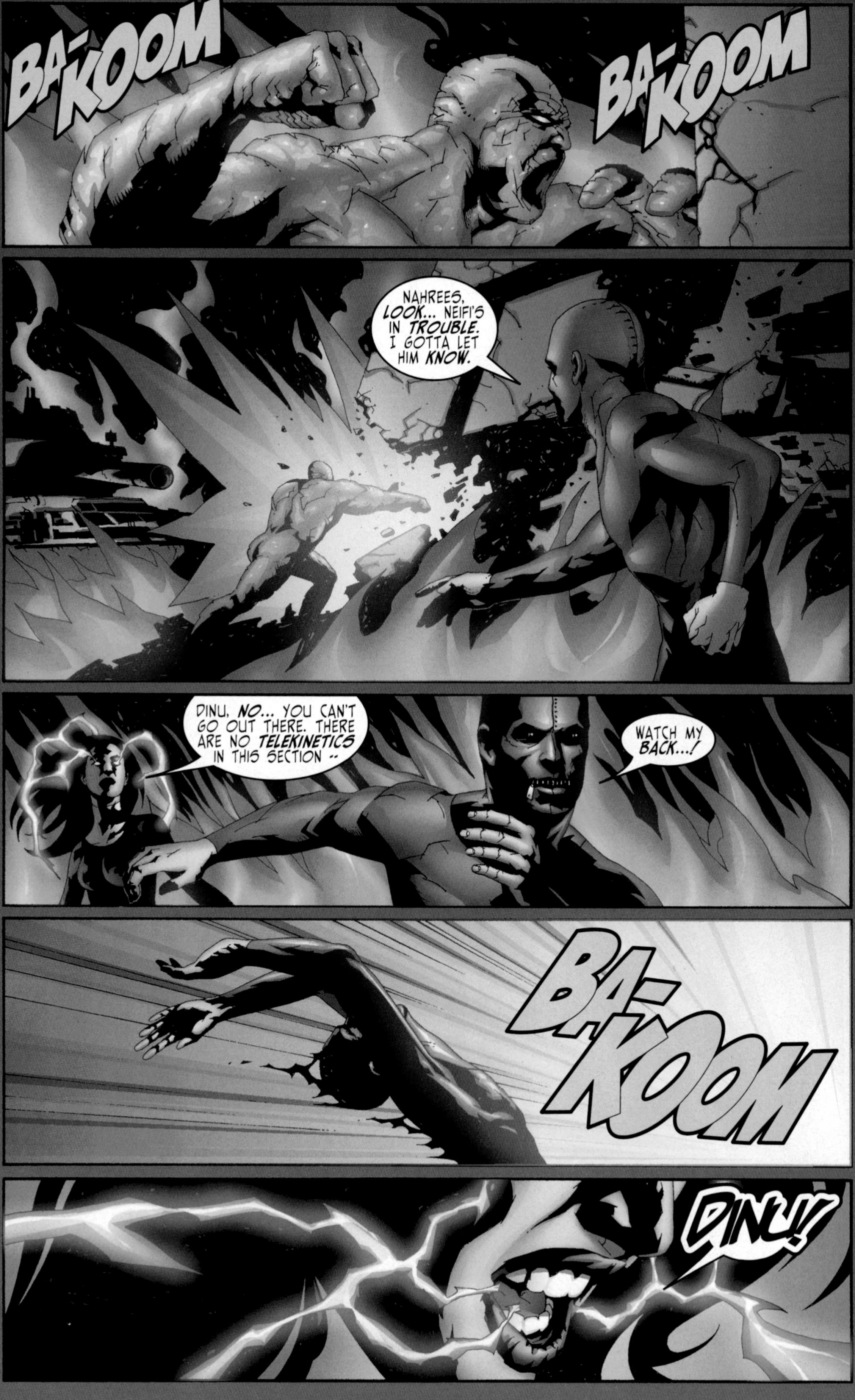
BA-KOOM
BA-KOOM
NAHREES, LOOK... NEIFI'S IN TROUBLE. I GOTTA LET HIM KNOW.
DINU, NO... YOU CAN'T GO OUT THERE. THERE ARE NO TELEKINETICS IN THIS SECTION --
WATCH MY BACK...!
BA-KOOM
DINU!!

NEIFI, WHAT HAPPENED?

THERE'S NOTHING MORE YOU CAN DO HERE --

-- WE'VE BEEN ORDERED TO FALL BACK BEHIND THE TELEKINETICS.

UNDERSTOOD. I'LL NEED SOME HELP HERE.

BA-KOOM

THEY GOT DINU... IT'S PRETTY BAD.

uhh...

C'MON, SOLDIER... I'VE GOT YOU.

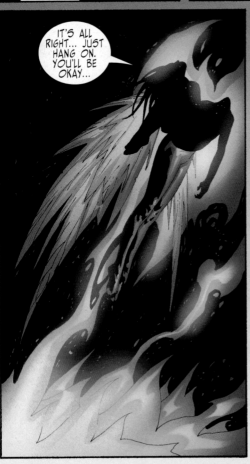

IT'S ALL RIGHT... JUST HANG ON. YOU'LL BE OKAY...

PLEASE BE OKAY.

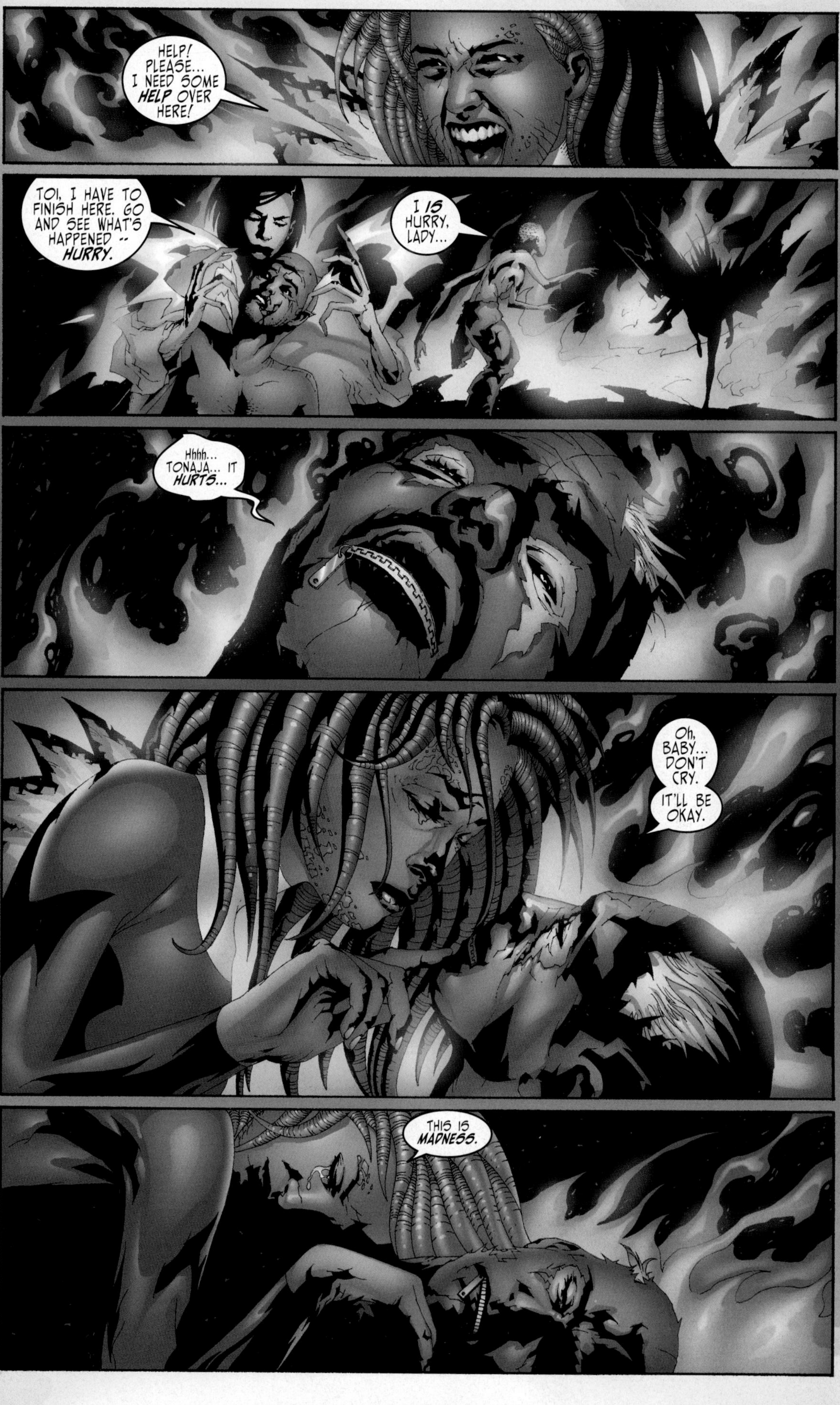
HELP! PLEASE... I NEED SOME HELP OVER HERE!
TOI, I HAVE TO FINISH HERE. GO AND SEE WHAT'S HAPPENED -- HURRY.
I IS HURRY, LADY...
Hhhh... TONAJA... IT HURTS...
Oh, BABY... DON'T CRY.
IT'LL BE OKAY.
THIS IS MADNESS.

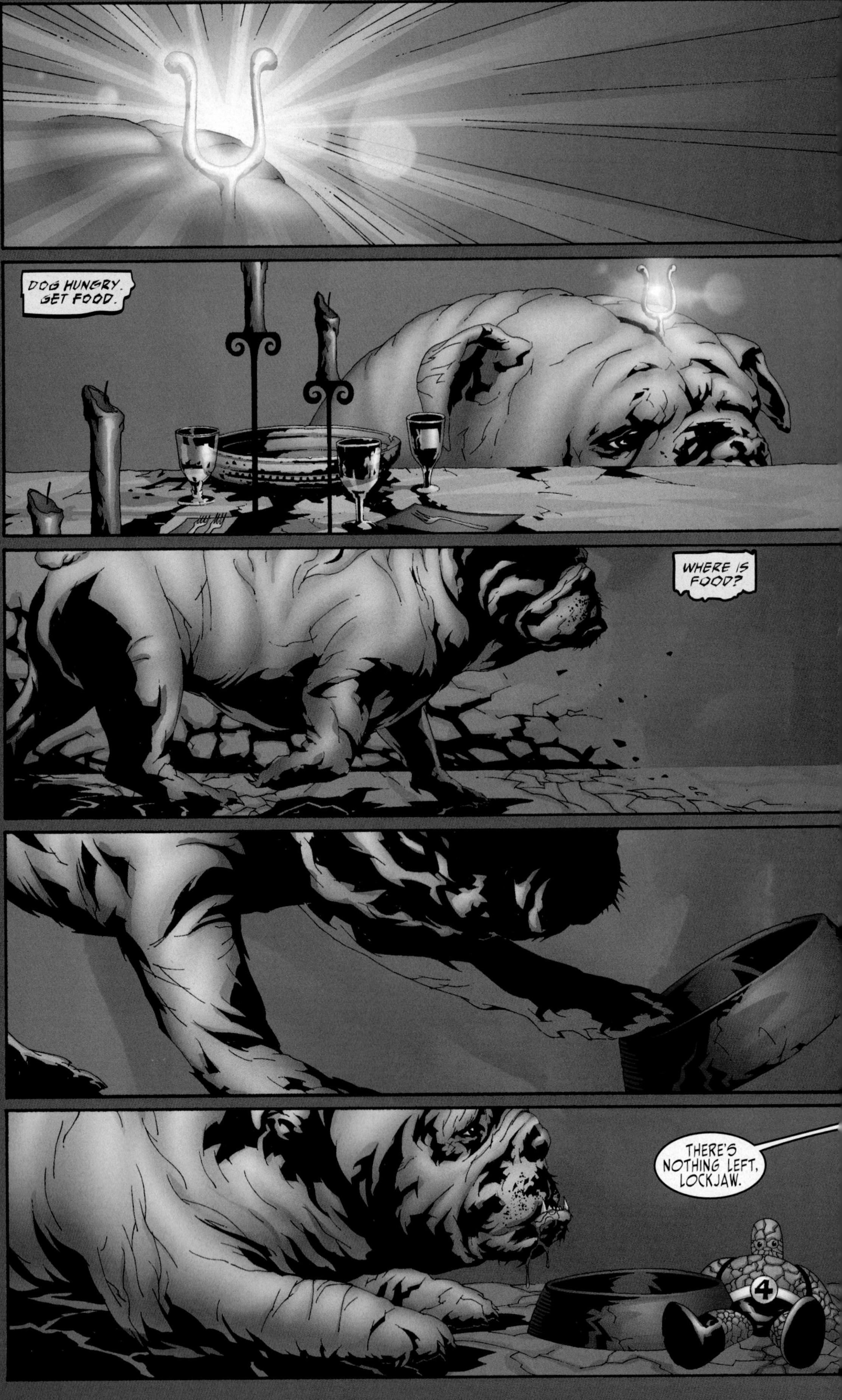
DOG HUNGRY. GET FOOD.
WHERE IS FOOD?
THERE'S NOTHING LEFT, LOCKJAW.

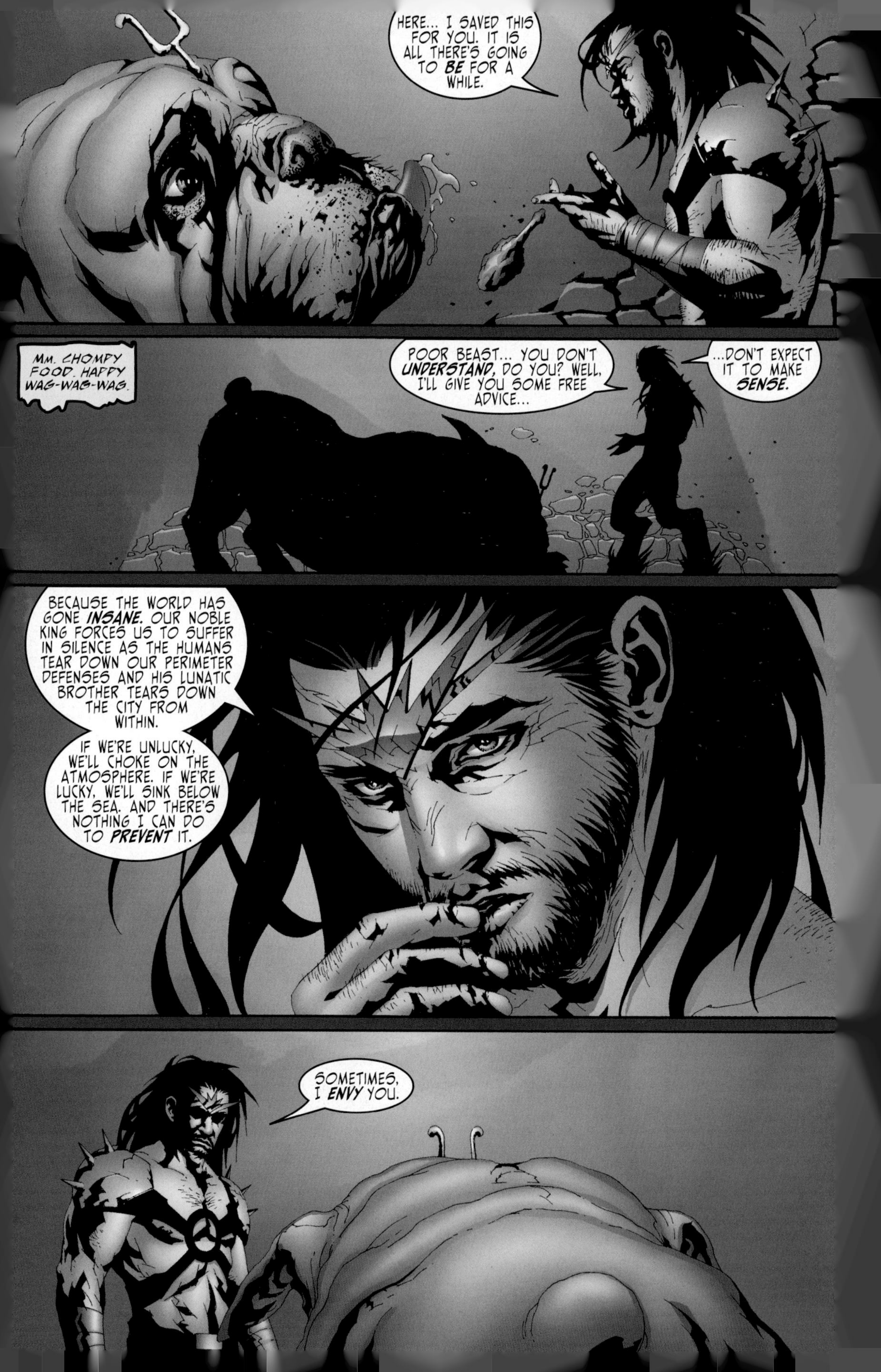
HERE... I SAVED THIS FOR YOU. IT IS ALL THERE'S GOING TO *BE* FOR A WHILE.
MM. CHOMPY FOOD. HAPPY WAG-WAG-WAG.
POOR BEAST... YOU DON'T *UNDERSTAND*, DO YOU? WELL, I'LL GIVE YOU SOME FREE ADVICE...
...DON'T EXPECT IT TO MAKE *SENSE*.
BECAUSE THE WORLD HAS GONE *INSANE*. OUR NOBLE KING FORCES US TO SUFFER IN SILENCE AS THE HUMANS TEAR DOWN OUR PERIMETER DEFENSES AND HIS LUNATIC BROTHER TEARS DOWN THE CITY FROM WITHIN.
IF WE'RE UNLUCKY, WE'LL CHOKE ON THE ATMOSPHERE. IF WE'RE LUCKY, WE'LL SINK BELOW THE SEA. AND THERE'S NOTHING I CAN DO TO *PREVENT* IT.
SOMETIMES, I *ENVY* YOU.

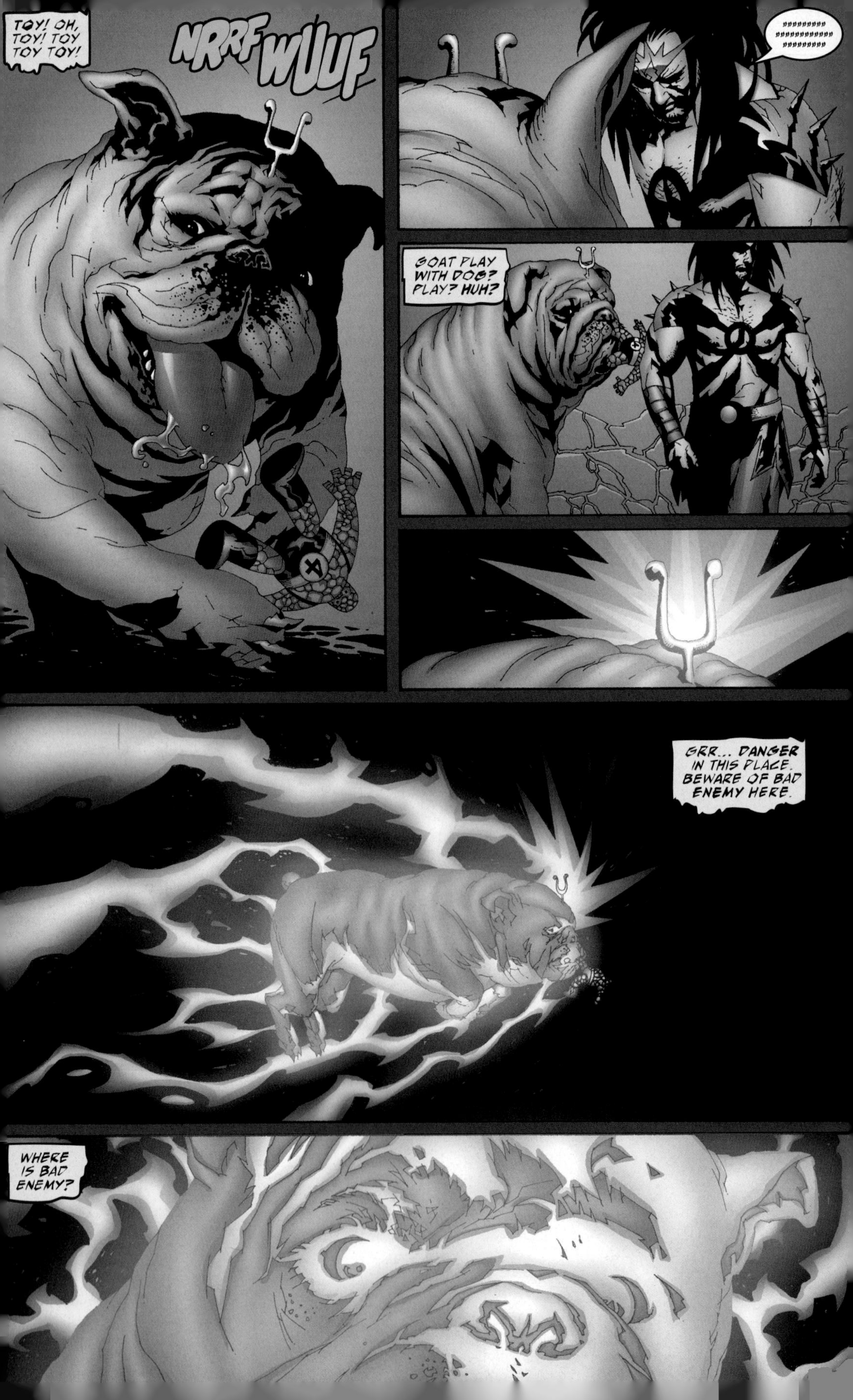
TOY! OH, TOY! TOY TOY TOY!
NRRF WUUF
GOAT PLAY WITH DOG? PLAY? HUH?
GRR... DANGER IN THIS PLACE. BEWARE OF BAD ENEMY HERE.
WHERE IS BAD ENEMY?

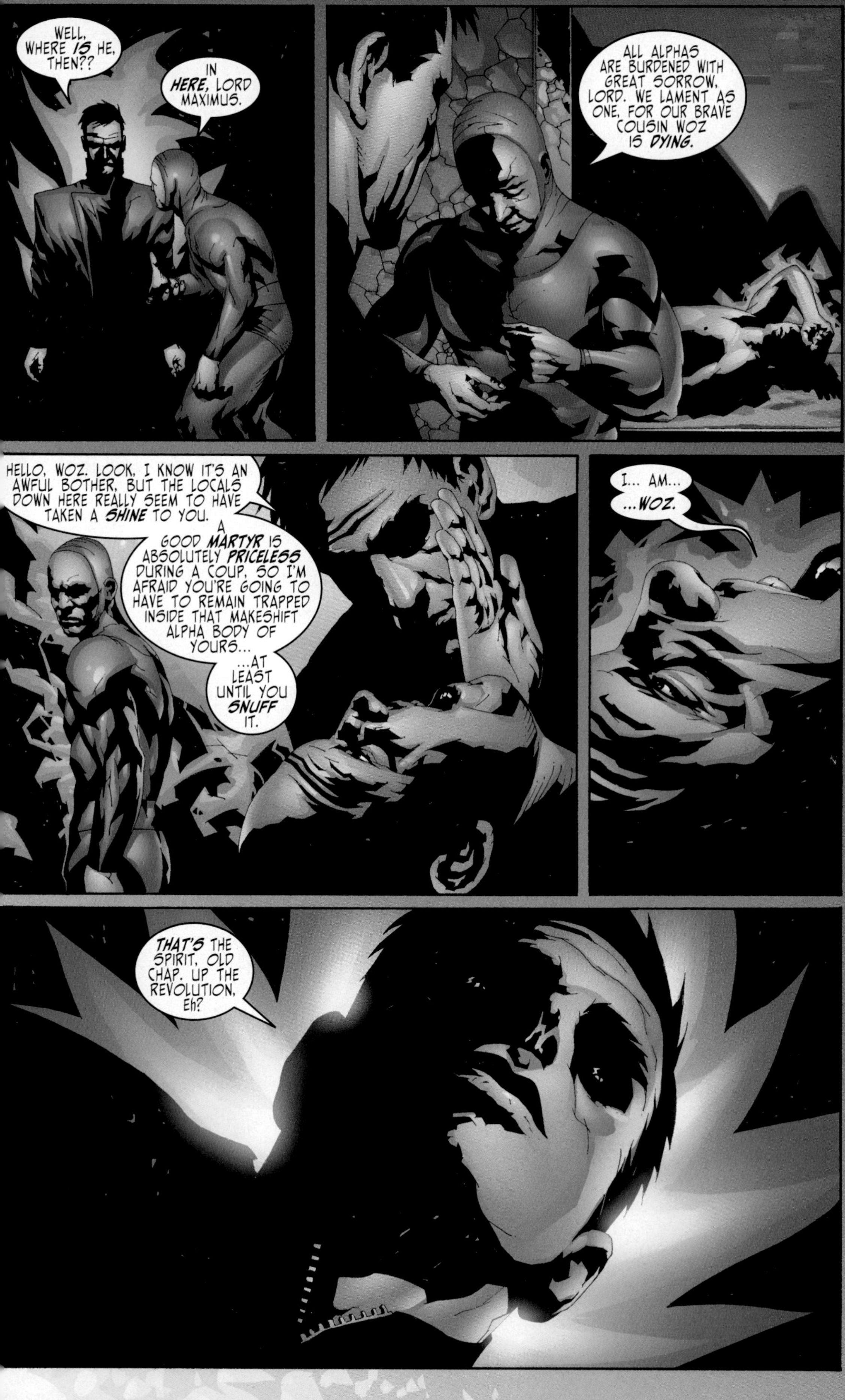

WELL, WHERE IS HE, THEN??
IN HERE, LORD MAXIMUS.
ALL ALPHAS ARE BURDENED WITH GREAT SORROW, LORD. WE LAMENT AS ONE, FOR OUR BRAVE COUSIN WOZ IS DYING.
HELLO, WOZ. LOOK, I KNOW IT'S AN AWFUL BOTHER, BUT THE LOCALS DOWN HERE REALLY SEEM TO HAVE TAKEN A SHINE TO YOU.
A GOOD MARTYR IS ABSOLUTELY PRICELESS DURING A COUP, SO I'M AFRAID YOU'RE GOING TO HAVE TO REMAIN TRAPPED INSIDE THAT MAKESHIFT ALPHA BODY OF YOURS...
...AT LEAST UNTIL YOU SNUFF IT.
I... AM... ...WOZ.
THAT'S THE SPIRIT, OLD CHAP. UP THE REVOLUTION, Eh?

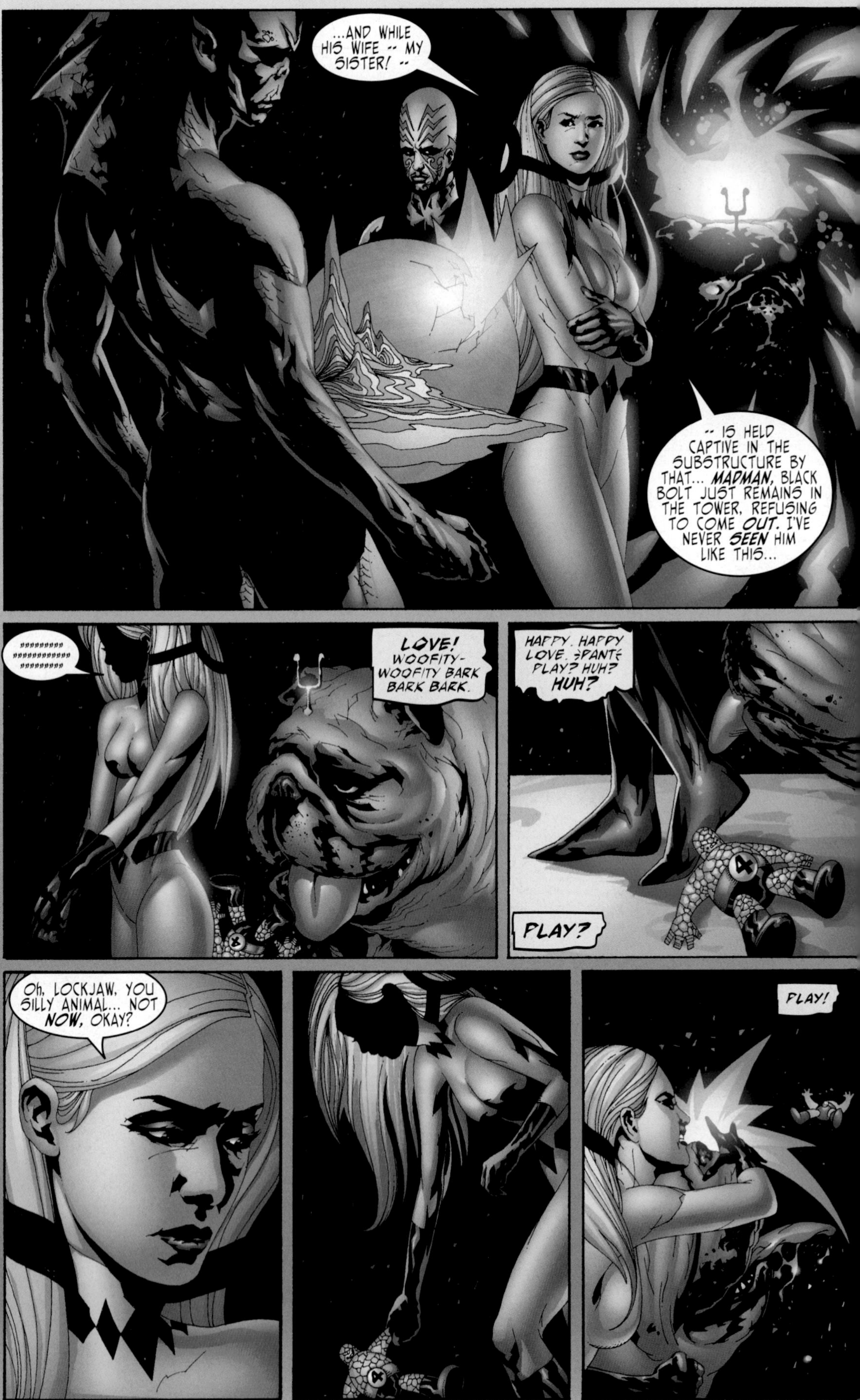
...AND WHILE HIS WIFE -- MY SISTER! --
-- IS HELD CAPTIVE IN THE SUBSTRUCTURE BY THAT... MADMAN, BLACK BOLT JUST REMAINS IN THE TOWER, REFUSING TO COME OUT. I'VE NEVER SEEN HIM LIKE THIS...
LOVE! WOOFITY-WOOFITY BARK BARK BARK.
HAPPY. HAPPY LOVE. PLAY? HUH? HUH?
PLAY?
Oh, LOCKJAW, YOU SILLY ANIMAL... NOT NOW, OKAY?
PLAY!

THIS IS A TIME OF MUCH EMERGENCY, I FEAR. HUMANS NOW ADVANCE RAPIDLY, MAKING GROUND *HERE*... AND *HERE*. WITH CITY *CONTROLS* LOST TO US, THIS NEWS IS DIRE INDEED.

AGREED. AND YET WE ARE ORDERED TO REMAIN PASSIVE EVEN AS OUR PROTECTIVE DOME DISINTEGRATES AROUND US.

"EVERY CITIZEN IS NOW EXPOSED TO THE TOXICITY IN THE AIR. WE HAVE A COUNTER AGENT, AND WE'VE DEVISED A SYSTEM OF DISTRIBUTION SO THAT EVERY CITIZEN RECEIVES A DAILY SUPPLY."

"BUT THE RESERVES ARE DWINDLING. WITH MAXIMUS CONTROLLING THE SUBSTRUCTURE WE CAN MANUFACTURE NO MORE. AT OUR CURRENT RATE OF USAGE, WE HAVE ENOUGH TO LAST FOUR DAYS AT *MOST*."

IF WE LAST THAT LONG. THE TELEKINETICS ARE OUR LAST LINE OF PASSIVE RESISTANCE, BUT THEY'RE RAPIDLY BEGINNING TO TIRE.

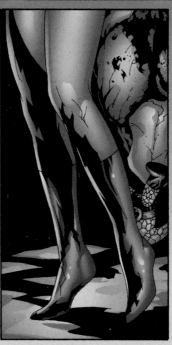

I... I CONFESS, COUSINS... ...IF I DIDN'T KNOW BLACK BOLT ANY BETTER, I WOULD BEGIN TO THINK HE HAS GONE THE WAY OF HIS *BROTHER*.

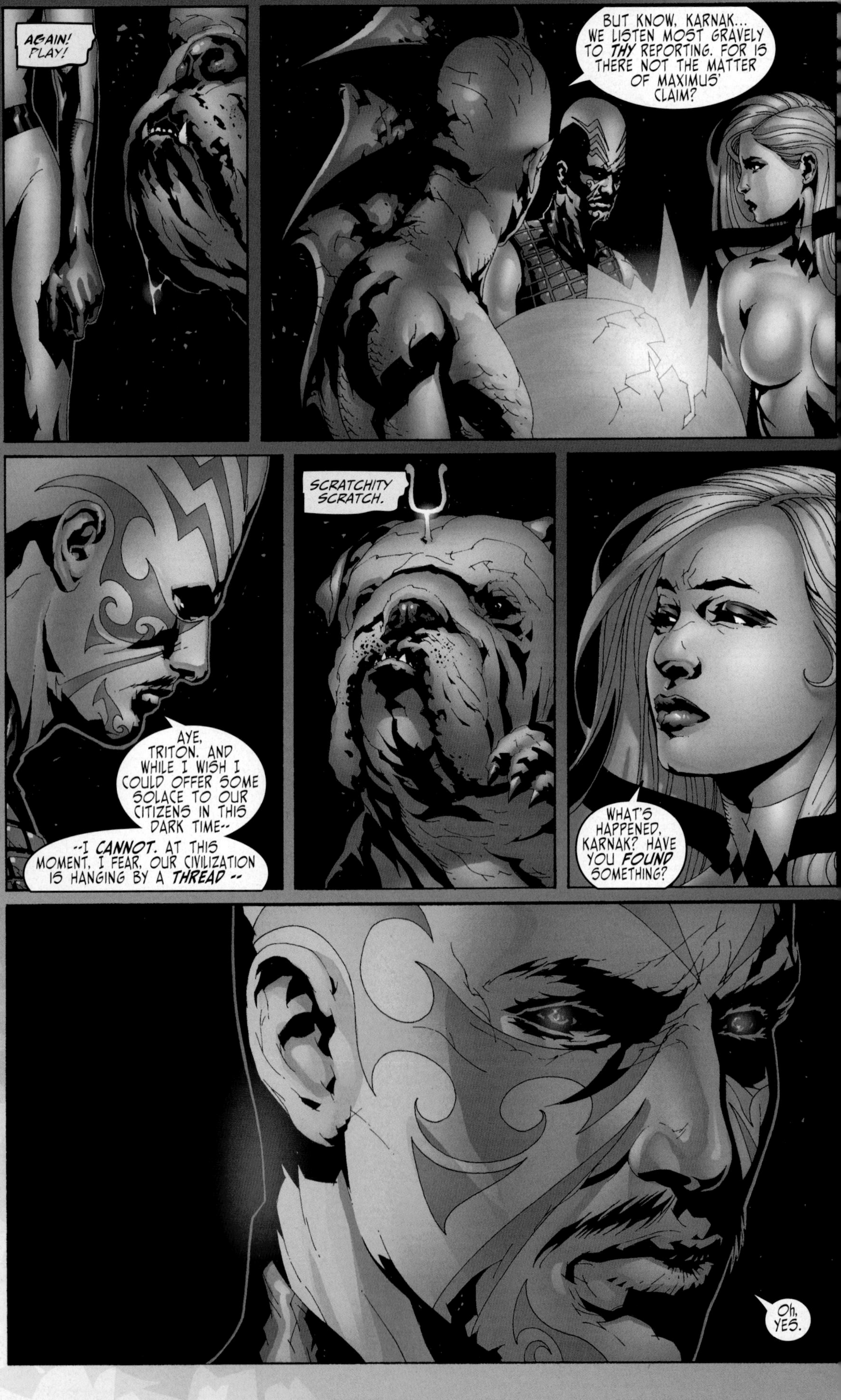
AGAIN! PLAY!
BUT KNOW, KARNAK... WE LISTEN MOST GRAVELY TO THY REPORTING. FOR IS THERE NOT THE MATTER OF MAXIMUS' CLAIM?
AYE, TRITON. AND WHILE I WISH I COULD OFFER SOME SOLACE TO OUR CITIZENS IN THIS DARK TIME--
--I CANNOT. AT THIS MOMENT, I FEAR, OUR CIVILIZATION IS HANGING BY A THREAD --
SCRATCHITY SCRATCH.
WHAT'S HAPPENED, KARNAK? HAVE YOU FOUND SOMETHING?
Oh, YES.

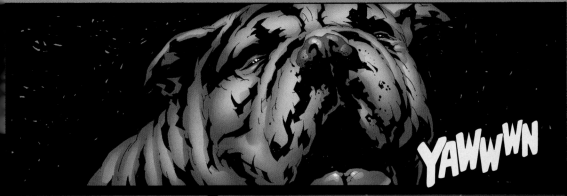

YAWWWN

"I SUSPECTED MAXIMUS' CLAIM OF A FAULT LINE NEAR ATTILAN TO BE SIMPLY THE RAVINGS OF A MADMAN. NEVERTHELESS, THIS MORNING, I PILOTED AN ANTIGRAV TO A VANTAGE POINT HIGH ABOVE THE CITY.

"NOTHING COULD HAVE PREPARED ME FOR WHAT I SAW..."

"THE FLAW IS THERE, JUST AS MAXIMUS SAID IT WOULD BE. AND IT'S *WEAKER* THAN WE COULD POSSIBLY HAVE IMAGINED."

"I SUSPECT A DIRECT HIT WILL SEND ATLANTIS ONCE AGAIN INTO DRAMATIC UPHEAVAL, SIMILAR TO THAT WHICH CONSIGNED THE ISLAND TO THE WAVES CENTURIES AGO."

THE SIMPLE TRUTH IS THIS: THE IMPACT OF ONE HUMAN SHELL MAY BE ENOUGH TO SINK US BELOW THE WAVES.

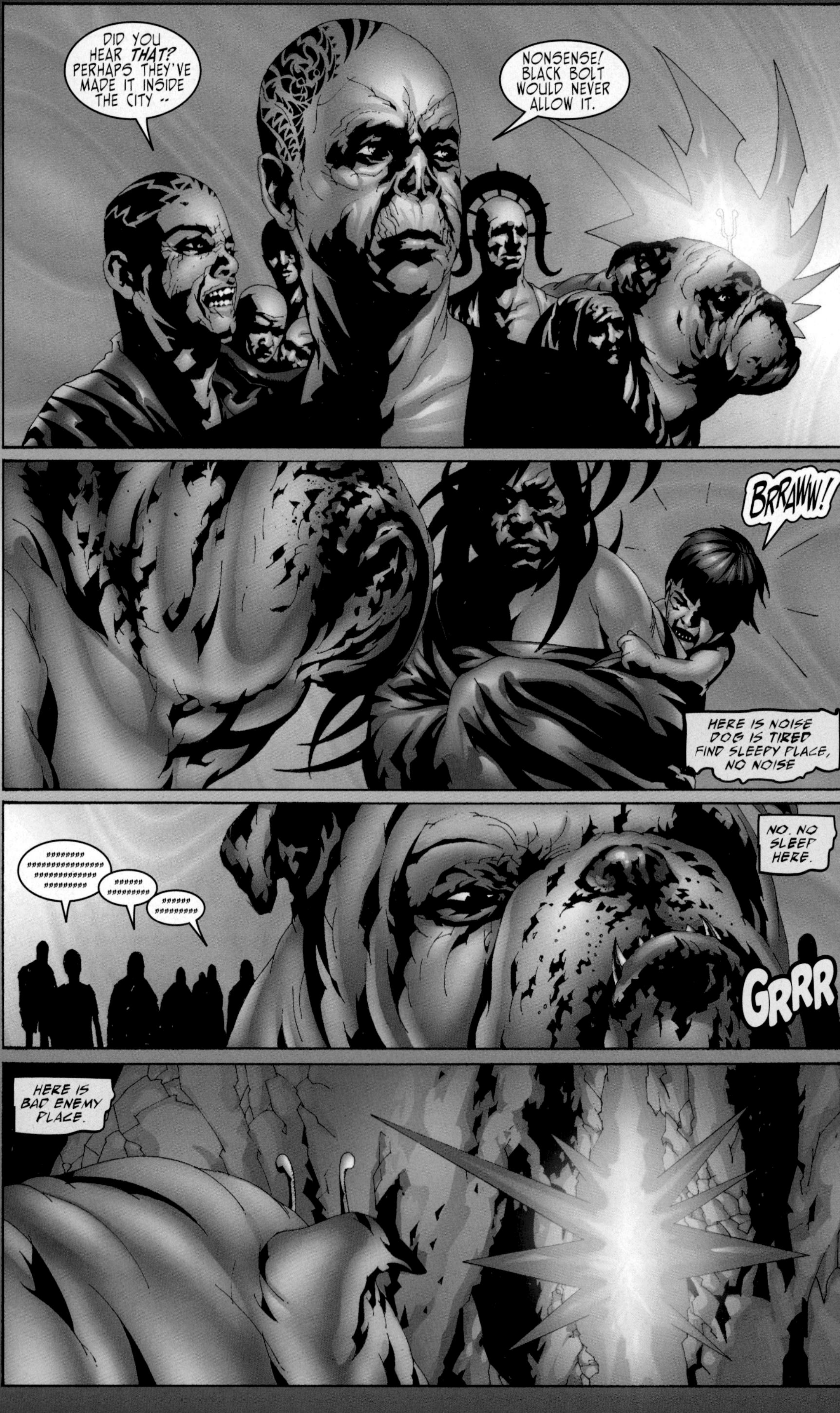
DID YOU HEAR THAT? PERHAPS THEY'VE MADE IT INSIDE THE CITY --
NONSENSE! BLACK BOLT WOULD NEVER ALLOW IT.
BRRAWW!
HERE IS NOISE
DOG IS TIRED
FIND SLEEPY PLACE, NO NOISE
NO. NO SLEEP HERE.
GRRR
HERE IS BAD ENEMY PLACE.

CENTRAL CITY CONTROL

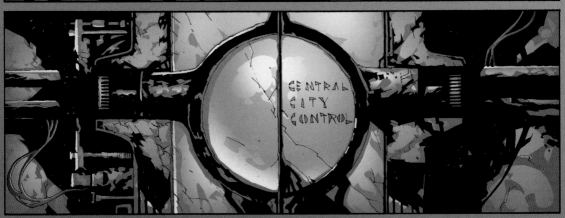

COMFY, DARLING?

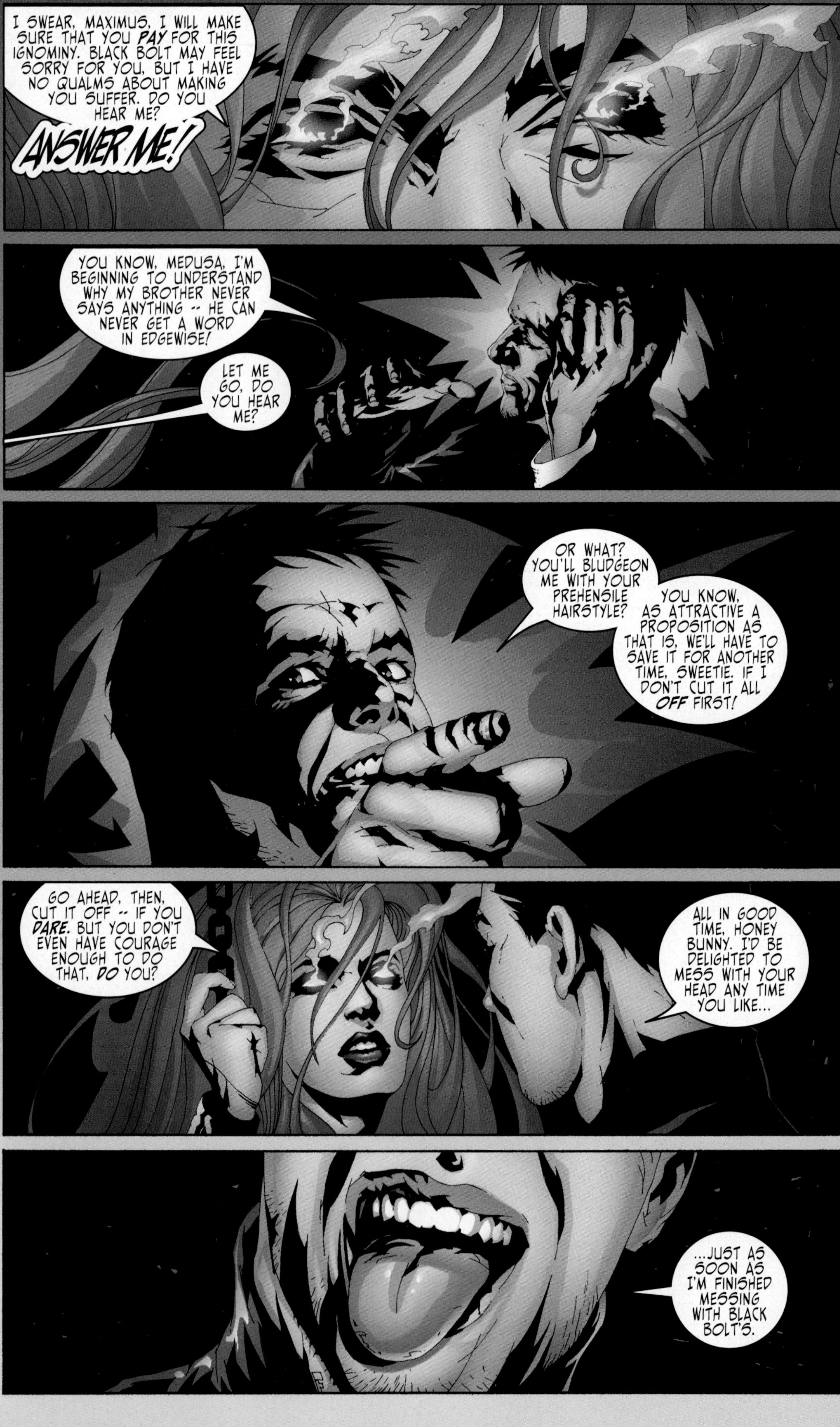
I SWEAR, MAXIMUS, I WILL MAKE SURE THAT YOU *PAY* FOR THIS IGNOMINY. BLACK BOLT MAY FEEL SORRY FOR YOU, BUT I HAVE NO QUALMS ABOUT MAKING YOU SUFFER. DO YOU HEAR ME?
ANSWER ME!
YOU KNOW, MEDUSA, I'M BEGINNING TO UNDERSTAND WHY MY BROTHER NEVER SAYS ANYTHING -- HE CAN NEVER GET A WORD IN EDGEWISE!
LET ME GO, DO YOU HEAR ME?
OR WHAT? YOU'LL BLUDGEON ME WITH YOUR PREHENSILE HAIRSTYLE?
YOU KNOW, AS ATTRACTIVE A PROPOSITION AS THAT IS, WE'LL HAVE TO SAVE IT FOR ANOTHER TIME, SWEETIE. IF I DON'T CUT IT ALL *OFF* FIRST!
GO AHEAD, THEN, CUT IT OFF -- IF YOU *DARE*. BUT YOU DON'T EVEN HAVE COURAGE ENOUGH TO DO THAT, *DO* YOU?
ALL IN GOOD TIME, HONEY BUNNY. I'D BE DELIGHTED TO MESS WITH YOUR HEAD ANY TIME YOU LIKE...
...JUST AS SOON AS I'M FINISHED MESSING WITH BLACK BOLT'S.

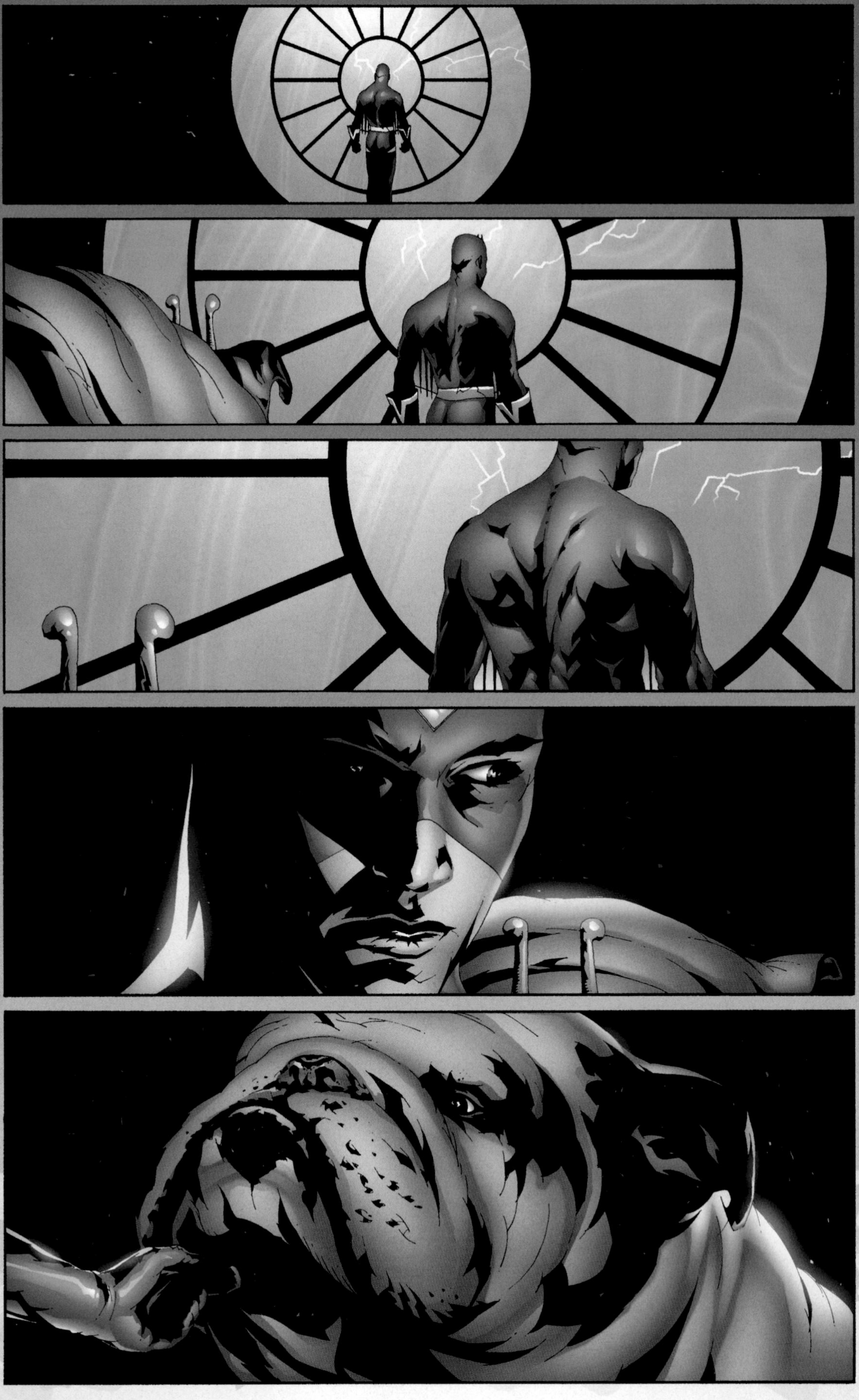

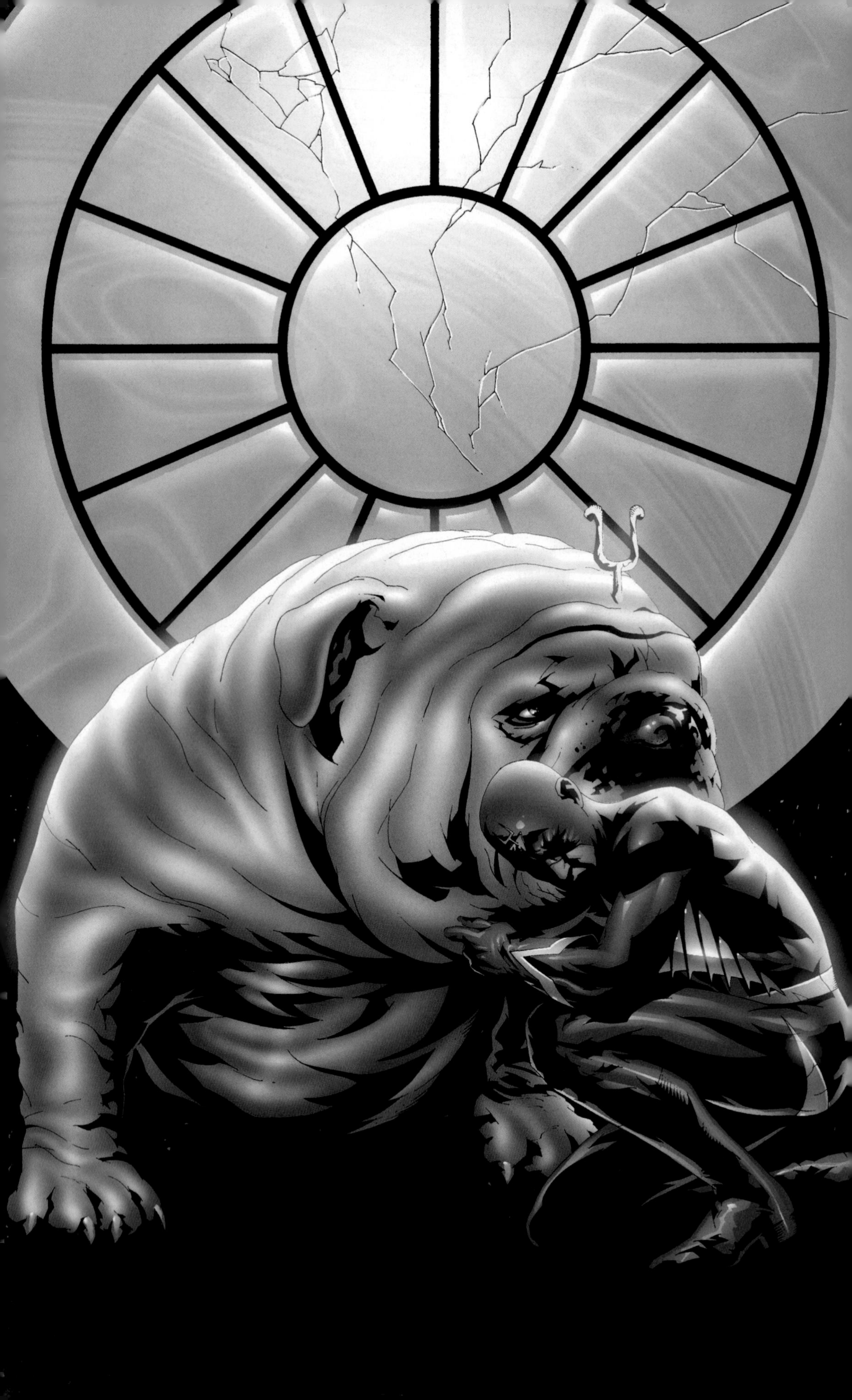

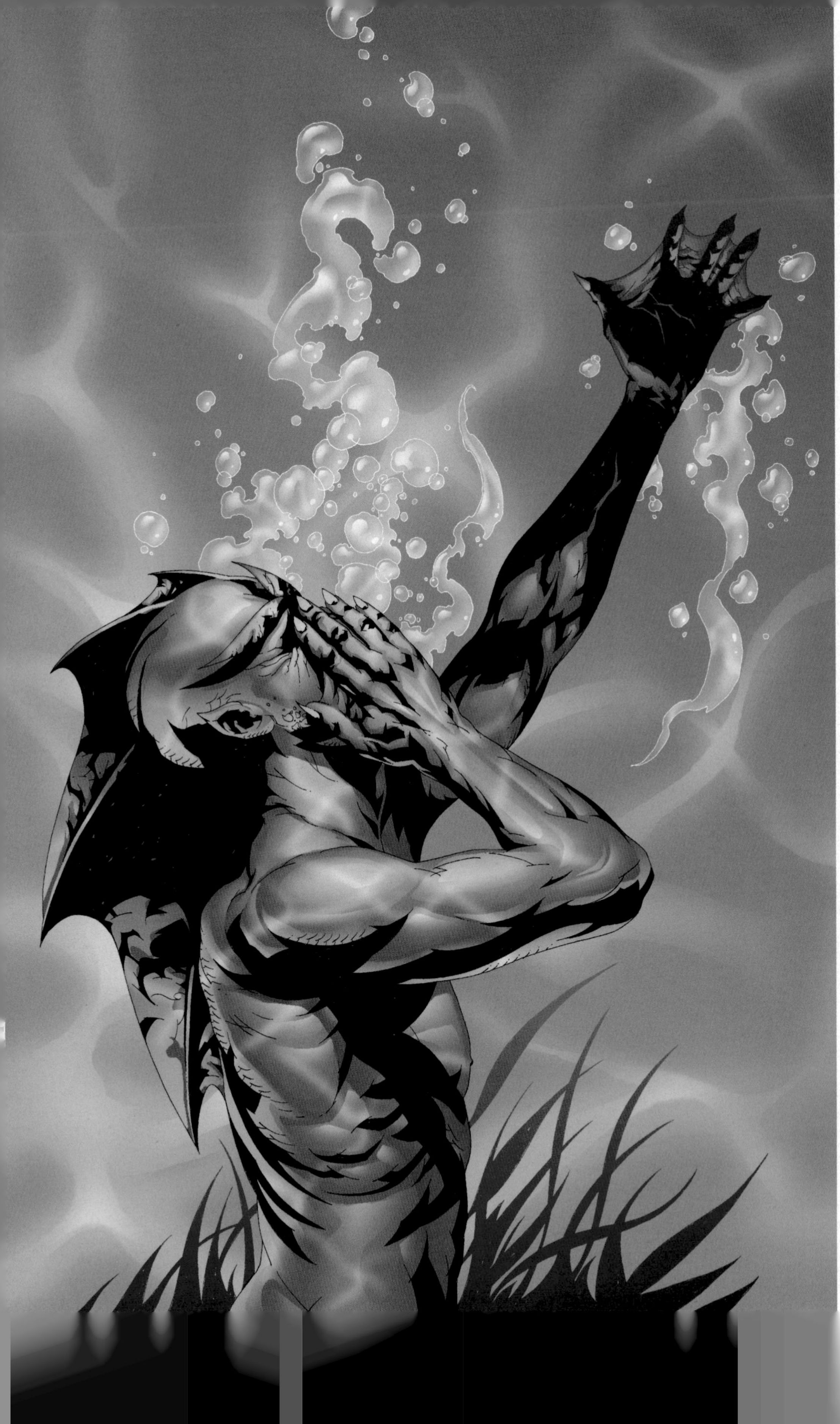

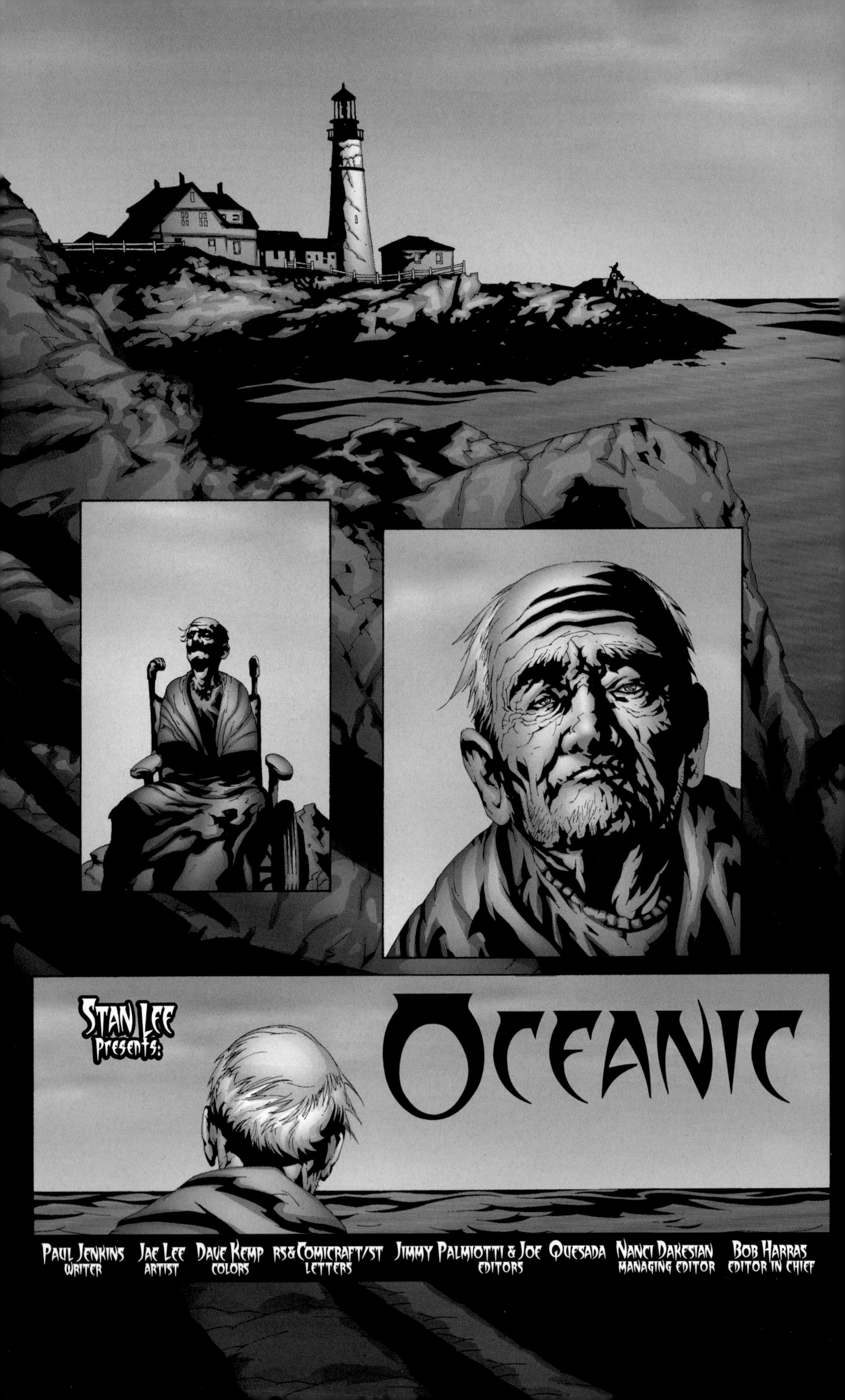

STAN LEE presents:
OCEANIC
PAUL JENKINS WRITER
JAE LEE ARTIST
DAVE KEMP COLORS
RS&COMICRAFT/ST LETTERS
JIMMY PALMIOTTI & JOE QUESADA EDITORS
NANCI DAKESIAN MANAGING EDITOR
BOB HARRAS EDITOR IN CHIEF

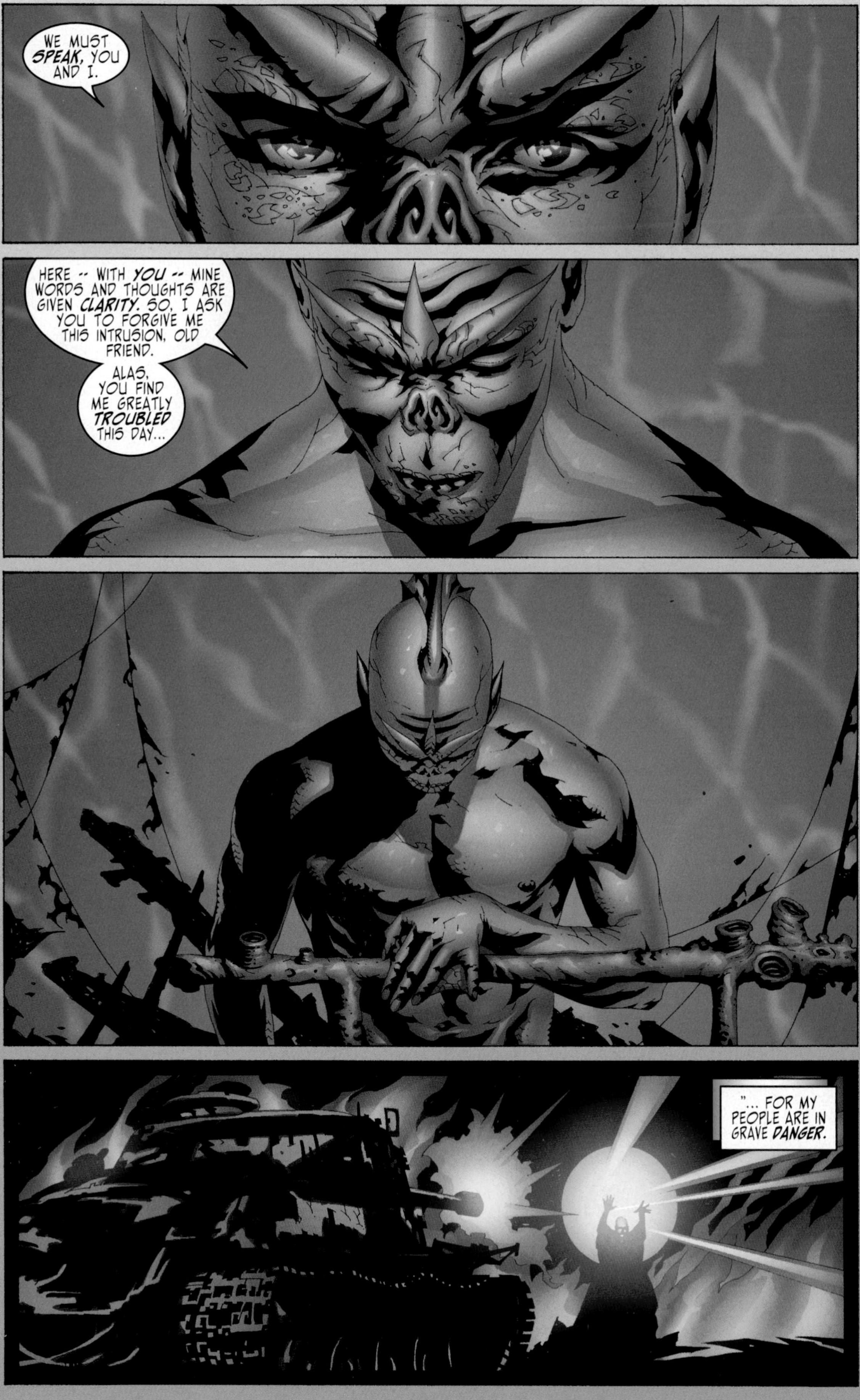
WE MUST SPEAK, YOU AND I.
HERE -- WITH YOU -- MINE WORDS AND THOUGHTS ARE GIVEN CLARITY. SO, I ASK YOU TO FORGIVE ME THIS INTRUSION, OLD FRIEND.
ALAS, YOU FIND ME GREATLY TROUBLED THIS DAY...
"... FOR MY PEOPLE ARE IN GRAVE DANGER.

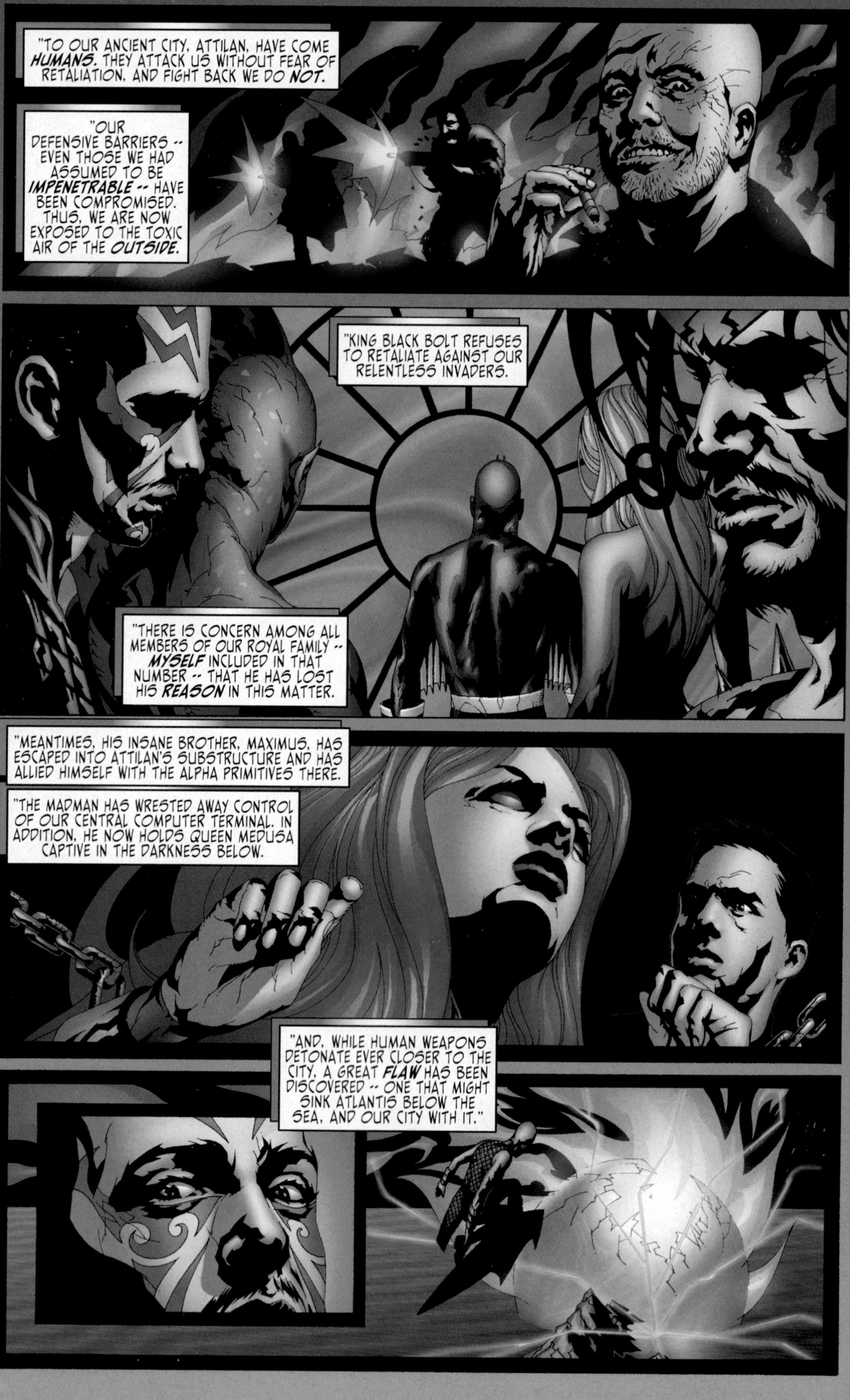
"TO OUR ANCIENT CITY, ATTILAN, HAVE COME HUMANS. THEY ATTACK US WITHOUT FEAR OF RETALIATION, AND FIGHT BACK WE DO NOT.
"OUR DEFENSIVE BARRIERS -- EVEN THOSE WE HAD ASSUMED TO BE IMPENETRABLE -- HAVE BEEN COMPROMISED. THUS, WE ARE NOW EXPOSED TO THE TOXIC AIR OF THE OUTSIDE.
"KING BLACK BOLT REFUSES TO RETALIATE AGAINST OUR RELENTLESS INVADERS.
"THERE IS CONCERN AMONG ALL MEMBERS OF OUR ROYAL FAMILY -- MYSELF INCLUDED IN THAT NUMBER -- THAT HE HAS LOST HIS REASON IN THIS MATTER.
"MEANTIMES, HIS INSANE BROTHER, MAXIMUS, HAS ESCAPED INTO ATTILAN'S SUBSTRUCTURE AND HAS ALLIED HIMSELF WITH THE ALPHA PRIMITIVES THERE.
"THE MADMAN HAS WRESTED AWAY CONTROL OF OUR CENTRAL COMPUTER TERMINAL. IN ADDITION, HE NOW HOLDS QUEEN MEDUSA CAPTIVE IN THE DARKNESS BELOW.
"AND, WHILE HUMAN WEAPONS DETONATE EVER CLOSER TO THE CITY, A GREAT FLAW HAS BEEN DISCOVERED -- ONE THAT MIGHT SINK ATLANTIS BELOW THE SEA, AND OUR CITY WITH IT."

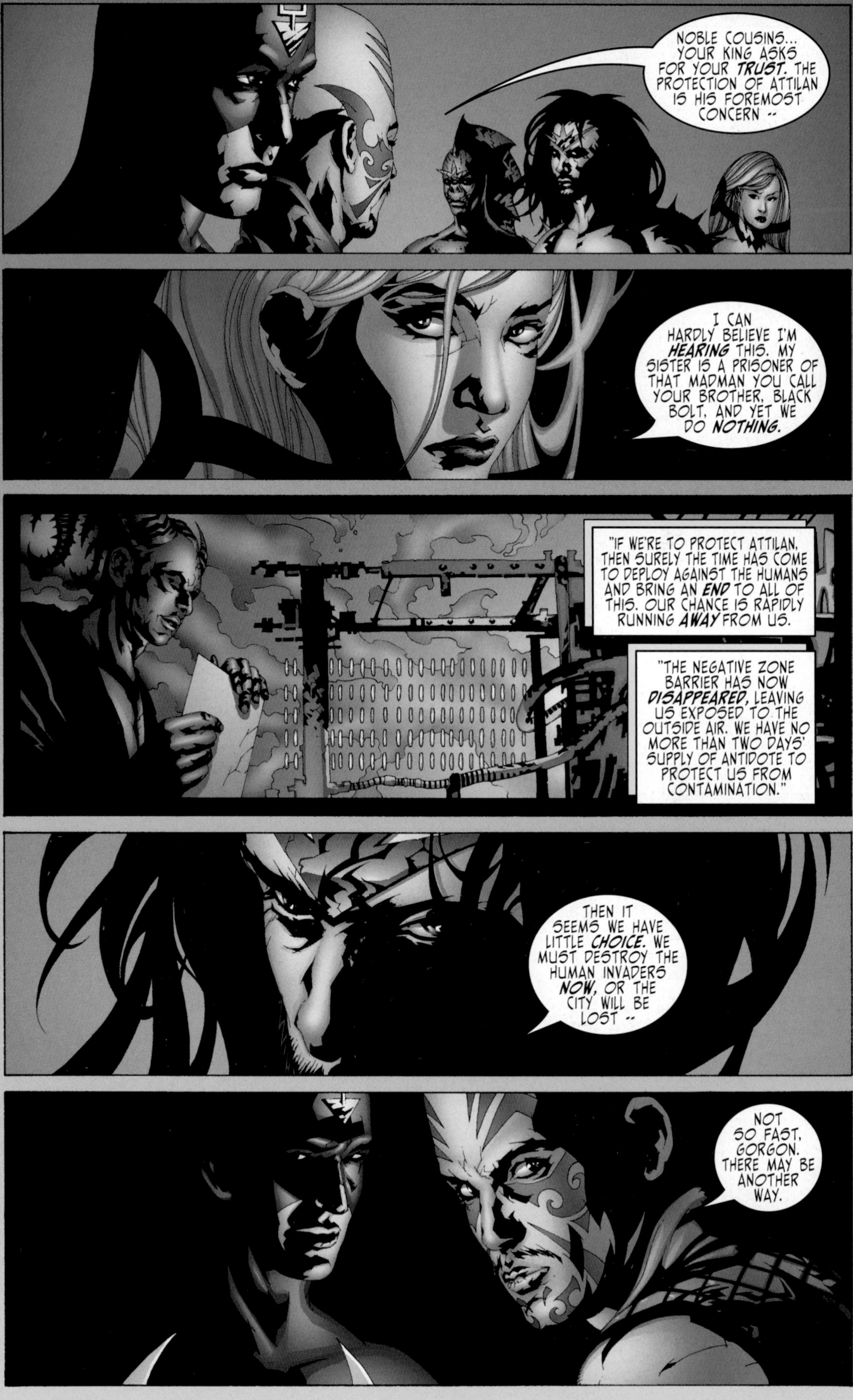
NOBLE COUSINS... YOUR KING ASKS FOR YOUR **TRUST**. THE PROTECTION OF ATTILAN IS HIS FOREMOST CONCERN --
I CAN HARDLY BELIEVE I'M **HEARING** THIS. MY SISTER IS A PRISONER OF THAT MADMAN YOU CALL YOUR BROTHER, BLACK BOLT, AND YET WE DO **NOTHING**.
"IF WE'RE TO PROTECT ATTILAN, THEN SURELY THE TIME HAS COME TO DEPLOY AGAINST THE HUMANS AND BRING AN **END** TO ALL OF THIS. OUR CHANCE IS RAPIDLY RUNNING **AWAY** FROM US.
"THE NEGATIVE ZONE BARRIER HAS NOW **DISAPPEARED**, LEAVING US EXPOSED TO THE OUTSIDE AIR. WE HAVE NO MORE THAN TWO DAYS' SUPPLY OF ANTIDOTE TO PROTECT US FROM CONTAMINATION."
THEN IT SEEMS WE HAVE LITTLE **CHOICE**. WE MUST DESTROY THE HUMAN INVADERS **NOW**, OR THE CITY WILL BE LOST --
NOT SO FAST, GORGON. THERE MAY BE ANOTHER WAY.

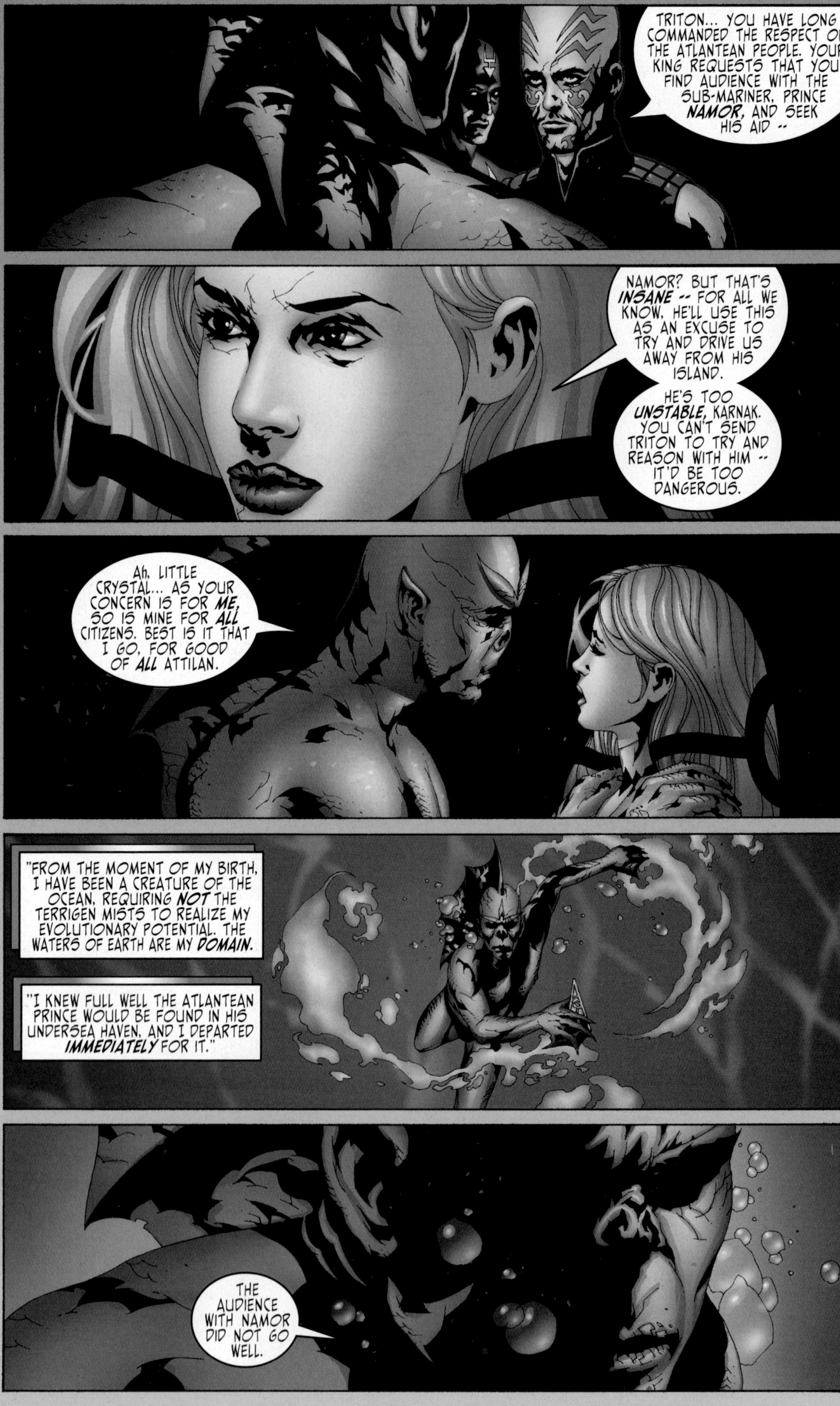
TRITON... YOU HAVE LONG COMMANDED THE RESPECT OF THE ATLANTEAN PEOPLE. YOUR KING REQUESTS THAT YOU FIND AUDIENCE WITH THE SUB-MARINER, PRINCE NAMOR, AND SEEK HIS AID --
NAMOR? BUT THAT'S INSANE -- FOR ALL WE KNOW, HE'LL USE THIS AS AN EXCUSE TO TRY AND DRIVE US AWAY FROM HIS ISLAND.
HE'S TOO UNSTABLE, KARNAK. YOU CAN'T SEND TRITON TO TRY AND REASON WITH HIM -- IT'D BE TOO DANGEROUS.
Ah, LITTLE CRYSTAL... AS YOUR CONCERN IS FOR ME, SO IS MINE FOR ALL CITIZENS. BEST IS IT THAT I GO, FOR GOOD OF ALL ATTILAN.
"FROM THE MOMENT OF MY BIRTH, I HAVE BEEN A CREATURE OF THE OCEAN, REQUIRING NOT THE TERRIGEN MISTS TO REALIZE MY EVOLUTIONARY POTENTIAL. THE WATERS OF EARTH ARE MY DOMAIN.
"I KNEW FULL WELL THE ATLANTEAN PRINCE WOULD BE FOUND IN HIS UNDERSEA HAVEN, AND I DEPARTED IMMEDIATELY FOR IT."
THE AUDIENCE WITH NAMOR DID NOT GO WELL.

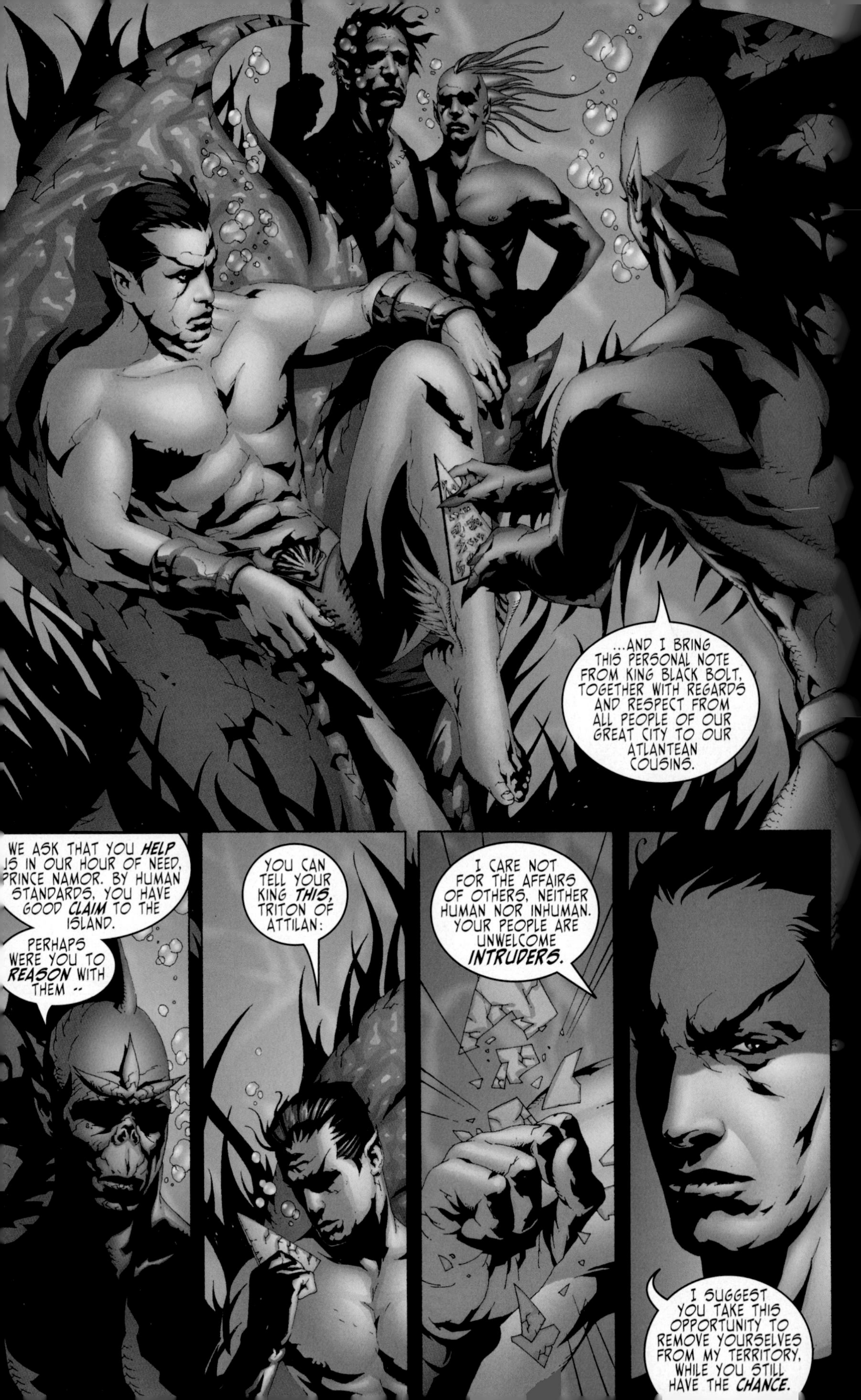
...AND I BRING THIS PERSONAL NOTE FROM KING BLACK BOLT, TOGETHER WITH REGARDS AND RESPECT FROM ALL PEOPLE OF OUR GREAT CITY TO OUR ATLANTEAN COUSINS.
WE ASK THAT YOU HELP US IN OUR HOUR OF NEED, PRINCE NAMOR. BY HUMAN STANDARDS, YOU HAVE GOOD CLAIM TO THE ISLAND.
PERHAPS WERE YOU TO REASON WITH THEM --
YOU CAN TELL YOUR KING THIS, TRITON OF ATTILAN:
I CARE NOT FOR THE AFFAIRS OF OTHERS, NEITHER HUMAN NOR INHUMAN. YOUR PEOPLE ARE UNWELCOME INTRUDERS.
I SUGGEST YOU TAKE THIS OPPORTUNITY TO REMOVE YOURSELVES FROM MY TERRITORY, WHILE YOU STILL HAVE THE CHANCE.

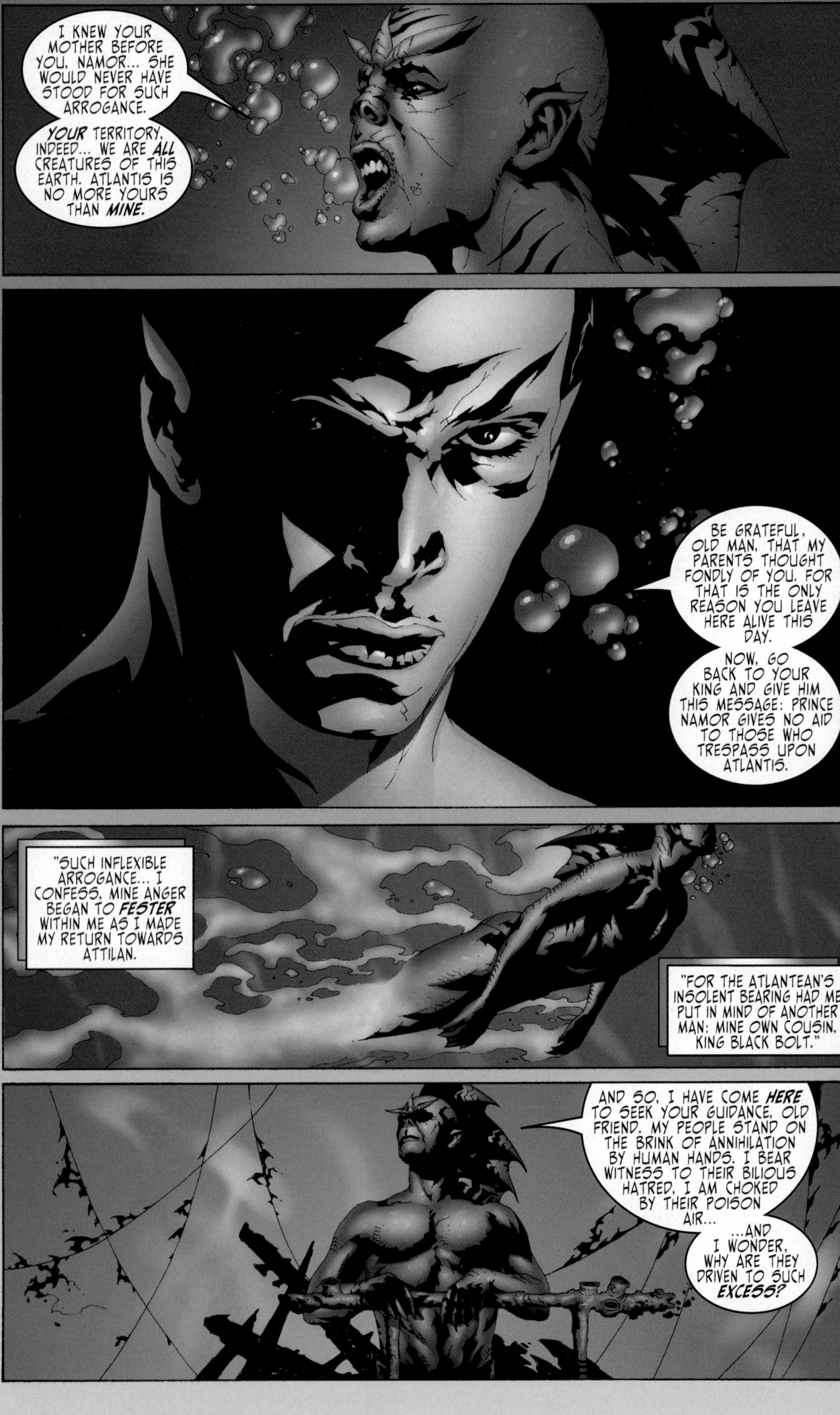
I KNEW YOUR MOTHER BEFORE YOU, NAMOR... SHE WOULD NEVER HAVE STOOD FOR SUCH ARROGANCE.
YOUR TERRITORY, INDEED... WE ARE ALL CREATURES OF THIS EARTH. ATLANTIS IS NO MORE YOURS THAN MINE.
BE GRATEFUL, OLD MAN, THAT MY PARENTS THOUGHT FONDLY OF YOU. FOR THAT IS THE ONLY REASON YOU LEAVE HERE ALIVE THIS DAY.
NOW, GO BACK TO YOUR KING AND GIVE HIM THIS MESSAGE: PRINCE NAMOR GIVES NO AID TO THOSE WHO TRESPASS UPON ATLANTIS.
"SUCH INFLEXIBLE ARROGANCE... I CONFESS, MINE ANGER BEGAN TO FESTER WITHIN ME AS I MADE MY RETURN TOWARDS ATTILAN.
"FOR THE ATLANTEAN'S INSOLENT BEARING HAD ME PUT IN MIND OF ANOTHER MAN: MINE OWN COUSIN, KING BLACK BOLT."
AND SO, I HAVE COME HERE TO SEEK YOUR GUIDANCE, OLD FRIEND. MY PEOPLE STAND ON THE BRINK OF ANNIHILATION BY HUMAN HANDS. I BEAR WITNESS TO THEIR BILIOUS HATRED, I AM CHOKED BY THEIR POISON AIR...
...AND I WONDER, WHY ARE THEY DRIVEN TO SUCH EXCESS?

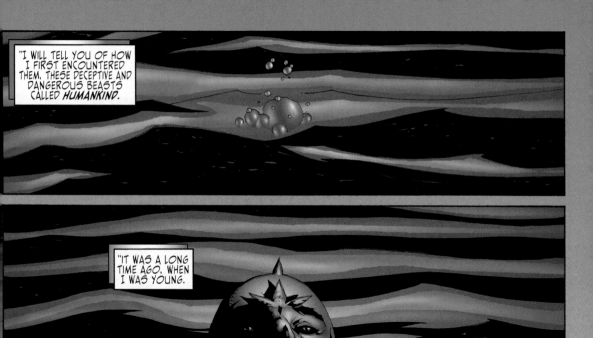

"I WILL TELL YOU OF HOW I FIRST ENCOUNTERED THEM, THESE DECEPTIVE AND DANGEROUS BEASTS CALLED *HUMANKIND.*"

"IT WAS A LONG TIME AGO. WHEN I WAS YOUNG."

"IT HAPPENED ON A CALM OCEAN..."

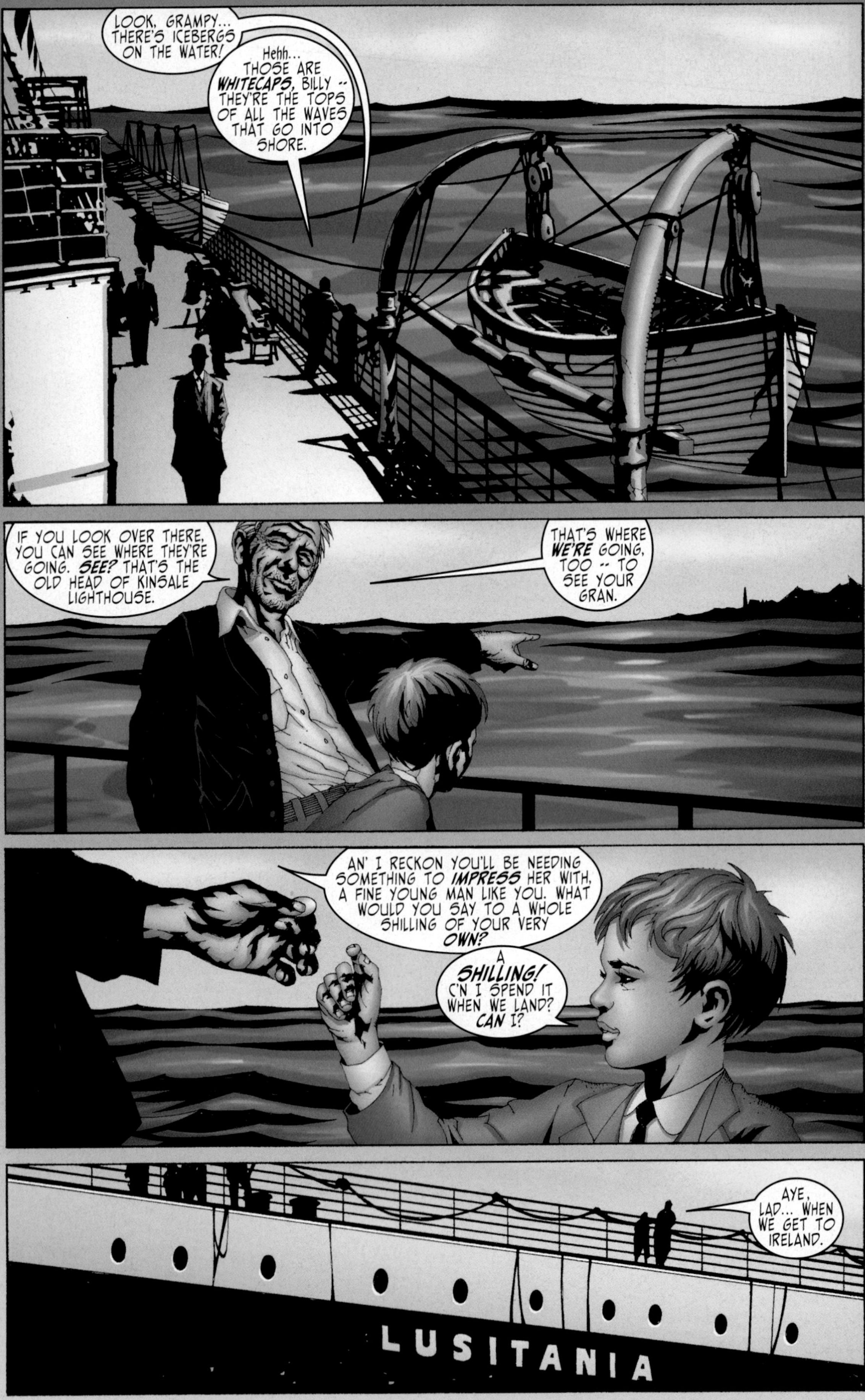
LOOK, GRAMPY... THERE'S ICEBERGS ON THE WATER!
Hehh... THOSE ARE WHITECAPS, BILLY -- THEY'RE THE TOPS OF ALL THE WAVES THAT GO INTO SHORE.
IF YOU LOOK OVER THERE, YOU CAN SEE WHERE THEY'RE GOING. SEE? THAT'S THE OLD HEAD OF KINSALE LIGHTHOUSE.
THAT'S WHERE WE'RE GOING, TOO -- TO SEE YOUR GRAN.
AN' I RECKON YOU'LL BE NEEDING SOMETHING TO IMPRESS HER WITH, A FINE YOUNG MAN LIKE YOU. WHAT WOULD YOU SAY TO A WHOLE SHILLING OF YOUR VERY OWN?
A SHILLING! C'N I SPEND IT WHEN WE LAND? CAN I?
AYE, LAD... WHEN WE GET TO IRELAND.
LUSITANIA

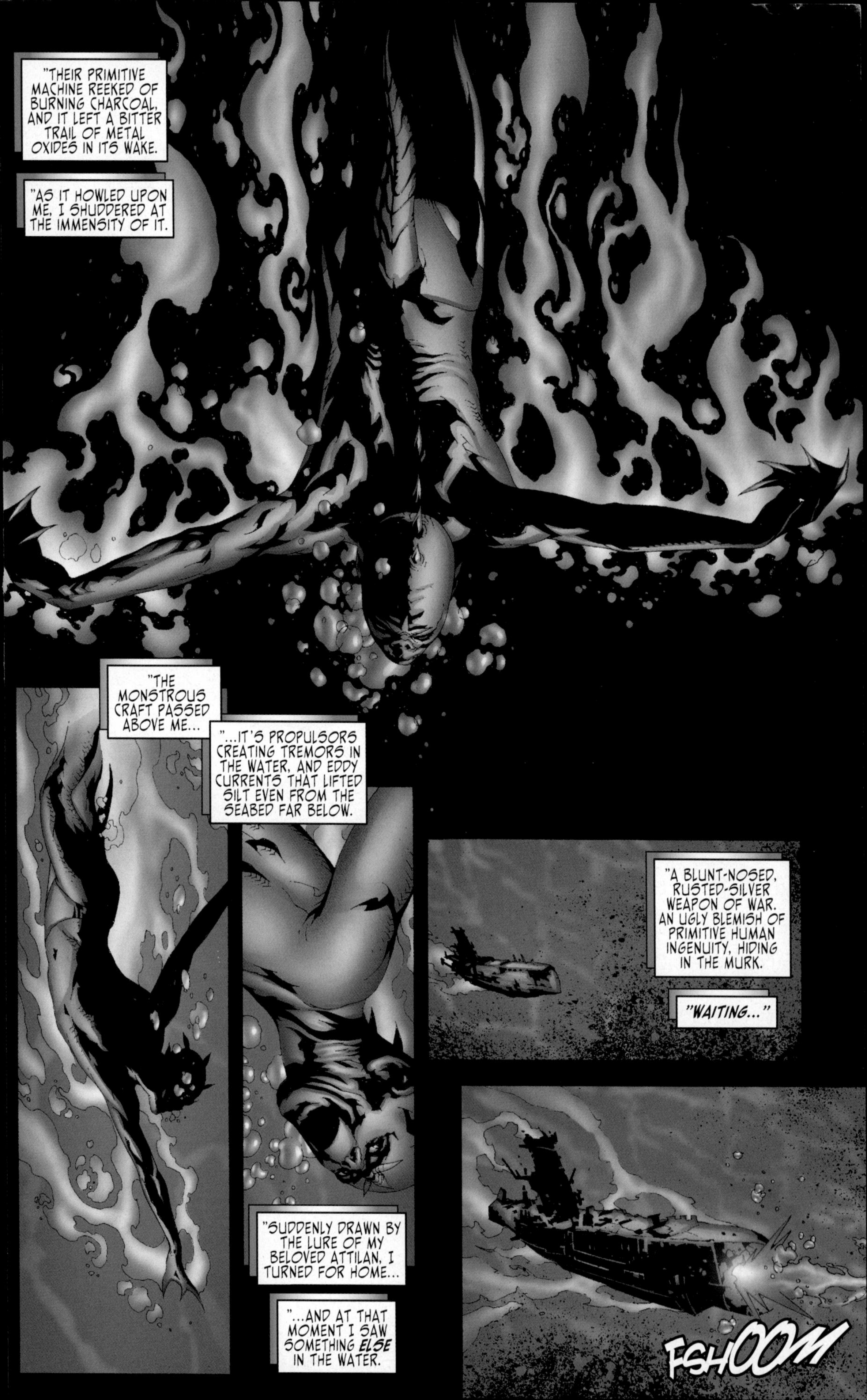
"THEIR PRIMITIVE MACHINE REEKED OF BURNING CHARCOAL, AND IT LEFT A BITTER TRAIL OF METAL OXIDES IN ITS WAKE.
"AS IT HOWLED UPON ME, I SHUDDERED AT THE IMMENSITY OF IT.
"THE MONSTROUS CRAFT PASSED ABOVE ME...
"...IT'S PROPULSORS CREATING TREMORS IN THE WATER, AND EDDY CURRENTS THAT LIFTED SILT EVEN FROM THE SEABED FAR BELOW.
"SUDDENLY DRAWN BY THE LURE OF MY BELOVED ATTILAN, I TURNED FOR HOME...
"...AND AT THAT MOMENT I SAW SOMETHING *ELSE* IN THE WATER.
"A BLUNT-NOSED, RUSTED-SILVER WEAPON OF WAR. AN UGLY BLEMISH OF PRIMITIVE HUMAN INGENUITY, HIDING IN THE MURK.
"*WAITING...*"
FSHOOM

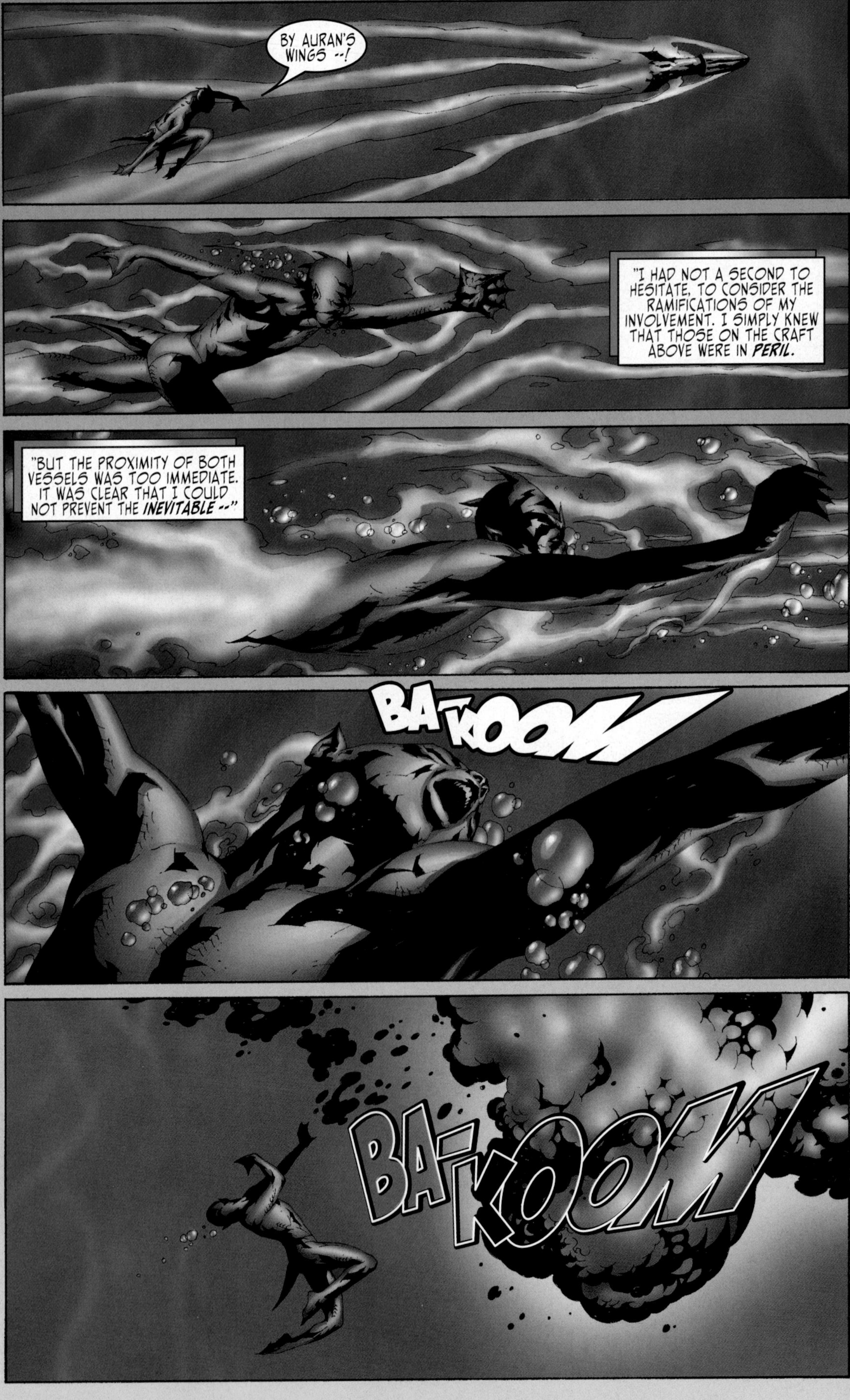
BY AURAN'S WINGS --!
"I HAD NOT A SECOND TO HESITATE, TO CONSIDER THE RAMIFICATIONS OF MY INVOLVEMENT. I SIMPLY KNEW THAT THOSE ON THE CRAFT ABOVE WERE IN PERIL.
"BUT THE PROXIMITY OF BOTH VESSELS WAS TOO IMMEDIATE. IT WAS CLEAR THAT I COULD NOT PREVENT THE INEVITABLE --"
BA-KOOM
BA-KOOM

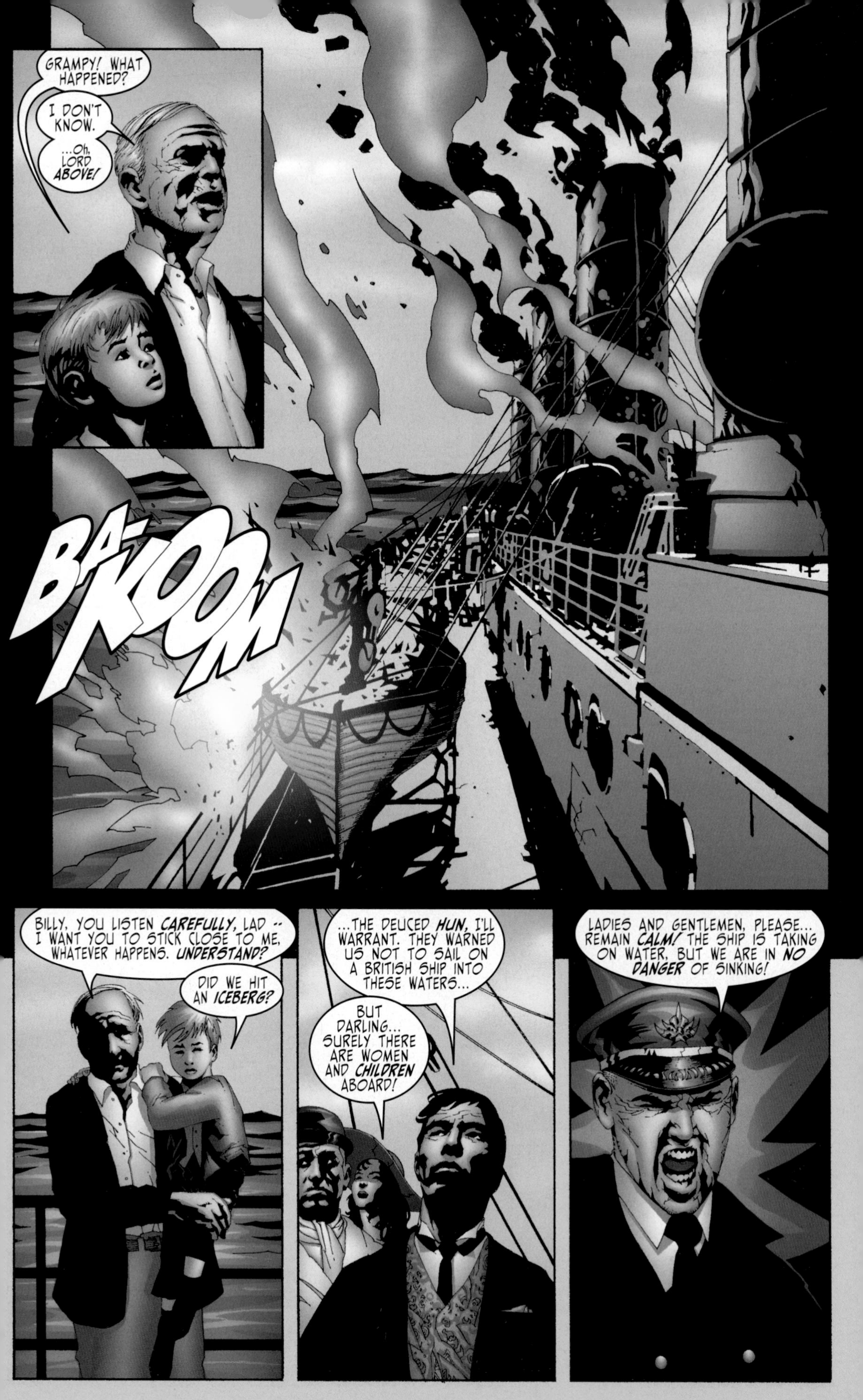
GRAMPY! WHAT HAPPENED?
I DON'T KNOW.
...Oh, LORD ABOVE!
BA-KOOOM
BILLY, YOU LISTEN CAREFULLY, LAD -- I WANT YOU TO STICK CLOSE TO ME, WHATEVER HAPPENS. UNDERSTAND?
DID WE HIT AN ICEBERG?
...THE DEUCED HUN, I'LL WARRANT. THEY WARNED US NOT TO SAIL ON A BRITISH SHIP INTO THESE WATERS...
BUT DARLING... SURELY THERE ARE WOMEN AND CHILDREN ABOARD!
LADIES AND GENTLEMEN, PLEASE... REMAIN CALM! THE SHIP IS TAKING ON WATER, BUT WE ARE IN NO DANGER OF SINKING!

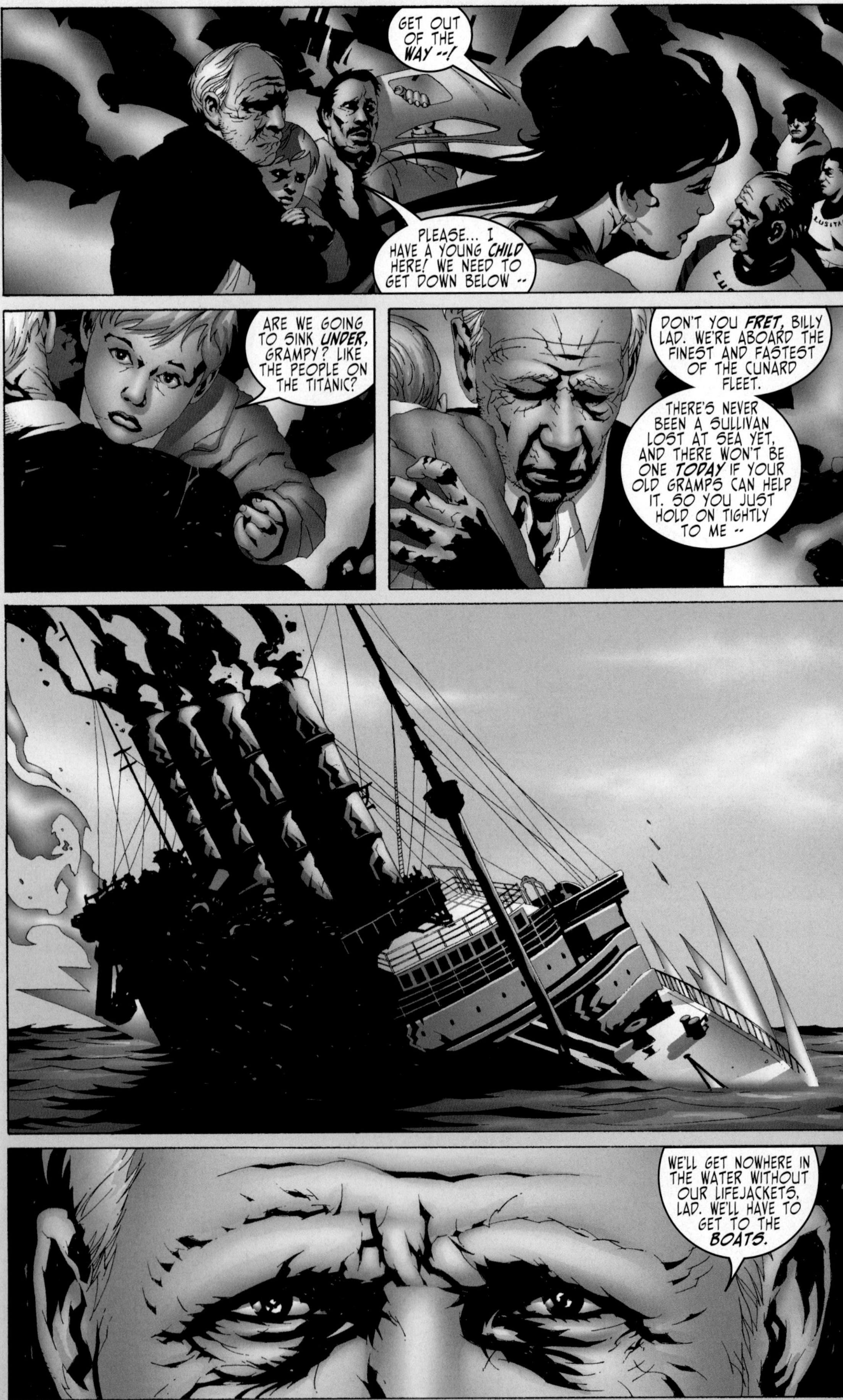
GET OUT OF THE WAY --!
PLEASE... I HAVE A YOUNG CHILD HERE! WE NEED TO GET DOWN BELOW --
LUSITANIA
ARE WE GOING TO SINK UNDER, GRAMPY? LIKE THE PEOPLE ON THE TITANIC?
DON'T YOU FRET, BILLY LAD. WE'RE ABOARD THE FINEST AND FASTEST OF THE CUNARD FLEET.
THERE'S NEVER BEEN A SULLIVAN LOST AT SEA YET, AND THERE WON'T BE ONE TODAY IF YOUR OLD GRAMPS CAN HELP IT. SO YOU JUST HOLD ON TIGHTLY TO ME --
WE'LL GET NOWHERE IN THE WATER WITHOUT OUR LIFEJACKETS, LAD. WE'LL HAVE TO GET TO THE BOATS.

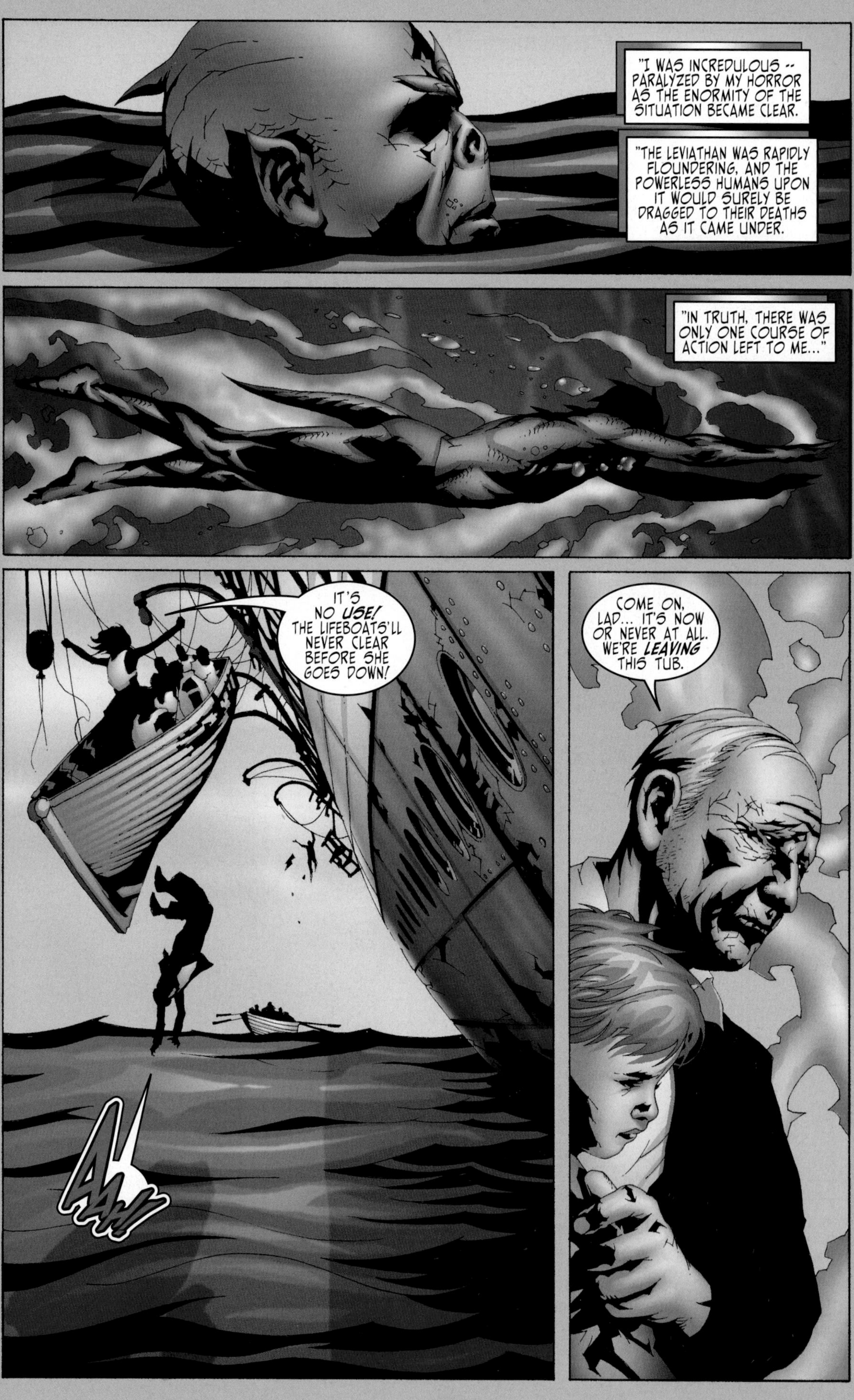
"I WAS INCREDULOUS -- PARALYZED BY MY HORROR AS THE ENORMITY OF THE SITUATION BECAME CLEAR.
"THE LEVIATHAN WAS RAPIDLY FLOUNDERING, AND THE POWERLESS HUMANS UPON IT WOULD SURELY BE DRAGGED TO THEIR DEATHS AS IT CAME UNDER.
"IN TRUTH, THERE WAS ONLY ONE COURSE OF ACTION LEFT TO ME..."
IT'S NO USE! THE LIFEBOATS'LL NEVER CLEAR BEFORE SHE GOES DOWN!
AAAH!
COME ON, LAD... IT'S NOW OR NEVER AT ALL. WE'RE LEAVING THIS TUB.

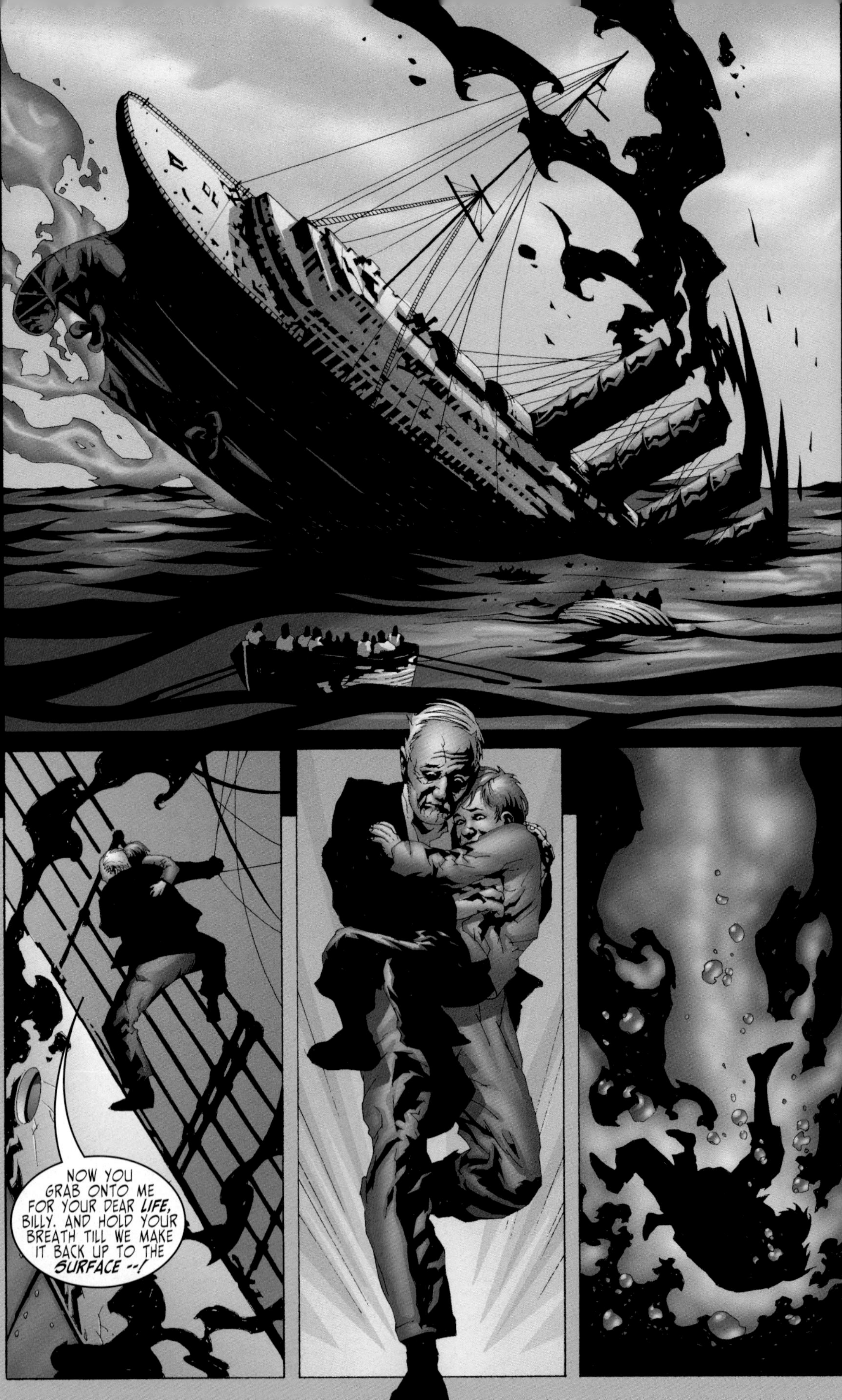
NOW YOU GRAB ONTO ME FOR YOUR DEAR LIFE, BILLY. AND HOLD YOUR BREATH TILL WE MAKE IT BACK UP TO THE SURFACE --!

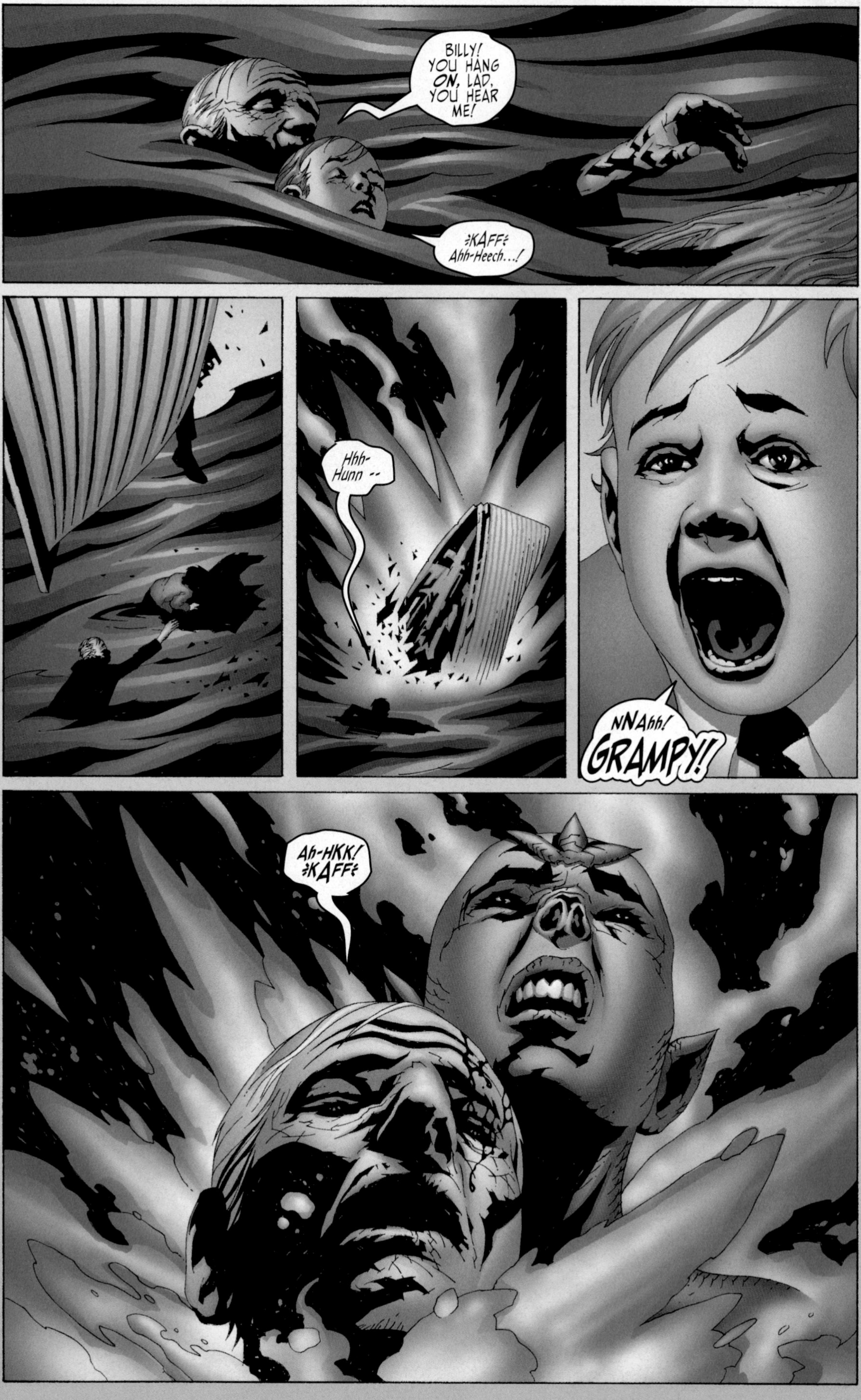

BILLY! YOU HANG ON, LAD, YOU HEAR ME!
⚡KAFF⚡ Ahh-Heech...!
Hhh-Hunn --
NNAhh! GRAMPY!!
Ah-HKK! ⚡KAFF⚡

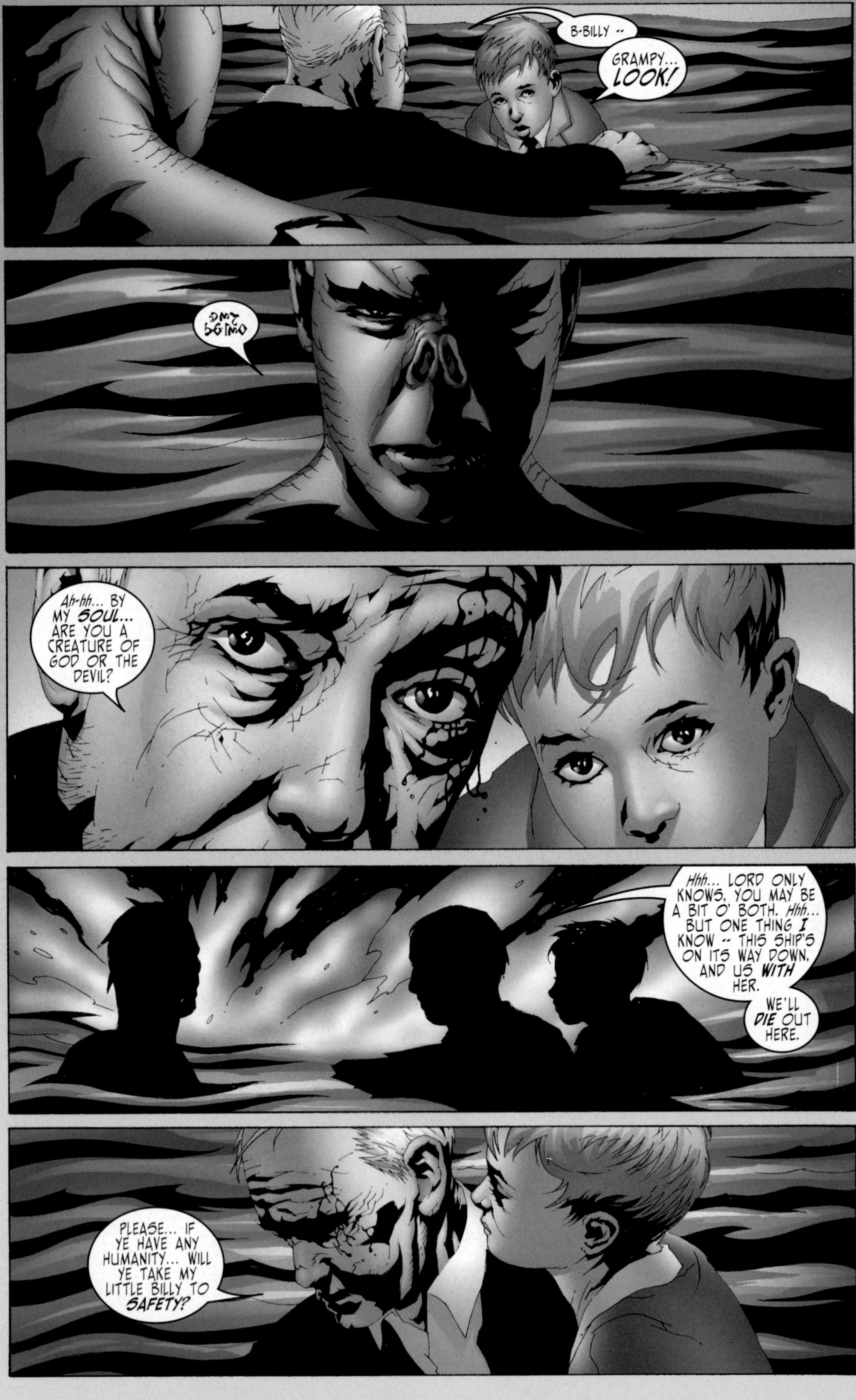
B-BILLY --
GRAMPY... LOOK!
Ah-hh... BY MY SOUL... ARE YOU A CREATURE OF GOD OR THE DEVIL?
Hhh... LORD ONLY KNOWS, YOU MAY BE A BIT O' BOTH. Hhh... BUT ONE THING I KNOW -- THIS SHIP'S ON ITS WAY DOWN, AND US WITH HER.
WE'LL DIE OUT HERE.
PLEASE... IF YE HAVE ANY HUMANITY... WILL YE TAKE MY LITTLE BILLY TO SAFETY?

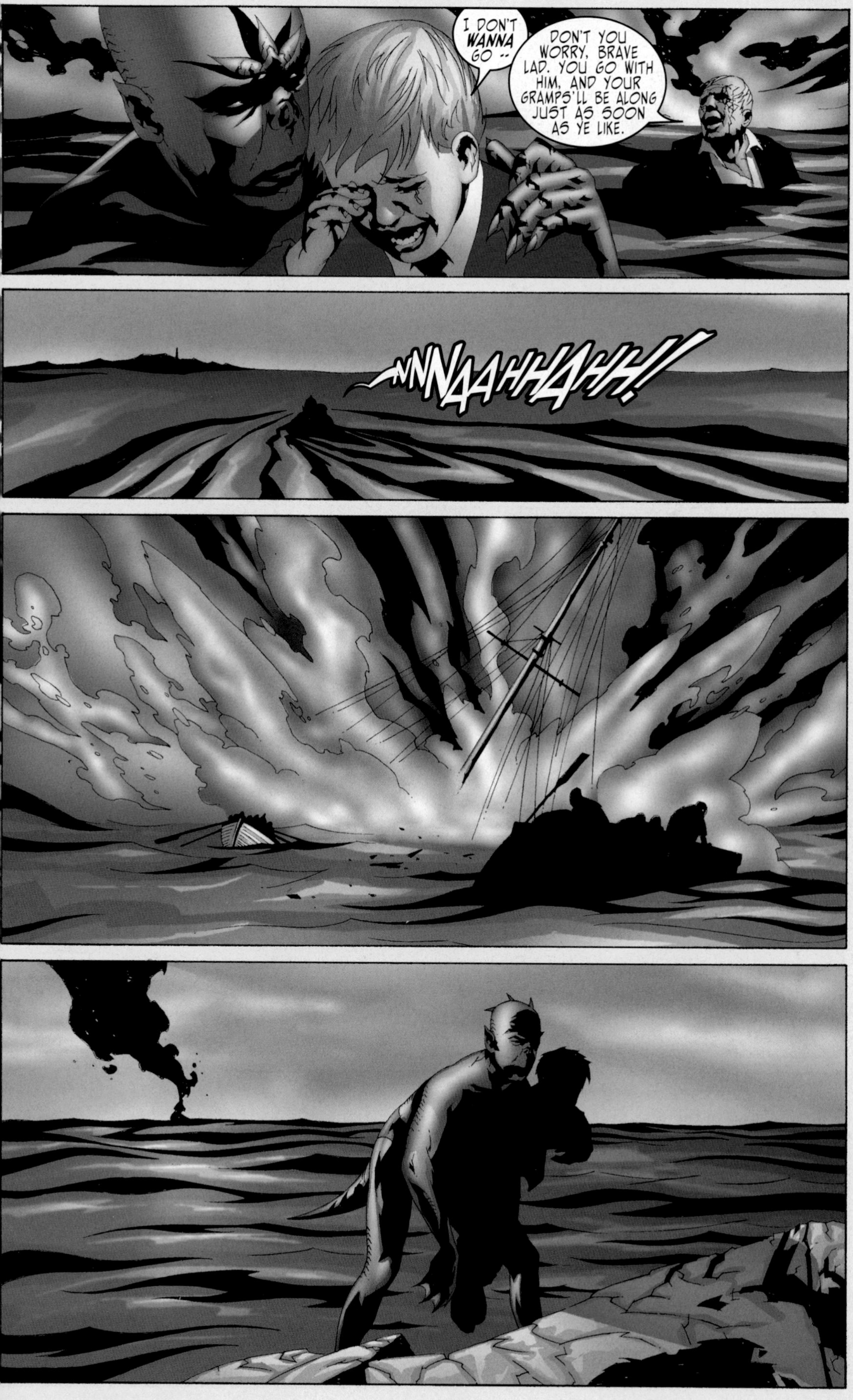
I DON'T WANNA GO --
DON'T YOU WORRY, BRAVE LAD. YOU GO WITH HIM, AND YOUR GRAMPS'LL BE ALONG JUST AS SOON AS YE LIKE.
NNNAAHHAHH!!

"I WAS *YOUNGER* THEN, AND HAD NOT THE STRENGTH TO TAKE MORE THAN ONE HUMAN TO SAFETY AT A TIME. AFTER I WAS CERTAIN THE HUMAN CHILDLING WOULD BE SAFE, I HASTENED BACK TO THE WATER AS QUICKLY AS I COULD.

"ALL FEAR OF CONTACT WITH THESE CREATURES -- ALL OF MY DISGUST AT THEIR TOXINATION OF THE WATER AND LAND --

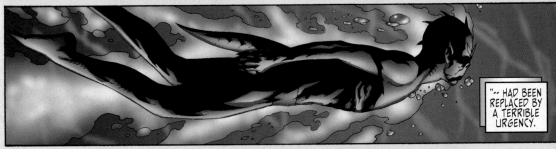

"-- HAD BEEN REPLACED BY A TERRIBLE URGENCY.

"I SAW MY BRETHREN, MY COUSINS, IN PERIL UPON THE SEA.

"BUT BY THE TIME I RETURNED, ALL THAT REMAINED OF THEM WAS DEBRIS, AND THE DISTANT CRIES OF DAMNED SOULS THAT ECHOED ACROSS THE DARK WATER.

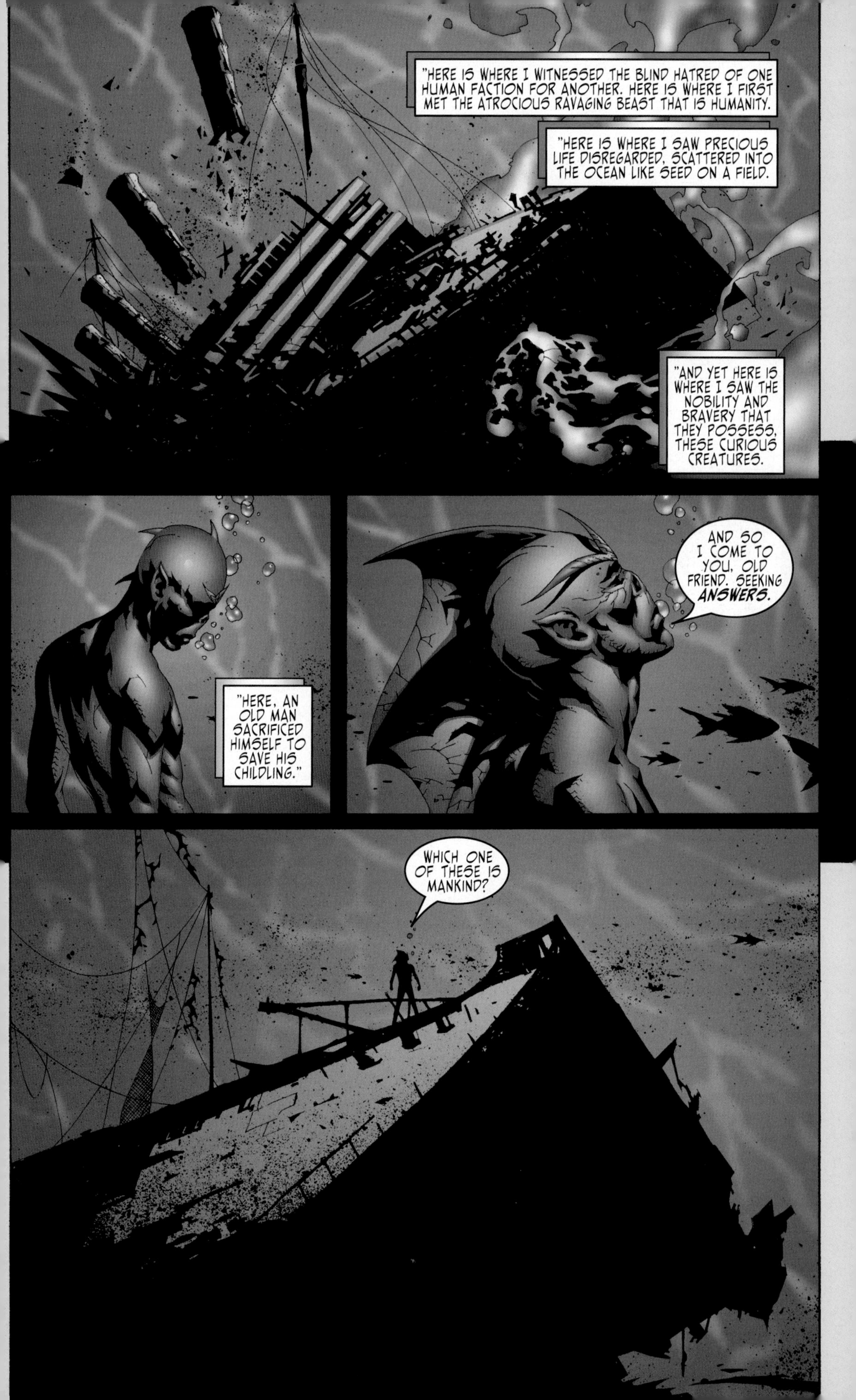
"HERE IS WHERE I WITNESSED THE BLIND HATRED OF ONE HUMAN FACTION FOR ANOTHER. HERE IS WHERE I FIRST MET THE ATROCIOUS RAVAGING BEAST THAT IS HUMANITY.
"HERE IS WHERE I SAW PRECIOUS LIFE DISREGARDED, SCATTERED INTO THE OCEAN LIKE SEED ON A FIELD.
"AND YET HERE IS WHERE I SAW THE NOBILITY AND BRAVERY THAT THEY POSSESS, THESE CURIOUS CREATURES.
"HERE, AN OLD MAN SACRIFICED HIMSELF TO SAVE HIS CHILDLING."
AND SO I COME TO YOU, OLD FRIEND. SEEKING ANSWERS.
WHICH ONE OF THESE IS MANKIND?

COME ON, YOUNG MAN... IT'S TIME TO GET YOU *INSIDE*...

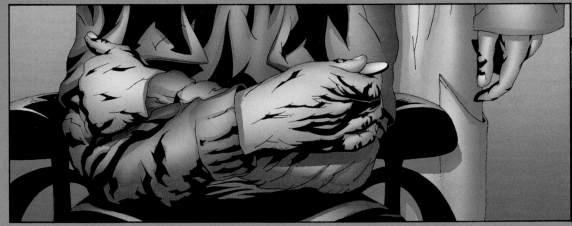

mmmh... mmuhh...

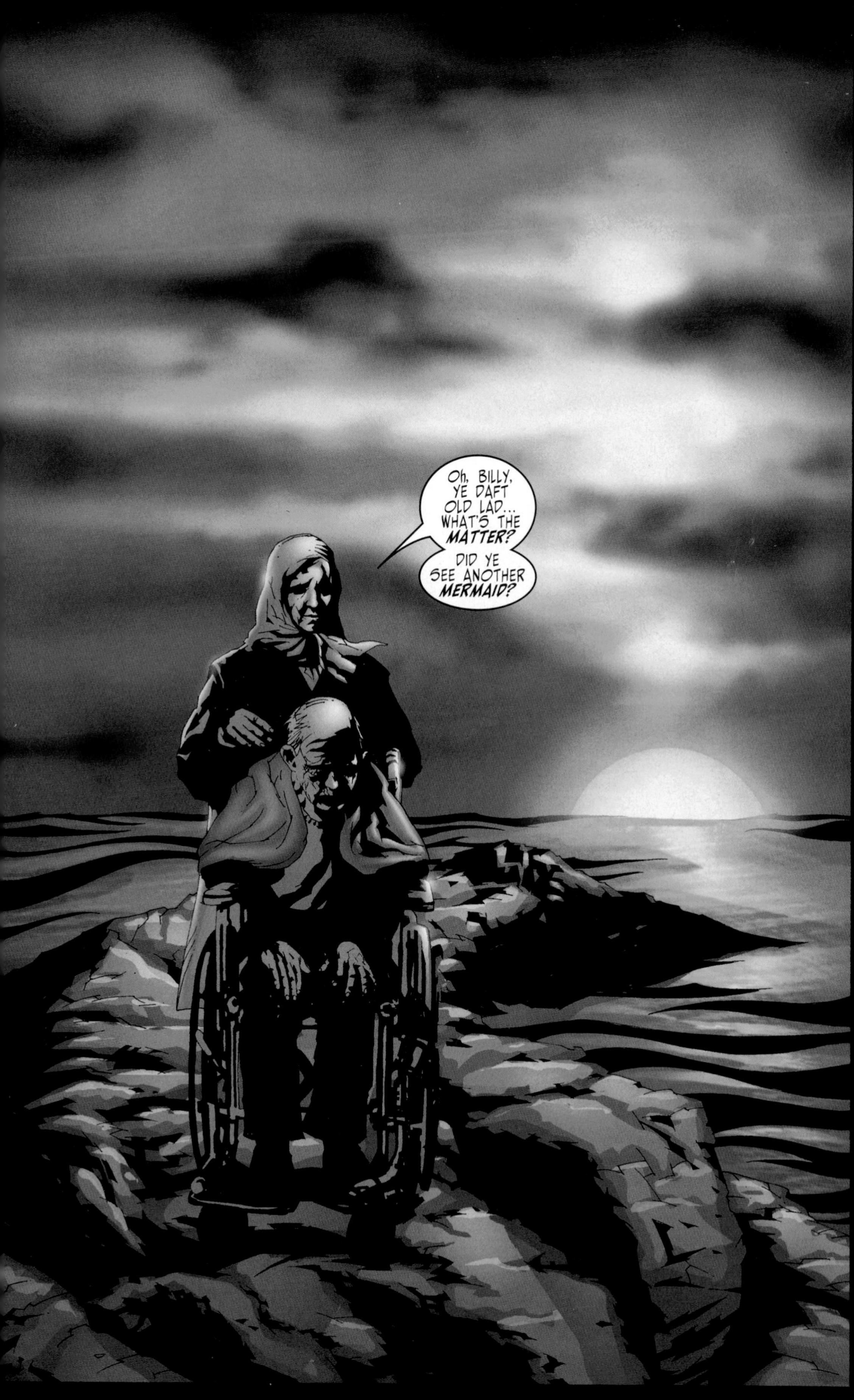
Oh, BILLY, YE DAFT OLD LAD... WHAT'S THE MATTER?
DID YE SEE ANOTHER MERMAID?

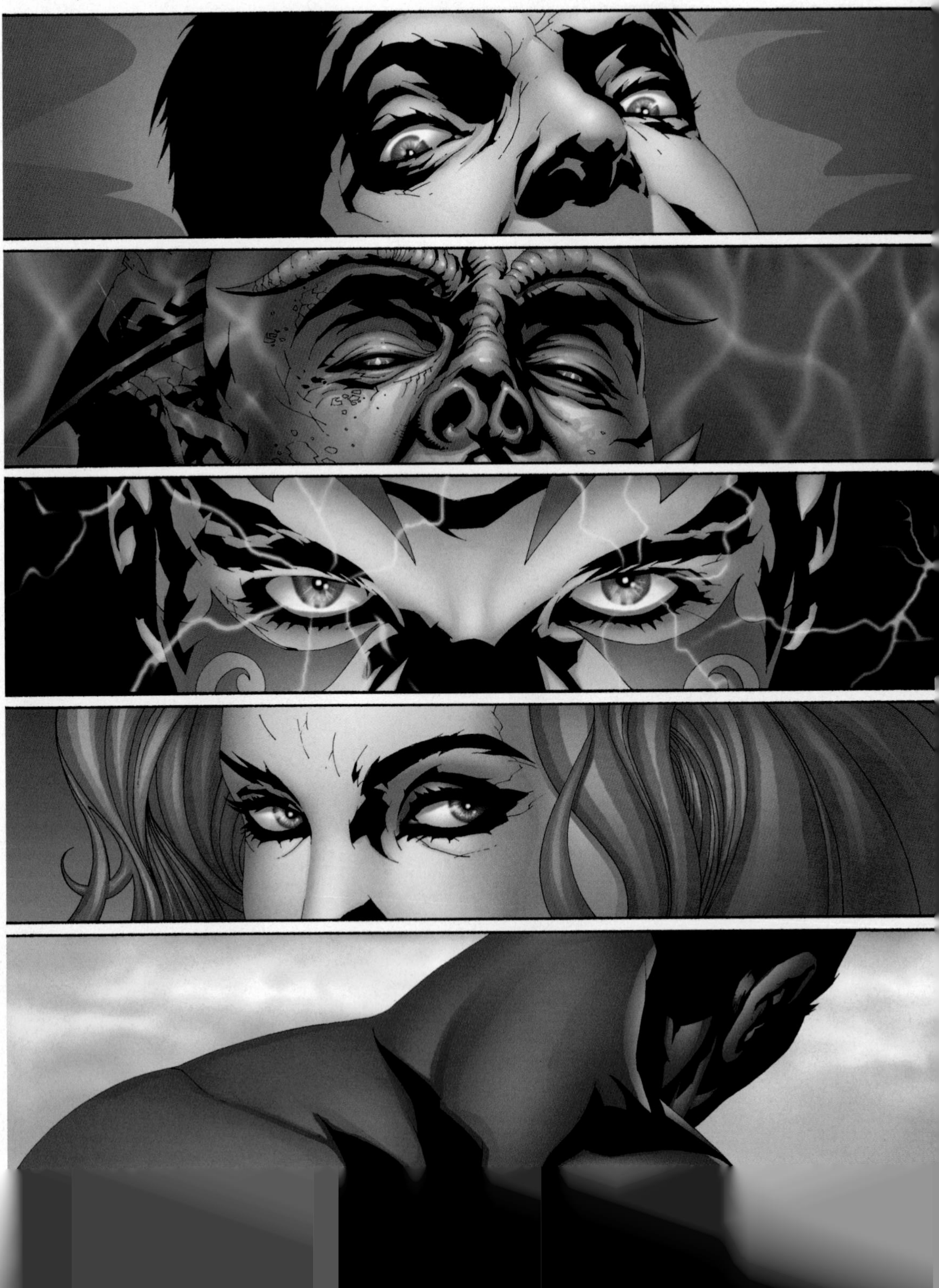

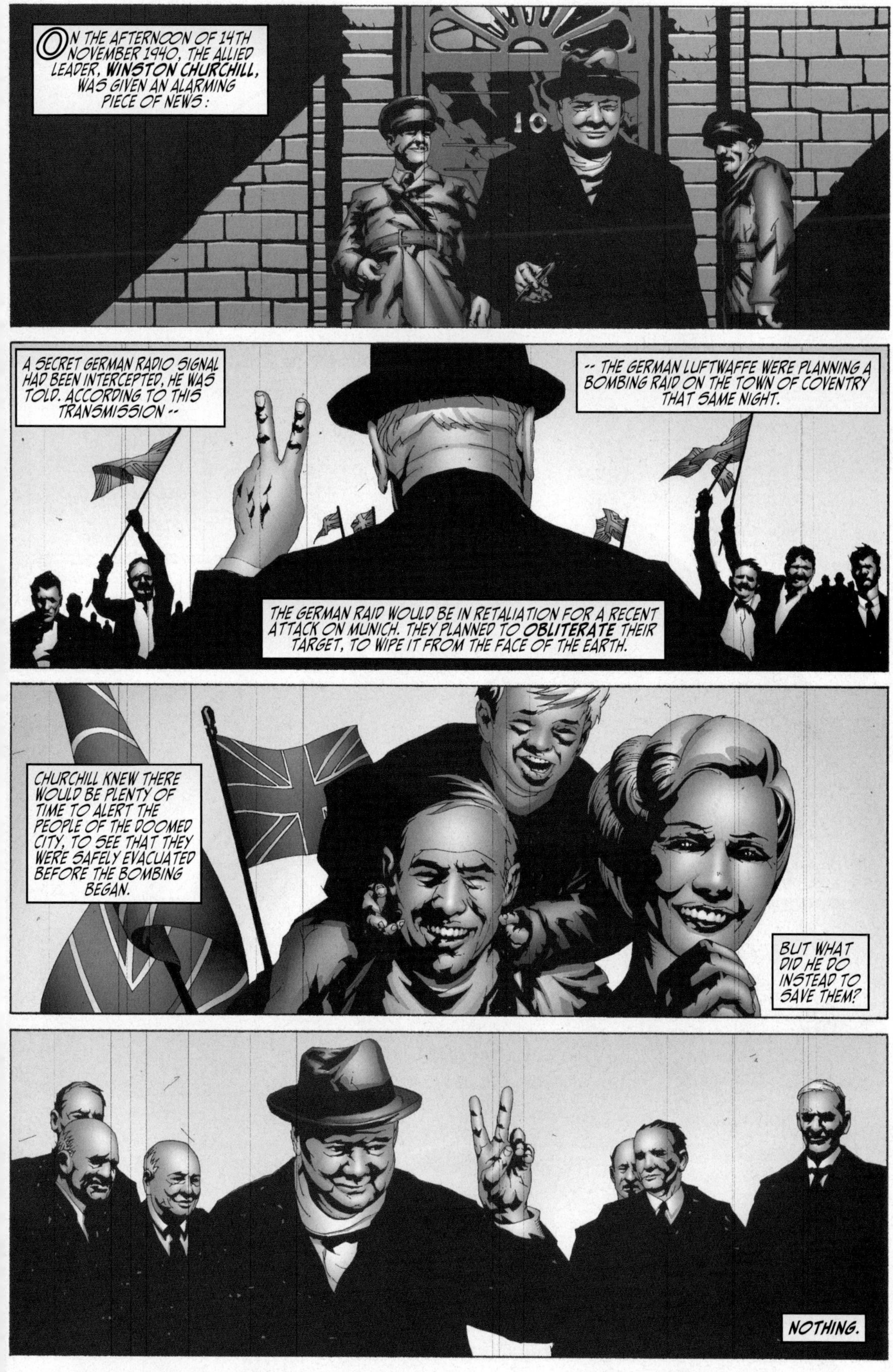
ON THE AFTERNOON OF 14TH NOVEMBER 1940, THE ALLIED LEADER, WINSTON CHURCHILL, WAS GIVEN AN ALARMING PIECE OF NEWS :
A SECRET GERMAN RADIO SIGNAL HAD BEEN INTERCEPTED, HE WAS TOLD. ACCORDING TO THIS TRANSMISSION --
-- THE GERMAN LUFTWAFFE WERE PLANNING A BOMBING RAID ON THE TOWN OF COVENTRY THAT SAME NIGHT.
THE GERMAN RAID WOULD BE IN RETALIATION FOR A RECENT ATTACK ON MUNICH. THEY PLANNED TO OBLITERATE THEIR TARGET, TO WIPE IT FROM THE FACE OF THE EARTH.
CHURCHILL KNEW THERE WOULD BE PLENTY OF TIME TO ALERT THE PEOPLE OF THE DOOMED CITY, TO SEE THAT THEY WERE SAFELY EVACUATED BEFORE THE BOMBING BEGAN.
BUT WHAT DID HE DO INSTEAD TO SAVE THEM?
NOTHING.

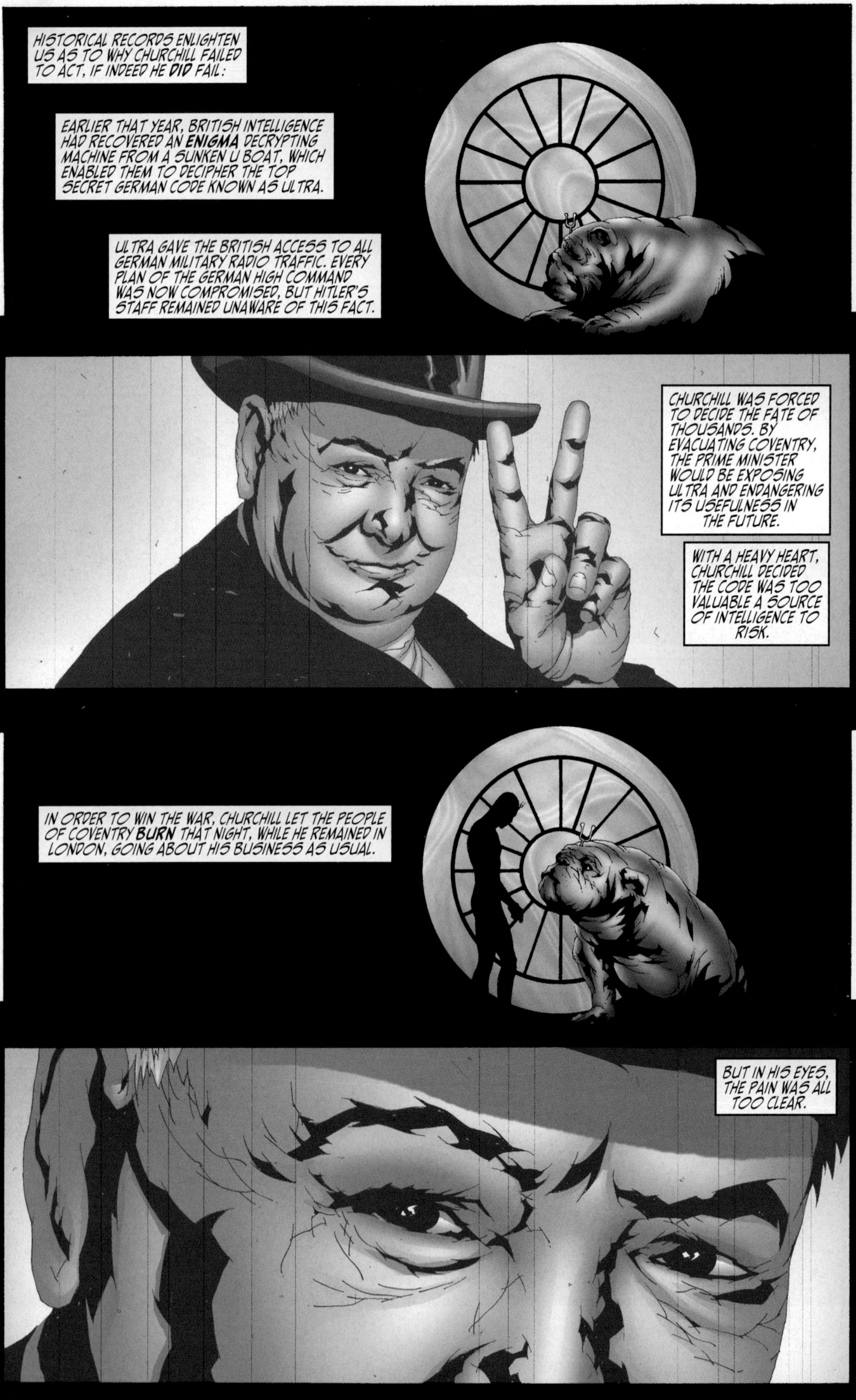
HISTORICAL RECORDS ENLIGHTEN US AS TO WHY CHURCHILL FAILED TO ACT, IF INDEED HE DID FAIL:
EARLIER THAT YEAR, BRITISH INTELLIGENCE HAD RECOVERED AN ENIGMA DECRYPTING MACHINE FROM A SUNKEN U BOAT, WHICH ENABLED THEM TO DECIPHER THE TOP SECRET GERMAN CODE KNOWN AS ULTRA.
ULTRA GAVE THE BRITISH ACCESS TO ALL GERMAN MILITARY RADIO TRAFFIC. EVERY PLAN OF THE GERMAN HIGH COMMAND WAS NOW COMPROMISED, BUT HITLER'S STAFF REMAINED UNAWARE OF THIS FACT.
CHURCHILL WAS FORCED TO DECIDE THE FATE OF THOUSANDS. BY EVACUATING COVENTRY, THE PRIME MINISTER WOULD BE EXPOSING ULTRA AND ENDANGERING ITS USEFULNESS IN THE FUTURE.
WITH A HEAVY HEART, CHURCHILL DECIDED THE CODE WAS TOO VALUABLE A SOURCE OF INTELLIGENCE TO RISK.
IN ORDER TO WIN THE WAR, CHURCHILL LET THE PEOPLE OF COVENTRY BURN THAT NIGHT, WHILE HE REMAINED IN LONDON, GOING ABOUT HIS BUSINESS AS USUAL.
BUT IN HIS EYES, THE PAIN WAS ALL TOO CLEAR.

DECADES LATER, THE INHUMAN LEADER, BLACK BOLT, FACES THE ANNIHILATION OF HIS CITY WITH THE SAME STOIC RESOLUTION.

WHILE HUMAN INVADERS ADVANCE TO THE VERY DOORS OF ATTILAN, HE ORDERS HIS DEFENSIVE TROOPS TO DO NOTHING -- THE TACTICS OF *SUICIDE*, IT SEEMS.

WHAT SECRET STRATEGIES DO BLACK BOLT'S EYES BETRAY? WHAT TURBULENT EMOTIONS ROIL UNDERNEATH HIS ENIGMATIC GAZE -- DOES HE FEEL *PAIN*, OR DESPAIR?

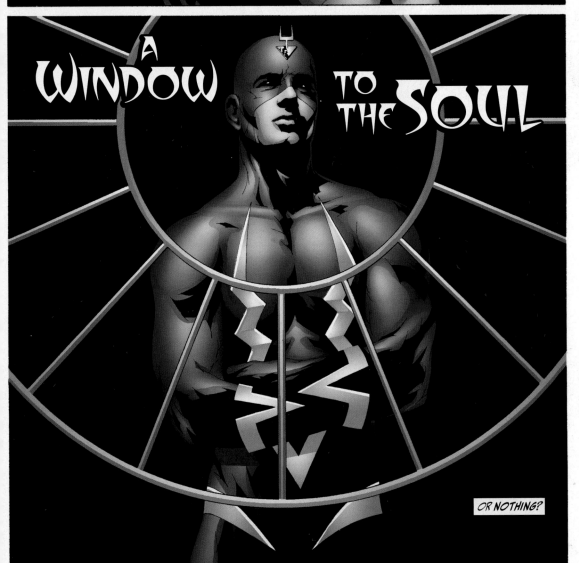

A WINDOW TO THE SOUL

OR *NOTHING?*

PAUL JENKINS
UNDERLING

JAE LEE
UNDERLING

DAVE KEMP
UNDERLING

RS & COMICRAFT/ST
UNDERLING

JOE QUESADA & JIMMY PALMIOTTI
OVERLORDS

NANCI DAKESIAN
OVERLORD

BOB HARRAS
OVERLORD

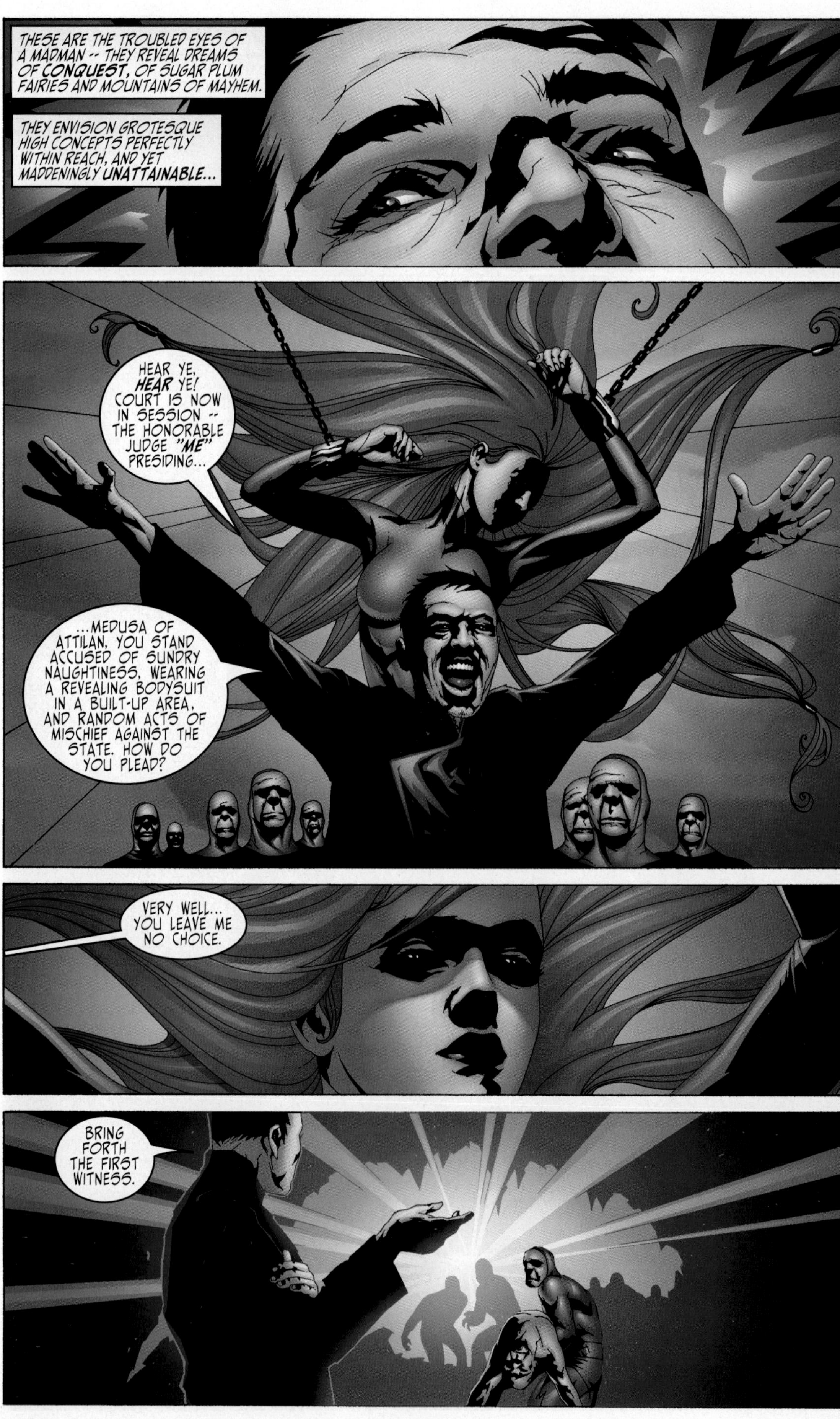
THESE ARE THE TROUBLED EYES OF A MADMAN -- THEY REVEAL DREAMS OF **CONQUEST**, OF SUGAR PLUM FAIRIES AND MOUNTAINS OF MAYHEM.
THEY ENVISION GROTESQUE HIGH CONCEPTS PERFECTLY WITHIN REACH, AND YET MADDENINGLY **UNATTAINABLE**...
HEAR YE, **HEAR** YE! COURT IS NOW IN SESSION -- THE HONORABLE JUDGE ***"ME"*** PRESIDING...
...MEDUSA OF ATTILAN, YOU STAND ACCUSED OF SUNDRY NAUGHTINESS, WEARING A REVEALING BODYSUIT IN A BUILT-UP AREA, AND RANDOM ACTS OF MISCHIEF AGAINST THE STATE. HOW DO YOU PLEAD?
VERY WELL... YOU LEAVE ME NO CHOICE.
BRING FORTH THE FIRST WITNESS.

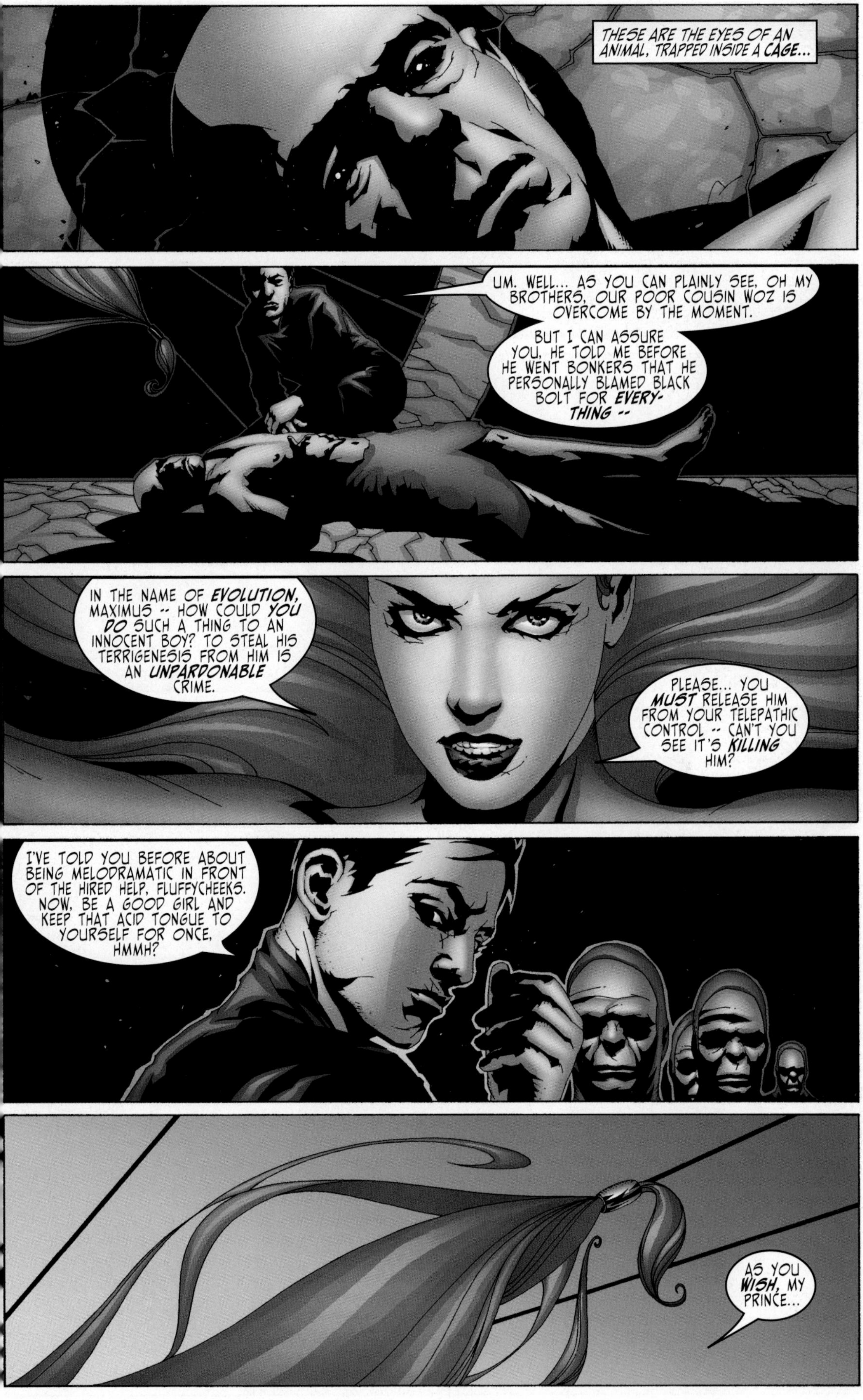

THESE ARE THE EYES OF AN ANIMAL, TRAPPED INSIDE A CAGE...
UM. WELL... AS YOU CAN PLAINLY SEE, OH MY BROTHERS, OUR POOR COUSIN WOZ IS OVERCOME BY THE MOMENT.
BUT I CAN ASSURE YOU, HE TOLD ME BEFORE HE WENT BONKERS THAT HE PERSONALLY BLAMED BLACK BOLT FOR EVERY-THING --
IN THE NAME OF EVOLUTION, MAXIMUS -- HOW COULD YOU DO SUCH A THING TO AN INNOCENT BOY? TO STEAL HIS TERRIGENESIS FROM HIM IS AN UNPARDONABLE CRIME.
PLEASE... YOU MUST RELEASE HIM FROM YOUR TELEPATHIC CONTROL -- CAN'T YOU SEE IT'S KILLING HIM?
I'VE TOLD YOU BEFORE ABOUT BEING MELODRAMATIC IN FRONT OF THE HIRED HELP, FLUFFYCHEEKS. NOW, BE A GOOD GIRL AND KEEP THAT ACID TONGUE TO YOURSELF FOR ONCE, HMMH?
AS YOU WISH, MY PRINCE...

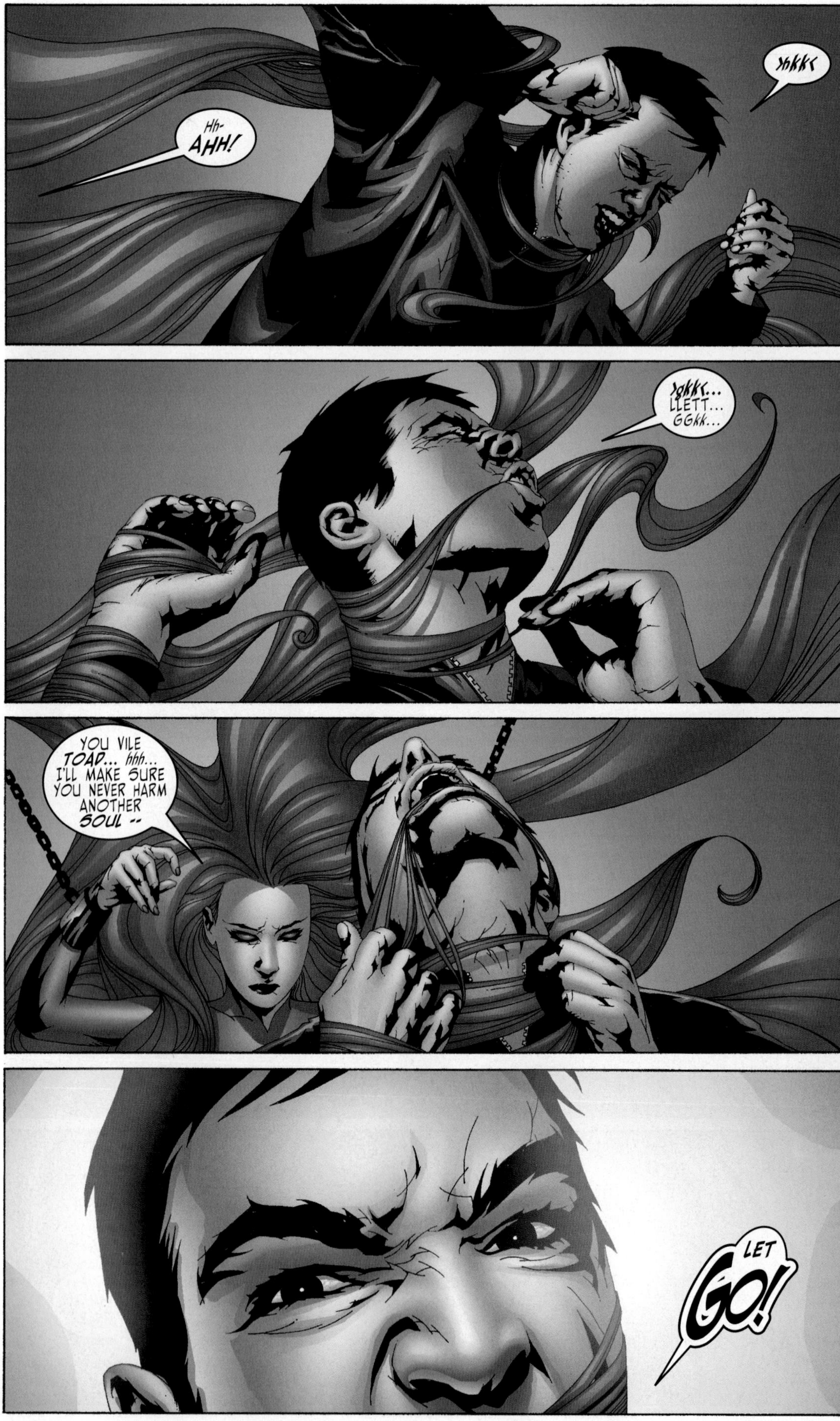
Hh- AHH!
LLETT... GGkk...
YOU VILE TOAD... hhh... I'LL MAKE SURE YOU NEVER HARM ANOTHER SOUL --
LET GO!

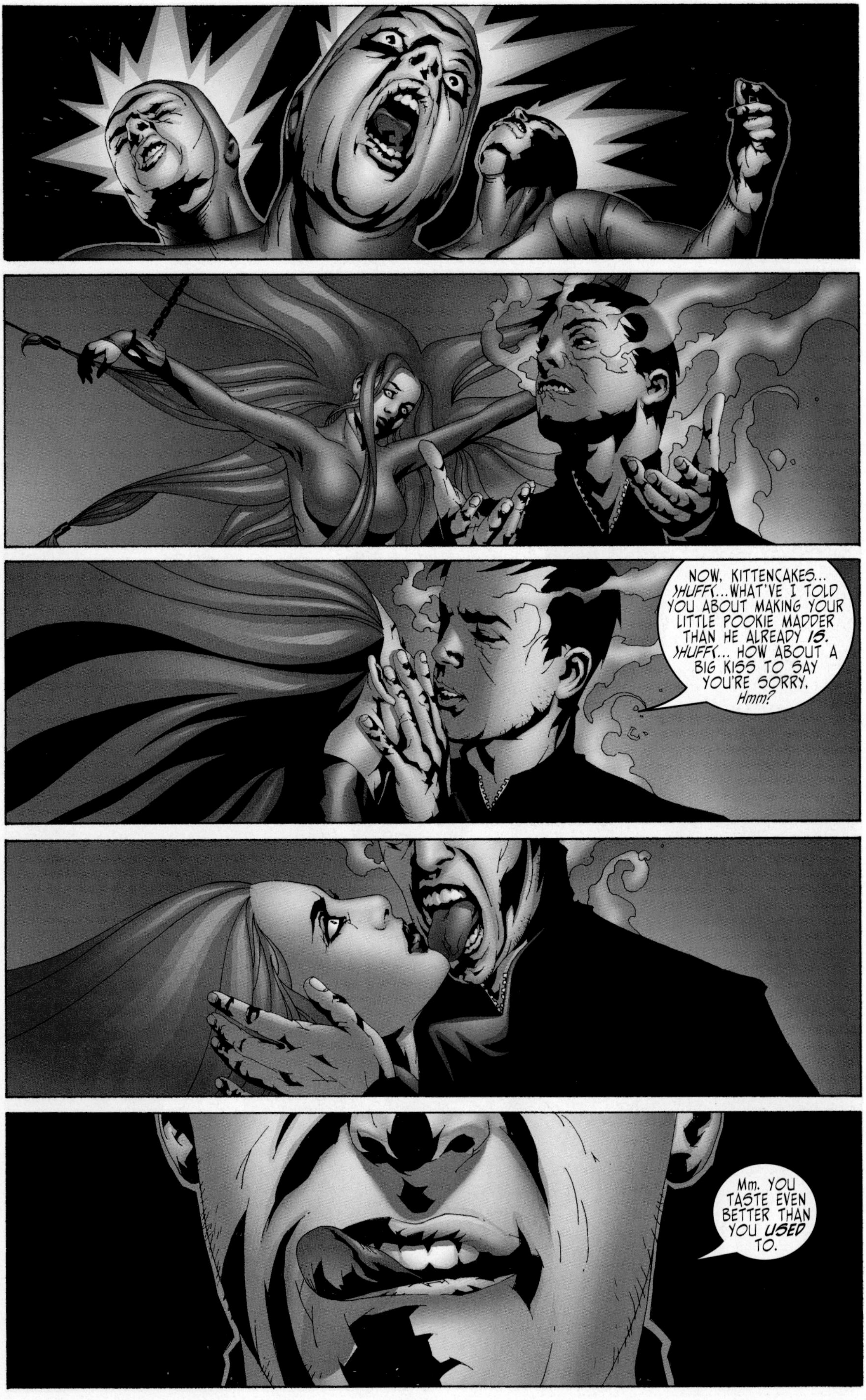
NOW, KITTENCAKES... *HUFF*...WHAT'VE I TOLD YOU ABOUT MAKING YOUR LITTLE POOKIE MADDER THAN HE ALREADY *IS*. *HUFF*... HOW ABOUT A BIG KISS TO SAY YOU'RE SORRY, *Hmm?*
Mm. YOU TASTE EVEN BETTER THAN YOU *USED* TO.

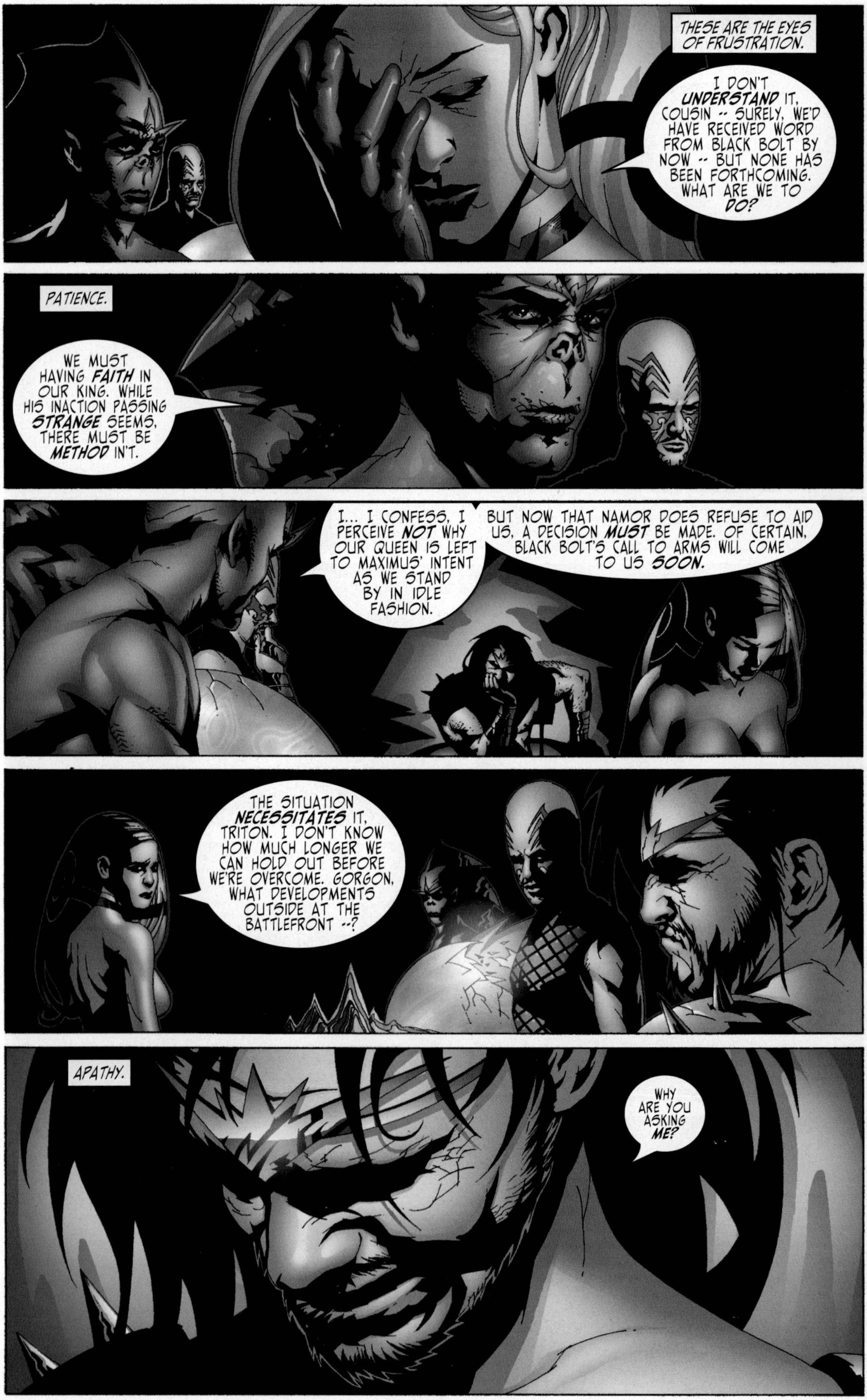
THESE ARE THE EYES OF FRUSTRATION.
I DON'T UNDERSTAND IT, COUSIN -- SURELY, WE'D HAVE RECEIVED WORD FROM BLACK BOLT BY NOW -- BUT NONE HAS BEEN FORTHCOMING. WHAT ARE WE TO DO?
PATIENCE.
WE MUST HAVING FAITH IN OUR KING. WHILE HIS INACTION PASSING STRANGE SEEMS, THERE MUST BE METHOD IN'T.
I... I CONFESS, I PERCEIVE NOT WHY OUR QUEEN IS LEFT TO MAXIMUS' INTENT AS WE STAND BY IN IDLE FASHION.
BUT NOW THAT NAMOR DOES REFUSE TO AID US, A DECISION MUST BE MADE. OF CERTAIN, BLACK BOLT'S CALL TO ARMS WILL COME TO US SOON.
THE SITUATION NECESSITATES IT, TRITON. I DON'T KNOW HOW MUCH LONGER WE CAN HOLD OUT BEFORE WE'RE OVERCOME. GORGON, WHAT DEVELOPMENTS OUTSIDE AT THE BATTLEFRONT --?
APATHY.
WHY ARE YOU ASKING ME?

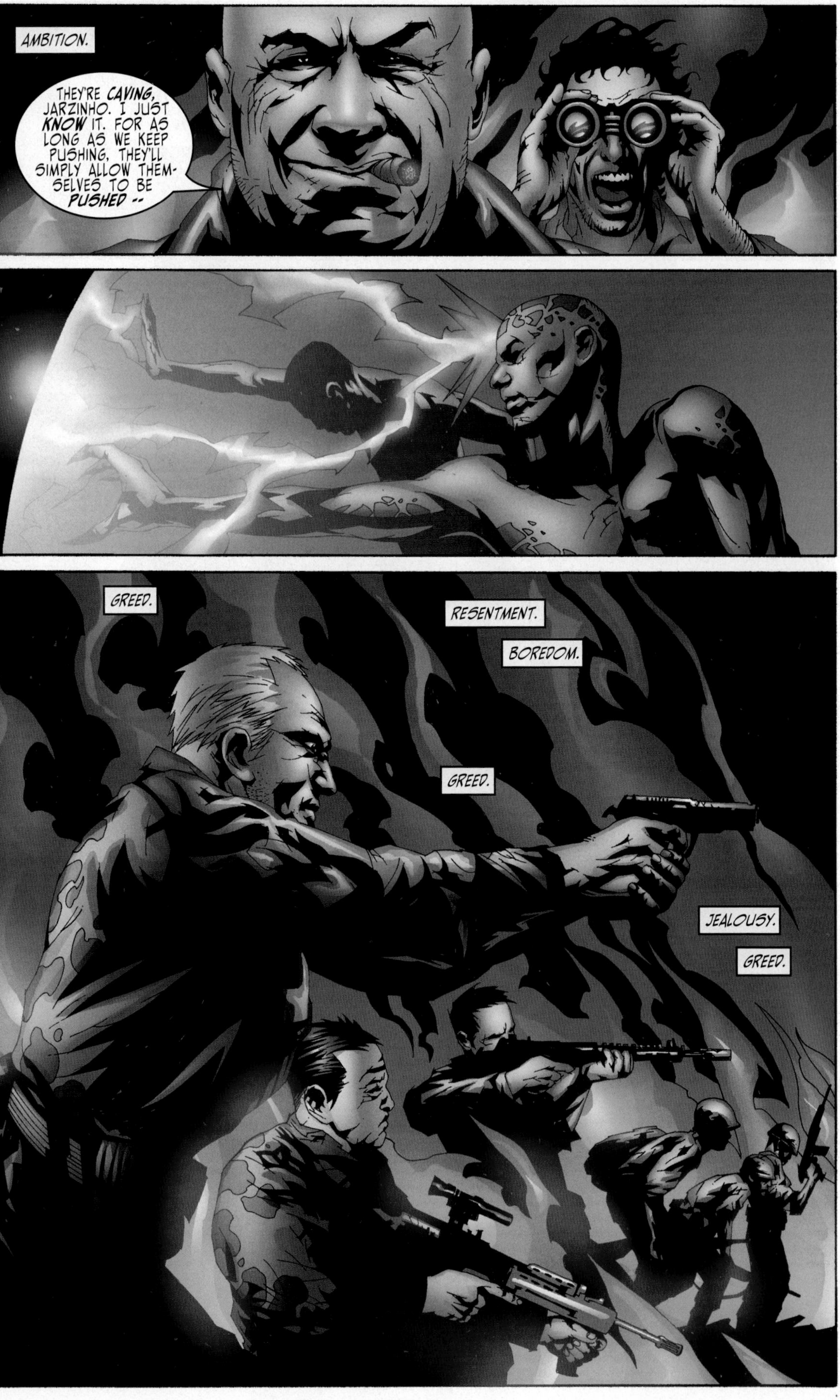
AMBITION.
THEY'RE CAVING, JARZINHO. I JUST KNOW IT. FOR AS LONG AS WE KEEP PUSHING, THEY'LL SIMPLY ALLOW THEMSELVES TO BE PUSHED --
GREED.
RESENTMENT.
BOREDOM.
GREED.
JEALOUSY.
GREED.

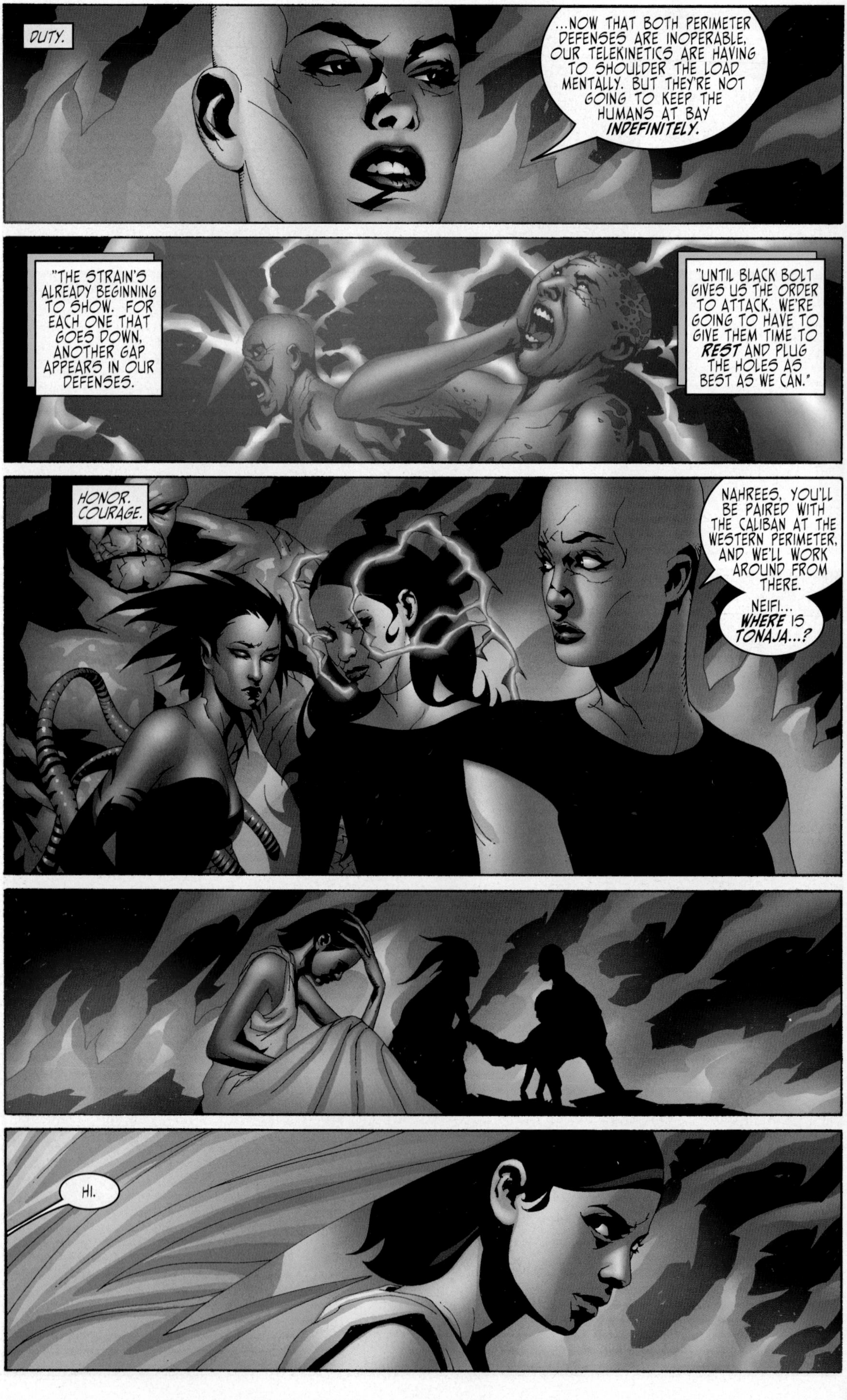
DUTY.
...NOW THAT BOTH PERIMETER DEFENSES ARE INOPERABLE, OUR TELEKINETICS ARE HAVING TO SHOULDER THE LOAD MENTALLY. BUT THEY'RE NOT GOING TO KEEP THE HUMANS AT BAY INDEFINITELY.
"THE STRAIN'S ALREADY BEGINNING TO SHOW. FOR EACH ONE THAT GOES DOWN, ANOTHER GAP APPEARS IN OUR DEFENSES.
"UNTIL BLACK BOLT GIVES US THE ORDER TO ATTACK, WE'RE GOING TO HAVE TO GIVE THEM TIME TO REST AND PLUG THE HOLES AS BEST AS WE CAN."
HONOR. COURAGE.
NAHREES, YOU'LL BE PAIRED WITH THE CALIBAN AT THE WESTERN PERIMETER, AND WE'LL WORK AROUND FROM THERE.
NEIFI... WHERE IS TONAJA...?
HI.

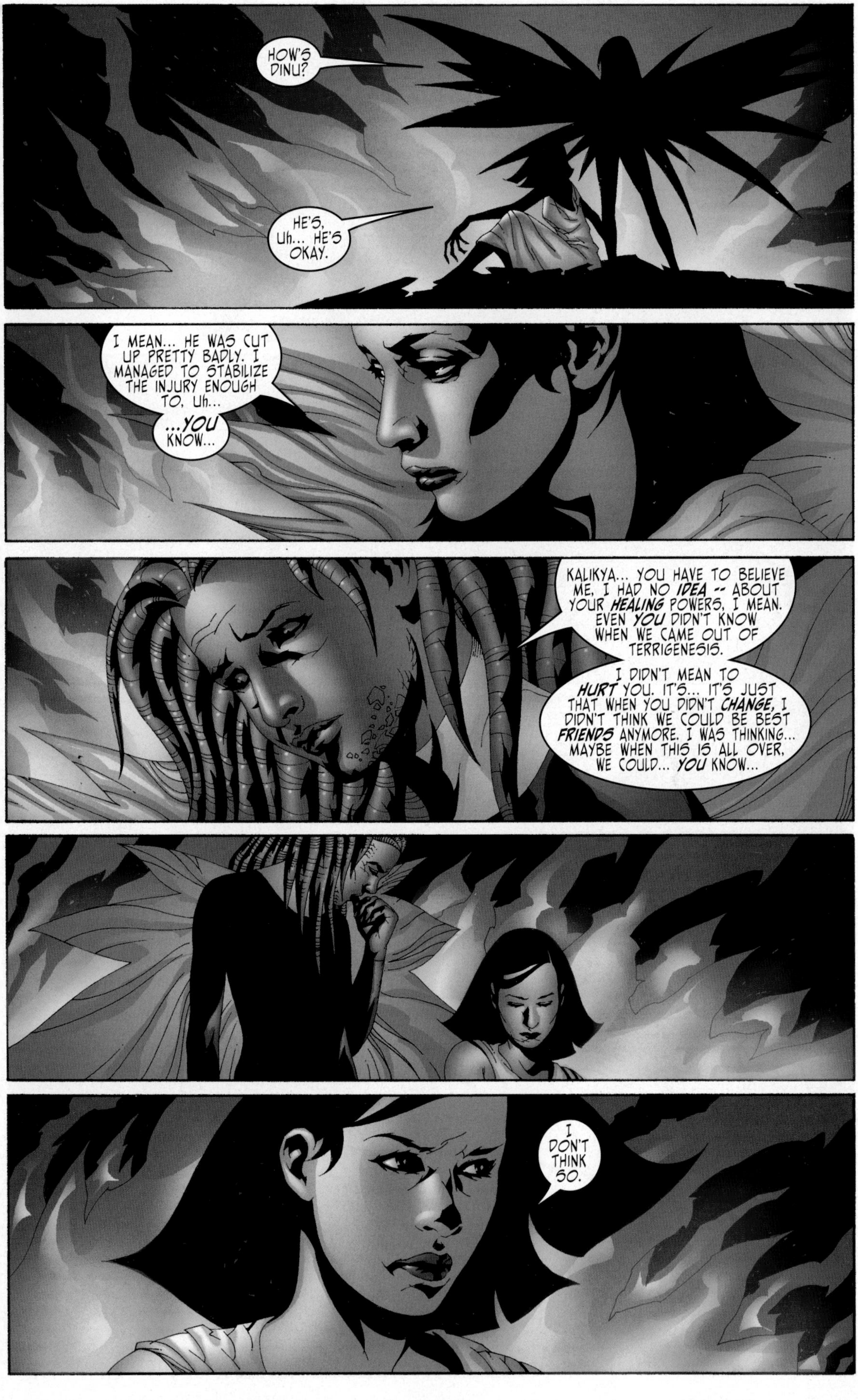
HOW'S DINU?
HE'S, Uh... HE'S OKAY.
I MEAN... HE WAS CUT UP PRETTY BADLY. I MANAGED TO STABILIZE THE INJURY ENOUGH TO, Uh...
...YOU KNOW...
KALIKYA... YOU HAVE TO BELIEVE ME, I HAD NO IDEA -- ABOUT YOUR HEALING POWERS, I MEAN. EVEN YOU DIDN'T KNOW WHEN WE CAME OUT OF TERRIGENESIS.
I DIDN'T MEAN TO HURT YOU. IT'S... IT'S JUST THAT WHEN YOU DIDN'T CHANGE, I DIDN'T THINK WE COULD BE BEST FRIENDS ANYMORE. I WAS THINKING... MAYBE WHEN THIS IS ALL OVER, WE COULD... YOU KNOW...
I DON'T THINK SO.

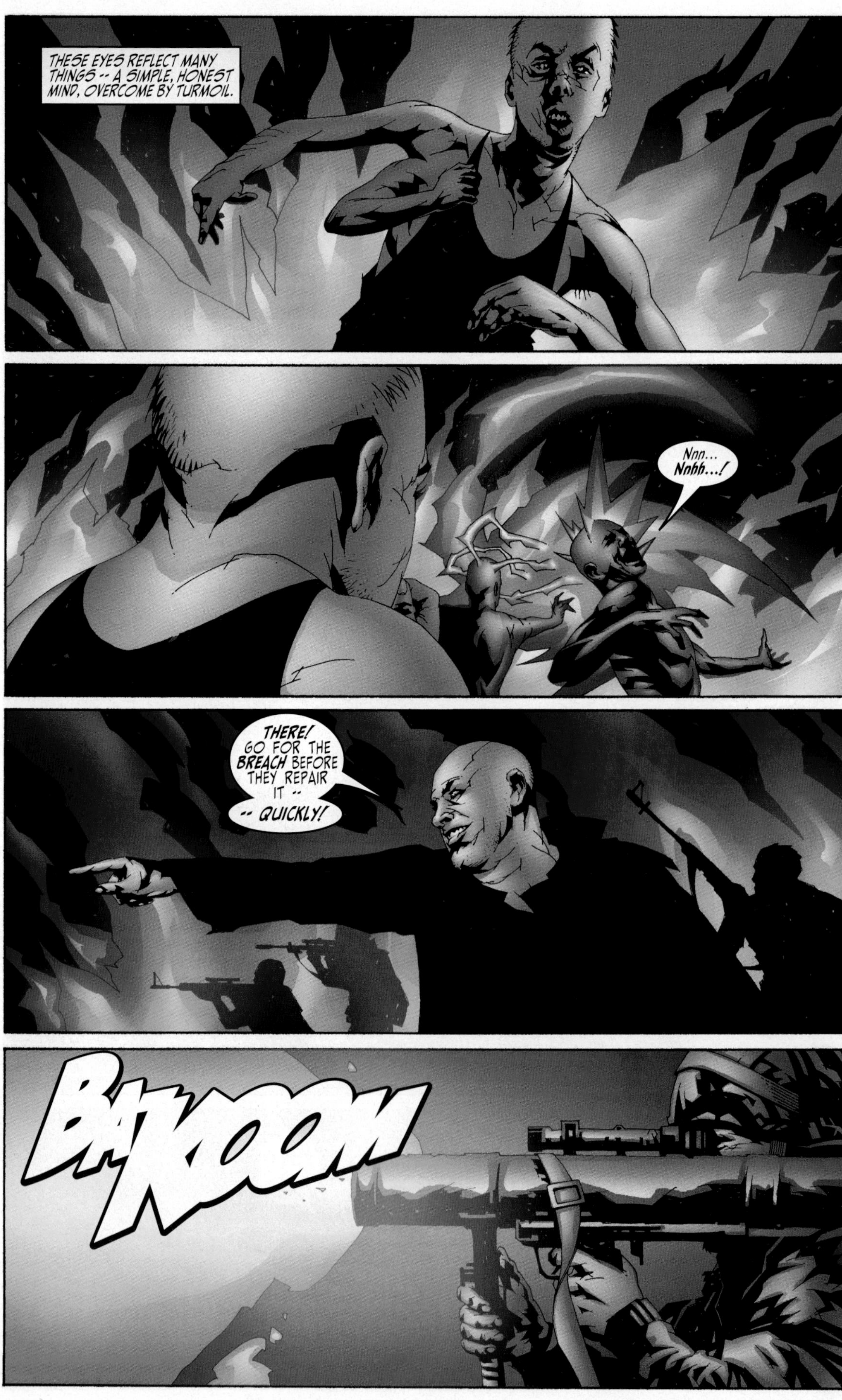
THESE EYES REFLECT MANY THINGS -- A SIMPLE, HONEST MIND, OVERCOME BY TURMOIL.
Nnn... Nnhh...!
THERE! GO FOR THE BREACH BEFORE THEY REPAIR IT --
-- QUICKLY!
BAKOOM

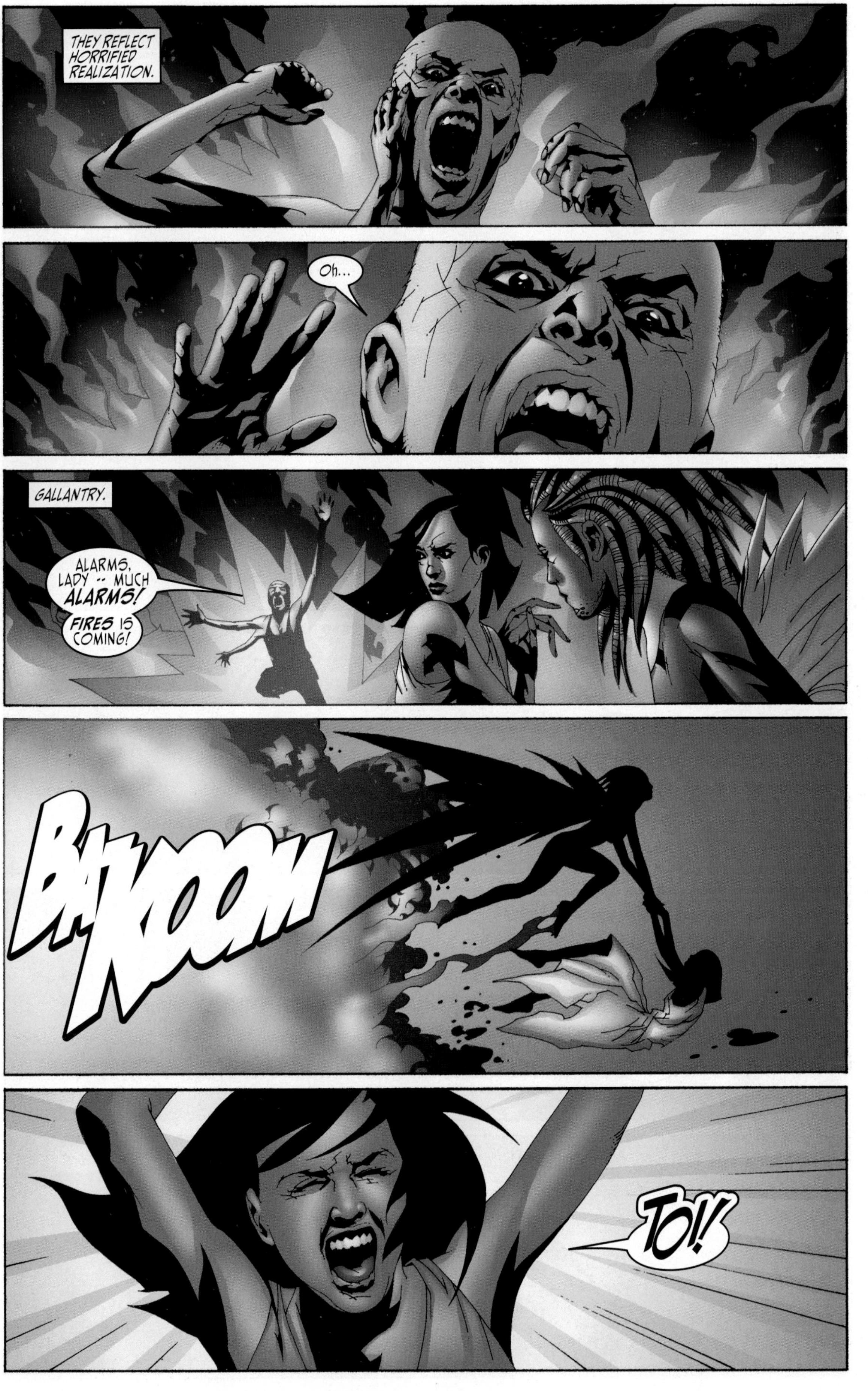

THEY REFLECT HORRIFIED REALIZATION.
Oh...
GALLANTRY.
ALARMS, LADY -- MUCH ALARMS!
FIRES IS COMING!
BAKOOM
TOI!

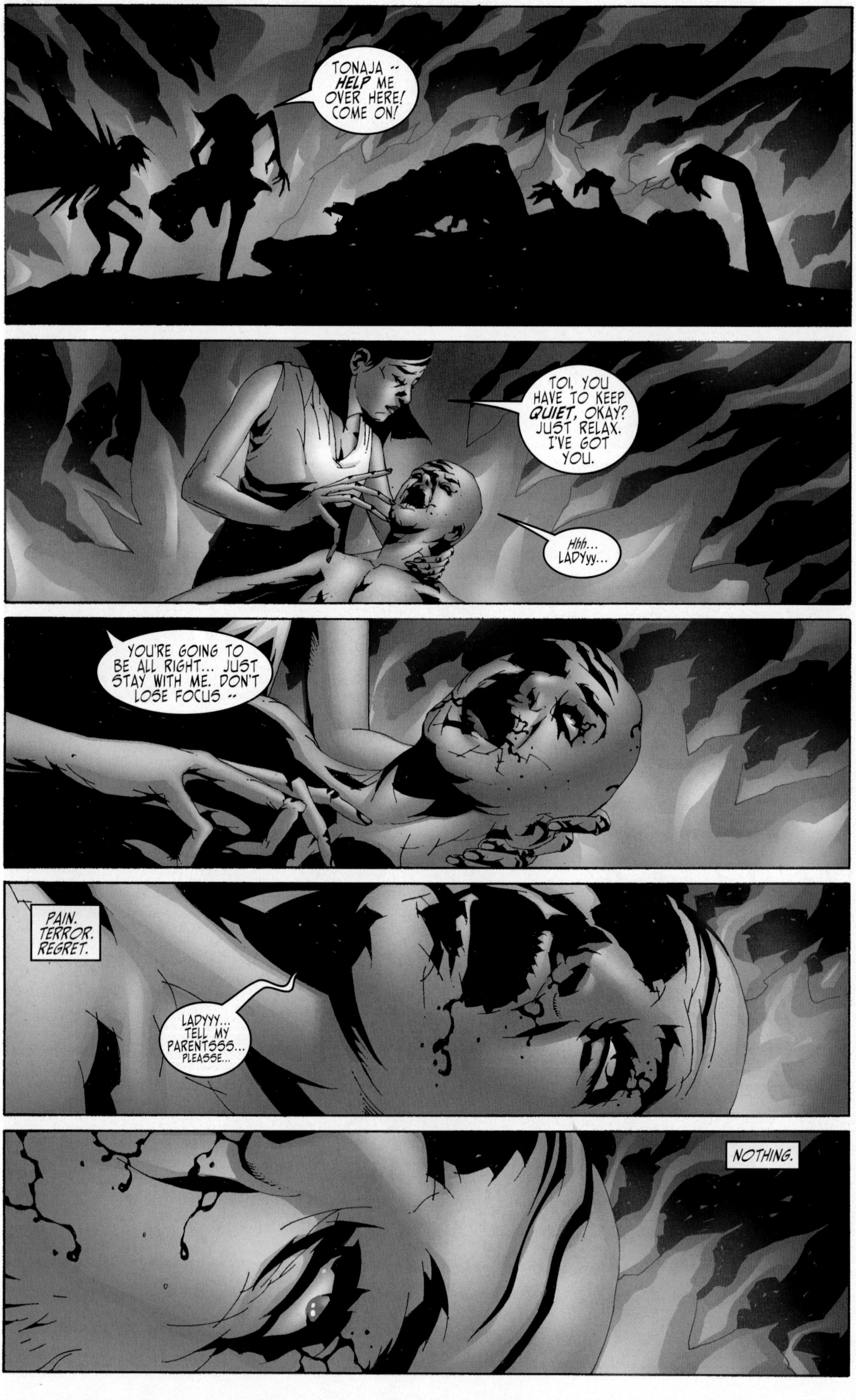
TONAJA -- HELP ME OVER HERE! COME ON!
TOI, YOU HAVE TO KEEP QUIET, OKAY? JUST RELAX. I'VE GOT YOU.
Hhh... LADYyy...
YOU'RE GOING TO BE ALL RIGHT... JUST STAY WITH ME. DON'T LOSE FOCUS --
PAIN. TERROR. REGRET.
LADYYY... TELL MY PARENTSSS... PLEASSE...
NOTHING.

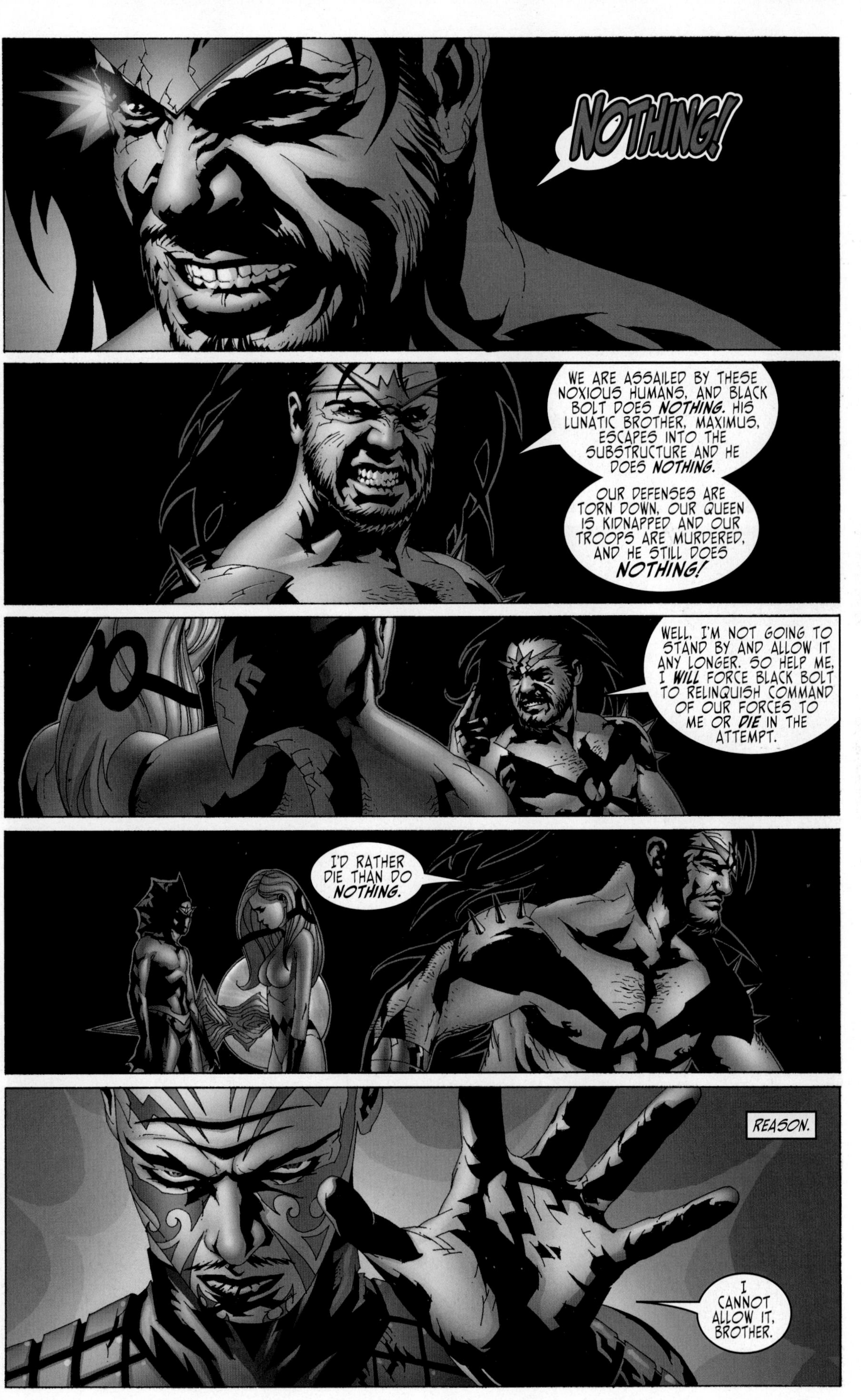
NOTHING!
WE ARE ASSAILED BY THESE NOXIOUS HUMANS, AND BLACK BOLT DOES NOTHING. HIS LUNATIC BROTHER, MAXIMUS, ESCAPES INTO THE SUBSTRUCTURE AND HE DOES NOTHING.
OUR DEFENSES ARE TORN DOWN, OUR QUEEN IS KIDNAPPED AND OUR TROOPS ARE MURDERED, AND HE STILL DOES NOTHING!
WELL, I'M NOT GOING TO STAND BY AND ALLOW IT ANY LONGER. SO HELP ME, I WILL FORCE BLACK BOLT TO RELINQUISH COMMAND OF OUR FORCES TO ME OR DIE IN THE ATTEMPT.
I'D RATHER DIE THAN DO NOTHING.
REASON.
I CANNOT ALLOW IT, BROTHER.

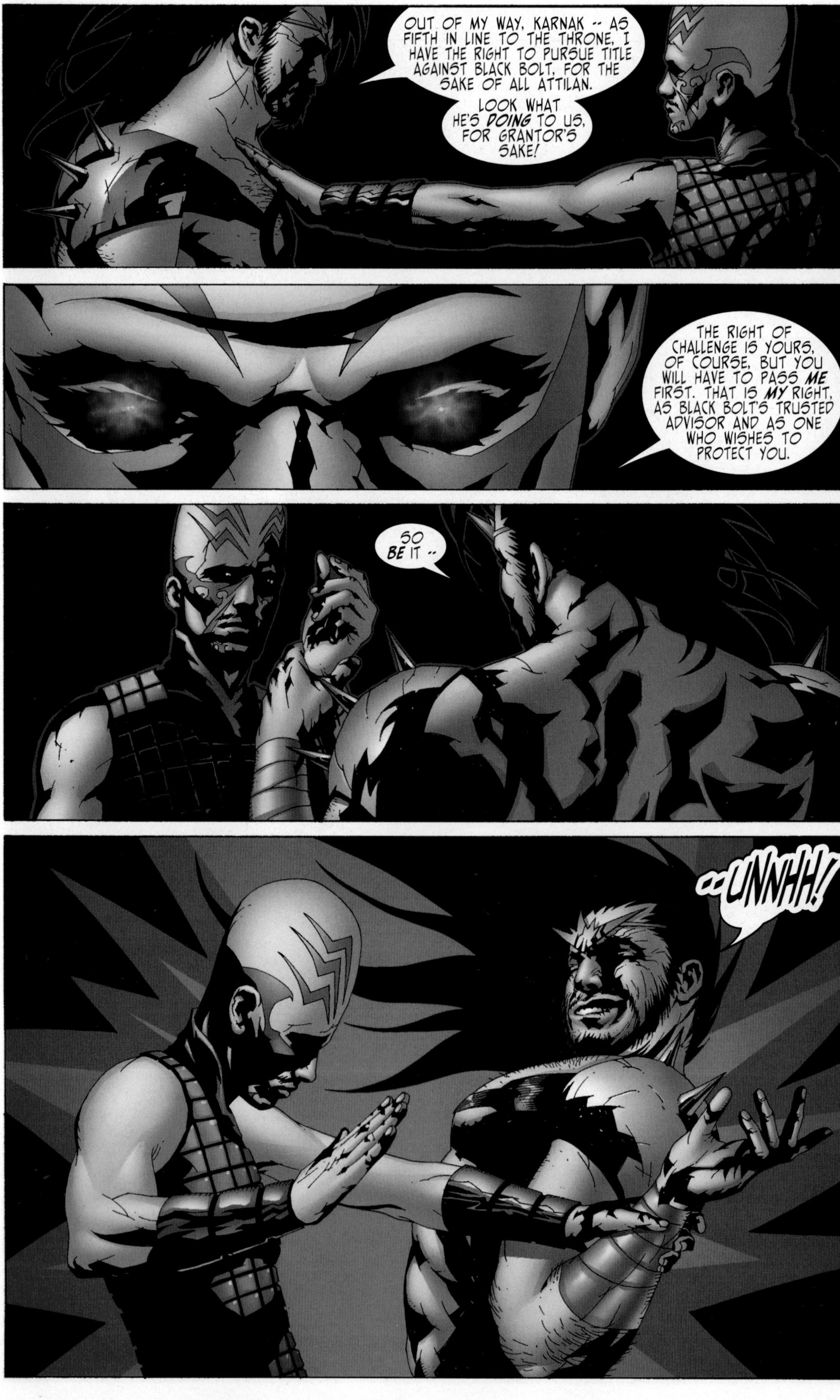
OUT OF MY WAY, KARNAK -- AS FIFTH IN LINE TO THE THRONE, I HAVE THE RIGHT TO PURSUE TITLE AGAINST BLACK BOLT, FOR THE SAKE OF ALL ATTILAN.
LOOK WHAT HE'S DOING TO US, FOR GRANTOR'S SAKE!
THE RIGHT OF CHALLENGE IS YOURS, OF COURSE, BUT YOU WILL HAVE TO PASS ME FIRST. THAT IS MY RIGHT, AS BLACK BOLT'S TRUSTED ADVISOR AND AS ONE WHO WISHES TO PROTECT YOU.
SO BE IT --
--UNNHH!

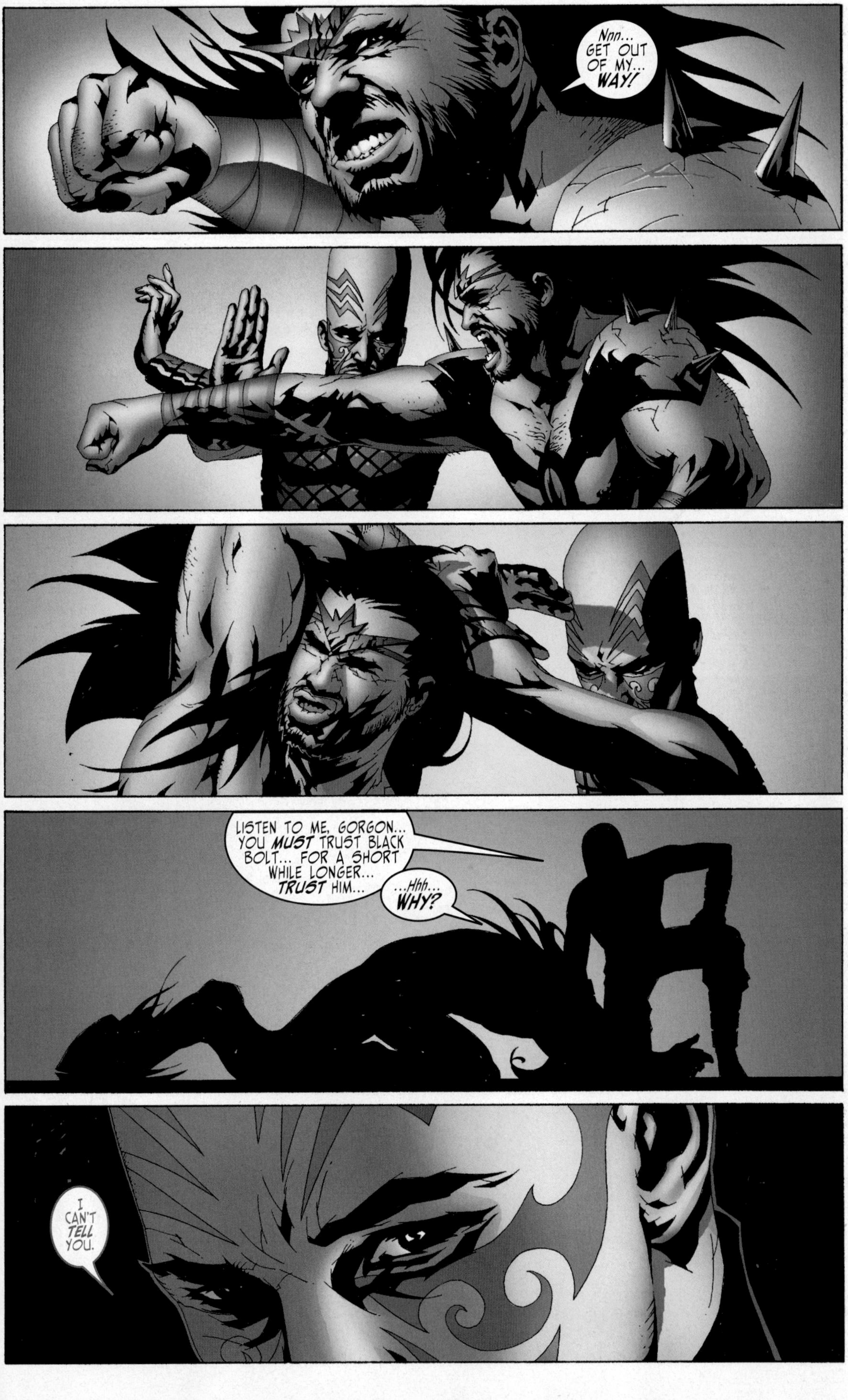
Nnn... GET OUT OF MY... WAY!
LISTEN TO ME, GORGON... YOU MUST TRUST BLACK BOLT... FOR A SHORT WHILE LONGER... TRUST HIM...
...Hhh... WHY?
I CAN'T TELL YOU.

THESE ARE THE EYES OF A BOY DYING OF A BROKEN HEART.

SORRY I HAD TO TAKE OUT ALL THE REFLECTIVE SURFACES, WOZ, OLD BEAN, BUT I CAN'T AFFORD TO HAVE YOU TELEPORTING YOUR WAY TO FREEDOM WITHOUT SO MUCH AS A BY-YOUR-LEAVE, NOW *CAN* I?

TELL YOU WHAT: JUST POP OFF QUICKLY -- MAKE SURE YOU DO IT *BRAVELY* IN FRONT OF THE ALPHAS -- AND WE'LL CALL IT *EVEN*, OKAY?

THE BOY HEARS HIS SENTENCE UTTERED, AND UNDERSTANDS THAT HE WILL NEVER ASSUME HIS PROPER FORM, DESIGNATED TO HIM BY THE TERRIGEN MISTS.

INSTEAD, HE WILL DIE *HERE* IN THIS DARKENED ROOM UNDER THE CITY. THE EYES OF THE MADMAN BETRAY THIS TRUTH.

BUT JUST AS WOZ MAKES READY TO MEET OBLIVION, A SUDDEN REALIZATION COMES -- THAT EYES ARE WINDOWS TO THE SOUL...

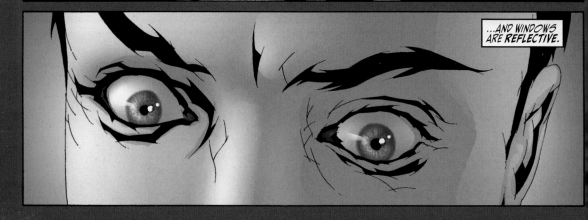

...AND WINDOWS ARE *REFLECTIVE*.

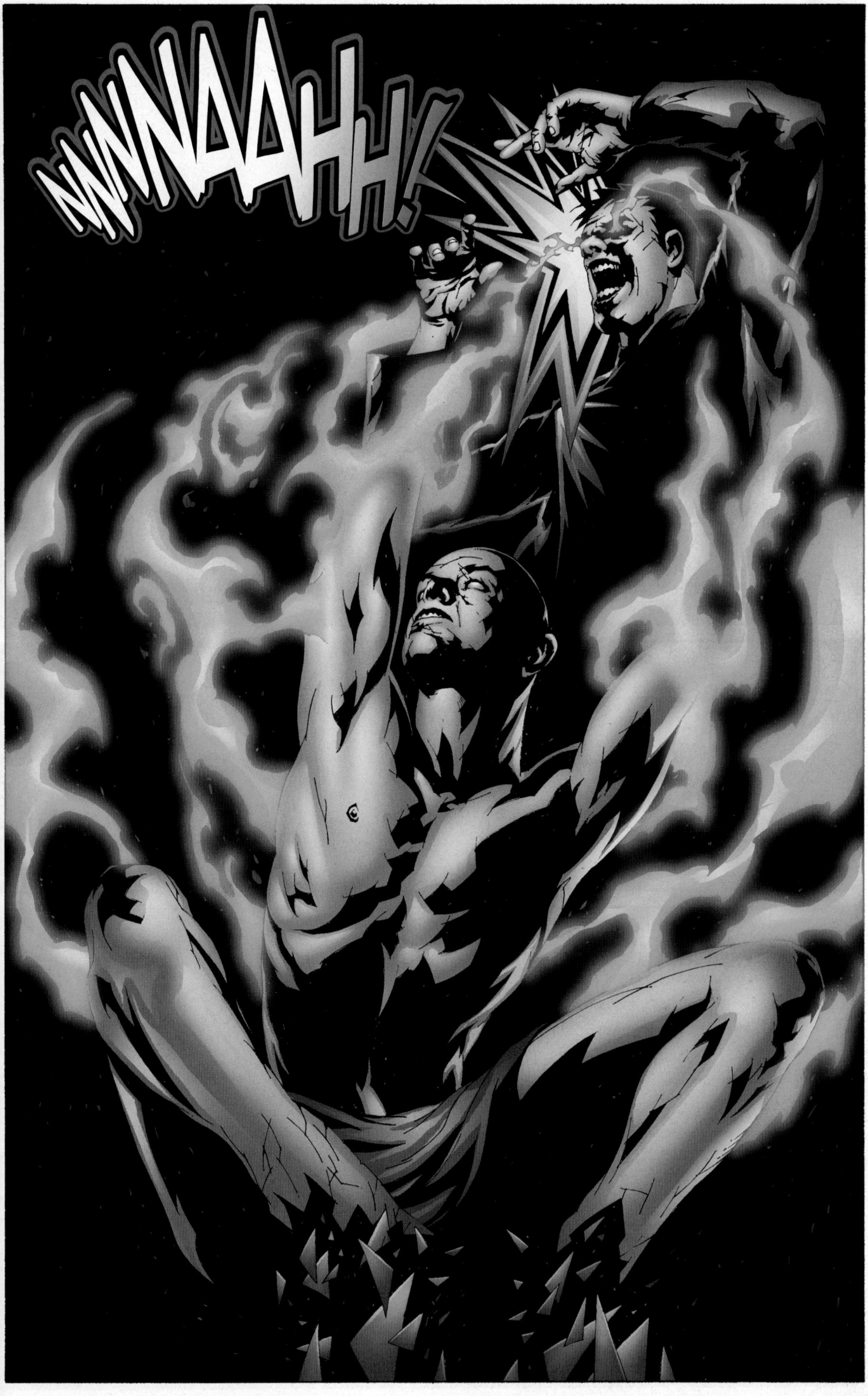
NNNNAAHH!

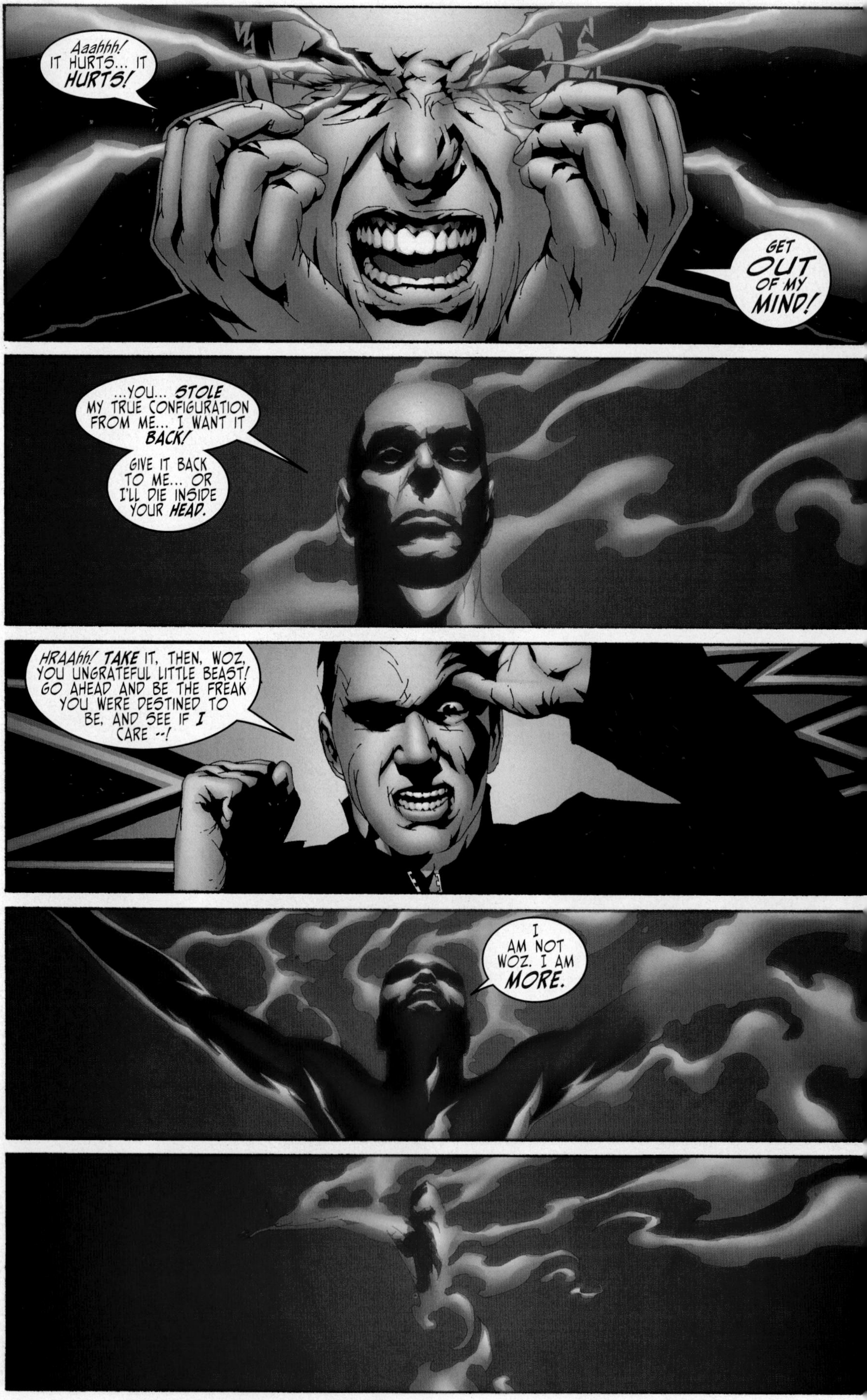
Aaahhh! IT HURTS... IT HURTS!
GET OUT OF MY MIND!
...YOU... STOLE MY TRUE CONFIGURATION FROM ME... I WANT IT BACK!
GIVE IT BACK TO ME... OR I'LL DIE INSIDE YOUR HEAD.
HRAAhh! TAKE IT, THEN, WOZ, YOU UNGRATEFUL LITTLE BEAST! GO AHEAD AND BE THE FREAK YOU WERE DESTINED TO BE, AND SEE IF I CARE --!
I AM NOT WOZ. I AM MORE.

ON THESE EYES,
EMPTINESS.
NOTHING AT ALL.

OR PERHAPS...

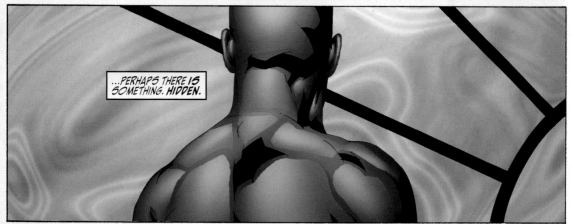

...PERHAPS THERE *IS*
SOMETHING. *HIDDEN.*

A *SECRET?*

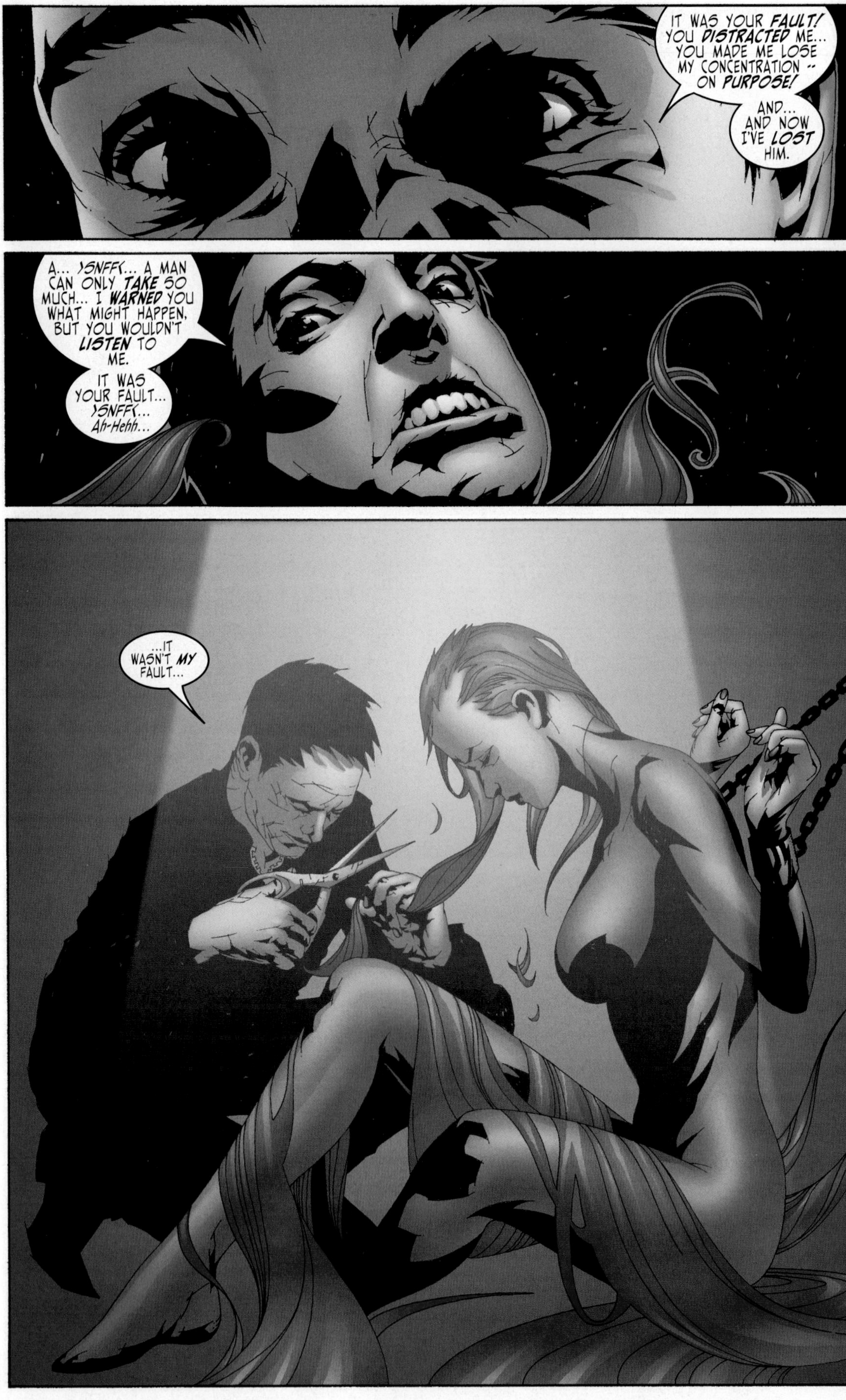
IT WAS YOUR FAULT! YOU DISTRACTED ME... YOU MADE ME LOSE MY CONCENTRATION -- ON PURPOSE!
AND... AND NOW I'VE LOST HIM.
A... >SNFF<... A MAN CAN ONLY TAKE SO MUCH... I WARNED YOU WHAT MIGHT HAPPEN, BUT YOU WOULDN'T LISTEN TO ME.
IT WAS YOUR FAULT... >SNFF<... Ah-Hehh...
...IT WASN'T MY FAULT...

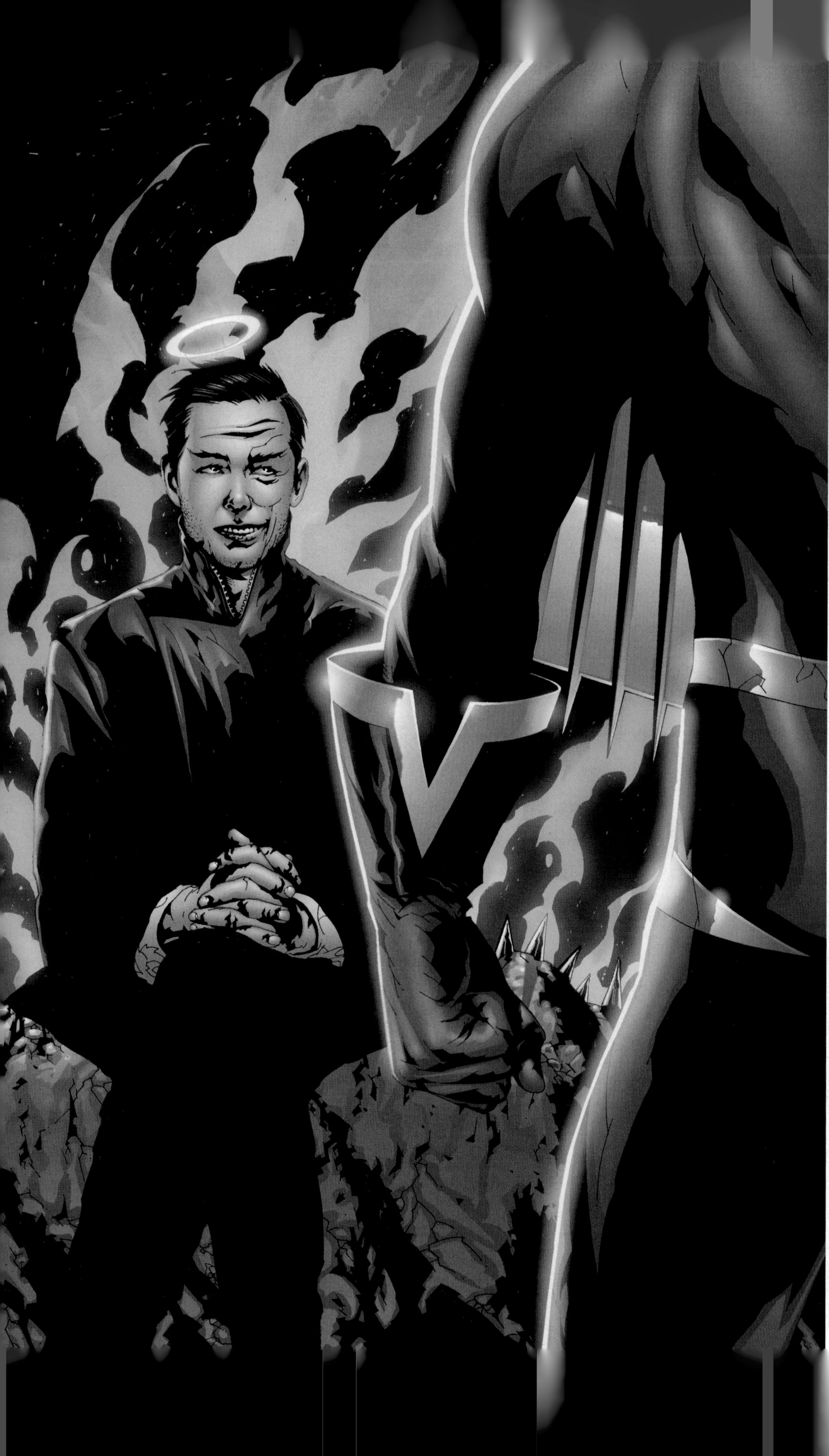

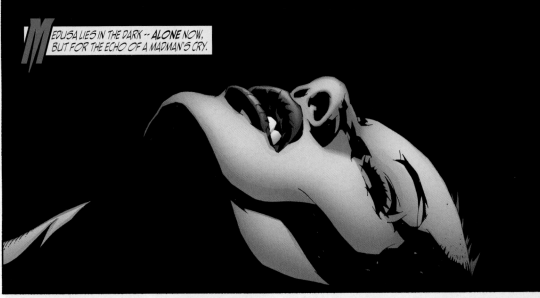

MEDUSA LIES IN THE DARK -- *ALONE* NOW, BUT FOR THE ECHO OF A MADMAN'S CRY.

MAXIMUS HAS LONG SINCE GONE, BUT SHE IMAGINES SHE HEARS HIM STILL; RANTING AND RAVING -- BLAMING HER FOR LOSING HIS FAVORITE TOY.

RUNNING DOWN THE CORRIDORS LIKE A PETULANT CHILD...

...WITH VERY SHARP SCISSORS.

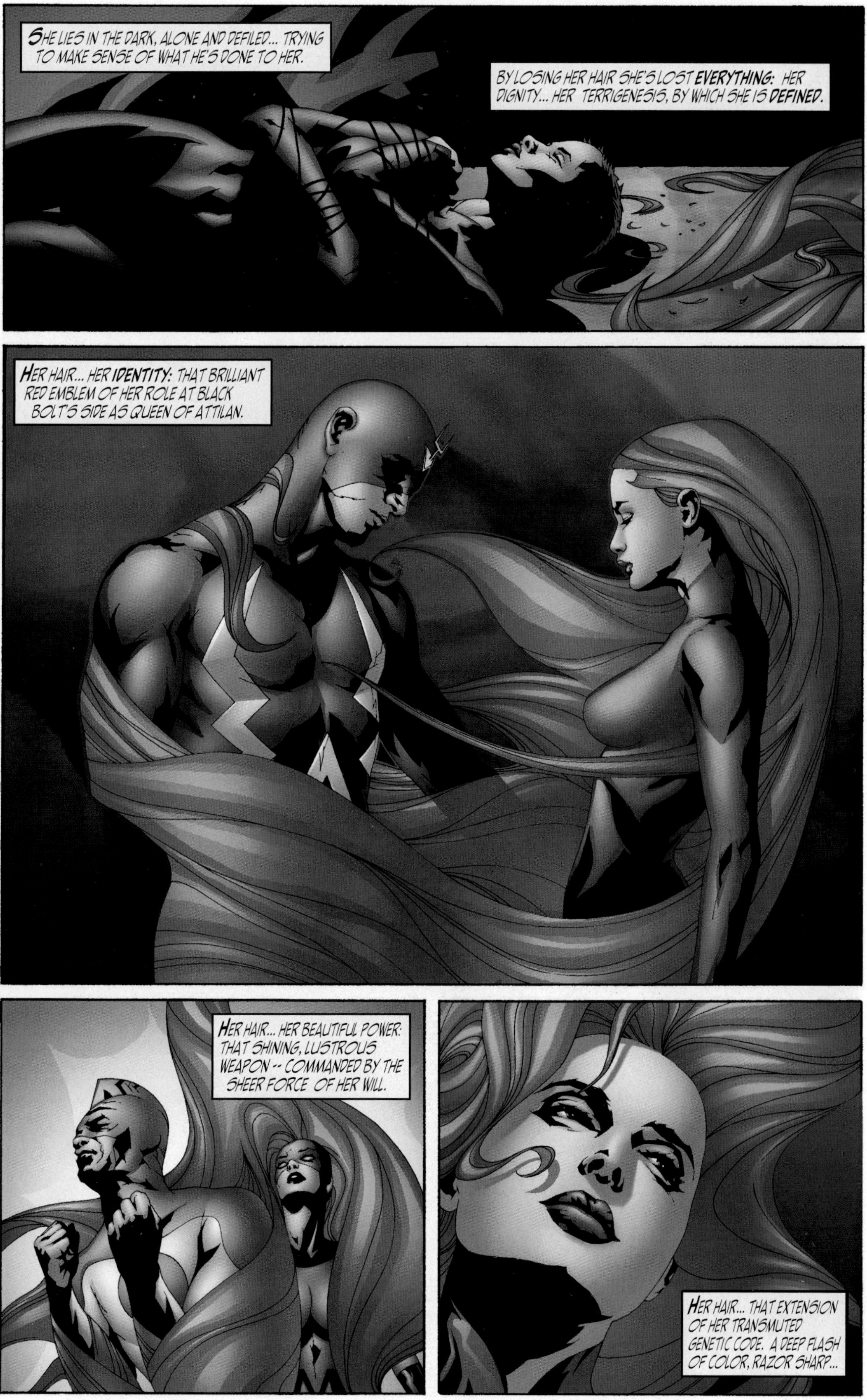
SHE LIES IN THE DARK, ALONE AND DEFILED... TRYING TO MAKE SENSE OF WHAT HE'S DONE TO HER.
BY LOSING HER HAIR SHE'S LOST EVERYTHING: HER DIGNITY... HER TERRIGENESIS, BY WHICH SHE IS DEFINED.
HER HAIR... HER IDENTITY: THAT BRILLIANT RED EMBLEM OF HER ROLE AT BLACK BOLT'S SIDE AS QUEEN OF ATTILAN.
HER HAIR... HER BEAUTIFUL POWER: THAT SHINING, LUSTROUS WEAPON -- COMMANDED BY THE SHEER FORCE OF HER WILL.
HER HAIR... THAT EXTENSION OF HER TRANSMUTED GENETIC CODE. A DEEP FLASH OF COLOR, RAZOR SHARP...

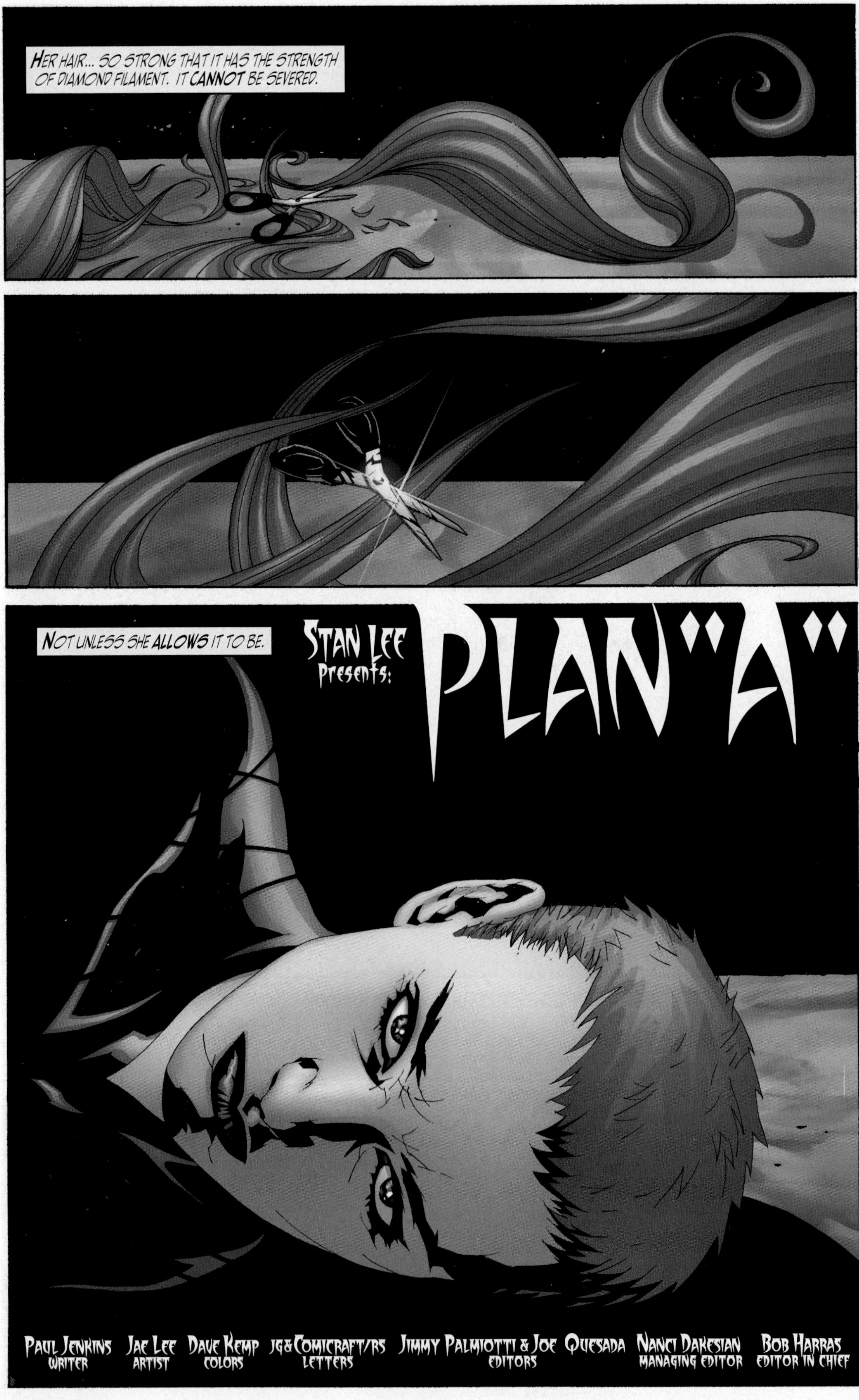
HER HAIR... SO STRONG THAT IT HAS THE STRENGTH OF DIAMOND FILAMENT. IT CANNOT BE SEVERED.
NOT UNLESS SHE ALLOWS IT TO BE.
STAN LEE Presents:
PLAN "A"
PAUL JENKINS WRITER
JAE LEE ARTIST
DAVE KEMP COLORS
JG&COMICRAFT/RS LETTERS
JIMMY PALMIOTTI & JOE QUESADA EDITORS
NANCI DAKESIAN MANAGING EDITOR
BOB HARRAS EDITOR IN CHIEF

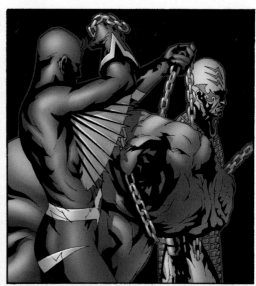
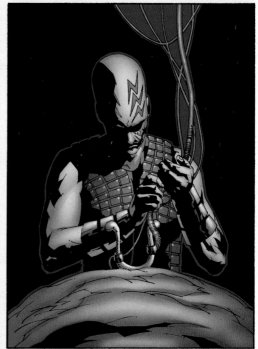

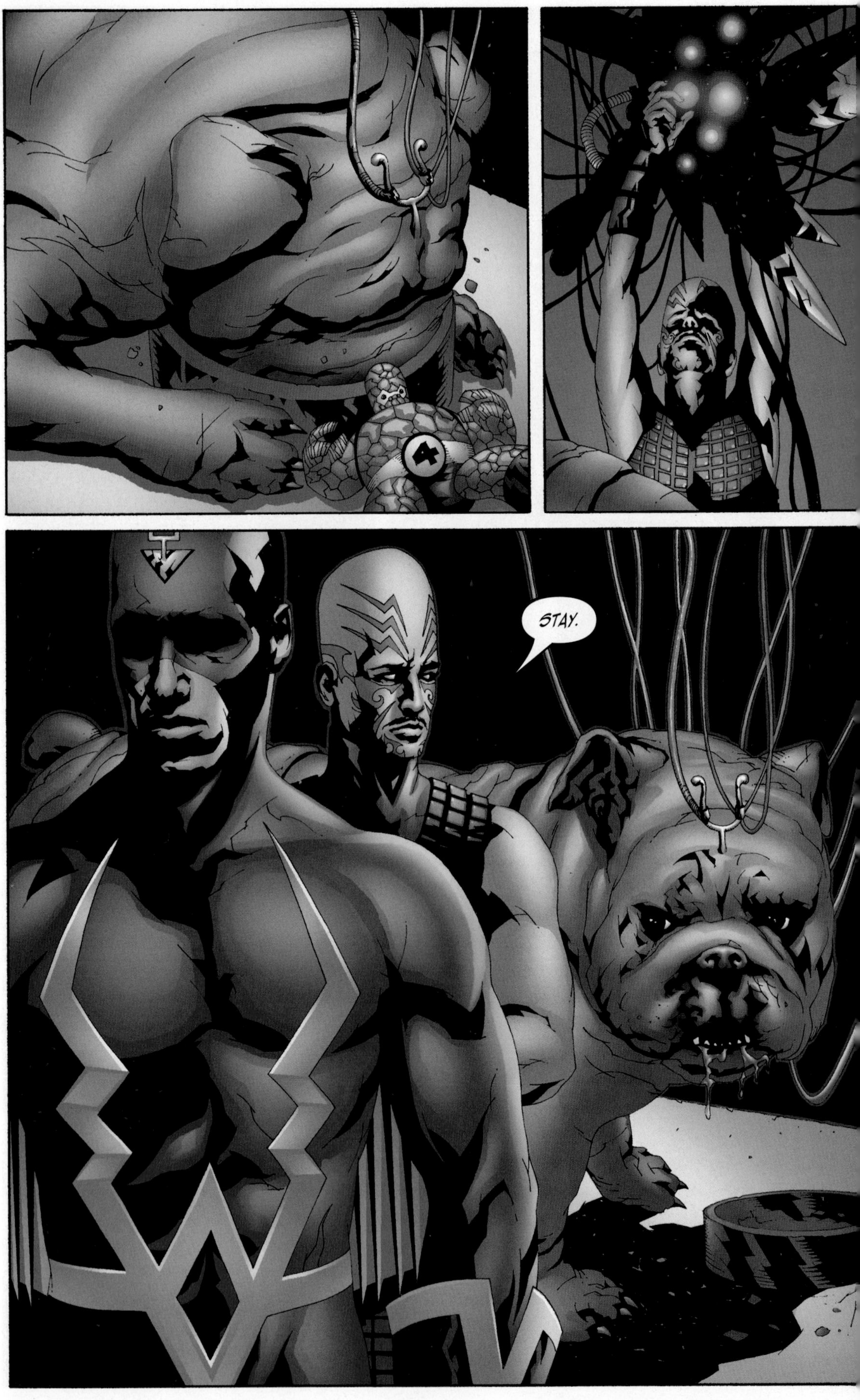
STAY.

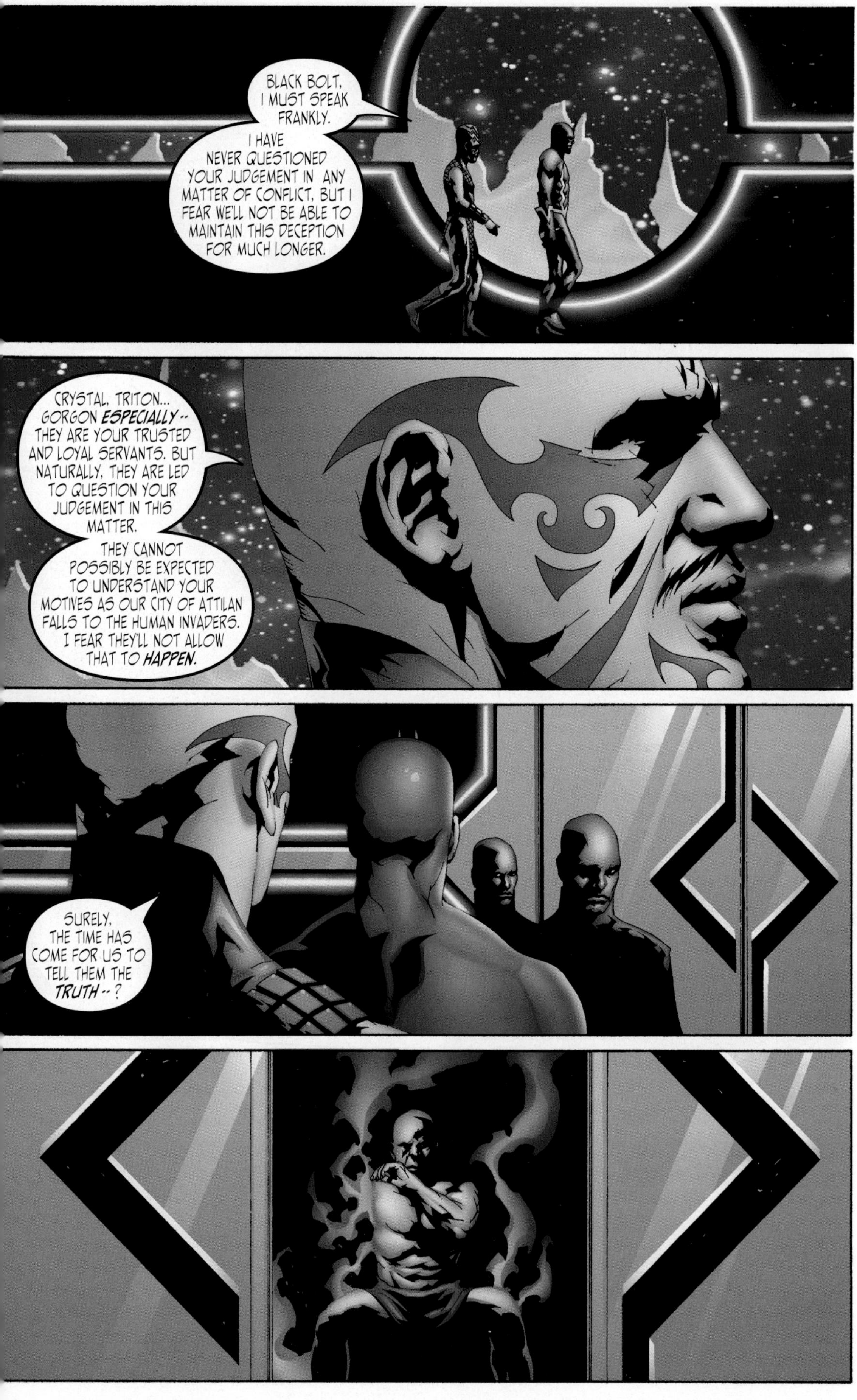

BLACK BOLT, I MUST SPEAK FRANKLY.
I HAVE NEVER QUESTIONED YOUR JUDGEMENT IN ANY MATTER OF CONFLICT, BUT I FEAR WE'LL NOT BE ABLE TO MAINTAIN THIS DECEPTION FOR MUCH LONGER.
CRYSTAL, TRITON... GORGON ESPECIALLY -- THEY ARE YOUR TRUSTED AND LOYAL SERVANTS. BUT NATURALLY, THEY ARE LED TO QUESTION YOUR JUDGEMENT IN THIS MATTER.
THEY CANNOT POSSIBLY BE EXPECTED TO UNDERSTAND YOUR MOTIVES AS OUR CITY OF ATTILAN FALLS TO THE HUMAN INVADERS. I FEAR THEY'LL NOT ALLOW THAT TO HAPPEN.
SURELY, THE TIME HAS COME FOR US TO TELL THEM THE TRUTH -- ?

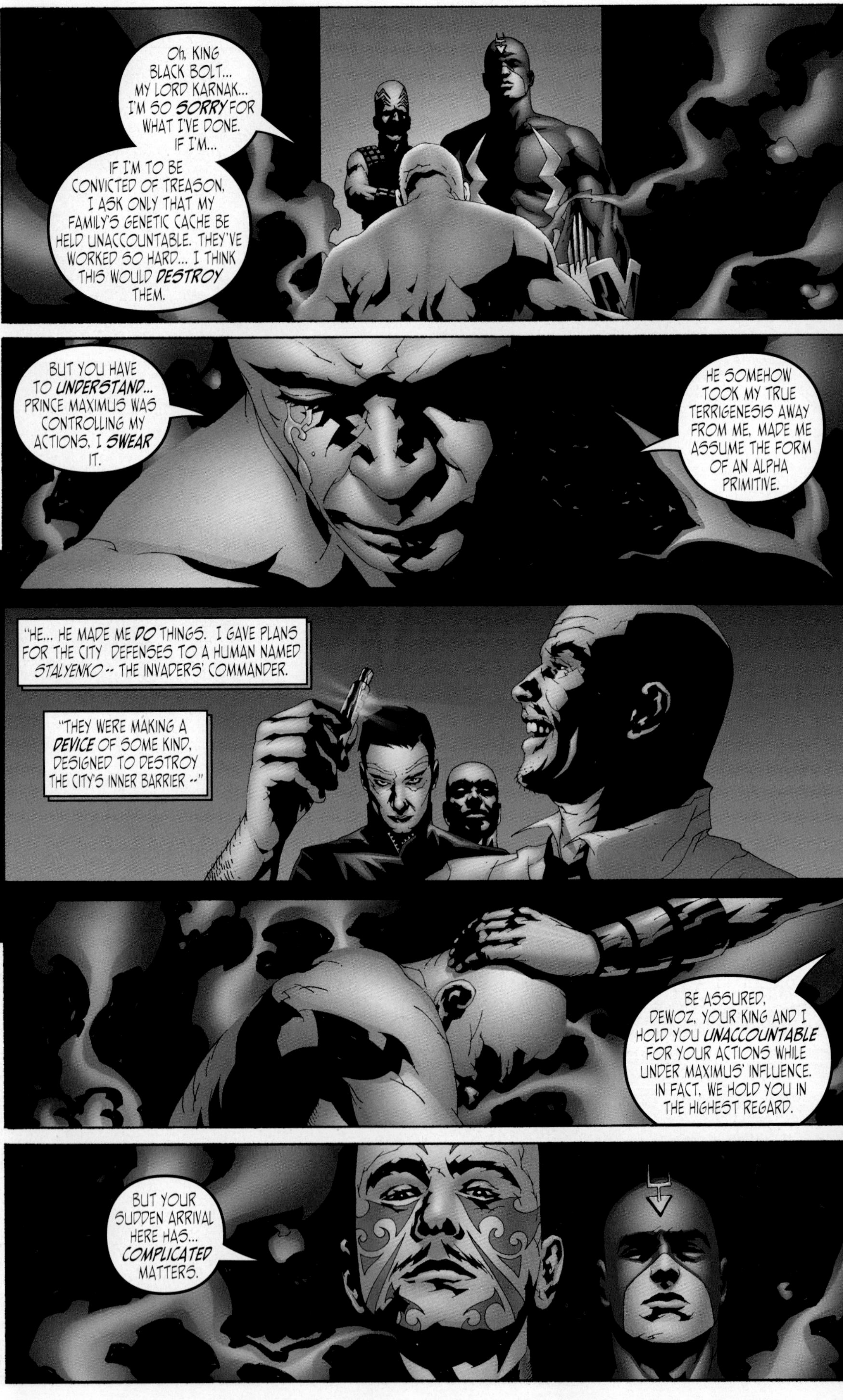

Oh, KING BLACK BOLT... MY LORD KARNAK... I'M SO SORRY FOR WHAT I'VE DONE. IF I'M...
IF I'M TO BE CONVICTED OF TREASON, I ASK ONLY THAT MY FAMILY'S GENETIC CACHE BE HELD UNACCOUNTABLE. THEY'VE WORKED SO HARD... I THINK THIS WOULD DESTROY THEM.
BUT YOU HAVE TO UNDERSTAND... PRINCE MAXIMUS WAS CONTROLLING MY ACTIONS, I SWEAR IT.
HE SOMEHOW TOOK MY TRUE TERRIGENESIS AWAY FROM ME, MADE ME ASSUME THE FORM OF AN ALPHA PRIMITIVE.
"HE... HE MADE ME DO THINGS. I GAVE PLANS FOR THE CITY DEFENSES TO A HUMAN NAMED STALYENKO -- THE INVADERS' COMMANDER.
"THEY WERE MAKING A DEVICE OF SOME KIND, DESIGNED TO DESTROY THE CITY'S INNER BARRIER --"
BE ASSURED, DEWOZ, YOUR KING AND I HOLD YOU UNACCOUNTABLE FOR YOUR ACTIONS WHILE UNDER MAXIMUS' INFLUENCE. IN FACT, WE HOLD YOU IN THE HIGHEST REGARD.
BUT YOUR SUDDEN ARRIVAL HERE HAS... COMPLICATED MATTERS.

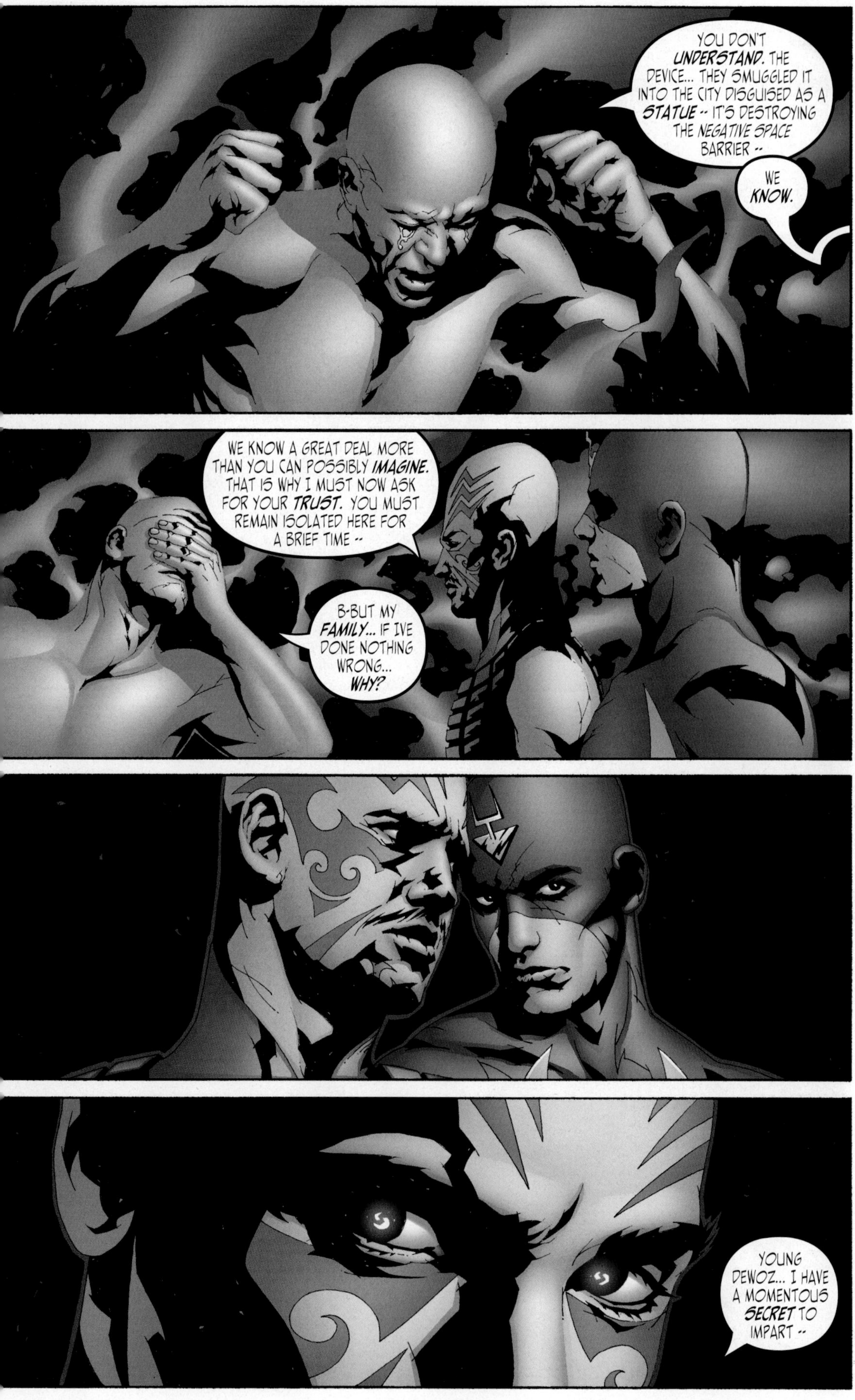
YOU DON'T *UNDERSTAND*. THE DEVICE... THEY SMUGGLED IT INTO THE CITY DISGUISED AS A *STATUE* -- IT'S DESTROYING THE *NEGATIVE SPACE* BARRIER --
WE *KNOW*.
WE KNOW A GREAT DEAL MORE THAN YOU CAN POSSIBLY *IMAGINE*. THAT IS WHY I MUST NOW ASK FOR YOUR *TRUST*. YOU MUST REMAIN ISOLATED HERE FOR A BRIEF TIME --
B-BUT MY *FAMILY*... IF IVE DONE NOTHING WRONG... *WHY?*
YOUNG DEWOZ... I HAVE A MOMENTOUS *SECRET* TO IMPART --

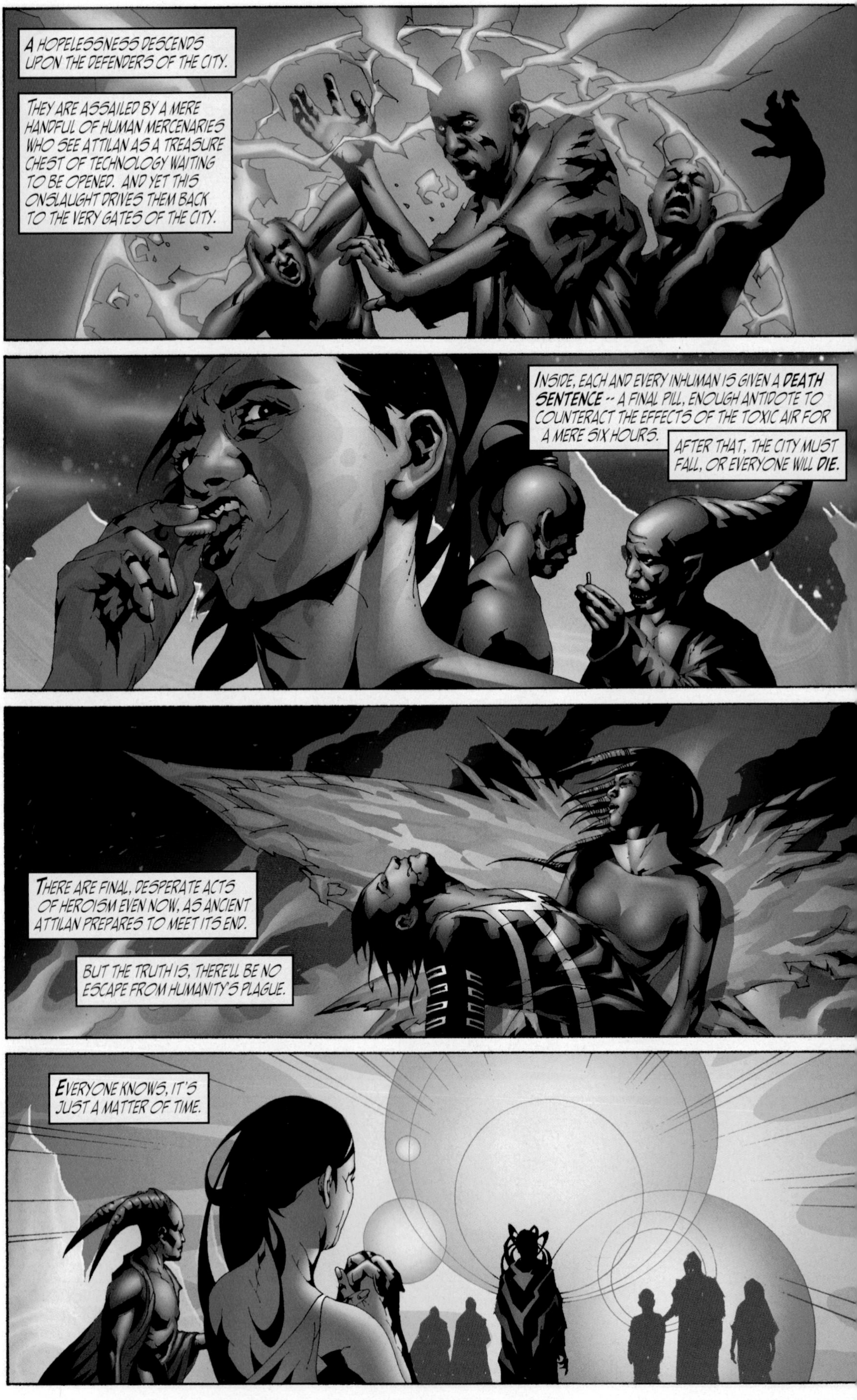
A HOPELESSNESS DESCENDS UPON THE DEFENDERS OF THE CITY.
THEY ARE ASSAILED BY A MERE HANDFUL OF HUMAN MERCENARIES WHO SEE ATTILAN AS A TREASURE CHEST OF TECHNOLOGY WAITING TO BE OPENED. AND YET THIS ONSLAUGHT DRIVES THEM BACK TO THE VERY GATES OF THE CITY.
INSIDE, EACH AND EVERY INHUMAN IS GIVEN A DEATH SENTENCE -- A FINAL PILL, ENOUGH ANTIDOTE TO COUNTERACT THE EFFECTS OF THE TOXIC AIR FOR A MERE SIX HOURS.
AFTER THAT, THE CITY MUST FALL, OR EVERYONE WILL DIE.
THERE ARE FINAL, DESPERATE ACTS OF HEROISM EVEN NOW, AS ANCIENT ATTILAN PREPARES TO MEET ITS END.
BUT THE TRUTH IS, THERE'LL BE NO ESCAPE FROM HUMANITY'S PLAGUE.
EVERYONE KNOWS, IT'S JUST A MATTER OF TIME.

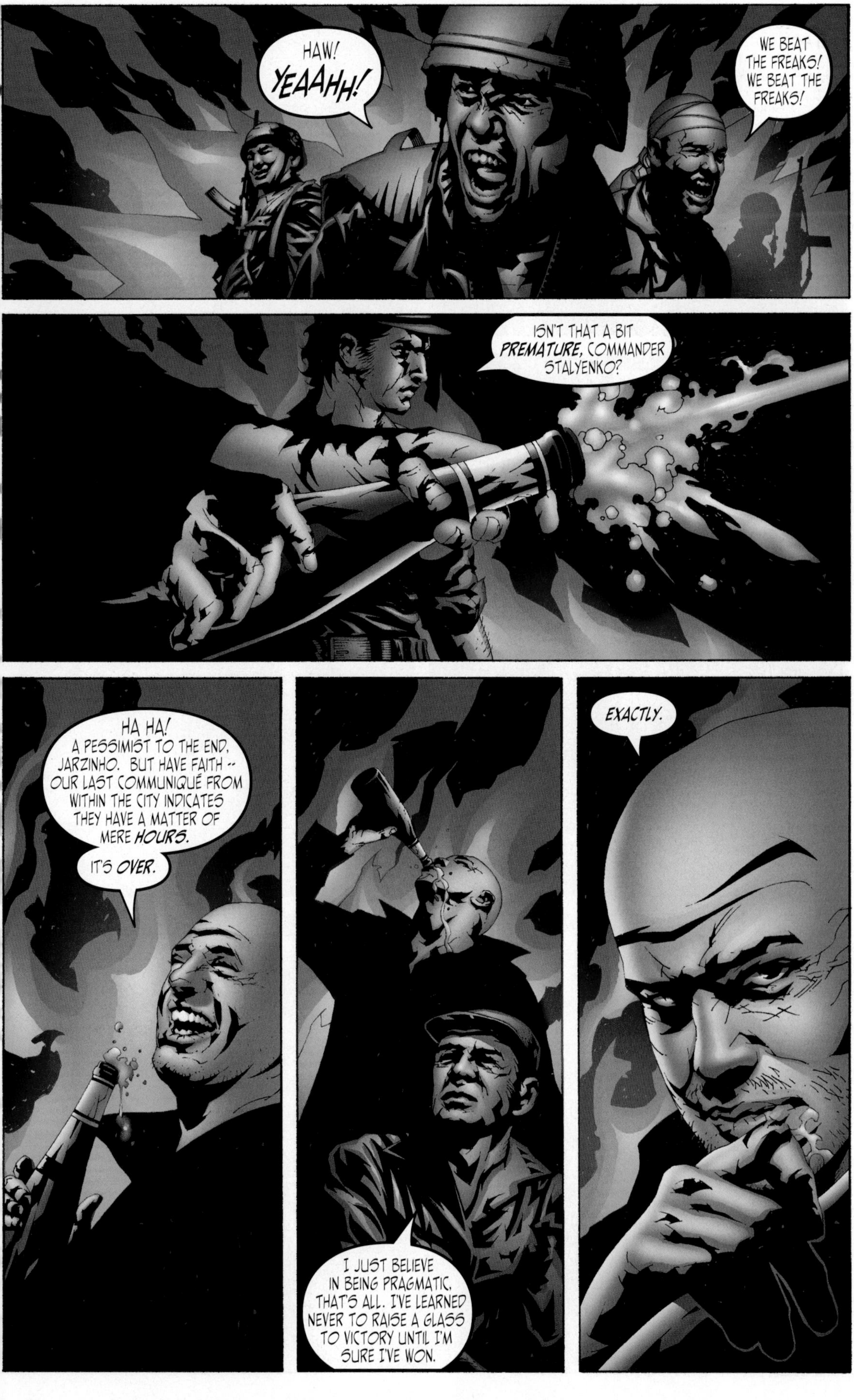
HAW! YEAAHH!
WE BEAT THE FREAKS! WE BEAT THE FREAKS!
ISN'T THAT A BIT PREMATURE, COMMANDER STALYENKO?
HA HA! A PESSIMIST TO THE END, JARZINHO. BUT HAVE FAITH -- OUR LAST COMMUNIQUÉ FROM WITHIN THE CITY INDICATES THEY HAVE A MATTER OF MERE HOURS.
IT'S OVER.
I JUST BELIEVE IN BEING PRAGMATIC, THAT'S ALL. I'VE LEARNED NEVER TO RAISE A GLASS TO VICTORY UNTIL I'M SURE I'VE WON.
EXACTLY.

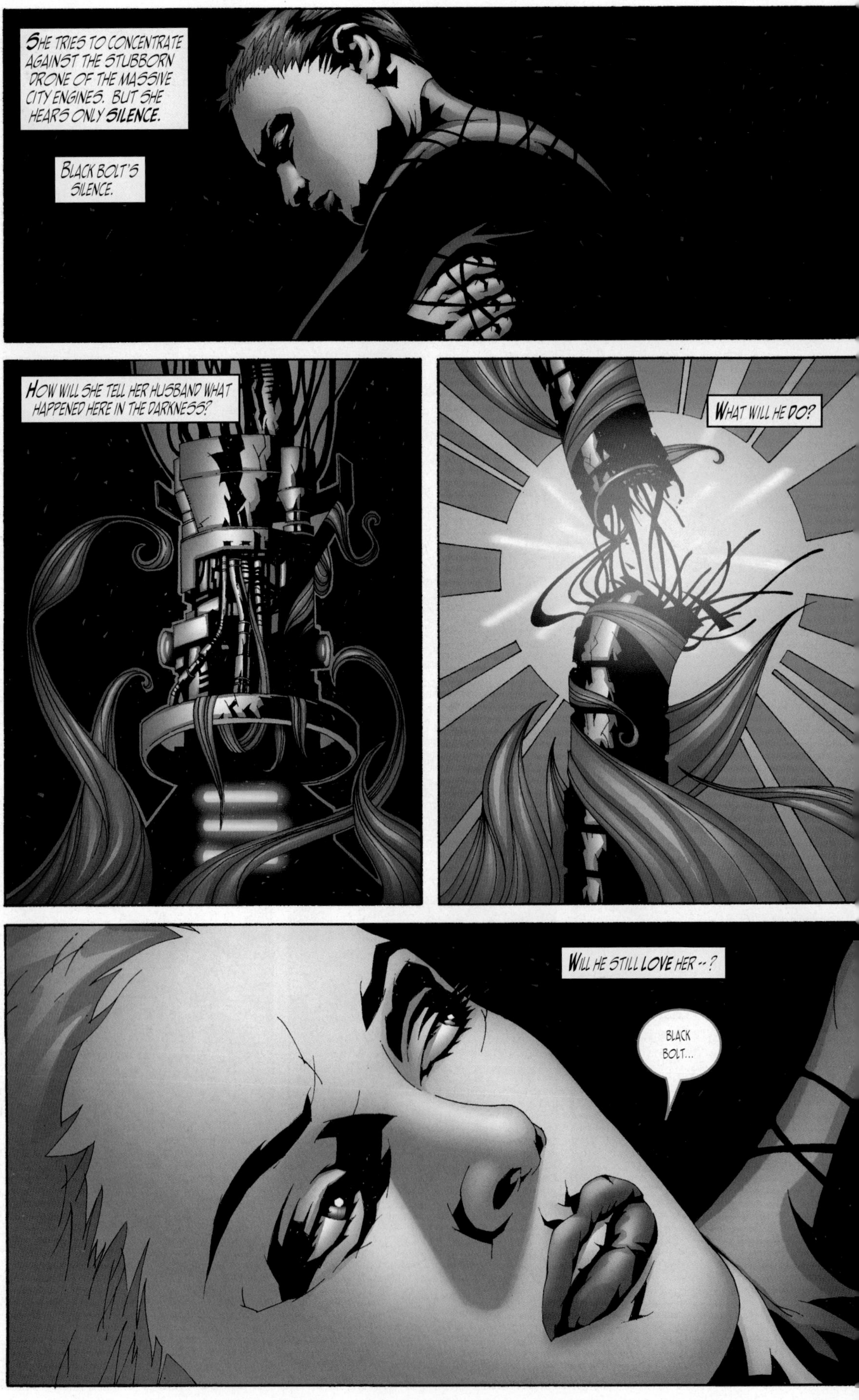
SHE TRIES TO CONCENTRATE AGAINST THE STUBBORN DRONE OF THE MASSIVE CITY ENGINES. BUT SHE HEARS ONLY SILENCE.
BLACK BOLT'S SILENCE.
HOW WILL SHE TELL HER HUSBAND WHAT HAPPENED HERE IN THE DARKNESS?
WHAT WILL HE DO?
WILL HE STILL LOVE HER--?
BLACK BOLT...

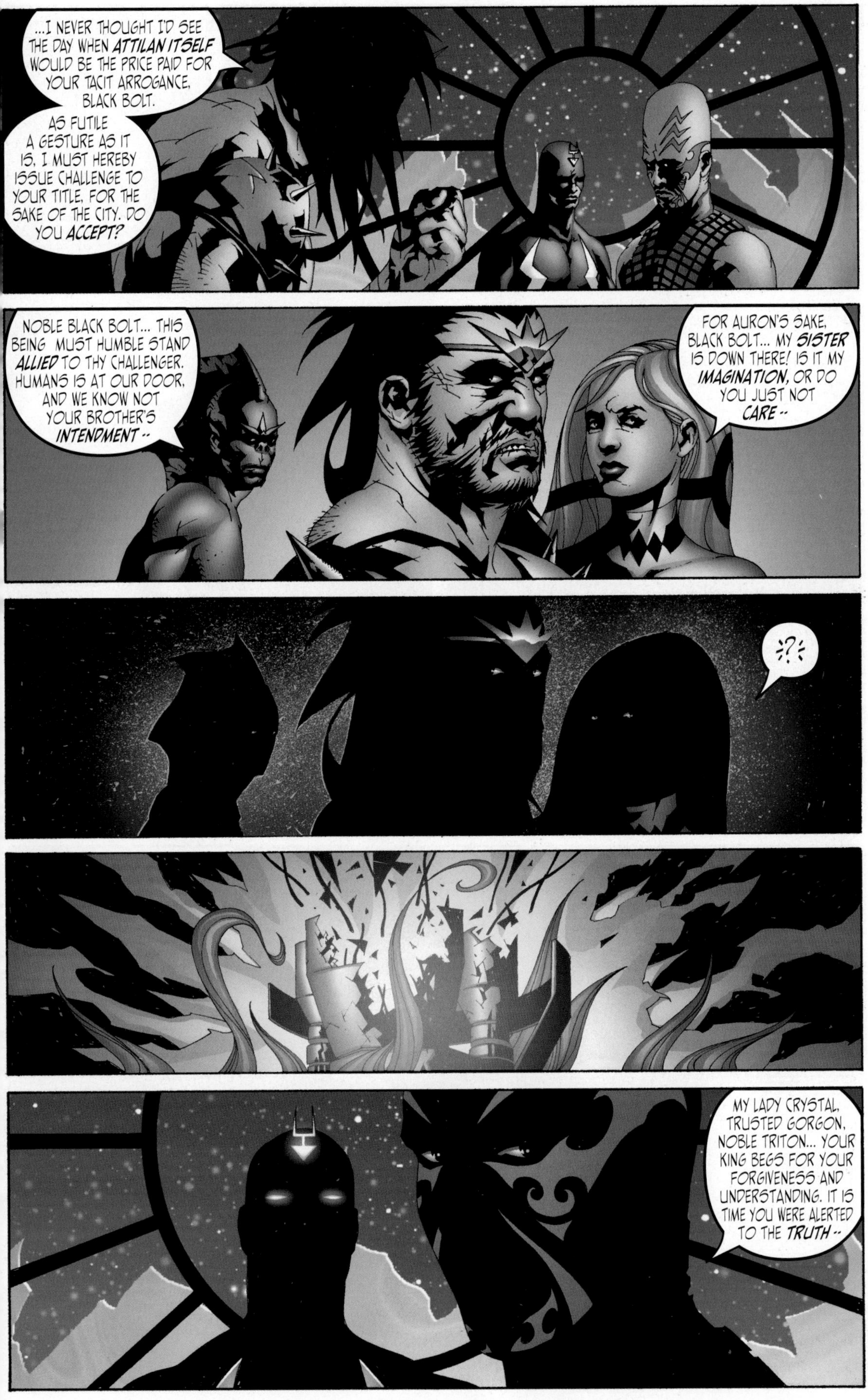

...I NEVER THOUGHT I'D SEE THE DAY WHEN ATTILAN ITSELF WOULD BE THE PRICE PAID FOR YOUR TACIT ARROGANCE, BLACK BOLT.
AS FUTILE A GESTURE AS IT IS, I MUST HEREBY ISSUE CHALLENGE TO YOUR TITLE, FOR THE SAKE OF THE CITY. DO YOU ACCEPT?
NOBLE BLACK BOLT... THIS BEING MUST HUMBLE STAND ALLIED TO THY CHALLENGER. HUMANS IS AT OUR DOOR, AND WE KNOW NOT YOUR BROTHER'S INTENDMENT --
FOR AURON'S SAKE, BLACK BOLT... MY SISTER IS DOWN THERE! IS IT MY IMAGINATION, OR DO YOU JUST NOT CARE --
?
MY LADY CRYSTAL, TRUSTED GORGON, NOBLE TRITON... YOUR KING BEGS FOR YOUR FORGIVENESS AND UNDERSTANDING. IT IS TIME YOU WERE ALERTED TO THE TRUTH --

WHAT *HAPPENED* -- ?

I DON'T KNOW. THE ENTIRE POWER GRID'S BEEN SHUT DOWN.

IT... IT'S NOT *POSSIBLE* -- I DIDN'T GIVE THE ORDER TO TURN OFF THE POWER. WHO IS RESPONSIBLE FOR THIS WANTON ACT OF INDEPENDENT THOUGHT?

Oh, PRINCE MAXIMUS... IT WAS NOT *WE* ALPHAS. WE ARE YOUR SERVANTS, GOOD AND TRUE.

FROM THE QUEEN'S QUARTERS COMES THIS DISTURBANCE --

THE TRUTH, KARNAK? WHAT DO YOU MEAN, "THE *TRUTH?*"

I DEMAND TO KNOW WHAT'S HAPPENING. YOU'RE UP TO SOMETHING -- I *KNOW* IT!

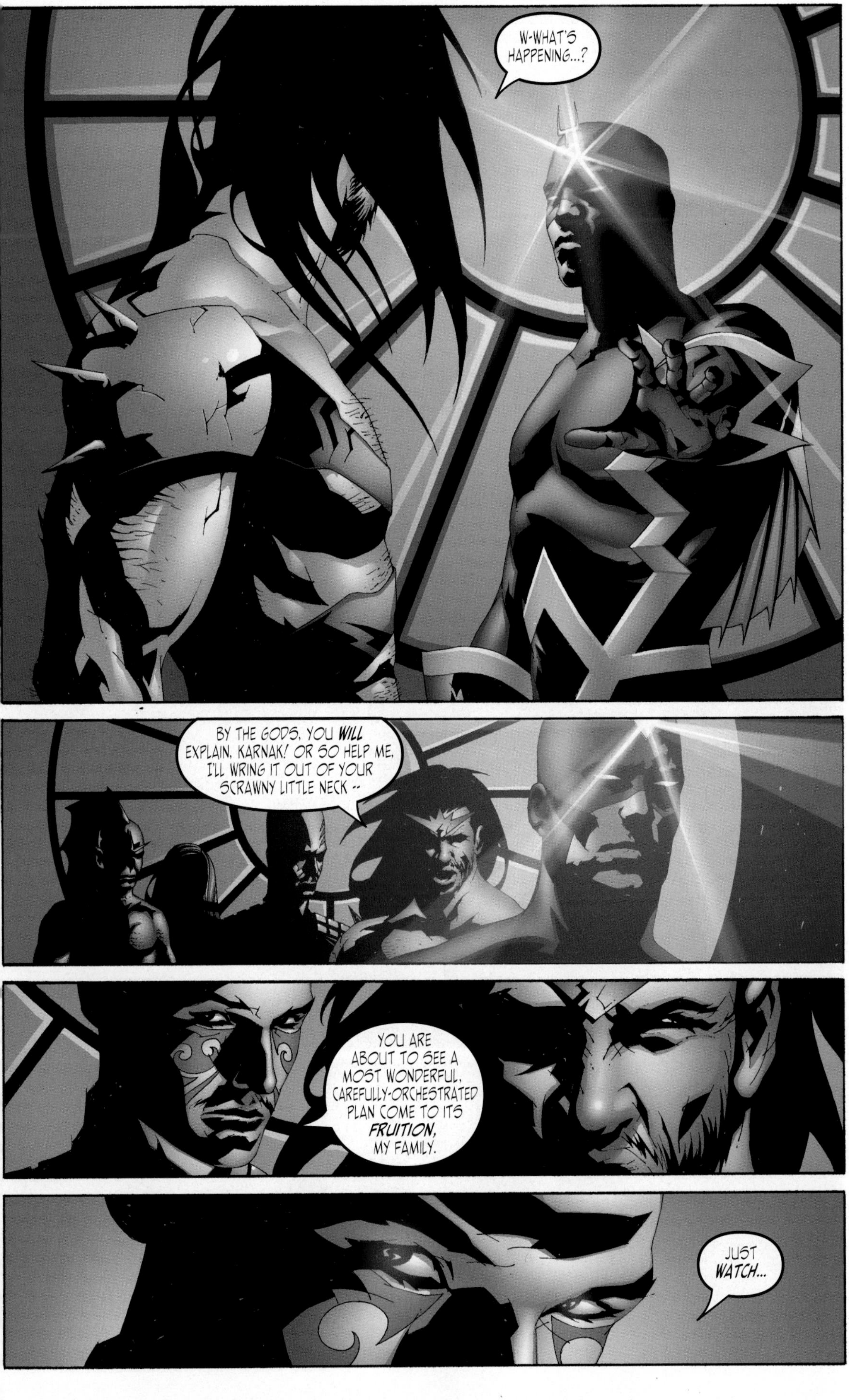
W-WHAT'S HAPPENING...?
BY THE GODS, YOU WILL EXPLAIN, KARNAK! OR SO HELP ME, I'LL WRING IT OUT OF YOUR SCRAWNY LITTLE NECK --
YOU ARE ABOUT TO SEE A MOST WONDERFUL, CAREFULLY-ORCHESTRATED PLAN COME TO ITS FRUITION, MY FAMILY.
JUST WATCH...

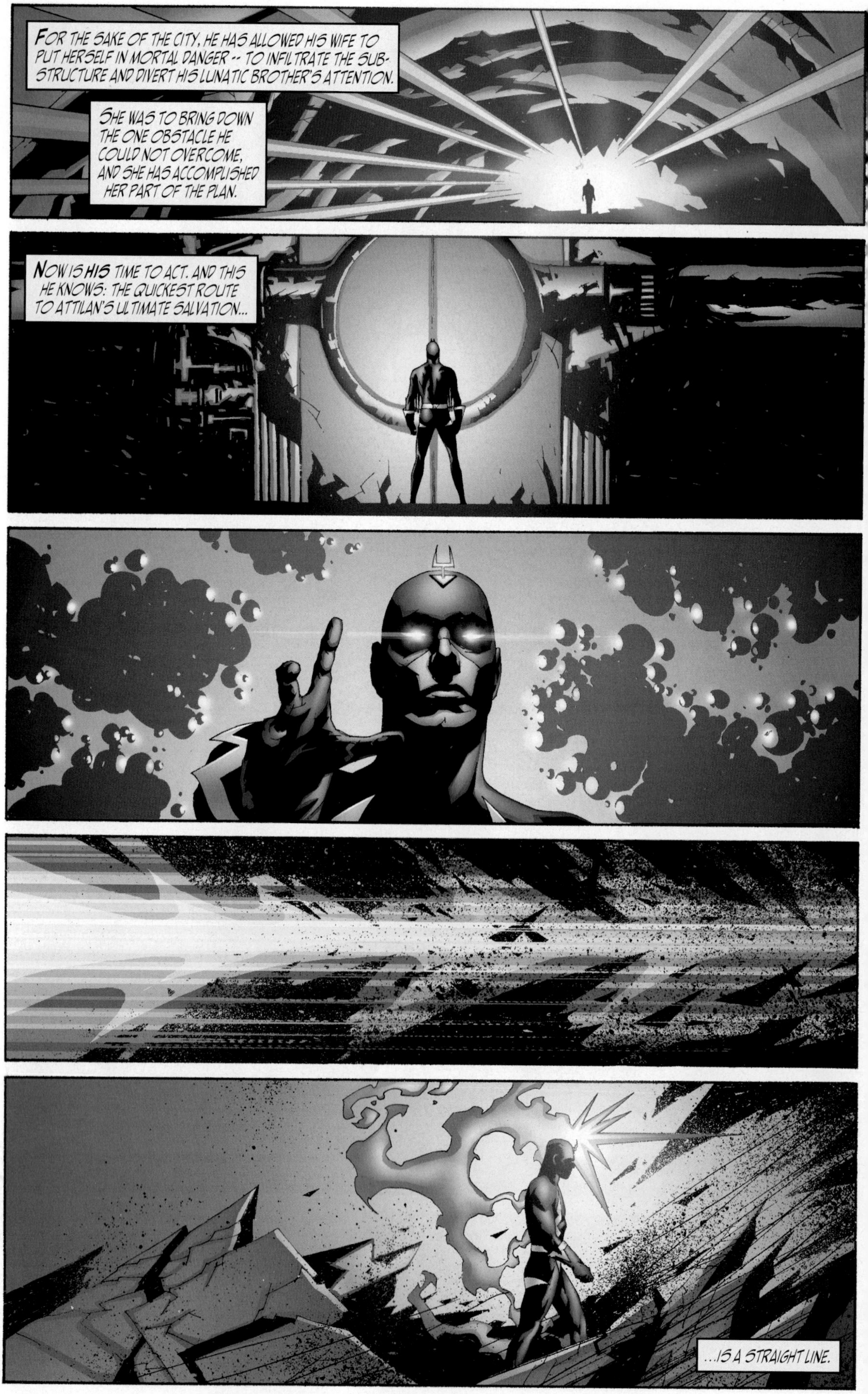
FOR THE SAKE OF THE CITY, HE HAS ALLOWED HIS WIFE TO PUT HERSELF IN MORTAL DANGER -- TO INFILTRATE THE SUB-STRUCTURE AND DIVERT HIS LUNATIC BROTHER'S ATTENTION.
SHE WAS TO BRING DOWN THE ONE OBSTACLE HE COULD NOT OVERCOME, AND SHE HAS ACCOMPLISHED HER PART OF THE PLAN.
NOW IS HIS TIME TO ACT. AND THIS HE KNOWS: THE QUICKEST ROUTE TO ATTILAN'S ULTIMATE SALVATION...
...IS A STRAIGHT LINE.

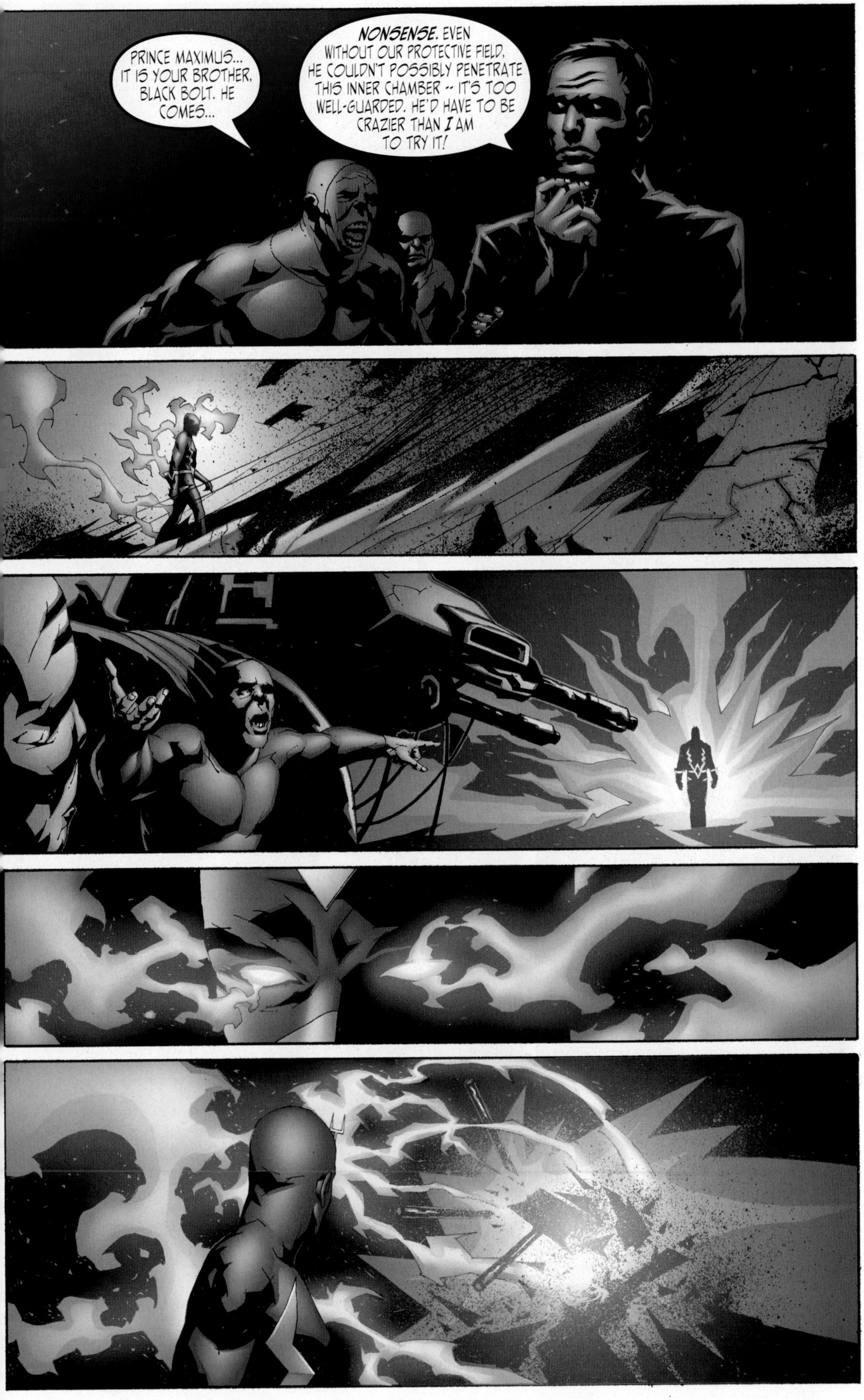
PRINCE MAXIMUS... IT IS YOUR BROTHER, BLACK BOLT. HE COMES...
NONSENSE. EVEN WITHOUT OUR PROTECTIVE FIELD, HE COULDN'T POSSIBLY PENETRATE THIS INNER CHAMBER -- IT'S TOO WELL-GUARDED. HE'D HAVE TO BE CRAZIER THAN I AM TO TRY IT!

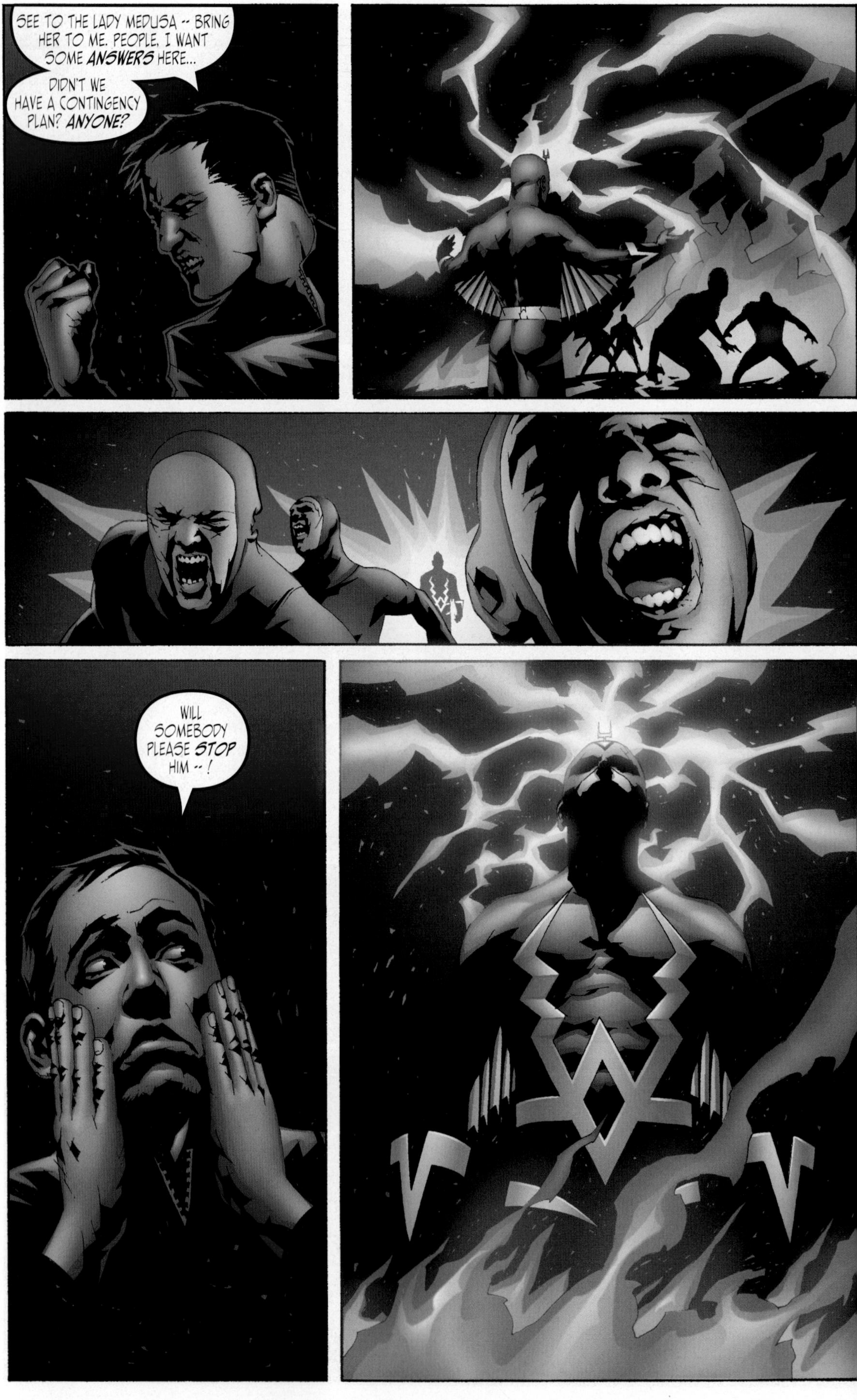
SEE TO THE LADY MEDUSA -- BRING HER TO ME. PEOPLE, I WANT SOME ANSWERS HERE...
DIDN'T WE HAVE A CONTINGENCY PLAN? ANYONE?
WILL SOMEBODY PLEASE STOP HIM -- !

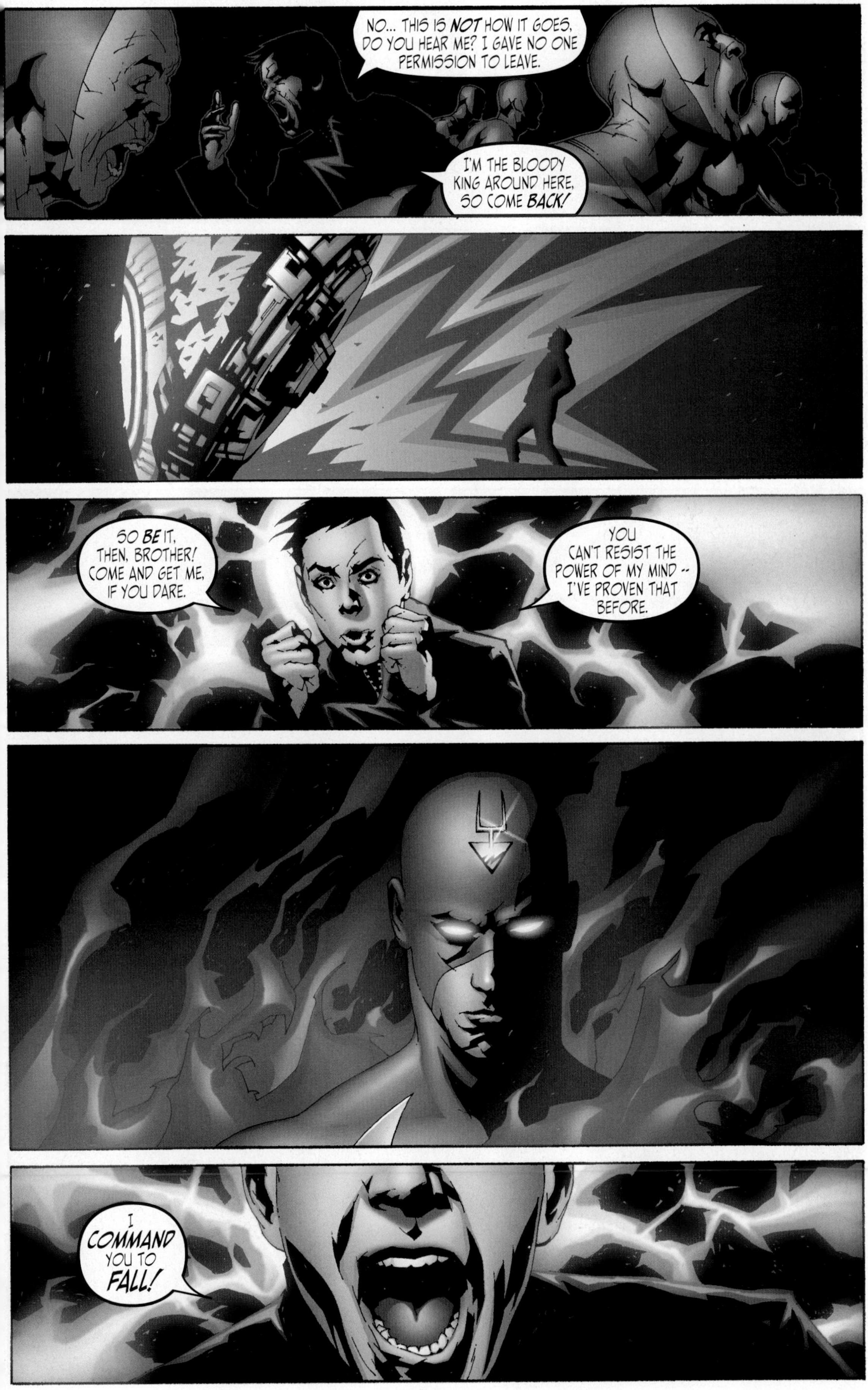
NO... THIS IS NOT HOW IT GOES, DO YOU HEAR ME? I GAVE NO ONE PERMISSION TO LEAVE.
I'M THE BLOODY KING AROUND HERE, SO COME BACK!
SO BE IT, THEN, BROTHER! COME AND GET ME, IF YOU DARE.
YOU CAN'T RESIST THE POWER OF MY MIND -- I'VE PROVEN THAT BEFORE.
I COMMAND YOU TO FALL!

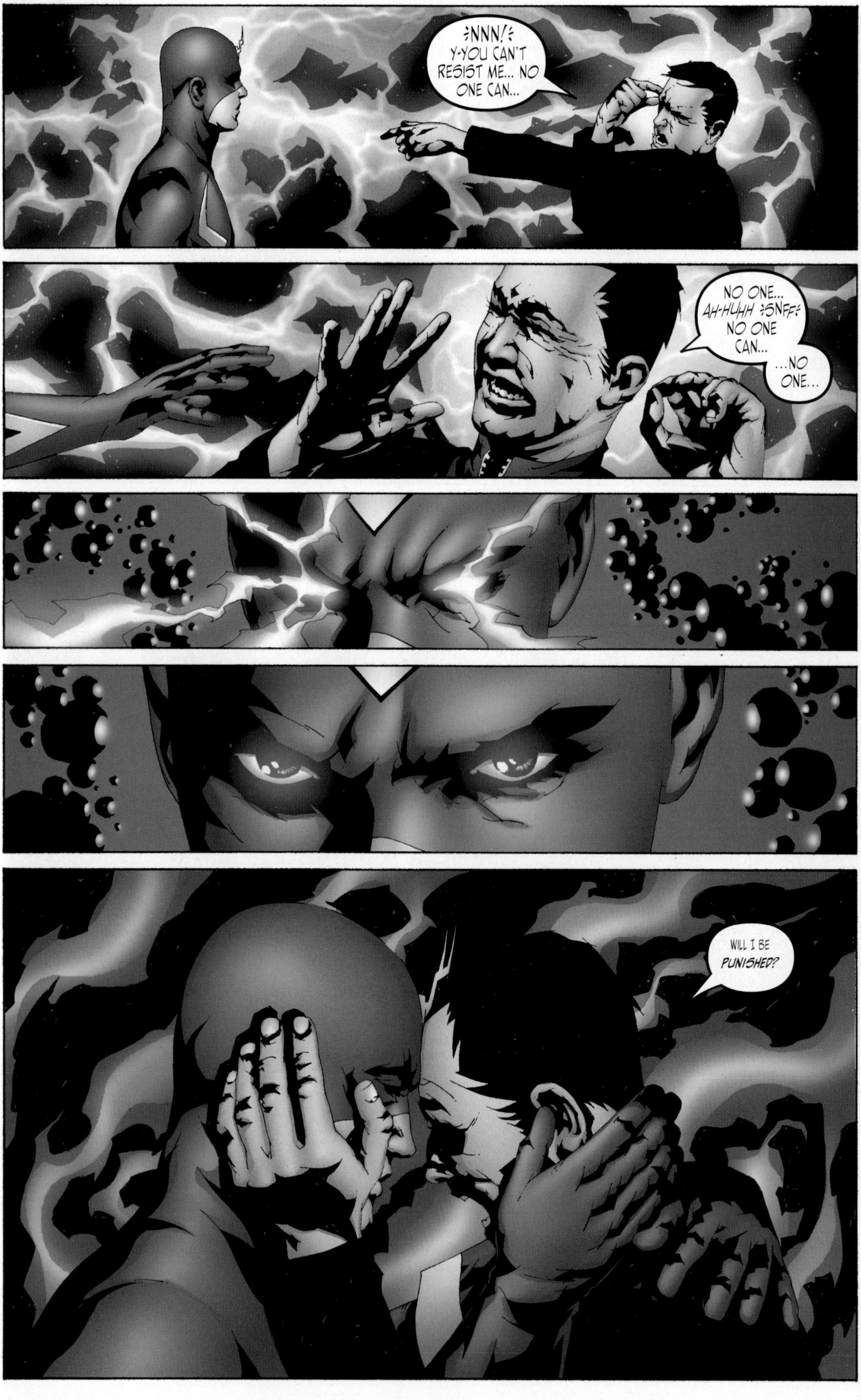

NNN! Y-YOU CAN'T RESIST ME... NO ONE CAN...
NO ONE... AH-HUHH SNFF NO ONE CAN...
...NO ONE...
WILL I BE PUNISHED?

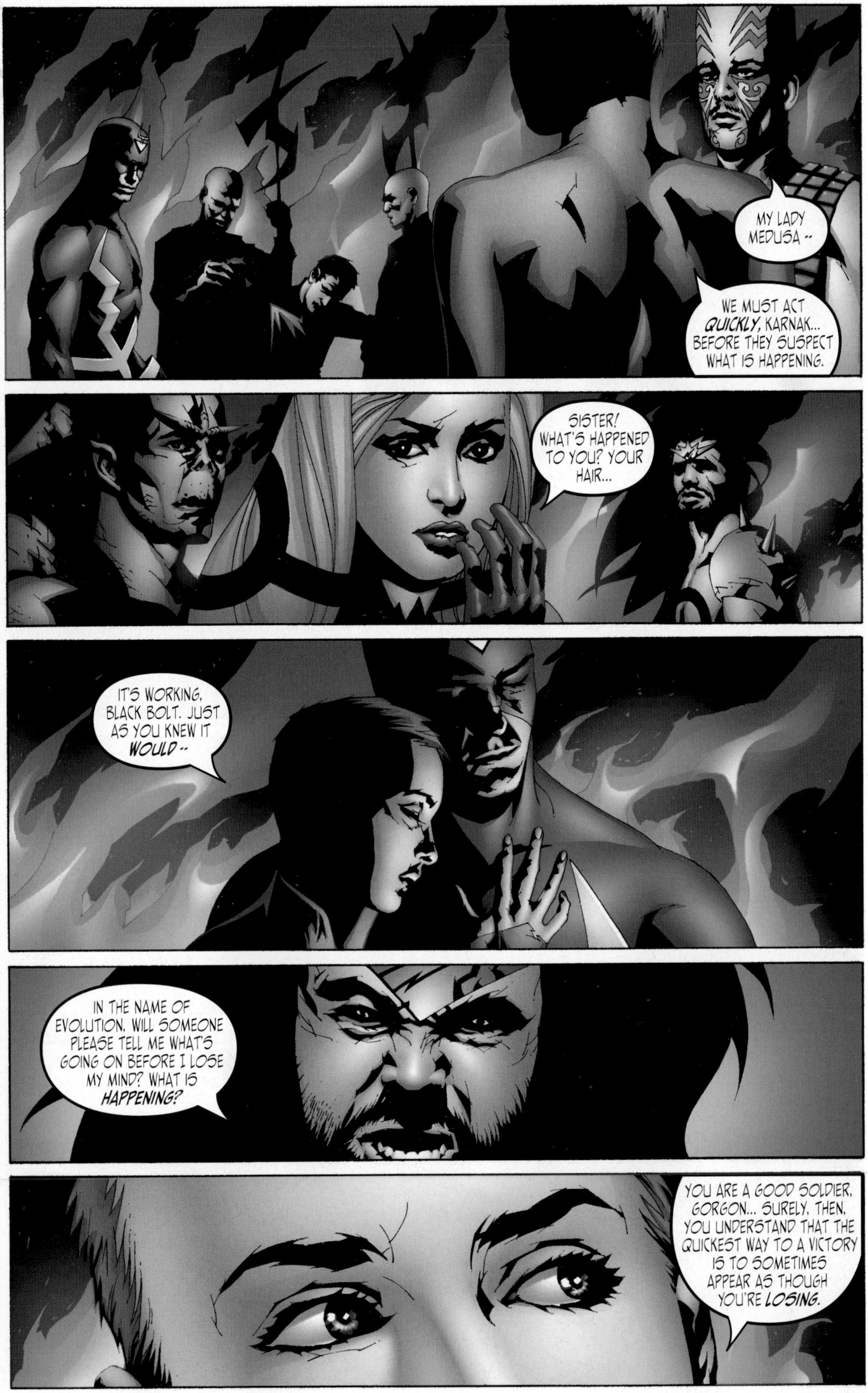
MY LADY MEDUSA --
WE MUST ACT QUICKLY, KARNAK... BEFORE THEY SUSPECT WHAT IS HAPPENING.
SISTER! WHAT'S HAPPENED TO YOU? YOUR HAIR...
IT'S WORKING, BLACK BOLT. JUST AS YOU KNEW IT WOULD --
IN THE NAME OF EVOLUTION, WILL SOMEONE PLEASE TELL ME WHAT'S GOING ON BEFORE I LOSE MY MIND? WHAT IS HAPPENING?
YOU ARE A GOOD SOLDIER, GORGON... SURELY, THEN, YOU UNDERSTAND THAT THE QUICKEST WAY TO A VICTORY IS TO SOMETIMES APPEAR AS THOUGH YOU'RE LOSING.

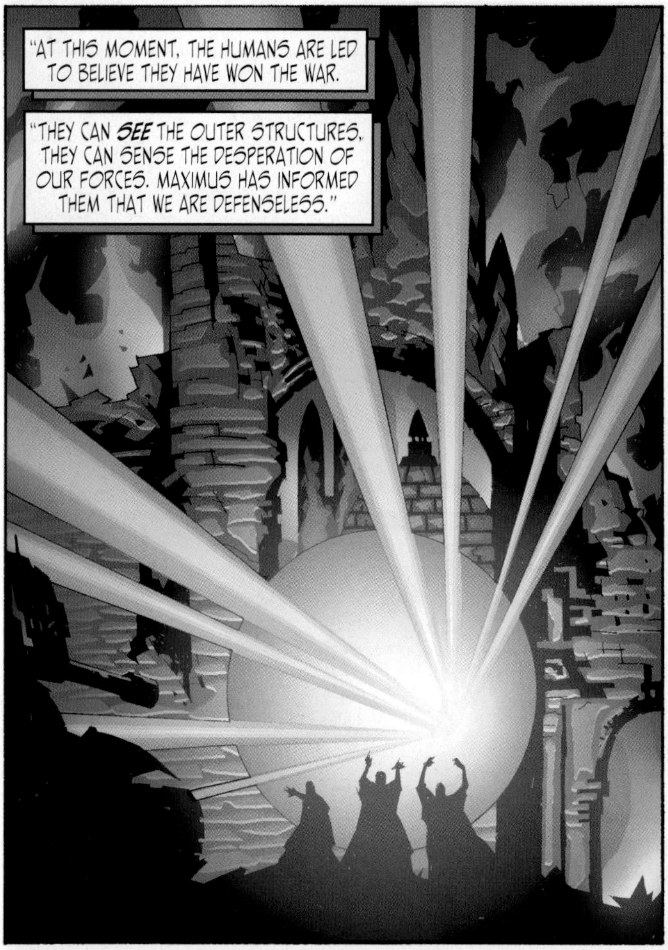
"AT THIS MOMENT, THE HUMANS ARE LED TO BELIEVE THEY HAVE WON THE WAR.
"THEY CAN SEE THE OUTER STRUCTURES, THEY CAN SENSE THE DESPERATION OF OUR FORCES. MAXIMUS HAS INFORMED THEM THAT WE ARE DEFENSELESS."

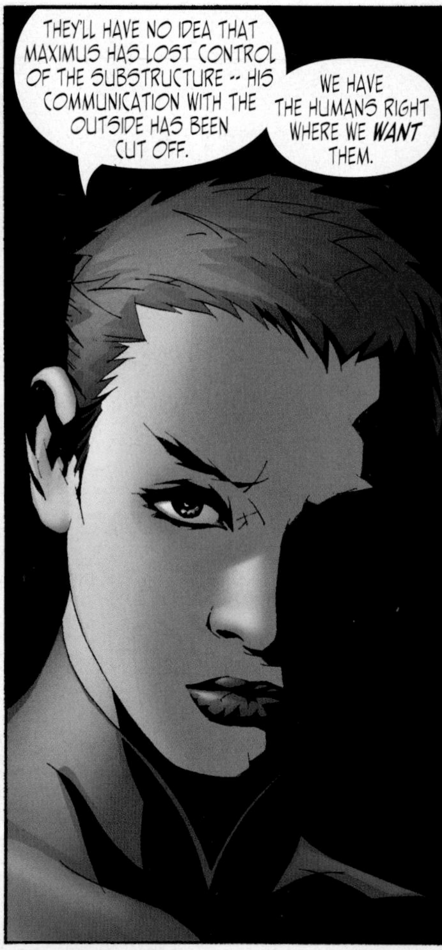
THEY'LL HAVE NO IDEA THAT MAXIMUS HAS LOST CONTROL OF THE SUBSTRUCTURE -- HIS COMMUNICATION WITH THE OUTSIDE HAS BEEN CUT OFF.
WE HAVE THE HUMANS RIGHT WHERE WE WANT THEM.

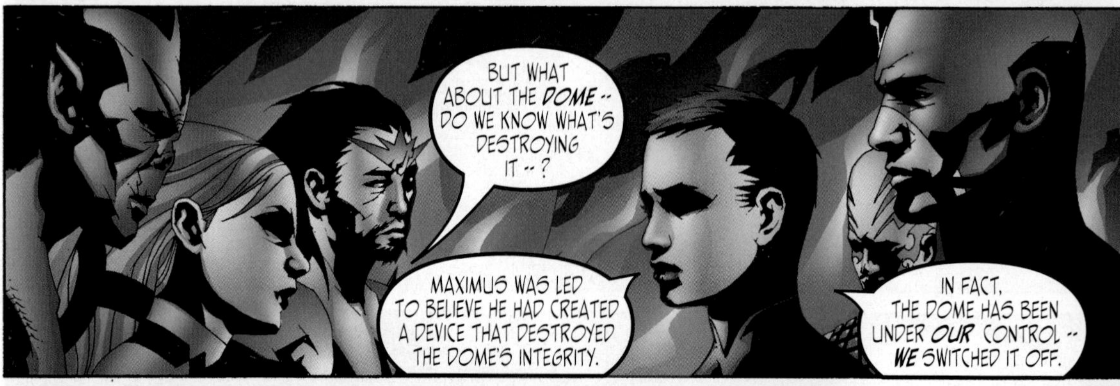
BUT WHAT ABOUT THE DOME -- DO WE KNOW WHAT'S DESTROYING IT -- ?
MAXIMUS WAS LED TO BELIEVE HE HAD CREATED A DEVICE THAT DESTROYED THE DOME'S INTEGRITY.
IN FACT, THE DOME HAS BEEN UNDER OUR CONTROL -- WE SWITCHED IT OFF.

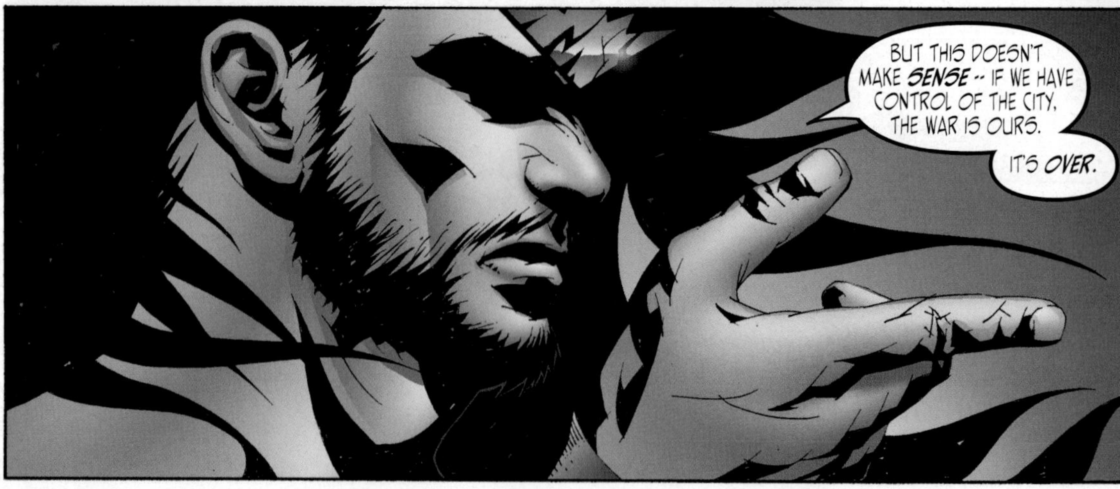
BUT THIS DOESN'T MAKE SENSE -- IF WE HAVE CONTROL OF THE CITY, THE WAR IS OURS.
IT'S OVER.

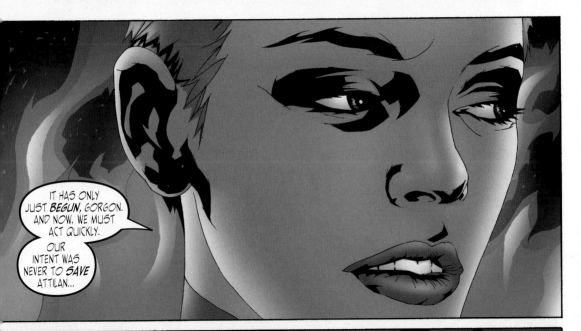

IT HAS ONLY JUST *BEGUN*, GORGON. AND NOW, WE MUST ACT QUICKLY.

OUR INTENT WAS NEVER TO *SAVE* ATTILAN...

... BUT TO *DESTROY* IT.

NEXT: PLAN "B"

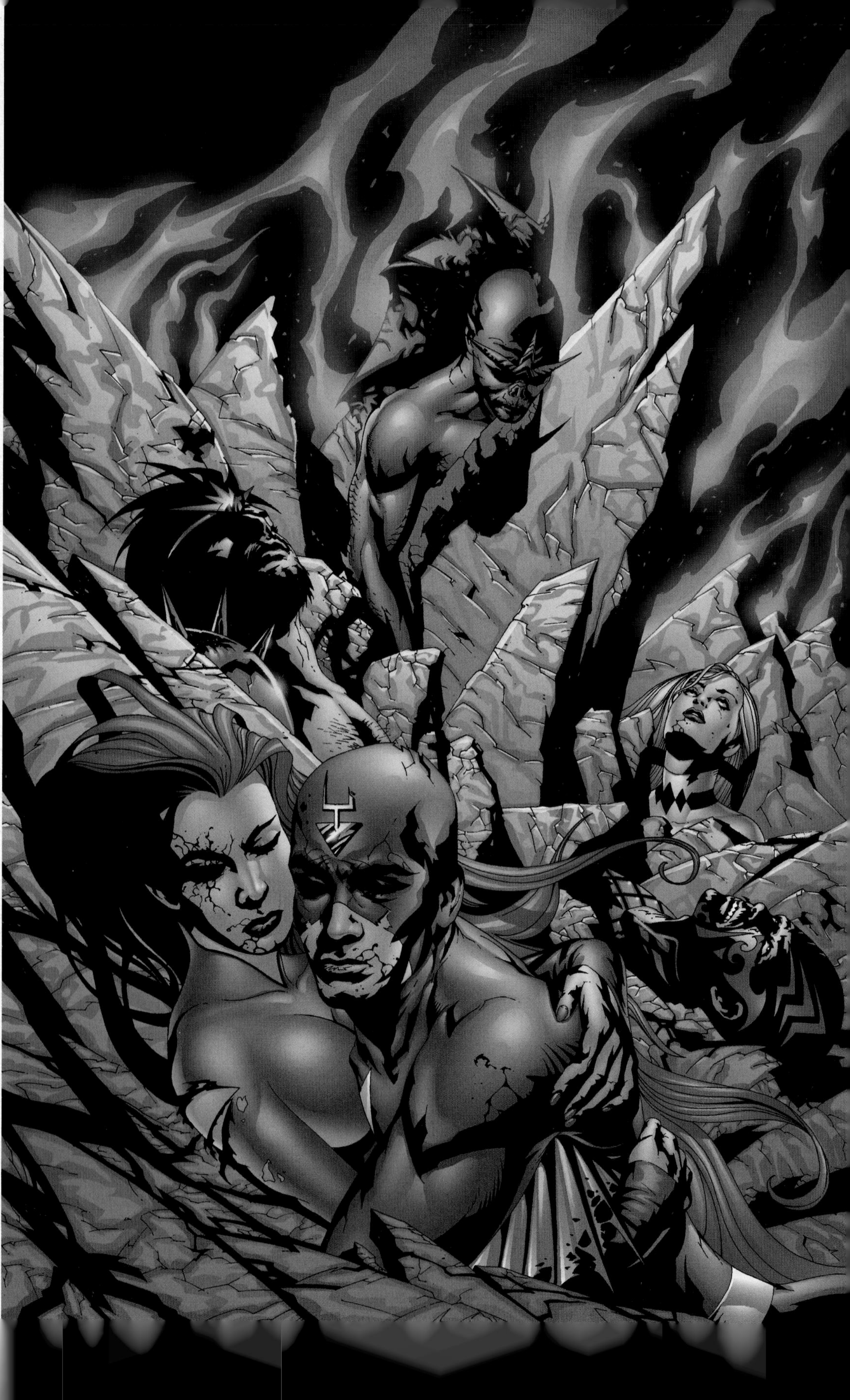

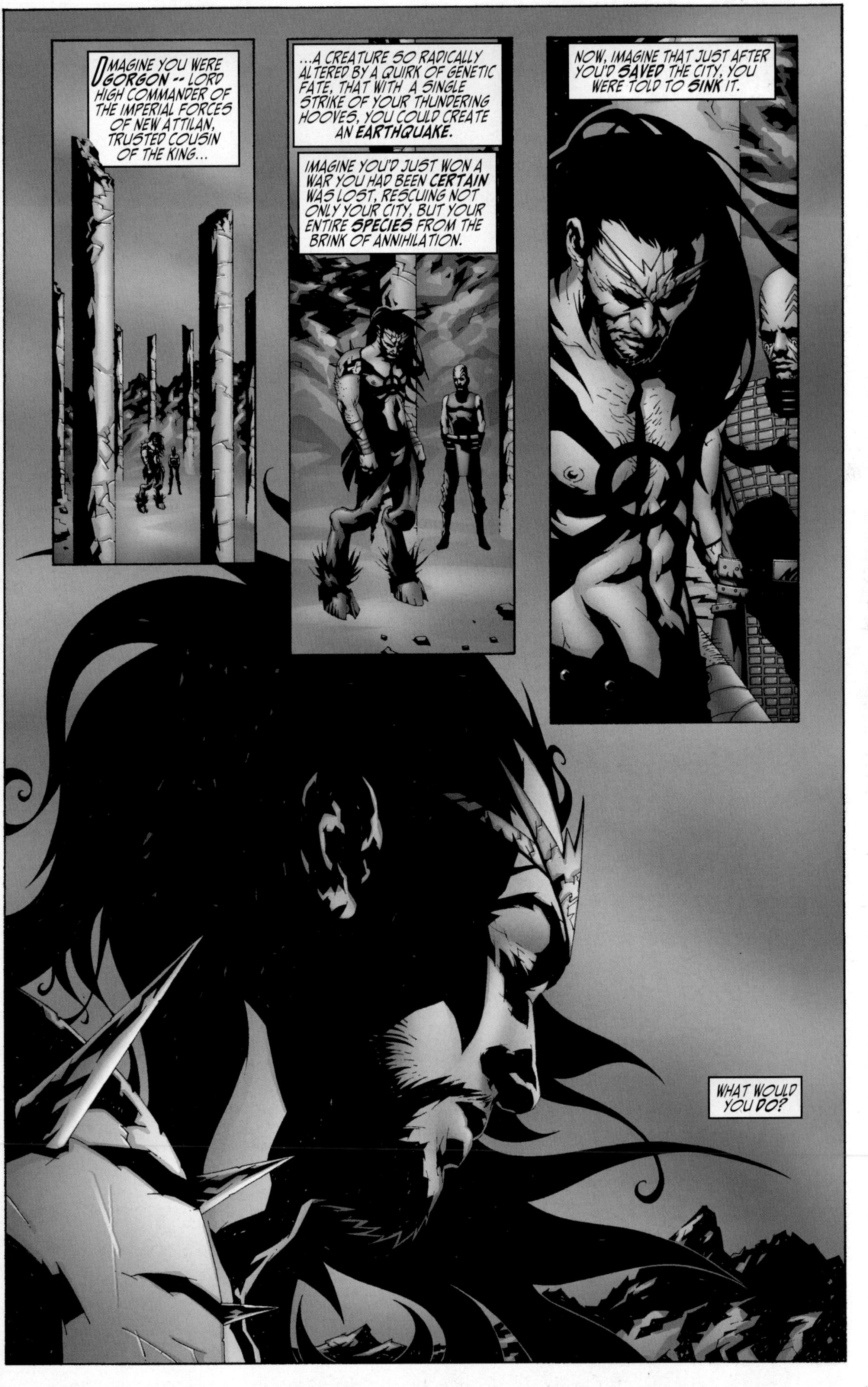
IMAGINE YOU WERE GORGON -- LORD HIGH COMMANDER OF THE IMPERIAL FORCES OF NEW ATTILAN, TRUSTED COUSIN OF THE KING...
...A CREATURE SO RADICALLY ALTERED BY A QUIRK OF GENETIC FATE, THAT WITH A SINGLE STRIKE OF YOUR THUNDERING HOOVES, YOU COULD CREATE AN EARTHQUAKE.
IMAGINE YOU'D JUST WON A WAR YOU HAD BEEN CERTAIN WAS LOST, RESCUING NOT ONLY YOUR CITY, BUT YOUR ENTIRE SPECIES FROM THE BRINK OF ANNIHILATION.
NOW, IMAGINE THAT JUST AFTER YOU'D SAVED THE CITY, YOU WERE TOLD TO SINK IT.
WHAT WOULD YOU DO?

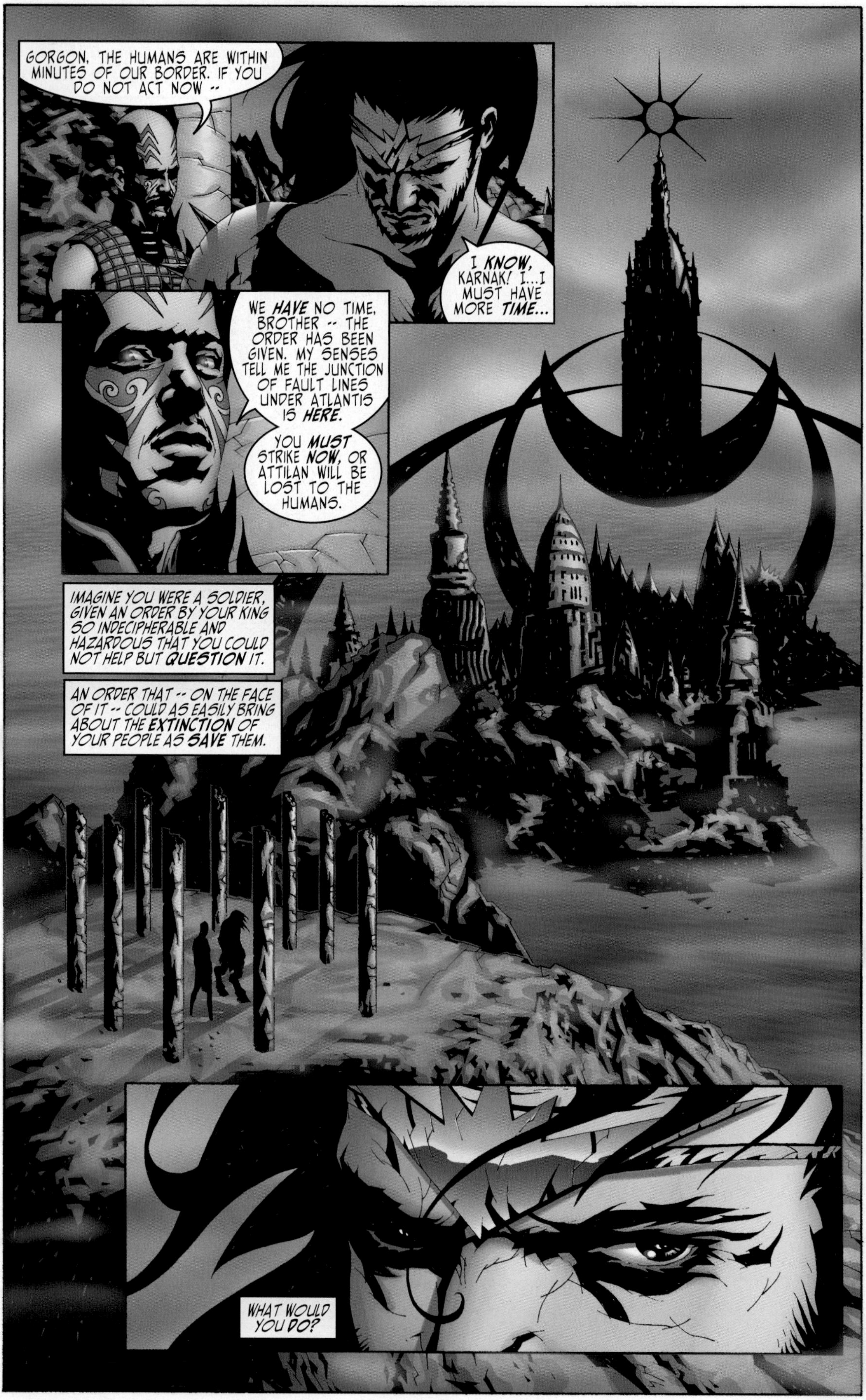
GORGON, THE HUMANS ARE WITHIN MINUTES OF OUR BORDER. IF YOU DO NOT ACT NOW --
I KNOW, KARNAK! I...I MUST HAVE MORE TIME...
WE HAVE NO TIME, BROTHER -- THE ORDER HAS BEEN GIVEN. MY SENSES TELL ME THE JUNCTION OF FAULT LINES UNDER ATLANTIS IS HERE.
YOU MUST STRIKE NOW, OR ATTILAN WILL BE LOST TO THE HUMANS.
IMAGINE YOU WERE A SOLDIER, GIVEN AN ORDER BY YOUR KING SO INDECIPHERABLE AND HAZARDOUS THAT YOU COULD NOT HELP BUT QUESTION IT.
AN ORDER THAT -- ON THE FACE OF IT -- COULD AS EASILY BRING ABOUT THE EXTINCTION OF YOUR PEOPLE AS SAVE THEM.
WHAT WOULD YOU DO?

Paul Jenkins — Dirty Rotten Plotter
Jae Lee — Con Artist
Dave Kemp — Coloring the Truth
RS&Comicraft/ST — Scheming
Joe Quesada & Jimmy Palmiotti — Planning a Coup
Nanci Dakesian — Managing Scoundrelette
Bob Harras — Naughtypersoninchief

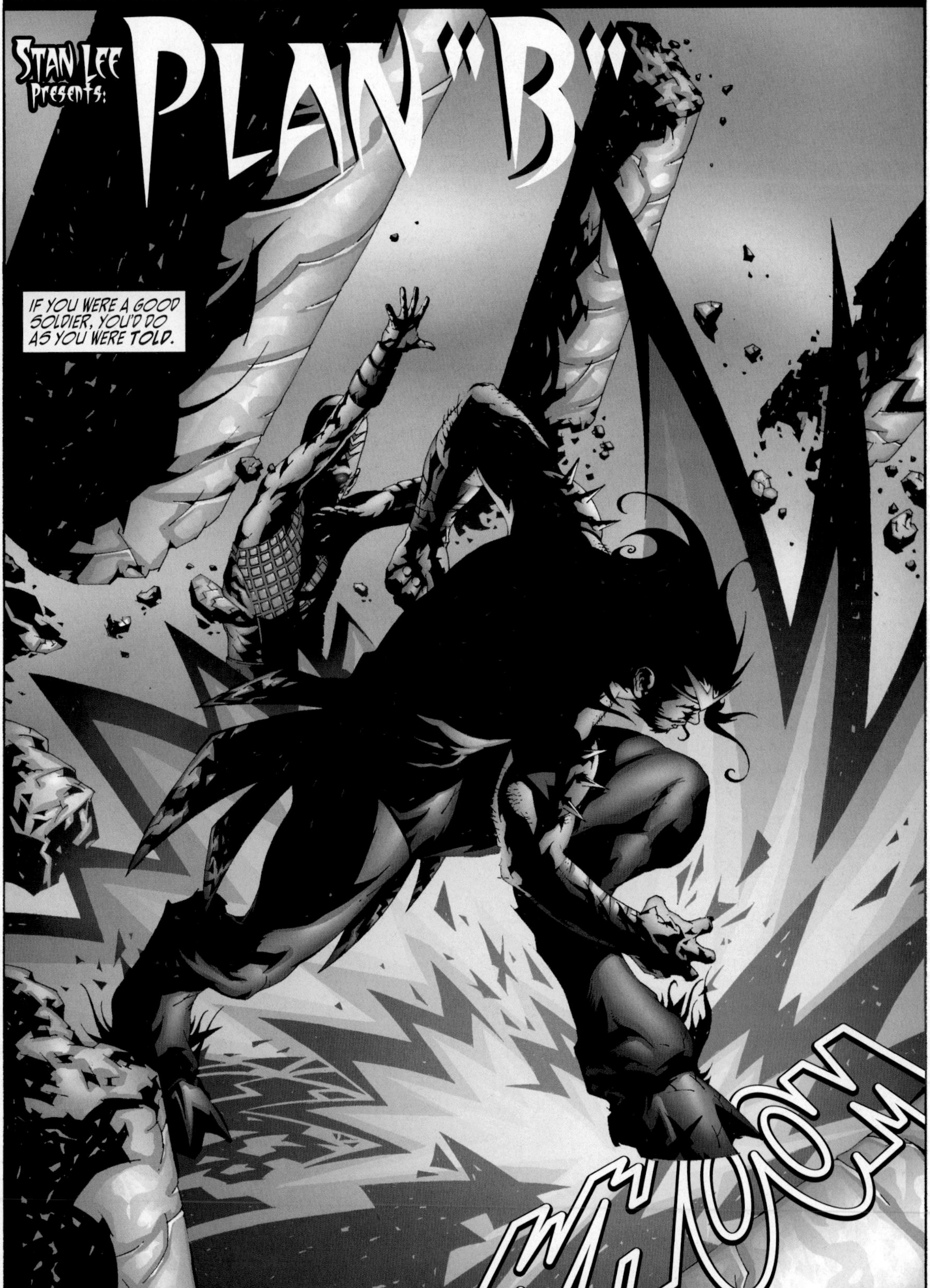

Stan Lee presents:
Plan "B"
IF YOU WERE A GOOD SOLDIER, YOU'D DO AS YOU WERE TOLD.

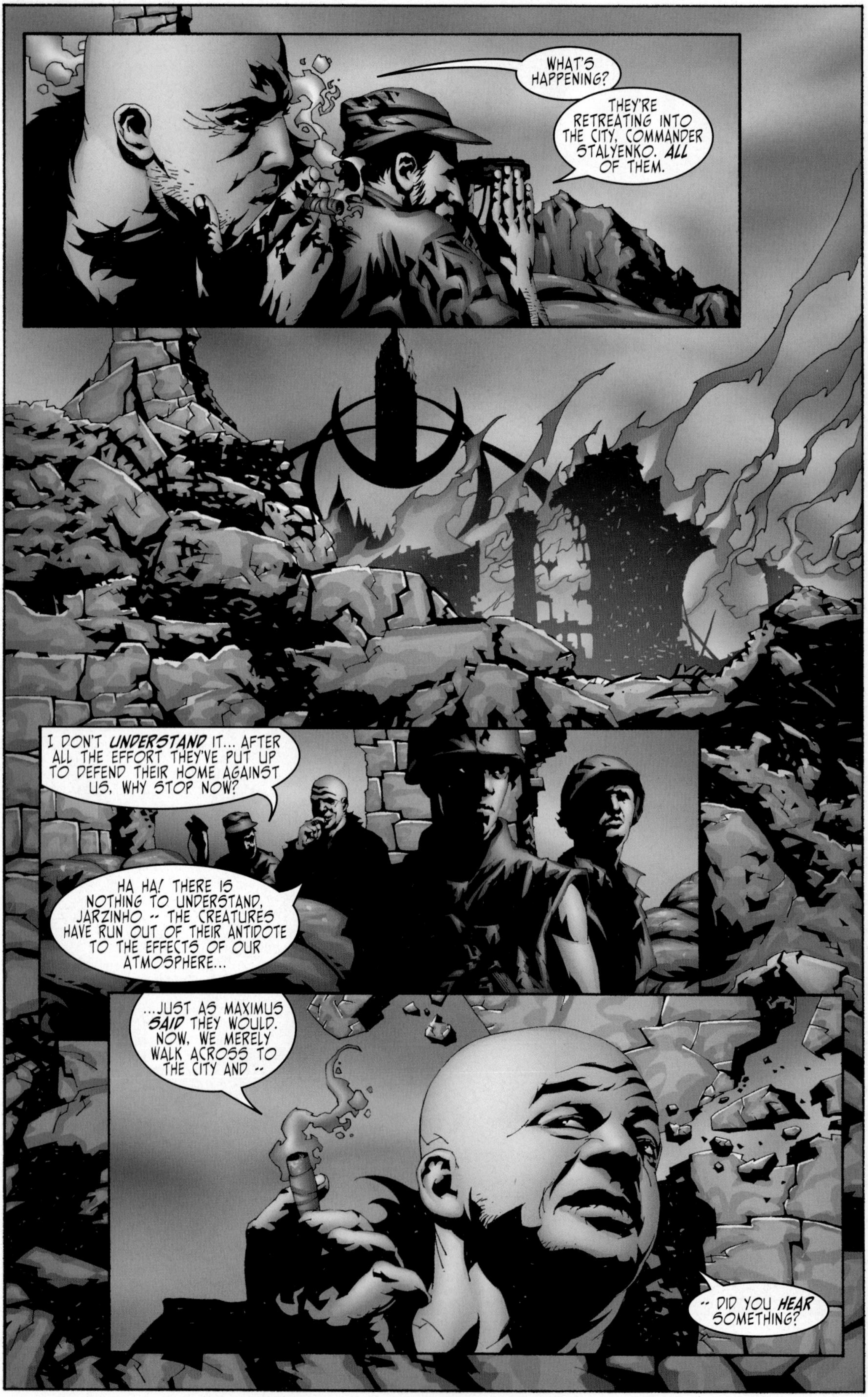
WHAT'S HAPPENING?
THEY'RE RETREATING INTO THE CITY, COMMANDER STALYENKO. *ALL* OF THEM.
I DON'T *UNDERSTAND* IT... AFTER ALL THE EFFORT THEY'VE PUT UP TO DEFEND THEIR HOME AGAINST US, WHY STOP NOW?
HA HA! THERE IS NOTHING TO UNDERSTAND, JARZINHO -- THE CREATURES HAVE RUN OUT OF THEIR ANTIDOTE TO THE EFFECTS OF OUR ATMOSPHERE...
...JUST AS MAXIMUS *SAID* THEY WOULD. NOW, WE MERELY WALK ACROSS TO THE CITY AND --
-- DID YOU *HEAR* SOMETHING?

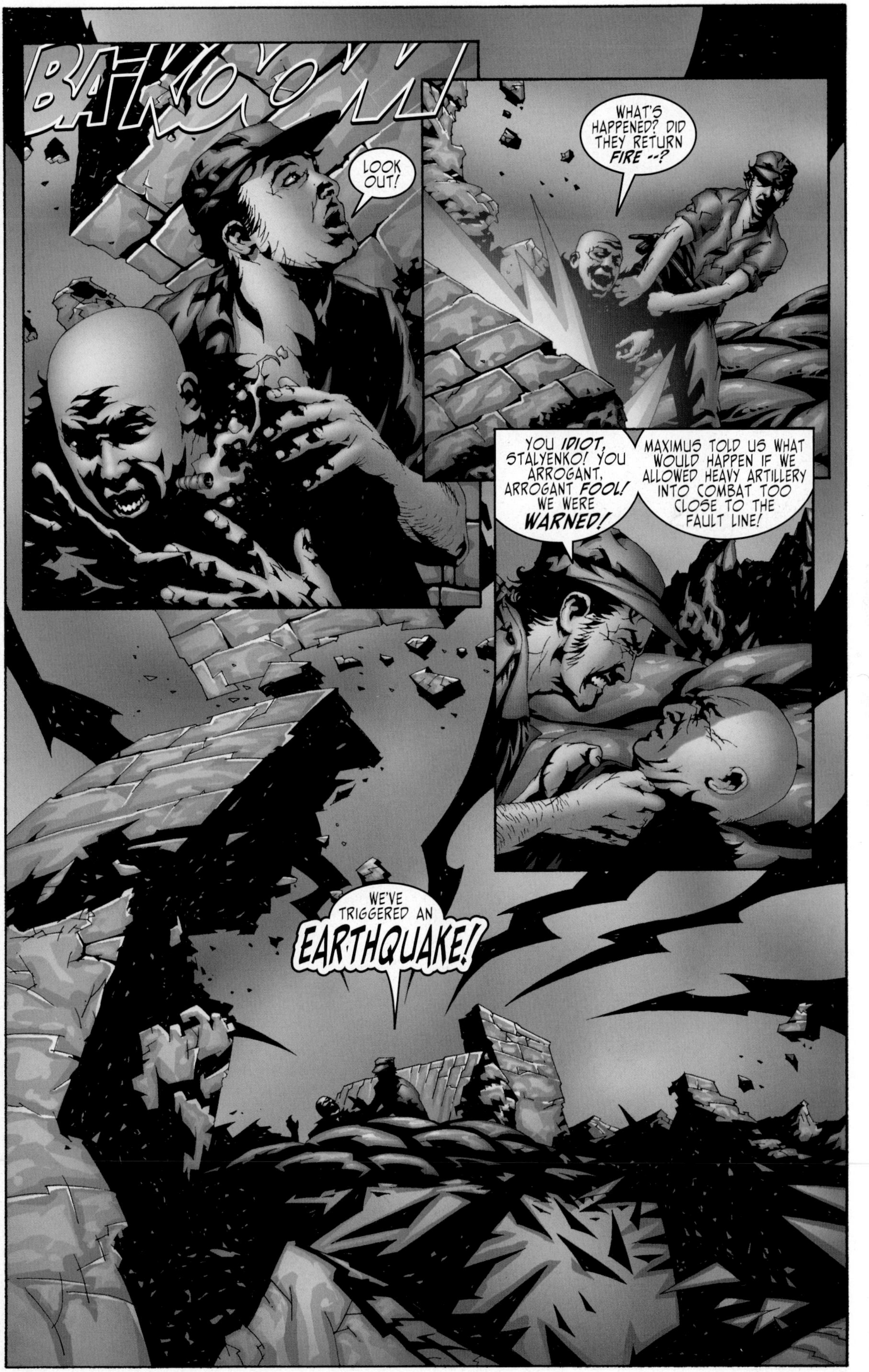
BAKOOOM
LOOK OUT!
WHAT'S HAPPENED? DID THEY RETURN FIRE --?
YOU IDIOT, STALYENKO! YOU ARROGANT, ARROGANT FOOL! WE WERE WARNED!
MAXIMUS TOLD US WHAT WOULD HAPPEN IF WE ALLOWED HEAVY ARTILLERY INTO COMBAT TOO CLOSE TO THE FAULT LINE!
WE'VE TRIGGERED AN EARTHQUAKE!

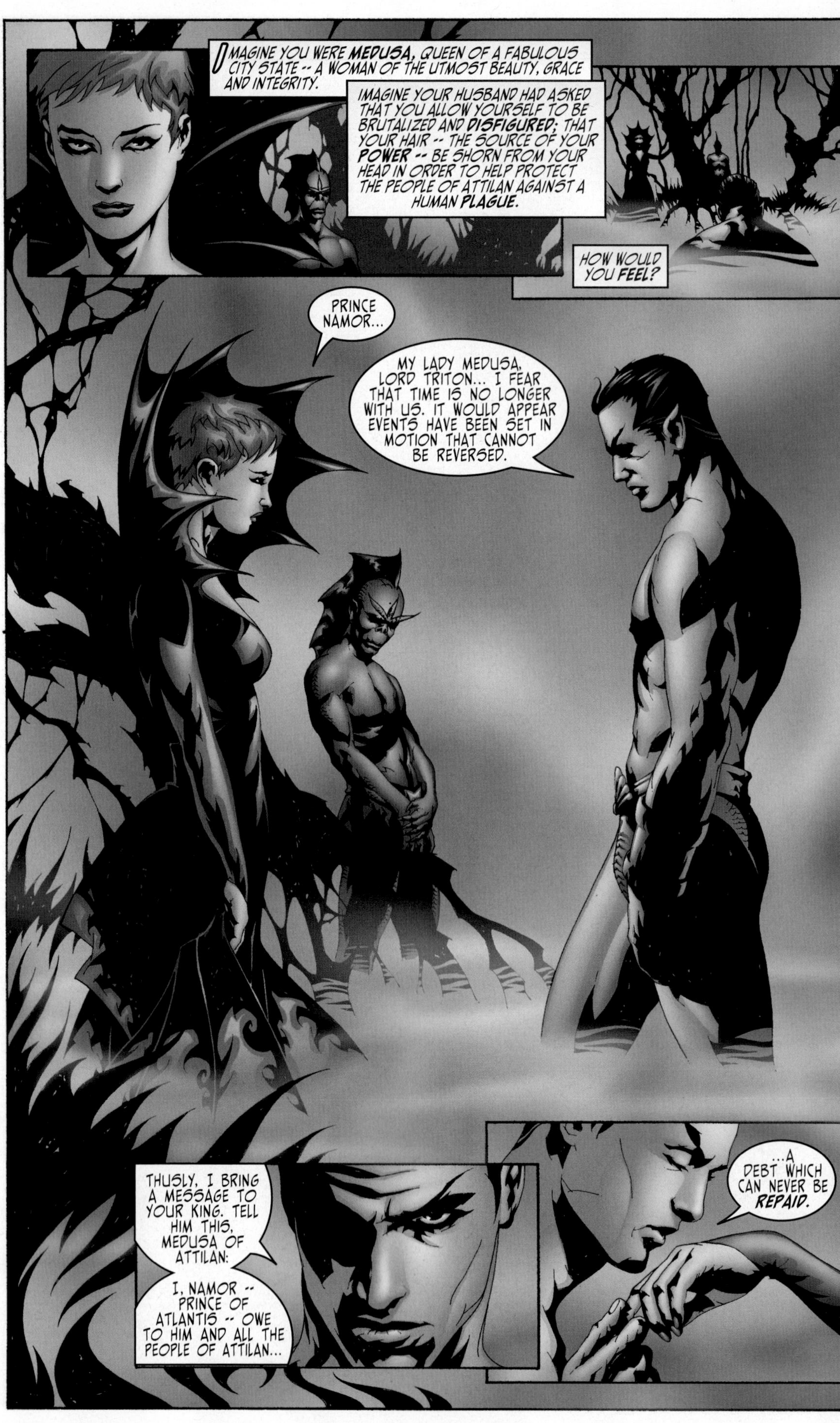
IMAGINE YOU WERE MEDUSA, QUEEN OF A FABULOUS CITY STATE -- A WOMAN OF THE UTMOST BEAUTY, GRACE AND INTEGRITY.
IMAGINE YOUR HUSBAND HAD ASKED THAT YOU ALLOW YOURSELF TO BE BRUTALIZED AND DISFIGURED; THAT YOUR HAIR -- THE SOURCE OF YOUR POWER -- BE SHORN FROM YOUR HEAD IN ORDER TO HELP PROTECT THE PEOPLE OF ATTILAN AGAINST A HUMAN PLAGUE.
HOW WOULD YOU FEEL?
PRINCE NAMOR...
MY LADY MEDUSA, LORD TRITON... I FEAR THAT TIME IS NO LONGER WITH US. IT WOULD APPEAR EVENTS HAVE BEEN SET IN MOTION THAT CANNOT BE REVERSED.
THUSLY, I BRING A MESSAGE TO YOUR KING. TELL HIM THIS, MEDUSA OF ATTILAN:
I, NAMOR -- PRINCE OF ATLANTIS -- OWE TO HIM AND ALL THE PEOPLE OF ATTILAN...
...A DEBT WHICH CAN NEVER BE REPAID.

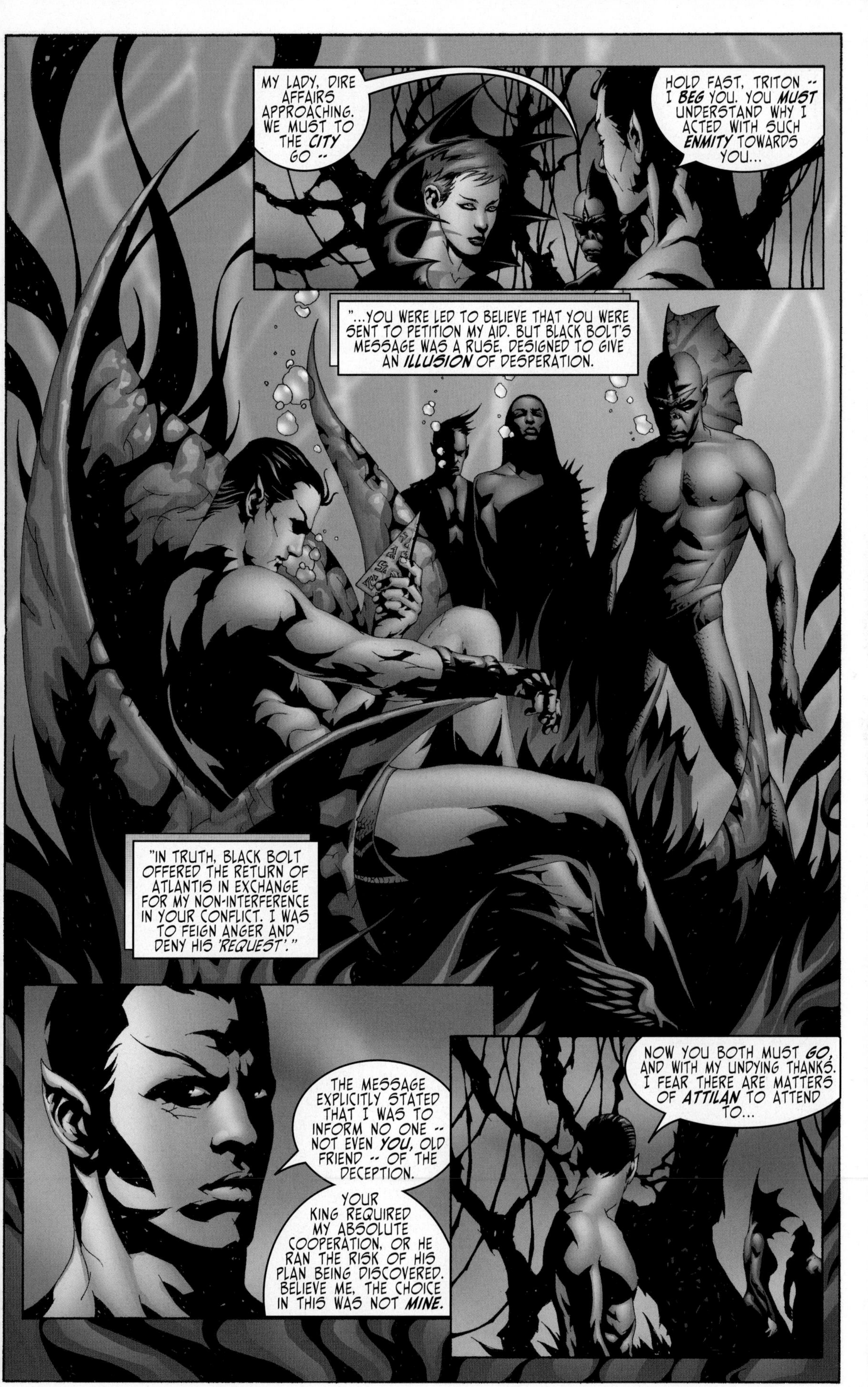
MY LADY, DIRE AFFAIRS APPROACHING. WE MUST TO THE CITY GO --
HOLD FAST, TRITON -- I BEG YOU. YOU MUST UNDERSTAND WHY I ACTED WITH SUCH ENMITY TOWARDS YOU...
"...YOU WERE LED TO BELIEVE THAT YOU WERE SENT TO PETITION MY AID. BUT BLACK BOLT'S MESSAGE WAS A RUSE, DESIGNED TO GIVE AN ILLUSION OF DESPERATION.
"IN TRUTH, BLACK BOLT OFFERED THE RETURN OF ATLANTIS IN EXCHANGE FOR MY NON-INTERFERENCE IN YOUR CONFLICT. I WAS TO FEIGN ANGER AND DENY HIS 'REQUEST'."
THE MESSAGE EXPLICITLY STATED THAT I WAS TO INFORM NO ONE -- NOT EVEN YOU, OLD FRIEND -- OF THE DECEPTION.
YOUR KING REQUIRED MY ABSOLUTE COOPERATION, OR HE RAN THE RISK OF HIS PLAN BEING DISCOVERED. BELIEVE ME, THE CHOICE IN THIS WAS NOT MINE.
NOW YOU BOTH MUST GO, AND WITH MY UNDYING THANKS. I FEAR THERE ARE MATTERS OF ATTILAN TO ATTEND TO...

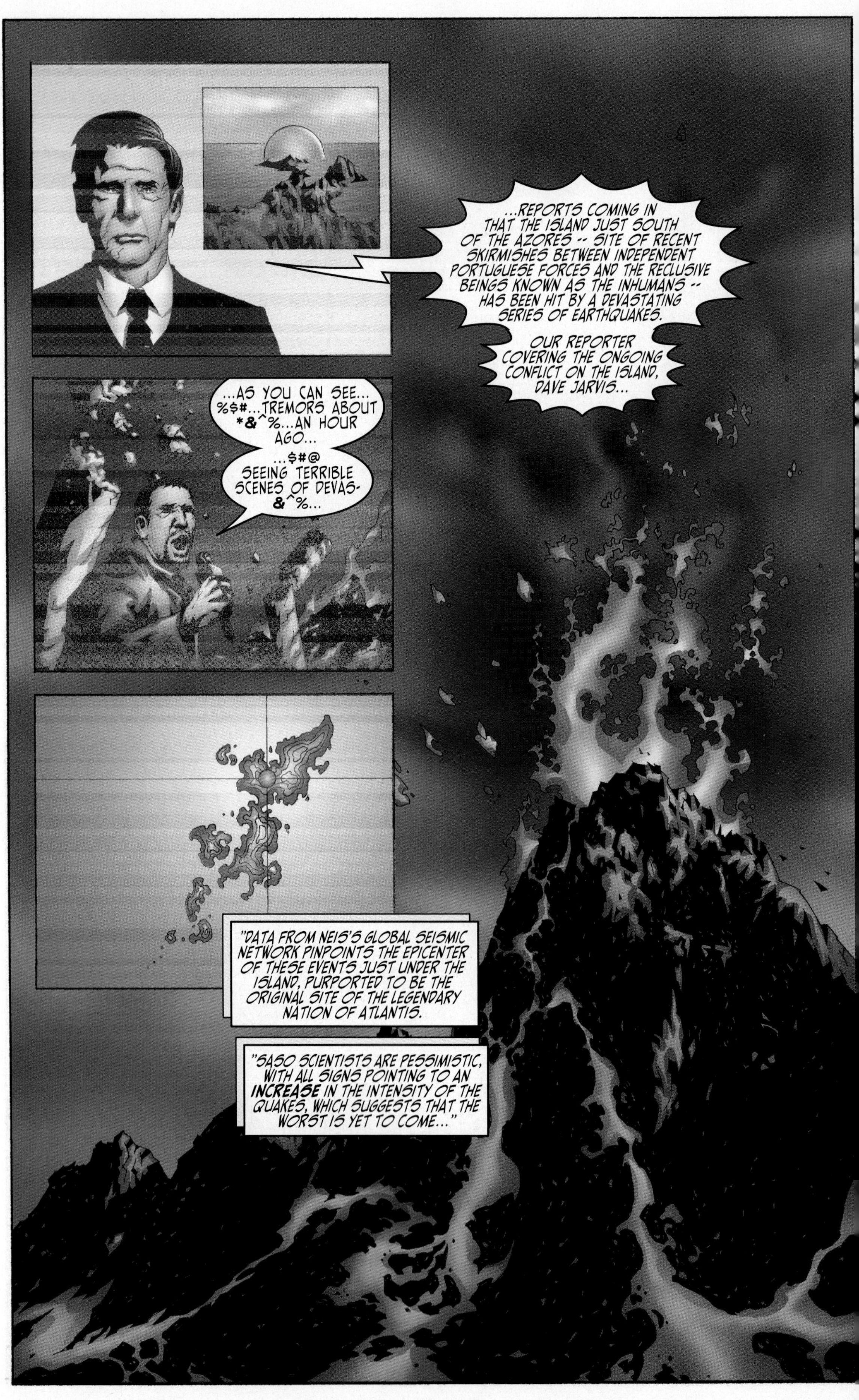
...REPORTS COMING IN THAT THE ISLAND JUST SOUTH OF THE AZORES -- SITE OF RECENT SKIRMISHES BETWEEN INDEPENDENT PORTUGUESE FORCES AND THE RECLUSIVE BEINGS KNOWN AS THE INHUMANS -- HAS BEEN HIT BY A DEVASTATING SERIES OF EARTHQUAKES.
OUR REPORTER COVERING THE ONGOING CONFLICT ON THE ISLAND, DAVE JARVIS...
...AS YOU CAN SEE... %$#...TREMORS ABOUT *&^%...AN HOUR AGO...
...$#@ SEEING TERRIBLE SCENES OF DEVAS- &^%...
"DATA FROM NEIS'S GLOBAL SEISMIC NETWORK PINPOINTS THE EPICENTER OF THESE EVENTS JUST UNDER THE ISLAND, PURPORTED TO BE THE ORIGINAL SITE OF THE LEGENDARY NATION OF ATLANTIS.
"SASO SCIENTISTS ARE PESSIMISTIC, WITH ALL SIGNS POINTING TO AN INCREASE IN THE INTENSITY OF THE QUAKES, WHICH SUGGESTS THAT THE WORST IS YET TO COME..."

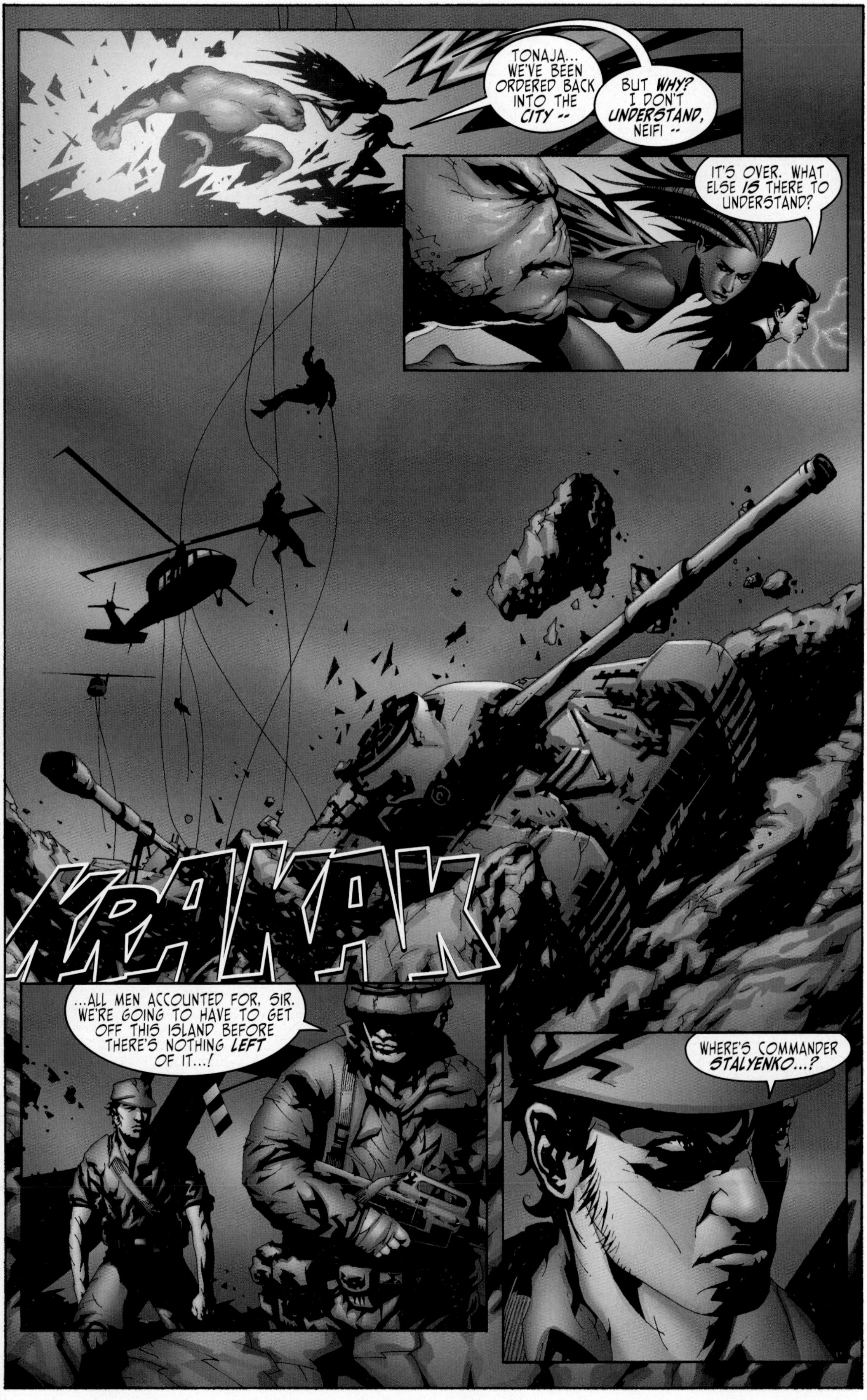
TONAJA... WE'VE BEEN ORDERED BACK INTO THE CITY --
BUT WHY? I DON'T UNDERSTAND, NEIFI --
IT'S OVER. WHAT ELSE IS THERE TO UNDERSTAND?
KRAKAK
...ALL MEN ACCOUNTED FOR, SIR. WE'RE GOING TO HAVE TO GET OFF THIS ISLAND BEFORE THERE'S NOTHING LEFT OF IT...!
WHERE'S COMMANDER STALYENKO...?

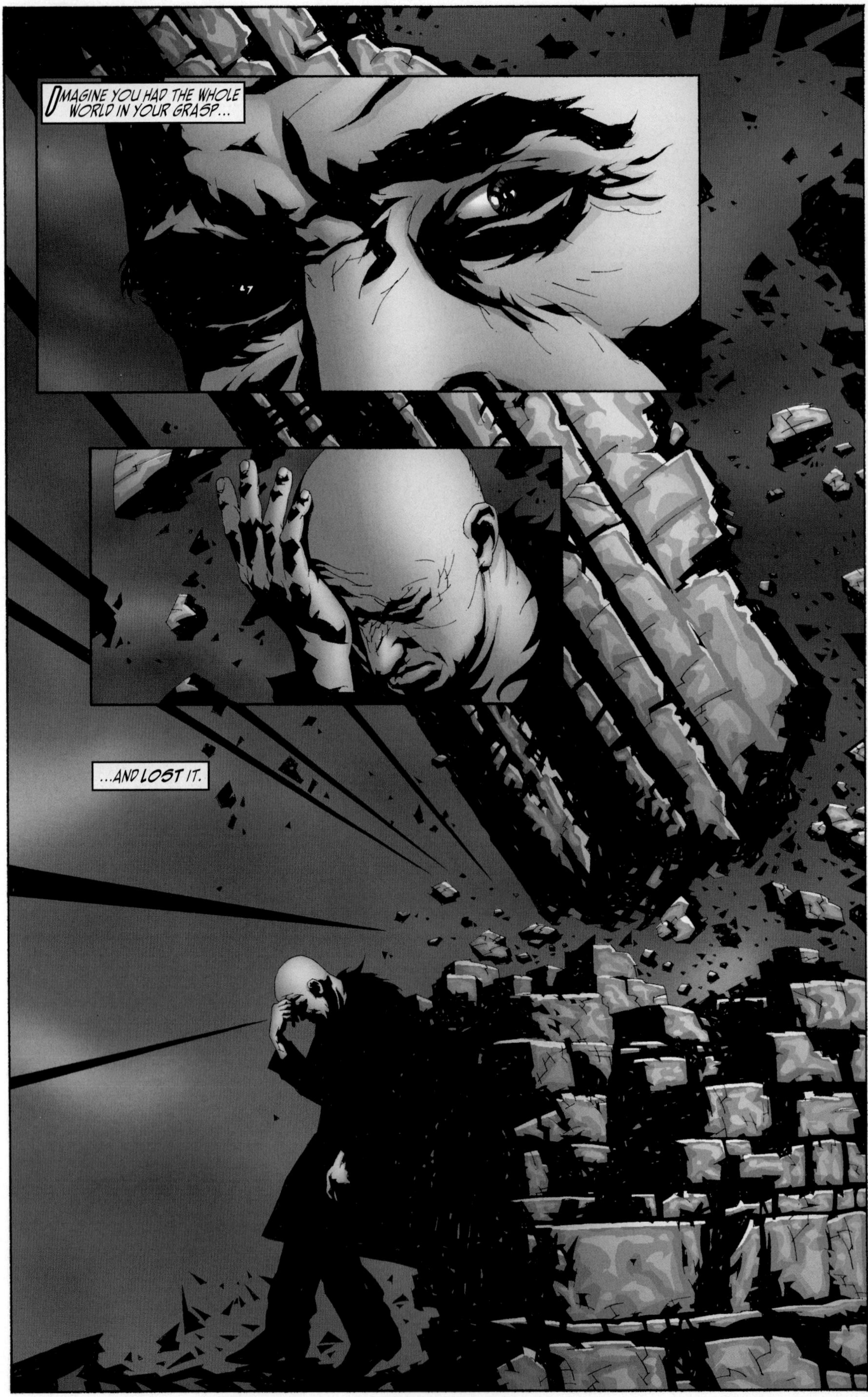
IMAGINE YOU HAD THE WHOLE WORLD IN YOUR GRASP...
...AND LOST IT.

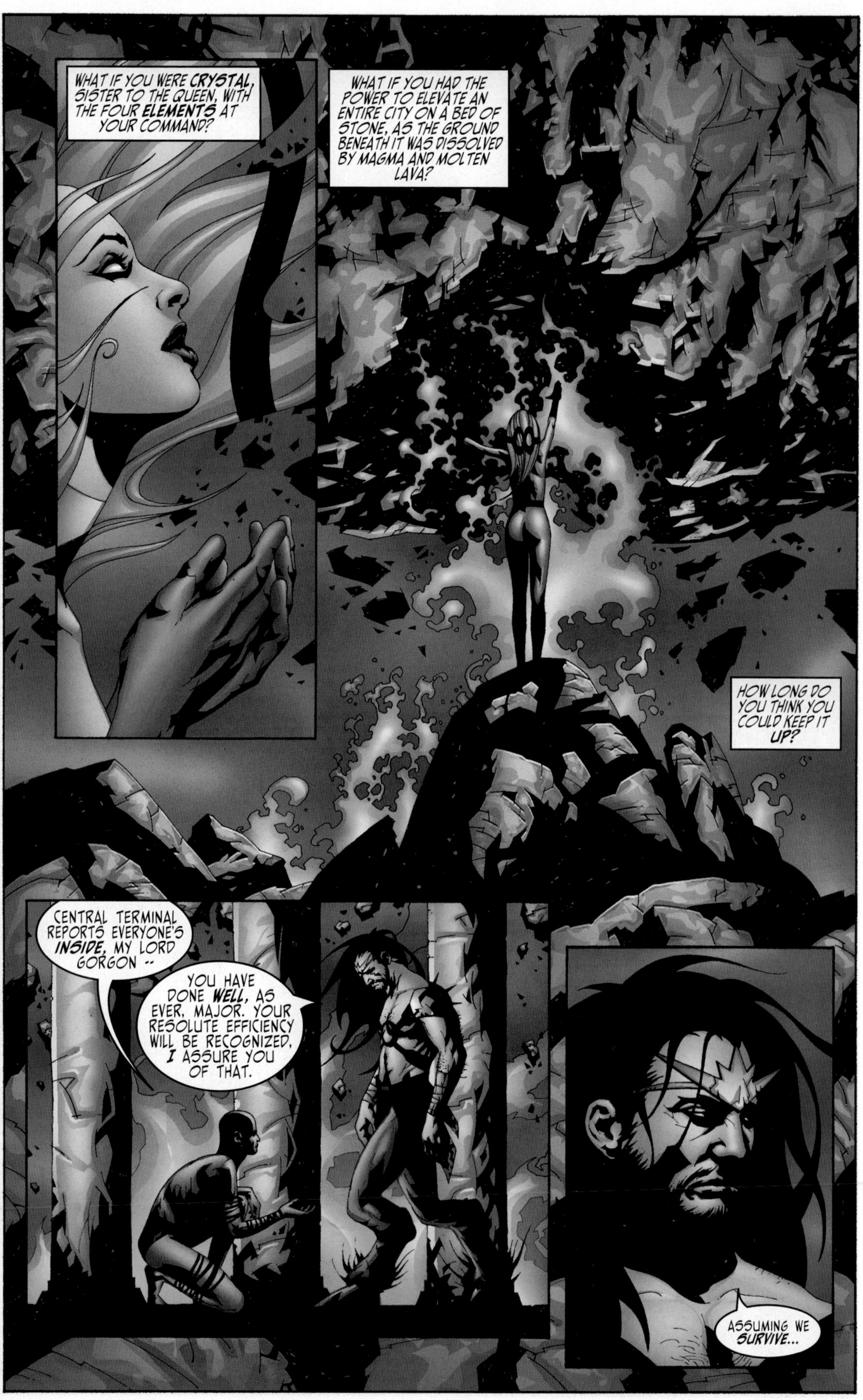

WHAT IF YOU WERE CRYSTAL, SISTER TO THE QUEEN, WITH THE FOUR ELEMENTS AT YOUR COMMAND?
WHAT IF YOU HAD THE POWER TO ELEVATE AN ENTIRE CITY ON A BED OF STONE, AS THE GROUND BENEATH IT WAS DISSOLVED BY MAGMA AND MOLTEN LAVA?
HOW LONG DO YOU THINK YOU COULD KEEP IT UP?
CENTRAL TERMINAL REPORTS EVERYONE'S INSIDE, MY LORD GORGON --
YOU HAVE DONE WELL, AS EVER, MAJOR. YOUR RESOLUTE EFFICIENCY WILL BE RECOGNIZED, I ASSURE YOU OF THAT.
ASSUMING WE SURVIVE...

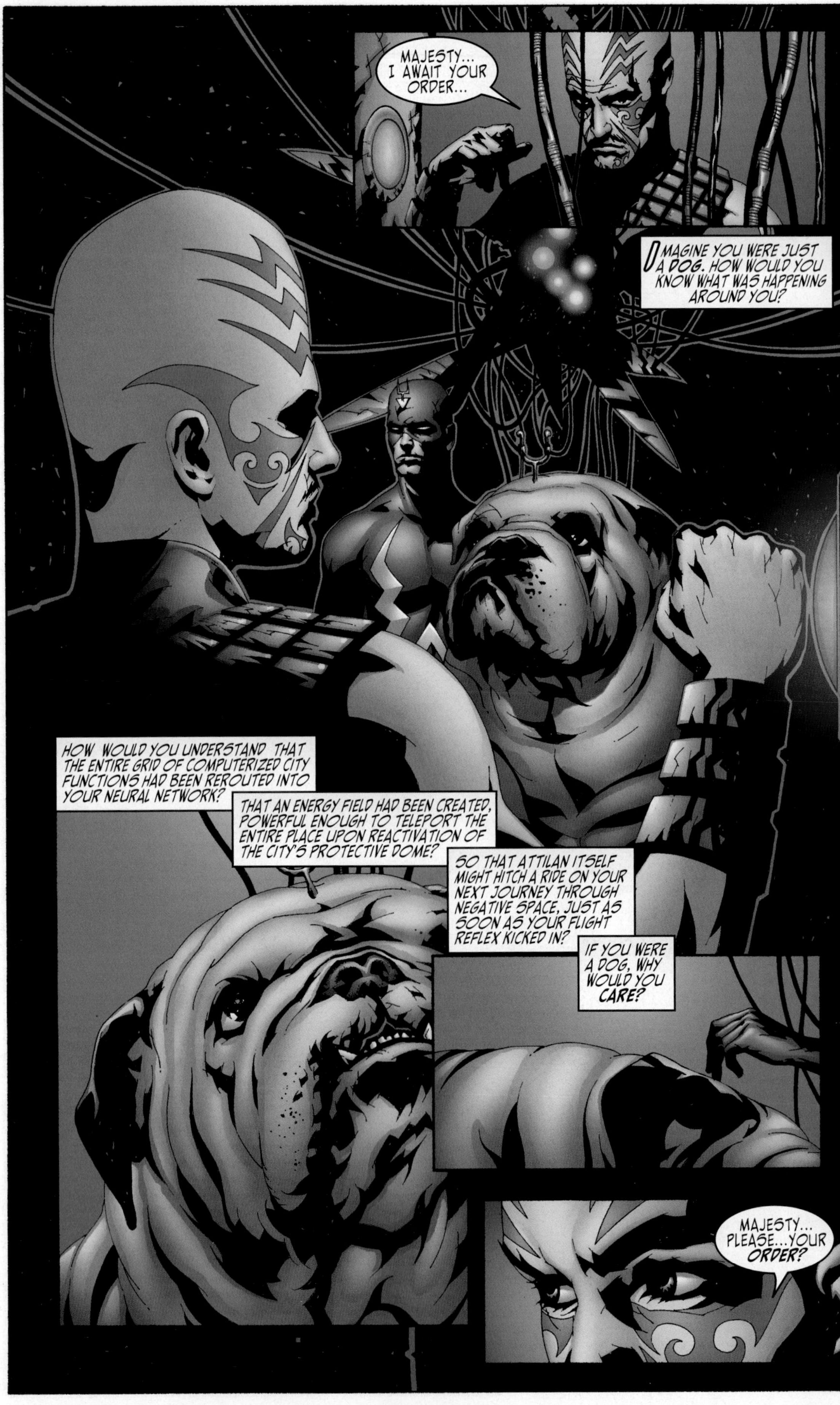
MAJESTY... I AWAIT YOUR ORDER...
IMAGINE YOU WERE JUST A DOG. HOW WOULD YOU KNOW WHAT WAS HAPPENING AROUND YOU?
HOW WOULD YOU UNDERSTAND THAT THE ENTIRE GRID OF COMPUTERIZED CITY FUNCTIONS HAD BEEN REROUTED INTO YOUR NEURAL NETWORK?
THAT AN ENERGY FIELD HAD BEEN CREATED, POWERFUL ENOUGH TO TELEPORT THE ENTIRE PLACE UPON REACTIVATION OF THE CITY'S PROTECTIVE DOME?
SO THAT ATTILAN ITSELF MIGHT HITCH A RIDE ON YOUR NEXT JOURNEY THROUGH NEGATIVE SPACE, JUST AS SOON AS YOUR FLIGHT REFLEX KICKED IN?
IF YOU WERE A DOG, WHY WOULD YOU CARE?
MAJESTY... PLEASE... YOUR ORDER?

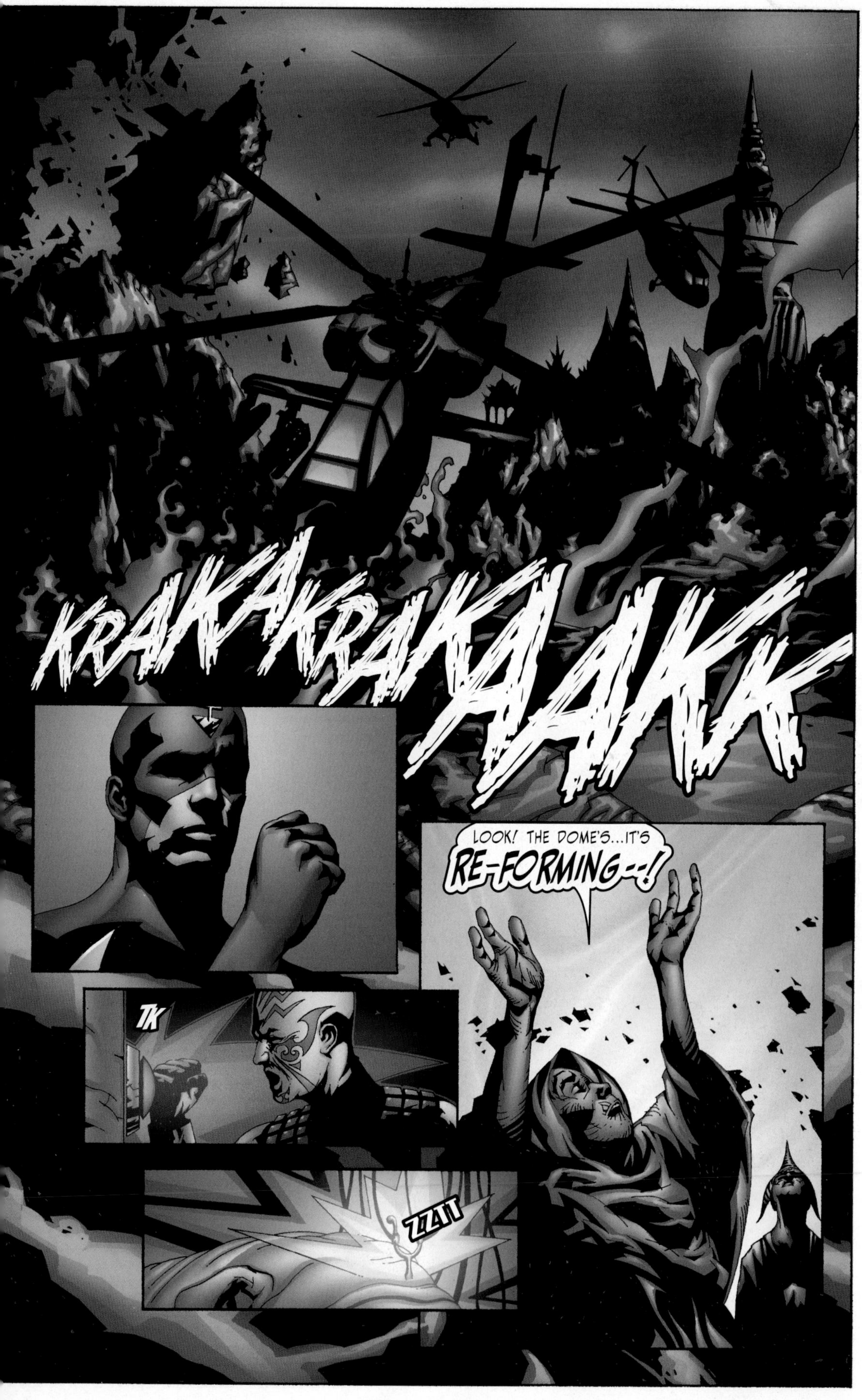
KRAKAKRAKAAKK
LOOK! THE DOME'S...IT'S RE-FORMING--!
TK
ZZATT

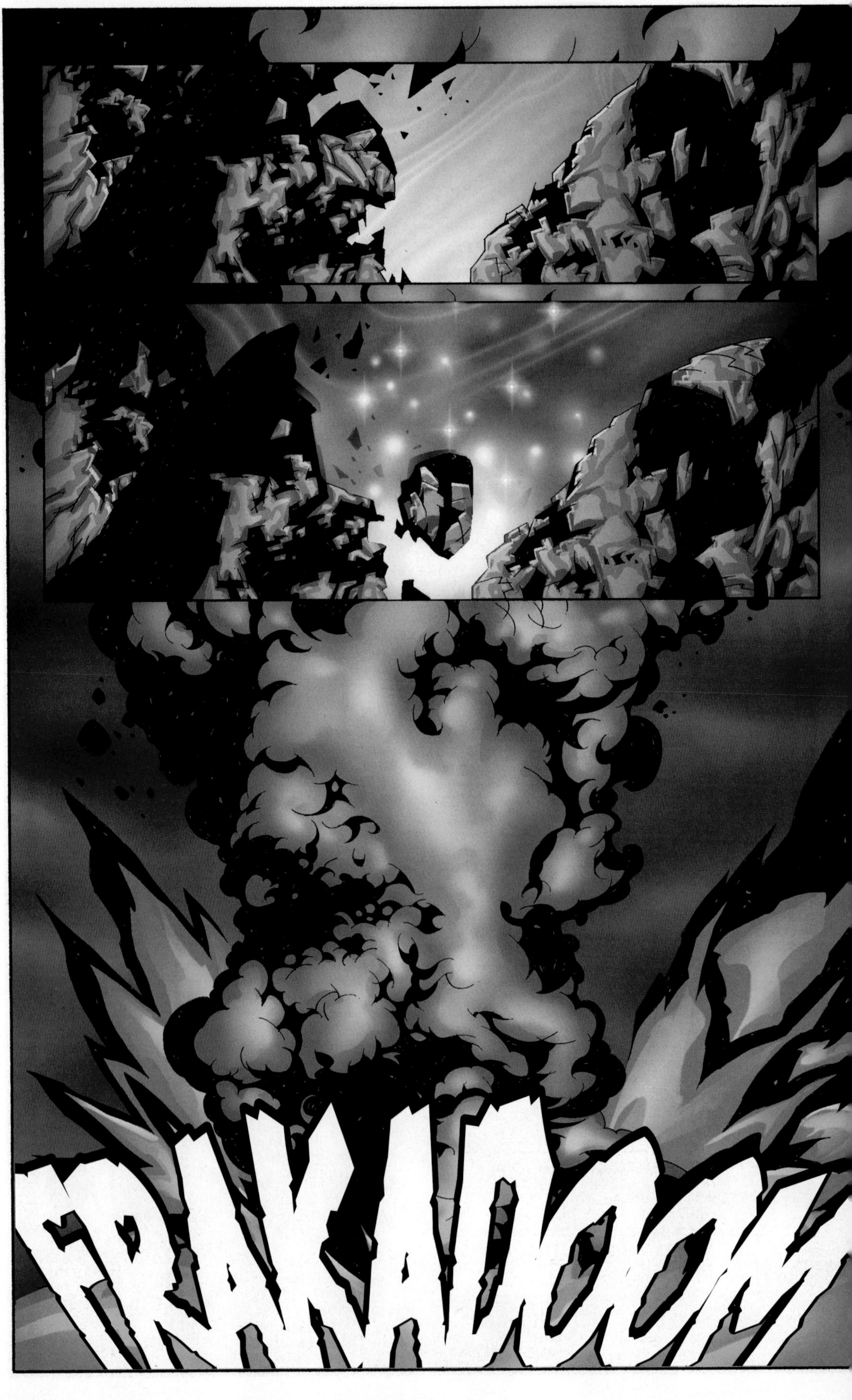
CRAKADOOM

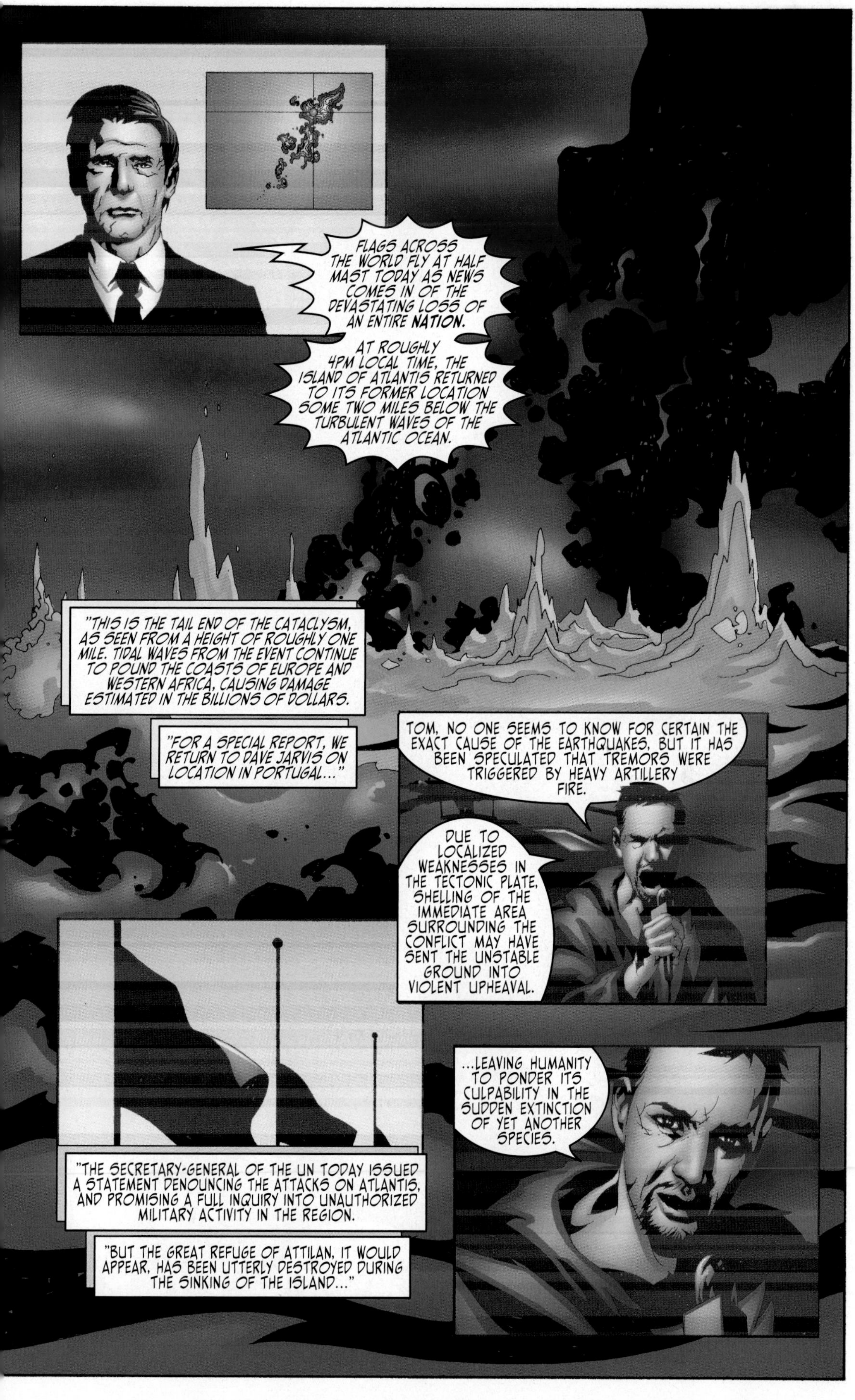

FLAGS ACROSS THE WORLD FLY AT HALF MAST TODAY AS NEWS COMES IN OF THE DEVASTATING LOSS OF AN ENTIRE NATION.
AT ROUGHLY 4PM LOCAL TIME, THE ISLAND OF ATLANTIS RETURNED TO ITS FORMER LOCATION SOME TWO MILES BELOW THE TURBULENT WAVES OF THE ATLANTIC OCEAN.
"THIS IS THE TAIL END OF THE CATACLYSM, AS SEEN FROM A HEIGHT OF ROUGHLY ONE MILE. TIDAL WAVES FROM THE EVENT CONTINUE TO POUND THE COASTS OF EUROPE AND WESTERN AFRICA, CAUSING DAMAGE ESTIMATED IN THE BILLIONS OF DOLLARS.
"FOR A SPECIAL REPORT, WE RETURN TO DAVE JARVIS ON LOCATION IN PORTUGAL..."
TOM, NO ONE SEEMS TO KNOW FOR CERTAIN THE EXACT CAUSE OF THE EARTHQUAKES, BUT IT HAS BEEN SPECULATED THAT TREMORS WERE TRIGGERED BY HEAVY ARTILLERY FIRE.
DUE TO LOCALIZED WEAKNESSES IN THE TECTONIC PLATE, SHELLING OF THE IMMEDIATE AREA SURROUNDING THE CONFLICT MAY HAVE SENT THE UNSTABLE GROUND INTO VIOLENT UPHEAVAL.
"THE SECRETARY-GENERAL OF THE UN TODAY ISSUED A STATEMENT DENOUNCING THE ATTACKS ON ATLANTIS, AND PROMISING A FULL INQUIRY INTO UNAUTHORIZED MILITARY ACTIVITY IN THE REGION.
"BUT THE GREAT REFUGE OF ATTILAN, IT WOULD APPEAR, HAS BEEN UTTERLY DESTROYED DURING THE SINKING OF THE ISLAND..."
...LEAVING HUMANITY TO PONDER ITS CULPABILITY IN THE SUDDEN EXTINCTION OF YET ANOTHER SPECIES.

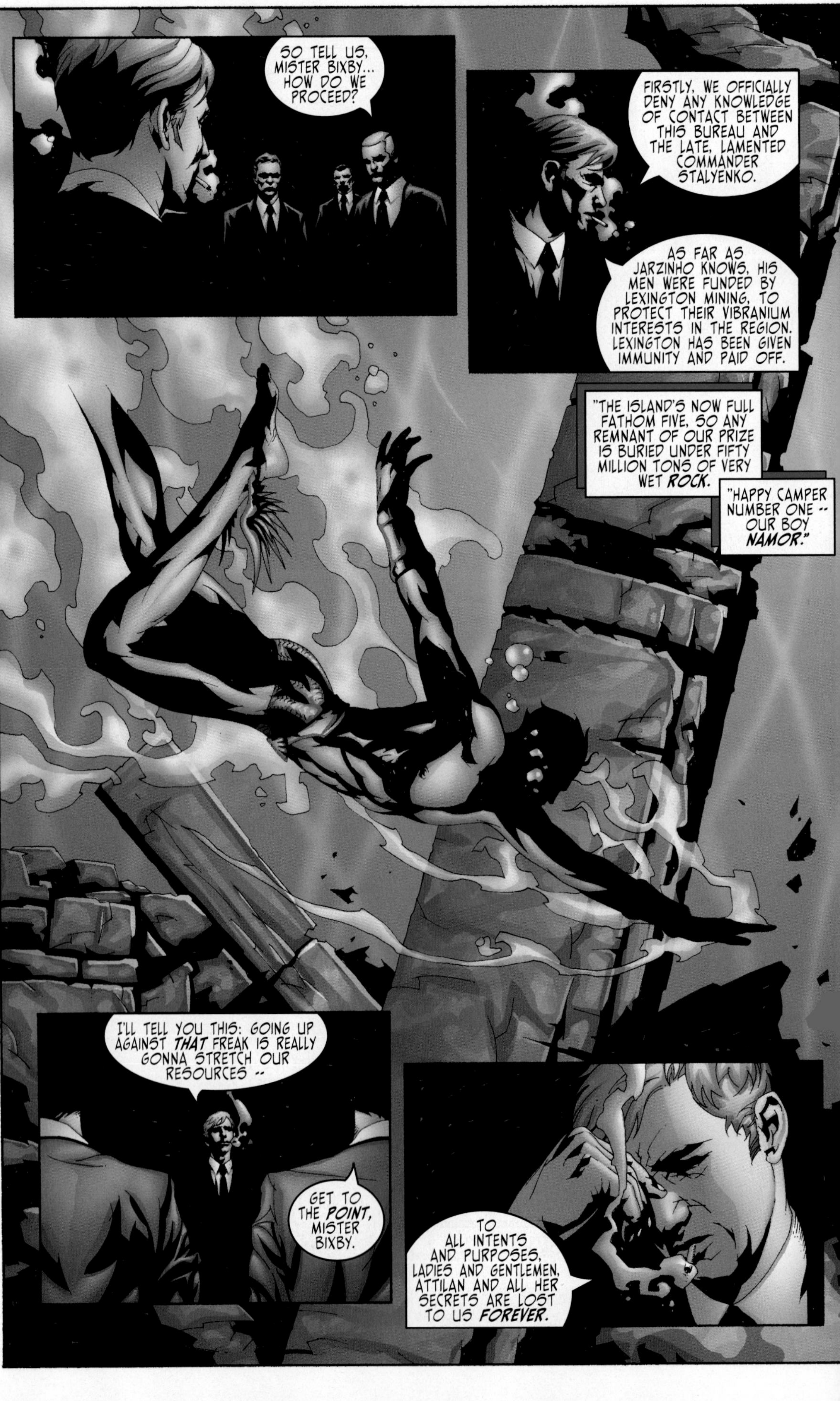
SO TELL US, MISTER BIXBY... HOW DO WE PROCEED?
FIRSTLY, WE OFFICIALLY DENY ANY KNOWLEDGE OF CONTACT BETWEEN THIS BUREAU AND THE LATE, LAMENTED COMMANDER STALYENKO.
AS FAR AS JARZINHO KNOWS, HIS MEN WERE FUNDED BY LEXINGTON MINING, TO PROTECT THEIR VIBRANIUM INTERESTS IN THE REGION. LEXINGTON HAS BEEN GIVEN IMMUNITY AND PAID OFF.
"THE ISLAND'S NOW FULL FATHOM FIVE, SO ANY REMNANT OF OUR PRIZE IS BURIED UNDER FIFTY MILLION TONS OF VERY WET ROCK.
"HAPPY CAMPER NUMBER ONE -- OUR BOY NAMOR."
I'LL TELL YOU THIS: GOING UP AGAINST THAT FREAK IS REALLY GONNA STRETCH OUR RESOURCES --
GET TO THE POINT, MISTER BIXBY.
TO ALL INTENTS AND PURPOSES, LADIES AND GENTLEMEN, ATTILAN AND ALL HER SECRETS ARE LOST TO US FOREVER.

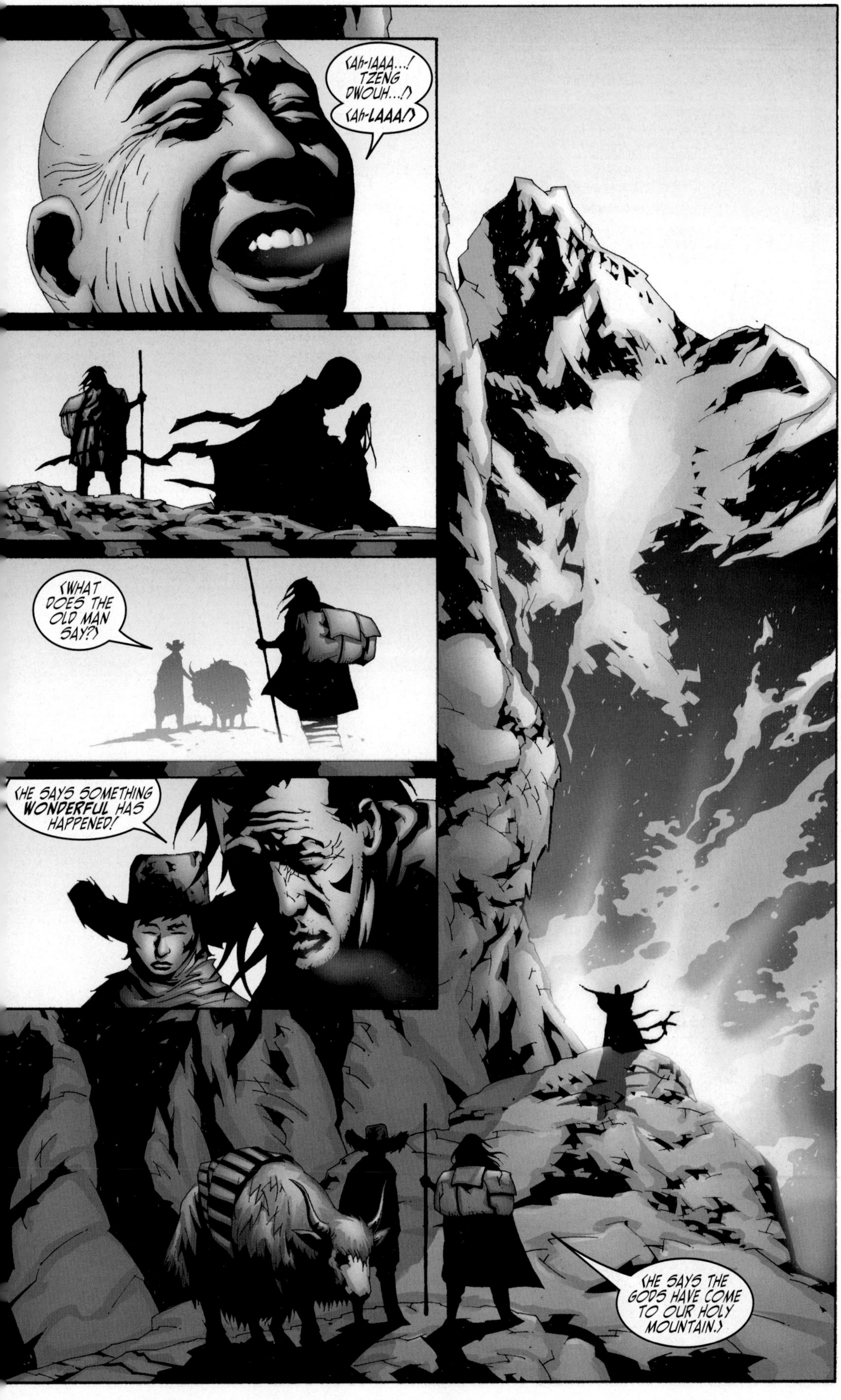
‹AH-IAAA...! TZENG DWOUH...!›
‹AH-LAAA!›
‹WHAT DOES THE OLD MAN SAY?›
‹HE SAYS SOMETHING **WONDERFUL** HAS HAPPENED!›
‹HE SAYS THE GODS HAVE COME TO OUR HOLY MOUNTAIN.›

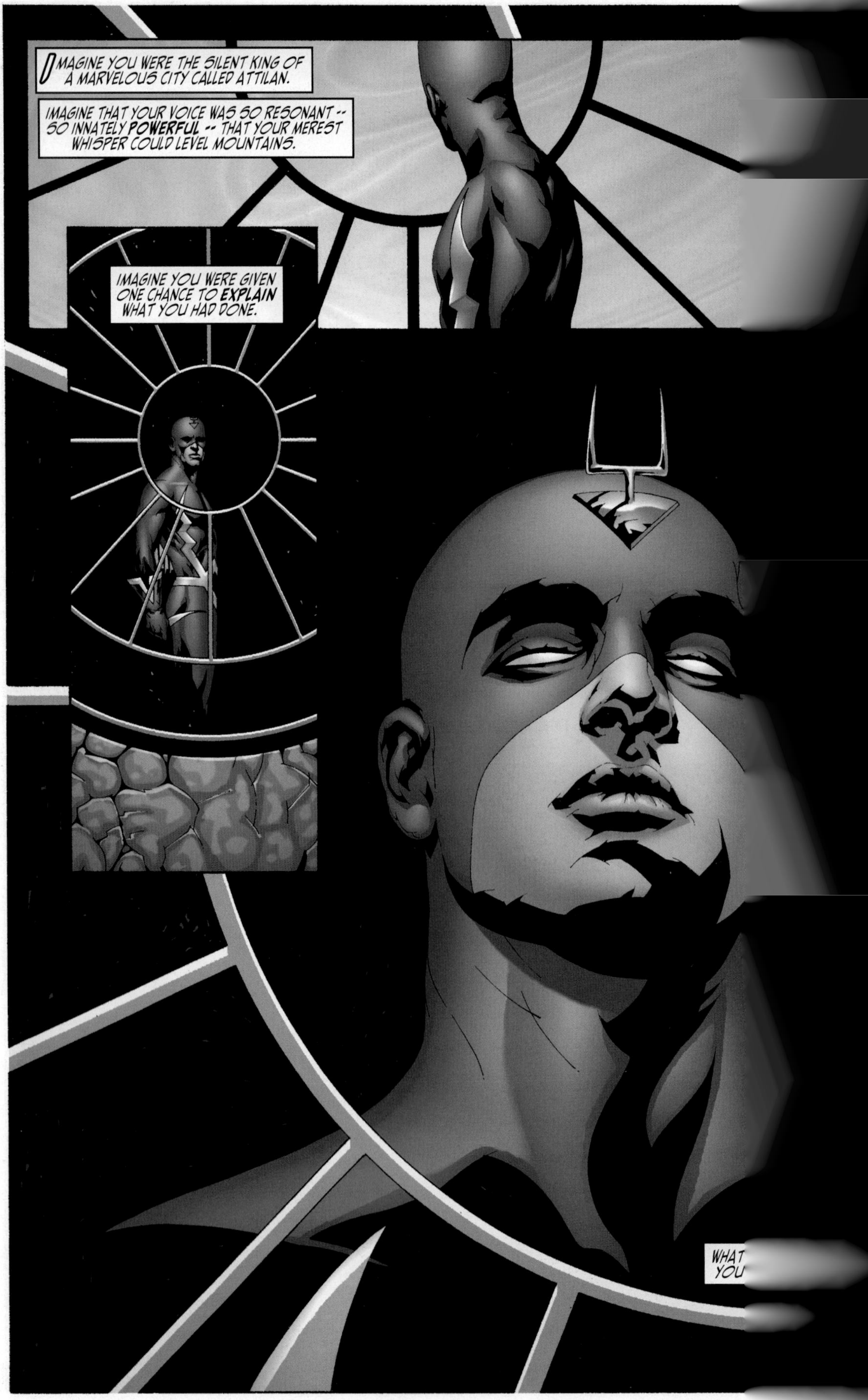
IMAGINE YOU WERE THE SILENT KING OF A MARVELOUS CITY CALLED ATTILAN.
IMAGINE THAT YOUR VOICE WAS SO RESONANT -- SO INNATELY **POWERFUL** -- THAT YOUR MEREST WHISPER COULD LEVEL MOUNTAINS.
IMAGINE YOU WERE GIVEN ONE CHANCE TO **EXPLAIN** WHAT YOU HAD DONE.
WHAT YOU

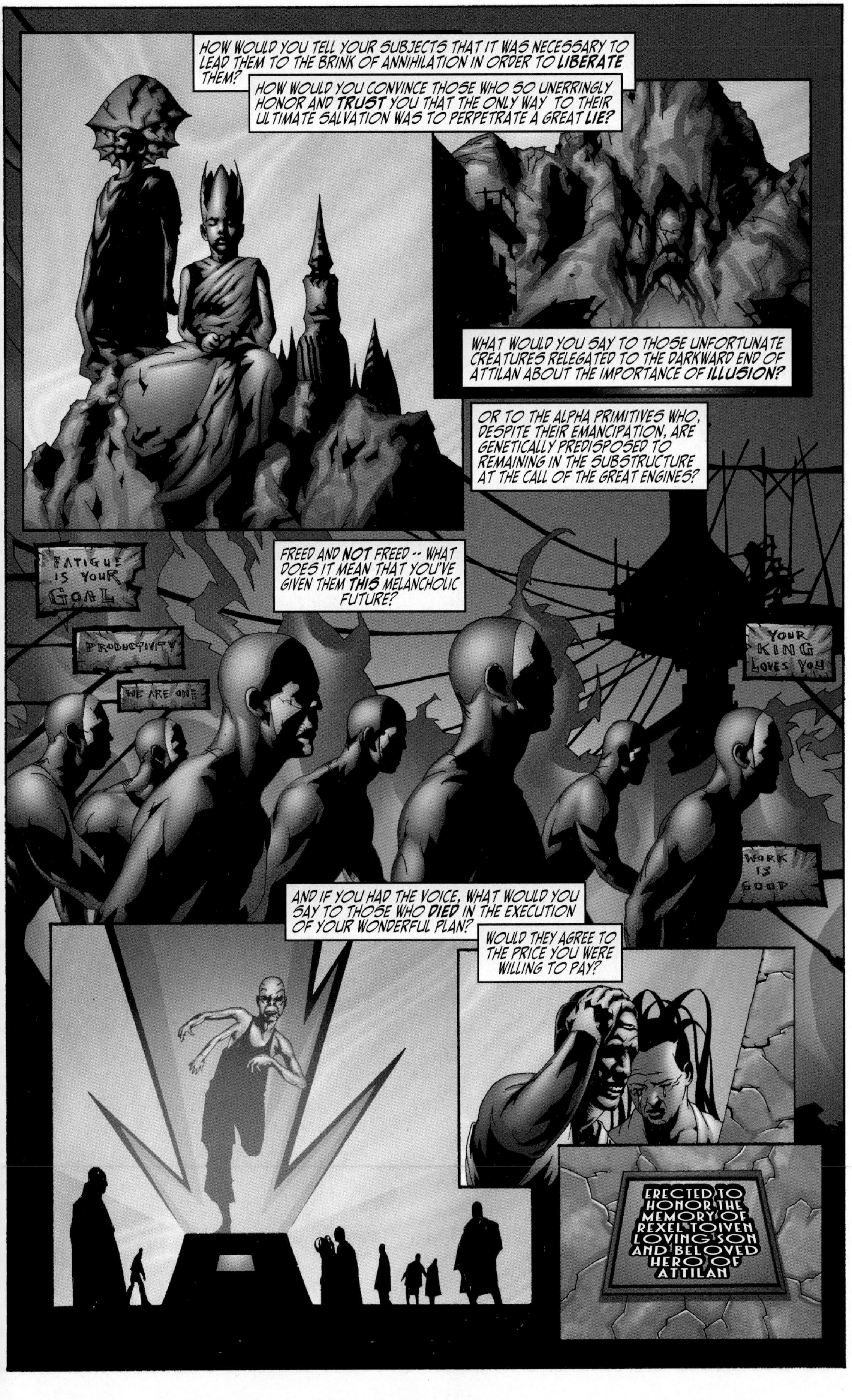
HOW WOULD YOU TELL YOUR SUBJECTS THAT IT WAS NECESSARY TO LEAD THEM TO THE BRINK OF ANNIHILATION IN ORDER TO LIBERATE THEM?
HOW WOULD YOU CONVINCE THOSE WHO SO UNERRINGLY HONOR AND TRUST YOU THAT THE ONLY WAY TO THEIR ULTIMATE SALVATION WAS TO PERPETRATE A GREAT LIE?
WHAT WOULD YOU SAY TO THOSE UNFORTUNATE CREATURES RELEGATED TO THE DARKWARD END OF ATTILAN ABOUT THE IMPORTANCE OF ILLUSION?
OR TO THE ALPHA PRIMITIVES WHO, DESPITE THEIR EMANCIPATION, ARE GENETICALLY PREDISPOSED TO REMAINING IN THE SUBSTRUCTURE AT THE CALL OF THE GREAT ENGINES?
FATIGUE IS YOUR GOAL
FREED AND NOT FREED -- WHAT DOES IT MEAN THAT YOU'VE GIVEN THEM THIS MELANCHOLIC FUTURE?
PRODUCTIVITY
WE ARE ONE
YOUR KING LOVES YOU
WORK IS GOOD
AND IF YOU HAD THE VOICE, WHAT WOULD YOU SAY TO THOSE WHO DIED IN THE EXECUTION OF YOUR WONDERFUL PLAN?
WOULD THEY AGREE TO THE PRICE YOU WERE WILLING TO PAY?
ERECTED TO HONOR THE MEMORY OF REXEL TOIVEN LOVING SON AND BELOVED HERO OF ATTILAN

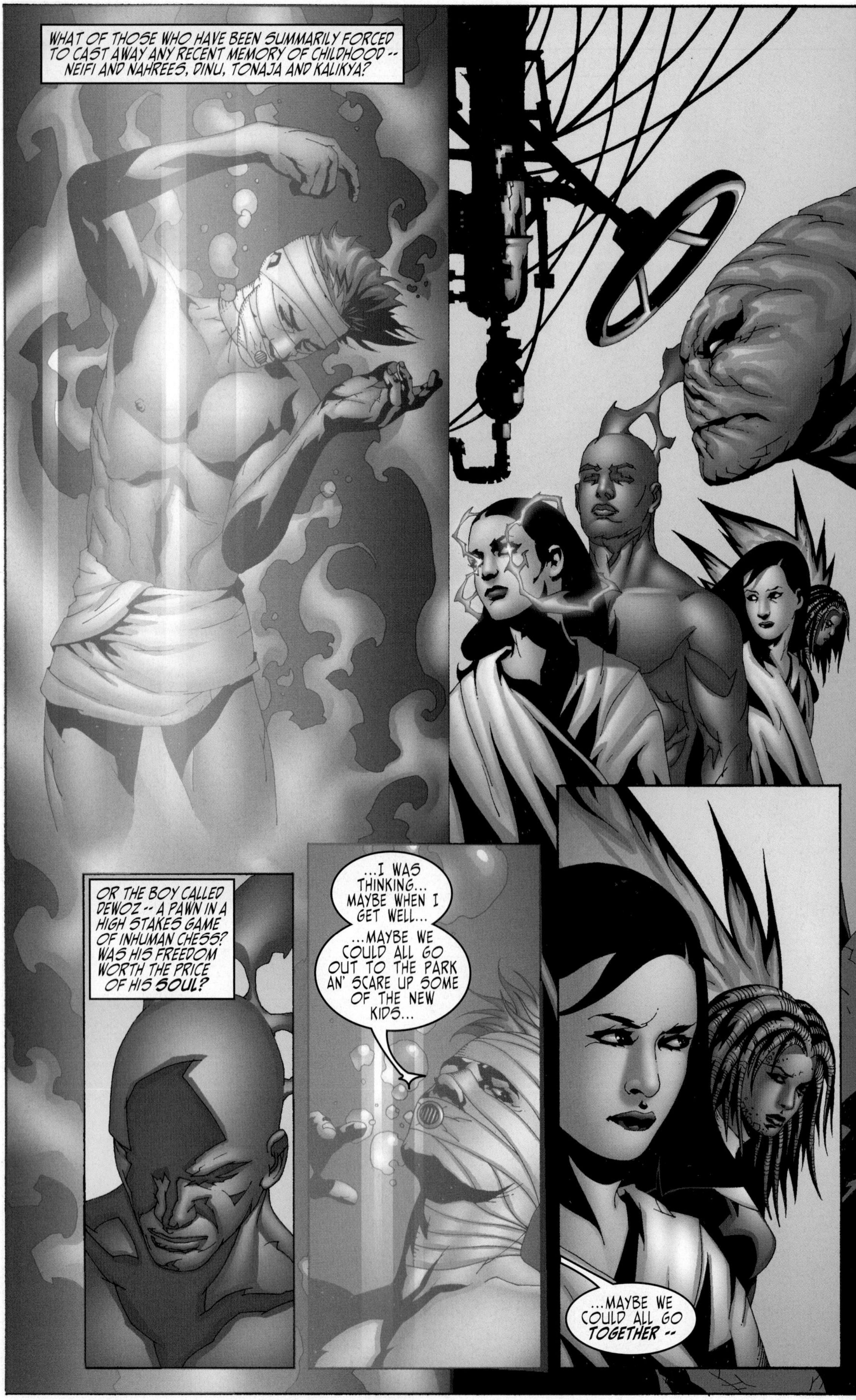
WHAT OF THOSE WHO HAVE BEEN SUMMARILY FORCED TO CAST AWAY ANY RECENT MEMORY OF CHILDHOOD -- NEIFI AND NAHREES, DINU, TONAJA AND KALIKYA?
OR THE BOY CALLED DEWOZ -- A PAWN IN A HIGH STAKES GAME OF INHUMAN CHESS? WAS HIS FREEDOM WORTH THE PRICE OF HIS SOUL?
...I WAS THINKING... MAYBE WHEN I GET WELL...
...MAYBE WE COULD ALL GO OUT TO THE PARK AN' SCARE UP SOME OF THE NEW KIDS...
...MAYBE WE COULD ALL GO TOGETHER --

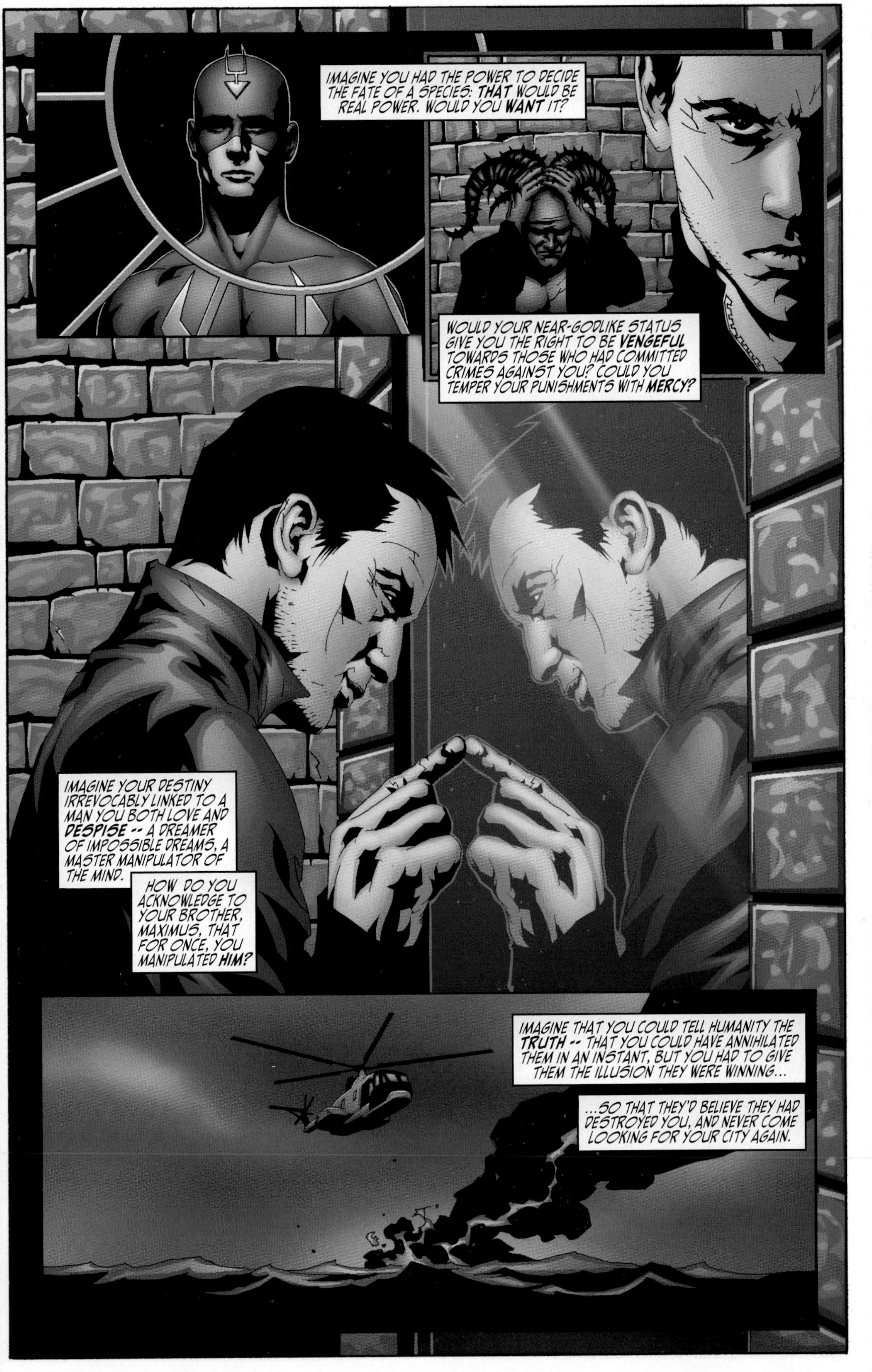
IMAGINE YOU HAD THE POWER TO DECIDE THE FATE OF A SPECIES: THAT WOULD BE REAL POWER. WOULD YOU WANT IT?
WOULD YOUR NEAR-GODLIKE STATUS GIVE YOU THE RIGHT TO BE VENGEFUL TOWARDS THOSE WHO HAD COMMITTED CRIMES AGAINST YOU? COULD YOU TEMPER YOUR PUNISHMENTS WITH MERCY?
IMAGINE YOUR DESTINY IRREVOCABLY LINKED TO A MAN YOU BOTH LOVE AND DESPISE -- A DREAMER OF IMPOSSIBLE DREAMS, A MASTER MANIPULATOR OF THE MIND.
HOW DO YOU ACKNOWLEDGE TO YOUR BROTHER, MAXIMUS, THAT FOR ONCE, YOU MANIPULATED HIM?
IMAGINE THAT YOU COULD TELL HUMANITY THE TRUTH -- THAT YOU COULD HAVE ANNIHILATED THEM IN AN INSTANT, BUT YOU HAD TO GIVE THEM THE ILLUSION THEY WERE WINNING...
...SO THAT THEY'D BELIEVE THEY HAD DESTROYED YOU, AND NEVER COME LOOKING FOR YOUR CITY AGAIN.

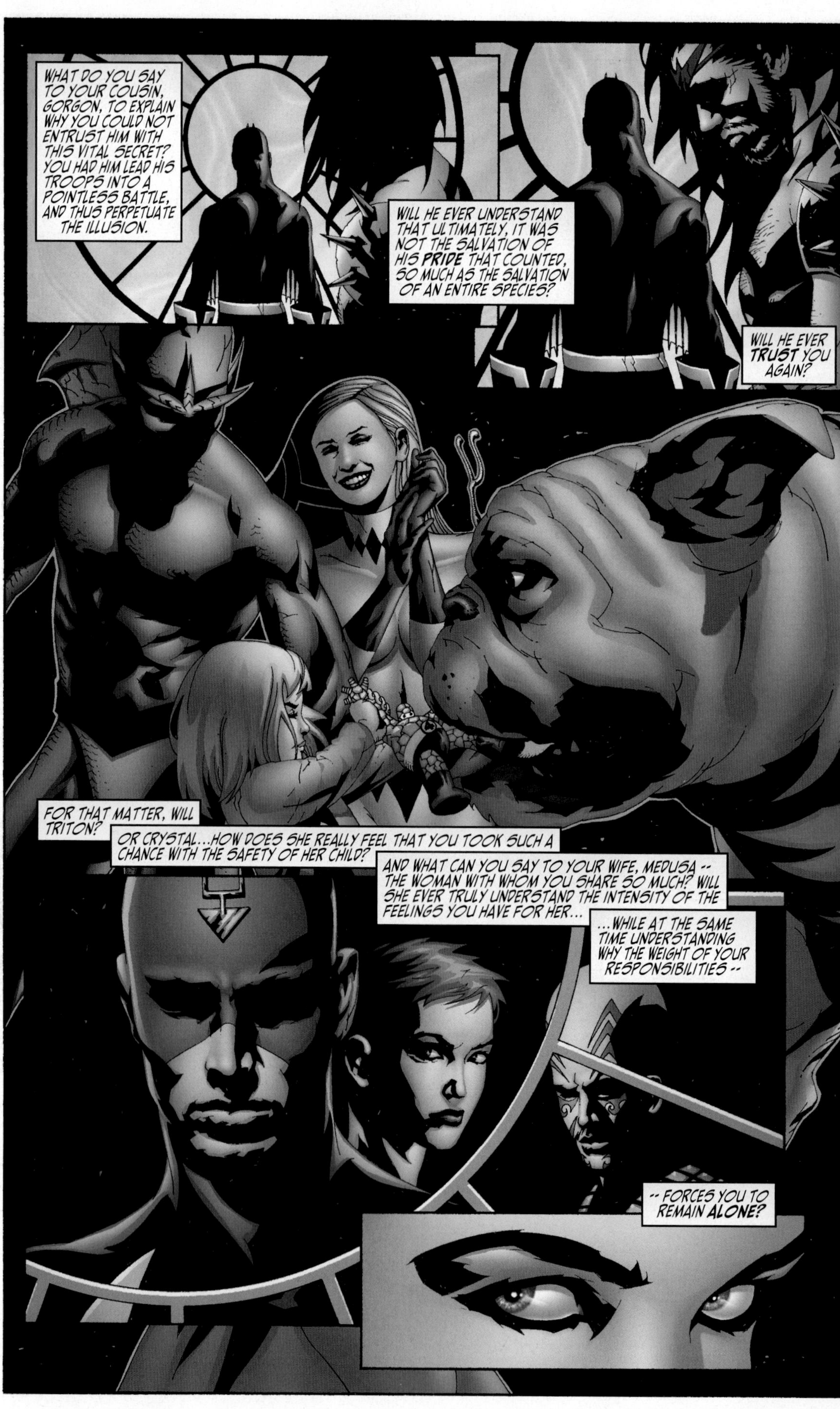
WHAT DO YOU SAY TO YOUR COUSIN, GORGON, TO EXPLAIN WHY YOU COULD NOT ENTRUST HIM WITH THIS VITAL SECRET? YOU HAD HIM LEAD HIS TROOPS INTO A POINTLESS BATTLE, AND THUS PERPETUATE THE ILLUSION.
WILL HE EVER UNDERSTAND THAT ULTIMATELY, IT WAS NOT THE SALVATION OF HIS PRIDE THAT COUNTED, SO MUCH AS THE SALVATION OF AN ENTIRE SPECIES?
WILL HE EVER TRUST YOU AGAIN?
FOR THAT MATTER, WILL TRITON?
OR CRYSTAL... HOW DOES SHE REALLY FEEL THAT YOU TOOK SUCH A CHANCE WITH THE SAFETY OF HER CHILD?
AND WHAT CAN YOU SAY TO YOUR WIFE, MEDUSA -- THE WOMAN WITH WHOM YOU SHARE SO MUCH? WILL SHE EVER TRULY UNDERSTAND THE INTENSITY OF THE FEELINGS YOU HAVE FOR HER...
...WHILE AT THE SAME TIME UNDERSTANDING WHY THE WEIGHT OF YOUR RESPONSIBILITIES --
-- FORCES YOU TO REMAIN ALONE?

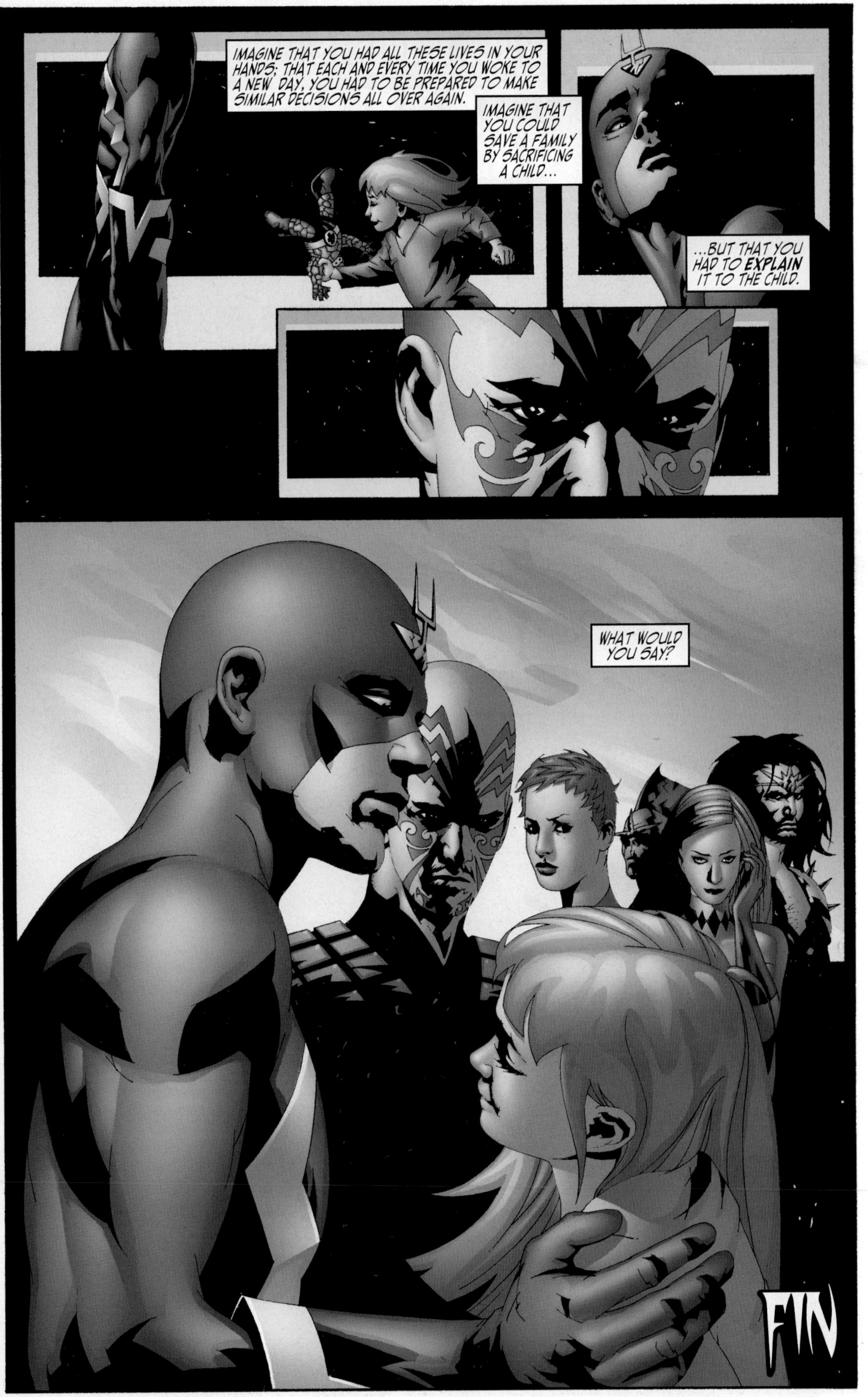
IMAGINE THAT YOU HAD ALL THESE LIVES IN YOUR HANDS; THAT EACH AND EVERY TIME YOU WOKE TO A NEW DAY, YOU HAD TO BE PREPARED TO MAKE SIMILAR DECISIONS ALL OVER AGAIN.
IMAGINE THAT YOU COULD SAVE A FAMILY BY SACRIFICING A CHILD...
...BUT THAT YOU HAD TO EXPLAIN IT TO THE CHILD.
WHAT WOULD YOU SAY?
FIN

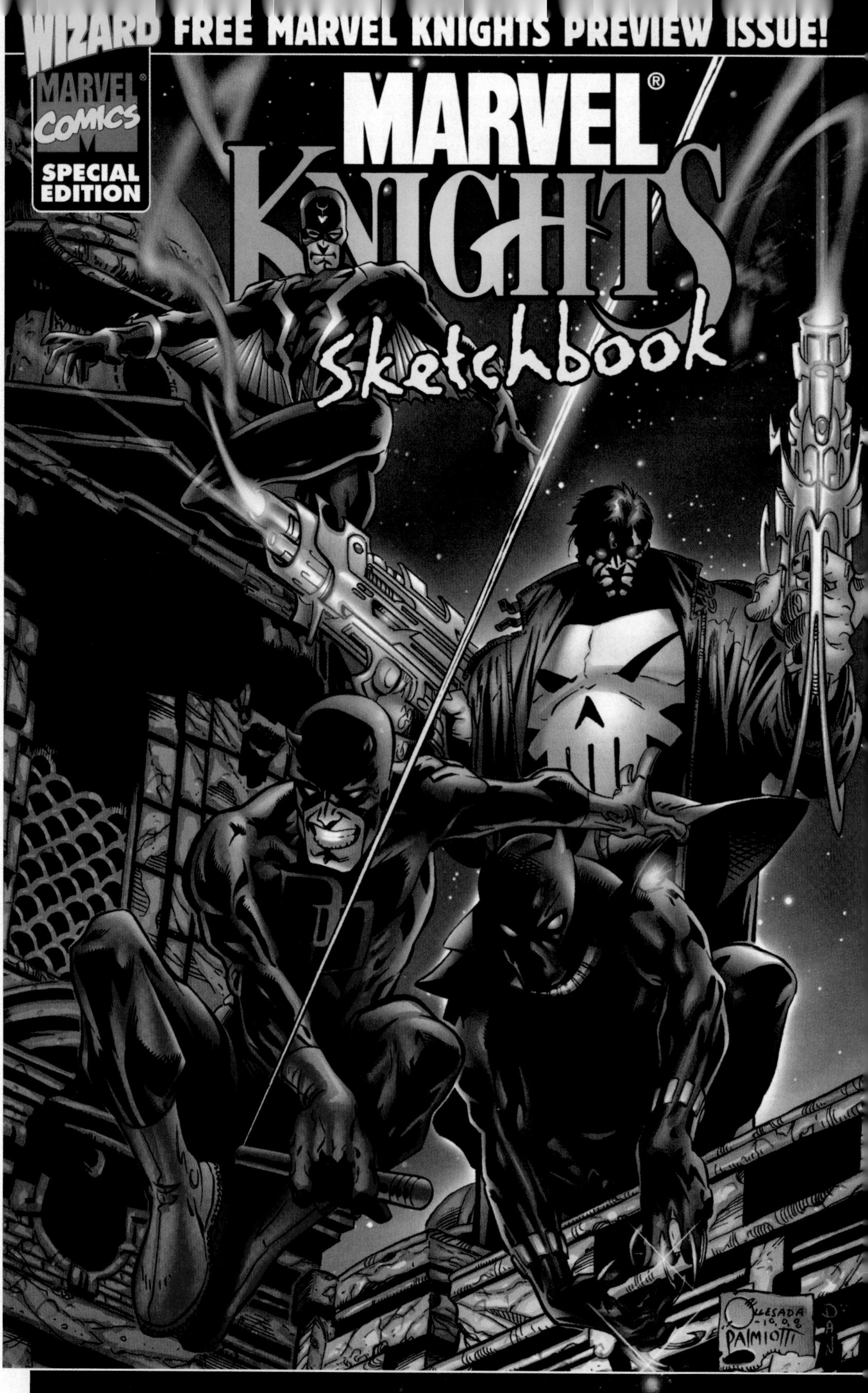
WIZARD FREE MARVEL KNIGHTS PREVIEW ISSUE!
MARVEL COMICS
SPECIAL EDITION
MARVEL® KNIGHTS
Sketchbook

PAUL JENKINS ON:

THE INHUMANS

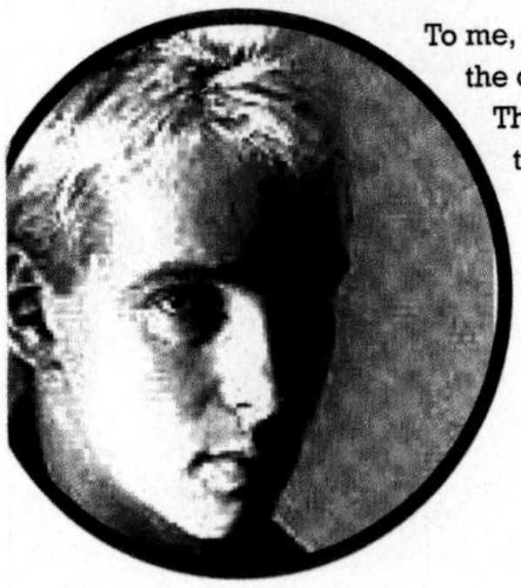

To me, the crux of the matter, the most appealing aspect of writing about The Inhumans, is the chance to examine the nature of humanity.

These are some pretty amazing supernatural creatures living in a remote super-city, and they couldn't be further removed socially from everyone else on the planet: They each develop some marvelous power that defines their class structure, their King has never been defeated in battle, and they have a bunch of troglodytes under the city that do all the hard graft while they sit about sipping Piña Coladas. A lot like real life, really, except that Bill Clinton couldn't punch his way out of a paper bag.

Oh, and they've got a teleporting dog with a tuning fork on his head. Bloody brilliant.

BLACK BOLT

MEDUSA

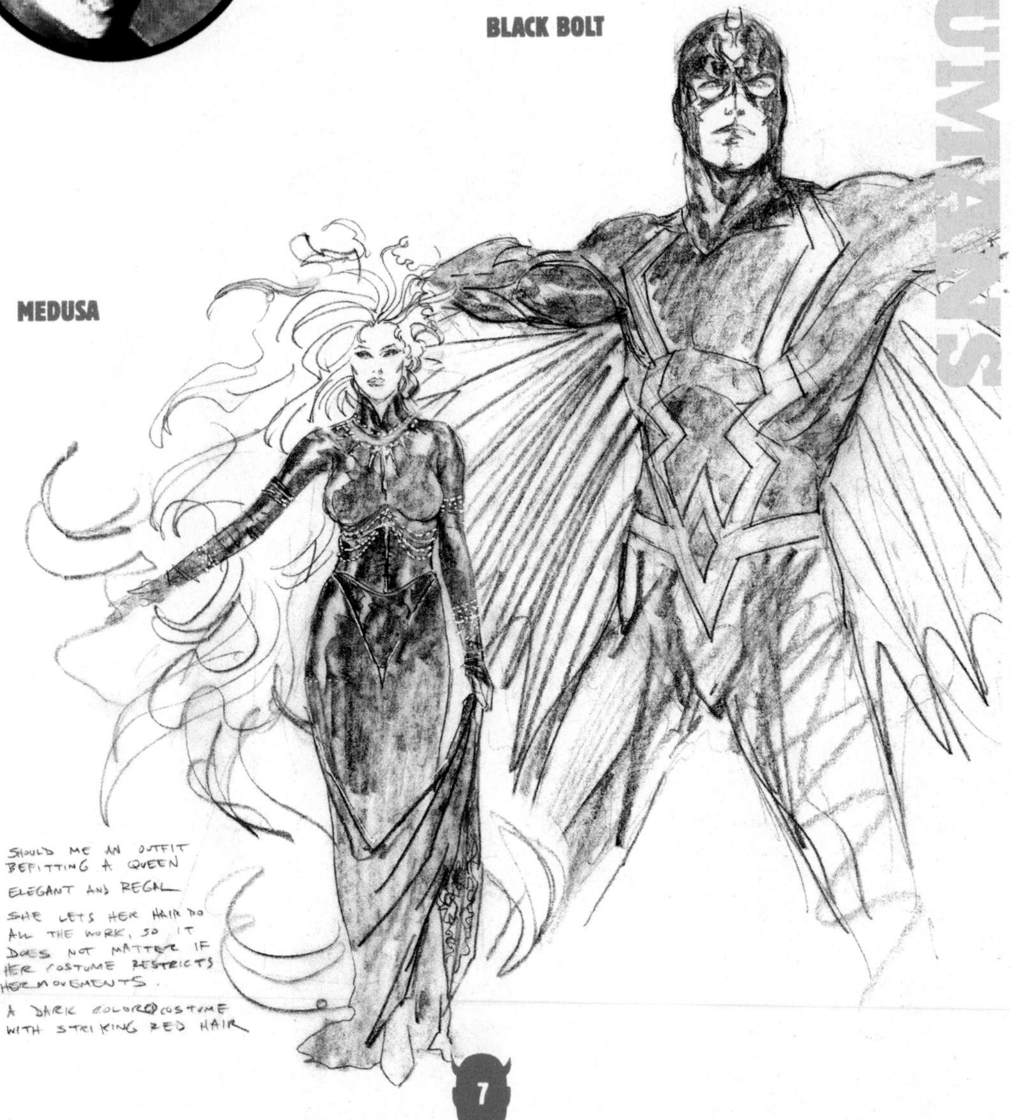
SHOULD ME AN OUTFIT BEFITTING A QUEEN
ELEGANT AND REGAL
SHE LETS HER HAIR DO ALL THE WORK, SO IT DOES NOT MATTER IF HER COSTUME RESTRICTS HER MOVEMENTS.
A DARK COLORED COSTUME WITH STRIKING RED HAIR

JAE LEE ON:
THE INHUMANS

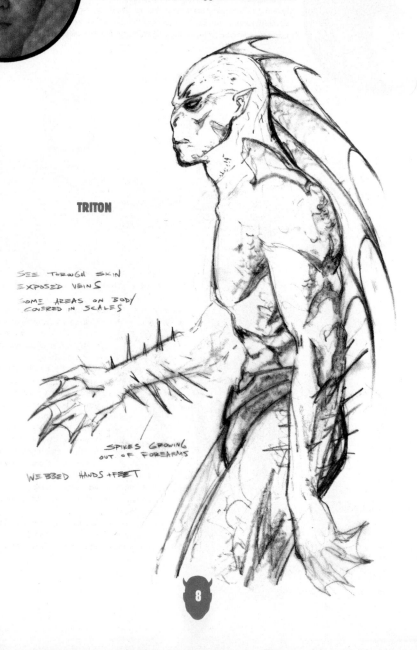

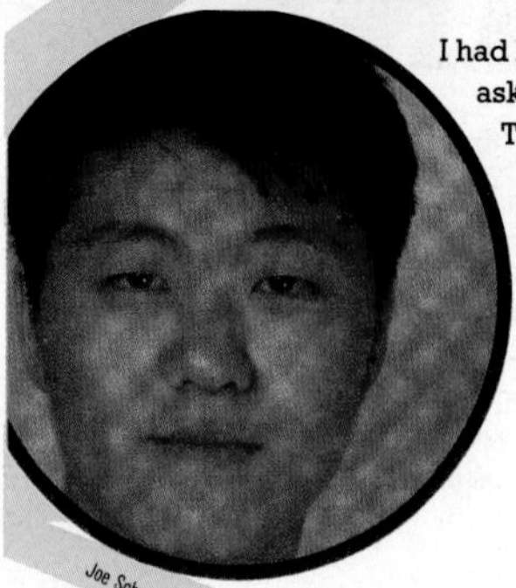

Joe Schuyler

I had heard Joey and Jimmy were up to no good. And when I heard that they were going to ask me to get involved, I was ready to say no.

This time their pitch was this: Take any existing Marvel characters without a book of their own and resurrect them. I started flipping through my old issues of *The Official Handbook of the Marvel Universe* to see my options. But this search bore no fruit. Later that week, I was talking with Jose Villarrubia, a collaborator on my creator-owned book *Hellshock*, and being much, MUCH older than me (he actually *remembers* the '60s and '70s), he suggested The Inhumans.

TRITON

SEE THROUGH SKIN
EXPOSED VEINS
SOME AREAS ON BODY
COVERED IN SCALES

SPIKES GROWING
OUT OF FOREARMS

WEBBED HANDS + FEET

8

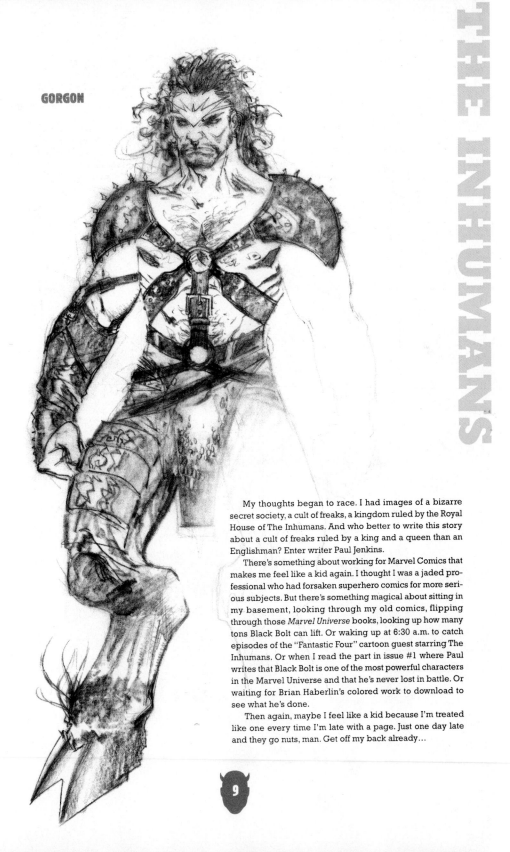

GORGON

My thoughts began to race. I had images of a bizarre secret society, a cult of freaks, a kingdom ruled by the Royal House of The Inhumans. And who better to write this story about a cult of freaks ruled by a king and a queen than an Englishman? Enter writer Paul Jenkins.

There's something about working for Marvel Comics that makes me feel like a kid again. I thought I was a jaded professional who had forsaken superhero comics for more serious subjects. But there's something magical about sitting in my basement, looking through my old comics, flipping through those *Marvel Universe* books, looking up how many tons Black Bolt can lift. Or waking up at 6:30 a.m. to catch episodes of the "Fantastic Four" cartoon guest starring The Inhumans. Or when I read the part in issue #1 where Paul writes that Black Bolt is one of the most powerful characters in the Marvel Universe and that he's never lost in battle. Or waiting for Brian Haberlin's colored work to download to see what he's done.

Then again, maybe I feel like a kid because I'm treated like one every time I'm late with a page. Just one day late and they go nuts, man. Get off my back already...

9

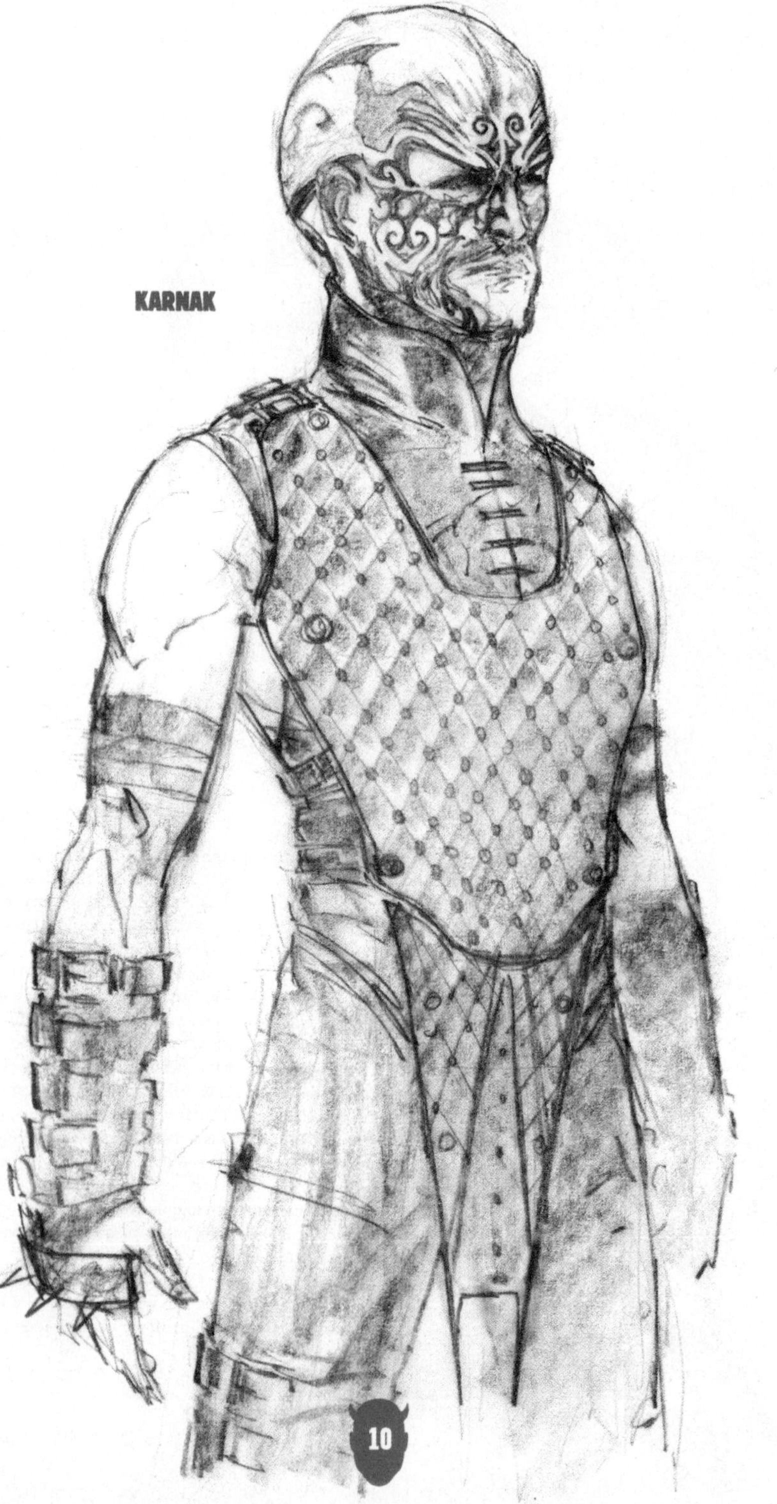

KARNAK

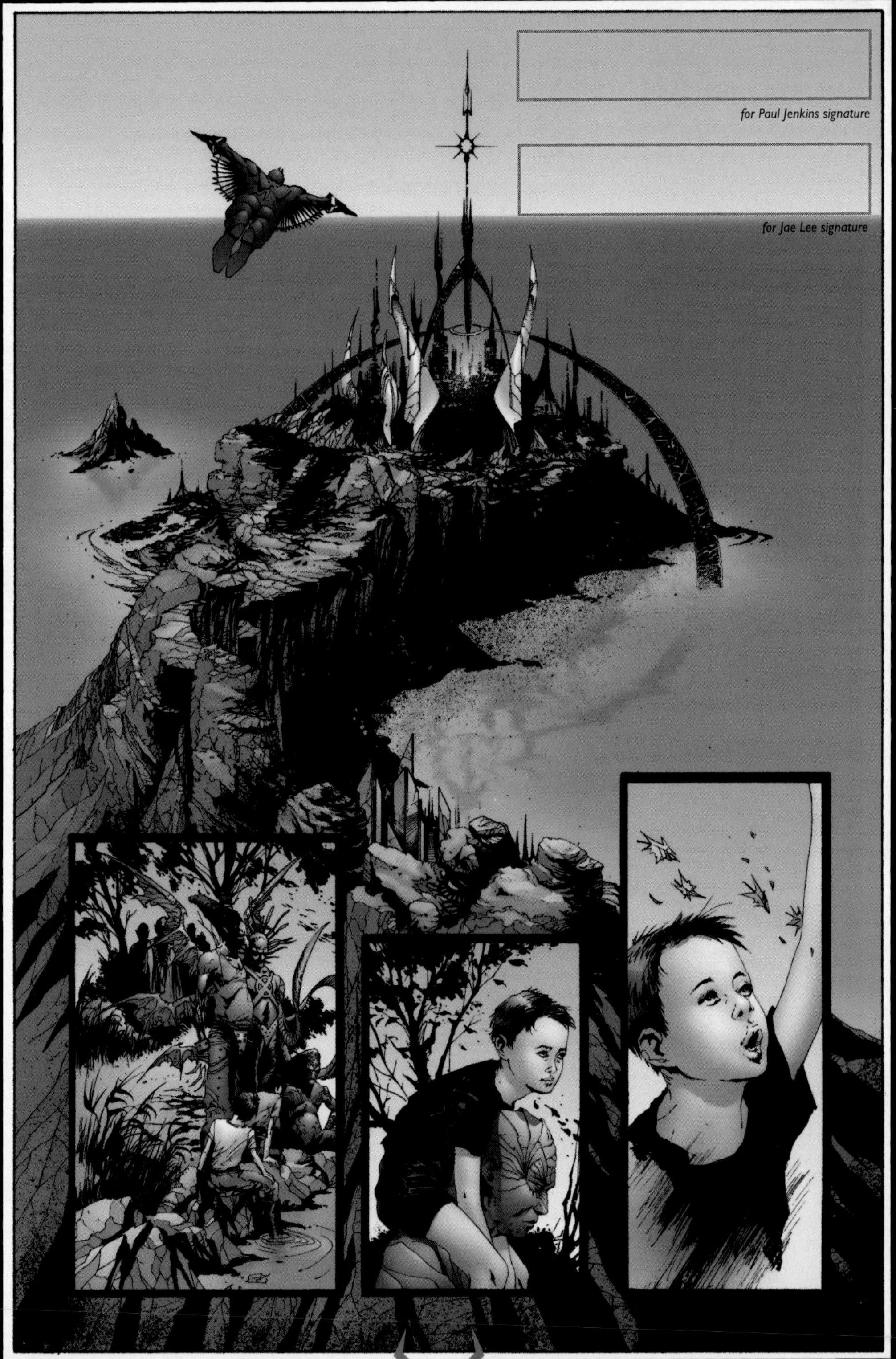

for Paul Jenkins signature
for Jae Lee signature

MARVEL KNIGHTS TOUR BOOK **(1998) — PRELIMINARY COLORS FOR** INHUMANS #1, **PAGE 2 BY AVALON STUDIOS**

The INHUMANS #1

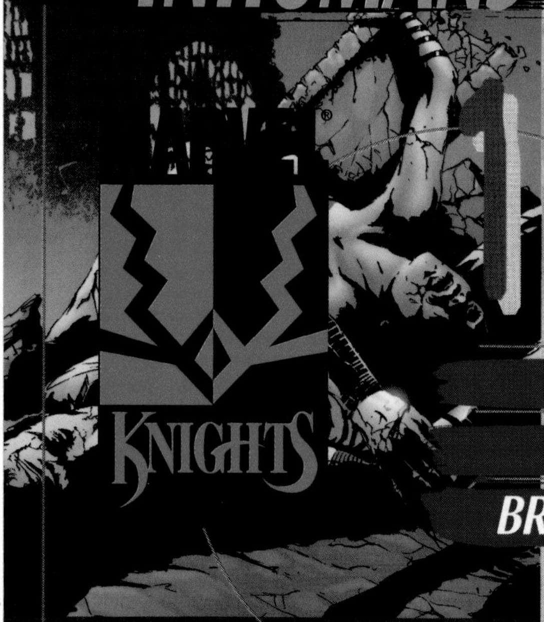
KNIGHTS

12 ISSUE MAXI SERIES

PAUL JENKINS - SCRIPT
JAE LEE - ART
BRIAN HABERLIN - COLORS

What does it mean to be an Inhuman?

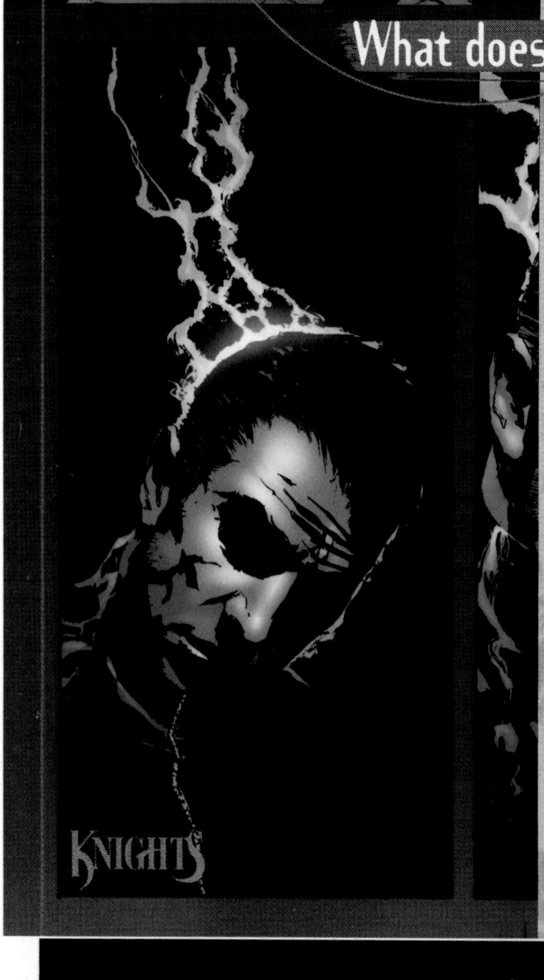
KNIGHTS

We explore this question through the eyes of its ruler, its Royal Family and in upcoming issues through the eyes of the people of Attilan. We explore the world of the Alpha Primitives, a genetically engineered race of slave workers who were designed to serve the upper cast of Inhumans, only later to be set free by their king Black Bolt. Does having one's freedom mean that one is free? The Inhumans series will be like looking in a mirror; we explore our own human condition through the Inhuman one.

INTERVIEW

PAUL JENKINS AND JAE LEE

ANY TREPIDATION ARISING FROM WORKING ON AND REVITALIZING SUCH "CLASSIC" MARVEL CHARACTERS?

Jae: Only when Bob Harras gave me a little friendly encouragement by telling me: "Don't blow it."

PAUL: I think it's vitally important that our readers will be able to relate to the dog, the one with the tuning fork on its head. It worries me that people will not find this character very believeable.

WHAT'S THE MOST ENJOYABLE PART ABOUT TACKLING THESE ESTABLISHED CHARACTERS?

Jae: Probably the backlash that we're bound to receive from irate fans who complain because we've messed up the characters they've grown up with.

PAUL: Jae and I are being given a tremendous opportunity to basically redefine these characters. If we do our jobs well, the Inhumans can be as popular as any other major Marvel characters; certainly, they have the potential for that. If you look to the early days of Marvel, everything was so fresh and exciting, and the characters were totally believeable in an unbelieveable context. As Ralph Macchio once pointed out to me, we weren't so obsessed with whether or not Spider-Man would defeat Doctor Octopus, but whether he'd have enough time afterwards to do his homework.

Believe me, there are going to be some pyrotechnics in this series—a major conflict, in fact. But before we get to them, we're going to make sure that the characters live and breathe. After all, if you don't care about them as people, you won't care about their conflicts.

DO YOU HOPE TO LEAVE A LASTING CREATIVE IMAGE ON THE BOOK/CHARACTERS YOU'RE WORKING ON?

PAUL: Again, these characters have so much untapped potential. By the time we finish, I want Attilan to be a real place. I want people to care as much about Black Bolt's hopes and fears as they do about whether or not he'd beat the Hulk in a fight.

Jae: Yes. If years from now, other writers and artists continued with our rendition of the Inhumans, that would be a sign that we didn't completely mess it up.

AFTER DRAWING A SOLO CHARACTER BOOK FOR A WHILE, HOW HAS IT BEEN ADJUSTING TO DRAWING A TEAM BOOK?

Jae: I've grown to hate the words: group shot.

WHAT DO YOU THINK WILL ULTIMATELY BE THE HOOK TO DRAW FANS TO A BOOK THAT HASN'T BEEN PUBLISHED IN TWO DECADES?

PAUL: (1) Jae's art, which is truly brilliant. (2) The fact that Black Bolt is so powerful, has never been defeated in battle, and also has a tuning fork on his head. (3) The chance to get acquainted with two thousand new super heroes, each of whom has a remarkable and unique power. (4) Marvel has my family held captive, and is promising to release one family member for each million copies sold.

WHAT TYPE OF SUPER HERO STORIES ARE YOU GOING TO TRY TO TELL WITH THE INHUMANS?

PAUL: A story with a moral: beware of Utopia... it comes with a huge price tag.

WHAT'S BEEN THE BIGGEST CHALLENGE(S) WORKING ON THE PROJECT SO FAR?

Jae: The obvious. Putting out a monthly book. But I've found a way to speed things along to ensure a trouble-free shipping schedule. After issue 1, all characters except for Black Bolt will be rendered in stick figure form. Hey, Dave McKean isn't the only one who can push the envelope.

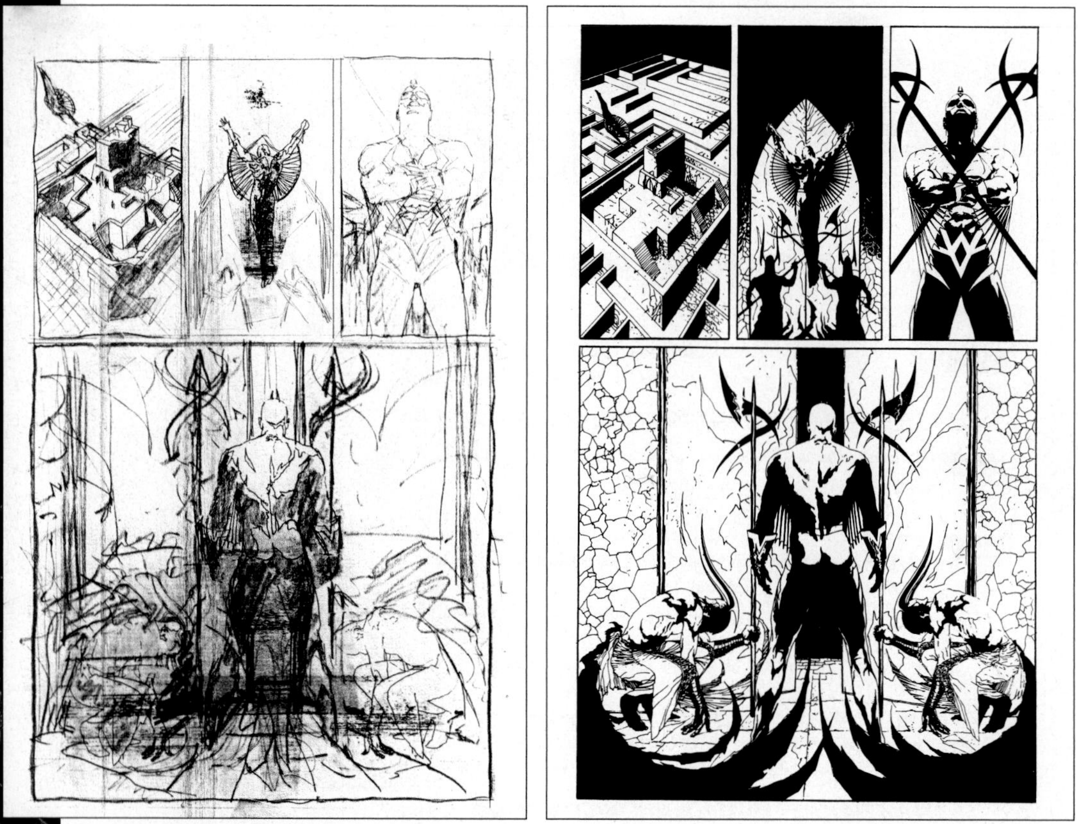

INHUMANS #1, **PAGE 4 PENCILS & INKS BY JAE LEE**

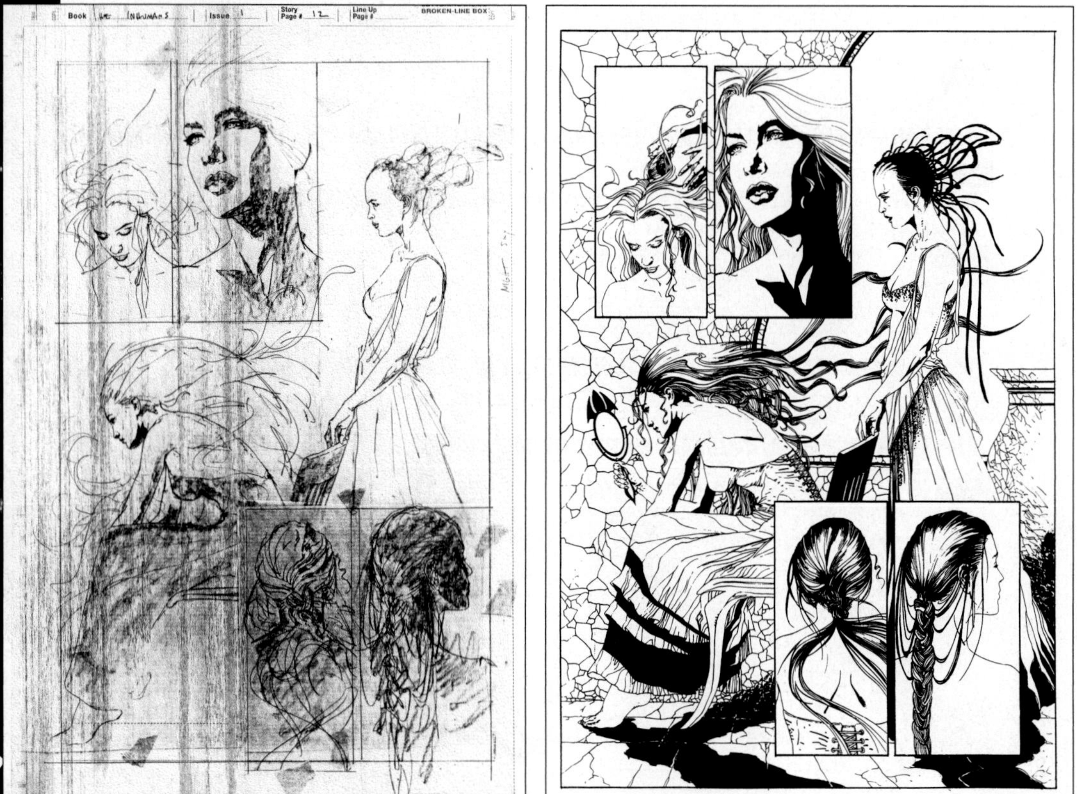
Book INHUMANS
Issue 1
Story Page # 12
Line Up Page #
BROKEN-LINE BOX

INHUMANS #1, **PAGE 12 PENCILS & INKS BY JAE LEE**

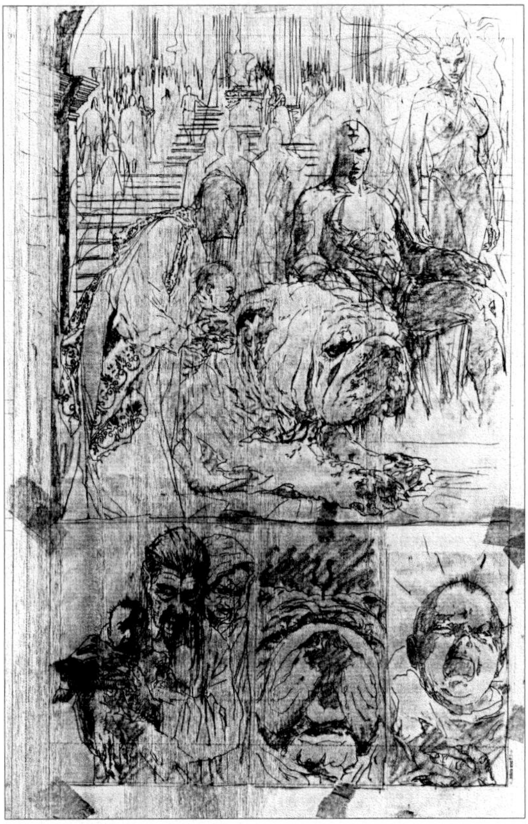

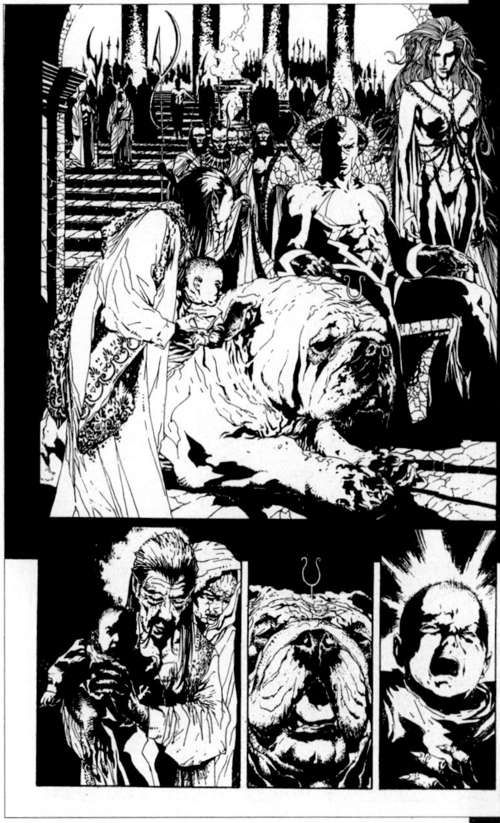

INHUMANS #1, **PAGE 14 PENCILS & INKS BY JAE LEE**

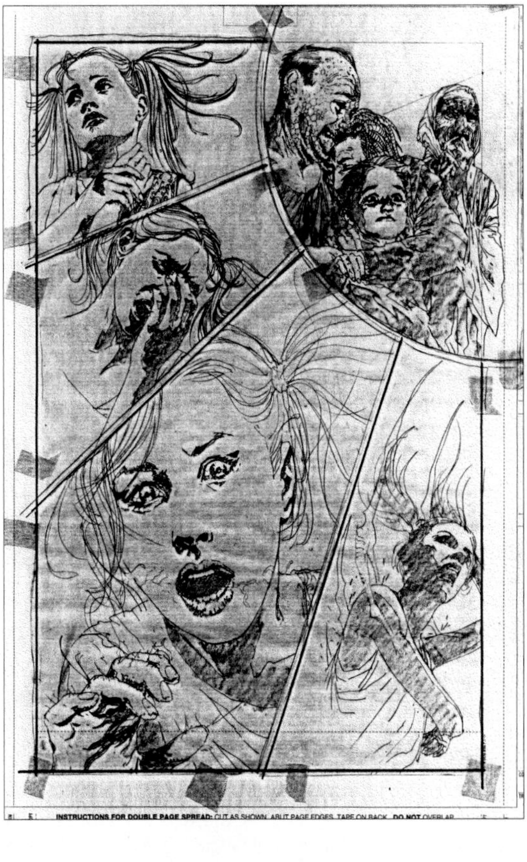
INSTRUCTIONS FOR DOUBLE PAGE SPREAD: CUT AS SHOWN. ABUT PAGE EDGES. TAPE ON BACK. DO NOT OVERLAP.

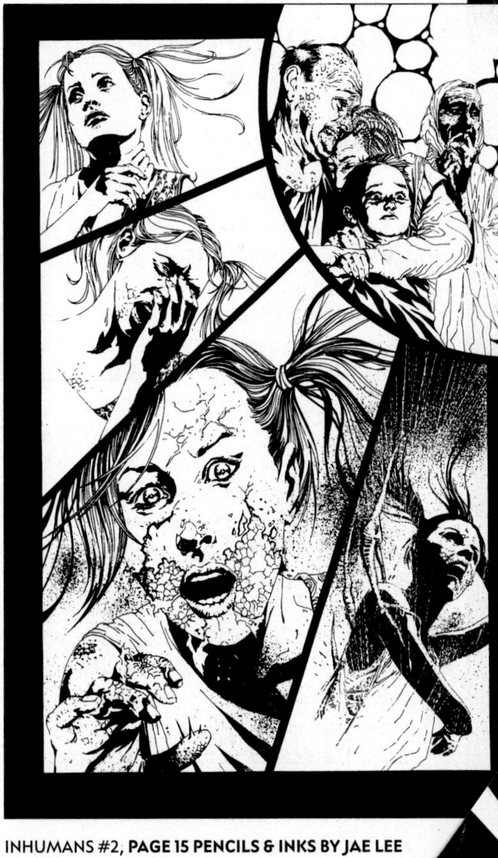

INHUMANS #2, **PAGE 15 PENCILS & INKS BY JAE LEE**

INHUMANS #8, **PAGE 4 PENCILS & INKS BY JAE LEE**

INHUMANS #1 SCRIPT
BY PAUL JENKINS

PAGE ONE (THREE PANELS)
Howay, the Jae!

Well then... here we jolly well go, eh? It's a fairly unusual experience for me, I finally get the Wizard treatment, good and proper. Joe, Nancy, Jimmy... I love yez. Superheroes, by gum. Lots of odd people flying about in their underwear, which is the way people really would behave if they could fly. I mean, if I could fly, I'd go bare naked and buzz the White House.

Just to reiterate the theme I mentioned in our phone conversation of the other day, this first issue is both a guided tour of the marvelous city of Attilan and a sneaky look into the mind of one of the most powerful characters in the Marvel pantheon: Black Bolt. With his bodysuit of shimmering ebon and a bloody great big tuning fork stuck in the middle of his head, our boy flits from venue to venue, acting regal and otherworldly and stoic without so much as a thought given to fashion sense. In a way, we're going to be setting him up as a sort of Icarus figure, both literally and figuratively speaking, since it may be that his downfall will come as a result of hubris. That's "pride" for those of you watching in black and white...

So, as you go through this first issue, bear in mind just how bloody difficult it would be to keep your mouth shut. Really. Imagine someone threatened your wife or your mum, or your cat... you'd want to at least say something as you

bashed aforementioned someone's head against a rock, wouldn't you? Imagine what a waste of a life it would be if you had to emotionally detach yourself from the sort of visceral experiences that everyone else is capable of enjoying. In a way, that isolates our boy, doesn't it? Me, I feel sorry for the poor sod. If I was king, I'd want to get away with practical jokes and eat what I wanted for dinner and give orders to the army and so on. So, for this first issue, let's try to have a certain air of mild despair hanging over the place, eh?

Author's note: This issue written to the strains of Mike Oldfield's "Songs of Distant Earth" and Enigma's "Le Roi est Mort," just so you know. Blimey, you can recreate the entire experience if you listen to the same CD's over and over again. Without further ado, then, read on, MacJae...

PANEL 1 Okay, laddie, we're going to begin with a wonderfully serene flying sequence, just to get people in the mood. It's a sort of Icarus thing we're going to set up, as I mentioned before.

As we come in on our first page, we're looking out across the very top of the fabled city of Attilan. You mentioned that you didn't want it to be domed any longer, so your wish is my command, oh exalted one: the "dome" is now going to be the negative zone barrier that protects the city from the outside world's pollution and disease. If you look at where Attilan is supposed to be from the outside, you see only this incredible dome of negative space... a special effect-y trick of the light, which we shall get into later. Inside the city, however, the sky appears almost like normal, and it should be noted that we can see the sun somewhere in the sky. If you want to suggest that there's something odd about the place, then perhaps the N-space somehow distorts the blue sky, sending colorful little rainbow blobs across it. It would make Attilan immediately come across as very different. (We're going to make the rules very unusual in here: lots of buggering about with gravity and waterfalls and Escher-type shennanigans. People happily perambulating along upside-down walkways, little airborne hovercraft, and large, bulky ones that defy gravity. If you look back at old pictures, Jack Kirby went totally nuts with his version, as far as sci-fi stuff was concerned. I suggest we follow his template, but only to a point: I'd like to add a suggestion that we make the architecture very foreign... buildings swoop outwards to impossible angles, and so on.)

Anyway, we catch some of the tops of these impressive buildings, and perhaps the side of one such building is in our foreground. This acts as a frame, sending our eyes into the sky, where we see a single flying dot.

Caption: Imagine you could never make another sound, not for the rest of your life.

Caption: Not a sigh, not a yawn. Not a single word. Ever.

PANEL 2 We close in on the dot in the sky, which is Black Bolt. He flies by the power of his mind, but swoops along with his arms out wide for reasons known only to misters Lee and Kirby. I like swooping anyway, so there you have it. Nice one, Jack and Stan...

Caption: Then, imagine you were given one chance to speak.

PANEL 3 Closing in on Black Bolt, so that we see the entirety of his body in this panel. He's swooping along so serenely, with the webbing of his costume billowing out, that you'd almost get to thinking he was actually enjoying himself. The poor lad, however, has only one single expression, at least for the first 21 pages of this book. He's enigmatic, man—in a very Mona Lisa sort of way. He's just so Jesus/Godlike, it's a bit disturbing...

Caption: What would you say?
PAGE TWO (FOUR PANELS)
PANEL 1 Okay, Jae... a chance to check out the wonderful city of Attilan below. Now, we are directly above Black Bolt, looking beyond him as he swoops along. (The following is suggestion, to spark your creative juices. Final version of Attilan is at your mercy, mate.) Down below, we can see the aforementioned walkways and triple spires. There are bulbous antigrav crafts hefting raw materials to be processed. Might be fun to show lightning playing around one building, so that energy crackles in the very center of this panel. The city's technology is very dense, I'd suggest, so that what we see goes down for perhaps half a mile. It's just layer upon layer of escalators and roadways and buildings in this section. Other sections will be different—this is Attilan's Manhattan, where the entire place is "Altered Earth New York City."

What dominates below, however, is a circular platform about a quarter of a mile across that is a park. There are various

Attilans on this raised dais, wandering around on the grass and along the pathways. We can see a small body of water, some fountains, what have you.

Caption: What would you say to the people of Attilan—this marvelous, isolated metropolis at the edge of human awareness—if you were their king?

PANEL 2 Looking down at some of the people in the park as if we're taking a snapshot of them, unawares. We're in a central area by a waterfall. The waterfall is odd in that it flows upwards, splashes into a strategically placed rock and splashes back downwards again. It's more antigravity at work, kids.

The people are, of course, going to be incredibly diverse. Here, a female reptilian creature walks hand in hand with a man who seems to glow at the end of each of his limbs. The man resembles your typical "Communion" Whitley Strieber alien, so he's a bit disturbing as well. There are more humanoids than any other form, but everyone seems quite unique. If you like, one person here might have extra limbs, and walks on them like a daddy long legs.

It's all hustle and bustle at the center of the park, with this incongruous group of people. Someone pushes a baby stroller that glides along through the air.

Caption: Your subjects are powder kegs of genetic potential, primed to detonate upon exposure to the Terrigen mists.

Caption: Each of them is truly unique—a subspecies of one.

PANEL 3 Moving away to where there are less people. In our foreground, a little child of about eight years old—therefore unchanged—is pointing up into the sky. The child is holding his daddy's hand. Daddy is a big, lumpy creature that looks extremely odd and alien next to his son. Mum (mom) might be a little wispy and pretty humanoid lady, if you want to show her. We're showing here the diversity in any given Attilan family.

The child is pointing at Black Bolt, who flies above.

Caption: Here, diversity is the rule of nature. Beings of pure energy mingle with shape-changers and dragons. To emerge from the mists transformed into a chimera is to conform.
PANEL 4 We're a few feet in the air, now looking down at the child as if from Black Bolt's angle. The child is excited to see his king flying above, and rather awestruck. He's still holding daddy's hand, but looking intently at us or past us. The kid's jaw is open...

Caption: So how do you govern these Inhumans—who are so divided by their individuality?

PAGE THREE (FIVE PANELS)
PANEL 1 Pulling away from a group of people, including the kid. They are shading their eyes to look up at us. Perhaps one adult is pointing BB out to another person nearby. Everyone has stopped, it seems, excited to see their king. Some are chatting animatedly...

Caption: You are their model of stoic consistency—their father, mother, priest and teacher. You have the capacity to destroy utterly, and to create profusely.

PANEL 2 Black Bolt has flown further from this built-up area of Attilan, so that he's now over relative Brooklyn. Here, the techno city isn't half a mile deep, so that people are actually walking on the ground. The buildings have spread out, suggesting that this is the area where most people make their homes. If you close your eyes tightly here in suburbia, you can just imagine some spotty little Attilan teenager asking dad if he can borrow the truck.

Caption: In such a place as Attilan, abnormality means power. Power affords status, which is why you are king.

PANEL 3 We're out of the city, pretty much. Black Bolt is a distant speck, albeit still visible. This is the section where Attilan meets the sea at a beautiful cove. Near us, water splashes against some rocks. I think it'd be very cool if we can show some sort of water-dwelling creature at work or play out here, Jae. Actually, you think it'd be out of order to show the back of some huge Nessie-like beast that's about to dip below the waves? I mean enormous.

Caption: You are the most powerful—an aberration of an anomaly who has never been defeated in battle.

PANEL 4 Okay, man... here, we show our hero framed by the sun. It's meant to evoke thoughts of Icarus and what have you, so there's no particular need for subtlety. With arms spread wide, Black Bolt soars. His form is somewhat obliterated by the intense corona of the sun.

Caption: You are so far removed from average that you seem more than inhuman.

PANEL 5 Another part of town altogether—a pretty dark and decrepit place, actually. As Black Bolt begins to come lower in the sky, we come across an ominous sight: the outskirts of town are a bit ghettoized. We see a very human-looking individual who simply sits on something, looking at his feet. Although he might be drunk for all we can tell. Here, there is less technology and everything's a bit scummy. Maybe there's the equivalent of trash on the streets here... perhaps some pretty unsavory individuals. There might be an Inhuman version of an ale house, and a couple of drunken sots outside laughing it up. What d'you think... would Inhumans have cats and dogs? A suspicious-looking cat perched on a fence would ground this place in reality, wouldn't it?
Whatever the case, this is the rough end of town.

Caption: Like a necessary God.

PAGE FOUR (FOUR PANELS)
PANEL 1 We're up with Black Bolt again, and he's coming in to land. Ahead of him, we can see the building he's approaching, which is the jail where he keeps his looney brother, Maximus. If we can see much of it, it's like the maze of Knossos, in Crete.
There's a pavement leading up to the entrance of this fortified building, which is on the outskirts of town. It's a pretty normal, block of a building. In fact, there's even an armed guard or two out front... one each side of the open entrance to the building.

Caption: You might well speak of the irony in this. But to do so would result in catastrophe.

PANEL 2 Holding his arms out wide, Black Bolt lands gently a few yards from the entrance. He's pretty graceful, landing on one foot.

Caption: Because your voice is so resonant that it reaches into some nameless, distant sonic range. Your slightest whisper has the power to level mountains.

PANEL 3 Same POV. Black Bolt folds his wings, having fully landed. Beyond, the guards hold their weapons to attention...

Caption: In truth, your people would scarcely hear your words...

PANEL 4 As Black Bolt walks regally into the front entrance of the jail, the two guards bow deeply to their king. It's a little absurdly formal, perhaps, but an indication of the esteem in which the people of Attilan hold their regent.

Caption: ... before the impact tore them into a million pieces.

SONIC YOUTH

Paul Jenkins Writer
Jae Lee Artist
Brian Haberlin Colorist
Richard Starkings & Comicraft Letterer
Joe Quesada, Jimmy Palmiotti Editors
Nanci Dakesian Managing Editor
Bob Harras Editor In Chief

PAGE FIVE (FOUR PANELS)
PANEL 1 Right, lad... this is a page you and I have talked about—we're going to visit the dark and dingy room where Maximus plies his evil trade. I'm suggesting three panels above, with the fourth as a larger bleed below. If you want to do it in more or less panels, be my guest. We just chop off a finger for each time you mess up, that's all...
Anyway, we are looking at the looney bugger form the side-on in silhouette here. Maximus sits on a sort of office chair—one that has arms so he can lean on them. He's looking at his feet, presumably thinking about escape plans and the price of fish. The room's pretty dark, 'cause that's the way Maximus likes it. A little hokey, perhaps, but it gets the point across.

No dialogue

PANEL 2 Still, Maximus looks at the ground. We can see he has a primitive, wooden-framed mirror in front of him in the room. The freestanding mirror is his only company these days, the poor sod. We can see his reflection in the glass, since we're looking from just behind him.
No dialogue

PANEL 3 Slowly, Maximus begins to raise his head. (Y'know, when I think of this character, I always think of Nero, the Roman Emperor. What do you say to giving him rather full lips, a weakish chin, etc?)

No dialogue

PANEL 4 And now, he is looking directly at us, albeit in a strained way out the top of his head. (You know... his head is slightly lowered still, and he's looking up at us. It's always unnerving, that is.) I should point out that even though Max appears to be looking up at us, we're looking at him from the angle of the mirror. He only ever talks to the mirror, y'see.

Max is either wet or sweating profusely... probably the latter. He is quite clearly off his rocker, even judging from this very first picture of him. Maximus grins, evilly, like the devil himself...

Maximus: I know you're there, brother.

PAGE SIX (FIVE PANELS)
PANEL 1 Okay, Jae... a smallish panel that shows Black Bolt as seen through an entire glass wall. This, I suppose, is an observation window, where the patient or prisoner is allowed to see the person they're talking to. Black Bolt, however, has chosen to keep his viewing room dark. It almost seems as though he wishes to hide in the shadows, and perhaps this tells us something about him. He's almost hidden, even more so because his outfit is black. That reserved silence of his is maddening...

No dialogue

PANEL 2 Now, we get the idea that Maximus is actually only talking to the mirror. His expression can change at any given second, from anger to calm to hilarity to sadness. And Max never does anything by halves, either... if he laughs, it's from the depths of his soul. His expressions and gestures are generally overdone, 'cause he's always playing to the crowd. Even if the only crowd is himself.

Max leans back in his chair, as if suddenly slightly amused at something or other. He rests his head in his hand in a very eccentric fashion, just to be a loon.

Maximus: There's something on your mind, isn't there? I can always tell.

Maximus: Unless you dropped by just to pass the time of day. Heaven forfend...

PANEL 3 Closing in on Black Bolt, still hidden partially in the shadows of the observation room. Black Bolt's expression, of course, hasn't changed at all, so he's an interesting contrast to his brother. Even though his face is probably mostly in darkness for the purposes of this scene, you know exactly what he looks like, but you never know what he's thinking. Perhaps, Jae, his mouth comes just slightly open. Could it be he wants to say something?

Caption: What do you say to your brother, Maximus—this twisted and remorseless lunatic to whom you are bound by the laws of fate and family?

PANEL 4 Looking at Max from another POV. Since we left him, Max seems to have had a sudden brain aneurysm. He's suddenly squeezing his head very hard with both palms, all the while looking at himself in the mirror. Therefore, Max's eyes are sorta squeezed and pulled and narrowed. I mean, he's off his bloody rocker.

Caption: How do you communicate with a man whose mind resonates on a plane twice removed from reality?

PANEL 5 Still looking at Max, who is still squeezing his temples with his palms. Perhaps we close in, perhaps we move to a different angle, perhaps we can see the observation room and Black Bolt behind Max. (Max has never looked around. Then again, maybe he sees his brother in the mirror.)

Caption: Are there words enough to satisfy a cannibal of the heart?

PAGE SEVEN (FOUR PANELS)
PANEL 1 Max now leans forwards in his chair, and again, his expression changes. He's now pretending to be very interested in his imaginary self's day. He's suddenly absorbed in a casual conversation with himself, although the words are all directed at Black Bolt.

Maximus: Mm? Oh... I'm enjoying my time here immensely, thank you for asking. So tell me, Blackagar, how have you been?

PANEL 2 More of Max speaking. He leans back, elbows resting on the armchair, and clasps his hands. This is a wonderful conversation he's having with himself...

Maximus: Hehh... ah. That's a rhetorical question, of course, so I'd prefer if you didn't answer it directly. After all, we wouldn't want a repeat of that other unpleasantry, now would we?

PANEL 3 Extreme close up of Max's face. He closes his eyes and smiles as he throws another couple of barbed taunts his brother's way.

Maximus: And don't pretend you don't understand (haven't a clue?) what I'm talking about... you know...

PANEL 4 And now, with Max's words appearing in a caption box above, we are shown an horrific image. We are looking at the rubble of an obliterated building, with little bits of burning stuff all over the place. Amongst the rubble, a woman (their mum) is lying face down and dead. If you like, she can be on fire, or her clothes burning, at least. We can see her only as clearly as the code permits, I guess, but let's try to make it somewhat shocking, eh? From under a piece of rubble, a hand protrudes... the hand of Agon, the boys' now deceased father. Something to do with Kree drunken driving and sonic booms and, well... read on and you'll get the picture. Suffice to say, we delve yet again into Greek tragedic devices. (Somewhere along the way someone always eats their father, plonks their mother and offends the bloody Gods by worshiping the wrong turnip. Daft bleedin' Greeks...)

Max (Caption): "... I mean that time you murdered our parents."

PAGE EIGHT (FIVE PANELS)
PANEL 1 Right, lad... this page is a flashback to events that took place when Black Bolt was a fresh-faced nineteen-year-old. It's a retelling of an old story, so by the time you get this, someone might have dredged up the reference.

**Note: Joe, Nancy... this is the reminder you asked for. Since we couldn't track down the reference for this bit, it needs to be run by Bob for the sake of accuracy, and amended if necessary.

As we come in, we're in the middle of some conflict

or other. Maximus stands on a building, looking insane, gesticulating wildly as a Kree ship takes off into the sky. Black Bolt himself is chained, and cannot break free.

Max (Caption): "It wasn't my fault—I didn't ask you to be there when the Kree came. You and that intractable, insufferable conscience of yours.

PANEL 2 Closing in on Black Bolt, who shouts up at the ship. We're looking at him as he delivers a sonic blast into the air.
     Beyond, Max grabs at his head in extreme pain.

Max (Caption): "You just couldn't leave me to my little faux pas, could you? You had to say something...

PANEL 3 Wham! The Kree ship breaks up in the sky, catching fire as it begins to disintegrate. The main bulk of the ship already looks as though it's falling in suspiciously space shuttle-type fashion. I give you full permission to draw in a sound effect.

SFX:

PANEL 4 Bakoom! (Hehh... this is fun.) Anyway, where was I? Oh yeah... bakoom.
     Bakoom! The ship has landed on the royal palace, coincidentally squashing the boys' mum and dad and a very nice royal cactus called Colin. Mum and dad have legs, but not enough time to outrun the fireball that engulfs them. Poor Colin, of course, is entirely screwed. And what I want to know is why Black Bolt never felt guilty about Colin.

SFX:

PANEL 5 Looking at Black Bolt, whose jaw sorta drops in horror at what he has done. We're simply looking at his face, perhaps lit by the light of the intense fire over in the distance.

Max (Caption): "... just to bring the whole party crashing down in flames."

PAGE NINE (FIVE PANELS)
PANEL 1 Okay... we're back in the present. You remember the last panel from page 8? Okay, we're going to show Black Bolt's face in the present, as seen from the same POV. Now, of course, he's a bit more stoic and so forth. He's in the observation booth, and slightly hidden by the shadows.
     Now, his face betrays no emotion as he remembers the past. It's that same old enigmatic expression, Jae, and we begin to wonder about him a little.

No dialogue

PANEL 2 Maximus is now scowling, extremely angry. He looks very frightening in this half light. Still, he jabbers on at the mirror, getting more and more worked up with each thing he says.

Maximus: I know you could speak if you wanted to, brother, but what would you possibly say?

Maximus: Would you tell everyone exactly what you did to mother and father, and run the risk of losing your precious

throne?

PANEL 3 Suddenly, Maximus is on his feet, and pointing right at the observation window. His face is full of venom as he suddenly lashes out at his brother. The fact that he's suddenly moved away from the mirror is doubly disconcerting.

Maximus: Well, it'd probably do you some good instead of standing around like a statue all day.

Maximus: You think you're fooling them, but you're not. There's a flaw, d'you hear me? A FLAW!

PANEL 4 We're in the observation room. Black Bolt has turned, and is walking away, going past us. Through the glass we can make out the dim figure of Maximus, cursing and shouting and carrying on.
     Black Bolt doesn't register any emotion—he's simply finished with his visit, it seems.

Caption: That's it... go on. Admit to your guilt, damn you! I know you want to!

PANEL 5 As we leave Maximus, he's now kneeling on the floor, with his face pressed right up against the mirror, babbling at his reflection again. This might be a pretty cool way to leave him, when you think about it, because when he talks about guilt, he's probably now referring to himself.

Caption: It's tearing you up inside.

PAGE TEN (FOUR PANELS)
PANEL 1 (Jae: I suggest stacking these four panels one upon the other, as a sort of progressive view of the island outside the dome. Just a suggestion.)
     Okay... we are a mile or so high above the fabled island of Atlantis. I suppose another continuity check is in order so that we can make sure of the size of the island. For the time being, I suggest it's the size of, say, Ireland. Most of what we can see here is brown, with the occasional patch of green. We're at the end of the island where Attilan lays, so we can see its size and shape relative to the rest of the place. Basically what we're seeing, then, is a stretch of coastline that leads away over either side of the panel. Just for the sake of future possibilities, make a very small little island just off the coast, slightly removed from the mainland, about two miles out to sea from the edge of Attilan. Maybe I'll find an opportunity to use it later.
     Attilan ought to be pretty frigging big, really. But we can only just see a distorted, rainbow-colored dome thingy where it stands.

Caption: When the great island of Atlantis was dredged from the sea you brought your city here.

Caption: So that your people might reestablish their roots, even though Earth's polluted air is deadly poison to all Inhumans.

PANEL 2 Moving in. We're looking at the city from a vantage point out to sea, and it's pretty weird. I think we ought to make something cool out of the Negative Zone barrier that protects the city. For instance, I imagine that if you try to get through the barrier, you walk into another dimension or something, and maybe that dimension is like hell. It'd be pretty cool that if you were close enough to the barrier, you'd be able to discern the images of trapped souls, screaming their torment from within. Certainly, it'd make one hell of a warning sign.

The set up of the barriers follows my description in the captions below. I think they could be sorta distorting, so that you might even get just a vague idea of the outline of Attilan by looking through. The rainbow effect could resemble oil in water, yes?

Caption: To safeguard Attilan, a series of protective barriers was devised. Five seperate defensive systems: a trillion volt pallisade, a progressive eco-filter to scrub the rancid air.

Caption: And the ultimate fortification—a dome of impenetrable Negative space surrounding it all.

PANEL 3 Outside, now on the island. Here, we are looking at an ancient Atlantean building—perhaps an amphitheatre—that is overgrown with grass. Its structure is something different again, even though its architecture is reminiscent of Attilan. Basically, this place is very ancient and mysterious and fragile.

Caption: You peered outside, but the looming, archaic structures of Atlantis seemed unwilling to divulge their long-kept secrets.

Caption: Silent ghosts. You resolved to talk to them one day, when the time was right.

PANEL 4 Moving to a different POV of the same place. We can now see something going on to one side of the amphitheatre. The humans are here... yahoo!

The ignorant humans are digging a quarry out of this place using a couple of enormous yellow Caterpillar excavators! They've simply torn out the side of some ancient building or other, and are going about wrecking the place to their hearts' content. We might see a few people in this, if you want. It's a very busy quarry.

Just an additional note that there are also a few Portuguese soldiers hanging around, ready to protect the workers from danger.

Caption: But before you could, the humans showed up and began fighting over the scraps.

PAGE ELEVEN (FIVE PANELS)
PANEL 1 We can see a couple of bored, hard-hatted workers milling about as they do their work, whatever it may be. These people are miners, by the look of it, and rather unsavory miners at that. Anyway, they are just destroying the place and polluting it while they go.

Caption: Where they are arrogant, they are also noble; divisive, and yet capable of unquestioning loyalty.

Caption: They hide their compassion beneath hostility.

PANEL 2 Nearby, some guys are taking a lunch break. (There can be some female workers, of course, and you must be sure to make them look like Russian shot- putters.) Anyway, most of the workers are smoking heavily and laughing raucously.

Caption: They are ozone eaters. Each of them harbors an apocalyptic array of viruses and bacterial infections, to which they have a Herculean resistance.

PANEL 3 Near a large drill bit which is currently tearing into the ground at a rate of knots. Chunks of earth spill out over the side. Over the noise, a foreman shouts to a technician who is trying to make notes, despite the terrific rumbling. The impression we get is of pollution and violation.

Caption: For months now, they have been raking the ancient island for metal and minerals. International conglomerates, supported by the occupying Portuguese army.

PANEL 4 Looking at a couple of Portuguese soldiers who are on guard next to some barbed wire. They are at attention, working hard as opposed to slacking off.

Caption: Whatever you say to them, it had better be good. Because these humans, who bring pestilence, disease and decay to your people, are back.

PANEL 5 A larger page-wide panel. Now, we can see exactly where on Atlantis we are. As a matter of fact, we're close to the protected city of Attlian, which we can see in the background. In the foreground we can the barbed wire and warning signs and a large tank. The Portuguese soldiers are on guard here. A multilingual sign near the barbed wire tells us that there is a minefield over the fence. We might also see the edge of a tractor or something, just to remind us why the soldiers are here.

Caption: And they're less than a mile away from your border.
PAGE TWELVE (FIVE PANELS)
PANEL 1 Okay, man... a two page scene with Black Bolt's lovely wife, Medusa. Loathe as I am to describe women as objects of lust with a gravity-defying figure, Medusa fits that description. I suppose you could model her on Brigitte Bardot... that'd make sense.

Anyway, as we come in, Medusa is in her dressing room with her personal servant girl whom we shall call Marista, after camarista. (Look it up. I did.) She's getting ready to retire for the night, so she might well be differently dressed than normal. Marista is Medusa's confidante and amiga, even though she's a servant. Marista is brushing her mistresses' hair, which is kinda interesting in itself. Medusa is looking at herself in a mirror.

Marista: Something troubles you, lady Medusa?
PANEL 2 They continue to talk, as Medusa confides in her maid. She seems pretty agitated, but it's a lot of pillow talk, I suppose.

Medusa: It's my husband, Marista. Sometimes, I wonder at the weight of his responsibility.

Medusa: Perhaps I'm being ridiculous... but it's hard to see where I fit into it all.

PANEL 3 Going around to look at both women. Marista chuckles at what she's been told, trying to cheer her boss up a little bit. Actually, this might look kinda cool.

Marista is putting the brush to one side on the table. Meanwhile, Medusa's hair is getting ready for bed by folding in on itself and tying itself up in a bun behind her head. This seems pretty normal to both women, but rather wild to us.

Marista: Isn't it the same with all of them, my lady?

Medusa: I suppose it is.

PANEL 4 More talking. The hair is tying itself quite nicely, and Marista has grabbed another small mirror from the dressing table. Meanwhile, Medusa is still studying herself in the mirror.

Medusa: It's just... sometimes, he's capable of looking at me in such a way that I'm so completely sure of what he feels. Other times, he's an enigma.

Medusa: I just wish... you know... sometimes, I need more than anything to hear the words.

PANEL 5 Closing in on Medusa, who looks rather sour. Behind her, Marista is holding up the mirror so that Medusa can see the now-finished hairstyle. We don't see Marista's face—only that she's holding the mirror.

Medusa: But he can't say them. And he never will.

Page Thirteen (Five panels)
PANEL 1 Moving into the adjacent bedroom, where we find Black Bolt, alone. He's stripped naked to the waist, and blindfolded in such a way that his face is as covered as when he wears his normal clothing. Black Bolt is doing a sort of yoga/martial arts concentration technique by standing on one foot and balancing. In fact, he's standing on the toes of one foot, since he can levitate, and his arms are held out just so... the poor man has to go through half an hour of this every night, just to make sure that he doesn't talk in his sleep.

Medusa (Caption): "Every night he goes ahead of me, to meditate alone. So that while he's sleeping he doesn't accidentally say something that might destroy us all.

PANEL 2 Closing in. Black Bolt hasn't moved. A slight breeze blows the bedroom curtain inwards.

Medusa (Caption): "For one hour every night, Marista... to purge all the thoughts of the day from his mind.

Medusa (Caption): "Can you imagine the sheer effort of will that it takes to force yourself to sleep in absolute silence?

PANEL 3 Closing in again, so that Black Bolt's face is in the extreme foreground. Even though his mouth betrays no expression under the blindfold, Black Bolt is sweating with the effort. Concentrating like this is very taxing, which means little or no nookie for Medusa...

Medusa (Caption): "To push away every sight and sound

you've experienced, to detach yourself from even the memory of your emotions—"

PANEL 4 Back with Medusa and Marista. Marista is holding up a nightgown for her mistress, who puts it on as she continues to complain about her relationship. Both women are near to the door, so it seems as though Medusa's about to join her husband for the night.

Marista: Are you afraid he's going to make a mistake, my lady?

Medusa: No... no. But don't you see, that's the problem?

Medusa: It terrifies me to think that my husband can so easily close the door to his mind, and lock everything and everyone out.

PANEL 5 Medusa pauses, and looks at the bedroom door sadly...

Medusa: Including me.

PAGE FOURTEEN (FIVE PANELS)
PANEL 1 It's another day, and this time we are inside Black Bolt's court. The setup is very Jacobean, with Black Bolt and Medusa strategically placed at the end of a long room so that they can officially receive people and do courtly things. As we come in, Black Bolt shows perhaps the first spark we've seen yet that he's not a robot—his enigmatic expression might almost be taken for boredom if you take into account that he's sorta slouched down, resting his chin on one fist. With his free hand, Black Bolt absent-mindedly scratches the head of Lockjaw, the dog, who is asleep next to his master.

Looking from a different angle, we can now see that a ceremony of sorts is taking place. In Attilan, childbirth is a rare occurence, so each newborn baby is brought before the king so that he can bestow some karma on it, or whatever. The gang's all here, so we can see Gorgon and Karnak and Crystal somewhere in the picture. (Not this one, necessarily... just around.) Triton's not here, but I'll explain in a bit.

The child is being held by two ever-so-loving-and-proud parents, who get this one chance to show off to the king. Dad is a hairy, lupine individual who works on the outskirts of town in an electronics repair workshop. He's very down to earth. He's holding the little girl, who's wrapped up quite nicely, thanks very much. Mom is some sort of semitransparent creature, albeit humanoid, and both parents are simply beaming with pride.

Dad: ... and so, we come to her paternal lineage, as is my duty, honor and privilege to recite, your majesty.

Dad: Um... beginning with me, obviously. And then onto my father, Grimal, also a carnivore...

PANEL 2 Dad kneels, holding the little dudette up for Black Bolt to see. The baby begins to squawk with the strangeness of it all. If we see Medusa, she might be smiling in a very maternal fashion.

Dad: ... whose father before him was Tauron, second cousin to Vel. Um... with whom your father dined often, as you may recall...

PANEL 3 Down at the foot of the throne, lazy old Lockjaw opens one eye, disturbed for a moment by the sound of the baby. Like any dog, though, he's mildly curious as to the source of the noise, but only 'cause he wishes it'd go away.

No dialogue

PANEL 4 Closing in on the (very human-looking) baby, held up for all the world to see. The little girl is now squealing at the very top of her lungs, so that her little face is going red with the effort.

Caption: What do you tell her, this child of infinite possibilities?

PAGE FIFTEEN (FIVE PANELS)
PANEL 1 Flashback: Suddenly, we are in the middle of a past conflict. Black Bolt is flying along and zooming through, while Gorgon is trying to knock the crap out of the Thing with his remarkable feet. In the meantime, the other Inhumans are having at it with other members of the FF.

Caption: Do you tell her that the world is a violent, angry place, populated by violent, angry people? That she is already misunderstood, just for the circumstances of her birth?

PANEL 2 Another scene from the past. This time, Black Bolt is facing off with his looney brother, Maximus. At the same time, a couple of hundred Alpha Primitives are spilling out of the bowels of the city, while things explode in the background. (These scenes are all taking place in the mind's eye, Jae. They are Black Bolt's recollections of a very mad world.)

Caption: That her home could collapse at any moment under the whim of a mad pretender to the throne?
PANEL 3 A larger panel. Um. Now, we're on the moon. Rather disconcertingly, old Galactus is filling up the sky in the background while he admonishes Earth about one thing or another. I dunno... doesn't he show up and blow up planets that aren't worthy, or something? I suggest, then, that he looks a mite annoyed.

Near us a couple of Attilans are pointing up into the sky, aghast.

Caption: That the universe is a cup of danger which can spill over at any second?

PANEL 4 Looking at the little baby, held in her daddy's arms. The father is still kneeling, but now looking up at us expectantly, so we can assume we're back in the present and seeing things from Black Bolt's POV.

No dialogue
PANEL 5 Black Bolt holds his hand up in some silent show of acknowledgement. The baby is still central to our picture, but Black Bolt approves of the little child.

Caption: How do you explain all of that?

PAGE SIXTEEN (FOUR PANELS)
PANEL 1 Yahoo! Okay, man... my favorite scene of this book, the one with Karnak and Gorgon. Now, I happen to think Karnak is one of the coolest comic characters ever next to the Silver Surfer (wild dude with an intergalactic surfboard?) and Batman (a hard bastard with a deathwish, in my opinion). Anyway, I want to accomplish a couple of things with this scene: (1) the major revelation about Black Bolt, which we'll get to in a second and (2) a basic description of how Karnak intuits the inherent flaw in people, places and things. It's gonna be cool, I am so excited.

Anyway, as we come in, Karnak and Gorgon are hanging about in the main banquet hall, where there is going to be a very large feast later on. For the moment, everything is in preparation, and old Gorgon is going about the business of getting pleasantly drunk. He and Karnak are at the far end of the table from the head chair, which is where Black Bolt will sit. There's enough room for, say, sixteen people at the table. One chair is quite remarkable, if we see it—it's where old Triton must sit. (Now, I also really like Triton, and we're going to treat him in rather a sympathetic way. Triton's a bit of an oddball, even by Inhuman standards... he needs to be kept wet if he is out of the water for any given length of time, so he has this special chair for banquets that sprays him with a continual mist of seawater. I also think the poor sod has a little trouble communicating, 'cause he's very old fashioned, but that's a story for another time.)

Anyway... back to the fray. Like I said, Gorgon is having a rollicking old time of it, drinking up all the beer before he's supposed to. He would've made a great Viking warrior, 'cause he likes living and fighting and partying. He ain't such a bad sort... in fact, he's going to have quite the sense of humor about him, I think. As we see him here, he's slurping down some ale with one hand and holding up a half full jug with the other. Beer slops over the side.

Karnak's glass sits, untouched, at the end of the table near to where Gorgon is sitting. Karnak himself is standing at a window about ten yards away at the end of the room. He has his arms behind his back, and is looking outside across the city. Outside, it's early evening and raining against the window pane...

Gorgon: ... and the goat says "I don't know, but the one in the middle is definitely a shapechanger!"

PANEL 2 Looking at Gorgon, who fills his glass up again with ale. It's a wild party of one, and his eyes sorta give the game away. We like him for this, though...
Gorgon: A shapechanger! Ah-hehh... Ha ha ha!

PANEL 3 (If you want, add a silent panel, where Gorgon waits for a reaction but doesn't get one.)

(Laughs fades into a nervous whimper)

PANEL 4 Gorgon rests his drunken head on the table and blearily looks at Karnak's glass which just sits there. Suddenly, the glass is all-consuming to old

Gorgon, who is a bit all-consuming himself. Gorgon sorta lazily looks at the glass with one eye open, and makes an offhanded comment.

Gorgon: Hmff... there's a crack in your glass, Karnak.

PANEL 5 Okay... first of all, I suggest that we have some sort of inset panel inside this panel, which is pretty big. The inset panel is an extreme close up of Karnak's eyes, which glow with an intense inner light. We've never seen them before, but you and I have talked about them, Jae.

As to the main panel, we are now outside the window, looking in at Karnak. He remains motionless, and like Black Bolt, his expression wavers very little. We can see the entire window pane, which fills up just about the entire panel, and we can see the glass in "Karnak vision." That is, we're looking at the flaws in the pane of glass between us and Karnak. A bunch of "invisible" cracks all converge at one single point—presumably, where one might push and have the window shatter. (Not sure how you want to show this... perhaps as whisper-thin little lines in the glass that glow?)

PANEL 6

Karnak: I know.

PAGE SEVENTEEN (FIVE PANELS)
PANEL 1 Gorgon now sits up, in our foreground, and looks directly over at his best buddy. In a way, he's goading Karnak a little, but in a relatively good-natured way. Karnak hasn't moved; he remains at the window, looking out across the city, as if he's waiting for something to happen.

Gorgon: I don't understand you, brother. You've been at that window for an hour now. You know how I hate it when somebody lets their ale get warm.

Gorgon: I'm serious. If you don't come over here right this minute, I'm going to drink it—

PANEL 2 Gorgon continues, gently chiding his buddy. Karnak's his best friend, so he clearly feels he can say anything, and we can tell that Karnak doesn't seem to mind. Gorgon's fairly hammered, of course.

Karnak is turning, interrupting Gorgon.

Karnak: I'm worried about our king.

PANEL 3 Gorgon erupts with laughter, thinking the whole thing is a little bit ridiculous. In so doing, Gorgon spills some of his beer.
Gorgon: You... worried? Ah hehh! You are a reprehensible being, dear Karnak.

PANEL 4

Gorgon: If I didn't know any better from watching you, I'd swear you were irrevocably drunk. If so, the world would never make sense to me again.

PANEL 5 Gorgon is looking drunkenly down at the table

and chuckling to himself at the thought of his staid brother having some reservations about Black Bolt. To him, the whole idea is quite preposterous.

Beyond, we can see that Karnak is wandering over to the table, coming towards us.

Gorgon: And about him, too... I never thought the day would come. In all the years I've known you, Karnak, you have never once so much as raised an eyebrow at the motives of our king.

Gorgon: Of all people, your loyalty to Black Bolt is beyond question. So tell me... what troubles you?

PANEL 6 Close up of Karnak, who is troubled. He looks down at his feet as he begins to explain.

Karnak: A secret, Gorgon. Something that I have never told anyone.

PAGE EIGHTEEN (FIVE PANELS)
PANEL 1 Even closer to Karnak. Really, we're concentrating on the lad's eyes, which again seem possessing an inner fire. As he launches into his explanation of the way things work, we almost detect his internal flaw-sensing mechanism going to work. It's pretty weird, and very cool...

Karnak: To interpret the secret, you must know what I know. You must understand my... gift.

PANEL 2 Flashback: We are with Karnak, who stands in front of a metal door with his hand held lightly towards it. We are shown things in Karnak-vision, so we can see what Karnak senses.

Okay, so... he's in front of the door, about to break it down, trying to pick out its weak spot. Like the window earlier, we see the flaws running through the door and converging at one point.

Karnak (Caption): "In everything, there hides a flaw—be it structural, geological, psychological. To me, these flaws appear like beacons that guide the way to weakness.

PANEL 3 Another flashback: Now, the Inhumans are battling against a tremendous amphibian creature. It towers above them, and while some of the regular crew keep it busy, Karnak's in our foreground, sensing the creature's weakness. Same rules apply.

Karnak (Caption): "The cracks appear at the periphery of my awareness, to be intuited... interpreted.
Karnak (Caption): "It matters not the size of the structure, nor the material from which it is made. Everything has an imperfection that can be traced to one single point and exploited."

PANEL 4 Back in the room. Gorgon doesn't seem too impressed. In fact, he's pretty sure he's flawless—typical Gorgon. Despite his mild protestation, Karnak is quite firm in his conviction.

Gorgon: Hmph. Are you saying that I am anything less than perfect, Karnak?

Karnak: Everything has a flaw, brother. Everything and everyone.

PANEL 5 Close up of Karnak again. He admits the big secret.
Karnak: Except for Black Bolt.

PAGE NINETEEN (FOUR PANELS)
PANEL 1 Flashing away for a second as Karnak's words continue in caption. We are at some royal gathering or other that takes place in the streets of Attilan. Here, Black Bolt and Medusa and the others are making a public appearance on some kind of raised dais. Just about every single Attilan is in attendance. Everyone's cheering and carrying on. It's like the ethereal Nuremberg rallies, 'cause just about every single Attilan citizen is in attendance.

Black Bolt just stands, emotionless, whereas Medusa and others wave to the crowd. But we can see that Karnak is standing nearby and slightly behind everyone else, his arms crossed, scrutinizing his regent very closely.

Karnak (Caption): "I have studied him constantly. He is surrounded by chaos and inconsistency, yet he gives no indication that it affects him in any way.

Karnak (Caption): "In all the time I've known him, he has never once wavered from his impossible duty."

PANEL 2 Back in the present. Gorgon seems to have sobered up immensely—he's taken Karnak's revelation very seriously indeed, and he looks mildly shocked. Karnak has now taken his glass of ale and is looking down at the liquid inside, avoiding making eye contact with Gorgon. You get the feeling that he's a bit guilty for spilling the beans...

Gorgon: And do you now detect flaws?

Karnak: No. No... but I should.

PANEL 3 Karnak holds up his glass to the light so that he can study it some more. He is extremely serious.

Karnak: Entropy is the way of the universe, Gorgon. One day, the cracks are going to appear—they must.

PANEL 4 Final close up of Karnak's face. He is grim indeed.

Karnak: And when they do, I fear for us all.

PAGE TWENTY (SIX PANELS)
PANEL 1 Okay, mate... our final scene of this first book, and it takes place in the same banquet hall. As we come in, it is now nighttime. We're some way away from the banquet room, outside the window, looking in. There are lights on inside, and it seems as though the dinner is in full swing. We can only see the hustle and bustle of the party, etc.

And guess what? Gorgon's voice appears from inside the room. The daft bastard is telling the same crappy joke that he told earlier.

Voice (inside): ... and the goat says "I don't know, but the one in the middle is definitely a shapechanger!"

PANEL 2 As we come inside, we now see the banquet is humming along. A couple of Alpha Primitives are glumly wandering around with serving plates, and maybe old Lockjaw is over in the corner somewhere, snoozing off a plate of pork. It'd be nice if Black Bolt were feeding him under the table, but I don't think he'd fit.

Anyway... Gorgon finishes up his joke to a mixed reaction. Next to him, Karnak is simply dabbing at the edge of his mouth with his napkin, leaving his plate of food pretty much intact. Whereas Gorgon's food is all over the shop, Karnak's part of the table is wonderfully neat and tidy. To the other side of Gorgon is a merchant-type fellow, quite human in appearance, a little bit like a fat old Viking. The merchant snorts with laughter.

However, we can see Lady Crystal on the other side of the table, and perhaps a couple of other people. Crystal looks pretty angry at Gorgon... others look slightly shocked at the drunken Inhuman's antics. It's actually kinda funny, when you think about it. (Um... remember that Gorgon and Co. are at the far end of the table from Black Bolt, okay?) Basically, all eyes turn towards Gorgon as he makes his faux pas.

Gorgon: A shapechanger! Ha ha ha!

Merchant: Hphsss... Ha ha ha!

PANEL 3 We are looking at Triton, who sits in his special chair over the table from Gorgon. Like I said, the chair sprays a mist of water over Triton, who is very different from the others in both the way he thinks and the way he acts. He has a tube running under his nose, similar to one you might find delivering oxygen to an emphysema patient.

Anyway... Triton looks across the table (directly at us, I suppose) and gently admonishes his drunken cousin. He's very similar to the Creature from the Black Lagoon, Jae... I'd like to make his lips very fishlike, and give him lidless eyes. Whatever... he's the oddest of an odd bunch.
*Note: let's give Triton a special font and word-balloon, okay?

Triton: Cousin Gorgon, well know you not ribaldry so close to ears of the king. Well known to any being, for if he laugh...

Triton: Tsk. Shame to you, for the risk you demolish us all—
PANEL 4 Looking at Medusa, who is sitting at this end of the table. Now, she pipes in—not to admonish Gorgon, but to admonish Triton. She is stern—a little too stern, we might think.

Medusa: Though my husband is incapable of speech, cousin Triton, I can assure you that his hearing is very acute.

Medusa: I would remind you that he is present at this table and would prefer not to be spoken about as if he isn't here.

PANEL 5 Poor Triton looks extremely crestfallen and begins to apologize. And with that, Lady Crystal takes his side and a right royal argument begins...

Triton: If it pleasing your Majesty... this being am poor foolish. I humble apologise.

Crystal: Hey! Don't you pick on poor Triton, sister. He can't help it if he's different... he doesn't know how to say things.

PANEL 6 ... Because the next thing you know, the entire thing erupts. Suddenly, Gorgon is to his feet and shouting drunkenly at Crystal, who is shouting back and pointing at him. Medusa, if we can see her, looks angry. Triton looks embarrassed, and others are either joining in or looking shocked. Just like my bloody family, really...

Gorgon: Hpmh! I may be smashed groggy, but at least I know my place, impetuous child.

PANEL 7

Crystal: I have the deepest respect for you, cousin Gorgon, but sometimes you can be such a bloated old oaf.

PAGE TWENTY ONE (SEVEN PANELS)
PANEL 1 Now, we go down to the other end of the table to see Black Bolt's reaction to everything. Guess what? He's just sitting there like a lemon, taking it all in. Poor sod is pretty good at being royal, really. For his reaction think "emotionally detached."
Again, that enigmatic look plays across his face.

Caption: What would you say, if you could only say just one simple phrase for the rest of your life?

PANEL 2 Over at the other end, world war three has broken out. Crystal, being a wilful sort of girl is throwing a glass of beer in Gorgon's face. The merchant ducks as it splashes all over everything. Others are joining in, as before.

Caption: What would you tell the people around you who are your subjects, your cousins, your allies?

PANEL 3 A very small panel in which Karnak's hand calmly folds his napkin at one edge.
Lockjaw: Rrr

PANEL 4 Over at the edge of the room, or wherever he is, Lockjaw bares his teeth in a growl. He doesn't like the atmosphere in the room—especially because it's too bloody noisy.

SFX: ptui

PANEL 5 Gorgon's looking a bit embarrassed and shocked as beer drips off him and onto the table and floor. He looks at his arms, which are dripping wet. Beyond, Medusa is still fuming, her arms crossed.

SFX: (Crinkle)

PANEL 6 Another very small panel, pulling away. Karnak folds another corner of his napkin.

Crystal: Sorry.

PANEL 7 Looking at Crystal, who looks very satisfied at the result of her bravery. Poor old Triton, sitting next to her, looks nervously up at her. He's a bit of a drip, is the best description.

Caption: What would you say?

PAGE TWENTY TWO (FOUR PANELS)
PANEL 1 Okay, man... for the last page we are going to zoom in on Black Bolt, who is sitting at the other end of the table. The last panel is larger than these three at the top, okay?
In this first panel, we are just behind Medusa's chair, looking down the entire length of the table. Gorgon and Crystal are either side of the table, pointing at each other and shouting. There are various other arguments breaking out, too. So much for a nice dinner.
Black Bolt hasn't moved at the other end of the table. The Alphas stand calmly to one side now, waiting for the lunacy to subside...

Caption: Just one thing...

PANEL 2 Now, Karnak is in our foreground. he holds his napkin in front of him on the table, neatly folded, while chaos reigns all around him. Rather than join in, he is studying the reaction of his king, who still hasn't moved.
So, it's a sort of fisheye lens shot as we look down the length of the table at Black Bolt. Karnak sends our gaze that way, despite the fact that everything's going nuts around him.

Caption: ... and you'd shout it across the world so that everyone could hear:

PANEL 3 Closing in on Black Bolt, who betrays absolutely no emotion. Is he bored? Angry? Tired?

No dialogue

PANEL 4 And finally, we are very close to Black Bolt. For the first time, we are given a glimpse of something other than emotional detachment in this enigmatic man's face.
Very slowly, at the edge of his mouth there is a slight turn. As he decides what he'd say, Black Bolt allows himself a tiny little smile...

Caption: Relax.